FREEDOM BY THE SWORD
THE U.S. COLORED TROOPS, 1862–1867

FERRO IIS LIBERTAS PERVENIET ("Freedom attained by the sword")

Inscription on medal struck for black soldiers in the Army of the James, 1864

ARMY HISTORICAL SERIES

FREEDOM BY THE SWORD
THE U.S. COLORED TROOPS, 1862–1867

by

William A. Dobak

MILITARY INSTRVCTION

CENTER OF MILITARY HISTORY
UNITED STATES ARMY
WASHINGTON, D.C., 2011

Library of Congress Cataloging-in-Publication Data

Dobak, William A., 1943–
  Freedom by the sword : the U.S. Colored Troops, 1862–1867 / by William A.
Dobak.
      p. cm. — (Army historical series)
  Includes bibliographical references and index.
  1. United States. Colored Troops. 2. United States. Army—African American
troops—History—19th century. 3. United States—History—Civil War, 1861–
1865—Participation, African American. 4. African American soldiers—History—
19th century. I. Title.
  E492.9.D63 2011
  973.7'415—dc22

                                                                        2011000365

First Printing—CMH Pub 30–24–1

For sale by the Superintendent of Documents, U.S. Government Printing Office
Internet: bookstore.gpo.gov   Phone: toll free (866) 512-1800;   DC area (202) 512-1800
Fax: (202) 512-2104 Mail: Stop IDCC, Washington, DC 20402-0001

ISBN 978-0-16-086695-1

ARMY HISTORICAL SERIES

Richard W. Stewart, General Editor

Advisory Committee
(As of December 2010)

Reina J. Pennington
Norwich University

William T. Allison
Georgia Southern University

James J. Carafano
The Heritage Foundation

Lt. Gen. Robert L. Caslen Jr.
U.S. Army Combined Arms Center

John F. Guilmartin Jr.
Ohio State University

Brig. Gen. Sean B. MacFarland
U.S. Army Command and
General Staff College

Michael S. Neiberg
University of Southern Mississippi

Gerald B. O'Keefe
Deputy Administrative Assistant
to the
Secretary of the Army

Mark P. Parillo
Kansas State University

Lt. Gen. John E. Sterling Jr.
U.S. Army Training
and
Doctrine Command

Col. Bobby A. Towery
U.S. Army War College

Brig. Gen. Timothy Trainor
U.S. Military Academy

Steve Vogel
Washington Post

Paul M. Wester Jr.
National Archives and Records Administration

U.S. Army Center of Military History
Col. Peter D. Crean, Acting Director

Chief Historian
Chief, Histories Division
Acting Chief, Publishing Division

Richard W. Stewart
Joel D. Meyerson
Beth F. MacKenzie

CONTENTS

TABLES

MAPS

ILLUSTRATIONS

Illustrations courtesy of the following sources: cover, 2, 4, 35, 38, 71, 73, 81, 84, 260, 276, 280, 293, 325, 327, 342 (*top* and *bottom*), 347, 350, 368, 374, 375, 379, 404, 417, 421, 467, Library of Congress; 27, 33, 62, 107, 118, 125, 163, 170, 200, 239 (*top*), 271, 288, 303, 311, 344, 412, 427, 449, *Frank Leslie's Illustrated Newspaper*; 12 (*bottom*), 46, 48, 321, 353, 360, 362, 486, 492, *Harper's Weekly*; 50, 56, 60, 77, 105, 126 (*top* and *bottom*), 130, 173, 193, 195, 211, 221, 245, 264, 306, 340, 356, 397, 406, 452, 459, U.S. Army Military History Institute; 53, Howard University, Washington, D.C.; 12 (*top*), 101, 146, 239 (*bottom*), 296, 339, 365, 391, 439, National Archives; 114, Western Reserve Historical Society Library and Archives, Cleveland, Ohio; 233, Special Collections, University of Arkansas Libraries, Fayetteville; 273, Chicago Public Library; 313, Philadelphia recruits (http://people.virginia.edu/~jh3v/retouching history/figure1.html); 382, J. H. Colton, *Colton's Illustrated Cabinet Atlas and Descriptive Geography;* 400, *Atlas to Accompany the Official Records of the Union and Confederate Armies* (vol. 1).

FOREWORD

The impetus for *Freedom by the Sword* came from Brig. Gen. (Ret.) John S. Brown, the U.S. Army's Chief of Military History from 1998 until his retirement in 2005. William A. Dobak, an authority on the history of black soldiers in the nineteenth century and an award-winning historian at the Center of Military History, took charge of the project beginning in 2003.

The years since then have seen the U.S. invasion of Iraq and our country's subsequent involvement there and in Afghanistan. These events, as well as a year that Dobak spent drafting chapters for a book in the Center's Vietnam series, helped to shape his view of the Civil War, the importance of guerrilla operations in that conflict, and the role of the U.S. Colored Troops in it.

This is primarily an operational history of the Colored Troops in action. Other works have dealt with such subjects as the Colored Troops and racial discrimination, the soldiers' lives in camp and at their homes, and how these men fared as veterans during Reconstruction and afterward. Instead, *Freedom by the Sword* tells what they did as soldiers during the war. This book is about American soldiers, fighting under the flag of the Union to preserve that Union and to free their enslaved brothers and sisters. Despite formidable obstacles of poor leadership and deep prejudices against the very idea of African Americans being armed and sent into battle, these men rallied to the colors in large numbers and fought. It is thus a quintessentially American story. It is also perhaps the only book to examine the Colored Troops' formation, training, and operations during the entire span of their service, and in every theater of the war in which they served. By doing so, it underscores the unique nature of their contributions both to Union victory and to their own liberation. That there are lessons here for the modern soldier goes without saying, for however much the technology of war evolves, its essence changes little.

Washington, D.C.   RICHARD W. STEWART
31 March 2011   Chief Historian

THE AUTHOR

William A. Dobak received his Ph.D. from the University of Kansas in American studies in 1995. His published dissertation, *Fort Riley and Its Neighbors: Military Money and Economic Growth, 1853–1895* (1998), won the Edward A. Tihen Award from the Kansas State Historical Society in 1999.

After receiving his degree, Dobak joined the staff at the National Archives. While there, he and coauthor Thomas D. Phillips worked on *The Black Regulars, 1866–1898* (2001). This work received the Western History Association's Robert M. Utley Award for 2003 as the best book on the military history of the frontier and western North America. In 2002, he joined the staff of the U.S. Army Center of Military History. In 2003, he began work on *Freedom by the Sword: The U.S. Colored Troops, 1862–1867*. Since completing the manuscript, he has retired from federal service and is now engaged in several other historical projects.

PREFACE

Edward L. Pierce was a special agent of the United States Treasury Department, appointed in 1862 to supervise the federal government's attempt at plantation management on the South Carolina Sea Islands. The aim of this project was to grow and market cotton to help defray the cost of waging the Civil War. Just as important in the eyes of the occupiers was the need to organize and regulate the labor of the local population, former slaves whose masters had fled the islands at the approach of a Union naval and military expedition the previous fall. After a year on the job, Pierce published his reflections in a magazine article. "Two questions are concerned in the social problem of our time," he wrote. "One is, Will the people of African descent work for a living? and the other is, Will they fight for their freedom?" By the end of the article, Pierce had answered both questions in the affirmative.[1]

That anyone in 1863 would have asked "Will they fight for their freedom?" shows how thoroughly white Americans had forgotten the service of black soldiers during the Revolutionary War and the War of 1812. Much the same thing happened after 1865. Although more than two hundred thousand black men served the Union as soldiers and sailors, and three contemporary black authors published books about them, the fact that black Americans had fought for the nation slipped once again from the public consciousness. Thus, by 1928 a biographer of Ulysses S. Grant could write: "The American negroes are the only people in the history of the world, so far as I know, that ever became free without any effort of their own." In the twenty-five years that followed, two historians devoted chapters of larger works to the black military role in the Civil War, but not until Dudley T. Cornish's *The Sable Arm* appeared in 1956 did the U.S. Colored Troops receive book-length treatment.[2]

Since then, historians have paid more attention to black troops' service. James M. McPherson's *The Negro's Civil War* (1965) and the massive documentary collection compiled by Ira Berlin and his colleagues, *The Black Military Experience* (1982), preceded Joseph T. Glatthaar's *Forged in Battle* (1990). The years since 1998 have seen the publication of a battle narrative, a study of the Colored Troops'

---

[1]Edward L. Pierce, "The Freedmen at Port Royal," *Atlantic Monthly* 12 (September 1863): 291–315 (quotation, p. 291).

[2]Bernard C. Nalty, *Strength for the Fight: A History of Black Americans in the Military*, pp. 10–26, gives a brief account of America's black soldiers from 1775 to 1815. The three books by nineteenth-century black authors are William W. Brown, *The Negro in the American Rebellion* (1867); George W. Williams, *A History of the Negro Troops in the War of the Rebellion, 1861–1865* (1888); and Joseph T. Wilson, *The Black Phalanx* (1890). Bell I. Wiley, *Southern Negroes, 1861–1865* (1938), and Benjamin Quarles, *The Negro in the Civil War* (1953), preceded Dudley T. Cornish, *The Sable Arm: Negro Troops in the Union Army, 1861–1865*. William E. Woodward, *Meet General Grant* (1928), p. 372 (quotation). David W. Blight's *Race and Reunion: The Civil War in American Memory* examines the process by which white Americans deleted black participation in the war from the national narrative. See Bibliography for full citations.

off-duty behavior, a book about black veterans, and an analysis of one subset of their white officers, as well as a collection of essays (*Black Soldiers in Blue*, edited by John David Smith). In addition, there have been regimental histories, studies of the atrocities Confederates committed on their black opponents, and a narrative of one of the earliest campaigns in which black troops took part.[3]

Nevertheless, the focus of scholarship has not changed a great deal since 1997, when Brooks D. Simpson observed that

> historians have concentrated on the consequences of military service for blacks and for the whites who commanded them. Scholars view the enlistment of blacks as a laboratory for social change. . . . Yet there were other dimensions to the role of black soldiers in the war. Generals had to answer questions involving their use as combat soldiers, as support personnel working behind the lines, and as an occupation force. These specific issues in turn place the issue of employing black troops in the wider context of civil and military policy during and after the war. . . . By examining . . . the deployment of black regiments within the context of large policies and problems of command, we gain a better sense of the conflicting pressures upon white commanders as they sought to grapple with the implications of arming African Americans.[4]

This book will tell the story of how the Union Army's black regiments came into being, what they accomplished when they took the field, and how their conduct affected the course of the war and the subsequent occupation of the defeated South. It will deal with matters such as the organization, pay, and health of black troops only so far as is necessary to tell this story. Most of the documentation comes either from *The War of the Rebellion: Official Records of the Union and Confederate Armies*, published between 1880 and 1901, or from official correspondence in the National Archives, most of it unpublished. Since state laws in the South prohibited teaching slaves to read and write and poor educational opportunities in the North had the same effect, the overwhelming majority of the source material was written by whites.

Freedom by the Sword begins with a chapter that sketches national factors that affected the formation of all-black regiments: the racial attitudes of white Americans, the symbiotic relationship that developed between soldiers and es-

---

[3] James M. McPherson, *The Negro's Civil War: How American Negroes Felt and Acted During the War for the Union*; Ira Berlin et al., eds., *The Black Military Experience*; Joseph T. Glatthaar, *Forged in Battle: The Civil War Alliance of Black Soldiers and White Officers*; Noah A. Trudeau, *Like Men of War: Black Troops in the Civil War, 1862–1865*; Keith P. Wilson, *Campfires of Freedom: The Camp Life of Black Soldiers During the Civil War*; Donald R. Shaffer, *After the Glory: The Struggles of Black Civil War Veterans*; Martin W. Öfele, *German-Speaking Officers in the U.S. Colored Troops, 1863–1867*; Richard M. Reid, *Freedom for Themselves: North Carolina's Black Soldiers in the Civil War Era*; John David Smith, ed., *Black Soldiers in Blue: African American Troops in the Civil War Era*; Gregory J. W. Urwin, ed., *Black Flag over Dixie: Racial Atrocities and Reprisals in the Civil War*; George S. Burkhardt, *Confederate Rage, Yankee Wrath: No Quarter in the Civil War*; Stephen V. Ash, *Firebrand of Liberty: The Story of Two Black Regiments That Changed the Course of the Civil War*. See bibliography for full citations.

[4] Brooks D. Simpson, "Quandaries of Command: Ulysses S. Grant and Black Soldiers," in *Union and Emancipation: Essays on Politics and Race in the Civil War Era*, eds. David W. Blight and Brooks D. Simpson (Kent, Ohio: Kent State University Press, 1997), pp. 123–49 (quotation, pp. 123–24).

caped slaves as Union armies moved south, and the development of federal policy in regard to emancipation and military recruiting. The balance of the book falls into five parts, arranged to correspond more or less with the advance of federal armies into Confederate territory. The first section therefore deals with the Department of the South, where a Union force secured a beachhead in November 1861. There, officers found more than thirty thousand black residents, whom they first organized as civilian laborers and later recruited as soldiers. The second section of the book treats the Department of the Gulf, where Union troops landed at New Orleans in April 1862. The sugar plantations of southern Louisiana furnished troops that eventually operated along the Gulf Coast, from the mouth of the Rio Grande to central Florida. The focus of the third section is on the rest of the Mississippi drainage basin. Four chapters cover the territory between Fort Scott, Kansas, and northwestern Georgia. North Carolina and Virginia are the subject of the fourth section. Most of the black regiments raised in the free states served in these two states; in other parts of the South, black soldiers' service seldom took them so far from home. The fifth section of the book deals with the black regiments' activities between the time of the Confederate surrender and their muster out. One chapter sketches their efforts on the lower Rio Grande in response to political turmoil in Mexico, while the other considers their responsibilities while the last regiments of Civil War volunteers turned over occupation duties in the defeated South to the Regular Army.

The narrative includes extensive quotations from contemporary documents, diaries, and private letters. These appear with the original spelling and punctuation as much as possible, with minimal use of bracketed explanation. Expressions of racial bigotry occur frequently; they illustrate the prevailing moral climate of nineteenth-century America and often shed light on the minds of the authors.

When referring to officers' ranks, I use the rank that appears beneath the writer's signature on a letter—often a brevet, or acting, rank. In the case of Winfield Scott, the commanding general in 1861, whose brevet as lieutenant general dated from the Mexican War, I use "Lt. Gen." Since the narrative describes military operations rather than the careers of individual officers, there is no attempt to distinguish between rank in the Regular Army and in the U.S. Volunteers.

Research for the book required a fair amount of travel. Librarians and archivists at the institutions named in the bibliography extended courteous and efficient assistance. Staff members of the National Archives, at both College Park, Maryland, and Washington, D.C., deserve special mention; without their expert and energetic help, research for this book would not have been possible. Also helpful were the staffs of the Abraham Lincoln Presidential Library (formerly the Illinois State Historical Library), the Bowdoin College Library, the Houghton and Widener Libraries at Harvard University, the Kansas State Historical Society, the New Bedford Free Public Library, the Rhode Island Historical Society, the libraries of the University of South Carolina and Syracuse University, the Historical Society of Washington, D.C., and the Western Reserve Historical Society. I visited all these sites, although the sources housed there do not appear in the final version of the text. W. Bart Berger, Richard B. Booth Sr., Lucy B.

Daoust, and John G. Saint, descendants of Civil War soldiers, made available typescripts of their ancestors' letters or diaries.

At the U.S. Army Center of Military History, William M. Hammond went through successive drafts of the manuscript with a sharp pencil. Among the author's colleagues, Bianka J. Adams, Andrew J. Birtle, and Edgar F. Raines each read one or more chapters and Mark L. Bradley read the entire first draft. Friends of the author—James N. Leiker, Thomas D. Phillips, and Frank N. Schubert—also read the first draft. Schubert served on the panel that reviewed the entire second draft, as did Leslie S. Rowland, of the Freedmen and Southern Society Project at the University of Maryland, and Col. Versalle F. Washington, U.S. Army. I would also like to acknowledge members of the Publishing Division who worked on this book, including editors Diane M. Donovan and Hildegard J. Bachman, cartographer S. L. Dowdy, and layout designer Michael R. Gill. Any errors or inaccuracies in the text are, of course, the responsibility of the author.

Patricia Ames, Lenore Garder, and James Knight were librarians at the U.S. Army Center of Military History during much of the time I spent researching and writing this book. I dedicate it to them.

Washington, D.C.   WILLIAM A. DOBAK
31 March 2011

FREEDOM BY THE SWORD
THE U.S. COLORED TROOPS, 1862–1867

CHAPTER 1

MUSTERING IN—FEDERAL POLICY ON EMANCIPATION AND RECRUITMENT

On 12 April 1861, Confederate shore batteries at Charleston opened a two-day bombardment of Fort Sumter, the federal outpost that commanded the harbor entrance. The day after the garrison surrendered, President Abraham Lincoln called on the loyal states to provide seventy-five thousand militia to put down the insurrection; he promised Unionist or undecided residents of the seven seceded states that Union armies would take "the utmost care . . . to avoid any . . . interference with property." Two days after Lincoln's call, the Virginia legislature passed an ordinance of secession, asserting that the federal government had "perverted" its powers "to the oppression of the Southern slaveholding states." Americans North and South knew what kind of "property" the president meant "to avoid . . . interference with."[1]

Some politicians and journalists were even more forthright. Addressing a secessionist audience at Savannah in March, the Confederate vice president, Alexander H. Stephens, called "African slavery . . . the immediate cause" of secession. The new government's "foundations are laid, its cornerstone rests, upon the great truth that the Negro is not equal to the white man; that slavery, subordination to the superior race, is his natural and moral condition." Four months later, just after the Union defeat at Bull Run, a *New York Times* editorial predicted that the war would result in the abolition of slavery. Charles Sumner, the senior U.S. senator from Massachusetts, was equally confident. By prolonging the war, he told his fellow abolitionist, Wendell Phillips, Bull Run "made the extinction of Slavery inevitable."[2]

The Army's senior officer, Lt. Gen. Winfield Scott, had been weighing possible responses to secession even before Lincoln took the oath of office. One course of action was to assert federal authority by force. To invade the South would require "300,000 disciplined men," Scott told Secretary of State Designate William H. Seward. The old general allowed one-third of this force for guard duty behind

---

[1] *The War of the Rebellion: A Compilation of the Official Records of the Union and Confederate Armies*, 70 vols. in 128 (Washington, D.C.: Government Printing Office, 1880–1901), ser. 3, 1: 68 ("the utmost"); ser. 4, 1: 223 ("perverted") (hereafter cited as *OR*).

[2] *New York Times*, 27 March ("African slavery"), and 29 July 1861; Beverly W. Palmer, ed., *Selected Letters of Charles Sumner*, 2 vols. (Boston: Northeastern University Press, 1990), 2: 70 ("made the extinction").

This photograph of the Union depot at City Point, Virginia, taken between 1864 and 1865, includes examples of the wind, steam, and animal muscle that powered the Union Army.

the advance and an even greater number for anticipated casualties, many of them caused by "southern fevers." The task might take three years to complete, followed by an occupation "for generations, by heavy garrisons." Soon after the surrender of Fort Sumter, Scott began making more definite plans. These involved Union control of the Mississippi River and a naval blockade of Confederate ports. Because this strategy promised to squeeze the Confederacy but did not offer the quick solution many newspaper editors clamored for, critics dubbed it the Anaconda. Despite its derisive name, Scott's plan furnished a framework for Union strategy throughout the war. Federal troops captured the last Confederate stronghold on the Mississippi River in the summer of 1863, while blockading squadrons cruised the Atlantic and Gulf coasts until the fighting ended.[3]

During the spring and summer of 1861, few Northerners would have predicted that black people would play a part in suppressing the rebellion. This attitude would change within the year, as large federal armies fielding tens of thousands of men assembled in the slaveholding border states and began probing southward, entering Nashville, Tennessee, in February 1862 and capturing New Orleans, Lou-

---

[3] *OR*, ser. 1, vol. 51, pt. 1, pp. 369–70, 386–87; Winfield Scott, *Memoirs of Lieut.-General Scott* (New York: Sheldon, 1864), pp. 626–28.

isiana, the South's largest city, in a maritime operation two months later. Armies of this size required thousands of tons of supplies in an era when any freight that did not travel by steam, wind, or river current had to move by muscle power, whether animal or human. Advancing Union armies depended from the war's outset on black teamsters, deckhands, longshoremen, and woodcutters.

Throughout the country, black people, both slave and free, were quick to fasten their hopes on the eventual triumph of the Union cause—hopes that federal officials, civilian and military, took every opportunity to dampen. As Southern states seceded, slaves began to suppose that the presence of a U.S. military or naval force meant freedom. Few, though, were rash enough to act on the notion and risk being returned to their masters, as happened to three escaped slaves at Pensacola, Florida, in March 1861; for even as militia regiments from Northern states moved toward Washington, D.C., to defend the capital, Northern generals assured white Southerners that their only aim was to preserve the Union and that slaveholders would retain their human property. Brig. Gen. Benjamin F. Butler of the Massachusetts militia told the governor of Maryland in April that his troops stood ready to suppress a slave rebellion should one occur. Residents of counties in mountainous western Virginia received assurances from Maj. Gen. George B. McClellan that his Ohio troops would refrain "from interference with your slaves" and would "with an iron hand crush any attempt at insurrection on their part."[4]

Whatever Northern generals promised, slaveholders were quick to imagine "interference" with the institution of slavery. Butler's force sailed to Annapolis and went ashore at the U.S. Naval Academy—on federal property, in order to avoid possible conflict with state authorities—rather than enter the state by rail and have to march from one station to another through the heart of Baltimore, where a mob had stoned federal troops on 19 April. Despite Butler's precautions, just eighteen days later the governor of Maryland passed along a constituent's complaint that "several free Negroes have gone to Annapolis with your troops, either as servants or camp followers . . . [and] they seek the company of and are corrupting our slaves." The idea of free black men "corrupting" slaves, which at first involved only a few officers' servants, would become widespread as the war progressed, a charge leveled against tens of thousands of black men who wore the uniform of the United States.[5]

Having helped to secure Washington's rail links to the rest of the Union by mid-May, General Butler received an assignment that took him nearly one hundred fifty miles south to command the Department of Virginia, with headquarters at Fort Monroe. Part of an antebellum scheme of coastal defenses, the fort stood at the tip of a peninsula near the mouth of the James River across from the port of Norfolk. Butler reached there on 22 May and soon made a decision that began to change the aim and meaning of the war. The day after his arrival, three black men approached the Union pickets and sought refuge. They had been held as slaves on the peninsula above the fort, they said, and were about to be sent south to work on

---

[4] *OR*, ser. 2, 1: 750, 753.

[5] *OR*, ser. 1, 2: 590, 604; *New York Times*, 25 April 1861; Benjamin F. Butler, *Private and Official Correspondence of Gen. Benjamin F. Butler During the Period of the Civil War*, 5 vols. ([Norwood, Mass.: Plimpton Press], 1917), 1: 78 (quotation) (hereafter cited as *Butler Correspondence*).

A sketch by William Waud shows slaves building a Confederate battery that bore on Fort Sumter in Charleston Harbor early in 1861.

Confederate coastal defenses in the Carolinas. Butler decided to put them to work at Fort Monroe instead. "Shall [the enemy] be allowed the use of this property against the United States," he asked the Army's senior officer, General Scott, "and we not be allowed its use in aid of the United States?" When a Confederate officer tried to reclaim the escaped slaves the next day, Butler told him that he intended to keep them as "contraband of war," as he would any other property that might be of use to the enemy. During the next two months, about nine hundred escaped slaves gathered at the fort.[6]

Scott was delighted with Butler's reasoning. Within days, use of the term *contraband* had spread to the president and his cabinet members. Newspapers nationwide took up its use. As a noun, it was applied to escaped slaves, at first as a joke but soon in official documents. The adoption and jocular use of the term as a noun illustrated a disturbing national attitude, for white Americans in the nineteenth century routinely expressed a shocking degree of casual contempt for black people. One instance was the habit of equating them with livestock, which was commonplace in the official and private correspondence of soldiers of every rank. In May 1863, a Union division commander in Mississippi ordered his cavalry "to

---

[6]*OR*, ser. 1, 2: 638–40, 643, 649–52 (p. 650, "Shall [the enemy]"); *Butler Correspondence*, 1: 102–03 ("contraband"), 116–17; Ira Berlin et al., eds., *The Destruction of Slavery* (New York: Cambridge University Press, 1985), p. 61.

Collect all Cattle and male negroes" from the surrounding country. On the same day, a private marching toward Vicksburg wrote to a cousin in Iowa that his regiment "took all the Horses Mules & Niggars that we came acrost."[7]

The term *racism* is inadequate to describe this attitude, for it verged on what twentieth-century animal rights activists would call speciesism. Thomas Jefferson had speculated at some length on perceived and imagined differences between black people and white; but "scientific" evidence, based on the study of human skulls, did not become accepted as proof that blacks and whites belonged to separate species of the genus *Homo* until the 1840s—the same decade in which Ulysses S. Grant, William T. Sherman, and other future leaders of the Union armies graduated from West Point. Famous Americans who took an interest in the "science" of phrenology included Clara Barton, Henry Ward Beecher, Horace Greeley, and Horace Mann. Even Louis Agassiz, the Swiss biologist who began teaching at Harvard in 1848, found the separate-species theory persuasive. Small wonder, then, that Union soldiers from privates to generals lumped draft animals and "the negro" together. This attitude pervaded the Union Army, even though many soldiers had seldom set eyes on a black person.[8]

As federal armies gathered in the border states before pushing south in the spring of 1862, escaped slaves thronged their camps. Union generals promised anxious slaveholders that federal occupation did not mean instant emancipation, but the behavior of troops in the field displayed a different attitude. Despite any aversion they may have entertained toward black people in the abstract, young Northern men away from home for the first time delighted in thwarting white Southerners who came to their camps in search of escaped slaves. At one camp near Louisville, Kentucky, a Union soldier wrote, "negro catchers were there waiting for us and . . . made a grab for them. The darkies ran in among the soldiers and begged at them not to let massa have them. The boys interfered" with the slave catchers until the commanding officer arrived and ordered the slave catchers to leave the camp "and do it d——d quick and they concluded to retreat . . . as their fugitive slave laws did not seem to work that day. That night for fear the general officers might order the darkies turned over to their masters some of the boys got some skiffs and rowed the darkies over the Ohio River into Indiana and gave some money and grub and told them where and how to go." An Illinois soldier wrote home from Missouri: "Now, I don't care a damn for the darkies, and know that they are better off with their masters 50 times over than with us, but of course you know

---

[7]John Y. Simon, ed., *The Papers of Ulysses S. Grant*, 30 vols. to date (Carbondale and Edwardsville: Southern Illinois University Press, 1967–), 8: 278 (hereafter cited as *Grant Papers*); Stephen V. Ash, *When the Yankees Came: Conflict and Chaos in the Occupied South, 1861–1865* (Chapel Hill: University of North Carolina Press, 1995), p. 55. Other examples of the "horses, mules, and Negroes" formula occur in *Grant Papers*, 8: 290, 349; 9: 571; 10: 143, 537; and 12: 97. See also Mark Grimsley, *The Hard Hand of War: Union Military Policy Toward Southern Civilians, 1861–1865* (New York: Cambridge University Press, 1995), pp. 152, 157–58.

[8]Thomas Jefferson, *Notes on the State of Virginia*, ed. William Peden (Chapel Hill: University of North Carolina Press, 1954), pp. 138–43; George M. Fredrickson, *The Black Image in the White Mind: The Debate on Afro-American Character and Destiny, 1817–1914* (Middletown, Conn.: Wesleyan University Press, 1971), pp. 75–96. On cranial research and the "science" of phrenology, see John S. Haller, *American Medicine in Transition, 1840–1910* (Urbana: University of Illinois Press, 1981), pp. 13–17.

I couldn't help to send a runaway nigger back. I'm blamed if I could." All across the border states, thousands of Union soldiers who directed coarse epithets at black people nevertheless took the initiative and helped slaves escape to freedom.[9]

Many of the fugitives stayed in the camps or nearby, and soldiers tolerated their presence because it relieved them of many domestic chores and labor details that otherwise would have been inseparable from army life. "If the niggers come into camp . . . as fast as they have been," one private wrote home from Tennessee in August 1862, "we will soon have a waiter for every man in the Reg[imen]t." His remark shows that the status of the new arrivals was as fixed and their degree of acceptance as limited in the Army as it was in civil life: the private's home state, Wisconsin, did not allow black people to vote. Other states in the Old Northwest had laws on the books and even constitutional provisions that barred blacks from residence. "We don't want the North flooded with free niggers," an Indiana soldier wrote soon after the Emancipation Proclamation became law. Clearly, anti-Negro sentiment was not confined to the working-class Irish who rioted in New York City in the summer of 1863.[10]

It should be no surprise, then, that the idea of recruiting black soldiers inspired revulsion. On the day after the Union defeat at Bull Run in July 1861, Representative Charles A. Wickliffe of Kentucky told Congress that he had not heard a current report that the Confederates "employed negroes" as soldiers. "I have," replied William M. Dunn, an Indiana Republican, "and that they were firing upon our troops yesterday." Later that week, the *Philadelphia Evening Bulletin* reported the presence of "two regiments of well-drilled negroes at Richmond." Not long afterward, another representative from Kentucky "expressed his profound horror at the thought of arming negroes" and a senator asked whether the U.S. Army had plans to recruit them. In the end, Secretary of War Simon Cameron had to reassure Congress that he had "no information as to the employment of . . . negroes in the military capacity by the so-called Southern Confederacy." Following a forty-year-old Army policy, Cameron continued to reject black Northerners' attempts to enlist.[11]

Despite official discouragement, black men across the North had begun trying to enlist soon after the first call for militia in 1861. A letter to the War Department dated 23 April 1861 offered the services of "300 reliable colored free citizens" of Washington to defend the city. Cameron replied that his department had "no intention at present" of recruiting black soldiers, but by the end of the year, his views had changed. "If it shall be found that the men who have been held by the rebels as

---

[9] *OR*, ser. 2, 1: 755–59; Terrence J. Winschel, ed., *The Civil War Diary of a Common Soldier: William Wiley of the 77th Illinois Infantry* (Baton Rouge: Louisiana State University Press, 2001), p. 22 ("negro catchers"); Charles W. Wills, *Army Life of an Illinois Soldier* (Carbondale and Edwardsville: Southern Illinois University Press, 1996 [1906]), p. 83 ("Now, I").

[10] Stephen E. Ambrose, ed., *A Wisconsin Boy in Dixie: The Selected Letters of John K. Newton* (Madison: Wisconsin State Historical Society, 1961), p. 28; Emma L. Thornbrough, *Indiana in the Civil War Era, 1850–1880* (Indianapolis: Indiana Historical Society, 1965), p. 197. On disenfranchisement and exclusion, see Leon F. Litwack, *North of Slavery: The Negro in the Free States, 1790–1860* (Chicago: University of Chicago Press, 1961), pp. 66–74, 92.

[11] *Congressional Globe*, 37th Cong., 1st sess., 22 July 1861, p. 224; *New York Times*, 26 July 1861; *Philadelphia Evening Bulletin*, 28 July 1861 ("expressed his," "no information"); Leon F. Litwack, *Been in the Storm So Long: The Aftermath of Slavery* (New York: Knopf, 1979), p. 60.

slaves are capable of bearing arms and performing efficient military service, it is the right . . . of this Government to arm and equip them, and employ their services against the rebels, under proper military regulations, discipline, and command," he wrote in a draft of his annual report, toward the end of a long passage in which he compared slave property with other property that might be used in rebellion or impounded by the government. Lincoln made Cameron rewrite the passage, eliminating all reference to black military service, before its publication.[12]

Still, the North was home to vocal abolitionists, although such radicals were themselves the object of other whites' suspicion and animosity. "Wicked acts of abolitionists have done the Union cause more harm . . . than anything the Rebel chief and his Congress could possibly have done," one Indiana legislator remarked while denouncing emancipation. Nevertheless, abolitionists thrived in Boston and Philadelphia, cities that were home to major publishers and magazines with national circulation. They campaigned untiringly to sway public opinion across the North by means of lectures, sermons, speeches, and newspaper editorials while in Congress men like Charles Sumner and Thaddeus Stevens wielded influence on behalf of their ideas.[13]

As Union armies began to penetrate Confederate territory in 1862, slaves fled to take refuge with the invaders. A few Northern generals with profound antislavery convictions tried to raise regiments of former slaves, but their efforts were thwarted by worries at the highest levels of government that such moves would alienate potentially loyal Southerners and drive the central border state, Kentucky, into the Confederacy. A quip attributed to Lincoln, "I would like to have God on my side, but I must have Kentucky," remains apocryphal, but it sums up nicely the predicament of Union strategists. What finally tipped the balance in favor of black recruitment was the Union Army's demand for men.[14]

During the first summer of the war, Congress authorized a force of half a million volunteers to suppress the rebellion. More than seven hundred thousand responded by the end of 1861, but in late June 1862, only 432,609 officers and men were present for duty—an attrition rate of almost 39 percent even before many serious battles had been fought. Lincoln mentioned this in his call to the state governors for another one hundred fifty thousand men on 30 June 1862. The governors responded so cordially that the president doubled the call the next day, but this

---

[12]*OR*, ser. 3, 1: 107 ("300 reliable"), 133 ("no intention"), 348; Edward McPherson, ed., *The Political History of the United States of America During the Great Rebellion* (Washington, D.C.: Philp & Solomons, 1864), p. 249 ("If it shall"). See *OR*, ser. 3, 1: 524, 609, for offers of enlistment from New York and Michigan during the summer and fall. For instances in Ohio, see Versalle F. Washington, *Eagles on Their Buttons: A Black Infantry Regiment in the Civil War* (Columbia: University of Missouri Press, 1999), pp. 2–3; for Pennsylvania, J. Matthew Gallman, *Mastering Wartime: A Social History of Philadelphia During the Civil War* (New York: Cambridge University Press, 1990), p. 45. Fredrickson, *Black Image in the White Mind*, pp. 53–55, outlines a view that was common among antebellum whites that the innate savagery of black people required forcible restraint.

[13]James M. McPherson, *The Struggle for Equality: Abolitionists and the Negro in the Civil War and Reconstruction* (Princeton: Princeton University Press, 1964), pp. 75–93; Thornbrough, *Indiana in the Civil War Era*, p. 197 (quotation).

[14]Richard M. McMurry, *The Fourth Battle of Winchester: Toward a New Civil War Paradigm* (Kent, Ohio: Kent State University Press, 2002), p. 94 (quotation).

time the volunteers proved slow to arrive, forcing Congress to entertain the idea of compulsory military service.[15]

The failure of a Union attempt to take Richmond in the early summer of 1862 prompted Congress to enlarge the scope of federal Emancipation policy. In August 1861, the First Confiscation Act had used contorted legalese to proclaim that a slaveholder who allowed his slaves to work on Confederate military projects forfeited his "claim" to those slaves without actually declaring the slaves free. On 17 July 1862, the Second Confiscation Act declared free any slave who left a disloyal owner and escaped to a Union garrison or who stayed at home in Confederate-held territory to await the arrival of an advancing federal army. Moreover, the act authorized the president "to employ as many persons of African descent as he may deem necessary . . . for the suppression of this rebellion, and . . . [to] organize and use them in such manner as he may judge best." On the same day, the Militia Act provided that "persons of African descent" could enter "the service of the United States, for the purpose of constructing intrenchments, or performing camp service, or . . . any military or naval service for which they may be found competent." The next section of the act fixed their pay at ten dollars per month. This was as much as black laborers earned at Fort Monroe and as much as the Navy paid its lowest-ranked beginning sailors, but it was three dollars less than the Army paid its white privates. The same section then contradicted itself by providing that "all persons who have been or shall be hereafter enrolled in the service of the United States under this act shall receive the pay and rations now allowed by law to soldiers, according to their respective grades." This ill-considered phrasing, rushed through Congress on the last day of the session, resulted in many complaints, disciplinary problems, and at least one execution for mutiny before a revised law two years later finally provided equal pay for both black and white soldiers.[16]

As Congress debated the employment of black laborers, Union battle casualties continued to mount: in April 1862, more than 13,000 in two days at Shiloh; at the beginning of summer, nearly 16,000 during the Seven Days' Battles outside Richmond; and in September, more than 12,000 in a single day at Antietam, the battle that turned the Confederates back across the Potomac and made possible Lincoln's preliminary announcement of the Emancipation Proclamation later that month. All the while, disease ate away at the Union ranks. The North was running out of volunteers.[17]

While leaders of the executive and legislative branches pondered conscription, they also considered the policy of enlisting black soldiers. Prospective recruits were many. The federal census of 1860 counted about one hundred thousand free

---

[15] *OR*, ser. 3, 1: 380–84, and 2: 183–85, 187–88.

[16] *OR*, ser. 2, 1: 774; ser. 3, 2: 276 ("to employ"), 281–82 ("the service"), and 4: 270–77, 490–93, 564–65. *Official Records of the Union and Confederate Navies in the War of the Rebellion*, 30 vols. (Washington, D.C.: Government Printing Office, 1894–1922), ser. 1, 6: 252; *U.S. Statutes at Large* 12 (1861): 319 ("claim"); Howard C. Westwood, "The Cause and Consequence of a Union Black Soldier's Mutiny and Execution," *Civil War History* 31 (1985): 222–36. Convenient summaries of the equal pay controversy are in Dudley T. Cornish, *The Sable Arm: Negro Troops in the Union Army, 1861–1865* (New York: Longmans, Green, 1956), pp. 184–96, and Joseph T. Glatthaar, *Forged in Battle: The Civil War Alliance of Black Soldiers and White Officers* (New York: Free Press, 1990), pp. 169–76.

[17] Casualty figures in *OR*, ser. 1, 10: 108; vol. 11, pt. 2, p. 37; vol. 19, pt. 1, p. 200.

black men and well over eight hundred thousand slaves who would be of military age by 1863—potentially a formidable addition to the Union's manpower pool. Most of the slave population lived in parts of the South still under Confederate control; but federal armies in 1862 had gained beachheads on the Atlantic Coast, seized New Orleans, marched through Arkansas, and ensconced themselves firmly in Nashville and Memphis. The new year was likely to bring further advances by Union armies and freedom to many more Southern slaves, opening up fertile fields for recruiters. On 1 January 1863, the Emancipation Proclamation declared free all slaves in the seceded states, except for those in seven Virginia counties occupied by Union troops, thirteen occupied Louisiana parishes, and the newly formed state of West Virginia. The proclamation omitted Tennessee entirely, exempting slaves there from its provisions. Toward the end of the document, the president announced cautiously that former slaves would "be received into the armed service of the United States to garrison forts . . . and other places, and to man vessels of all sorts in said service."[18]

Among troops who were already in the field, opinions of the government's plans to enlist black soldiers varied from unfavorable to cautious. "I am willing to let them fight and dig if they will; it saves so many white men," wrote a New York soldier. Lt. Col. Charles G. Halpine, a Union staff officer in South Carolina, published some verses in Irish dialect entitled "Sambo's Right to Be Kilt." The burden of the poem was what an Iowa infantry soldier expressed in one sentence of his diary: "If any African will stand between me and a rebel *bullet* he is *welcome* to the honor and the *bullet too*." Maj. Gen. William T. Sherman took a different view: "I thought a soldier was to be an active machine, a fighter," he told his brother John, a U.S. senator from Ohio. "Dirt or cotton will stop a bullet better than a man's body."[19]

Sherman is often cited as an exemplar of racial bigots who occupied high places in the Union Army, and with good cause: "I won't trust niggers to fight yet," he told his brother the senator. "I have no confidence in them & don't want them mixed up with our white soldiers." Even so, Sherman had sound military reasons for his disinclination to raise black regiments. He was the only Union general who had seen untried soldiers stampede both at Bull Run in July 1861 and, nine months later, on the first day at Shiloh. Two years' experience in the field had bred in him a distrust of new formations. In 1863, he implored both his brother John and Maj. Gen. Ulysses S. Grant, his immediate superior, to warn the president against creating new, all-conscript regiments. Drafted men should go to fill up depleted regiments that had been in the field since 1861, Sherman urged. "All who deal with troops in fact instead of theory," he told Grant, "know that the knowledge of the little details of Camp Life is

---

[18] *OR*, ser. 3, 3: 2–3; James W. Geary, *We Need Men: The Union Draft in the Civil War* (DeKalb: Northern Illinois University Press, 1991), pp. 50–52; U.S. Census Bureau, *Historical Statistics of the United States: Colonial Times to 1970*, 2 vols. (Washington, D.C.: Government Printing Office, 1975), 1: 18.

[19] Harry F. Jackson and Thomas F. O'Donnell, *Back Home in Oneida: Hermon Clarke and His Letters* (Syracuse: Syracuse University Press, 1965), p. 100. Halpine's poem is printed in Cornish, *Sable Arm*, pp. 229–30. Mildred Throne, ed., *The Civil War Diary of Cyrus F. Boyd, Fifteenth Iowa Infantry, 1861–1863* (Baton Rouge: Louisiana State University Press, 1998), p. 119; Brooks D. Simpson and Jean V. Berlin, eds., *Sherman's Civil War: Selected Correspondence of William Tecumseh Sherman, 1860–1865* (Chapel Hill: University of North Carolina Press, 1999), p. 628.

absolutely necessary to keep men alive. New Regiments for want of this knowledge have measles, mumps, Diarrhea and the whole Catalogue of Infantile diseases." He was referring to white troops, but the new regiments of Colored Troops suffered from the same diseases.[20]

Moreover, Sherman realized something that fervent abolitionists may have been reluctant to admit: not all newly freed black men were keen to enlist. He raised this point in both personal and official correspondence. "The first step in the liberation of the Negro from bondage will be to get him and family to a place of safety," he told the Adjutant General, Brig. Gen. Lorenzo Thomas, "then to afford him the means of providing for his family, . . . then gradually use a proportion—greater and greater each year—as sailors and soldiers." Nevertheless, from the South Carolina Sea Islands to the Mississippi Valley, enlistment of Colored Troops went on apace through 1863. "Bands of negro soldiers [operating as press gangs] have hunted these people like wild beasts—driven them out of their homes at night, shooting at them and at their women; hunting them into the woods," an officer in South Carolina told the department commander. Many men of military age reacted to these efforts by taking refuge in forests and swamps. They preferred to provide for their families by farm work or civilian employment with Army quartermasters rather than by donning a uniform.[21]

By the time orders to recruit black soldiers came in early 1863, a few generals had already taken steps in that direction. Commanding the Department of the Gulf since the capture of New Orleans in April 1862, General Butler had already accepted the services of several Louisiana regiments that were made up largely of "free men of color," some of whose ancestors had served with Andrew Jackson in 1815. Union officers in Beaufort, South Carolina, and Fort Scott, Kansas, resumed premature recruiting efforts that had fallen into abeyance for want of official support from Washington. Massachusetts raised one all-black infantry regiment and then quickly added another. States across the North from Rhode Island to Iowa also began raising black regiments, for their governors were deeply interested in officers' appointments as a tool of political patronage. In March 1863, Secretary of War Edwin M. Stanton sent Adjutant General Thomas to organize regiments of U.S. Colored Troops in the Mississippi Valley. Army camps sprang up near Baltimore, Philadelphia, and Washington that produced seventeen infantry regiments between them by the end of the war.[22]

The process of organizing the Colored Troops was disjointed, even ramshackle. Many regiments raised in the South received state names at first, whether or not they were organized within the particular state. In Louisiana, General Butler

---

[20] Simpson and Berlin, *Sherman's Civil War*, pp. 397, 458, 461 ("I won't"), 463 ("I have"), 474–75 ("All who"). For negative views of Sherman, see Glatthaar, *Forged in Battle*, p. 197; Anne J. Bailey, "The USCT in the Confederate Heartland," in *Black Soldiers in Blue: African American Troops in the Civil War Era*, ed. John David Smith (Chapel Hill: University of North Carolina Press, 2002), pp. 227–48.

[21] *OR*, ser. 3, 4: 454 ("The first"); Lt Col J. F. Hall to Maj Gen J. G. Foster, 27 Aug 1864 ("Bands of negro"), Entry 4109, Dept of the South, Letters Received (LR), pt. 1, Geographical Divs and Depts, Record Group (RG) 393, Rcds of U.S. Army Continental Cmds, National Archives (NA). See also Ira Berlin et al., *Slaves No More: Three Essays on Emancipation and the Civil War* (New York: Cambridge University Press, 1992), pp. 39, 43, 98–100, 106–09.

[22] Michael T. Meier, "Lorenzo Thomas and the Recruitment of Blacks in the Mississippi Valley, 1863–1865," in *Black Soldiers in Blue*, ed. Smith, pp. 249–75, esp. p. 254. On the new black regiments as a source of patronage appointments, see Maj C. W. Foster to W. A. Buckingham (Connecticut),

accepted the services of the Native Guards, black New Orleans regiments that had begun the war on the Confederate side. The first two black infantry regiments organized in Tennessee were numbered the 1st and 2d United States Colored Infantries (USCIs), even though 1st and 2d USCIs had already been raised in Washington, D.C., earlier in the year. Although the main impetus for recruiting black soldiers was federal, state governments and private organizations played a part, as they had done in raising white regiments during the first two years of the war.[23]

The force known generally as the U.S. Colored Troops was organized in regiments that represented the three branches of what was then known as the line of the Army: cavalry, artillery, and infantry. It grew to include seven regiments of cavalry, more than a dozen of artillery, and well over one hundred of infantry. The precise number of these infantry regiments is hard to determine, as the histories of two regiments, both numbered 11th USCI, indicate. The 11th USCI (Old) was raised in Arkansas during the winter of 1864 but consolidated in April 1865 with the 112th and 113th, also from that state, as the 113th USCI. The other 11th USCI, organized in Mississippi and Tennessee, began as the 1st Alabama Siege Artillery (African Descent [AD]), then became in succession the 6th and 7th U.S. Colored Artillery (Heavy) before being renumbered in January 1865 as the 11th USCI (New). The simultaneous existence for three months of two regiments with the same designation, one east of the Mississippi River and one west of it, is an extreme instance of the ambiguities and difficulties that stemmed from a regional, decentralized command structure. The authority of Union generals in Louisiana, Tennessee, and the Carolinas to raise regiments and to nominate officers equaled that of the Colored Troops Division of the Adjutant General's Office in Washington or of state governors throughout the North.[24]

The composition of the new regiments was much more uniform than their numbering and was the same as that of white volunteer organizations. Ten companies made up an infantry regiment, each company composed of a captain, 2 lieutenants, 5 sergeants, 8 corporals, 2 musicians, and from 64 to 82 privates. A colonel, lieutenant colonel, major, surgeon, two assistant surgeons, chaplain, and noncommissioned staff constituted regimental headquarters, or, as it was called, "field and staff." Cavalry and artillery regiments included twelve companies and employed two additional majors because of tactical requirements. The minimum and maximum strength of cavalry companies was slightly smaller than those of the infantry, that of artillery companies considerably larger (122 privates). A volunteer regiment had no formal battalion structure; any formation of two companies or more, but less than an entire regiment, constituted a battalion. Generals commanding geographical departments, especially Maj. Gen. Nathaniel P. Banks in the Department of the Gulf, might have

---

23 Jan, 2 Feb 1864; to R. Yates (Illinois), 19 Feb 1864; to O. P. Morton (Indiana), 19 Feb 1864; to J. Brough (Ohio), 7 Mar 1864; all in Entry 352, Colored Troops Div, Letters Sent, RG 94, Rcds of the Adjutant General's Office (AGO), NA.

[23]The Tennessee regiments eventually received the numbers 12 and 13, but some of their early papers are still misfiled with those of the 1st and 2d United States Colored Infantries (USCIs). Entry 57C, Regimental Papers, RG 94, NA. They are easily distinguishable by their Tennessee datelines and by comparing signatures with officers' names in *Official Army Register of the Volunteer Force of the Unites States Army*, 8 vols. (Washington, D.C.: Adjutant General's Office, 1867), 8: 169–70, 183–84 (hereafter cited as *ORVF*).

[24]*ORVF*, 8: 181–82; Frederick H. Dyer, *A Compendium of the War of the Rebellion* (New York: Thomas Yoseloff, 1959 [1909]), pp. 997, 1721–22, 1725–26.

A Harper's Weekly *artist thought that a photograph of the escaped slave Hubbard Pryor made a good "before enlistment" image. After Pryor enlisted in the 44th U.S. Colored Infantry, the artist found the squat, scowling soldier less appealing and substituted an idealized figure to show the transformative effect of donning the Union blue.*

had their own ideas about a smaller optimum size for Colored Troops regiments, but the War Department eventually ordered them to conform to the national standard.[25]

A new black regiment usually recruited its men and completed its organization in one place. Along the edge of the Confederacy, cities and army posts from Baltimore, Maryland, to Fort Scott, Kansas, drew tens of thousands of black people seeking refuge from slavery and were good recruiting grounds. So were towns in the Confederate interior that Union troops had occupied by the summer of 1863, such as La Grange, Tennessee, and Natchez, Mississippi. As Union armies expanded their areas of operation, large posts also sprang up at places like Camp Nelson, Kentucky, and Port Hudson, Louisiana, in territory previously untouched by Union recruiters. Regiments organized in the free states secured volunteers without resorting to impressment or disturbing the local labor market, as sometimes happened in the occupied South when recruiters competed for men with Army quartermasters and engineering officers and the Navy, as well as with plantation owners and lessees. This rivalry caused friction between officials who wore the same uniform and strove for the same cause.[26]

Prevailing racial attitudes dictated that white men would lead the new regiments. An important practical consideration was the need for men with military experience, and identifiably black men had been barred from enlistment until late in 1862. Political advantage also weighed heavily with governors who appointed officers in regiments raised in Northern states. In most of these states, black residents lacked the vote and other civil rights and were of little consequence politically. All these factors, especially the possibility that white soldiers might have to take orders from a black man of superior rank, pointed toward an all-white officer corps.

The first step in becoming an officer of Colored Troops was to secure an appointment. Most applicants came directly from state volunteer regiments or had previous service in militia or short-term volunteer units. Those who were already officers attained field grade in the Colored Troops, while noncommissioned officers and privates became company officers. At Lake Providence, Louisiana, Adjutant General Thomas addressed two divisions of the XVII Corps in April 1863 and asked each to provide enough officer candidates for two Colored Troops regiments. The vacancies filled within days. Two years later, when the XVII Corps had marched through the Carolinas and was about to reorganize its black road builders as the 135th USCI,

---

[25]AGO, General Orders (GO) 110, 29 Apr 1863, set the standards for volunteer regiments. *OR*, ser. 3, 3: 175; see also 4: 205–06 (Banks); Maj C. W. Foster to Col H. Barnes, 7 Jan 1864, Entry 352, RG 94, NA; Brig Gen J. P. Hawkins to Brig Gen L. Thomas, 19 Aug 1864 (H–48–AG–1864), Entry 363, LR by Adj Gen L. Thomas, RG 94, NA. Because regiments of infantry far outnumbered all other types throughout the federal army, state infantry regiments will be referred to simply as, for instance, "the 29th Connecticut" (black) or "the 8th Maine" (white). Other regiments will receive more complete identification, as with "the 5th Massachusetts Cavalry" (black) or "the 1st New York Engineers" (white).

[26]The 4th, 7th, and 39th USCIs organized at Baltimore; the 1st and part of the 2d Kansas Colored Infantry, which became the 79th (New) USCI and 83d (New) USCI, at Fort Scott. Natchez was home to the 6th United States Colored Artillery (USCA) and the 58th, 70th, and part of the 71st USCIs; La Grange, to the 59th, 61st, and part of the 11th (New) USCIs. The 5th and 6th U.S. Colored Cavalry; 12th and 13th USCAs; and 114th, 116th, 119th, and 124th USCIs organized at Camp Nelson. The 78th, 79th (Old), 80th, 81st, 82d, 83d (Old), 84th, 88th (Old), and 89th USCIs organized at Port Hudson. *ORVF*, 8: 145–46, 154, 161–63, 172, 176, 182, 212, 231–32, 234, 243–44, 254–63, 269, 271, 295, 297, 300, 305.

thirty-one of the new regiment's thirty-five officers came from within the corps. Local availability was a principle that guided officer appointments in the Colored Troops throughout the war.[27]

In the immense volunteer army of the Civil War, regimental commanders as well as state governors could have a good deal to say about officer appointments. Their personal preferences were influential in staffing the Colored Troops. In one instance, the new colonel of the 3d U.S. Colored Cavalry objected to the officers he had been assigned and asked for others from his old regiment, the 4th Illinois Cavalry, to replace them. His request was granted. In North Carolina, the officers of "Wild's African Brigade"—the 35th, 36th, and 37th USCIs—were overwhelmingly from Massachusetts. They had been nominated by their leader, Brig. Gen. Edward A. Wild, who was himself from that state. Ten of the company officers of the 1st South Carolina —exactly one-third of the original captains and lieutenants—came from the 8th Maine Infantry, a white regiment that happened to be serving in the Department of the South, where the 1st South Carolina was organized.[28]

A fragmented and contradictory command structure impeded the appointment process. Col. Thomas W. Higginson, a Massachusetts abolitionist who commanded the 1st South Carolina, described one such instance. Brig. Gen. Rufus Saxton had charge of plantations in the Sea Islands that had been abandoned by secessionist owners and was responsible for those black residents who had stayed on the land. Saxton "was authorized to raise five regiments & was going successfully on," Higginson wrote, when Col. James Montgomery arrived from Washington

> with independent orders . . . entirely ignoring Gen. Saxton. At first it all seemed very well; but who was to *officer* these new regiments? Montgomery claimed the right, but allowed Gen. Saxton by courtesy to issue the commissions & render great aid, the latter supposing [Montgomery's to be] one of his five regiments. Presently they split on a Lieutenant Colonelcy—Gen. S. commissions one man, Col. M. refuses to recognize him & appoints another; the officers of the regiment take sides, & the question must go to Washington. All the result of *want of unity of system.*

The problem existed wherever Union armies went. The War Department had to improvise a force that many civilian officials and soldiers of every rank thought was more of a gamble than an experiment.[29]

To select officers for the Colored Troops and confirm appointments in the new regiments, examining boards convened in Washington, Cincinnati, St. Louis, and a few other cities. Maj. Charles W. Foster, head of the adjutant gen-

---

[27] *OR*, ser. 3, 3: 121; Maj A. F. Rockwell to Capt H. S. Nourse, 8 Apr 1865, Entry 352, RG 94, NA. See also Thomas' report to the secretary of war in *OR*, ser. 3, 5: 118–24.

[28] Col E. D. Osband to Brig Gen L. Thomas, 10 Oct 1863 (O–4–AG–1863), Entry 363, RG 94, NA; Brig Gen E. A. Wild to Maj T. M. Vincent, 4 Sep 1863, lists of officers, E. A. Wild Papers, U.S. Army Military History Institute (MHI), Carlisle, Pa.; William E. S. Whitman, *Maine in the War for the Union* (Lewiston, Me.: Nelson Dingley Jr., 1865), p. 197.

[29] Col. T. W. Higginson to Maj. G. L. Stearns, 6 Jul 1863, Entry 363, RG 94, NA. On the fragmented authority among officers organizing regiments of Colored Troops, see *OR*, ser. 3, 3: 111–15.

eral's Colored Troops Division, wanted "as high a standard as possible [to] be maintained for this branch of the service." He instructed the president of one examining board that lieutenants were required to "understand" individual and company drill, "know how to read and write," and have a fair grasp of arithmetic. Captains should be "perfectly familiar" with company and battalion tactics and "reasonably proficient" in English. Field officers, besides having the attainments required of company officers, should be "conversant" with brigade tactics. "A fair knowledge of the U.S. Army Regulations should be required for all grades." Boards were also to consider evidence of "good moral character" such as the "standing in the community" of applicants from civil life. For those already in the service, officers' recommendations were necessary: "Each applicant shall be subjected to a fair but rigorous examination as to physical, mental, and moral fitness to command troops."[30]

The boards were far from equally rigorous. Irregularities were especially common among temporary and local boards. "In one instance, an officer . . . was examined and was recommended for Major," the commissioner organizing black regiments in Tennessee reported. "He was afterwards informed by the Board, that he would have passed for Colonel, had he been taller!" The commissioner did not think that the candidates approved by examiners in Tennessee were as good as those passed by the board in Washington.[31]

Whatever applicants' origins might be, their motives for joining the U.S. Colored Troops varied. Some college-educated New Englanders and Ohioans held abolitionist views, but contemporary public opinion about race guaranteed that opportunists would far outnumber abolitionists in the officer corps as a whole. After Adjutant General Thomas addressed a division of western troops, explaining the government's aim in organizing Colored Troops and encouraging officer applicants, one Illinois soldier was amused "to see men who have bitterly denounced the policy of arming negroes . . . now bending every energy to get a commission."[32]

Officers who reported for duty and helped to recruit and organize companies were not eligible for pay until the company was accepted for service and mustered in. Consequently, some new officers took a cautious approach toward assuming their duties. "Our Reg[imen]t is six miles below guarding cotton pickers," 2d Lt. Minos Miller wrote home from Helena, Arkansas, while the 54th USCI was organizing in the fall of 1863. "They send up an order ev[e]ry few days for . . . officers to report to the reg[imen]t but . . . let them that has Companies and has been mustered in do the duty is my motto. . . . When I am mustered then I will do duty." Miller anticipated a problem that would plague the Colored Troops, one that Congress did not resolve until the summer of 1866. During the last months of 1863, queries from unpaid officers constituted

[30] *OR*, ser. 3, 3: 215–16 ("Each applicant," p. 216); Maj C. W. Foster to Brig Gen J. B. Fry, 18 Jul 1864 ("as high"), and to Maj T. Duncan, 15 Mar 1864 (other quotations), both in Entry 352, RG 94, NA.

[31] Col R. D. Mussey to Col C. W. Foster, 8 Feb 1865, filed with (f/w) S–63–CT–1865, Entry 360, Colored Troops Div, LR, RG 94, NA.

[32] Mary A. Andersen, ed., *The Civil War Diary of Allen Morgan Geer, Twentieth Regiment, Illinois Volunteers* (Denver: R. C. Appleman, 1977), p. 89.

more than 60 percent of correspondence in the Colored Troops Division. One former officer of the 54th USCI was still trying to collect six months' back pay as late as 1884. Miller's reluctance to report for duty no doubt saved him a lot of paperwork, but it shifted to others the burden of recruiting and organizing the new regiment.[33]

In addition to administrative challenges, a new Colored Troops officer could be prey to conflicting emotions about his situation. An appointment in the 29th Connecticut instead of the 30th disappointed 1st Lt. Henry H. Brown because the senior regiment would complete its organization and head south first and he had hoped to have a long stay in his home state. When the 29th arrived at Beaufort, South Carolina, in April 1864, Brown told friends, "The move suits me better than any move I have made in the army . . . for . . . in jumping from [Maj. Gen. Ambrose E.] Burnside's command [we] have jumped I think a very hard peninsular campaign in Va." Still, Brown scanned newspaper casualty lists anxiously for the names of friends who were advancing on Richmond with Burnside's IX Corps. "Poor boys to have such hard times when I am taking so much comfort," he wrote.[34]

By the end of 1863, examining boards had interviewed 1,051 candidates and approved 560, enough to staff fully only sixteen infantry regiments. Maj. Gen. Silas Casey, the author of a book of infantry tactics and a former division commander in the Army of the Potomac, served as president of the Washington, D.C., examining board. Thomas Webster of Philadelphia was chairman of that city's Supervisory Committee for Recruiting Colored Regiments, which organized eleven all-black infantry regiments at nearby Camp William Penn during the war. Together, the two men conceived the idea of a free preparatory school for officer applicants, which the Supervisory Committee opened in Philadelphia in December 1863. The students included soldiers on special furlough, veterans whose enlistments had ended, members of the militia, and civilians with no military experience at all. They studied tactics, mathematics, and other subjects covered by the examining board. Parade-ground drill was not neglected, and the course included a practicum with the black recruits at Camp William Penn.[35]

Only thirty-day furloughs were available for soldiers to attend the school. This time limit meant that the student body was confined to civilians and men from the Army of the Potomac. Since Pennsylvania was the nation's second most populous state in 1860, it is not surprising that nearly 40 percent of the soldier-students came from Pennsylvania regiments, many of them organized

[33] M. Miller to Dear Mother, 15 Oct 1863 ("Our Reg[imen]t"), M. Miller Papers, University of Arkansas, Fayetteville; Public Resolution 68, 26 Jul 1866, published in AGO, GO 62, 11 Aug 66, Entry 44, Orders and Circulars, RG 94, NA; Entry 352, vol. 6, pp. 1–25, RG 94, NA; J. W. Stryker to Maj O. D. Greene, 25 Sep 1884, f/w S–11–CT–1863, Entry 360, RG 94, NA.

[34] H. H. Brown to Dear Mother, 22 Feb 1864; to Dear Friends at Home, 13 Apr 1864 ("The move"); to Dear Mother, 15 May 1864 ("Poor boys"); all in H. H. Brown Papers, Connecticut Historical Society, Hartford.

[35] Free Military School for Applicants for Command of Colored Troops, 2d ed. (Philadelphia: King and Baird, 1864), pp. 3, 7, 18–19. This edition of the school's brochure includes the names of graduates who had successfully passed the Washington board's examination, as well of those still enrolled on 31 March 1864.

in Philadelphia itself. The school's brochure boasted that ninety of its first ninety-four graduates passed the examining board, but according to the list of names, only seventy-three received appointments. Of the 205 names listed as still attending at the end of March 1864, fewer than half appear in the volume of the *Official Register of the Volunteer Force* that includes the Colored Troops. It would appear, therefore, that the graduates' rate of success was less than the school's brochure intimated. Most graduates' appointments were in one of the regiments formed at Camp William Penn or in one of the Kentucky regiments that began to form rapidly in 1864 as federal armies penetrated so far south that there was little need any longer for the Lincoln administration to placate the slaveholders of that state. Nearly all these regiments served in Virginia and the Carolinas. The school's influence, therefore, was mainly regional.[36]

In other parts of the country, appointment as an officer of Colored Troops came before—often, long before—a candidate's appearance before an examining board. While inspecting the 74th USCI in the fall of 1864, an officer in New Orleans commented on the regiment's adjutant, 1st Lt. Dexter F. Booth: "If he was examined by the Board, he certainly was not by the Surgeon." Booth's ill health was one of the factors that resulted in his dismissal. In the winter of 1865, an inspector warned the commanding officer of the 116th USCI, one of the new Kentucky regiments, that his company officers "must be compelled to see that the men are kept clean and made as comfortable as possible." An inspector in the Department of the South noted that the 104th and 128th USCIs, "which were enlisted near the close of the war, . . . became utterly worthless, owing to the inefficiency of most of the commissioned officers." In another instance, the 125th USCI, which was raised in Kentucky in the winter and spring of 1865, received orders early in 1866 to march to New Mexico for at least a year's stay. An examination of the regiment's officers resulted in four resignations and discharges, including that of the colonel. Running out of suitable officers, of course, was not a problem peculiar to the Civil War or to American armies.[37]

Proponents of the Colored Troops hoped that the selection process would assure a better type of officer than prevailed in the other volunteer regiments of the Union Army. Some observers believed that these hopes had been realized. Col. Randolph B. Marcy, a West Point graduate of 1832 and the Army's inspector general, thought that officers of the Colored Troops he saw in the lower

---

[36] *Free Military School*, pp. 9, 28–31, 33–43. Pennsylvania regiments' cities of origin are in Dyer, *Compendium*, pp. 214–28. Officers' names can be found in *ORVF*, vol. 8. Of the 204 names of Free Military School graduates, only 101 appear in *ORVF*, 8: 343–411, even making allowance for typographical errors and variant spellings like "Brown" and "Browne."

[37] Lt Col W. H. Thurston to Maj G. B. Drake, 29 Oct 1864 ("If he was"), 74th USCI, Entry 57C, RG 94, NA; Maj C. W. Foster to Maj Gen W. T. Sherman, 12 Apr 1866, Entry 352, RG 94, NA; Capt W. H. Abel to Brig Gen W. Birney, 6 Feb 1865 ("must be"), Entry 533, XXV Corps, Letters . . . Rcd by Divs, pt. 2, Polyonymous Successions of Cmds, RG 393, NA; Maj J. P. Roy to Maj Gen D. E. Sickles, 10 Nov 1866 ("which were"), Microfilm Pub M619, LR by the AGO, 1861–1870, roll 533, NA; *ORVF*, 8: 249, 255, 261, 306. Jeffrey J. Clarke and Robert R. Smith note the problem of U.S. Army infantry leadership late in the Second World War in *Riviera to the Rhine*, U.S. Army in World War II (Washington, D.C.: U.S. Army Center of Military History, 1993), pp. 570–73. David French, *Military Identities: The Regimental System, the British Army, and the British People, c. 1870–2000* (New York: Oxford University Press, 2005), p. 321, tells how the problem affected the British Army during the same period.

Mississippi Valley in 1865 were "generally . . . much better instructed in their duties than the officers of the white regiments that I have inspected." Marcy attributed their greater proficiency to the examining boards, "and although this has not uniformly been the case and many inefficient officers were at first appointed," he thought that most of those had been cleared out by the end of the war. "All that . . . is required to make efficient troops of negroes is that their officers should be carefully selected," he concluded.[38]

Despite the improvements that Marcy reported, problems with the Colored Troops officers persisted, partly because appointment so often came before examination. Sometimes, misconduct or inability became so apparent that authorities recommended the examination of all of a regiment's officers. In June 1865, a board convened in Arkansas "to examine into the capacity, qualifications, propriety of conduct and efficiency" of all officers of the 11th USCI. That same month, a board in New Orleans recommended that all but two of the officers in the 93d USCI be "summarily discharged" as "a disgrace to the service." Later that year, an inspector in Alabama recommended examinations for all officers of the 110th USCI. Meanwhile, state governors continued to meddle in the appointment process, demanding reasons for the dismissal of constituents. In one instance, Major Foster had to explain to the governor of Illinois that a "totally worthless" Capt. James R. Locke had been discharged from the 64th USCI for "utter incompetency."[39]

One problem especially prevalent in black regiments was fraud by officers. From the Ohio River to the Gulf Coast, officers schemed to separate men from their enlistment bonuses or their pay by promising to bank the money or invest it in government bonds. Brig. Gen. Ralph P. Buckland, whose command at Memphis included six black regiments, thought it worthwhile to issue an order forbidding the practice. Fraud seemed especially prevalent in the Kentucky regiments, which were among the last to be raised. Three lieutenants of the 114th USCI were detected before they could abscond with $1,700 of their men's money. Lt. Col. John Pierson of the 109th USCI received $2,200 in trust for soldiers when the regiment was first paid in September 1864. He resigned that December and was far beyond the reach of military justice when questions about the money arose as the regiment mustered out fifteen months later. The chief paymaster of the Department of the Gulf observed that the "conduct of these officers . . . seems to have become practice with certain officers of Colored Regiments whose terms of service are about to expire."[40]

Yet, despite a selection process that admitted many officers who then could be removed only by resignation or dismissal, the Colored Troops ran short of officers. In the spring of 1864, Major Foster in Washington was able to assure

---

[38]Col R. B. Marcy to Maj Gen E. D. Townsend, 16 May 1865 (M–352–CT–1865), Entry 360, RG 94, NA.

[39]Maj C. W. Foster to Maj. Gen. G. H. Thomas, 6 Jun 1865 ("to examine"); Col H. W. Fuller to Maj W. Hoffman, 19 Jun 1865 ("summarily discharged"); Maj E. Grosskopf to Major, 1 Nov 1865; Maj C. W. Foster to R. Yates, 13 Oct 1864 ("totally worthless"); all in Entry 352, RG 94, NA. James R. Locke had been chaplain of the 2d Illinois Cavalry before becoming a captain in the 64th USCI. *ORVF*, 6: 178.

[40]Dist Memphis, Special Orders (SO) 264, 30 Oct 1864, Entry 2844, Dist of Memphis, SO, pt. 2, RG 393, NA; Col T. D. Sedgwick to Adj Gen, 18 Feb 1867 (S–53–DG–1867), Entry 1756,

Adjutant General Thomas, who was still in the field west of the Appalachians, that "the supply" of men available for appointment as lieutenant was "at present greater than the demand."[41] Six months later, Foster reported that more than twenty new black regiments had gobbled up the surplus and that between fifteen and twenty new second lieutenants were required each week "to fill the vacancies occasioned by the promotion of senior officers."[42]

The inability to fill vacancies, added to the detachment of line officers to fill staff jobs, meant that many regiments had to function with only half their normal complement of officers. In July 1863, three companies of the 74th USCI manned Fort Pike, a moated brick fort overlooking Lake Pontchartrain in Louisiana. The garrison had only two officers for 255 enlisted men, and one of the two was described as "neither mentally or physically qualified to hold a commission." A few weeks later, the entire regiment reported having only seven officers for its ten companies. In September 1865, the 19th USCI had nine officers on detached service, with three of the regiment's captains commanding two companies each. A year later, the 114th USCI had only four captains for its ten companies.[43]

The consequent increase in officers' paperwork is easily documented in official and personal correspondence. "Much of the time which should be devoted to the men . . . is necessarily spent with the Books and Papers of the Company," the commanding officer of the 55th USCI reported from Corinth, Mississippi, in September 1863. Two years later, as the 102d USCI prepared to muster out and go home to Michigan, Capt. Wilbur Nelson and another officer spent seven days preparing the necessary paperwork. "It is a very tedious job," Nelson recorded in his diary. "I hope they will be right, so that we will not have to do them over again." Col. James C. Beecher of the 35th USCI, who came from a family famous for its literacy, told his fiancée that he would "rather fight a battle any day than make a Quarterly Ordnance Return."[44]

The deleterious effect on discipline of officers' absences is unclear but may be inferred from numerous civilian complaints of the troops' misbehavior. When a provost marshal in Huntersville, Arkansas, alleged that men of the 57th USCI had stolen seventy chickens, the regiment's commanding officer—a captain—admitted that "men from every Co. in the Regt. were engaged" in the

---

Dept of the Gulf, LR, pt. 1, RG 393, NA; Col O. A. Bartholomew to Col W. H. Sidell, 7 Mar 1866 (B–136–CT–1866), Entry 360, RG 94, NA. For similar instances, see HQ 12th USCA, GO 6, 22 Jan 1866, 12th USCA, Regimental Books; HQ 19th USCI, GO 19, 15 Nov 1865, 19th USCI, Regimental Books; both in RG 94, NA.

[41] Maj C. W. Foster to Brig Gen L. Thomas, 13 May, 8 Jun 1864, Entry 352, RG 94, NA.

[42] Maj C. W. Foster to W. A. Buckingham, 23 Nov 1864, and to T. Webster, 22 Nov 1864 (quotation), both in Entry 352, RG 94, NA.

[43] Capt P. B. S. Pinchback to Maj Gen N. P. Banks, 15 Jul 1863; Inspection Rpt, n.d., but reporting the same number of troops in garrison (quotation); Lt Col A. G. Hall, Endorsement, 4 Aug 1863, on Chaplain S. A. Hodgman to Maj Gen N. P. Banks, 5 Aug 1863; all in 74th USCI, Entry 57C, RG 94, NA. Col T. S. Sedgwick to Asst Adj Gen, Dept of Texas, 5 Oct 1866, 114th USCI, Entry 57C, RG 94, NA; 1st Div, XXV Corps, GO 60, 18 Sep 1865, Entry 533, pt. 2, RG 393, NA.

[44] Col J. M. Alexander to Lt Col J. H. Wilson, 11 Sep 1863, 55th USCI, Entry 57C, RG 94, NA; W. Nelson Diary, 17–24 Aug 1865, Michigan State University Archives, East Lansing; J. C. Beecher to My Beloved, 9 Apr 1864, J. C. Beecher Papers, Schlesinger Library, Harvard University, Cambridge, Mass.

theft but that he had just learned of it. "At the time, I was not on duty with my Co. or Regt.," he explained.[45]

Without officers attending to their needs through official channels, enlisted men were forced to take care of themselves, staving off scurvy, for instance, by pillaging vegetable gardens. Civilians across the occupied South, from South Carolina to Mississippi, complained of these raids. When it came to taking food, soldiers did not care whether the growers were white or black. Men of the 26th USCI were accused of taking "Corn, Watermelons, etc.," from black residents of Beaufort, South Carolina, those of the 108th USCI of robbing "colored men who are planting in the vicinity of Vicksburg." It is not surprising to see scurvy reported at remote posts in Texas, but to find it in the heart of Kentucky in the spring or Louisiana at harvest time is startling.[46]

Besides a tendency to "wander about the neighborhood" in search of food and firewood, the Colored Troops' discipline suffered from carelessness with firearms, both those that the government issued them and those that they carried for their own protection. The propensity of black soldiers to carry personal weapons is revealed in dozens of regimental orders forbidding the practice. The need for protection is plain from the historical record. When Emancipation caused black people to lose their cash value, their lives became worth nothing in the eyes of many Southern whites. Assaults and murders became every-day occurrences, especially as Confederate veterans returned from the war. A Union officer serving in South Carolina after the war observed: "My impression is that most of the murders of the negroes in the South are committed by the poor-whites, who . . . could not shoot slaves in the good old times without coming in conflict with the slave owner and getting the worst of it." Black people in the North were well acquainted with antagonism—the New York Draft Riot was only an extreme instance—and many of them carried weapons to discourage assailants. In garrison at Jeffersonville, Indiana, men of the 123d USCI were "daily subject to abuse and violent treatment from white soldiers" and civilians. When the men armed themselves, their officers confiscated the weapons. Black Southerners, as soon as they were able to, also began to carry concealed weapons. At Natchez, men of the 6th U.S. Colored Artillery owned enough pistols by 1864 to inspire a ban and confiscation.[47]

Regimental orders issued in all parts of the South attest to the prevalence of un-authorized weapons. Just as disturbing for discipline was the troops' mishandling of their Army-issue firearms. "The men must be cautioned repeatedly," the adjutant of

---

[45] Capt P. J. Harrington to Col W. D. Green, 4 Aug 1864, 57th USCI, Entry 57C, RG 94, NA.

[46] Capt S. M. Taylor to Commanding Officer (CO), 26th USCI, 20 Aug 1864, 26th USCI; HQ 12th USCA, Circular, 4 May 1865, 12th USCA; 1st Lt C. S. Sargent to CO, 65th USCI, 17 Oct 1864, 65th USCI; A. F. Cook to CO, 108th USCI, 30 Aug 1865, 108th USCI; all in Entry 57C, RG 94, NA. 1st Div, XXV Corps, GO 60, 18 Sep 1865, Entry 533, pt. 2, RG 393, NA.

[47] HQ 75th USCI, GO 8, 6 Mar 1864 ("wander about"), 75th USCI, Entry 57C; Capt D. Bailey to Maj J. H. Cole, 1 Jul 1865 ("daily subject"), 123d USCI, Entry 57C; Capt G. H. Travis to CO, 123d USCI, 14 Aug 1865, 123d USCI, Entry 57C; HQ [6th USCA], GO 6, 28 Jan 1864, 6th USCA, Regimental Books; all in RG 94, NA. Brackets in a citation mean that the order was issued under the regiment's earlier state designation, in this case the 2d Mississippi Artillery (African Descent [AD]). John W. DeForest, *A Union Officer in the Reconstruction* (New Haven: Yale University Press, 1948), pp. 153–54 ("My impression"). Ira Berlin et al., eds., *The Black Military*

the 107th USCI warned officers, "against the habit of snapping the hammers of Guns against the Cones [on which the percussion cap was placed]; which oftentimes renders the arm unserviceable." Carelessness could also take the more dangerous form of playing with a capped and loaded weapon or indiscriminate firing in camp at night. "Too much attention cannot be paid by the men in handling their arms," the commanding officer of the 59th USCI wrote when his regiment mustered in. "So much unnecessary suffering has been caused by the careless manner in which so many soldiers have heretofore handled their arms." While the 60th USCI was organizing in St. Louis, Pvt. Jasper Harris shot and killed Pvt. Peter Gray as "they were playing with their guns knowing they were loaded." Of course, black soldiers of that era were not alone in their disregard of precautions, which was widespread in American society. The author of one antebellum travelers' guidebook warned readers that careless handling of firearms was a major cause of deaths in wagon trains headed west.[48]

A further disability that afflicted the U.S. Colored Troops had its origin in the history and geography of the war itself. By the time organization of the Colored Troops got under way, the North had begun to sort out its winning and losing generals, and these categories became sharper as the war went on. Less competent commanders tended to become sidetracked away from the major theaters of operations; some finished their military careers in parts of the South where many black regiments were raised and also served. Nathaniel P. Banks, a former governor of Massachusetts who was one of the first three major generals of volunteers Lincoln appointed in 1861, became the subject of doggerel verse after his defeat in Virginia by the Confederate Maj. Gen. Thomas J. Jackson in 1862. Late that year, Banks went to Louisiana to command the Department of the Gulf, which furnished the Union Army with nearly three dozen regiments of U.S. Colored Troops. Some of these regiments took part in the disastrous Red River Campaign of 1864 and in Banks' other failures. A soldier on one of Banks' Texas expeditions in 1864 parodied William Cowper's hymn: "Banks moves in a mysterious way, / His blunders to perform."[49]

Brig. Gen. Truman Seymour, an 1846 graduate of West Point, was another Union general whose incompetence caused repeated failures. He commanded the disastrous assault on Fort Wagner, South Carolina, in July 1863, when the

---

Experience (New York: Cambridge University Press, 1982), pp. 799–810, reprints firsthand accounts of assaults on black Union veterans and their families in Georgia, Kentucky, Maryland, North Carolina, and Virginia.

[48] HQ 107th USCI, Regimental Orders 1, 1 Jan 1865 ("The men"), 107th USCI, Regimental Books, RG 94, NA; HQ 12th USCA, Circular, 27 Jan 1865, 12th USCA, Regimental Books, RG 94, NA (Bowling Green, Ky.); HQ 2d USCI, GO 10, 20 Aug 1863, 2d USCI, Regimental Books, RG 94, NA (Alexandria, Va.); HQ 14th USCI, GO 11, 19 Mar 1865, 14th USCI, Regimental Books, RG 94, NA (Chattanooga, Tenn.). 3d Div, VII Corps, Circular, 5 Apr 1865, 57th USCI, Entry 57C, RG 94, NA (Fort Smith, Ark.), and Post Orders 88, Corinth, Miss., 9 Nov 1863, and HQ Dept of the Tenn, GO 17, 19 Sep 1865, both in 59th USCI, Regimental Books, RG 94, NA, show that the problem was wide ranging and recurring. HQ [59th USCI], SO 10, 28 June 1863 ("Too much"), 59th USCI, Regimental Books, RG 94, NA. Similar orders from Virginia and Mississippi are HQ 2d USCI, GO 5, 31 Jul 1863, 2d USCI, Regimental Books, and HQ [6th USCA], GO 4, 3 Dec 1863, 6th USCA, Regimental Books, both in RG 94, NA. 1st Lt G. H. Brock to 1st Lt W. H. Adams, 5 Nov 1863 ("they were"), 60th USCI, Entry 57C, RG 94, NA; John D. Unruh Jr., *The Plains Across: The Overland Emigrants and the Trans-Mississippi West, 1840–1860* (Urbana: University of Illinois, 1979), pp. 410–13, 517.

[49] Stephen A. Townsend, *The Yankee Invasion of Texas* (College Station: Texas A&M University Press, 2006), p. 18.

54th Massachusetts came under fire for the first time. Seven months later in northern Florida, none of Seymour's superiors or subordinates was sure why he pushed his force so far forward, resulting in the defeat at Olustee in February 1864. This time, his troops included three black regiments, the 8th and 35th USCIs, as well as the 54th Massachusetts. He was relieved from command and sent to Virginia, where he fell into Confederate hands during the spring offensive there. "They are welcome to him," wrote Capt. John W. M. Appleton of the 54th Massachusetts when news of Seymour's capture reached him. "Incompetence, rashness and imbecility" were the traits Appleton saw in Seymour.[50]

A letter that Maj. Gen. Henry W. Halleck sent to Lt. Gen. Ulysses S. Grant in April 1864, when the two were considering possible commanders for the Department of the South and the Union garrison at Memphis, exemplifies the difficulty of finding suitable generals. "To defend [the Sea Islands] properly we want a general there of experience and military education," Halleck wrote:

> My own opinion of [Maj. Gen. Stephen A.] Hurlbut has been favorable, but I do not deem him equal to the command of the Department of the South. . . . [Brig. Gen. John P.] Hatch is hardly the man for the place, but probably he is the best that can now be spared from the field. . . . I think [Maj. Gen. David] Hunter . . . is even worse than [Maj. Gen. John A.] McClernand in creating difficulties. If you had him in the field under your immediate command perhaps things would go smoothly. Before acting on General Hunter's case it would be well for you to see his correspondence while in command of a department.

Hurlbut was an Illinois politician who commanded the garrison of Memphis, which included many locally recruited black soldiers; General Sherman was unwilling to have him as a subordinate in the field. Hatch was a professional soldier who had commanded a division in the Army of the Potomac and who, at the time Halleck wrote, was commanding the District of Florida in the Department of the South. Hunter was a lifelong soldier who had already commanded the Department of the South twice and been relieved twice; his unauthorized enlistment of black South Carolinians in 1862 had embarrassed the Lincoln administration. McClernand was another political general from Illinois whose penchant for lying and boasting had led Grant to relieve him during the Vicksburg Campaign. Such were the senior officers available to command the geographical departments and districts where many black soldiers served. Problems of administration, personnel, and national politics exacerbated the trials the new black regiments faced.[51]

Despite these difficulties, the U.S. Colored Troops managed to field more than 101,000 officers and enlisted men on average during the spring of 1865— nearly 15 percent of the Union's total land force as the fighting drew to a close. Far from performing only garrison duty, as the president and Congress first imagined they would, black soldiers' service included every kind of operation that Union armies undertook during the war: offensive and defensive battles,

---

[50] *OR*, ser. 1, vol. 35, pt. 1, pp. 277, 285–86, 290–91; J. W. M. Appleton Jnl photocopy, pp. 175, 225, MHI.
[51] *OR*, ser. 1, vol. 35, pt. 2, pp. 46, 48 ("To defend").

sieges, riverine and coastal expeditions, and cavalry raids. The fluid nature of the war that both sides conducted and the vast and varied country that they fought over guaranteed something more active than garrison duty.[52]

---

[52]Mean strength calculated from figures in *Medical and Surgical History of the War of the Rebellion*, 2 vols. in 6 (Washington, D.C.: Government Printing Office, 1870), vol. 1, pt. 1, pp. 605, 685.

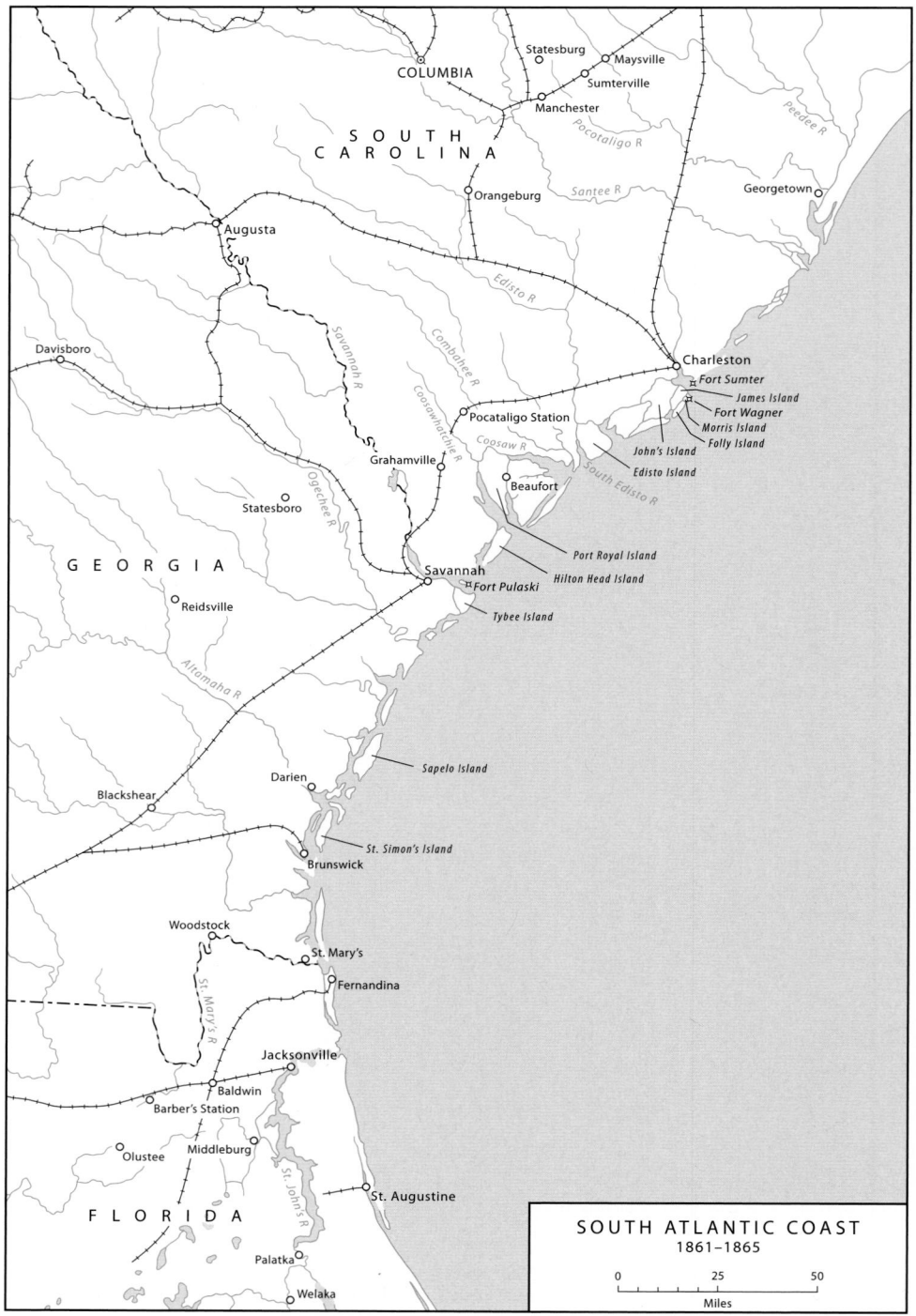

SOUTH ATLANTIC COAST
1861–1865

0   25   50
Miles

Map 1

CHAPTER 2

THE SOUTH ATLANTIC COAST 1861–1863

Enforcement of a naval blockade was a mainstay of Lt. Gen. Winfield Scott's plan for subduing the Confederacy. Since the seceded states were almost entirely rural and agricultural, it was necessary to prevent them from selling their products—chiefly cotton—to foreign buyers in exchange for the manufactured goods necessary to field Southern armies. Therefore, the North's first carefully planned offensive movement of the war was the occupation of a Southern beachhead to sustain the U.S. Navy's blockading fleet. Vessels cruising off the coast of Florida, Georgia, and the Carolinas needed a depot for food, fresh water, and naval stores and a dockyard for repairs. After considering half a dozen landing sites, Union strategists settled on Port Royal Sound in South Carolina. One of the finest harbors on the Atlantic seaboard, it lay between the ports of Charleston and Savannah. Coincidentally, the planners had settled on a region that was home to one of the South's highest concentrations of black people. More than 33,000 black residents—32,530 of them slaves—constituted 83 percent of the population on the sound and along the small rivers that emptied into it (*see Map 1*).[1]

Coastal South Carolina was plantation country. Around Port Royal, the cash crop was Sea Island cotton, the long, silky fiber of which was even more valuable than the short-fiber variety grown inland. The region's population consisted of a tiny minority of white planters and an enormous majority of slaves. The slaves' numerical predominance and the absence of their owners during the unhealthy coastal summers allowed them some measure of independence. The "task system" under which they tended Sea Island cotton left them more time at the end of the day than the sunup-to-sundown "gang system" practiced on the vast plantations on which cotton grew throughout most of the South. After completing their daily assigned tasks, slaves in coastal South

---

[1] Robert M. Browning Jr., *Success Is All That Was Expected: The South Atlantic Blockading Squadron During the Civil War* (Washington, D.C.: Brassey's, 2002), pp. 7–17; U.S. Census Bureau, *Population of the United States in 1860* (Washington, D.C.: Government Printing Office, 1864), p. 452. The Blockade Strategy Board's report on three South Carolina harbors is in *The War of the Rebellion: A Compilation of the Official Records of the Union and Confederate Armies*, 70 vols. in 128 (Washington, D.C.: Government Printing Office, 1880–1901), ser. 1, 53: 67–73 (hereafter cited as *OR*).

Carolina were able to raise their own garden crops and poultry and often sold the products of their labor.[2]

Outnumbered by their slaves, South Carolina planters had lived for generations in fear of bloody revolt. In 1739, the Stono Rebellion may have involved as many as one hundred slaves. Denmark Vesey's 1822 conspiracy in Charleston had occurred within living memory. More than a generation later, when the Union fleet bombarded Confederate shore defenses on 7 November 1861, whites on the South Carolina Sea Islands seized what movable belongings they could and sailed, steamed, or rowed for the mainland, fearing for their lives more than for their property. As federal troops went ashore the next day, they found the islands' black residents in possession of the town of Beaufort and the surrounding country. Planters' houses had been looted and, on some plantations, cotton gins smashed. Former slaves wanted nothing more to do with the cotton crop that they had just finished picking. They intended to devote their energies to growing food instead.[3]

Union authorities saw the future differently. Cotton would help to pay for the war and at the same time turn slaves into wage workers. Northern manufacturers wanted to assure a steady supply of cotton, and their employees feared that a northward migration of newly freed Southern blacks would depress wages. The landing in the Sea Islands thus had support from important sections of the Northern public, besides representing one of the first Union victories of the war.[4]

The Department of the Treasury assumed responsibility for enemy property—real estate and cotton, around Port Royal Sound—and Treasury agents soon swarmed on Hilton Head and other islands. Leading them was Lt. Col. William H. Reynolds, who had been a Rhode Island textile manufacturer before the war. His state's governor had introduced him to Secretary of the Treasury Salmon P. Chase (the governor's future father-in-law), who appointed Reynolds to head the agency's cotton gatherers. Also active in the Sea Islands was William H. Nobles. Although Nobles had resigned his commission as lieutenant colonel of the 79th New York Infantry, other Northern administrators still addressed him by his old rank. Reynolds, Nobles, and their assistants moved at once to seize goods, including wagons and draft animals, that might contribute to federal revenues. Their avidity riled Brig. Gen. Isaac I. Stevens, commanding the District of Port Royal, who allowed the Treasury agents a free hand in collecting cotton while warning them not to touch "such quartermaster and commissary stores as my parties may take possession of."[5]

To superintend the Sea Islands' black residents, Chase named the Massachusetts abolitionist lawyer Edward L. Pierce, who already had several months of experience working with Maj. Gen. Benjamin F. Butler's original "contrabands" at Fort Mon-

---

[2] Ira Berlin, *Generations of Captivity: A History of African-American Slaves* (Cambridge: Harvard University Press, 2003), pp. 177–78.

[3] *OR*, ser. 1, 6: 6; William Dusinberre, *Them Dark Days: Slavery in the American Rice Swamps* (New York: Oxford University Press, 1996), p. 389; Eugene D. Genovese, *Roll, Jordan, Roll: The World the Slaves Made* (New York: Pantheon Books, 1974), pp. 588–97; Willie Lee Rose, *Rehearsal for Reconstruction: The Port Royal Experiment* (Indianapolis: Bobbs-Merrill, 1964), pp. 16, 104–07.

[4] John Niven, *Salmon P. Chase: A Biography* (New York: Oxford University Press, 1995), pp. 323–25.

[5] *OR*, ser. 1, 6: 200–201 (quotation, p. 201); Rose, *Rehearsal for Reconstruction*, p. 19; Ira Berlin et al., eds., *The Wartime Genesis of Free Labor: The Lower South* (New York: Cambridge

SCENE IN THE MILITARY MARKET AT BEAUFORT, S. C.
FROM A SKETCH BY W. T. CRANE.

This scene at a market in Beaufort, South Carolina, shows the makeup of the Sea Islands population in 1862—black residents in civilian clothing, white men in uniform. Local slaveholders had fled the approaching Yankee invaders the previous fall.

roe, Virginia. Pierce surveyed the islands' remaining population and reported to the Treasury secretary "what could be done," as he put it, "to reorganize the laborers, prepare them to become sober and self-supporting citizens, and secure the success-ful culture of a cotton crop, now so necessary to be contributed to the markets of the world." Pierce was as much concerned with the home lives of the former slaves as he was with their ability to grow cotton. "They [should] attend more to the cleanliness of their persons and houses, and . . . , as in families of white people, . . . take their meals together at table—habits to which they will be more disposed when they are provided with another change of clothing, and when better food is furnished and a proper hour assigned for meals." Pierce also noted approvingly that "I have heard among the negroes scarcely any profane swearing—not more than twice—a striking contrast with my experience among soldiers in the army."[6]

Reynolds' and Nobles' single-minded intent to gather cotton soon brought the two men and their subordinates into conflict with the benevolent authoritarian Pierce and the band of philanthropic New Englanders, dubbed Gideonites, whom he had recruited to oversee, educate, and improve the freedpeople. The attitudes

---

University Press, 1990), p. 90 (hereafter cited as *WGFL: LS*). *Official Army Register of the Volunteer Force of the United States Army*, 8 vols. (Washington, D.C.: Adjutant General's Office, 1867), 1: 246 (Reynolds), 2: 551 (Nobles) (hereafter cited as *ORVF*).

[6]*WGFL: LS*, pp. 141 ("what could be"), 128 ("They [should]"), 131 ("I have heard").

and methods of the Gideonites were at odds with those of the overbearing cotton agents, and the two groups soon came into conflict. On one occasion, Nobles punched Pierce "and knocking me down, continued to beat me," Pierce told Secretary Chase. Resignations by Pierce and Reynolds in the spring of 1862 removed conflicting personalities, but this contest between two appointed agents of the Treasury Department portended the troubles the Army would soon have as recruiters for the U.S. Colored Troops vied with Army staff officers for the South's limited supply of black manpower. That summer, the Army's commissary of subsistence at Hilton Head had to request authority to raise the wages of the Sea Islanders in his workforce by 50 percent, from eight dollars a month to twelve. This was necessary, he wrote, because some of his most able hands had already left for other, better-paying jobs.[7]

Superintendent Pierce left South Carolina, but the Gideonites remained. Due partly to their inexperienced planning and supervision, the next cotton crop failed, yielding less than 25 percent of that produced the previous year. The Sea Islands' black residents, about eight thousand in all, came to rely more and more on employment with Northern occupiers, military and naval, or on handouts from the Army. Meanwhile, at least as great a number of escaped slaves from the mainland thronged the contraband camps on the islands. The Army's commissary of subsistence at Beaufort soon complained that he was unable to keep up with the work of feeding indigent civilians.[8]

Unlike the Gideonites, Northern soldiers had not come south to free slaves but to crush secession. During the war's first year, the means toward this end included reassurances aimed at white residents to encourage their cooperation. When Union troops landed at Hilton Head in November 1861, Brig. Gen. Thomas W. Sherman, joint commander of the expedition, issued a proclamation addressed "To the People of South Carolina" in which he disavowed any intention to "interfere with . . . social and local institutions." Sherman's orders from the War Department allowed him to employ "the services of any persons, whether fugitives from labor or not," but he did not concern himself much with fugitive slaves, other than to find fault with them.[9]

After a month ashore, Sherman wrote to Quartermaster General Montgomery C. Meigs:

> Thus far the negroes have rendered us but little assistance. Many come in and run off. They have not yet been organized to the extent we desire. The large families they bring with them make a great many useless mouths. Before long— after they have consumed all they have on the plantations—they will come in

---

[7]Capt G. Scull to Capt M. R. Morgan, 25 Jun 1862, Entry 4109, Dept of the South, Letters Received (LR), pt. 1, Geographical Divs and Depts, Record Group (RG) 393, Rcds of U.S. Army Continental Cmds, National Archives (NA); John Niven et al., eds., *The Salmon P. Chase Papers*, 5 vols. (Kent, Ohio: Kent State University Press, 1993–1998), 3: 188 ("and knocking") (hereafter cited as *Chase Papers*); Rose, *Rehearsal for Reconstruction,* pp. 24–25, 67–69; *WGFL: LS*, pp. 92–96.

[8]Capt L. A. Warfield to Capt L. J. Lambert, 26 Jul 1862, Entry 4109, pt. 1, RG 393, NA; Niven, *Salmon P. Chase: A Biography*, p. 326; Rose, *Rehearsal for Reconstruction*, pp. 69–70, 128, 204–05, 302; *WGFL: LS*, pp. 88–89.

[9]*OR*, ser. 1, 6: 5, 176.

greater numbers, and no doubt will give us many laborers; but where we get one good, able-bodied man, we have five or six women and children. They are a most prolific race.

Here Sherman broached two topics that would vex Southern black people and Union administrators, military and civil, for the duration of the war and long into the peace that followed: organization of the black workforce, which involved difficult economic and political choices, and the welfare of black families.[10]

A few days later, Sherman wrote to Adjutant General Lorenzo Thomas in an even more pessimistic vein. "The negro labor expected to be obtained here is so far almost a failure," he complained. "They are disinclined to labor, and will evidently not work to our satisfaction without those aids to which they have ever been accustomed, viz., the driver and the lash. A sudden change of condition from servitude to apparent freedom is more than their intellects can stand, and this circumstance alone renders it a very serious question what is to be done with the negroes who will hereafter be found on conquered soil." The next day, for "the information of the proper authorities," Sherman sent Thomas a note with some statistics: three hundred twenty former slaves had come within the Union lines; of these, only sixty were "able-bodied male hands, the rest being decrepit, and women and children." He then repeated his remarks about laziness and "the lash; an aid we do not make use of." A West Point graduate of 1836, Sherman had been an officer for twenty-five years before Congress banned flogging in the Army during the first summer of the war.[11]

Whatever their usefulness as laborers, Sea Island residents at once became an important source of military intelligence. "From what I can gather from negroes," the expedition's chief engineer wrote on the day of the landing, "there are no rebel troops on any of the northern portions of Hilton Head Island." Most of the former slaves viewed the invaders with caution, if not outright suspicion. Their absconding masters had told them that the Yankees would turn a dollar by kidnapping them and selling them in Cuba. Nevertheless, within a month of the troops' landing, black Sea Islanders were coming forward to volunteer information. Some of it was mere hearsay about troop movements, but some was expert advice about the country in which the soldiers would live and fight.[12]

Capt. Quincy A. Gillmore, the chief engineer, became acquainted with a recent arrival named Brutus, "the most intelligent slave I have met here, . . . quite familiar with the rivers & creeks, between Savannah city and Tybee Island. He made his escape . . . last week in a canoe." Brutus told Gillmore that boats drawing ten feet or less could pass at high tide from one part of the Savannah estuary to another, avoiding Confederate guns that commanded a narrow stretch of river. "I place great reliance on Brutus' statement," Gillmore told General Sherman, "for everything he said of Big Tybee inlet was verified with

---

[10] Ibid., p. 202.

[11] Ibid., pp. 204–05; ser. 3, 1: 401.

[12] *OR*, ser. 1, 6: 31 ("From what"), 240; Maj O. T. Beard to Brig Gen T. W. Sherman, 20 Nov 1861; Capt Q. A. Gillmore to Brig Gen T. W. Sherman, 7 Jan 1862; both in Entry 2254, South Carolina Expeditionary Corps, LR, pt. 2, Polyonymous Successions of Cmds, RG 393, NA.

remarkable accuracy by my examination. What he says is moreover confirmed by other slaves at Tybee Island."[13]

Fortunately, both for the Union position in the Sea Islands and for black residents of the islands, Sherman had an able assistant in the expedition's chief quartermaster, Capt. Rufus Saxton. The captain soon had black men organized into work gangs unloading supplies and building fortifications. A West Point graduate of 1849, Saxton persevered with his quartermaster duties until April 1862, when a promotion to brigadier general of U.S. Volunteers placed him in charge of all abandoned plantations in the department and their residents. Secretary of War Edwin M. Stanton directed him to issue rations and clothing to the indigent while "encouraging industry . . . and general self-improvement." A military emergency took Saxton north to command the defense of Harpers Ferry during Stonewall Jackson's Valley Campaign, but he returned to the islands in June. Again, he received orders direct from Stanton "to take such measures . . . for the cultivation of the land, and for protection, employment, and government of the inhabitants as circumstances may seem to require." Saxton was to assume many of the functions earlier exercised by Pierce and Reynolds. Men and materiel to back this project would come from Brig. Gen. David Hunter, the commander who succeeded General Sherman. Hunter was a West Pointer of the generation before Saxton's but a man much more in sympathy with the freedpeople than Sherman had been.[14]

Sherman was no abolitionist, but his successor most emphatically was. In March 1862, Hunter took command of the newly created Department of the South, which included, on paper, all of South Carolina, Georgia, and Florida, although federal troops controlled only tiny beachheads. Adjutant General Thomas told him to abide by the instructions Sherman had received for dealing with "contrabands, or persons heretofore held to involuntary servitude by rebel masters," but he allowed Hunter "large discretion . . . for the purpose of vigorously prosecuting the war to a successful result."[15]

Congress had recently enacted a new Article of War that barred federal troops from returning escaped slaves to their former masters, and Hunter saw in it a chance to smite the Slave Power. To that end, in early April he asked Secretary of War Stanton for "50,000 muskets . . . to arm such loyal men as I can find in the country"—clearly meaning former slaves, who were the only "loyal" South Carolinians within Union lines. Hunter wanted a distinctive uniform for them, too; "scarlet pantaloons," he thought, would be right. When the War Department failed to act, he seized the initiative. In the second week of April, he freed the slaves near Fort Pulaski, Georgia, with the intention of putting the able-bodied men to work for the quartermaster. Early in May, he declared free

[13] Capt Q. A. Gillmore to Brig Gen T. W. Sherman, 30 Dec 1861, Entry 2254, pt. 2, RG 393, NA.

[14] *OR*, ser. 1, 6: 186–87; ser. 3, 2: 28 ("encouraging"), 152–53 ("to take"). *WGFL: LS*, p. 88.

[15] Brig Gen L. Thomas to Maj Gen D. Hunter, 15 Mar 1862 ("contrabands"), Entry 159GG, Generals' Papers and Books (Hunter), RG 94, NA.

all slaves in the Department of the South, but the President quickly overruled this decision.[16]

On the same day that Hunter issued his department-wide emancipation proclamation, he clarified his recruitment policy and reasserted his determination to bring former slaves into the Union service. He ordered the impressment of "all the able-bodied negroes capable of bearing arms" in the department. Attempts to enforce the order brought the Army into sharp conflict with Treasury Department agents in charge of abandoned plantations who objected to disruption of their workforce, as well as with former slaves who objected to the unexpected and unwelcome draft. The conflict between recruiters trying to organize regiments; Army quartermasters, engineers, and other officers of support services who required labor; and civilians in charge of the plantations and contraband camps that housed the dependents of black soldiers recruited in the South was a constant source of friction between administrators and a hindrance to the Union war effort.[17]

Despite the president's reversal of Hunter's emancipation pronouncements, the department commander was operating only slightly in advance of federal policy. The First Confiscation Act, which Congress passed in August 1861, allowed federal officers to receive escaped slaves who reached Union lines and to put them to work while keeping careful records against the day when peace was restored and loyal masters might claim compensation for their slaves' labor. In March 1862, Congress settled the question of soldiers' assisting slaveholders to recover escaped slaves by adopting an article of war that forbade the practice.[18]

By the time of Hunter's attempts at emancipation, Congress had been debating for months the terms of another and far more sweeping confiscation act. Signed into law on 17 July 1862, the Second Confiscation Act prescribed death or imprisonment for "every person who shall hereafter commit the crime of treason against the United States . . . and all his slaves, if any, shall be declared and made free." The act further declared that any slaves who escaped to Union lines or were captured by advancing federal armies "shall be forever free of their servitude, and not again held as slaves." Moreover, the president might "employ as many persons of African descent as he may deem necessary for the suppression of this rebellion, and for this purpose he may organize and use them in such manner as he may judge best for the public welfare." The way lay open at last for the enlistment of black soldiers.[19]

The Second Confiscation Act came too late to save General Hunter's black regiment. In May 1862, soon after Hunter issued his order to recruit "able-bodied negroes," soldiers began to round them up, "marching through the islands

---

[16]*OR*, ser. 1, 6: 248, 263, 264 ("50,000 muskets"); 14: 333, 341; ser. 3, 2: 42–43. Edward A. Miller Jr., *Lincoln's Abolitionist General: The Biography of David Hunter* (Columbia: University of South Carolina Press, 1997), pp. 44–49.

[17]*OR*, ser. 1, 6: 258; ser. 3, 2: 31 (quotation).

[18]*OR*, ser. 2, 1: 761–62. The Articles of War, numbering 101 before the addition of the fugitive-slave article, formed the code of regulations that governed the military justice system. *OR*, ser. 2, 1: 810.

[19]*OR*, ser. 3, 2: 275–76.

during the night," as Superintendent Pierce reported to Secretary Chase. The shrewder black residents hid in the woods. Others "were taken from the fields without being allowed to go to their houses even to get a jacket. . . . On some plantations the wailing and screaming were loud and the women threw themselves in despair on the ground. . . . The soldiers, it is due to them to say, . . . conducted themselves with as little harshness as could be expected." Northern civilians, both plantation superintendents and teachers, thought that Hunter's abrupt military action impeded their efforts to win the confidence of black Sea Islanders.[20]

The men of the 1st South Carolina Infantry, as Hunter's regiment was called, performed fatigues, mostly unloading cargo and preparing fortifications, under the direction of locally appointed officers. Former enlisted men themselves, the regiment's officers "were subjected to all kinds of annoyances and insult from Non-Com Off[icer]s and Privates of the White Regiments & some of them getting quite disheartened at the continual persecution . . . waited on General Hunter . . . and asked permission to go back to their Regiments." The general assured them that he would put a stop to the abuse and that all would be well.[21]

Meanwhile, word of Hunter's activities had reached Washington. Eleven months earlier, Representative Charles A. Wickliffe of Kentucky had asked whether the Confederates used black troops at Bull Run. In June 1862, he addressed the question of black men in arms by demanding that the secretary of war tell Congress whether Hunter was organizing a regiment of "fugitive slaves." With a sarcasm intended for public consumption, Hunter told Stanton:

> No regiment of "fugitive slaves" has been or is being organized in this department. There is however a fine regiment of persons whose late masters are "fugitive rebels"—men who everywhere fly before the appearance of the national flag, leaving their servants behind them to shift as best they can for themselves. So far indeed are the loyal persons composing this regiment from seeking to avoid the presence of their late owners that they are now one and all working with remarkable industry to place themselves in a position to go in full and effective pursuit of their fugacious and traitorous proprietors.[22]

One New England officer at Beaufort thought that Hunter's retort was "the best thing that has been written since the war commenced." The mood of most soldiers in the department was far different. "General Hunter is so carried away by his idea of negro regiments as . . . to write flippant letters . . . to Secretary Stanton," another New England officer wrote late in July. "The negroes should be organized and officered as soldiers; they should have arms put in their hands and be drilled simply with a view to their moral elevation and the effect on their self-respect, and for the rest they

---

[20]Ibid., p. 57 ("marching through"); Elizabeth W. Pearson, ed., *Letters from Port Royal, 1862–1868* (New York: Arno Press, 1969 [1906]), p. 39.

[21]Cpl T. K. Durham to Maj W. P. Prentice, 27 Sep 1862, 33d United States Colored Infantry (USCI), Entry 57C, Regimental Papers, RG 94, NA. Durham had been adjutant of the 1st South Carolina and was writing to protest the lack of commissions and pay for nearly three months' service.

[22]*OR*, ser. 2, 1: 821.

Members of Company A, 1st South Carolina, take the oath at Beaufort, South Carolina, late in 1862.

should be *used* as fatigue parties and on all fatigue duty." On 9 August 1862, having been unable to pay the men or issue commissions to the officers, Hunter disbanded the regiment. He then went north on leave. Maj. Gen. Ormsby M. Mitchel arrived in September to take command of the Department of the South and its troops.[23]

One company of the 1st South Carolina had managed to escape disbanding. The recently promoted Brig. Gen. Rufus Saxton, the military superintendent of plantations, had dispatched Capt. Charles T. Trowbridge's Company A to St. Simon's Island, Georgia. Saxton was worried about raids from the mainland on all the Sea Islands, but especially St. Simon's, with its four hundred self-sustaining and armed black residents. These had recently driven off a party of rebel marauders, Saxton told Secretary of War Stanton. A Confederate general had urged that the defenders of St. Simon's, if captured, "should be hanged as soon as possible at some public place as an example," as though he were suppressing a slave rebellion. Saxton requested authority to enroll five thousand quartermaster's laborers "to be uniformed, armed, and officered by men detailed from the Army." When permission arrived, he set to work at once.[24]

The problem, as Saxton saw it, was that the number of potential recruits on the islands was limited. "In anticipation of our action," he told Stanton in mid-October, "the rebels are moving all their slaves back from the sea-coast as fast as they can." In response, federal troops would reach the slaves by raiding up the region's numerous rivers. These raids would constitute an important part of military

[23] *OR*, ser. 1, 14: 376, 382; A. H. Young to My Dear Susan, 12 Jul 1862 ("the best"), A. H. Young Papers, Dartmouth College, Hanover, N.H.; Dudley T. Cornish, *The Sable Arm: Negro Troops in the Union Army, 1861–1865* (New York: Longmans, Green, 1956), pp. 48–49 ("General Hunter"). Joel Williamson, *After Slavery: The Negro in South Carolina During Reconstruction, 1861–1877* (Chapel Hill: University of North Carolina Press, 1965), pp. 13–15, tells the story of Hunter's early efforts to recruit black troops.
[24] *OR*, ser. 1, 6: 77–78 ("should be hanged"), 81; 14: 374–76 ("to be uniformed").

operations in the Department of the South during the next two years. They would provide the Union Army with new black recruits while depriving the Confederacy of labor, military supplies, and marketable commodities.[25]

In recruiting, Saxton had to compete for men with Army quartermasters and engineers, the Navy, and private employers. The work went slowly. Meanwhile, he dispatched Company A of the 1st South Carolina on the first raid. Starting from St. Simon's on 3 November, sixty-two men and three officers aboard the steamer *Darlington* traveled forty miles south to St. Mary's, Georgia, where they destroyed a salt-works and removed two slave families. During the next four days, they carried out three more raids north of St. Simon's, meeting the enemy and holding their ground each time while losing four men wounded. They destroyed eight more saltworks, burned buildings, and carried off stores of corn and rice. Lt. Col. Oliver T. Beard, the expedition's leader, estimated the damage at twenty thousand dollars. "I started . . . with 62 colored fighting men and returned . . . with 156," Beard reported. "As soon as we took a slave . . . we placed a musket in his hand and he began to fight for the freedom of others." Besides the additional recruits, the raids freed sixty-one women and children. "Rarely in the progress of this war," Saxton exulted, "has so much mis-chief been done by so small a force in so short a space of time."[26]

His first objective in ordering the raid, Saxton admitted, was "to prove the fighting qualities of the negroes (which some have doubted)." Having done this to his own satis-faction, he suggested to the secretary of war a system of riverine warfare. "I would pro-pose to have a number of light-draught steamers . . . well armed and barricaded against rifle-shots, and place upon each one a company of 100 black soldiers," he wrote:

> Each boat should be supplied with an abundance of spare muskets and ammu-nition, to put in the hands of the recruits as they come in. These boats should then go up the streams, land at the different plantations, drive in the pickets, and capture them, if possible. The blowing of the steamer's whistle the ne-groes all understand as a signal to come in, and no sooner do they hear it than they come in from every direction. In case the enemy arrives in force at any landing we have either to keep him at a proper distance with shells or quietly move on to some other point and repeat the same operation long before he can arrive with his forces by land. In this way we could very soon have complete occupation of the whole country.

This plan was pursued to some extent by black regiments in the Department of the South, but it was thwarted from time to time by negligent Army officers and in-competent river pilots. In any case, no southern river system was extensive enough to permit "the entire occupation of States," as Saxton projected. At most, it would have brought parts of the tidewater region under a degree of federal control.[27]

Meanwhile, Saxton continued to recruit for the 1st South Carolina. By mid-November, the regiment had five hundred fifty men; by the end of the month, it had a colonel, Thomas W. Higginson, formerly a captain in the 51st

---

[25] *OR*, ser. 3, 2: 663.
[26] *OR*, ser. 1, 14: 190, 192 (quotation); ser. 3, 2: 695.
[27] *OR*, ser. 1, 14: 189 ("to prove"), 190 ("I would").

This cypress swamp on Port Royal Island typified the half-land, half-water environment in which troops operated along the South Atlantic coast.

Massachusetts Infantry, a two-month-old regiment that had just arrived at Beaufort. Urged by the regiment's chaplain, who had suggested his name for the vacancy in the first place, Higginson accepted. The 1st South Carolina was already partly staffed with New England abolitionists. Higginson, a former associate of John Brown, brought other like-minded officers with him to the regiment.[28]

The new colonel began recording impressions of his command soon after he arrived: "There is more variety than one would suppose even in the different companies. . . . Some are chiefly made up of men who have been for months under drill . . . & have been in battle. There is a difference even in the color of the companies. When the whites left [the Sea Islands] they took all the house servants & mixed bloods with them; so that the blacks of this region are very black." Some recent recruits from northeastern Florida were "much lighter in complexion & decidedly more intelligent—so that the promptness with which they are acquiring the drill is quite astounding." Like most white people of that era, Higginson associated light skin with intelligence, although by intelligence he may have meant education or mere worldliness, the result of growing up near a seaport rather than on a plantation. The Floridians were among the

---

[28] Ibid., p. 190; Christopher Looby, ed., *The Complete Civil War Journal and Selected Letters of Thomas Wentworth Higginson* (Chicago: University of Chicago Press, 2000), pp. 243–45.

ninety-odd escaped slaves who had joined Captain Trowbridge's raid earlier that month. They had not yet had time for much drill, but they had certainly come under fire.[29]

The 1st South Carolina's camp, as Chaplain James H. Fowler put it, was to be "a field for *work*." It is clear from the context of the chaplain's remark that he meant philanthropic and missionary work, but Higginson began "tightening reins" and imposing a training regimen that within a month brought his command to a pitch that won Saxton's approval. "I stood by General Saxton—who is a West Pointer—the other night," the regiment's surgeon wrote home, "witnessing the dress parade and was delighted to hear him say that he knew of no other man who could have magically brought these blacks under the military discipline that makes our camp one of the most enviable." Although volunteers came in "tolerably fast," by early December their number was still two hundred short of the minimum required to organize a regiment. Higginson decided to send two of his officers "down the coast to Fernandina and St. Augustine" to recruit in northeastern Florida.[30]

The least populous state in the Confederacy, Florida remained an afterthought of federal military policy throughout the war. Except for the Union advance in the Mississippi Valley, operations outside Virginia were of secondary importance to the Army's leaders. Least important in their eyes were coastal operations. After Maj. Gen. George B. McClellan failed to capture Richmond in the spring of 1862, he drew reinforcements from North Carolina and the Department of the South. The decrease amounted to more than half the Union troops in North Carolina and one-third of those farther south.[31]

Florida's east coast lay within the Department of the South. Beginning at the St. Mary's River, which formed part of the state's border with Georgia, a series of anchorages stretched some eighty miles south, as far as St. Augustine. These had attracted the attention of Union strategists during the war's first summer. South of the St. Mary's, the estuary of the St. John's River led to Jacksonville, the state's third-largest town. From there, a railroad ran west to Tallahassee, and beyond that to St. Mark's on the Gulf Coast.[32]

Production of Sea Island cotton in Florida had expanded greatly during the 1850s. Toward the end of the decade, the crop nearly equaled that of South Carolina. The three counties along the coast between the St. Mary's River and St. Augustine were home to 4,602 slaves (39 percent of the region's total popula-

---

[29] Looby, *Complete Civil War Journal*, p. 47. For more on nineteenth-century ideas about intelligence, see William A. Dobak and Thomas D. Phillips, *The Black Regulars, 1866–1898* (Norman: University of Oklahoma Press, 2001), p. 295n42.

[30] Looby, *Complete Civil War Journal*, pp. 47 ("tightening"), 245 ("a field"), 250 ("down the coast"), 252 ("tolerably fast"); "War-Time Letters from Seth Rogers," pp. 1–2 ("I stood"), typescript at U.S. Army Military History Institute (MHI), Carlisle, Pa.

[31] *OR*, ser. 1, 9: 406, 408–09, 414; 14: 362, 364, 367. Stephen A. Townsend, *The Yankee Invasion of Texas* (College Station: Texas A&M University Press, 2006), shows that from late 1863 to the end of the war, Union troop strength on the Gulf Coast of Texas fluctuated according to manpower needs elsewhere. The Department of the South was subject to similar demands from the summer of 1862 through the summer of 1864.

[32] *OR*, ser. 1, 6: 100. Pensacola's population was 2,876; Key West's 2,832; Jacksonville's 2,118. Census Bureau, *Population of the United States in 1860*, p. 54. The strategists' conclusions about northeastern Florida are in *OR*, ser. 1, 53: 64–66.

tion). Just beyond the river lay Camden County, Georgia, with another 4,143 black residents. Union garrisons at Fernandina and St. Augustine offered a refuge for fleeing slaves, and the first effort to enlist black soldiers in the region provided nearly half the men needed to fill the regiment to minimum strength. The 1st South Carolina reached minimum strength by the end of December. "I don't suppose this quiet life will last many weeks longer," Higginson wrote to his mother.[33]

Before action, though, came the presentation of the regimental colors and a celebratory feast. "Some of our officers and men have been off and captured some oxen, and today all hands have been getting ready for a great barbecue, which we are to have tomorrow," Dr. Seth Rogers, the regiment's surgeon, wrote on the last day of 1862. "They have killed ten oxen which are now being roasted whole over great pits containing live coals made from burning logs in them," Rogers explained to his New England relatives, to whom this was alien cuisine. Colonel Higginson, another Massachusetts man, showed in his journal entry that he, too, was unused to the idea of barbecue: "There is really nothing disagreeable about the looks of the thing, beyond the scale on which it is done."[34]

Two steamboats appeared about 10:00 on New Year's morning bringing visitors from neighboring islands. General Saxton and his retinue arrived from the nearby town of Beaufort, "& from that time forth the road was crowded with riders & walkers—chiefly black women with gay handkerchiefs on their heads & a sprinkling of men," Colonel Higginson wrote:

> Many white persons also, superintendents & teachers. . . . My companies were marched to the neighborhood of the platform & collected sitting or standing, as they are at Sunday meeting; the band of the 8th M[ain]e regiment was here & they & the white ladies & dignitaries usurped the platform—the colored people from abroad filled up all the gaps, & a cordon of officers & cavalry visitors surrounded the circle. Overhead, the great live oak trees & their trailing moss & beyond, a glimpse of the blue river.

The regimental chaplain offered a prayer. A former South Carolina slaveholder turned abolitionist read the president's Emancipation Proclamation, which took effect that day. Mansfield French, a confidant of Treasury Secretary Chase, presented the colors, a gift from the congregation of a church in New York City. "At the close of my remarks," French wrote to Chase the next day, "a most wonderful thing happened. As I passed the flag to Col. Higginson & before he could speak the colored people with *no previous* concert whatever & without

---

[33]Lewis C. Gray, *History of Agriculture in the Southern United States to 1860* (Gloucester, Mass.: Peter Smith, 1958 [1932]), p. 734; Census Bureau, *Population of the United States in 1860*, p. 54; Daniel L. Schafer, "Freedom Was as Close as the River: African-Americans and the Civil War in Northeast Florida," in *The African American Heritage of Florida*, ed. David R. Colburn and Jane L. Landers (Gainesville: University Press of Florida, 1995), pp. 157–84, 170–71; Looby, *Complete Civil War Journal*, pp. 255 (quotation), 260.

[34]"War-Time Letters from Seth Rogers," p. 4; Looby, *Complete Civil War Journal*, p. 75.

Brig. Gen. Rufus Saxton's headquarters at Beaufort stood between two other large planters' houses.

any suggestion from any person, broke forth in the song, 'My country tis of thee.'"[35]

Some of the white visitors on the speakers' platform began to sing, too, but Higginson hushed them. "I never saw anything so electric," he wrote:

> It made all other words cheap, it seemed the choked voice of a race, at last unloosed; nothing could be more wonderfully unconscious; art could not have dreamed of a tribute to the day of jubilee that should be so affecting; history will not believe it. . . . Just think of it; the first day they had ever had a country, the first flag they had ever seen which promised anything to their people,—& here while others stood in silence, waiting for my stupid words these simple souls burst out in their lay, as if they were squatting by their own hearths at home.

---

[35] Looby, *Complete Civil War Journal*, pp. 75–76 ("& from"); *Chase Papers*, 3: 352. Higginson wrote that "a strong but rather cracked & elderly male voice, into which two women's voices immediately blended," began the singing. Looby, *Complete Civil War Journal*, pp. 76–77. Surgeon Rogers first heard a woman's voice, as did Harriet Ware, one of the "Gideonite" teachers on the Sea Islands. "War-Time Letters from Seth Rogers," p. 5; Pearson, *Letters from Port Royal*, p. 130. For Brisbane's career, see Looby, *Complete Civil War Journal*, p. 176; *Chase Papers*, 3: 354.

When they stopped there was nothing to do for it but to speak, & I went on; but the life of the whole day was in those unknown people's song.

After Higginson spoke, he presented the colors to Cpls. Prince Rivers and Robert Sutton, who replied to the colonel's remarks. Rivers expressed a desire to show the flag to "all the old masters" of the men in the regiment, and even to Jefferson Davis in Richmond. Sutton declared that they must not rest while any of their kin remained in bondage. Speeches by General Saxton and other dignitaries followed. Then the men sang "John Brown's Body" and all sat down to eat.[36]

By mid-January 1863, Colonel Higginson thought that his new regiment was sufficiently drilled to appear in public and the 1st South Carolina marched from its camp to Beaufort, played through the town by the band of the 8th Maine. On 21 January, General Hunter visited to inspect the regiment and bring word of its first assignment—"a trip along shore to pick up recruits & lumber," as Higginson wrote in his journal. Two days after Hunter delivered the order, 462 officers and men of the 1st South Carolina went aboard three steamboats at Beaufort and steered for the mainland. They were gone ten days.[37]

The steamers took them south along the coast to the mouth of the St. Mary's River and then forty miles upstream, as far as the town of Woodstock, Georgia. Part of the expedition's purpose was, literally, to show the flag—the regiment had brought its colors along—but the vessels returned to Beaufort laden with "250 bars of the best new railroad iron, valued at $5,000, . . . about 40,000 large-sized bricks, valued at about $1,000, in view of the present high freights," and about $700 worth of yellow pine lumber. "We found no large number of slaves anywhere," Higginson reported, "yet we brought away several whole families, and obtained by this means the most valuable information." Just as important, the regiment met the enemy for the first time.[38]

"Nobody knows anything about these men who has not seen them under fire," Higginson told General Saxton. "It requires the strictest discipline to hold them in hand." Yet, whether they were enduring fire from shore as the armed steamer *John Adams* went up the St. Mary's or meeting Confederate horsemen unexpectedly in a pine forest at night, the men of the 1st South Carolina held their own. The raid "will establish past question the reputation of the regiment," Higginson wrote to his mother the night before the expedition returned to Beaufort. In his report to Saxton, he went on at greater length:

No officer in this regiment now doubts that the key to the successful prosecution of this war lies in the unlimited employment of black troops. Their superiority lies simply in the fact that they know the country, while white troops do not, and, moreover, that they have peculiarities of . . . motive which belong to them alone. Instead of leaving their homes and families to fight they are fighting for

[36]Looby, *Complete Civil War Journal*, p. 77 ("I never"); Pearson, *Letters from Port Royal*, pp. 131–32; *Chase Papers*, 3: 352 (quotation).

[37]*OR*, ser. 1, 14: 195; Looby, *Complete Civil War Journal*, p. 92 (quotation).

[38]*OR*, ser. 1, 14: 196 ("250 bars"), 197 ("We found").

their homes and families, and they show the resolution and sagacity which a personal purpose gives. It would have been madness to attempt, with the bravest white troops what I have successfully accomplished with black ones. Everything, even to the piloting of the vessels and the selection of the proper points for cannonading, was done by my own soldiers. Indeed, the real conductor of the whole expedition up the St. Mary's was Corpl. Robert Sutton, . . . formerly a slave upon the St. Mary's River, a man of extraordinary qualities, who needs nothing but a knowledge of the alphabet to entitle him to the most signal promotion. In every instance when I followed his advice the predicted result followed, and I never departed from it, however, slightly, without finding reason for subsequent regret.

Higginson summarized aptly the value of locally recruited soldiers as federal armies penetrated the Confederacy. Although white Southerners served the Union cause in seventy-two regiments and battalions and often were valuable in the kind of operation that Higginson and his men had just completed, their numbers never approached those of the U.S. Colored Troops.[39]

The month after Higginson and his men returned from their first raid, another colonel of black troops appeared at Beaufort with 125 recruits to begin organizing the 2d South Carolina Infantry. James Montgomery, a veteran of the "Bleeding Kansas" conflict in the 1850s, had been active in Missouri and Kansas during the first summer and autumn of the war; and the Confederates there held him in such dread that they discussed raising units of American Indians to counteract his "jayhawking bands." A month after the new colonel's arrival in the Department of the South, one of his Confederate opponents referred to him as "the notorious Montgomery."[40]

Another expedition to Florida was soon in preparation. At 9:00 on the morning of 5 March 1863, Colonel Higginson asked one of his company commanders, "with the coolness of one who . . . expected you had been making preparations for a month," how long it would take to break camp at Beaufort and board ship for Jacksonville. "About an hour," Capt. James S. Rogers replied. "The boys had to fly around lively," Rogers recalled: "Knapsacks were packed, tents struck and everything was ready for moving. All that afternoon my men were on board the Boston [transport] waiting for the vessels to be loaded with camp equipage and provisions. About nine p.m. they relieved another company which had been hard at work all the afternoon, and from then till nearly one they worked with a will, wheeling and

---

[39] Ibid., pp. 196 ("Nobody knows"), 198 ("No officer"); Looby, *Complete Civil War Journal*, p. 261 ("will establish"); Frederick H. Dyer, *A Compendium of the War of the Rebellion* (New York: Thomas Yoseloff, 1959 [1909]), pp. 21, 24, 28, 30, 33–35.

[40] *OR*, ser. 1, 3: 624, 8: 707 ("jayhawking"); 14: 238 ("the notorious"); 53: 676–77. See also Brian Dirck, "By the Hand of God: James Montgomery and Redemptive Violence," *Kansas History* 27 (2004): 100–15; Looby, *Complete Civil War Journal*, p. 104; Daniel E. Sutherland, *A Savage Conflict: The Decisive Role of Guerrillas in the American Civil War* (Chapel Hill: University of North Carolina Press, 2009), pp. 11, 15–16. The jayhawk is an imaginary bird, the embodiment of rapacity, which became associated in Kansas Territory with armed and dangerous Free Soilers, opponents of the pro-slavery Border Ruffians. By the time of the Civil War, the word had become a verb, meaning to forage aggressively and lawlessly. J. E. Lighter, ed., *Random House Historical Dictionary of American Slang*, 2 vols. (New York: Random House, 1994–1997), 2: 257–58.

carrying, rowing and 'toting' goods." Despite what Higginson called "the usual uncomfortable delays which wait on military expeditions," the small force, consisting of his own regiment and two companies of Colonel Montgomery's 2d South Carolina, was ready to cast off by sunrise the next day.[41]

On the morning of 10 March, Higginson's expedition went ashore at Jacksonville and occupied the town without opposition. The troops found "fine rows of brick houses, all empty, along the wharf" and "streets shaded with fine trees." Soldiers felled some of these trees to block streets at the edge of town. Beyond the outskirts, they cleared a field of fire to a distance of about two miles, partly by burning houses occupied by the families of Confederate soldiers. Confederate cavalry appeared each day to trade long-range shots with Union pickets. The occupiers found about five hundred residents, nearly one-fourth of the prewar population, still in town. Captain Rogers became provost marshal, in charge of law enforcement.[42]

Colonel Montgomery exercised his troops while he organized them. Arriving at Beaufort late in February, he had two companies mustered in when the expedition left for Jacksonville. Northern Florida was reportedly full of potential black recruits. During the expedition, Montgomery took his two companies seventy-five miles up the St. John's River to Palatka and captured twelve thousand dollars' worth of cotton; "but just as I was getting into position for recruiting, we were recalled from Florida," he reported. The small number of Florida slaves who escaped to Union lines and joined the black regiments during this expedition gives a hint of how the course of Emancipation and black recruiting might have differed if the first federal landing force had carved out an enclave in northeastern Florida rather than in the densely populated South Carolina Sea Islands.[43]

Several men of the 1st and 2d South Carolina were from Florida and had joined the Army during earlier raids. "My men have behaved perfectly well," Colonel Higginson recorded in his journal, "though many were owned here and do not love the people." Disloyal Southerners "fear . . . our black troops infinitely more than they do the white soldiers," Captain Rogers wrote, "because they know that our men know them, know the country, and are willing to give all the information in their power. We get recruits for no other bounty than conferring on them the precious boon of liberty."[44]

The presence of black soldiers infuriated the city's slaveholders. Captain Rogers met one of them when a soldier in his company told him that a Jacksonville resident owned one of the soldier's daughters, "and he would like to get her if possible. I had him pilot me to the house," Rogers wrote. "The lady was at home and before I had a chance to state my mission she said: 'I know what you are after, you dirty Yank. You are after that nigger's girl. Well, she is safe beyond the lines where

[41] J. S. Rogers typescript, p. 48 (quotation), Sophia Smith Collection, Smith College, Northampton, Mass.; Thomas W. Higginson, *Army Life in a Black Regiment* (East Lansing: Michigan State University Press, 1960 [1870]), p. 75 ("the usual").

[42] "War-Time Letters from Seth Rogers," p. 67 (quotation); Looby, *Complete Civil War Journal*, p. 109; J. S. Rogers typescript, p. 49.

[43] *OR*, ser. 1, 14: 423; Col J. Montgomery to Brig Gen J. P. Hatch, 2 May 1864, 34th USCI, Regimental Books, RG 94, NA; Stephen V. Ash, *Firebrand of Liberty: The Story of Two Black Regiments That Changed the Course of the Civil War* (New York: W. W. Norton, 2008), pp. 144–62.

[44] Looby, *Complete Civil War Journal*, p. 109 ("My men"); J. S. Rogers typescript, p. 50 ("fear").

you can't get her. I expected you Yanks would want to steal her so I sent her off yesterday. You are too late.'" Rogers tried to explain the effects of the Emancipation Proclamation to the woman. "'Well, you'll have to fight your way out there before you can get that wench,' she said. 'Is this your child?' I said as a flaxen haired boy came toward me. 'Yes, he is, and what of it?'" Rogers told one of his soldiers to take the boy to the guardhouse and keep him there until the girl returned.

> [The soldier] looked at me with a half frightened, half questioning expression on his black face, but when he saw I was in earnest his look changed to one of triumph, and grasping the little fellow by the arm he started off for the guard house before either mother or child could recover from their surprise. Then the "lady" gave me a volley of abuse which I will not repeat, nor did I stop to hear the end of the tirade. Finding she could get no satisfaction from the colonel she was advised to hunt up the provost marshal and get a pass [to go beyond Union lines]. Imagine her chagrin and disgust when she found I was the man she was seeking. She asked for the pass. I did not ask her what for, nor did I pretend to know her. She got it and also an escort of four of my best looking "nasty niggers" dressed in their best.

The next day the woman returned, bringing with her the soldier's daughter. "The soldier's heart was made glad, the white child was exchanged for the black one, and with another blast at the nasty Yankees the haughty 'lady' returned to her home."[45]

While the black soldiers' presence annoyed white Southerners, it alarmed Confederate authorities. Brig. Gen. Joseph Finegan, commanding the Confederate District of East Florida, thought that there might be as many as four thousand armed blacks arrayed against him. He predicted that Union troops would "hold the town of Jacksonville and then . . . advance up the Saint John's in their gunboats and establish another secure position higher up the river, whence they may entice the slaves. That the entire negro population of East Florida will be lost and the country ruined there cannot be a doubt, unless the means of holding the Saint John's River are immediately supplied." Finegan asked for reinforcements and four heavy cannon with which to engage the Union gunboats: "The entire planting interest of East Florida lies within easy communication of the river; . . . intercourse will immediately commence between negroes on the plantations and those in the enemy's service; . . . this intercourse will be conducted through swamps and under cover of the night, and cannot be prevented. A few weeks will suffice to corrupt the entire slave population of East Florida." Aside from Finegan's use of the verb corrupt to describe the effect of black soldiers on slaves, which expressed a typical Southern attitude, his account of the aims and methods of the U.S. Colored Troops could have issued from the most fervid abolitionist in the United States service.[46]

As it turned out, Finegan need not have worried. On 23 March, two white infantry regiments, the 6th Connecticut and the 8th Maine, arrived at Jacksonville to secure the town so that Colonel Higginson could move his black troops up the

---

[45]Looby, *Complete Civil War Journal*, p. 109; J. S. Rogers typescript, pp. 50–51 (quotation).
[46]*OR*, ser. 1, 14: 228.

St. John's River and institute exactly the kind of program Finegan feared. But just five days later, orders came from department headquarters to abandon the entire project and evacuate Jacksonville again. General Hunter, commanding the Department of the South, had begged the War Department for a greater force to move against Charleston just after he initiated the Jacksonville expedition. When the War Department failed to cooperate, Hunter found it necessary to withdraw troops from Florida.[47]

While the orders were in transit from South Carolina to Jacksonville, scouts of the 8th Maine reported discovering a Confederate camp of twenty-two tents not far from the town. Four companies of the 1st South Carolina set out to investigate. "After going about four miles through the open pine woods and over fields carpeted with an immense variety of wild flowers we found the 'tents of the enemy' were merely some clothes belonging to a 'cracker' hut, hung on a fence," Captain Rogers wrote. "Had our black men made such a fool report we should never hear the last of it. We drove in a herd of poor scrawny cows, which was all we gained by this adventure." Colonel Higginson expressed no fears for his regiment's reputation, but he wrote in his journal that the only thing that saved the 8th Maine from being the butt of unending mockery was the imminent breakup of the Jacksonville expedition.[48]

As federal troops boarded the transports, fires broke out in the town. Officers of the 1st South Carolina blamed the white troops for setting them; the colonel of the 8th Maine blamed Confederate arsonists. The evacuation of Jacksonville was Higginson's "first experience of the chagrin which officers feel from divided or uncertain council in higher places." The withdrawing federals took with them yet more Florida Unionists. This time, the troops would be gone for more than ten months.[49]

General Hunter had resumed command of the Department of the South in January 1863, after General Mitchel's death from malaria the previous October. Hunter was ready to move against Charleston, where Secessionists had first fired on the United States flag. He thought that the city would fall within a fortnight. To augment his force in South Carolina, he summoned north part of the garrisons of Fernandina and St. Augustine and evacuated Jacksonville altogether. Since racial animosity, mistrust, and contempt continued to dictate a subordinate role for black soldiers, Higginson's and Montgomery's regiments would secure the islands around Port Royal Sound while white troops operated against Charleston. The black regiments could not, Hunter wrote, "consistently with the interests of the service (in the present state of feeling) be advantageously employed to act in concert with our other forces."[50]

The 1st and 2d South Carolina manned a picket line along the Coosaw River, a part of the Coosawhatchie estuary that separated Port Royal Island from the mainland. By mid-May, Montgomery had organized six companies of his regiment; at the begin-

---

[47] Ibid., pp. 232–33, 424–25, 428–29.

[48] J. S. Rogers typescript, p. 52 (quotation); Looby, *Complete Civil War Journal*, p. 118.

[49] *OR*, ser. 1, 14: 233; Looby, *Complete Civil War Journal*, p. 120; "War-Time Letters from Seth Rogers," p. 82.

[50] *OR*, ser. 1, 14: 388, 390, 411, 424 ("consistently"), 432; ser. 3, 2: 695. Charleston's "symbolic significance was greater than its strategic importance." James M. McPherson, *Battle Cry of*

ning of June, he took three hundred men on a raid twenty-five miles up the Combahee River. A Confederate inspector later condemned the defenders' "confusion of counsel, indecision, and great tardiness of movement" that allowed Montgomery's men to free 725 slaves in one day and return with them to Port Royal. The indecisive and tardy Confederates, the inspector fumed, "allowed the enemy to come up to them almost unawares, and then retreated without offering resistance or firing a gun, allowing a parcel of negro wretches, calling themselves soldiers, with a few degraded whites, to march unmolested, with the incendiary torch, to rob, destroy, and burn a large section of country." The raiders burned four plantation residences and six mills during the day and destroyed a pontoon bridge. Among the newly freed people, Montgomery found enough recruits to organize two more companies of his regiment.[51]

The 2d South Carolina was not the only black regiment organizing for service at that time. On 26 January 1863, Governor John A. Andrew of Massachusetts received authority to enlist as three-year volunteers "persons of African descent, organized into separate corps." Andrew, who counted many abolitionists among his political supporters, asked Secretary of War Stanton whether the appointment of black company officers, assistant surgeon, and chaplain would be acceptable. Stanton replied that an answer would have to wait until Congress acted and might finally depend on "the discretion of the President." Five weeks after the secretary rebuffed the governor, an abolitionist minister in Pittsburgh wrote to him, asking, "Can the colored men here raise a regiment and have their own company officers?" Stanton agreed, demonstrating clearly the unfinished state of federal policy at this stage of the war.[52]

As it turned out, residents of Pittsburgh organized no black regiment and few black men ever became officers. Even in the Massachusetts regiments, Governor Andrew appointed only a few and those received promotion only after the fighting was over. In other black regiments, prospects for promotion were more dismal still. This was a source of discontent among the minority of black sergeants who were fully literate when the war broke out and thought themselves able to shoulder greater responsibilities. If Stanton had given the governor of Massachusetts the same offhand assent that he gave the Pennsylvania minister, events might have taken a different course. Appointment of black officers by the energetic governor of a state with two powerful U.S. senators, Charles Sumner and Henry Wilson, backed by influential abolitionists and a national magazine, the *Atlantic Monthly*, might have swayed War Department policy during the war and created a precedent for the promotion of black soldiers in the postwar period. As it was, aside from the officers of the original three regiments of Louisiana Native Guards, only thirty-two black men received appointments in the U.S. Colored Troops. Thirteen of the thirty-two were chaplains.[53]

Governor Andrew began recruiting at once. When his own state fell far short of yielding enough men to fill the 54th Massachusetts, he sent recruiters across the North, stripping some states of their most educated and patriotic black men. Pennsylvania

---

Freedom: The Civil War Era (New York: Oxford University Press, 1988), p. 646.

[51] *OR*, ser. 1, 14: 304–05 ("confusion," "allowed the enemy"), 306, 463; Col J. Montgomery to Brig Gen J. P. Hatch, 2 May 1864, 34th USCI, Regimental Books, RG 94, NA; Looby, *Complete Civil War Journal*, p. 123.

[52] *OR*, ser. 3, 3: 20 ("persons of"), 36, 38, 47 ("the discretion"), 72 ("Can the"), 82.

[53] Joseph T. Glatthaar, *Forged in Battle: The Civil War Alliance of Black Soldiers and White Officers* (New York: Free Press, 1990), pp. 180, 279–80. For the way in which Andrew and Wilson,

furnished 294, New York 183, and Ohio 155. The nationally famous abolitionist author and orator Frederick Douglass encouraged enlistment, and two of his sons served in the regiment. Capt. Robert G. Shaw of the 2d Massachusetts, a veteran of nearly two years' service that included several battles, would lead the new regiment. Governor Andrew had the 54th organized, armed, and aboard ship for South Carolina by the end of May.[54]

On 5 June, the 2d South Carolina embarked for St. Simon's Island. From there, boats took the men fifteen miles up the Turtle River, where they dismantled part of a railroad bridge but found that the trestle was too waterlogged to burn. On 9 June, the 54th Massachusetts arrived on St. Simon's. Two days later, accompanied by the 2d South Carolina, the new regiment steamed up the Altamaha River on its first expedition. "We saw many Rice fields along the shores and quite a number of alligators," Capt. John W. M. Appleton of the 54th Massachusetts recalled. "The water was so charged with soil as to give it an orange color. We kept running aground," and Appleton found himself sometimes at the head of the squadron, sometimes in its rear. At Darien, near the river's mouth, they captured a forty-ton schooner loaded with cotton, which they sent back to Port Royal Sound.[55]

Montgomery ordered the troops to "take out anything that can be made useful in camp." Besides poultry and livestock, they gathered furnishings from private residences. "Some of our officers got very nice carpets," an officer of the 54th Massachusetts wrote home. Then, despite the entire lack of armed resistance, Montgomery decided to burn Darien. The glare of the flames could be seen on St. Simon's Island fifteen miles away. Colonel Shaw protested the order, and only one company of his regiment took part in the arson.[56]

Higginson had suspected from the start that Montgomery's "system of drill & discipline may be more lax & western than mine." After four months of observation, Higginson wrote: "Montgomery's raids are dashing, but his brigand practices I detest and condemn. . . . I will have none but civilized warfare in *my* reg[imen]t." In June, the same month in which Higginson deplored "brigand practices," General Hunter felt obliged to send Montgomery a copy of the War Department's General Orders 100, issued that spring, which published "Instructions for the Government of Armies of the United States in the Field." The legal scholar Francis Lieber had prepared "Instructions" as a code of conduct for U.S. soldiers. It distinguished, for instance, between partisans (uniformed troops operating behind enemy lines), guerrillas, and "armed prowlers." Hunter called Montgomery's "particular attention" to sections of the "Instructions" headed "Military necessity—Retaliation," "Public and private property of the enemy,"

---

who chaired the Senate Military Affairs Committee, worked together, see James W. Geary, *We Need Men: The Union Draft in the Civil War* (DeKalb: Northern Illinois University Press, 1991), pp. 16–31.

[54]Edwin S. Redkey, "Brave Black Volunteers: Profile of the Fifty-fourth Massachusetts Regiment," in *Hope and Glory: Essays on the Legacy of the Fifty-fourth Massachusetts Regiment,* ed. Martin H. Blatt et al. (Amherst: University of Massachusetts Press, 2001): 21–34, p. 24 (statistics).

[55]J. W. M. Appleton Jnl photocopy, p. 22 (quotation), MHI; *Anglo-African,* 27 June 1863.

[56]Appleton Jnl, p. 23 ("take out"); Russell Duncan, *Where Death and Glory Meet: Colonel Robert Gould Shaw and the 54th Massachusetts Infantry* (Athens: University of Georgia Press, 1999), p. 94 ("Some of"); Luis F. Emilio, *A Brave Black Regiment: History of the Fifty-fourth Regiment of Massachusetts Volunteer Infantry* (New York: Arno Press, 1969 [1894]), pp. 42–44. Emilio was captain of the regiment's Company E and a participant in most of the events he described.

Col. James Montgomery's raid up the Combahee River in early June 1863, as imagined by a Harper's Weekly *artist.*

and "Prisoners of war—Hostages—Booty on the battle-field." "Not that in any manner [do] I doubt the justice or generosity of your judgment," Hunter told Montgomery:

> But . . . it is particularly important . . . to give our enemies . . . as little ground as possible for alleging any violation of the laws and usages of civilized warfare as a palliative for these atrocities which are threatened against the men and officers of commands similar to your own. If, as is threatened by the rebel Congress, this war has eventually to degenerate into a barbarous and savage conflict . . . , the infamy of this deterioration should rest exclusively and without excuse upon the rebel Government. It will therefore be necessary for you to exercise the utmost strictness in . . . compliance with the instructions herewith sent, and you will avoid any devastation which does not strike immediately at the resources or material of the armed insurrection.[57]

That summer, the black regiments began to take part in operations on a larger scale than the raids that so suited them. After months of begging reinforcements from the War Department and quarreling with subordinates, General Hunter was relieved from

---

[57] *OR*, ser. 1, 14: 466 ("Not that"); Looby, *Complete Civil War Journal*, pp. 105 ("system of drill"), 288 ("Montgomery's"); Sutherland, *Savage Conflict*, pp. 127–28. General Orders 100

command of the Department of the South in June. The recently promoted Maj. Gen. Quincy A. Gillmore, a man twenty-three years younger than Hunter, would lead the land assault on Charleston. A West Point classmate of Saxton, Gillmore had distinguished himself as chief engineer of the Port Royal Expedition in 1861 (when the escaped slave Brutus taught him the geography of the Sea Islands) and in the siege of Fort Pulaski, at the mouth of the Savannah River, during the winter and spring of 1862.[58]

Gillmore gathered his troops. He recalled the 2d South Carolina from St. Simon's Island and put Montgomery in charge of a brigade of two regiments: his own and the 54th Massachusetts. The plan of attack was to land troops on Morris Island at the south side of the entrance to Charleston Harbor. When they had taken Fort Wagner, near the northern end of the island, Union artillery fire could reach and demolish Fort Sumter, which stood on an island in the middle of the harbor entrance. Naval vessels could then run past the remaining Confederate forts to bombard the city itself.[59]

Brig. Gen. George C. Strong's brigade of six white regiments would carry out the landing. All were veterans of the original Port Royal Expedition in October 1861, although the question of race undoubtedly was important in their selection, too. "I was the more disappointed at being left behind," Colonel Shaw wrote to Strong:

> I had been given to understand that we were to have our share of the work in this department. I feel convinced too that my men are capable of better service than mere guerrilla warfare. . . . It seems to me quite important that the colored soldiers should be associated as much as possible with the white troops, in order that they may have other witnesses besides their own officers to what they are capable of doing.

The black regiments would play subsidiary roles in the attack.[60]

While the main landing went forward on Morris Island, a division led by Brig. Gen. Alfred H. Terry diverted the Confederates' attention with a demonstration against James Island, just to the west, and up the Stono River. Montgomery's and Shaw's regiments were attached to Terry's force. Higginson's 1st South Carolina was to ascend the South Edisto River, about halfway between Port Royal Sound and Charleston Harbor, and cut the line of the Charleston and Savannah Railroad by destroying its bridge across the river.

Higginson loaded two hundred fifty men and two cannon in three boats and embarked on the afternoon of 9 July. By dawn the next morning, the expedition had steamed twenty miles upstream through rice-growing country. Higginson's cannon routed a small Confederate garrison at Willstown with three shots; but a row of pilings in the river blocked his boats long enough to cost them the tide, delaying further progress till afternoon. Soldiers pulled up the pilings while Captain Rogers and a few men set fire to storehouses of corn and rice and broke the sluice that provided the rice fields with water. When the tide began to flow, the boats moved on, but two of them ran aground. By the time they floated again, the Confederates had placed six guns

---

remained the basic law of war for American soldiers through the twentieth century. The text is in *OR*, ser. 3, 3: 148–64 (quotations, pp. 148, 151, 154).

    [58]*OR*, ser. 1, 14: 464; Miller, *Lincoln's Abolitionist General*, pp. 129–36, 141–46. Gillmore's reports of the siege of Fort Pulaski are in *OR*, ser. 1, 6: 144–65.

    [59]*OR*, ser. 1, 14: 462–63; vol. 28, pt. 1, pp. 6–7, and pt. 2, pp. 15–16.

    [60]Emilio, *Brave Black Regiment*, p. 49.

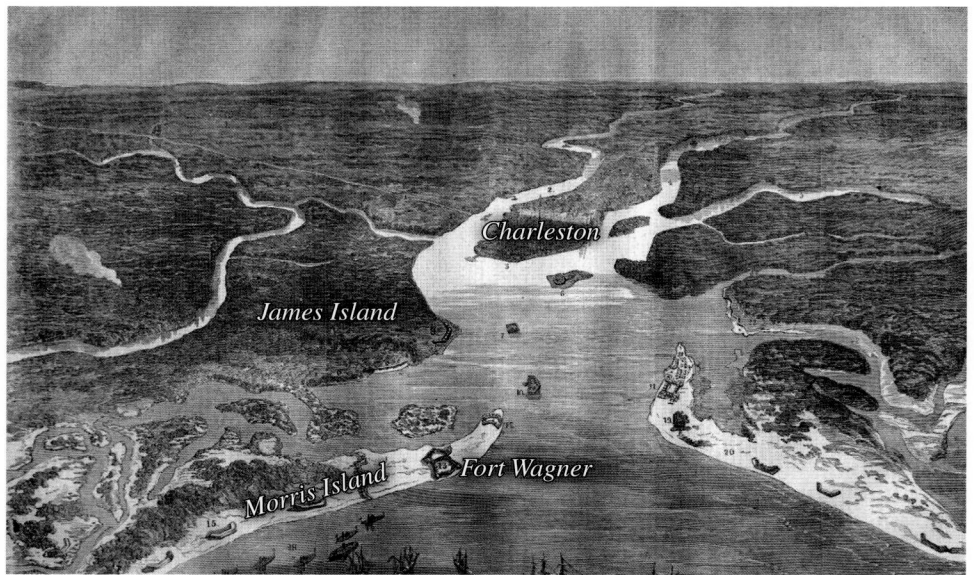

Bird's-eye view of Charleston Harbor, with Morris Island and Fort Wagner at the bottom of the picture. James Island is the large wooded island just above Morris Island; across the harbor is the city of Charleston.

to defend the railroad bridge and the expedition was unable to approach. Running downstream, the smallest of Higginson's boats grounded again. "Her first engineer was killed and the second engineer was wounded," Rogers wrote:

> We were perfectly helpless, hard and fast. . . . We could not use our guns. One [paddle] wheel of the boat was playing in the mud and high grass of the river bank, and we pushed and rolled the vessel for some time. . . . I remained on the upper deck with the colonel and pilots and did what I could to make the latter do their duty and to keep the captain of the boat away from them, for he was so frightened that he was almost crazy. Once when the steam nearly gave out . . . the firemen were all so scared that they were lying on their faces on the floor and not until I had thrown the wood at them did they turn and go to work. . . . The only thing to keep her from falling into the hands of the rebs was to burn her, and accordingly it was done after spiking the guns and taking off all we could of value.

The expedition was able to free two hundred slaves, who escaped with the retreating troops, but the railroad bridge remained undamaged.[61]

In the meantime, federal troops farther east were moving forward. On 10 July, General Strong's six regiments landed on Morris Island but failed to capture Fort Wagner by assault the next day. Terry's demonstration up the Stono River

---

[61]*OR*, ser. 1, vol. 28, pt. 1, pp. 194–95; J. S. Rogers typescript, pp. 102, 103–04 ("Her first").

was successful; one Confederate general felt "certain of an attack, both from the Stono and from bays in rear, before or by daylight" on 11 July, but the Union troops settled down in the rain and heat to "the usual picket and fatigue duty," protected by the guns of naval vessels offshore. Confederate pickets were in sight but too far off for them to tell black Union soldiers from white: they called the 54th Massachusetts "Flat-headed Dutchmen." "We stood under arms this morning from just before dawn until half an hour after daylight," Captain Appleton recorded on 13 July. "Then I found a clean puddle, took a drink from it and then bathed in it, and felt better."[62]

To counter the Union move against Charleston, the Confederate command summoned reinforcements from neighboring states. General Pierre G. T. Beauregard thought the James Island position "most important," and it was there that his troops attacked on 16 July. Union soldiers on the island had gone a week without tents or a change of clothing. Three companies of the 54th Massachusetts manned the right of the Union picket line. They fell back, but their resistance allowed men of the 10th Connecticut on the left of the picket line to move closer to the water, where the entire force came under covering fire from Union gunboats. When the Confederates retreated, Union troops recovered the ground they had lost. Men of the 54th Massachusetts thought at first that the fourteen dead they had left on the field had been mutilated by the Confederates but eventually concluded that fiddler crabs had eaten the corpses' ears and eyelids. Going over the ground, officers could tell by the position of discarded cartridge papers that the pickets of the 54th Massachusetts had retired in good order. "It was pleasing . . . to see the Connecticut boys coming over to thank our men for their good fighting," Captain Appleton noted. General Terry praised "the steadiness and soldierly conduct" of the 54th, but Beauregard summarized the day's events in one sentence: "We attacked part of the enemy's forces on James Island . . . and drove them to the protection of their gunboats . . . with small loss on both sides." The successful defense put the men of the 54th Massachusetts in good spirits, but it was no substitute for potable water. What was available on James Island came "from horse ponds covered with a green scum," was "almost coffee colored and [had] a taste that coffee cannot disguise," Captain Appleton wrote.[63]

General Gillmore ordered the evacuation of James Island. The men withdrew through the swamp during the night, "over narrow dikes and bridges . . . mostly of three planks, but sometimes one and sometimes another would be missing." The 54th Massachusetts went two days without food, except for a box of hardtack that was cast up on the beach. Boats took the regiment first to Folly Island, then to Morris Island, where a Union force had been preparing for another assault on

---

[62] *OR*, ser. 1, vol. 28, pt. 1, pp. 428 ("certain of"), 584 ("the usual"); Appleton Jnl, pp. 45, 46 ("Flat-headed"), 47 ("We stood").

[63] *OR*, ser. 1, vol. 28, pt. 1, p. 755 (Terry), and pt. 2, pp. 192, 194 ("most important"), 203 (Beauregard). Appleton Jnl, pp. 48, 51, 52 ("It was pleasing," "from horse ponds"). Fiddler crabs are members of the genus *Uca*. Three species, *U. minax, U. pugilator,* and *U. pugnax,* range from Florida to Cape Cod. Austin B. Williams, *Shrimps, Lobsters, and Crabs of the Atlantic Coast of the Eastern United States, Maine to Florida* (Washington, D.C.: Smithsonian Institution Press, 1984), pp. 472–81.

Like most officers of black regiments, Capt. John W. M. Appleton had served as an enlisted man in a white regiment. These photographs show him as a private in the Massachusetts militia and as an officer of the 54th Massachusetts.

Fort Wagner. General Gillmore concentrated his artillery; by nightfall on 17 July, twenty-five rifled cannon and fifteen siege mortars were trained on the Confederate works. A heavy rain during the night delayed the opening bombardment until late the next morning. By the time the 54th Massachusetts landed, late on the afternoon of 18 July, two Union brigades—a little more than four thousand men—had been under arms for anywhere from four to seven hours.[64]

Gillmore's report, written weeks later, called Morris Island "an irregular mass of sand, which, by continued action of wind and sea (particularly the former)," had accumulated on top of the mud of a salt marsh. The buildup had been gradual: sixty years earlier, the island had not existed, but wind and sea could subtract as well as add. Only after the attack of 18 July did Army officers learn that beach erosion had

---

[64] *OR*, ser. 1, vol. 28, pt. 1, pp. 345–46; vol. 53, pp. 8, 10, 12; Appleton Jnl, pp. 53 ("over narrow"), 54; Emilio, *Brave Black Regiment*, pp. 65–68. Strength calculated by averaging the strengths of the 6th Connecticut, 9th Maine, 7th New Hampshire, and 100th New York in *OR*, ser. 1, vol. 28, pt. 1, p. 357, and vol. 53, pp. 10–13, and multiplying by nine, the number of regiments in the two brigades (*OR*, ser. 1, vol. 28, pt. 1, pp. 346–47). A third brigade that included Montgomery's 2d South Carolina was present but did not come into action. Stephen R. Wise, *Gate of Hell: Campaign for Charleston Harbor 1863* (Columbia: University of South Carolina Press, 1994), pp. 232–33, reckons the "Estimated Effective Strength" of the regiments that took part in the attack as 5,020. But the commanders of the four regiments named above listed a total strength of 1,820, while Wise gives 2,140 (an overestimate of nearly 17.6 percent).

narrowed the island "to about one-fourth or one-third of the width shown on the latest Coast Survey charts, and that . . . the waves frequently swept entirely over it, practically isolating that position defended by Fort Wagner . . . , thus greatly augmenting the difficulty to be overcome in capturing the position, whether by assault or gradual approaches." In a few places, Morris Island was less than one hundred yards wide.[65]

What moved Brig. Gen. Truman Seymour, commanding the attack, to put the tired, hungry men of the 54th Massachusetts in the lead is unclear. Perhaps it was the regiment's strength—with 624 officers and men, it was the largest on Morris Island. Seymour called it a "regiment of excellent character, well officered, with full ranks." Seven months after the attack, a witness before the American Freedmen's Inquiry Commission testified that he had heard Seymour tell General Gillmore: "Well, I guess we will . . . put those d——d niggers from Massachusetts in the advance; we may as well get rid of them, one time as another"; but there is no corroborating evidence for this.[66]

The commander of the leading brigade, General Strong, told the men of the 54th Massachusetts that the enemy was tired and hungry, too, and ordered them forward: "Don't fire a musket on the way up, but go in and bayonet them at their guns." The 54th Massachusetts advanced at the head of Strong's brigade, with rifles loaded but percussion caps not set, in order to prevent accidental discharges. It was about 7:45 in the evening, still light enough for the attackers to see their way but dim enough, the generals hoped, to spoil the enemy's aim.[67]

The course of the attack lay along a spit of land between the Atlantic Ocean and a salt marsh. The distance to be covered was about sixteen hundred yards, the last hundred to be taken at the double. The 54th Massachusetts formed two lines of five companies abreast; each company was in two ranks, so the regiment's front was roughly one hundred fifty men wide. The regiments that followed, which numbered fewer men, formed in column of companies from twenty to twenty-five men wide. As the marsh widened and the beach narrowed, the 54th, in the lead, became disarranged, veering around the edge of the wet ground and hitting Fort Wagner at an angle that carried the attackers past part of the fortifications before they could turn in the right direction. In passing the narrow stretch between the harbor and the salt marsh, the men of the first-line flank companies became mixed with the companies of the second line and the men of the second-line flank companies fell even farther to the rear. "We came to a line of shattered palisades, how we passed them we can hardly tell," Captain Appleton wrote. "Then we passed over some rifle pits and I can dimly remember seeing some men in them, over whom we ran." By this time, the supporting naval gunfire had ceased and the fort's defenders opened fire on their attackers with short-barreled

---

[65]*OR*, ser. 1, vol. 28, pt. 1, pp. 13 ("to about"), 15 ("an irregular"); Wise, *Gate of Hell*, p. 2.

[66]*OR*, ser. 1, vol. 28, pt. 1, p. 347 ("regiment of"); Ira Berlin et al., eds. *The Black Military Experience* (New York: Cambridge University Press, 1982), pp. 534–35 ("Well, I guess").

[67]*OR*, ser. 1, vol. 28, pt. 1, p. 357; Appleton Jnl, pp. 56–57 ("Don't fire," p. 57). A percussion-cap weapon fired when the hammer struck the cap, which ignited the charge of black powder that propelled the bullet. The United States did not adopt standard time zones until 1883 and daylight-saving time until the First World War. Dusk in July 1863 therefore came an hour earlier than we are accustomed to think of it.

carronades, artillery that fired canister shot containing twenty-seven two-inch balls. "Just a brief lull, and the deafening explosions of cannon were renewed. . . . A sheet of flame, followed by a running fire, like electric sparks, swept along the parapet," hitting the regiment from the front and left flank. Some of the defenders were too panicked to man the ramparts: "Fortunately, too," as the senior surviving officer of the 54th Massachusetts remarked, or the attackers would never have reached the fort.[68]

As they stopped at the water-filled ditch in front of the wall, guns in the bastions fired into them, one from either flank. "I could hear the rattle of the balls on the men & arms," Captain Appleton wrote:

> [I] leaped down into the water, followed by all the men left standing. On my left the Colonel with the colors, and the men of the companies on the left, waded across abreast with me. We reached the base . . . and climbed up the parapet, our second battalion right with us. On the top of the work we met the Rebels, and by the flashes of their guns we looked down into the fort, apparently a sea of bayonets, some eight or ten feet below us. . . . In my immediate front the enemy were very brave and met us eagerly.

The Confederate garrison was much stronger than Generals Gillmore and Seymour had guessed, and the attackers could only hope to hold part of the wall until the second brigade came to their support. The other regiments of their own brigade, they knew, were in some other part of the fort; Captain Appleton found men of the 48th New York "and some other regiments" fighting on his right. "We join[ed] them and [took] part. Just before leaving our old position I found my Revolver cylinder would not turn, as it was full of sand. I took it apart, cleaned it on my blouse . . . and reloaded. Where we now were we had a stubborn lot of men to contend against."[69]

During the hour that the 54th Massachusetts held the rim of Fort Wagner, the regiment's colonel, 2 company commanders, and 31 enlisted men died and 11 officers and 135 enlisted men were wounded. By the end of the hour, the commanders of both brigades were out of action. One was already dead; the other would linger till the end of the month. When the survivors of the 54th Massachusetts were finally driven from Fort Wagner, about 9:00, Capt. Luis F. Emilio, the regiment's junior captain but the senior officer still on his feet, brought them together about halfway between the fort and the place from which they had started. By the next day, about four hundred men had assembled. Besides the previous night's killed and wounded, ninety-two men were listed as missing. "The splendid 54th is cut to pieces," Sgt. Maj. Lewis Douglass told his parents. The regiment suffered the highest total casualties of any regi-

---

[68] *OR*, ser. 1, vol. 28, pt. 1, pp. 372, 417–18; Appleton Jnl, pp. 57, 58 ("We came"); Emilio, *Brave Black Regiment*, p. 80 ("Just a brief," "Fortunately"), and map facing. Appleton mentions two guns firing. The map in Wise, *Gate of Hell*, p. 98, shows one 42-pounder carronade and two 32-pounder carronades bearing on the edge of the ditch where the 54th Massachusetts stood. *Instructions for Heavy Artillery, Prepared by a Board of Officers for the Use of the Army of the United States* (Washington, D.C.: Gideon, 1851), pp. 251–52, describes carronades and their ammunition.

[69] Appleton Jnl, pp. 58–59 ("I could"), 61 ("and some," "we joined").

ment in the attack, but not by much: the 7th New Hampshire and 48th New York, with strengths that were about three-quarters and two-thirds that of the 54th Massachusetts, lost 216 and 242—smaller totals, but just as large, or larger, percentages. Total Union losses were 246 killed, 880 wounded, and 389 missing.[70]

The missing men represented a worry for the 54th Massachusetts, as other black soldiers taken prisoner would for their regiments throughout the war. The Confederacy's first official reaction to the Union's raising black regiments had been to declare that captured officers and men of those regiments would be tried in state courts on charges of insurrection, a capital offense. The federal government soon announced policies of retaliation for mistreatment of prisoners; and for the rest of the war, the matter depended largely on the judgment of the generals on both sides who commanded field armies and geographical departments.[71]

Officers and men of the 54th Massachusetts learned eventually that twenty-nine of the men reported missing at Fort Wagner had been taken prisoner; the rest had been killed. Word reached the regiment in December that two of the prisoners, Sgt. Walter A. Jeffries and Cpl. Charles Hardy, were to have stood trial for insurrection but that a prominent Charleston

Sgt. Maj. Lewis Douglass of the 54th Massachusetts was a son of the abolitionist Frederick Douglass.

attorney, Nelson Mitchell, had volunteered to defend them. Mitchell, according to rumor, pointed out that the court would have to try Jeffries and Hardy at the place where they had committed the offense of insurrection and that Fort

---

[70]*OR*, ser. 1, vol. 28, pt. 1, pp. 10–12, 362–63; Emilio, *Brave Black Regiment*, p. 105; Peter C. Ripley et al., eds., *The Black Abolitionist Papers*, 5 vols. (Chapel Hill: University of North Carolina Press, 1985–1992), 5: 241 (quotation).

[71]Glatthaar, *Forged in Battle*, pp. 201–03. For examples of discussion at the local level, see correspondence of Brig. Gen. Q. A. Gillmore, commanding the Union Department of the South, and General P. G. T. Beauregard, commanding the Confederate Department of South Carolina, Georgia, and Florida, July–August 1863. *OR*, ser. 1, vol. 28, pt. 2, pp. 11–13, 21, 25–26, 37–38, 45–46.

Wagner, which was still under bombardment by federal guns, was too "warm [a] spot for a court to sit."[72]

What really happened was different. The court tried only four of the prisoners, who were thought to have been slaves before the war. Distinguished counsel represented both sides: Mitchell the defense, the state attorney general the prosecution. After extensive correspondence between Confederate and South Carolina officials, both civil and military, the court ruled that "persons engaged as soldiers in the act of war" were not subject to state slave statutes and the four prisoners rejoined their comrades. The 54th Massachusetts' captives spent the rest of the war in a camp at Florence, South Carolina. At least twelve of the twenty-nine died in captivity.[73]

The second assault on Fort Wagner had been a failure. The 54th Massachusetts' role did not go unremarked, but the comment was mixed. A *New York Times* editorialist noted that the idea that "negroes won't fight at all" had been "knocked on the head" but that "the great mistake now is that more is expected of these black regiments than any reasonable man would expect of white ones." A black regiment, the writer went on, "freshly recruited and which had never been under fire, [was] assigned the advance, which nobody would have dreamed of giving to equally raw white troops." Within the Army itself, rumor ran that when the 54th Massachusetts formed up on the morning after the failed attack, half of the survivors had lost their rifles.[74]

Missing arms or not, there were several reasons for the defeat. In the first place, Generals Gillmore and Seymour had entertained too great hopes of an easy capture of Fort Wagner. Gillmore's artillery had shattered Fort Pulaski's masonry the year before, but Fort Wagner's earthworks were more durable. General Strong, the brigade commander, was a Massachusetts man and heeded a plea for active service from another Massachusetts man, Colonel Shaw. In so doing, Strong placed in advance a regiment so tired that when one of its officers was wounded in the attack he "went to sleep on the rampart" of the fort. Moreover, being the largest regiment in the brigade, the 54th Massachusetts formed two five-company lines, a front too wide to negotiate the spit of land it had to cross on the way to the fort. This broad front on a narrow beach disarranged both lines and threw the rearmost men into the regiments immediately behind. Finally, neither the men nor the officers of the 54th Massachusetts had been under heavy fire before and some of the officers were very young. Captain Appleton's memoir names one who was 19 years old, another who was 18, and two who were 17. This combination of factors meant that the assault on Fort Wagner would have required a miracle to succeed. As it was, the Confederates were able to repel an attacking force that outnumbered them nearly three to one, even though many of the defenders were too demoralized to offer much resistance. The men of one

---

[72] Appleton Jnl, p. 125 (quotation); Emilio, *Brave Black Regiment*, p. 97.

[73] Howard C. Westwood, "Captive Black Union Soldiers in Charleston—What To Do?" *Civil War History* 28 (1982): 28–44 (quotation, p. 40); Emilio, *Brave Black Regiment*, pp. 298–99.

[74] *New York Times*, 31 July 1863; John C. Gray and John C. Ropes, *War Letters, 1862–1865* (Boston: Houghton Mifflin, 1927), p. 184.

regiment, the Confederate commander reported, "could not be induced to occupy their position, and ingloriously deserted the ramparts."[75]

After the failure of the attempt to take Fort Wagner by storm, Union soldiers settled down to siege warfare. Black soldiers performed many, but not all, of the fatigues, filling sandbags and wrestling logs for gun emplacements built to house enormous pieces of ordnance, at least one of which fired 200-pound rounds that could reach the city of Charleston itself. What dismayed men and officers alike in the black regiments was being required "to lay out camps, pitch tents, dig wells, etc., for white regiments who have lain idle until the work was finished for them," Capt. Charles P. Bowditch of the newly arrived 55th Massachusetts Infantry wrote in September. "If they want to keep up the self-respect and discipline of the negroes they must be careful not to try to make them perform the work of menials for men who are as able to do the work themselves as the blacks." The colonels of the 55th Massachusetts and 1st North Carolina took the matter to their brigade commander, Brig. Gen. Edward A. Wild. "They have been slaves and are just learning to be men," Col. James C. Beecher of the 1st North Carolina wrote. "When they are set to menial work doing for white Regiments what those Regiments are entitled to do for themselves, it simply throws them back where they were before and reduces them to the position of slaves again." General Wild told his colonels to disregard orders to perform fatigues for white regiments and passed Beecher's letter to their divisional commander, Brig. Gen. Israel Vogdes. On the same day, Captain Bowditch noted that only twenty-five of the eighty-six men in his company turned out for drill; the rest were sick, on guard, or performing fatigues. General Vogdes thought that menial employment would "exercise an unfavorable influence with the minds both of the white and black troops" and that ample time should be allowed "to drill and instruct the colored troops in their duties as soldiers." Two days later, General Gillmore issued a department-wide order banning the use of black regiments to perform fatigues for whites. Meanwhile, the Confederates evacuated Fort Wagner on 7 September, leaving all of Morris Island in federal hands and ending the active phase of the year's operations against Charleston.[76]

An unlooked-for result of the summer's siege was a questionnaire survey—probably the first on the subject—to evaluate the performance of black troops. Five questions, put to six engineer officers who had supervised labor details from both black and white regiments, covered such topics as black soldiers' behavior under fire, the quality and quantity of their work, and comparisons of black troops generally with whites and of Northern blacks with Southern blacks. The survey was the brainchild of Maj. Thomas B. Brooks, an engineer officer during the siege, and

---

[75]*OR*, ser. 1, vol. 28, pt. 1, p. 418 ("could not be"); vol. 53, p. 10; Appleton Jnl, pp. 60–61, 69, 91 ("went to sleep"). Wise, *Gate of Hell*, p. 233, estimates Fort Wagner's garrison at 1,621. The attackers, including the 54th Massachusetts, could not have numbered fewer than 4,700. Wise estimates the regiment's strength at 425, or 26.2 percent of Fort Wagner's defenders.

[76]*OR*, ser. 1, vol. 28, pt. 1, pp. 27–30, and pt. 2, p. 95; Col J. C. Beecher to Brig Gen E. A. Wild, 13 Sep 1863 ("They have been"), with Endorsement, Brig Gen E. A. Wild, 14 Sep 1863, and Endorsement, I. Vogdes, 15 Sep 1863, 35th USCI, Entry 57C, RG 94, NA. "War Letters of Charles P. Bowditch," *Proceedings of the Massachusetts Historical Society* 57 (1924): 414–95, are letters home from an officer of the 55th Massachusetts, describing the day-to-day progress of the siege (sandbags and logs, pp. 427, 430, 442; "to lay," p. 444). Emilio, *Brave Black Regiment*, pp. 106–27, also describes the siege (artillery, pp. 108–09).

*Men of the 54th Massachusetts and the 1st New York Engineers in a trench on
James Island, Charleston Harbor, during the summer of 1863*

may have included only officers from his own regiment, the 1st New York Engineers.[77] He summarized the results of the survey:

> To the first question, all answer that the black is more timorous than the white, but is in a corresponding degree more docile and obedient, hence, more completely under the control of his commander, and much more influenced by his example. . . . All agree that the black is less skillful than the white soldier, but still enough so for most kinds of siege work. . . . The statements unanimously agree that the black will do a greater amount of work than the white soldier, because he labors more constantly. . . . The whites are decidedly superior in enthusiasm. The blacks cannot be easily hurried in their work, no matter what the emergency. . . . All agree that the colored troops recruited from free States are superior to those recruited from slave States.

Brooks also included with his report two of the replies in their entirety. One of the officers found that black troops "compare favorably with the whites; they are easily handled, true and obedient; there is less viciousness among them; they are more patient; they have greater constancy." The other respondent answered all the questions but observed that since "the degree of efficiency peculiar to any

---

[77] *OR*, ser. 1, vol. 28, pt. 1, pp. 328–31 ("To the first"). Dobak and Phillips, *Black Regulars*, pp. 16–19, discusses a similar survey conducted in 1870.

company of troops depends so much upon the character of their officers," it would be impossible to arrive at any firm conclusion about the worth of a particular type of enlisted man.[78]

Throughout the siege of Charleston, whether Colored Troops were attending to purely military siege duties or performing menial tasks for white regiments, the effect was to reduce their clothing to rags. The clothing allowance was inadequate, and many soldiers actually found themselves in debt to the government. This was because black soldiers' pay during most of the war was less than that of white soldiers.[79]

The pay difference resulted from the piecemeal way in which the Army had accepted black soldiers. In August 1862, General Saxton had asked permission to issue army rations and uniforms to five thousand quartermaster's laborers in the Department of the South; unskilled hands were to be paid five dollars a month and mechanics eight. Secretary of War Stanton agreed to this, as well as to the workers' "organization, by squads, companies, battalions, regiments, and brigades." He also told Saxton to enlist five thousand black soldiers "to guard the plantations and settlements occupied by the United States . . . and protect the inhabitants thereof from captivity and murder by the enemy." These soldiers would "receive the same pay and rations" as white volunteers. Only later did the War Department learn that Congress, a month earlier, had established the pay of black troops as "ten dollars per month . . . , three dollars of which . . . may be in clothing," as part of the act that authorized President Lincoln "to receive into the service of the United States, for the purpose of constructing intrenchments, or performing camp service, . . . or any military or naval service for which they may be found competent, persons of African descent." The executive branch, in the person of Secretary Stanton, thus promised what Congress had already denied.[80]

Governor Andrew of Massachusetts also promised soldiers', not laborers', pay to the two black infantry regiments that organized in his state during the spring of 1863. By the time these regiments arrived in South Carolina, locally recruited black regiments had been taking part in coastal raids for more than six months— far different duty from digging trenches, "camp service," or guarding plantations, the role that had been prescribed for them at first. Events had taken a turn unforeseen by policymakers.

---

[78] OR, ser. 1, vol. 28, pt. 1, pp. 329, 330 ("compare favorably"), 331 ("the degree").

[79] Edwin S. Redkey, *A Grand Army of Black Men: Letters From African-American Soldiers in the Union Army, 1861–1865* (New York: Cambridge University Press, 1992), p. 238.

[80] OR, ser. 1, 14: 377 ("organization," "to guard," "receive the"); ser. 3, 2: 282 ("ten dollars"), 281 ("to receive").

CHAPTER 3

THE SOUTH ATLANTIC COAST
1863–1865

By the first week of September 1863, Union troops on Morris Island had dug their trenches close enough to Fort Wagner's earthworks to risk another assault. Just after midnight on the morning of 7 September, a Confederate deserter brought word that the defenders had slipped away by rowing out to steamers that took them to other sites around Charleston Harbor. Federal troops moved into the battered fort before dawn. The eight-week siege of Fort Wagner had ended, but operations against the city itself would go on.[1]

Two days later, a small party of men from the 1st and 2d South Carolina set out on one of the riverine expeditions they were becoming expert in, a foray that depended on the men's local knowledge. The object was to ascend the Combahee River to the Charleston and Savannah Railroad, a little more than twenty miles from the mouth of the river, and tap the telegraph line that ran beside the tracks for enemy messages.[2] The party numbered nearly one hundred men led by two officers, 1st Lt. William W. Sampson of the 1st South Carolina and 1st Lt. Addison G. Osborn of the not-yet-mustered 4th South Carolina. Chaplain James H. Fowler, 1st South Carolina, and Capt. John E. Bryant, 8th Maine Infantry, the originator of the expedition, went along. The chaplain was a remarkable character who sometimes accompanied troops on expeditions heavily armed; Bryant was "one of the most daring scouts in these parts," Col. Thomas W. Higginson wrote. The lieutenants were both former enlisted men of Bryant's company who had been appointed to South Carolina regiments. On the night of 10 September, Lieutenant Osborn, ten enlisted men, and Chaplain Fowler left the base camp along with a civilian telegraph operator and headed for the railroad.[3]

Osborn's party reached the railroad on 11 September, found a hiding place in the woods about 275 yards from the track, and laid a wire from the woods to the telegraph line. Unfortunately, the telegraph operator's connection was so

---

[1] *The War of the Rebellion: A Compilation of the Official Records of the Union and Confederate Armies*, 70 vols. in 128 (Washington, D.C.: Government Printing Office, 1880–1901), ser. 1, vol. 28, pt. 1, p. 27, and pt. 2, p. 86 (hereafter cited as *OR*).

[2] Capt J. E. Bryant to Brig Gen R. Saxton, 29 Sep 1863, filed with (f/w) Brig Gen R. Saxton to Maj Gen Q. A. Gillmore, 10 Nov 1863 (S–518–DS–1863), Entry 4109, Dept of the South, Letters Received, pt. 1, Geographical Divs and Depts, Record Group (RG) 393, Rcds of U.S. Army Continental Cmds, National Archives (NA).

[3] "War-Time Letters from Seth Rogers," p. 65, typescript at U.S. Army Military History Institute (MHI), Carlisle, Pa.; William E. S. Whitman, *Maine in the War for the Union* (Lewiston,

Men of the 54th Massachusetts stand inside Fort Wagner, September 1863

sloppy that it left a length of wire dangling to the ground and attracted the attention of passengers on the first train to pass after dawn the next day. The train stopped and began to blow its whistle as an alarm. The Union soldiers packed up their equipment and started to withdraw toward the Combahee River. Confederate cavalry caught them before they reached the base camp and chased them into a swamp. They captured Lieutenant Osborn, Chaplain Fowler, and some others. Two enlisted men managed to reach the river and find the base camp. Captain Bryant pointed out that despite the failure of the intelligence-gathering mission, the expedition had penetrated fifteen miles beyond Union lines and the advance party a farther ten. They had moved mostly at night, "by long rows upon the Rivers, dangerous and difficult marches . . . in the enemies country, yet no man failed in his duty," Bryant told Brig. Gen. Rufus Saxton. "No troops could have behaved better than did the Colored Soldiers under my command."[4]

Lieutenant Osborn disappears from the historical record at this point. Like scores of other soldiers during the months when black regiments were organizing, he went into action before being mustered into service and his published

---

Me.: Nelson Dingley Jr., 1865), p. 199; Christopher Looby, ed., *Complete Civil War Journal and Selected Letters of Thomas Wentworth Higginson* (Chicago: University of Chicago Press, 2000), p. 171 (quotation). Captain Bryant's report gives the lieutenant's name as Osborn, which does not fit any commissioned officer in the South Carolina regiments, according to the *Official Army Register of the Volunteer Force of the United States Army*, 8 vols. (Washington, D.C.: Adjutant General's Office, 1867).

[4]Bryant to Saxton, 29 Sep 1863.

service record notes that he was discharged to accept an appointment in the 4th South Carolina. A later, end-of-the-war report by the state adjutant general lists him as "died in rebel prison" but assigns him to the 8th Maine. The report of Captain Bryant, his former company commander, mentioned him as "H. E. Osborn" and assigned him to the 2d South Carolina. Since Osborn had not yet mustered in as an officer of his new regiment, there is no record of his service with the U.S. Colored Troops. Such mishaps occurred whenever black regiments went into battle before the Army's clerical processes were complete and helped to swell the war's sum of unknown soldiers.[5]

On 24 November, Bryant led another expedition, sixty men of the 1st South Carolina, toward Pocotaligo Station on the Charleston and Savannah Railroad. The object was to free several families of slaves in the neighborhood and to capture a few Confederate pickets. Sgt. Harry Williams led a small party beyond the rail line to the plantation where the slaves lived and returned with twenty-seven of them. Meanwhile, a dense fog had gathered on the river and the boats that were to embark the successful raiders could not find the landing place. Some of the troops waiting on shore for the fog to lift were discovered by a Confederate cavalry patrol accompanied by five bloodhounds of the kind used to catch escaped slaves. A rifle volley and bayonet charge killed three of the dogs and scattered the cavalry. As the Confederates dispersed, another small party of Union soldiers fired on them, killing the last two bloodhounds. General Saxton thought that the expedition was "a complete success" and that it would prove "startling" to persons who still, in the fall of 1863, "doubt whether the negro soldiers will fight." The 1st South Carolina kept the body of one of the hounds, skinned it, and sent the hide to a New York City taxidermist to preserve as a trophy.[6]

Such small expeditions typified the sort of operation in which locally recruited troops excelled. Black troops recruited in the North, poorly trained before being thrust into a pitched battle, tended to do poorly at first but improved with practice. The dilemma that faced recruiters of Colored Troops in the Department of the South was that Union beachheads in Florida and South Carolina afforded them limited opportunities. Only those former slaves who had escaped on their own or had left with a Union raiding party came within the recruiters' reach. By 1864, black troops from the North would predominate in the department, with two-thirds of the black regiments coming from outside the region: from Maryland and Michigan, New England and New York City, and from Camp William Penn near Philadelphia. They were intended to replace white regiments that had served in the South for two years or more; the Army had plans to use these veteran regiments elsewhere.

Late in 1863, with most Union troops in the Department of the South engaged in the siege of Charleston, interest in the Florida theater of operations revived. The cause was twofold: Confederates were driving Florida cattle north to feed the garrison at Charleston, and the administration in Washington hoped that more active operations in the state might lead to formation of a Unionist government, thus providing Republican electors for the presidential contest of 1864. Both the incum-

---

[5] *Annual Report of the Adjutant General of the State of Maine* (Augusta: Stevens and Sayward, 1863), p. 291; *Appendix D of the Report of the Adjutant General of the State of Maine for the Years 1864 and 1865* (Augusta: Stevens and Sayward, 1866), p. 314.

[6] *OR*, ser. 1, vol. 28, pt. 1, pp. 745–46 (quotation, p. 746); Looby, *Complete Civil War Journal*, p. 329.

This Frank Leslie's Illustrated Newspaper *picture shows twice the number of dogs mentioned in the official report of an encounter between Confederates and the 1st South Carolina. The regiment sent one of the dead dogs to a New York taxidermist for preservation.*

bent Abraham Lincoln and Secretary of the Treasury Salmon P. Chase, who hoped to supplant Lincoln as the party's standard bearer, took an interest in Florida.[7] On 6 February 1864, a 6,000-man expedition boarded transports in the rain at Hilton Head, South Carolina, and steered for the mouth of the St. John's River. Brig. Gen. Truman Seymour, who had organized the assault on Fort Wagner in July, was in command—"a man we have no confidence in," wrote the newly promoted Maj. John W. M. Appleton, "and believe so prejudiced that he would as soon see us slaughtered as not." Appleton and three companies of the 54th Massachusetts would share the steamer *Maple Leaf* with General Seymour and his staff.[8]

Four of the expedition's ten infantry regiments were black. One brigade, led by the veteran raider Col. James Montgomery, included the 54th Massachusetts, Montgomery's own 2d South Carolina, and the 3d United States Colored Infantry (USCI), the first of a series of black regiments organized at Philadelphia and Camp William

---

[7] Robert A. Taylor, *Confederate Storehouse: Florida in the Confederate Economy* (Tuscaloosa: University of Alabama Press, 1995), pp. 133, 136; Jerrell H. Shofner, *Nor Is It Over Yet: Florida in the Era of Reconstruction, 1863–1877* (Baton Rouge: Louisiana State University Press, 1967), pp. 8–9. On Chase's interest in Florida, see John Niven et al., eds., *The Salmon P. Chase Papers*, 5 vols. (Kent, Ohio: Kent State University Press, 1993–1998), 4: 234–35, 307 (quotation, p. 235).

[8] J. W. M. Appleton Jnl photocopy, pp. 157 (quotation), 158, MHI. Estimate of the expedition's strength is a fraction of the 10,092 officers and men listed as present for duty in "Seymour's

Penn. Col. Edward N. Hallowell now led the 54th Massachusetts and Col. Benjamin C. Tilghman the 3d USCI. The 8th USCI, recently arrived from Philadelphia, served in an otherwise white brigade; the regiment's commander was Col. Charles W. Fribley. All of the black regiments' colonels had held commissions in white volunteer regiments and were veterans of the first two years of fighting in the eastern theater of war. The entire Union force numbered about seven thousand men.[9]

On 7 February 1864, the expedition steamed and sailed through the mouth of the St. John's River, passing white sandy beaches and continuing upstream to the burnt ruins of Jacksonville. Confederate pickets were waiting on shore and opened fire as soon as the *Maple Leaf*, bearing General Seymour, Major Appleton, and three companies of the 54th Massachusetts, moored at the city's fish market wharf. The men disembarked at once and moved away from the waterfront. "The sand was deep, and we could not keep our alignment, but Seymour kept calling to me to have the men dress up," Appleton recalled. His men drove the Confederates off quickly, wounding and capturing one of them. The rest of the expedition disembarked and the next day began to move into the country outside the town. The 3d USCI occupied Baldwin, a railroad junction eighteen miles west of Jacksonville that consisted of a depot and warehouse, a hotel, and a few shabby houses. Seymour arrived on 9 February and pushed on to the west, following the mounted troops of his command. The telegraph line between Baldwin and Jacksonville was in working order two days later.[10]

At this point, the expedition began to show the first signs of falling apart. Early on the morning of 11 February, Seymour sent a telegram from Baldwin to Maj. Gen. Quincy A. Gillmore, the department commander, who had accompanied the expedition as far as Baldwin but had returned to Jacksonville en route to his headquarters in South Carolina. The message claimed that Seymour had learned much during his four days ashore that cast doubt on both the methods and aims of the expedition. The Florida Unionist refugees "have misinformed you," he told Gillmore:

> I am convinced that . . . what has been said of the desire of Florida to come back [into the Union] now is a delusion. . . . I believe I have good ground for this faith, and . . . I would advise that the force be withdrawn at once from the interior, that Jacksonville alone be held, and that Palatka be also held, which will permit as many Union people . . . to come in as will join us voluntarily. This movement is in opposition to sound strategy. . . . Many more men than you have here now will be required to support its operation, which had not been matured, as should have been done.

Seymour also warned his superior officer against "frittering away the infantry of your department in such an operation as this." Besides questioning Floridians' ability to form a Unionist government (one of the expedition's fundamental aims),

Command" on 31 January 1864, since not all of the regiments went to Florida. *OR*, ser. 1, vol. 35, pt. 1, pp. 303, 315, 463.

[9]Charles W. Fribley had served in the 84th Pennsylvania, Edward N. Hallowell in the 20th Massachusetts, William W. Marple in the 104th Pennsylvania, and Benjamin C. Tilghman in the 26th Pennsylvania. Luis F. Emilio, *A Brave Black Regiment: History of the Fifty-fourth Regiment of Massachusetts Volunteer Infantry* (New York: Arno Press, 1969 [1894]), p. 150.

[10]*OR*, ser. 1, vol. 35, pt. 1, p. 276; Appleton Jnl, pp. 159–60; *New York Times*, 20 February 1864; Emilio, *Brave Black Regiment*, pp. 151, 155.

Seymour recommended in one sentence both occupying Jacksonville "alone" and "also" Palatka to the south, more than sixty miles up the St. John's River from Jacksonville. Gillmore had told Seymour the day before to "push forward as far as you can toward the Suwanee River," nearly one hundred miles west of Jacksonville and more than halfway to Tallahassee. In reply to Seymour's telegram, Gillmore told him to advance no farther than Sanderson, a station some twenty miles west of Jacksonville on the Florida Atlantic and Gulf Central Railroad.[11]

Seymour's message was a symptom of behavior that puzzled people besides Gillmore. Lincoln's personal secretary John Hay was in Florida that winter helping to organize the state's Unionists. "Seymour has seemed very unsteady and queer since the beginning of the campaign," Hay wrote. "He has been subject to violent alternations of timidity & rashness now declaring Florida loyalty was all bosh— now lauding it as the purest article extant, now insisting that [General Pierre G. T.] Beauregard was in his front with the whole Confederacy & now asserting that he could whip all the rebels in Florida with a good Brigade." Indeed, a few days after Gillmore returned to South Carolina, Seymour reversed his earlier opinion of Florida Unionists' temper and abilities and decided to move toward the Suwanee. Gillmore expressed himself "surprised at the tone" of Seymour's letter and "very much confused" by Seymour's views. He told Seymour to hold the line of the St. Mary's River, which ran from Jacksonville through Baldwin to Palatka, but the message arrived too late.[12]

Seymour had under his command fifteen regiments of infantry (one of them mounted) with a sixteenth still in transit; one battalion of cavalry; and several batteries of light artillery. Nearly all of the infantry regiments were veterans of the siege of Charleston the year before, and three of them had come south with the Port Royal Expedition in the fall of 1861. Seymour's black regiments included the 54th and 55th Massachusetts, 1st North Carolina, 2d and 3d South Carolina, and the 3d and 8th USCIs. All together, the federal force included some nine thousand men.[13]

The soldiers skirmished forward, built defensive works, and repaired the telegraph line, which Confederate guerrillas attacked continually. They also seized $75,000 worth of cotton and foraged liberally on livestock and poultry. When one farmer asked for military aid in recovering a flock of turkeys, the soldiers learned that he kept his slaves locked in the smokehouse lest they hear of the Emancipation Proclamation. "Your men have brought back my turkeys but have taken all my servants," the farmer complained to Major Appleton of the 54th Massachusetts. "The men beg me to allow them to scout for slaves to free," Appleton wrote in his diary. Most of the people the soldiers freed headed for Jacksonville. On 15 February, Appleton saw a railroad flatcar moving in that direction "with a lot of our wounded cavalry on cotton bales & three rebel prisoners of note, and filled in all around them negro children and their mammas, while a long train of freed slaves

---

[11] *OR*, ser. 1, vol. 35, pt. 1, pp. 281–83 (Seymour), 473 (Gillmore).

[12] Ibid., pp. 284–86 (quotations, pp. 285, 286); Michael Burlingame and John R. T. Ettlinger, eds., *Inside Lincoln's White House: The Complete Civil War Diary of John Hay* (Carbondale and Edwardsville: Southern Illinois University Press, 1997), p. 169.

[13] Estimate of total strength derived from averaging the strength of four regiments and multiplying by ten. *OR*, ser. 1, vol. 35, pt. 1, pp. 303, 315. Seymour estimated the strength of his advance as "near 5,500" (p. 288).

walked and pushed the car. Many of the freed slaves belonged to the three prisoners." Despite the invasion's apparent success, some veterans entertained a sense of foreboding. Colonel Fribley of the 8th USCI told Appleton that the army in Florida was "beginning just as we first did in Virginia, knowing nothing, with everything to learn."[14]

The Confederates had not been idle since the Union landing at Jacksonville. General Beauregard, commanding the three-state department, ordered reinforcements to Brig. Gen. Joseph Finegan's District of East Florida from as far away as Charleston. "Do what you can to hold enemy at bay and prevent capture of slaves," he telegraphed Finegan. Beauregard's other concern was to preserve Florida for the Confederate commissary department. "The supply of beef from the peninsula will of course be suspended until the enemy is driven out," Finegan warned. Insufficient rolling stock and a 26-mile gap between the Georgia and Florida rail systems hindered troop movements, but on 13 February, Finegan advanced with barely two thousand men to look for a defensible position east of Lake City. He found one at Olustee Station, thirteen miles down the track. By the time Union troops approached a week later, Finegan's force had grown to nearly fifty-three hundred men.[15]

General Seymour announced his plan to advance toward the Suwanee River on 17 February. If successful, the move would take him two-thirds of the way to the port of St. Mark's on the Gulf Coast. His striking force of fifty-five hundred men—eight infantry regiments, a mounted command, and four batteries of artillery—trudged through the piney woods of northeast Florida. Accompanying two white regiments in the lead brigade was the untried 8th USCI, which had arrived from Philadelphia just two weeks before Seymour's expedition sailed for Florida. The 1st North Carolina and 54th Massachusetts marched together at the rear of the force.[16]

The right of way of the Florida Atlantic and Gulf Central Railroad afforded the easiest route west. By the early afternoon of 20 February, Seymour's force had been on the move since 7:00 a.m., with no rest of more than a few minutes in each hour and no food. The sixteen-mile march had led "over a road of loose sand, or boggy turf, or covered knee-deep with muddy water." Just short of Olustee Station, skirmishers of the 7th Connecticut Infantry met the enemy.[17]

The Confederates withdrew to trenches they had begun digging the day before and brought reinforcements forward rapidly. As the Union skirmishers fell back, their ammunition nearly exhausted, they met the other two regiments of their brigade. Col. Joseph R. Hawley, the brigade commander, tried to deploy the 7th New Hampshire Infantry as skirmishers but gave the order incorrectly. He then tried to correct him-

---

[14]*New York Tribune*, 20 February 1864; Appleton Jnl, pp. 164 ("turkeys"), 168, 169 ("men beg," "with a lot"), 170, 176 ("beginning").

[15]*OR*, ser. 1, vol. 35, pt. 1, pp. 323, 325 ("The supply"), 331, 579 ("Do what").

[16]*New York Tribune*, 1 March 1864; Emilio, *Brave Black Regiment*, p. 158.

[17]*New York Times*, 1 March 1864 (quotation). The 7th Connecticut's commanding officer reported "at 1.30." *OR*, ser. 1, vol. 35, pt. 1, p. 310. The commander of another brigade said "at 2 p.m. precisely" (p. 301); General Seymour, "about 3 p.m." (p. 288). The name of the railroad is taken from the map in George B. Davis et al., eds., *The Official Military Atlas of the Civil War* (New York: Barnes and Noble, 2003 [1891–1895]), pp. 334–35. Other sources call it by shorter variants of the name. *OR*, ser. 1, vol. 35, pt. 1, p. 299 (Florida Central); Emilio, *Brave Black Regiment*, map facing p. 160 (Florida Atlantic and Gulf).

self while the regiment was still attempting to obey his first order. "All semblance of organization was lost in a few moments," Hawley wrote, "save with about one company, which faced the enemy and opened fire. The remainder constantly drifted back, suffering from the fire which a few moments' decision and energy would have checked, if not suppressed. Most of the officers went back with their men, trying to rally them." Of the first brigade in the line of march, only the 8th USCI remained in position with full cartridge boxes.[18]

"An aide came dashing through the woods to us and the order was—'double quick, march!'" 1st Lt. Oliver W. Norton told his sister after the battle. "We . . . ran in the direction of the firing for half a mile. . . . Military men say that it takes veteran troops to maneuver under fire, but our regiment with knapsacks on and unloaded pieces . . . formed a line under the most destructive fire I ever knew." Before being appointed to the 8th USCI, Norton had taken part as an enlisted man in every campaign of the Army of the Potomac, from the spring of 1862 through the summer of 1863.[19]

"You must not be surprised if I am not very clear in regard to what happened for the next two or three hours," 2d Lt. Andrew F. Ely, another Army of the Potomac veteran in the 8th USCI, wrote in a letter home. "I can now tell but little more than what transpired in my own Company for my own 1st Lieut was killed within five minutes . . . and I had so much to attend to that I did not have time to look around much. We were the second company from the colors," which stood in the center of the regimental line, "and so fearful was the decimation that in a short time I dressed the left of my company up to the colors." The company on Ely's left had disintegrated, and he moved to close the gap. His own company went into action with sixty-two men in the ranks, he wrote, and ended with ten present for duty. "Four times our colors went down but they were raised again for *brave men* were guarding them although their skins were black."[20]

The 8th USCI had received its colors only the previous November and had come south two months later. The men had not fired their weapons often, although Colonel Fribley had asked repeatedly that more time be devoted to training. While the regiment was organizing near Philadelphia, Fribley ordered that members of the guard going off duty discharge their weapons at targets, with a two-day pass awarded to the best shot; but an occasional display of individual marksmanship was no substitute for drill in the volley fire that was basic to Civil War tactics. Like many other Civil War soldiers, the men of the 8th USCI entered battle with little practical training. At the time of the battle, the Union garrison of St. Augustine included fifty recruits (nearly 20 percent of the entire force) "who [had] never been initiated into the mysteries of handling a musket."[21]

The men of the 8th USCI "were stunned, bewildered, and . . . seemed terribly scared, but gradually they recovered their senses and commenced firing," Lieutenant Norton wrote. They had little room to maneuver. The road behind

---

[18] *OR*, ser. 1, vol. 35, pt. 1, pp. 304 (quotation), 308, 339, 343–44; William H. Nulty, *Confederate Florida: The Road to Olustee* (Tuscaloosa: University of Alabama Press, 1990), pp. 137–39.

[19] Oliver W. Norton, *Army Letters, 1861–1865* (Chicago: privately printed, 1903), p. 198.

[20] A. F. Ely to Hon A. K. Peckham, 27 Feb 64, A. K. Peckham Papers, Rutgers University, New Brunswick, N.J.

[21] *OR*, ser. 1, vol. 35, pt. 1, p. 489 (quotation); Camp William Penn, Special Orders 16, 16 Nov 1863, and General Orders 13, 8 Nov 1863, both in 8th United States Colored Infantry (USCI),

them was blocked by troops of the next brigade coming into action, and thick woods impeded movement on either side. Colonel Fribley was killed and his second in command received two wounds. Taking over the regiment, Capt. Romanzo C. Bailey ordered what men he could to support an artillery battery that was under attack, but out-of-control battery horses spoiled the movement by charging the infantry and the artillery men had to abandon their guns. It seemed to Norton that "the regiment had no commander . . . , and every officer was doing the best he could with his squad independent of any one else." Learning that his men had run out of ammunition, Bailey withdrew them behind the 54th Massachusetts, which had hurried forward. The 8th USCI had suffered more than 50 percent casualties in less than three hours: more than three hundred killed, wounded, and missing out of fewer than six hundred men. "From all I can learn . . . the regiment was under fire for more than two hours," Lieutenant Norton told his father, "though it did not seem to me so long. I never know anything of the time in a battle, though." As the Union Army began its retreat that evening, the 8th USCI survivors, along with those of the 7th New Hampshire, guarded the wagon train.[22]

While the 8th USCI was losing more than half its strength, Col. William B. Barton's brigade, three white regiments from New York, advanced on the right and engaged the Confederates for four hours. "It was soon apparent that we were greatly outnumbered," Barton reported afterward. "For a long time we were sorely pressed, but the indomitable and unflinching courage of my men and officers at length prevailed, and . . . the enemy's left was forced back, and he was content to permit us to retire. . . . The enemy were . . . too badly punished to feel disposed to molest us."[23] Barton's report was a remarkable piece of writing, an assertion that he had beaten the Confederates so badly that they had to let him retreat. In fact, his brigade lost more than eight hundred men, including all three regimental commanders, before it got away.[24]

As the fight continued, word went to the rear of the Union column for the two black regiments there to hurry forward. The 54th Massachusetts and 1st North Carolina doubled up the road, shedding knapsacks and blanket rolls as they ran past "hundreds of wounded and stragglers" who announced a Union defeat and predicted their imminent deaths. By the time the two regiments arrived at the front, Barton's brigade was withdrawing and the 7th Connecticut, one of the first regiments in action that day, had just received orders to fall back. Expecting a Confederate attack on his left flank, Seymour sent the 54th Massachusetts into the line on the left of the 7th Con-

Regimental Books, RG 94, Rcds of the Adjutant General's Office, NA; Norton, *Army Letters*, pp. 198, 202. On Civil War tactics, see Paddy Griffith, *Battle Tactics of the Civil War* (New Haven: Yale University Press, 1987), pp. 74, 87–89, 101.

[22]*OR*, ser. 1, vol. 35, pt. 1, pp. 312–14; Norton, *Army Letters*, p. 198 ("were stunned"), 204 ("the regiment," "From all"); *New York Times*, 1 March 1864. According to Captain Bailey, the 8th USCI took 565 officers and men into battle and lost a total of 343 killed, wounded, and missing. Col J. R. Hawley, the brigade commander, gave the regiment's strength as 575; Seymour put the loss at 310. *OR*, ser. 1, vol. 35, pt. 1, pp. 298, 303, 312. These figures indicate casualties somewhere between 53.9 and 60.7 percent. Surgeon Charles P. Heichhold estimated the length of the fight at "2 1/2 hours." *Anglo-African*, 12 Mar 1864.

[23]*OR*, ser. 1, vol. 35, pt. 1, p. 302.

[24]Seymour gave the figure as 824, Barton as 811. *OR*, ser. 1, vol. 35, pt. 1, pp. 298, 303.

necticut, with the 1st North Carolina on the right between the Connecticut regiment and Barton's brigade.[25]

The 54th took a position in pine woods about four hundred yards from the Confederates. Branches cut by artillery fire crashed to the ground, injuring some soldiers. The men of the 54th fired quickly; before the day was over, they had exhausted their forty cartridges per man, a total of about twenty thousand rounds for the regiment. It grew dark in the woods by 5:30 p.m., and the diminishing sounds of battle made it clear that the rest of the Union Army had retired. Colonel Montgomery gave the order to fall back; as Colonel Hallowell phrased it in his report, "the men of the regiment were ordered to retreat." Hallowell, though, had become separated from the 54th by this time and did not rejoin it till later in the evening. Officers and men of the regiment who were present heard Montgomery's words differently: "Now, men, you have done well. I love you all. Each man take care of himself." Rather than follow this advice, Lt. Col. Henry N. Hooper called the men together and put them through the manual of arms to calm them. He then ordered the men to cheer heartily, as though they were being reinforced, and afterward withdrew them until he ran into other Union troops "some considerable distance" to the rear. Then, with the 7th Connecticut and the expedition's mounted command, the 54th Massachusetts covered the army's retreat. Major Appleton halted stragglers and looked into their cartridge boxes. Those who still had ammunition joined the rearguard, goaded by Appleton's revolver or by his soldiers' bayonets.[26]

About midnight, the main body of Seymour's expedition reached Barber's Station, where the railroad crossed the St. Mary's River some eighteen miles east of the battlefield. The men of the rearguard caught up an hour or two later, early in the morning of 21 February. They continued on through Baldwin, sometimes pushing boxcars loaded with stores from evacuated posts, until they reached positions outside Jacksonville late the next day. They brought with them about eight hundred sixty wounded, having left forty at the ambulance station on the battlefield under the care of one of the regimental assistant surgeons and twenty-three more at another place on the railroad. When the retreating column reached Jacksonville, the transport *Cosmopolitan* took 215 of the wounded aboard at once and made steam for department headquarters in Port Royal Sound.[27]

The wounded who were left behind fell into the hands of the enemy. Confederate soldiers wrote several firsthand accounts of murdering wounded black soldiers on the battlefield, and their commander reported having taken one hundred fifty unwounded Union prisoners, of whom only three were black. Yet he also wrote to headquarters, "What shall I do with the large number of the enemy's wounded in my hands? Many of these are negroes." Presumably,

[25] *OR*, ser. 1, vol. 35, pt. 1, p. 305; Emilio, *Brave Black Regiment*, p. 162 (quotation).

[26] *OR*, ser. 1, vol. 35, pt. 1, p. 315 (Hallowell); Appleton Jnl, pp. 176, 178; Emilio, *Brave Black Regiment*, pp. 167–69 (Montgomery, p. 168, quotation, p. 169).

[27] *OR*, ser. 1, vol. 35, pt. 1, p. 300; Capt. B. F. Skinner, commanding the 7th Connecticut, reported 3:00 a.m. (p. 309). Col. E. N. Hallowell, commanding the 54th Massachusetts, reported "one hour after midnight" (p. 315).

those prisoners who survived the first few minutes after their capture were not molested further.[28]

Colonel Higginson was attending a ball in Beaufort when the *Cosmopolitan* arrived with its cargo of wounded on the night of 23 February. His regiment, the 1st South Carolina, had almost embarked for Florida earlier in the month, but a report of smallpox in the ranks led to its retention on the Sea Islands. Rumors reached the dancers of a defeat in Florida and of the hospital ship's arrival. All of the island's surgeons were at the ball, along with the ambulances that had carried them and other officers there, but they managed to start bringing the wounded ashore within the hour.[29]

Although Higginson thought that the department commander, General Gillmore, would blame Seymour for the defeat at Olustee, he held Gillmore equally responsible. It was Gillmore who had sent about 40 percent of his entire force on what Higginson and others saw as a political errand—to create a few more Republican electors that fall. Moreover, Gillmore had left in camp near Jacksonville the 2d South Carolina, which had recruited in Florida when Colonel Montgomery organized the regiment a year earlier. Some men of the 2d South Carolina had special knowledge of the country that regiments raised in the North, such as the 54th Massachusetts and the 8th USCI, lacked. This would have been useful on the march inland. Altogether, Higginson thought, the Olustee Campaign was "an utter & ignominious defeat."[30]

Lieutenant Norton, in Florida with the 8th USCI, summed up his impressions of the regiment's role at Olustee twelve days afterward in a letter to his father. "I think no battle was ever more wretchedly fought," the young veteran wrote:

> I was going to say planned, but there was no plan. No new regiment ever went into their first fight in more unfavorable circumstances. . . . I would have halted . . . out of range of the firing, formed my line, unslung knapsacks, got my cartridge boxes ready, and loaded. Then I would have moved up in support of a regiment already engaged. I would have had them lie down and let the balls and shells whistle over them till they got a little used to it. Then I would have moved them to the front.

Instead, Norton told his father:

> We were double-quicked for half a mile, came under fire by the flank, formed line with empty pieces under fire, and, before the men had loaded, many of them were shot down. . . . [A]s the balls came hissing past or crashing through heads, arms and legs, they curled to the ground like frightened sheep in a hailstorm. The officers

---

[28] *OR*, ser. 1, vol. 35, pt. 1, p. 328 (quotation). Accounts of killings on the battlefield are in George S. Burkhardt, *Confederate Rage, Yankee Wrath: No Quarter in the Civil War* (Carbondale: Southern Illinois University Press, 2007), pp. 88–89, and Nulty, *Confederate Florida*, pp. 210–13.

[29] Looby, *Complete Civil War Journal*, pp. 194–98.

[30] On 31 January 1864, troops for the Florida expedition included 11,829 listed as "aggregate present"; for the Sea Islands garrisons, 19,133. *OR*, ser. 1, vol. 35, pt. 1, pp. 281, 285, 463; Looby, *Complete Civil War Journal*, p. 199.

finally got them to firing, and they recovered their senses somewhat. But . . . they did not know how to shoot with effect.

Seymour mismanaged the troops, Norton went on: "Coming up in the rear, . . . as they arrived, they were put in, one regiment at a time, and whipped by detail. . . . If there is a second lieutenant in our regiment who couldn't plan and execute a better battle, I would vote to dismiss him for incompetency."[31]

The defeat at Olustee put out of action one-third of the fifty-five hundred Union troops who were present at the battle. Their losses amounted to 203 killed, 1,152 wounded, and 506 missing. The federal force in northeastern Florida kept to a defensive posture for most of the remainder of the war, but the reasons for this lay outside the state and even outside the Department of the South. The Union's major offensives of 1864 were in preparation, and the District of Florida would be reduced to a coastal toehold.[32]

Preparations for those offensives began even before Lt. Gen. Ulysses S. Grant received orders in March 1864 to report to Washington, D.C., to assume command of all the Union's field armies and to begin planning campaigns for the coming spring. In February, Grant's predecessor in Washington, Maj. Gen. Henry W. Halleck, had asked whether General Gillmore planned any major operations against Charleston for the coming year and how many troops the Department of the South could release for coastal operations elsewhere, perhaps at Mobile or somewhere in North Carolina. Gillmore thought that he might spare between seven and eleven thousand men and still be able to maintain a "safe quiescent defense."[33]

At that time, the Department of the South made the nomenclature of its black regiments conform to the pattern that was being adopted across the country. Colonel Higginson's 1st South Carolina became the 33d USCI; Colonel Montgomery's 2d South Carolina became the 34th USCI; and Col. James C. Beecher's 1st North Carolina became the 35th USCI. The next month, word reached the department that it would lose a number of veteran regiments. The three-year white regiments that had first enlisted in 1861 and had recently reenlisted in sufficient numbers to retain their designations and go home on furlough together would not return to the Department of the South but would report to Washington at the end of their furloughs.[34]

Early in April 1864, when General Grant had decided on troop dispositions, Gillmore received orders to send as many troops "as in your judgment can be safely spared" from the department to Fort Monroe, Virginia, to join Maj. Gen. Benjamin F. Butler's command there. Gillmore himself would go as commander of the X Corps, the field organization to which the regiments would belong. Having received a command he wanted, Gillmore immediately increased the number of troops he thought his old department could spare and took with him more than 40 percent of its total strength

[31] Norton, *Army Letters*, pp. 201–03.

[32] *OR*, ser. 1, vol. 35, pt. 1, p. 298. On 31 January 1864, the number of troops present in the Department of the South was 33,297 and on 31 October 1864, 14,070, a decline of 57.7 percent. In Florida, troops on those dates numbered 14,024 (including "Seymour's command") and 2,969, a decline of 85.9 percent. *OR*, ser. 1, vol. 35, pt. 1, p. 463, and pt. 2, p. 320.

[33] *OR*, ser. 1, vol. 35, pt. 1, p. 494, and pt. 2, p. 23 (quotation).

[34] *OR*, ser. 1, vol. 35, pt. 2, p. 23; Frederick H. Dyer, *A Compendium of the War of the Rebellion* (New York: Thomas Yoseloff, 1959 [1909]), p. 1729.

rather than the maximum of one-third that he had suggested to Halleck earlier.[35]

The Department of the South had always been near the bottom of the list of Union strategists' priorities; and within the department the District of Florida, at the tail end of the Atlantic Coast supply line, mattered least. Gillmore's move north withdrew nine white regiments from the District of Florida and sent the 21st and 34th USCIs and the 54th and 55th Massachusetts north to the islands around Charleston Harbor. By the end of April, only nine regiments remained in northeastern Florida. Four of them were black: the 3d, 8th, and 35th USCIs and the recently arrived 7th USCI. The 7th had come from Baltimore with the new district commander, Brig. Gen. William Birney, who had been organizing black regiments in Maryland. Gillmore's successors complained about the department's loss of troops to no avail. Scarce manpower would preclude any major Union operations until Maj. Gen. William T. Sherman's western armies, still bearing the title Military Division of the Mississippi, approached Savannah late that fall.[36]

Col. James C. Beecher of the 1st North Carolina (later the 35th U.S. Colored Infantry)

Capt. Luis F. Emilio of the 54th Massachusetts referred to the spring of 1864 in the Department of the South as a period of "utter stagnation," but there was more going on than Emilio could see from his post on Morris Island. By the end of April, fourteen black and fourteen white infantry regiments as well as one of artillery and one of cavalry (both white) were serving in the department. The transports that took the X Corps north had returned with two new regiments, the 29th Connecticut Infantry (Colored) and the 26th USCI from New York City. "When we were ordered here we all expected it would be to go into fighting immediately," the 26th's Assistant Surgeon Jonathan L. Whitaker told his wife; "but we find that the white troops who were here are leaving to go north, and we are to take their place, from which we . . . infer that our business will be simply to guard the place, an idea of course very acceptable to all of us."[37]

At Beaufort, where the new regiments landed, General Saxton called the newcomers "perfectly raw recruits, uninstructed in any of their duties." The interim department commander, Brig. Gen. John P. Hatch, was also concerned. He

---

[35] *OR*, ser. 1, vol. 35, pt. 1, p. 463, and pt. 2, pp. 34, 77, 203. Gillmore's requests for field command are in pt. 2, pp. 24, 29.

[36] *OR*, ser. 1, vol. 35, pt. 1, pp. 11 (Maj Gen J. G. Foster, 11 Jun 1864), 463, and pt. 2, pp. 77, 92 (Brig Gen J. P. Hatch, 13 May 1864), 130 (Foster, 15 Jun 1864), 142 (Foster, 21 Jun 1864), 251 (Foster, 19 Aug 1864).

[37] *OR*, ser. 1, vol. 35, pt. 2, pp. 37, 52, 78–79; J. L. Whitaker to My dear Wife, 13 Apr 1864, J. L. Whitaker Papers, Southern Historical Collection, University of North Carolina, Chapel Hill; Emilio, *Brave Black Regiment*, p. 192.

protested to the Adjutant General's Office that "mere raw colored troops . . . do not add to our efficiency; on the contrary, [they] are an element of weakness." Hatch's successor, Maj. Gen. John G. Foster, sought to remedy the problem by establishing a camp of instruction for new regiments. By mid-June, he was able to assure General Halleck that in "two or three months, at the farthest, I will have these colored regiments so set up that they can be taken into battle with confidence."[38]

Although the enlisted men in the new black regiments were unschooled, many of their officers had spent the previous two or three years in the Army and agreed with their generals about the need for instruction and discipline. One of them was 1st Lt. Henry H. Brown, 29th Connecticut, who expounded his views to friends and family in letters from Beaufort during the spring of 1864. "You don't see any need of white gloves & c.," he wrote to his mother, who scoffed at military niceties. "'They never will put down the rebellion.' Well which have you found to be the best workmen[,] the sloven or the one that took pride & kept himself clean?" Brown asked. "The cleanest & proudest man in personal dress & carriage, is the best & most faithful soldier. . . . Moreover health demands neatness & the higher the degree of neatness the better the health of the men." Comparing inspections at Beaufort with those he had undergone in his previous regiment, Brown reflected:

> I used to think Fort McHenry inspections something but they did not equal this. I did not like them, but I like these[.] [I]t is just what the men need to make them soldiers. . . . I look through different eyes somewhat now for my position enables me to judge better what is best for the welfare and discipline of the regt. . . . [W]ere our volunteer regts. officered differently & under more strict diciphine our army would be more effective. All troops in this department have invurbly done nobly. Witness Pulaski Charleston & even at Olustee though a defeat yet for the discipline of the men it would have been a rout.

So the men of the new regiments settled down to drill among the magnolias and mosquitoes.[39]

News of a Confederate naval project caused a brief flurry of activity early in the summer. According to a report from the U.S. Navy Department, South Carolina planters had built an ironclad ram in the Savannah River with which they intended to distract Rear Adm. John A. Dahlgren's South Atlantic Blockading Squadron while blockade runners put to sea with twenty-two thousand bales of cotton valued at $8 million. Dahlgren consulted with General Foster, who thought the best role for his troops would be to march inland and cut the Charleston and Savannah Railroad. On their way, they might capture or damage some Confederate gun emplacements that hindered the movement of Dahlgren's vessels. If all went well, Foster told General Halleck in Washington, he then intended to march on Savan-

---

[38] *OR*, ser. 1, vol. 35, pt. 2, pp. 55 (Saxton), 92 (Hatch), 130 (Foster).
[39] H. H. Brown to Dear friends at Home, 29 Apr 1864 ("I used," "mosquitoes"); H. H. Brown to Dear Mother, 24 May 1864 ("You don't," "magnolias"); both in H. H. Brown Papers, Connecticut Historical Society, Hartford.

*Newly arrived Union troops found the South full of strange plants and animals.
Here, officers and men of the 29th Connecticut stand beneath a large tree
apparently festooned with Spanish moss.*

nah, "where I think we can make a 'ten strike.'"[40] Officers in some of the black
regiments had been worried that spring about the possibility of mutinies because
of the men's dissatisfaction with their low pay and Congress' inattention to the
matter; but when the men of the 54th Massachusetts received orders on 30 June
to leave their insect- and vermin-ridden camp on Morris Island and prepare for a
campaign, they were "jubilant, cheerful as can be, joking each other and anxious
to meet the Rebs."[41]

General Foster ordered three separate Union brigades to head inland during
the first week of July, a process that on the South Carolina coast amounted to
island hopping. A brigade of white troops led by Col. William W. H. Davis steamed
north from Hilton Head Island to disembark on John's Island, about ten miles
from Charleston and a stretch of the railroad that ran west from the city parallel
to the Stono River. General Saxton's brigade, which included the 26th USCI, left
Beaufort, on Port Royal Island, to join Davis' brigade. General Birney's brigade,
brought from Florida and composed of the 7th, 34th, and 35th USCIs, went up the
North Edisto River and landed on the mainland, some distance west of the first
two brigades but far enough inland to be about the same distance as the others

---

[40]*OR*, ser. 1, vol. 35, pt. 2, pp. 146–47, 155–58 (quotations, p. 157); *Official Records of the
Union and Confederate Navies in the War of the Rebellion*, 30 vols. (Washington, D.C.: Government
Printing Office, 1894–1922), ser. 1, 15: 514–15 (hereafter cited as *ORN*).

[41]Appleton Jnl, p. 249. Complaints about insects and vermin on Morris Island are on pp. 216,
221, 237, and 245.

from the railroad. At the same time, the 33d USCI; the 55th Massachusetts; and a white regiment, the 103d New York, crossed from Folly Island to James Island in order to strike from that direction. The 54th Massachusetts left Morris Island to join the force on James Island.[42]

Birney's twelve hundred men camped just a mile from their landing place on the evening of 2 July. The next morning, they ran into Confederate skirmishers guarding a bridge over the Dawho River. This forced Birney's men off the road and offered them the alternatives of advancing through a "miry and deep" swamp or attempting to ford a salt creek thirty-seven yards wide and flanked on either side by fifty yards of marsh. Faced with equally unsatisfactory choices, the brigade withdrew and boarded ships for James Island, taking with it six wounded men who were its only casualties. Birney called the operation "an excellent drill" for his troops "preparatory to real fighting," but General Foster attributed the failure to Birney's dawdling on the first day.[43]

At John's Island, shallow water prevented Saxton's and Davis' brigades from getting ashore before 3 July; "intense heat" the next day prevented them from moving far. "We commenced marching at 3 O'clk and marched about 4 hours," Assistant Surgeon Whitaker told his wife. "On the march the men threw away many blankets, knapsacks &c which they were unable to carry, some were sunstruck on the way. The roads were narrow & sandy & dust flew & sweat poured till we were all of a color," enlisted men and officers alike. For the 26th USCI, three months after leaving New York City, the march was torturous. "The men done very well for the first 2 or 3 hours & then they began to fall out, . . . men by dozens began to fall down by the sides of the road unable to go another step," Whitaker wrote. "Of course if we left them behind the rebs would get them & so we had to keep them up some way. . . . [T]he very worst cases we put in ambulances. . . . Right in the midst of it all the rebel pickets fired upon us & we did not know but we should have a battle right away. They fell back however & did not molest us any more."[44]

On 5 July, the Union force advanced with Saxton's brigade guarding against Confederate attempts to cut the road to the landing. The next day, Navy vessels opened a supply line between the troops on John's Island and those on James Island and Saxton's men joined Davis' brigade in the advance. "We were now entirely out of everything to eat," Whitaker wrote. "All I had this day was some hard tack I picked up on the ground where the men had camped the night before. I also picked up a small piece of lean salt beef which I considered quite a prize. The next day by noon we managed to get some bread & coffee issued & a little meat." About 5:00 in the afternoon of 7 July, the 26th USCI attacked the Confederate position. General Hatch, temporarily commanding the department once more, thought that the men "behaved very handsomely, advancing steadily in open ground under a heavy fire, and driving the enemy from the line." According to the Confederate commander's report, the 26th carried the position on its fifth

---

[42]OR, ser. 1, vol. 35, pt. 1, pp. 104–06, and pt. 2, pp. 14, 78–79, 84–86, 408–09; Appleton Jnl, p. 248.
[43]OR, ser. 1, vol. 35, pt. 1, pp. 14, 408–09 (quotations, p. 409).
[44]Ibid., pp. 84 ("intense heat"), 105; J. L. Whitaker to My dear Wife, 12 Jul 1864 ("We commenced").

attempt and with the help of the 157th New York of Davis' brigade, at the cost of 11 men killed, 71 wounded, and 12 missing. "Had the advance been supported," Hatch wrote, "the enemy's artillery would have been captured; as it was, both artillery and infantry were driven from the field" by a regiment that had arrived from the North only three months earlier. The attack had not been arranged well, but the troops' performance must have benefited from the weeks spent at General Foster's camp of instruction at Beaufort.[45]

Two days later, the Confederates attacked early in the morning about 4:30 and again about 6:00, but the federal troops stopped both assaults. Then, having decided that Confederate batteries on the Stono River were too well positioned to storm, Union commanders declared the operation a success and reembarked the two brigades. Their demonstration on John's Island alarmed the Confederates and caused them to reinforce Charleston's defenders, but federal troops had not come within miles of their announced goal, the railroad.[46]

The third part of Union operations during early July consisted of a landing on the south end of James Island that was meant to draw Confederate defenders away from a projected federal attack on Fort Johnson, which overlooked Charleston Harbor at the island's northeastern tip. The force responsible for the southern landing was a brigade led by Col. Alfred S. Hartwell of the 55th Massachusetts. After a series of orders and counterorders that kept the troops up for two nights, the 55th Massachusetts, 103d New York, and 33d USCI landed on James Island early on the morning of 2 July. Trying to get ashore, men sank above their waists in mud. Soon after emerging from the thick woods and underbrush that lined the shore, the advancing troops came under fire from two Confederate cannon. This killed seven men in the lead regiment, the 103d New York, and caused it either to "fall back a few yards and reform," as its commanding officer reported, or to become "panic-stricken," as Sgt. James M. Trotter of the 55th Massachusetts put it. The 55th came out of the woods and moved through a marsh toward the Confederate guns. "This gave Johnny a great advantage over us as we could only advance very slowly and the men were continually sinking," Trotter wrote. "We had now got beyond the jungle [and] was within 200 yds of the battery when we made a desperate rush yelling unearthly. Here the Rebels broke . . . and by the time we had gained the parapet were far down the road leading to Secessionville. . . . We had been out two days and nights wading through the mud and water and were too tired to pursue." Meanwhile, the 1,000-man landing force at Fort Johnson missed the tide by an hour, grounded its boats, and lost 5 officers and 132 enlisted men captured by the Confederates. Like the troops on John's Island, Hartwell's brigade stayed put until Generals Foster and Hatch, after conferring with Admiral Dahlgren on 8 July, decided that the Confederate defenses were too formidable to assault with the force at their command. Union troops evacuated the inshore islands by

---

[45] *OR*, ser. 1, vol. 35, pt. 1, pp. 85 (quotations), 264; Whitaker to My dear Wife, 12 Jul 1864; Dyer, *Compendium*, p. 834.
[46] *OR*, ser. 1, vol. 35, pt. 1, p. 85.

the afternoon of 10 July. Naval vessels watched the estuaries and tidal creeks until daylight the next day to pick up stragglers.[47]

None of the three Union columns had come close to accomplishing General Foster's objective of damaging the Charleston and Savannah Railroad, but Foster declared himself satisfied with the result and withdrew the troops to the camps they had occupied before the operation. "The late movements have had a decidedly beneficial effect on the troops, both white and black," he told General Halleck in Washington. "The latter, especially, improved every day that they were out, and, I am happy to say, toward the last evinced a considerable degree of pluck and good fighting qualities. I am now relieved of apprehension as to this class of troops, and believe, with active service and drill, they can be made thorough soldiers." Foster must have found his new confidence in the black regiments reassuring, for their number had grown until they constituted half of his entire infantry force.[48]

The bombardment of Charleston and its forts wore on through the summer, its intensity lessening as ordnance depots in the Department of the South emptied to supply the Virginia Campaign. In August, three white infantry regiments and General Birney's brigade, the 7th, 8th, and 9th USCIs, sailed for Virginia. As summer passed into autumn, the troops that remained near Charleston toiled on gun emplacements, preparing for the day when more ammunition for the artillery would arrive.[49]

On 2 September, while Foster's reduced force remained entirely on the defensive, General Sherman's armies occupied the city of Atlanta, two hundred sixty miles west of Charleston. They then maneuvered against the Confederate General John B. Hood's Army of Tennessee for six weeks while Sherman readied his force for the March to the Sea. Whether the destination would be the Gulf of Mexico by way of the Chattahoochee River and Alabama or the Atlantic by way of Georgia and the Savannah River, no one outside Atlanta was sure. Then, on 11 November, Sherman telegraphed General Halleck, "To-morrow our wires will be broken, and this is probably my last dispatch. I would like to have General Foster to break the Savannah and Charleston road about Pocotaligo about December 1." The need to prevent Confederate reinforcements from annoying the left flank of his March to the Sea was the reason behind Sherman's instruction, which marked the beginning of the last Union offensive movement in the Department of the South.[50]

Halleck was still not quite sure of Sherman's route when he wrote to Foster on 13 November, but he emphasized that in any event "a demonstration on [the railroad] will be of advantage. You will be able undoubtedly to learn [Sherman's] movements through rebel sources . . . and will shape your action accordingly." General Hatch, commanding the Union force in the siege of Charleston, judged from activity in the Confederate defenses that Sherman was headed there. By the time Halleck's order arrived, Foster had a vague idea that Sherman had passed Macon, Georgia. He

---

[47] Ibid., pp. 14–15, 78, 79 ("fall back"); *ORN*, ser. 1, 15: 554–56; J. M. Trotter to E. W. Kinsley, 18 Jul 1864, E. W. Kinsley Papers, Duke University (DU), Durham, N.C.

[48] *OR*, ser. 1, vol. 35, pt. 1, pp. 16–17 (quotation, p. 17), and pt. 2, p. 204; *ORN*, ser. 1, 15: 556.

[49] *OR*, ser. 1, vol. 35, pt. 1, pp. 21–23, and pt. 2, p. 202.

[50] Ibid., pt. 1, p. 25, and pt. 2, p. 258; vol. 39, pt. 3, p. 740.

wrote to Halleck on 25 November that he would "move on the night of the 28th, and . . . attack on the next day."[51]

Foster assembled a striking force of five white and six black infantry regiments—among them the 34th and 35th USCIs from Florida—as well as other white troops—a cavalry regiment and sections of three artillery batteries. Left to look after Charleston Harbor and to man posts in the Sea Islands and Florida were five white and four black infantry regiments; some white engineers and artillery; and Battery G, 2d U.S. Colored Artillery. Foster's force, called the Coast Division, amounted to five thousand soldiers. An additional body of five hundred sailors and marines was termed the Naval Brigade.[52]

The division boarded ships at Hilton Head on 28 November. The transports cast off at about 2:30 the next morning and headed for a landing place on the south bank of the Broad River. A dense fog soon descended. Some vessels dropped anchor to wait for daylight, others ran aground, and still others steered a mistaken course up the

James M. Trotter was one of the few black men who rose above the enlisted ranks. This photograph shows him as a second lieutenant of the 55th Massachusetts.

nearby Chechesse River. It was 11:00 a.m. before the Naval Brigade began to go ashore. A small steamer carrying building material for a solid surface on which to land the artillery went up the wrong river and did not arrive until 2:00 p.m. Late that afternoon, Foster turned command over to General Hatch and returned to department headquarters at Hilton Head.[53]

The Naval Brigade began moving inland, its men pulling their own artillery support, eight twelve-pounder howitzers. "Unfortunately the maps and guides proved equally worthless," Hatch reported, and the naval force took a wrong turn while following some retreating Confederates. The nearest town was Grahamville, which Union troops had hoped to reach on the first day, but

---

[51] *OR*, ser. 1, vol. 35, pt. 2, p. 328 ("a demonstration"); 44: 505, 525, 547 ("move on").
[52] *OR*, ser. 1, 44: 420–21, 591.
[53] Ibid., pp. 420–21, 586–87.

the sailors and marines went two or three miles out of their way. A brigade of infantry commanded by Brig. Gen. Edward E. Potter landed by 4:00 p.m. and pushed after the Naval Brigade. Not until the soldiers caught up with the sailors did anyone discover the mistake.[54]

The troops retraced their steps to the crossroads where they had gone astray. There the infantry left the exhausted sailors and their cannon and went on. By this time it was dark. The soldiers took a road that led them six miles off course. They then turned around and made their way back, not stopping for the night until about 2:00 a.m. on 30 November. "The men had then marched fifteen miles, had been up most of the previous night, had worked hard during the day, and were unable to march farther," Hatch reported. "The distance marched, if upon the right road, would have carried us to the railroad, and I have since learned we would have met, at that time, little or no opposition." By daybreak, the sailors had found horses to draw all but two of their cannon. They left that pair at the crossroads along with an infantry guard of four companies from the 54th Massachusetts and moved to join Potter's brigade a few miles up the road. The other infantry brigade, commanded by Colonel Hartwell of the 55th Massachusetts Infantry, had spent all night getting ashore. Little more than one regiment had joined the main body when the Union force moved forward at 9:00 a.m. Fifteen minutes later, it met the enemy.[55]

The Confederate leader, Maj. Gen. Gustavus W. Smith of the Georgia State Troops, had decided to disregard his governor's order not to take his command beyond the state line. Smith delivered some twelve hundred Georgia militia and a few cannon by rail at Grahamville about 8:00 a.m. on 30 November. It was these men who met the Union advance. Other Confederate troops arrived during the day, but they never numbered more than fourteen hundred in the line of battle. Outnumbered three to one by the federal force, the Confederates fell back gradually for some three-and-a-half miles until they reached a hastily selected position on Honey Hill. The Union troops followed them up a narrow road through dense woods that more than one officer called "thick jungle," stopping whenever the retreating Confederates did and exchanging artillery shots. The 35th USCI "was ordered up, to move through the thicket along the right side of the road," Colonel Beecher told his fiancée. Orders were to flank the Confederate cannon and charge them. "I did so," Beecher continued:

> But the enemy ran the guns off & I came right in front of a strong earth work that nobody knew anything about. . . . The boys opened fire without orders, and the bushes were so thick that the companies were getting mixed. I halted and reformed the companies. Then got orders to move to the left of the earthwork and try to carry it. I led off by the left flank, the boys starting finely & crying out "follow de cunnel." It was a perfect jungle all laced with grape vines, & when I got on the left of the earth work and closed up I found that another regiment had marched right through mine & cut it off, so that I only had about 20 men. We could see the rebel gunners load. I told the boys to fire on them & raise a yell, hoping to make them think I had

---

[54] Ibid., pp. 422 (quotation), 436, 587.
[55] Ibid., pp. 422 (quotation), 435.

a force on their flank. We fired & shouted & got a volley or two in return. A rascally bullet hit me just below the groin & ranged down nearly through my thigh. Then I went back with my twenty to the road again, found 35th, 55th [Massachusetts], 54th [Massachusetts] men all mixed together.[56]

By late morning, Colonel Hartwell had come up with companies of the 54th and 55th Massachusetts. As they approached the Confederate position on Honey Hill, the woods fell away and Hartwell's command went into line in a cornfield to the left of the road. Lt. Col. Stewart L. Woodford offered to lead the 127th New York against the Confederate works if another regiment would charge on the other side of the road. Hartwell led part of the 55th Massachusetts forward until Confederate fire stopped them. He received a bullet wound in the hand and a stunning blow in the side from a spent grapeshot. Neither regiment reached the Confederate position. The 55th Massachusetts suffered casualties of 27 killed, 106 wounded, and 2 missing.[57]

With ammunition running out, Union soldiers rummaged the cartridge boxes of the dead and wounded. About 1:00 p.m., Col. Henry L. Chipman arrived on the field with his regiment, the 102d USCI. They had come ashore just two hours earlier and had marched straight to the battle. Chipman posted two companies on the road through the woods to round up stragglers. About 3:00 p.m., word reached him that men were needed to recover a pair of guns belonging to Battery B, 3d New York Artillery. Two of the battery's ammunition chests had exploded, injuring one officer and three enlisted men. One of its other officers had been killed and another wounded and eight enlisted men killed or seriously wounded. Eight of the battery's horses were out of action. One company of the 102d USCI tried to recover the guns. In the attempt, its commanding officer was killed and the only other officer wounded twice. The ranking noncommissioned officer, not having been told what the objective was, merely put the company in line of battle facing the enemy. Another company then moved toward the guns and retrieved them.[58]

By 4:00 p.m., the field artillery batteries had nearly run out of ammunition and had to be replaced by the sailors' twelve-pounder howitzers, which continued firing until long after dark. A withdrawal began at dusk, with the 102d USCI, the last regiment to arrive, remaining on the field with the 127th New York and two naval howitzers until 7:30 p.m. Striving to cast the day's events in a favorable light, General Hatch noted that the retreat "was executed without loss or confusion; . . . not a wounded man was left on the field, except those who fell at the foot of the enemy's works . . . ; no stores or equipments fell into the hands of the enemy." General Foster called Honey Hill "a drawn battle." Nevertheless, the expedition had failed to reach the Charleston and Savannah Railroad, let alone damage it. The day's losses amounted to 89 killed,

---

[56] J. C. Beecher to My beloved, 2 Dec 1864, J. C. Beecher Papers, Schlesinger Library, Harvard University, Cambridge, Mass.

[57] *OR*, ser. 1, 44: 415–16, 426, 428, 431–32, 911.

[58] Ibid., pp. 432–36.

629 wounded, and 28 missing on the Union side. Confederate casualties were 8 killed and 42 wounded.[59]

The Coast Division retired to Boyd's Neck, where it had come ashore. During the following weeks, several forays inland took its troops close to the railroad but inflicted no damage on the line. Meanwhile, Sherman's army continued to move from Atlanta toward the sea at the rate of about nine miles a day. On 4 December, General Foster received a report that the western army was in sight of Savannah. On 12 December, one of Sherman's scouts reached Beaufort and established communication with the Department of the South. Nine days later, Sherman's troops entered Savannah as the city's Confederate garrison abandoned it and dispersed toward Augusta and Charleston. The war had entered its final phase.[60]

It was a phase in which the Colored Troops of the Department of the South played only a minor part. The day before Savannah fell to Sherman's troops, Col. Charles T. Trowbridge led three hundred men of the 33d USCI on a reconnaissance from the Coast Division's base to a point two miles beyond the Union picket line toward the Pocotaligo Road. There they met a Confederate force of about equal size. "Formed line of battle and charged across the open field into the woods and routed the enemy," Trowbridge reported. "My observations yesterday," he added, "have convinced me that the only way to reach the railroad with a force from our present position is by the way of the Pocotaligo road, as the country on our left is full of swamps, which are impassable for anything except light troops." These were the same swamps, made worse by "the late heavy rains" that Sherman's XVII Corps encountered three weeks later when it moved by sea from Savannah to Beaufort and marched inland to cut the railroad.[61]

The XVII Corps numbered about twelve thousand soldiers. They impressed the Department of the South's seventy-five hundred officers and men by their appearance and their reputation. "Sherman's men appear gay and happy," Capt. Wilbur Nelson of the 102d USCI recorded in his diary. "They are a rough set of men, but good fighters." The new arrivals had marched across Tennessee, Mississippi, and Georgia during the past three years and now felt that they were in the home stretch. Pvt. Alonzo Reed of Captain Nelson's regiment agreed that the westerners "look[ed] very Rough." Captain Emilio of the 54th Massachusetts called them "a seasoned, hardy set of men. . . . Altogether they impressed us with their individual hardiness, powers of endurance, and earnestness of purpose, and as an army, powerful, full of resources and with staying powers unsurpassed." By 8 February 1865, the XVII Corps had "heavy details" of men at work destroying eight miles of track on the Charleston and Savannah Railroad, a goal that had eluded the Department of the South for months. The materiel and manpower available to one of the Union's principal armies and the high morale of its troops that came from their having continually beaten their

---

[59] Ibid., pp. 416, 424 ("was executed"), 425, 433, 665 ("a drawn").
[60] Ibid., pp. 12, 420–21, 708; vol. 47, pt. 1, p. 1003.
[61] *OR*, ser. 1, 44: 451 ("Formed line"); vol. 47, pt. 1, p. 375 ("late heavy rains").

This wagon track through woods was typical of country roads throughout the South—indeed, the United States—in the mid-nineteenth century. Along such roads, Union troops in South Carolina advanced inland in April 1865.

Confederate opponents overcame obstacles that had long baffled the troops of a backwater beachhead.[62]

The need to recruit more black soldiers was much on the mind of General Foster that winter as he prepared to relinquish command of the Department of the South to go on medical leave. Thousands of black Georgians had followed Sherman's army to the sea, and Foster saw a chance to "raise two or three regiments" from the men among them. By mid-January, he had filled his existing regiments of U.S. Colored Troops to the statutory minimum and recruited "several hundred" men besides. He asked the adjutant general to assign him numbers for "at least four" new regiments. Yet Foster had to admit on 1 February that "recruiting of negroes does not progress well." Only four hundred fifty men had enlisted, for which Foster blamed General Saxton, who had "created some disorder by his harangues before mass meetings of negroes, which he called in Savannah." The Union occupying force would prohibit any more mass meetings, Foster promised. Meanwhile,

---

[62] *OR*, ser. 1, 44: 848, 855; vol. 47, pt. 1, p. 377 ("heavy details"). W. Nelson Diary, 13 Jan 1865, Michigan State University Archives, East Lansing; A. Reed to Dear Mother, 11 Jan 1865, A. Reed Papers, DU; Emilio, *Brave Black Regiment*, pp. 269–70.

Foster's superintendent of volunteer recruiting, Brig. Gen. Milton S. Littlefield, would continue his work in the department.[63]

General Saxton's role in recruiting, and the conflict it generated, stemmed from a meeting on 12 January between General Sherman, Secretary of War Edwin M. Stanton, and twenty black clergymen and lay leaders in Savannah. They answered questions from the general and the secretary about their opinions regarding slavery, the war, black enlistment in the Union Army, and how black people would prefer to live after the war. In response to their answers, Sherman published his Special Field Orders No. 15 four days later. The orders restricted residence on the Sea Islands and nearby abandoned farms on the mainland to former slaves only, except for "military officers and soldiers detailed for duty." General Saxton became "inspector of settlements and plantations," charged with assuring residents' title to their land pending final action by Congress. His other duties included "enlistment and organization of the negro recruits and protecting their interests while [they were] absent from their settlements." The Department of the South, however, already had a superintendent of volunteer recruiting in General Littlefield. Not until 14 February was the difficulty straightened out, with Saxton succeeding Littlefield as superintendent. Even this late in the war, the government seemed incapable of organizing the U.S. Colored Troops without creating overlapping and conflicting authorities. As a result of this confusion, the first of the new regiments in the Department of the South, the 103d USCI, did not complete its organization until March 1865 and the other two, the 104th and 128th USCIs, until April.[64]

Long before spring, while the XVII Corps was moving inland to rejoin the rest of Sherman's army in its march north, the Union force that had been watching Charleston Harbor for the previous two years finally occupied the city. On the morning of 18 February, Lt. Col. Augustus G. Bennett, 21st USCI, sent Capt. Samuel Cuskaden, 52d Pennsylvania, to reconnoiter the ruins of Fort Sumter. Rowing toward the fort, Cuskaden met a boatload of Confederate bandsmen from Fort Moultrie on Sullivan's Island, who told him that they had been left behind in the evacuation of the city and its defenses. Cuskaden sent his original boat crew on to raise a U.S. flag over Fort Moultrie and had the Confederates row him back to Morris Island to report to Bennett. After securing the harbor forts, a small Union force landed in Charleston itself about 10:00 a.m. While Bennett sent for the mayor to arrange the city's surrender, he heard explosions as the Confederates blew up supply depots and warships. Late that afternoon, his own regiment, the 21st USCI, came ashore to begin patrolling Charleston as a provost guard.[65]

Meanwhile, the small force that remained in Florida tried to stay active. "I've just popped in here with 7 Cos. of my Regt after a raid of eight days," Colonel Beecher wrote from St. Augustine in May 1864. "We took a steamer up St. John's River. . . . Then across the County to east side. . . . Got out of rations–Shot beef & stole potatoes & Horses—Scared Secesh into fits . . . & played the mischief generally." In official correspondence, Beecher was more subdued, noting the condition

---

[63] *OR*, ser. 1, vol. 47, pt. 1, p. 1002 ("raise two"), 1005 ("at least"), 1007 ("recruiting").

[64] Ibid., pp. 61 ("military officers"), 62 ("enlistment"); vol. 47, pt. 2, pp. 37–41, 186, 424. Dyer, *Compendium*, pp. 252–53.

[65] *OR*, ser. 1, vol. 47, pt. 1, pp. 1018–20; vol. 53, pp. 60–61.

of railroads reconnoitered, a steam sawmill with a boiler in apparently good condition, salvageable naval stores, "live oak ship knees, about fifty above water, easy of access. . . . I suppose the lot to be valuable." He reported the suspected presence of a "considerable rebel force scattered round" and recommended a raid to disperse it and to secure about six hundred head of cattle that roamed outside Union lines.[66]

Nothing came of Beecher's proposal. General Foster, commanding the department, needed reinforcements for his move against the Charleston and Savannah Railroad (see pp. 72–76, above), and he ordered General Birney at Jacksonville to join him with the 7th and 35th USCIs. After the unsuccessful conclusion of Foster's South Carolina operation, Birney and both regiments returned to Florida and at once mounted an operation from the beachhead to which a defeated Union army had withdrawn after the Battle of Olustee. The 7th, 8th, and 35th USCIs, accompanied by two white infantry regiments (one of them mounted), a battalion of cavalry, and a battery of artillery, both white, attacked the railroad south of Baldwin, the town through which they had passed five months earlier while advancing toward and retreating from Olustee. To reach the railroad, they boated twenty-five miles up the St. John's River to Black Creek and another four miles up Black Creek to "an obscure landing concealed by woods" so small that it took three nights to disembark the entire force. By 24 July, all the troops were ashore and building a "frail and floating" bridge, "made mostly of fence rails," across a branch of Black Creek south of Middleburg. There, a force of nearly one hundred mounted Confederates attacked them. The 35th USCI drove them off, and the cavalry battalion gave chase. The next day, the Union troops continued their drive. The infantry built a bridge over the swollen North Fork of Black Creek while the horses swam the stream. Once across, the mounted troops dashed ahead to destroy trestles on the two rail lines that intersected at Baldwin. "It was after midnight when the work at the railroad ceased," General Birney reported. "The day's work had been enormous." On 27 July, Union troops occupied the railroad junction at Baldwin for the first time since their retreat from Olustee in February.[67]

The 3d USCI occupied the town of Palatka on the St. John's River some sixty miles upstream from Jacksonville. Its commanding officer was encouraged to patrol to the south and west, to go even as far as Ocala, two-thirds of the way to the Gulf, if he encountered no opposition. The 9th, 26th, 34th, and 102d USCIs and the 29th Connecticut were ready to embark at Hilton Head to reinforce that effort when word arrived that Generals Grant and Halleck had already agreed to move a brigade of black infantry from the Department of the South to the siege of Petersburg. Instead of sending five black regiments to march halfway across Florida, the Department of the South ordered General Birney with the 7th, 8th, and 9th USCIs and the 29th Connecticut to Virginia.[68]

General Hatch arrived on 3 August to take Birney's place as commander of the District of Florida. He brought with him the 34th and 102d USCIs. Hatch conferred with Birney, whom he thought "very sanguine" about the prospects of offen-

---

[66] J. C. Beecher to Frankie darling, 5 May 1864, Beecher Papers; Col J. C. Beecher to Capt M. Bailey, 22 Jun 1864 (quotations), and 24 Jun 1864, 35th USCI, Regimental Books, RG 94, NA.

[67] *OR*, ser. 1, vol. 35, pt. 1, pp. 420–21 (quotations, p. 420), and pt. 2, p. 195.

[68] Ibid., pt. 2, pp. 199, 202–03.

Ruins of Charleston after the Confederate evacuation

sive operations in the district, and began to ponder a raid toward Gainesville. On 15 August, the 34th, 35th, and 102d USCIs left Baldwin at daybreak accompanied by twenty mounted infantry and three artillery pieces. They marched south along the railroad for about ten miles and destroyed half a mile of track before camping for the night. Continuing south along the line for the next three days, they burned an estimated fourteen tons of cotton and a large steam-powered cotton gin and mill. On 19 August, the expedition turned northeast and marched to Magnolia on the St. John's River, arriving toward sundown. It brought with it, General Hatch noted, "about 75 contrabands, and some few horses and mules."[69]

Even before Hatch's raid got under way, Grant had demanded more troops from the Department of the South for his operations in Virginia. General Foster sent three white regiments from South Carolina, but he in turn demanded that Hatch, in Florida, return the 102d USCI. This reduced Hatch's command to the

---

[69]Ibid., pt. 1, pp. 428 ("about 75"), 430, and pt. 2, pp. 212, 215 ("very sanguine").

3d, 34th, and 35th USCIs and five white organizations: three infantry regiments, a battalion of cavalry, and a battery of artillery. The department remained "purely on the defensive," as Halleck advised. The scale of operations dwindled until, late in January 1865, the commanding officer of the 3d USCI thought it worthwhile to report that he had sent out forty men "to bring in a [Unionist] family and household goods, and hoping to capture a rebel soldier lurking about the neighborhood of the house to which the party was sent." He did not report whether his patrol succeeded in finding the lone Confederate.[70]

As Charleston's besiegers finally occupied the city, other troops from the Department of the South moved inland behind Sherman's XVII Corps. Colonel Beecher had recovered from the wounds he received at Honey Hill, and he rejoined the 35th USCI on 18 February. The regiment crossed the Edisto River on a mile-long railroad trestle that had been burned for fifty yards in the middle. The troops brought planks, laid them end to end, and then moved in single file across the gap. Succeeding days brought them to more bridges, some burned before Beecher's regiment reached them, others burned by the regiment after it crossed. Private dwellings suffered too. "It grieves me to see such splendid houses and such furniture burnt up," Beecher told his fiancée. "But we can't take it along, and up they go. Tonight the whole horizon is [lighted?] up splendidly. No less than four grand conflagrations going on at once. I shall get to be a regular brigand. . . . These planters have lived most luxuriously, but they have got to rough it now." Not far from Beecher, Captain Nelson and the 102d USCI were approaching Charleston from the southwest, out-marching the wagon trains that bore their rations. "The men did not suffer much for want of them," Nelson wrote, "as there is enough to eat in the country, which they helped themselves to pretty freely." After a long time in a coastal enclave, the troops of the Department of the South adapted easily to the ways of Sherman's army. "We have ransacked every plantation on our way and burnt up every thing we could not carry away," Private Reed told his mother.[71]

Still operating as the Military Division of the Mississippi, Sherman's force moved into North Carolina. From near Fayetteville, Sherman wrote to General Gillmore in mid-March, telling him of "a vast amount of rolling stock" in northeastern South Carolina that the federal advance had left undamaged. Burned railroad bridges had immobilized the cars and locomotives, but Sherman wanted them destroyed before the Confederates could repair the bridges and rescue them. Gillmore was to send a force of about twenty-five hundred men, Sherman wrote, taking them from the garrisons of Charleston and Savannah if necessary. "All real good soldiers must now be marching," he told Gillmore. "The men could march without knapsacks, with a single blanket, and carry eight days' provisions, which, with what is now in the country, will feed the command two weeks." Gillmore sent two brigades, one of white regiments from New York and Ohio, the other, commanded by Colonel Hallowell of the 54th Massachusetts, composed of Hallowell's own regiment and the 32d and 102d USCIs. With them went part of a battery of artillery, a detachment of cavalry, and some men of the 1st New York

---

[70] Ibid., pt. 2, pp. 231 ("purely on the defensive"), 247, 321; vol. 47, pt. 2, p. 142 ("to bring in").

[71] J. C. Beecher to Dearest, 19 Feb 1865, Beecher Papers; Nelson Diary, 24 Feb 1865; A. Reed to Dear Mother, 25 Feb 1865, Reed Papers.

Engineers, long in the trenches before Charleston but now ready to march cross-country, building bridges or destroying them. The entire force numbered some twenty-seven hundred men.[72]

The two brigades and their supporting troops moved by sea to Georgetown, farther north on the South Carolina coast than Union troops had operated before. On 5 April, they struck inland toward Columbia, destroying any cotton gins and cotton they found and exchanging shots with Confederate skirmishers from time to time. They reached the town of Manning three days later. Along the way, they received rations and ammunition from naval vessels in the Santee River. At Manning, they discovered a mile-long causeway with six bridges across the Pocotaligo River and an adjoining swamp, all of the bridges more or less burned. By midnight, the men of Hallowell's brigade had the bridges repaired sufficiently to bear the weight of infantry. They crossed at once and bivouacked two miles farther on. At dawn on 9 April, they moved ahead while the engineers finished repairing the bridges to allow the passage of horses and guns.[73]

Since the main Confederate force in the region was confronting Sherman's army in North Carolina, Hallowell's brigade reached Sumterville on the Wilmington and Manchester Railroad "without serious opposition" that evening. The next day, the regiments dispersed to begin their work. Moving east toward Maysville, the 32d USCI burned seven railroad cars and a bridge. To the west of Sumterville, the 102d USCI destroyed a bridge, four railroad cars, two hundred bales of cotton, and a gin. In Sumterville itself, the 54th Massachusetts wrecked a machine shop, disabled three locomotives, and burned fifteen cars. During the next two days, soldiers of the brigade destroyed an estimated $300,000 worth of property.[74]

By the end of another week, General Gillmore's two brigades had driven their Confederate opponents beyond Statesburg, a distance of some one hundred miles inland. The Union raiders then retraced their steps to Georgetown on the coast, having destroyed or disabled 32 locomotives, 250 railroad cars, and 100 cotton gins and presses while burning five thousand bales of cotton. More than three thousand slaves had left their plantations to accompany the expedition. On their way back to the seacoast, the soldiers learned on 21 April that the opposing armies in North Carolina had concluded a cease-fire. The next day came word of the Confederate surrender in Virginia and on the day after that news of Lincoln's assassination. On 25 April, the expedition reached Georgetown and went into camp. The Colored Troops' last operation in the Department of the South was over.[75]

A striking feature of officers' reports of this final raid is the extent to which Northern troops, black and white alike, continued to rely on information from black Southerners while conducting local operations. The 54th Massachusetts had been recruited across the North, the 32d USCI at Philadelphia, and the 102d USCI in Michigan. All three were, in varying degrees, alien to the South. Captain Emilio

---

[72] *OR*, ser. 1, vol. 47, pt. 1, pp. 1027–28, and pt. 2, pp. 856 ("vast amount"), 857 ("All real").

[73] *OR*, ser. 1, vol. 47, pt. 1, p. 1028; Emilio, *Brave Black Regiment*, pp. 292–94.

[74] Emilio, *Brave Black Regiment*, pp. 295–98 (quotation, p. 295).

[75] Ibid., pp. 307–08. "About three thousand negroes came into Georgetown with the division, while the whole number released was estimated at six thousand." Ibid., pp. 308–09. "The number of negroes who followed the column may be estimated at 5,000," Brig. Gen. E. E. Potter reported. *OR*, ser. 1, vol. 47, pt. 1, p. 1027.

of the 54th Massachusetts credited "contrabands" with telling his regiment's commanding officer about the extent of a swamp that lay in its path. The regiment got through "under the guidance of an old white-headed negro." General Potter directed a successful move against the enemy on 9 April after another black Carolinian told him "that [a] swamp could be crossed on the enemy's right." Nine days later, "a negro guide" helped to assure another victory for Union troops by leading them through another swamp. Federal soldiers' dependence on the local knowledge of black Southerners began the day of the Port Royal landing in November 1861 and continued through the raid from Georgetown to Sumterville forty-three months later. This collaboration was essential to Union operations during the entire war, not only on the Atlantic Coast but throughout the South.[76]

During the war's final months, little of note happened in northeastern Florida. In March 1865, Sgt. Maj. Henry James of the 3d USCI led a raid up the St. John's River. Twenty-four men of his own regiment and the 34th USCI, one soldier from a white regiment, and "7 civilians (colored)" made up the party. Past Welaka, they hid their boats in a swamp and struck westward about forty-five miles until they came near Ocala. On the way, besides burning a sugar mill and a distillery, they managed to take four white prisoners and set free ninety-one black Floridians. Returning, they drove off more than fifty Confederate cavalry who attacked them about twenty miles short of the river. The party's loss during the five-day expedition was two killed and four wounded. "I think that this expedition, planned and executed by colored Soldiers and civilians, reflects great credit upon the parties engaged in it," the regiment's commanding officer wrote to General Gillmore, "and I respectfully suggest that some public recognition of it, would have a good effect upon the troops." The letter went to department headquarters, where, on 20 April, Gillmore praised the raid in general orders: "This expedition, planned and executed by colored men under the command of a colored non-commissioned officer, reflects great credit upon the brave participants and their leader. The major-general commanding thanks these courageous soldiers and scouts, and holds up their conduct to their comrades in arms as an example worthy of emulation." This collaboration between 16 mostly Northern black soldiers (the 3d USCI was the first black regiment organized in Philadelphia), 6 Southern black soldiers from the 34th USCI, 1 soldier from a white regiment, and 7 black civilians, combining military training and local knowledge, exemplified the kind of success that the U.S. Colored Troops could achieve.[77]

A few days after Gillmore issued his order, the Confederate commander in Florida began negotiating a surrender with his Union opponent, Brig. Gen. Israel Vogdes. By 12 May, arrangements were complete. Vogdes "found it necessary," he told his adjutant general, to send seventy-five men of the 3d USCI to Baldwin to guard surrendered property until it could be brought to Jacksonville. "I have given them instructions to confine themselves exclusively to guarding the property and to preserve the strictest discipline, not to interfere with citizens in any way unless

---

[76]*OR*, ser. 1, vol. 47, pt. 1, pp. 1028 ("swamp"), 1030 ("negro guide"); Emilio, *Brave Black Regiment*, pp. 301 ("contrabands"), 302 ("white-headed negro").

[77]*OR*, ser. 1, vol. 47, pt. 3, p. 190; Col B. C. Tilghman to Capt T. J. Robinson, 20 Mar 1865, 3d USCI, Regimental Books, RG 94, NA.

attacked, and it be necessary to protect the public property." The tone of these orders, delivered just a week after the Confederate surrender, typified the restraint that would be enjoined on the U.S. Colored Troops as they took up occupation duties across the recalcitrant South.[78]

[78] *OR*, ser. 1, vol. 47, pt. 3, p. 514.

CHAPTER 4

SOUTHERN LOUISIANA AND THE GULF COAST, 1862–1863

Control of the Mississippi River was an objective that federal officials bore in mind even before hostilities began. Commercially important since the days of the first trans-Appalachian settlements, the river was the route by which a large part of the South's chief export, cotton, reached the world. Toward the end of its course, the Mississippi meets the Red River in low, flat land between Natchez and Baton Rouge. Because of the level terrain, parts of the flow of both rivers join to form a distributary stream called the Atchafalaya River, which flows south to empty into the Gulf of Mexico at Atchafalaya Bay while the Mississippi itself turns gradually to the southeast. Every landowner's lot in southeastern Louisiana included river frontage, a vestige of the region's French colonial heritage. Rivers and bayous substituted for roads, carrying planters' produce and purchases to and from market. They also provided routes for escaping slaves and, later, for raiding parties from both sides in the Civil War. Throughout the region, levees and drainage canals were, and still are, prominent features of the landscape (*see Map 2*).[1]

Around the confluence of the Red River and the Mississippi and to the west and south of it lay the "sugar parishes" of Louisiana. North of there, and up the Mississippi past Memphis, the planters grew cotton. Both crops required plenty of land and labor, and the lower Mississippi Valley was home to large plantations and some of the highest concentrations of black people in the United States. In the cotton-growing "Natchez District"—the five Mississippi counties south of Vicksburg and the three Louisiana parishes across the river—nearly 106,000 black residents outnumbered the region's whites by more than four to one. Only 407 of the 106,000 were free.[2]

The population of New Orleans was quite different. The city's 168,675 residents made it the nation's sixth largest and the only thing approaching a metropolis in the Confederacy. Charleston, the next most populous, was less than one-quarter

[1] Ira Berlin et al., eds., *The Destruction of Slavery* (New York: Cambridge University Press, 1985), p. 190; Martin Reuss, *Designing the Bayous: The Control of Water in the Atchafalaya Basin* (Alexandria, Va.: U.S. Army Corps of Engineers, 1998), pp. 19–23.

[2] Sam B. Hilliard, *Atlas of Antebellum Southern Agriculture* (Baton Rouge: Louisiana State University Press, 1984), pp. 34, 36, 38, 43, 71, 77; Ira Berlin, *Generations of Captivity: A History of African-American Slaves* (Cambridge: Harvard University Press, 2003), pp. 174–88; U.S. Census Bureau, *Population of the United States in 1860* (Washington, D.C.: Government Printing Office, 1864), pp. 194, 270. Michael Wayne, *The Reshaping of Plantation Society: The Natchez District,*

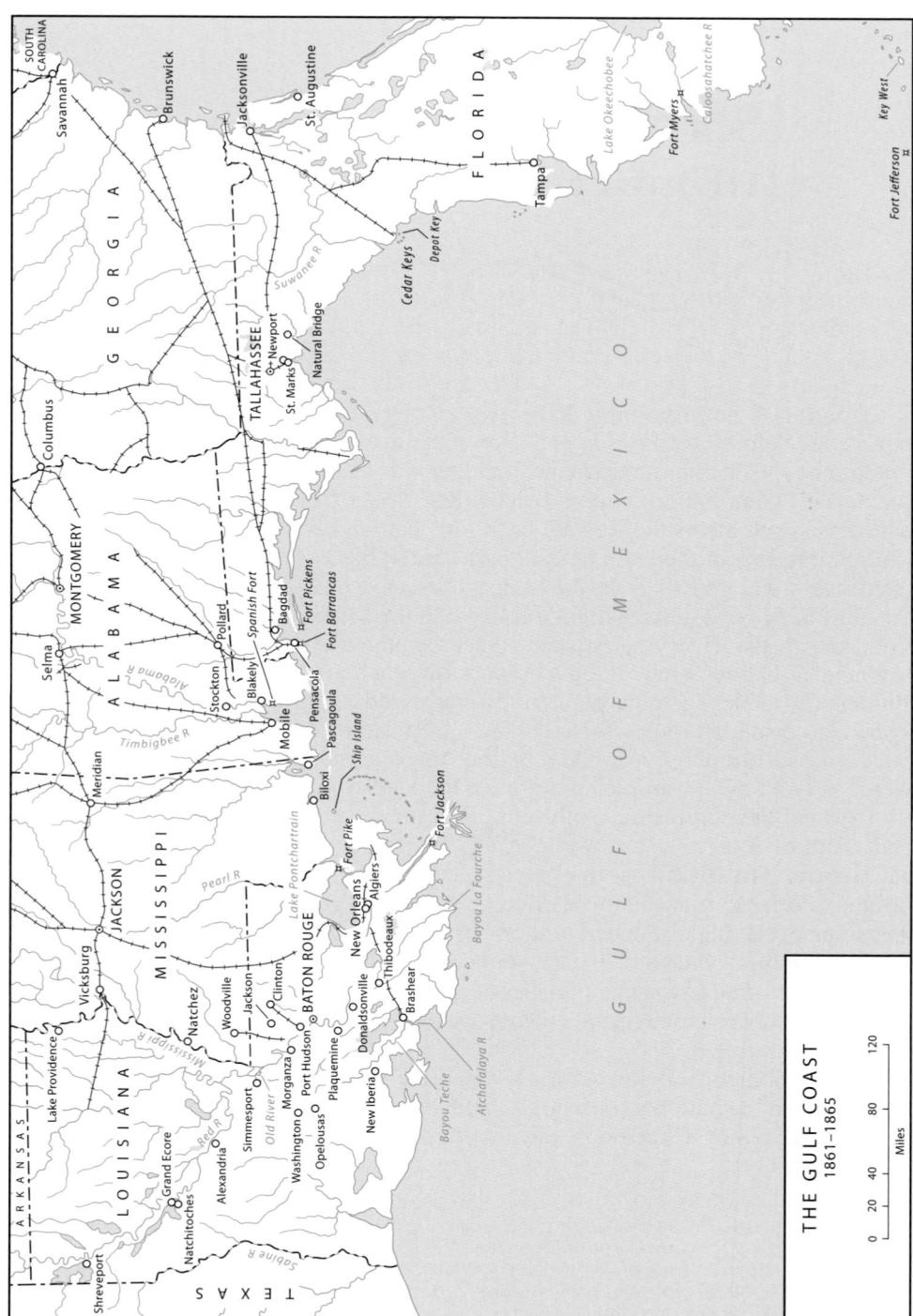

THE GULF COAST
1861–1865

Miles

0   20   40   80   120

Map 2

its size. In New Orleans, only every seventh resident was black, but the city's 10,689 "free people of color" constituted nearly half of the black population. Not only did these free people form a community larger than most Louisiana towns; Northern-born white residents of New Orleans far outnumbered the entire population of Baton Rouge, the state capital. Apart from its site near the mouth of the Mississippi, New Orleans' heterogeneous population made it an attractive target for a federal offensive.[3]

Outside New Orleans, in the sugar parishes, another set of circumstances differentiated southeastern Louisiana from the cotton-growing region. Planters whose wealth derived from sugar were in competition with the sugar-producing Caribbean colonies of Great Britain, France, Spain, the Netherlands, and Denmark. Unlike cotton producers, they never dreamed of having the European powers over a barrel. Louisiana sugar planters sent 78 percent of their product to the Northern states. They advocated high tariffs and tended to vote Whig. Half of the sugar parishes favored Douglas or Bell in the 1860 presidential election and sent anti-secession delegations to the state convention that winter. A large black population, an unusual proportion of which was free; a Northern- and foreign-born white population that was the largest in the Confederacy; and a commercial interest that was in large part anti-secessionist all combined to make southeastern Louisiana unique among Southern regions where Union forces tried to gain a beachhead.[4]

In New Orleans and throughout the French-speaking part of Louisiana, many "free people of color" belonged to families that traced their liberty back to the colonial eighteenth century, when European slave owners often freed their mixed-race offspring. The 1860 federal census described 15,158 of the state's "free colored" residents as "mulatto" and only 3,489 as "black." The legal status of these people and their descendants was somewhere between that of whites and enslaved black people. "Free people of color" could travel without the passes that were required of slaves and could own property (some, indeed, were slaveholders themselves), but they did not enjoy full civil and political rights. Among Louisiana's other legal oddities, it was the only state that admitted men of African ancestry to its militia. Some of the ancestors of these men had belonged to the American force that repelled a British invasion in 1815, and their descendants in 1861 had not forgotten it. Full of civic zeal, they organized a regiment called the Native Guards soon after the fall of Fort Sumter. Its officers came from the elite of "free colored" society. When they asked the secessionist state government for a chance to guard Union prisoners of war that September, though, Louisiana declined with thanks. Then, in January 1862, the state legislature passed a new militia act, inserting the word "white" as a qualification for membership. The disbanded Native Guards went home to await developments. Two months later, nearly to the day, they were recalled to duty when a federal fleet appeared in the mouth of the Mississippi

---

1860–80 (Baton Rouge: Louisiana State University Press, 1983), p. 17, explains the extent of the district and the origins of the term.

[3] Census Bureau, *Population of the United States in 1860*, pp. 195, 452, 615.

[4] "Unlike cotton planters, sugar planters had no delusions about sugar being king." Ted Tunnell, *Crucible of Reconstruction: War, Radicalism and Race in Louisiana, 1862–1877* (Baton Rouge: Louisiana State University Press, 1984), p. 17. Maps showing the votes of the sugar parishes in the 1860 presidential election and the secession convention are on pp. 11 and 12.

River. As had their ancestors, Louisiana's "free men of color" stood ready to protect "their homes [and] property . . . from the pollution of a ruthless invader."[5]

By 24 March, when the Native Guards rallied to Louisiana's defense for the second time, the potential invaders had been gathering off the Gulf Coast for sixteen weeks. Two Union regiments had landed on Ship Island, a spit of land about ten miles south of Biloxi, Mississippi, in early December 1861. The island lay halfway between Mobile Bay and Lake Pontchartrain, and its occupiers could threaten either Mobile or New Orleans. By the end of March, more than ten thousand federal troops were poised to attack the Confederate mainland.[6]

Their leader was a politician of no previous military experience but with a national reputation gained while he commanded a Union beachhead in Virginia during the spring and summer of 1861. Massachusetts had awarded Benjamin F. Butler a state commission a few days after Fort Sumter's surrender, and the president appointed him a major general of U.S. Volunteers in May. He avoided the debacle at Bull Run, spending the late spring and summer in command of Fort Monroe, across the James River estuary from the port of Norfolk. While there, Butler admitted escaped slaves into the Union lines and won national fame for terming them contrabands.[7]

By midsummer, Butler yearned for an independent command. That August, with Brig. Gen. Thomas W. Sherman already assigned to lead the land force in an expedition to Port Royal Sound, South Carolina, Butler secured authority from the War Department to raise five thousand men—six infantry regiments—in New England for a maritime venture. A pro-Union, pro-war Democrat, he aimed to revive his region's flagging military recruiting by offering command of the new regiments to other leading Democrats. State governors awarded field officer commissions in their states' volunteer regiments; and Butler believed that Republicans had received most of them thus far, which discouraged New England's many Democratic voters from enlisting. In late autumn, when the force was well on its way to completion, authorities in Washington decided to use it to occupy Ship Island and eventually to seize the port of New Orleans. While Butler attended to the final details of organization in New England, he asked for the assignment of Brig. Gen. John W. Phelps, a West Point graduate with twenty-three years' service, to lead the Ship Island landing. He had known Phelps at Fort Monroe, he told the secretary of war, and had "great confidence in him."[8]

Phelps, a Vermonter, was one of the few avowed abolitionists among the Army's career officers. Once ashore on Ship Island, he issued a manifesto addressed to "the loyal citizens of the South-West" in which he announced his

---

[5] Of the state's "slave" inhabitants, 32,623 were "mulatto" and 299,103 "black." Census Bureau, *Population of the United States in 1860*, p. 194. *The War of the Rebellion: A Compilation of the Official Records of the Union and Confederate Armies*, 70 vols. in 128 (Washington, D.C.: Government Printing Office, 1880–1901), ser. 1, 15: 556, 557 (quotation); ser. 4, 1: 625, 869 (hereafter cited as *OR*).

[6] *OR*, ser. 1, 6: 463–68, 707.

[7] Francis B. Heitman, *Historical Register and Dictionary of the United States Army*, 2 vols. (Washington, D.C.: Government Printing Office, 1903), 1: 268.

[8] *OR*, ser. 1, 6: 677; ser. 3, 1: 423, 637 (quotation), 815. Benjamin F. Butler, *Autobiography and Personal Reminiscences of Major-General Benj. F. Butler* (Boston: A. M. Thayer, 1892), pp. 295–309; *OR*, ser. 3, 1: 820–21.

opinion "that every State that has been admitted as a slave State into the Union since the adoption of the Constitution, has been admitted in direct violation of that Constitution." He traced the political history of slavery at length, including events such as the annexation of Texas; inserted three paragraphs in which he likened the abolition of slavery to the French Revolution's overthrow of the Catholic Church; and ended with a ringing declaration: "Our motto and our standard shall be, here and everywhere, and on all occasions, Free Labor and Workingmen's Rights." When the naval flag officer commanding the West Gulf Blockading Squadron refused Phelps a vessel to bear his proclamation to the mainland, the general had to content himself with releasing it through the New York newspapers.[9]

Phelps' address to Gulf Coast residents was premature as far as the administration's policy toward slavery went. Butler disavowed it as soon as he learned of it. A *New York Times* editorial predicted that Phelps and his statement would be "subjected to severe criticism" and was "likely to do the Union cause more harm than good." Whatever the official reaction, it did not take long for word of the federal presence to circulate among black people on the mainland. By the first week of February 1862, Phelps was able to report that some two dozen escaped slaves had made their way to Ship Island in small boats. Federal quartermasters put them to work unloading cargo.[10]

In late February, the War Department finally issued orders to Butler for the capture of New Orleans. At Ship Island on 10 April, the general embarked eight infantry regiments and three batteries of artillery to accompany Flag Officer David G. Farragut's fleet toward the mouth of the Mississippi River. When six days of bombardment failed to reduce the two forts that guarded the lower river, Farragut decided to cut the boom with which the Confederates had blocked the channel and to run his vessels past the forts and up the river to New Orleans. This he did. During the last week of April, most Confederate troops withdrew from the city, leaving the mayor to offer its surrender. Once again, the Native Guards returned to their homes.[11]

Leaving a few troops to occupy the forts, Butler began to land the bulk of his force at New Orleans on 1 May. Across the river from the city, he occupied the town of Algiers, the terminus of the New Orleans, Opelousas, and Great Western Railroad. Within the week, his troops had run a train as far as Brashear City, some eighty miles to the west, and were using the line's rolling stock to bring provisions from the country to New Orleans, where food was in short supply. During his first day ashore, Butler also issued a proclamation that condemned the rebellion, defined acceptable public behavior, and set forth pro-

---

[9] *Official Records of the Union and Confederate Navies in the War of the Rebellion*, 30 vols. (Washington, D.C.: Government Printing Office, 1894–1922), ser. 1, 17: 17–21 (hereafter cited as *ORN*); *New York Tribune*, 17 December 1861. The same ship that bore the *Tribune* correspondent's dispatch carried letters from *New York Times* and *New York Herald* reporters. Those papers printed the news of Phelps' proclamation on the same day.

[10] *OR*, ser. 1, 6: 465, 680; *New York Times*, 17 December 1861 (quotation).

[11] *OR*, ser. 1, 6: 694–95, 705–06; *ORN*, ser. 1, 18: 134–39, 148. A succinct description of the boom and its construction is in John D. Winters, *The Civil War in Louisiana* (Baton Rouge: Louisiana State University Press, 1963), p. 66; on pp. 96–102, Winters describes the chaotic last week of April in New Orleans.

cedures for trials and revenue collection. The proclamation's ninth paragraph read, in its entirety: "All rights of property, of whatever kind, will be held inviolate, subject only to the laws of the United States." Union soldiers had not come south to free slaves.[12]

Butler's proclamation also offered amnesty to former Confederates "who shall lay down and deliver up their arms" to the occupiers "and return to peaceful occupations." A delegation of four officers from the Native Guards soon called on him to determine their status and that of their men under the new regime. The delegates impressed Butler favorably: "in color, nay, also in conduct, they had much more the appearance of white gentlemen than some of those who have favored me with their presence claiming to be the 'chivalry of the South,'" he told Secretary of War Edwin M. Stanton soon afterward. Still, Butler declined to enroll the Native Guards in the Union cause, offering a variety of reasons: if he needed troops who were used to the Louisiana climate, he could enlist five thousand white men in New Orleans alone; black people, he claimed, had "a great horror of firearms, sometimes ludicrous in the extreme." Moreover, they made poor soldiers, anyway, and West Indian troops had badly hindered the British advance on the city in 1815. Butler made clear that he had no use for the Native Guards.[13]

Restoring a surface calm in New Orleans did not mean that the surrounding country was pacified. Long before Farragut's fleet appeared, the city's Confederate garrison, except for some ninety-day state troops, had been ordered to join the force concentrating at Corinth, Mississippi, which would soon take part in the battle of Shiloh. As the Union ships approached New Orleans, Confederate Maj. Gen. Mansfield Lovell sent the militia home and ordered the garrisons of the city's outlying forts to join him north of Lake Pontchartrain. In accordance with a recent act of the Confederate Congress, state authorities began organizing independent companies called Partisan Rangers "to prevent marauding excursions of small parties of the enemy." By the first week of July, recruiters had organized nine companies of Partisan Rangers and one was already in the field.[14]

The first encounter came within two weeks of federal troops' coming ashore. In Terrebonne Parish, about fifty miles west of New Orleans, a party of fifteen or twenty men who may have belonged to the militia stopped two wagons that were carrying four sick Union soldiers. They killed two of the soldiers and wounded the others. When federal troops arrived on 12 May, they were unable to make any arrests or even to find the men they wanted to question. After a few days, they burned or impounded the property of the missing suspects. General Butler "most fully" approved the retribution and warned his troops as

---

[12] *OR*, ser. 1, 6: 506, 719 (quotation), 720, 724; 15: 437.

[13] Ibid., 6: 718 ("who shall"); 15: 441 ("a great horror"), 442 ("in color"). James G. Hollandsworth Jr., *The Louisiana Native Guards: The Black Military Experience During the Civil War* (Baton Rouge: Louisiana State University Press, 1995), pp. 17–18.

[14] *OR*, ser. 1, 6: 512–18; 15: 735 (quotation), 773; Daniel E. Sutherland, *A Savage Conflict: The Decisive Role of Guerrillas in the American Civil War* (Chapel Hill: University of North Carolina Press, 2009), pp. 71–75.

far north as Baton Rouge to "punish with the last severity every guerrilla attack and burn the property of every guerrilla found murdering your soldiers."[15]

With the nearest Confederate army several days' march from the area of Union occupation and irregular warfare just beginning, federal authorities devoted a great deal of time to civil affairs. Much of this attention involved the international commerce that was New Orleans' lifeblood, especially the cotton trade, but part had to do with relations between white slaveholders and their black labor force. Sometimes the two spheres seemed to overlap, as when the consul who represented the commercial interests of Prussia and Hamburg in New Orleans asked for help in retrieving two of his slaves, who had escaped to Camp Parapet just west of the city. Phelps had opened the camp to escaped slaves since the earliest days of the occupation.[16]

Butler had asserted on the day he landed that "property, of whatever kind, will be held inviolate." He now found his force of some ten thousand men occupying "a tract of country larger than some States of the Union," as he explained to Secretary of War Stanton, and he wanted to avoid disturbing the "planters, farmers, mechanics, and small traders [who] have been passive rather than active in the rebellion." After receiving complaints about Phelps and Camp Parapet, Butler ordered him to drive out "all unemployed persons, black and white." To do so would put escaped slaves in danger of capture by their former masters.[17]

Fortunately for Camp Parapet's black residents, a flood threatened and the army needed their labor to avert a disaster. General Butler's chief of engineers, 1st Lt. Godfrey Weitzel, inspected the levees upriver from New Orleans on 23 May. He found "water running over at some points, and at a great many others . . . nearly level with the top." Any further rise, or a heavy wind, could cause a breach. Camp Parapet would be "completely untenable," New Orleans would be inundated "and upon the receding of the water . . . so unhealthy, as to endanger our occupation of it." Weitzel recommended that Butler should use one hundred laborers, presumably white, and "all the negroes now at Camp Parapet," to shore up the levees.[18]

While the residents of Camp Parapet struggled against the rising river, new arrivals swelled their numbers. During the first six months of Union occupation, some twenty thousand black refugees converged on New Orleans and drew Army rations. "My commissary is issuing rations to the amount of nearly double the amount required by the troops. This to the blacks," Butler told Army Chief of Staff Maj. Gen. Henry W. Halleck on 1 September. A planter on Bayou La Fourche, west of New Orleans, called the exodus "a perfect stampede." General Phelps saw the men among them as potential recruits for the Union Army. At the end of July, he submitted requisitions for clothing, equipment, and ordnance to outfit "three regi-

---

[15]*OR*, ser. 1, 15: 25 ("punish"), 447 ("most fully"), 450–57.

[16]Benjamin F. Butler, *Private and Official Correspondence of Gen. Benjamin F. Butler During the Period of the Civil War*, 5 vols. ([Norwood, Mass: Plimpton Press], 1917), 1: 564–65 (hereafter cited as *Butler Correspondence*).

[17]*OR*, ser. 1, 6: 707, 719 ("property"); 15: 439 ("a tract of country"), 440 ("planters, farmers"), 443 ("all unemployed").

[18]1st Lt G. Weitzel to Maj G. C. Strong, 23 May 1862 (no. 319), Entry 1756, Dept of the Gulf, Letters Received (LR), pt. 1, Geographical Divs and Depts, Record Group (RG) 393, U.S. Army Continental Cmds, National Archives (NA).

ments of Africans" to defend Camp Parapet. He claimed to have more than three hundred men organized in five companies.[19]

Instead of filling the requisition, Butler told Phelps to put the men to work cutting trees in order to clear a field of fire north of the camp. Phelps submitted his resignation rather than obey the order. "I am not willing to become the mere slave-driver which you propose, having no qualifications that way," he told Butler. When the resignation arrived in Washington, the president quickly accepted it. Phelps left Louisiana in September.[20]

Butler had refused to countenance Phelps' organization of black troops at the end of July, but before August was out, a Confederate attack on Baton Rouge made him withdraw the Union garrison from the town and consider seriously where he was to find more men. He had filled existing regiments with Unionist Louisiana whites, he told Stanton in mid-August, and would accept the Native Guards into the federal service. On 22 August, Butler called on "all the members of the Native Guards . . . and all other free colored citizens" to enlist. A few weeks later, he boasted to Stanton that he would soon have "a regiment, 1,000 strong, of Native Guards (colored), the darkest of whom will be about the complexion of the late [Daniel] Webster." By "accepting a regiment which had already been in Confederate service," as Collector of Customs George S. Denison pointed out, the general "left no room for complaint (by the rebels) that the Government were arming the negroes." Even so, Butler was disingenuous in his letter to Stanton; only 108 of the free men of color who served in the old regiment reenlisted; and as the new regiment filled up, no one inquired whether a recruit was an escaped slave. "As a consequence," Denison reported to Secretary of the Treasury Salmon P. Chase, "the boldest and finest fugitives have enlisted," and most of the enlisted men in the reorganized Native Guards, as it turned out, were not "free men of color." On 27 September 1862, the 1st Louisiana Native Guard mustered into federal service. A second regiment was ready in October and a third the month after. The 4th Native Guards took the field in February 1863.[21]

There was not much inquiry, either, into the backgrounds of officer candidates for the Native Guards. One of them, 2d Lt. Augustus W. Benedict of the 75th New York Infantry, wrote directly to Lt. Col. Richard B. Irwin, the department adjutant general, to propose himself for the major's position in the 4th Native Guards, which was then organizing. Benedict had served in the 75th New York with 1st Lt. Charles W. Drew, the 4th Native Guards' newly appointed colonel, he told Irwin,

---

[19]*OR*, ser. 1, 15: 534 ("three regiments"), 558 ("My commissary"), 572. J. Carlyle Sitterson, *Sugar Country: The Cane Sugar Industry in the South, 1753–1950* (Lexington: University of Kentucky Press, 1953), p. 209 ("a perfect"). Department of the Gulf commissary records from this period have not survived, but troop strength before Banks' arrival was more than ten thousand. *OR*, ser. 1, 6: 707, and 15: 613. A "contraband ration," issued to black refugees not employed by the Army, was less than a soldier's daily ration. 1st Lt G. H. Hanks to Capt R. O. Ives, 17 Jan 1863 (H–24–DG–1863); requisitions filed with Brig Gen J. W. Phelps to Capt R. S. Davis, 30 Jul 1862 (no. 19); both in Entry 1756, pt. 1, RG 393, NA.

[20]*OR*, ser. 1, 15: 535 (quotation), 542–43.

[21]Ibid., pp. 549, 557 ("all the members"), 559 ("a regiment"); Hollandsworth, *Louisiana Native Guards*, p. 18; "Diary and Correspondence of Salmon P. Chase," in *Annual Report of the American Historical Association for . . . 1902*, 57th Cong., 2d sess., H. Doc. 461, pt. 2 (serial 4,543), p. 313 ("accepting"); Frederick H. Dyer, *A Compendium of the War of the Rebellion* (New York: Thomas Yoseloff, 1959 [1909]), p. 1214.

and Drew had urged him to apply for the vacancy. The colonel of the 75th New York forwarded Benedict's application to the brigade commander, who commented, "I have no objection except that it deprives one of my regiments of an officer." The appointment was made. Others were more reluctant to apply. Capt. John W. DeForest of the 12th Connecticut heard that the Native Guards were destined to garrison "unhealthy positions" and to perform "fatigue duty, . . . making roads, building bridges and draining marshes" and decided not to try for a colonelcy in one of the new regiments. As it turned out, the 1st and 2d Native Guards were ready in time for a Union expedition to the La Fourche District west of New Orleans.[22]

Butler had succeeded in getting Lieutenant Weitzel, his chief engineer, appointed a brigadier general of U.S. Volunteers. Weitzel had been the second-ranking cadet in West Point's class of 1855, and he enjoyed wide esteem for his achievements before and during the war. "A majority of his classmates are now Generals, Colonels, and Lieut. Colonels, and he is still a Lieutenant," Butler told Secretary of War Stanton. "It is unjust." Stanton agreed, and the 26-year-old officer made the jump from lieutenant of engineers to brigadier general of Volunteers in August 1862.[23]

Weitzel led a force of more than three thousand men to clear Confederates out of the Bayou La Fourche. Butler's idea was to secure what he thought was "by far the richest" part of the state and to assure the loyalty of Unionist planters by allowing them to use the railroad from Opelousas to move their cotton and sugar to New Orleans while at the same time preventing the passage of Texas cattle to feed Confederate armies farther east. The 1st Native Guards and a New England infantry regiment moved along the railroad toward Thibodeaux and Brashear City. In less than a week, the two regiments opened fifty-two miles of the line, built nine culverts, and repaired a 435-foot bridge that the Confederates had burned, while clearing the track of grass and weeds that grew so thick they impeded the locomotives. By the beginning of November, the 1st and 2d Native Guards had taken up stations protecting bridges along the railroad.[24]

As Union troops advanced into the La Fourche District, escaped slaves flocked to their camps. "I have already twice as many negroes in and around my camp as I have soldiers within," General Weitzel complained. The Union move had been so sudden that retreating Confederates had abandoned "over 400 wagon loads of negroes," he wrote on 1 November. Planters who had stayed behind to take the required loyalty oath were "in great terror, fearing trouble with the negroes." Five days later, Weitzel reported that "symptoms of servile insurrection" were apparent in the district since the Native Guards had arrived. "I cannot command these negro regiments," he complained. When Weitzel wrote that "women, children, and even men, are in terror," it was quite evident that he did not refer to the district's black residents, and just as evident that he did not assign equal value to the opinions, well-being, and lives of whites and blacks. He begged the assistant adjutant gen-

[22]2d Lt A. W. Benedict to Lt Col R. B. Irwin, 2 Feb 1863, and Endorsement, Brig Gen G. Weitzel, n.d. ("I have") (B–163–DG–1863), Entry 1756, pt. 1, RG 393, NA; John W. DeForest, *A Volunteer's Adventures: A Union Captain's Record of the Civil War* (New Haven: Yale University Press, 1946), pp. 50 ("unhealthy positions"), 51 ("fatigue duty").

[23]*OR*, ser. 1, 15: 685; *Butler Correspondence*, 2: 43 (quotation).

[24]*OR*, ser. 1, 15: 159 (quotation), 161, 170, 587.

eral of the Department of the Gulf "to keep the negro brigade directly under your own command or place some one over both mine and it."[25]

General Butler had been a successful lawyer and politician in civilian life. A few months earlier, Secretary of War Stanton, another lawyer, had urged him to exercise his "accustomed skill and discretion" in dealing with the abolitionist General Phelps. Butler now set out to allay his subordinate's lack of confidence in the Native Guards. He pointed out that Weitzel had not complained that the Native Guards were unable to protect the railroad, the duty to which he had assigned them; neither had Weitzel given them a chance to test his privately expressed belief "that colored men will not fight." As for the Native Guards' unsettling influence on local black residents, the regiments had arrived at the same time as the rest of Weitzel's force. Was it the presence of the Native Guards, Butler asked, "or is it the arrival of United States troops, carrying, by the act of Congress, freedom to this servile race? . . . You are in a country where now the negroes outnumber the whites ten to one, and these whites are in rebellion against the Government or in terror seeking its protection." The solution, Butler told Weitzel, was to tell white Louisianans to lay down their arms, take the oath of allegiance, and pursue their private affairs. Then, U.S. troops would offer them "the same protection against negro or other violence" that had been available without interruption in states that had not seceded. It was the same course of action Butler had taken in the spring of 1861 when he arrived in Maryland, where white residents feared a slave rebellion. These remarks apparently placated Weitzel, for he remained in command of the La Fourche District and the Native Guards continued to protect the railroad.[26]

Col. Spencer H. Stafford, commander of the 1st Native Guards, also objected to his regiment's presence on the railroad, but for far different reasons. Being "scattered along the road for the space of twenty-eight miles," he wrote to department headquarters, prevented drill and degraded discipline. His recently organized regiment, acting as a unit, would be best employed in the field while the "highly important" duty of guarding the railroad was "confided to . . . veteran and well disciplined troops." Stafford wished to settle doubts about black soldiers' courage at "as early an opportunity as possible. . . . The acquaintance which I have formed with the characteristics, mental, moral and physical[,] of these men, satisfies me . . . that when tried, they will not be found wanting." He ended his letter by asserting that if his men were not "fit to fight," they must be "equally unfit for the delicate and important duty" of guarding lines of communication.[27]

Stafford's letter of 3 January 1863 was ill timed, arriving at headquarters during a period of tumult caused by a change in command of the Department of the Gulf. General Butler's time in the department was at an end. The cause of his removal was not his management of racial issues but another part of his civil duties involving commerce. "I believe the present military authorities are so corrupt that they will take all means to make money," Collector of Customs Denison told Treasury Secretary Chase. "Many officers and soldiers want to go home, not wishing to

---

[25] Ibid., pp. 170–72 (quotations, p. 172).
[26] Ibid., pp. 164–66 (Butler quotations, pp. 164–65), 516 ("accustomed skill").
[27] Col S. H. Stafford to Maj Gen N. P. Banks, 3 Jan 1863, 73d United States Colored Infantry (USCI), Entry 57C, Regimental Papers, RG 94, Rcds of the Adjutant General's Office (AGO), NA.

risk their lives to make fortunes for others." The general's brother Andrew, known by the courtesy title of colonel although he held no military rank, bought and sold cotton, sugar, and anything else of value, becoming several hundred thousand dollars richer by his dealings. Whether Butler himself profited by his brother's activities is uncertain, but, as Denison remarked, the general was "such a smart man, that it would . . . be difficult to discover what he wished to conceal." Furthermore, Butler's high-handed management of consular affairs had alienated representatives of the European powers in New Orleans during a year when the State Department was working hard to assure that France and Great Britain did not enter the war on the side of the Confederacy. In the circumstances, it was clear that Butler had to be removed.[28]

Butler's replacement in command of the Department of the Gulf was another Massachusetts politician whose commission as major general bore the same date as his own: 16 May 1861. Nathaniel P. Banks had begun public life as a Democrat, had served three terms in Congress during which he changed from Democrat–Free Soiler to Know-Nothing to Republican, and had been elected to three one-year terms as a Republican governor of Massachusetts. During his last term as governor, he vetoed a bill that would have removed the word "white" from the list of qualifications for membership in the state militia. Banks was a figure of national prominence—in 1856 he had become the first Republican speaker of the U.S. House of Representatives—and seemed a natural candidate for high military appointment in the early weeks of the war. Even so, political skills did not guarantee military ability. Troops led by Banks lost three battles to the Confederate Army of Northern Virginia during the spring and summer of 1862. Injured in the last of those battles, Banks spent September in command of the defenses of Washington, D.C. He used the time to lobby for command of an expedition to the coast of Texas. Seeing a chance to replace Butler in New Orleans, the president sent him there instead.[29]

Banks reached Louisiana in mid-December 1862. His expedition included thirty-nine infantry regiments, six batteries of artillery, and a battalion of cavalry. That twenty-one of the infantry regiments had mustered in that fall for only nine months' service showed the lengths to which Union authorities were willing to go to attract volunteers after little more than one year of war. The new arrivals brought Union strength in the department to more than thirty-one thousand soldiers. Banks found that his predecessor had established "an immense military government, embracing every form of civil administration, the assessment of taxes, . . . trade, . . . and the working of plantations, in addition to the ordinary affairs of a military department."[30]

While the new commander wrestled with the problems of civil administration, he set his staff officers to investigating the state of "ordinary affairs" in their branches. The new chief of ordnance found that the confusing way in which arms

---

[28] "Diary and Correspondence of Salmon P. Chase," p. 313 ("such a smart"), 325 ("Many officers").

[29] *OR*, ser. 1, 15: 590–91; Fred H. Harrington, *Fighting Politician: Major General N. P. Banks* (Philadelphia: University of Pennsylvania Press, 1948), p. 47; Heitman, *Historical Register*, 1: 28.

[30] *OR*, ser. 1, 15: 627, 639 ("an immense"); Frank J. Welcher, *The Union Army, 1861–1865: Organization and Operations*, 2 vols. (Bloomington: Indiana University Press, 1989–1993), 2: 44, 314.

and ammunition were stored made it hard to tell the quantity on hand and had to "make an entire change" in his department's personnel. The chief of artillery confessed that he "was unable to procure any information whatever" from his predecessor but ventured the opinion that none of the batteries could take the field for want of spare parts. To make matters worse, Banks' inspector general declared that not one of the newly arrived infantry regiments was fit for active service. Three of them in particular had antiquated or defective weapons. Offensive operations were out of the question in any case, for the country along the principal rivers was flooded and driftwood blocked the main channels.[31]

A Confederate force led by Maj. Gen. John C. Breckinridge had driven Union occupiers from Baton Rouge in August 1862, but they had not been able to hold the town and federal troops returned in December. The Union Army did not go on to retake Port Hudson, some twenty-five miles upstream. The Confederates hung on there through the fall and winter, increasing in strength from about 1,000 men present for duty at the end of August to 16,287 at the end of March 1863. The tiny village, which in peacetime was a shipping point for cotton and sugar, stood at the north end of a range of bluffs from which artillery could command a bend in the river. Breckinridge thought that Port Hudson's position was one of the strongest defensive sites on the Mississippi, more advantageous than either Baton Rouge or Vicksburg.[32]

Banks agreed, so when his troops, organized as the Union Army's XIX Corps, finally took the field they moved not against Port Hudson itself but up the Bayou Teche toward Opelousas. In that way, Banks intended to find a route that would allow federal vessels to reach the Red River without passing under the guns of Port Hudson. The move would also cut off Confederate armies east of the Mississippi from their sources of rations to the west. By 20 April, Union troops had reached Opelousas; by 9 May, they were in Alexandria. Banks reported taking two thousand prisoners and routing the Confederate force opposed to him, but General Halleck in Washington urged him to concentrate on capturing Port Hudson while Maj. Gen. Ulysses S. Grant, farther north, attacked Vicksburg. Control of the Mississippi River "is the all-important objective of the present campaign," Halleck told Banks. "It is worth to us forty Richmonds."[33]

The Native Guards, meanwhile, had moved from the Opelousas Railroad to other stations. The 1st, 3d, and 4th Regiments were with Maj. Gen. Christopher C. Augur's 1st Division, XIX Corps, at Baton Rouge. The 2d Regiment had seven companies on Ship Island and three at Fort Pike, near the mouth of Lake Pontchartrain, northeast of New Orleans. The first three Native Guards regiments were in turmoil as General Banks conducted a purge of the seventy-five company officers and one major whom Butler had appointed from among New Orleans' "free men of color." To Banks, their race alone was enough to make them "a source of constant embarrassment and annoyance." When he had begun organizing the 4th Native Guards, only white men received appointments as officers. So it would be with

---

[31] *OR*, ser. 1, 15: 242, 649 ("was unable"), 676; 1st Lt R. M. Hill to Maj Gen N. P. Banks, 15 Jan 1863 ("make an") (H–122–DG–1863), Entry 1756, pt. 1, RG 393, NA.
[32] *OR*, ser. 1, 15: 81 (quotation), 804, 1000.
[33] Ibid., pp. 299–300, 726 (quotation); vol. 26, pt. 1, pp. 8, 10–11.

the other black regiments raised by his orders.[34]

Apart from Maj. Francis E. Dumas, who was one of only two black men to attain that high a grade during the war, Butler had appointed white field officers in the first three Native Guards regiments. Col. Nathan W. Daniels, 2d Native Guards, protested an order that convened a board "to examine into the capacity, propriety of conduct and efficiency" of seven of his black officers at Fort Pike. The board found three of them deficient in one respect or another. Daniels explained to Banks that, "Believing as I do that the Policy of our country is to give this race an opportunity to manifest their Patriotism, Ability and intelligence by aiding in crushing the Rebellion, thus demonstrating their own capacity and at the same time rend[er]ing us valuable assistance," he felt bound to decry "an attempt . . . by the enemies of [this] organization to paralyze its power by overthrowing its

Col. Nathan W. Daniels alleviated the boredom of duty on Ship Island by leading his regiment, the 2d Louisiana Native Guards (later the 2d Corps d'Afrique Infantry and the 74th U.S. Colored Infantry) in raids on the Confederate mainland.

officers." Despite this objection, the three deficient officers were discharged on 24 February 1863 and the other four submitted their resignations nine days later. Most of the rest of the regiment's original company officers were gone by late summer. Just seven held on into the next year, the last of them mustering out of service on 18 July 1865, well after the Confederate surrender. By that time, all of the original company officers of the other two regiments had long since resigned or suffered discharge or dismissal.[35]

Colonel Daniels did not let personnel matters divert him from the business of fighting. Small parties of refugees from the mainland—mostly black, but many of them white—arrived on Ship Island every few days and kept him apprised of events there. Learning from them that part of Mobile's garrison would be sent to reinforce Charleston, South Carolina, Daniels decided that a raid on the port

---

[34] *OR*, ser. 1, 15: 711–14, and ser. 3, 3: 46 ("a source"); Hollandsworth, *Louisiana Native Guards*, pp. 117–24.

[35] Dept of the Gulf, Special Orders (SO) 34, 3 Feb 1863 ("to examine"); Col N. W. Daniels to Maj Gen N. P. Banks, 2 Mar 1863 ("Believing"); both in 74th USCI, Entry 57C, RG 94, NA. *Official Army Register of the Volunteer Force of the United States Army*, 8 vols. (Washington, D.C.: Government Printing Office, 1867), 8: 246–47, 250–51 (hereafter cited as *ORVF*); Hollandsworth, *Louisiana Native Guards*, p. 122; *ORVF*, 8: 248; Heitman, *Historical Register*, 1: 861.

of Pascagoula, Mississippi, some thirty miles west of Mobile Bay, would upset Confederate plans. He left Ship Island early on the morning of 9 April 1863 with one hundred eighty men of his regiment and reached Pascagoula about 9:00 a.m. Soon after Daniels' force went ashore, Confederate troops arrived and eventually managed to drive the Union pickets back from the outskirts of town before retiring themselves to the surrounding woods. Later in the morning, the enemy returned to the attack but was driven back again. When Daniels learned that Confederate reinforcements were on the way, he reembarked his force and returned to Ship Island. Union losses in four hours of intermittent fighting amounted to two killed and eight wounded by the enemy and six killed and two wounded by a shell from the U.S. Navy gunboat *Jackson* nearly a mile offshore. Daniels estimated more than twenty Confederates killed "and a large number wounded." The expedition took three Confederate prisoners but accomplished little else, although it may have contributed to civilian anxiety in nearby seaports. In May, a committee of Mobile residents complained to the governor of Alabama about the small size of the city's garrison and the possibility of coastal raids.[36]

Colonel Daniels' report mentioned by name Major Dumas; Capt. Joseph Villeverde; 1st Lt. Joseph Jones; 1st Lt. Theodule Martin; and the regimental quartermaster, 1st Lt. Charles S. Sauvenet. They were "constantly in the thickest of the fight," he wrote, and "their unflinching bravery and admirable handling of their commands contributed to the success of the attack." Four of these officers would be gone from the regiment in the next sixteen months, although it is not certain that General Banks' desire to remove black officers was manifest in each instance. Dumas and Jones would resign that July, almost certainly the result of official pressure; Martin and Villeverde would receive discharges in August 1864, one ostensibly for medical reasons, the other perhaps because of muddled property accounts. Only Sauvenet would manage to hold on until the end of the war.[37]

At the same time that Banks was purging black officers from existing regiments in the Department of the Gulf, the Lincoln administration had settled on a policy of recruiting black enlisted men in all parts of the occupied South. While the War Department sent no less a figure than Adjutant General Lorenzo Thomas to organize black troops in General Grant's command, which included parts of Arkansas, northeastern Louisiana, Mississippi, and Tennessee, it sent a Know-Nothing politician turned Republican, Brig. Gen. Daniel Ullmann, to the Department of the Gulf. Ullmann's rank reflected his assignment to recruit a brigade of five all-black

---

[36] *OR*, ser. 1, vol. 52, pt. 1, p. 61, and pt. 2, p. 471; Col N. W. Daniels to Brig Gen T. W. Sherman, 11 Apr 1863, Entry 1860, Defenses of New Orleans, LR, pt. 2, Polyonymous Successions of Cmds, RG 393, NA. Daniels apparently filed two reports, on 10 and 11 April. The earlier, shorter report appears in *OR*, ser. 1, vol. 52, pt. 1, p. 61, and in his diary, published as C. P. Weaver, ed., *Thank God My Regiment an African One: The Civil War Diary of Colonel Nathan W. Daniels* (Baton Rouge: Louisiana State University Press, 1998), pp. 79–87. The diary contains hints of the racial composition of Ship Island refugees on pp. 58, 62, 68, 71–73, 75–77. The report of 11 April was published in William W. Brown, *The Negro in the American Rebellion: His Heroism and His Fidelity* (Boston: Lee and Shepard, 1867), pp. 94–96. Daniels listed several different casualty figures in his reports and diary; the numbers given here are those that seem most consistent.

[37] Daniels to Sherman, 11 Apr 1863; *ORVF*, 8: 248; Hollandsworth, *Louisiana Native Guards*, pp. 72–76.

infantry regiments. As colonel of a New York regiment, he had served with Banks in Virginia the year before; Banks thought him "a poor man . . . [who] will make all the trouble he can." Banks was not alone in his low opinion; after observing Ullmann for a few months, Collector of Customs Denison told Treasury Secretary Chase that he was "not the right kind of man for the position." Ullmann's appointment to a department where the commanding general was already organizing black troops was one of the first occasions when authorities in Washington ordained two conflicting authorities for black recruiting in the same jurisdiction. It would not be the last.[38]

Politicians in New England were deeply interested in the organization of Ullmann's brigade. Governor John A. Andrew was prepared to recommend as officers "several hundreds" of deserving Massachusetts soldiers. The governor of Maine had his own candidates to propose. Vice President Hannibal Hamlin, another Maine man, proclaimed a special interest in Ullmann's nomination as brigadier general. The vice president's son would become Col. Cyrus Hamlin of Ullmann's third regiment, eventually numbered as the 80th United States Colored Infantry (USCI). The field officers, adjutant, and quartermaster of the first regiment Ullmann raised in Louisiana had been captains and lieutenants in his previous command, the 78th New York. In an age when reliable personnel records did not exist, there was no substitute for personal acquaintance.[39]

Banks ordered Ullmann to set up his depot at New Orleans, where there were many potential recruits and where Ullmann would be out of the way of "active operations." Banks also countered Ullmann's instructions from the War Department on 1 May by announcing his intention to organize an all-black Corps d'Afrique of eighteen regiments, including artillery, cavalry, and infantry, "with appropriate corps of engineers." The regiments that Ullmann had planned to number the 1st through the 5th U.S. Volunteers would bear the numbers 6th through 10th Corps d'Afrique Infantry. The new regiments would start small, no more than five hundred men each, "in order to secure the most thorough instruction and discipline and the largest influence of the officers over the troops." Banks cited precedent from the Napoleonic Wars, when the French Army organized recruits in small battalions. He did not add that in regiments made up of former slaves the burden of clerical tasks would fall entirely on the officers and that smaller regiments would mean less paperwork. In order to avoid any hint of radicalism, the former governor who had barred black men from the Massachusetts militia denied "any dogma of equality or other theory." Instead, recruiting black soldiers for the war was merely "a practical and sensible matter of business." "The Government makes use of mules, horses, uneducated and educated white men, in the defense of its institutions," he declared. "Why should not the negro contribute whatever is in his power for the cause in which he is as deeply

---

[38] *OR*, ser. 3, 3: 14, 100–103; James G. Hollandsworth Jr., *Pretense of Glory: The Life of General Nathaniel P. Banks* (Baton Rouge: Louisiana State University Press, 1998), p. 151 ("a poor man"); "Diary and Correspondence of Salmon P. Chase," p. 393 ("not the right").

[39] J. A. Andrew to Brig Gen D. Ullmann, 2 Feb 1863, D. Ullmann Papers, New-York Historical Society; A. Coburn to Brig Gen D. Ullmann, 3 Feb 1863, and H. Hamlin to Brig Gen D. Ullmann, 14 Feb 1863, both in Entry 159DD, Generals' Papers and Books (Ullmann), RG 94, NA; *ORVF*, 2: 550, 8: 254.

interested as other men? We may properly demand from him whatever service he can render."[40]

While Ullmann began to recruit his brigade, Banks issued orders to the three divisions of the XIX Corps that had reached Alexandria on 9 May 1863. From that town, in the middle of the state, they moved by road and river some eighty miles southeast to the Mississippi. There, on 25 May, they met the corps' fourth division coming north from Baton Rouge and laid siege to the Confederates at Port Hudson. Banks' army numbered well over thirty thousand men on paper at the beginning of the siege, but he reported that its actual strength was less than thirteen thousand.[41]

As the Union force approached, Confederate troops hastily completed a months-long effort to turn the artillery post that commanded the river into a defensible fort able to withstand assault from inland. Felling trees obstructed the attackers' path and cleared a field of fire for the defenders. The Confederates also dug rifle pits for skirmishers well to the front of their main line of trenches. Port Hudson's garrison had been tapped to furnish reinforcements for Vicksburg, which by that time was threatened by Grant's army, and so numbered only about seven thousand men, roughly one-third of the troops the town's four-and-a-half miles of trenches required.[42]

Banks wanted to capture the place at once and go north to join Grant. On 26 May, he decided on an assault to take place the next morning. The 1st and 3d Native Guards were part of the force that marched to Port Hudson from Baton Rouge. On the day Banks made his decision, the two regiments found themselves posted on the extreme right of the Union line, part of a collection of brigades from different divisions commanded by General Weitzel. These brigades were to lead the next day's attack on the Confederate position. It was the only part of the Union force that received definite orders. Other division commanders were merely to "take instant advantage of any favorable opportunity, and . . . if possible, force the enemy's works," or "hold [themselves] in readiness to re-enforce within the right or left, if necessary, or to force [their] own way into the enemy's works." Despite the vague wording of the order, which left the timing of the assault to the discretion of his subordinates, Banks ended with the exhortation: "Port Hudson must be taken to-morrow."[43]

Sunrise came at 5:00. The Union artillery opened fire "at daybreak"—one of the few unequivocal parts of Banks' order—and Weitzel's infantry, fourteen white regiments mostly from New England and New York, advanced from north and northeast of the town about one hour later. Crossing obstructions of felled timber and ravines as deep as thirty feet, they drove the Confederate skirmishers from their rifle pits and finally confronted the enemy's main line, some two hundred yards farther on. There, the attack stalled. One regiment, the 159th New York, had spent an hour advancing half a mile. Another, the 8th New Hampshire, had lost 124 of its 298 men killed and wounded. At 42 percent, this was twice the percentage of casualties of any other regi-

---

[40]*OR*, ser. 1, 15: 717 ("in order," "any dogma"); vol. 26, pt. 1, p. 684 ("with appropriate"); ser. 3, 4: 205–06. Maj Gen N. P. Banks to Brig Gen D. Ullmann, 29 Apr 1863 ("active operations"), Entry 159DD, RG 94, NA.

[41]*OR*, ser. 1, vol. 26, pt. 1, pp. 12–13, 526–28.

[42]Lawrence L. Hewitt, *Port Hudson, Confederate Bastion on the Mississippi* (Baton Rouge: Louisiana State University, 1987), p. 133; Hollandsworth, *Pretense of Glory*, pp. 121–22.

[43]*OR*, ser. 1, 15: 732; vol. 26, pt. 1, pp. 492–93, 504, 508–09 (quotation, p. 509); Richard B. Irwin, *History of the Nineteenth Army Corps* (New York: G. P. Putnam's Sons, 1892), p. 166.

Terrain across which Union troops advanced to attack the Confederate trenches at Port Hudson, 27 May 1863

ment in Weitzel's force. The attackers rested before renewing their assault, wondering when, or if, the rest of the Union line would move forward.[44]

About 7:00, the Louisiana Native Guards received an order to advance at a point about a mile to the southwest of the stalled attack near where the opposing lines approached the river. Six companies of the 1st Native Guards—perhaps as many as four hundred men—crossed a small creek and advanced toward the enemy position near the crest of a steep bluff about four hundred yards long. Four Confederate cannon and about three hundred sixty infantry awaited them there. Under fire from the time they crossed the creek, the Native Guards received a blast of canister shot from the cannon as they came within two hundred yards of the Confederate trenches. The shock sent the survivors down the slope in retreat. At the creek, they ran into and through the men of the 3d Regiment advancing to their support. Both regiments fell back into some woods on the far side of the stream, where they reorganized. The Confederate commander, who had been present since he heard of the impending attack early that morning, reported seeing several attempts to rally the survivors; "but all were unsuccessful and no effort was afterwards made to charge the works during the entire day." A captain in the Native Guards told an officer of Ullmann's brigade that his regiment "went into action about 6 a.m. and [was] under fire most of the time until sunset"; but he did not mention any renewed attack. Union casualties amounted to at least 112 officers and men killed and wounded, nearly all of them in the 1st Na-

---

[44]*OR*, ser. 1, vol. 26, pt. 1, p. 508 (quotation); Hewitt, *Port Hudson*, pp. 138–47; Irwin, *Nineteenth Army Corps*, pp. 170–72, 174.

tive Guards. The Confederate commander reported "not one single man" of his own troops killed "or even wounded."[45]

Sporadic, uncoordinated attacks occurred elsewhere along the Union line later in the day but accomplished nothing at a cost to Banks' army of 1,995 of all ranks killed, wounded, and missing. The loss of the 1st Native Guards that day was one of the heaviest, amounting to 5.2 percent of the total among some forty regiments taking part. In the failed attack and the six-week siege that followed, only seven regiments suffered greater casualties. Among the 1st Native Guards' twenty-six dead on 27 May were Capt. André Cailloux and seventeen-year-old 2d Lt. John H. Crowder. Both were black. Cailloux, born a slave but freed in 1846, was a native Louisianan. Crowder had come downriver from Kentucky, working as a cabin boy on a riverboat. Weeks after the battle, Cailloux received a public funeral in New Orleans that occasioned comment nationwide and an illustration in *Harper's Weekly*. Crowder's mother buried him in a pauper's grave.[46]

Not all the officers of the 1st Native Guards acted creditably during the engagement. The day after the failed assault, Capt. Alcide Lewis was in arrest for cowardice. Crowder, who had disagreements with Lewis, thought he was "a coward and no jentleman." On 4 June, 2d Lt. Hippolyte St. Louis found himself in arrest on the same charge. By the end of June, 2d Lt. Louis A. Thibaut was also in arrest. For officers, "arrest" meant relief from duty pending disposition of the case by court-martial or other administrative action. It did not mean "close confinement," which, *Army Regulations* specified, was not to be imposed on officers "unless under circumstances of an aggravated character." The action in these cases was a special order declaring the three officers "dishonorably dismissed the service for cowardice, breach of arrest, and absence without leave." Despite their commanding officer's request for a general court-martial, there was no trial; General Banks' recommendation sufficed.[47]

In describing the failed assault on Port Hudson, Banks had nothing but praise for the Native Guards. "The position occupied by these troops was one of importance, and called for the utmost steadiness and bravery," he reported:

It gives me pleasure to report that they answered every expectation. In many respects their conduct was heroic. No troops could be more determined or more daring. They made during the day three charges upon the batteries of the enemy,

---

[45]The only estimate of the total strength of the attacking force, from the *New York Times*, 13 June 1863, is 1,080: 6 companies of the 1st Native Guards and 9 companies of the 3d. Hollandsworth, *Louisiana Native Guards*, pp. 53, 57. Capt E. D. Strunk to Brig Gen D. Ullmann, 29 May 1863 ("went into"), Entry 159DD, RG 94, NA; Hewitt, *Port Hudson*, p. 149; Irwin, *Nineteenth Army Corps*, pp. 173–74; Jane B. Hewett et al., eds., *Supplement to the Official Records of the Union and Confederate Armies*, 93 vols. (Wilmington, N.C.: Broadfoot Publishing, 1994–1998), pt. 1, 4: 761 ("but all," "not one").

[46]*OR*, ser. 1, vol. 26, pt. 1, pp. 47, 67–70; Stephen J. Ochs, *A Black Patriot and a White Priest: André Cailloux and Claude Paschal Maistre in Civil War New Orleans* (Baton Rouge: Louisiana State University Press, 2006), pp. 16, 29, 155–63; Joseph T. Glatthaar, "The Civil War Through the Eyes of a Sixteen-Year-Old Black Soldier: The Letters of Lieutenant John H. Crowder of the 1st Louisiana Native Guards," *Louisiana History* 35 (1994): 201–16.

[47]Compiled Military Service Records (CMSRs), Alcide Lewis, 73d USCI, and Hippolyte St. Louis, 73d USCI, both in Entry 519, Carded Rcds, Volunteer Organizations: Civil War, RG 94, NA. Dept of the Gulf, SO 111, 26 Aug 1863 ("dishonorably"), Entry 1767, Dept of the Gulf, SO, pt. 1, RG 393, NA; Lt Col C. J. Bassett to Capt G. B. Halsted, 5 Aug 1863, 73d USCI, Entry 57C, RG 94,

A Frank Leslie's illustrator let his imagination run riot in this depiction of the Louisiana Native Guards' assault on Port Hudson. The Confederate reported that the assault petered out at some distance from their trenches and inflicted no casualties on the defenders.

suffering very heavy losses. . . . Whatever doubt may have existed heretofore as to the efficiency of organizations of this character, the history of this day proves conclusively . . . that the Government will find in this class of troops effective supporters and defenders. The severe test to which they were subjected, and the determined manner in which they encountered the enemy, leaves upon my mind no doubt of their ultimate success. They require only good officers . . . and careful discipline, to make them excellent soldiers.[48]

Banks' description of the battle—"They made during the day three charges"—was exaggerated. Banks had been nowhere near the extreme right of the Union line, where the Native Guards were; and in writing his report just three days after the attack he must have relied on oral accounts, as did the reporters who described the battle for Northern newspapers. His report bore a date, 30 May 1863, earlier than those written by regimental commanders who had taken part in the attack. It had been only a month since Banks had issued his order establishing the Corps d'Afrique, with its 500-man regiments intended "to secure the most thorough instruction and discipline and the largest influence of the officers over the troops." He could hardly undercut his new venture by faint praise for the Native Guards' performance, even if an honest appraisal would have called it no worse than that of the white soldiers that day.[49]

Outside the Department of the Gulf, the Native Guards' willingness to face fire at all—no matter that they had barely come within two hundred yards of the Confederate trenches—led to wild excesses in the Northern press. The steamer *Morning Star*

NA; Glatthaar, "Letters of Lieutenant John H. Crowder," p. 214 ("a coward"); *Revised United States Army Regulations of 1861* (Washington, D.C.: Government Printing Office, 1863), p. 38 ("unless under").

[48] *OR*, ser. 1, vol. 26, pt. 1, pp. 44–45.

[49] Ibid., 15: 717 ("to secure"); vol. 26, pt. 1, pp. 123–25, 128–29.

arrived in New York early on 6 June bearing a garbled report that the 2d Native Guard regiment, which was actually stationed on Ship Island, had suffered six hundred casualties at Port Hudson on 27 May. The Democratic *Herald*, no friend to the idea of black soldiers, emphasized the attackers' brutality: "It is said on every side that they fought with the desperation of tigers. One negro was observed with a rebel soldier in his grasp, tearing the flesh from his face with his teeth, other weapons having failed him. . . . After firing one volley they did not deign to load again, but went in with bayonets, and wherever they had a chance it was all up with the rebels." In fact, the Native Guards inflicted no casualties on the enemy. Horace Greeley's antislavery *Tribune* attributed the supposed six hundred casualties to the 3d Native Guards, which had at least been present at Port Hudson. "Their bearing upon this occasion has forever settled in this Department all question as to the employment of negro troops," the *Tribune* correspondent wrote. Two days later, a *Tribune* editorialist reverted to the earlier misidentification of the regiment: "Nobly done, Second Regiment of Louisiana Native Guard! . . . That heap of six hundred corpses, lying there dark and grim and silent before and within the Rebel works, is a better Proclamation of Freedom than even President Lincoln's." The project of putting black men in uniform inspired modest hopes, at best, in most white Americans. Any evidence of black soldiers' courage and resolve led to wild enthusiasm among their supporters and often to gross exaggeration. Coverage of the Native Guards at Port Hudson tended to bear out Captain DeForest's observation that "bayonet fighting occurs mainly in newspapers and other works of fiction."[50]

At least one black editor took a more practical view. "It is reported that the 2d Louisiana native guard, a regiment of blacks which lost six hundred in the gloriously bloody charge at Port Hudson, were placed in front, while veteran white troops brought up the rear. Great God, why is this?" demanded the *Christian Recorder*, the weekly organ of the African Methodist Episcopal Church. "We care not so much for the loss of men, however bravely they may die, but we damn to everlasting infamy, those who will thus pass by *veteran troops of any color*, and place a regiment of raw recruits in the front of a terrible battle." The editor was apparently unaware that more than one-fourth of the Union infantry force at Port Hudson consisted of nine-month men enlisted in the fall of 1862 and due for discharge in a few months. Only eleven of Banks' forty-five infantry regiments in the attack of 27 May had been in Louisiana for as long as a year. Port Hudson's besiegers did not constitute an army of vast experience.[51]

The Louisiana summer soon set in. Colonel Irwin, the officer in charge of all organizational returns, recalled its effects years later:

> The heat, especially in the trenches, became almost insupportable, the stenches quite so, the brooks dried up, the creek lost itself in the pestilential swamp, the springs gave out, and the river fell, exposing to the tropical sun a wide margin of

---

[50]The news stories appeared in the *New York Herald*, the *New York Times*, and the *New York Tribune* of 6 June 1863; editorial comment from the *Herald* of 6 June and the *Tribune* of 6 and 8 June. DeForest, *A Volunteer's Adventures*, p. 66. William F. Messner, *Freedmen and the Ideology of Free Labor: Louisiana, 1861–1865* (Lafayette: University of Southwest Louisiana, 1978), pp. 133–35, quotes other overwrought accounts of the Native Guards' performance.

[51]*Christian Recorder*, 13 June 1863; regiments listed in *OR*, ser. 1, 6: 706; *OR*, ser. 1, vol. 26, pt. 1, pp. 529–30, and Welcher, *Union Army*, 2: 728. Terms of service can be found in *ORVF* and Dyer, *Compendium*.

festering ooze. The illness and mortality were enormous. The labor of the siege, extending over a front of seven miles, pressed so severely . . . that the men were almost incessantly on duty; and as the numbers for duty diminished, of course the work fell more heavily upon those that remained[,] . . . while even of these every other man might well have gone on the sick-report if pride and duty had not held him to his post.[52]

Much of that labor fell to the men of General Ullmann's brigade. Soon after the failed attack of 27 May, General Banks ordered Ullmann to send all the men he had recruited, "whether armed or unarmed," to Port Hudson. Ullmann was able to send fourteen hundred. Banks put them to work at once in twelve-hour shifts. One month later, Maj. John C. Chadwick, commanding the 9th Corps d'Afrique Infantry of Ullmann's brigade, reported 231 men present for duty out of a total of 381. All were privates. Chadwick had not appointed any noncommissioned officers, he explained, because they were not needed: "We cannot drill any at present, being worked night and day." Half of the regiment's men were "unfit for the trenches," Brig. Gen. William Dwight reported. "The difficulty with this Regt. is that 2/3 of its officers are sick, and the other third inefficient." During the siege, Ullmann's five understrength regiments lost thirty-one men and officers killed, wounded, and missing in action.[53]

The Confederate garrison managed to hold out for forty-two days. On 7 July, a dispatch from Grant told Banks of Vicksburg's surrender. Word soon spread through the Union force and reached the Confederates in the trenches opposite. The two sides concluded terms of surrender the next day. Six weeks after the initial assault on Port Hudson, the Union Army that received the surrender of 6,408 eight Confederates could muster barely 9,000 men. Despite heat and sickness, it had gained its objective. The last Confederate stronghold on the Mississippi had fallen, and navigation of the river was open.[54]

With Port Hudson captured, recruiting the Corps d'Afrique took on new importance. The nine-months regiments that Banks had brought to Louisiana the previous winter made up nearly one-third of his infantry force, and they were bound for New England and New York in a few weeks to muster out. Apart from the river parishes below Port Hudson, Louisiana was by no means secure. Confederate troops had reoccupied the areas that Banks had abandoned in order to mass his divisions for the siege. Even along the river, bushwhacking snipers and the occasional Confederate cannon annoyed federal vessels. Banks used the same dispatch to Grant in which he told of Port Hudson's capture to ask for the loan of "a division of 10,000 or 12,000 men" to help chase the Confederates out of southern Louisiana. About the same time, he established the Corps d'Afrique's headquarters at Port Hudson and ordered General Ullmann to report there with his five regiments. The commander of the post, and of the

---

[52]Richard B. Irwin, "The Capture of Port Hudson," in *Battles and Leaders of the Civil War*, 4 vols. (New York: Century Co., 1887–1888), 3: 586–98 (quotation, p. 595).

[53]*OR*, ser. 1, vol. 26, pt. 1, pp. 70, 533 ("whether armed"); Brig Gen W. Dwight to Lt Col R. B. Irwin, 5 Jul 1863 ("unfit for") (D–361–DG–1863), Entry 1756, pt. 1, RG 393, NA; Maj J. C. Chadwick to Capt G. C. Getchell, 2 Jul 1863, 81st USCI, Entry 57C, RG 94, NA.

[54]*OR*, ser. 1, vol. 26, pt. 1, pp. 17, 52–54.

Corps d'Afrique, was Banks' former chief of staff, Brig. Gen. George L. Andrews, a Massachusetts man and a West Pointer who had superintended military construction in Boston Harbor while Banks was governor. At the end of August, Banks issued an order to enroll "all able-bodied men of color, in accordance with the law of conscription." A new "commission to regulate the enrollment, recruiting, employment, and education of persons of color" would draft as many men as it saw fit. The order also provided for the arrest of vagrants and "camp loafers" who would be assigned to public works and restricted the off-duty movements of black soldiers, forbidding them to "wander through the parishes," while promising to protect soldiers' families from retaliation for the soldiers' joining the Union Army.[55]

Filling extant regiments of the Corps d'Afrique and raising additional ones offered the best opportunity to replenish Union manpower in Louisiana. Union recruiters employed the method known as impressment. General Andrews called it "collecting negroes." One technique was to sweep the streets of New Orleans for "vagrant contrabands prowling about." The problem was that overzealous press gangs, whether black soldiers or city police, seized anyone they could, including civilians employed by the Army, prompting protests from quartermasters as cargo sat on the waterfront and unrepaired levees threatened to give way. "You ask if the Colored Troops are not enlisting fast," an officer in a white regiment at Port Hudson wrote to his wife that September. "In answer I can say that they are not enlisting at all but as fast as our folks can catch them they enlist them with the Bayonet for a persuader. Many of them are Deserting every night and they don't have a very good Story to tell those not yet initiated."[56]

The other technique was to send small expeditions to scour the countryside and collect any men who seemed sufficiently healthy. Capt. Francis Lyons and 1st Lt. George W. Reynolds led a recruiting party of the 14th Corps d'Afrique Infantry from New Orleans, where the regiment was organizing, and visited several plantations in the occupied parishes that had been exempted from the provisions of the Emancipation Proclamation. They "sent to [the] woods & collected the hands cutting wood, stripped & examined all the negroes, selected 11 & took them off. . . . The negroes say that these officers told them that now was the time for them to decide about being free or being slaves for life—that they could take their families to N.O. & they would be supported at Govt expense." Captain Lyons' black soldiers told the plantation hands "that they had

[55]Ibid., pp. 621, 624–25 ("a division," p. 625), 632, 704; S. M. Quincy to My dear Grandfather, 8 Dec 1863, S. M. Quincy Papers, Library of Congress (LC); George W. Cullum, *Biographical Register of the Officers and Graduates of the U.S. Military Academy*, 3d ed., 3 vols. (Boston: Houghton Mifflin, 1891), 2: 436.

[56]*OR*, ser. 1, vol. 26, pt. 1, p. 238 ("collecting"). P. F. Mancosas to Maj Gen N. P. Banks, 7 Aug 1863 ("vagrant contrabands") (M–372–DG–1863); Capt J. Mahler to Lt Col J. G. Chandler, 1 Aug 1863 (M–375–DG–1863); Col S. B. Holabird to Lt Col R. B. Irwin, 4 Aug 1863 (H–479–DG–1863); Brig Gen W. H. Emory to Lt Col R. B. Irwin, 13 Aug 1863 (E–141–DG–1863); all in Entry 1756, pt. 1, RG 393, NA. H. Soule to My Darling Mary, 24 Sep 1863 ("You ask"), H. Soule Papers, Bentley Historical Library, University of Michigan, Ann Arbor. See also C. Peter Ripley, "The Black Family in Transition: Louisiana, 1860–1865," *Journal of Southern History* 41 (1975): 369–80, p. 374.

better enlist voluntarily, as otherwise they would be forced in." In all, the expedition netted fifty-two potential soldiers.[57]

These recruiting drives, which seemed more like raids to planters and field hands alike, disrupted the economic routine of the sugar parishes. With everyday activities like woodcutting threatened, it became impossible to collect the fuel necessary to boil sugarcane. Each hogshead of sugar required three or four cords of firewood. With the fuel supply threatened, many planters switched to cotton the next year, as much because of the uncertain labor force as because of the "fabulous price" cotton fetched. In Terrebonne Parish, cotton constituted "almost the entire crop." Women and children could weed the rows, a task that did not require the strength of a man capable of wielding an axe: the kind of man Union recruiters sought.[58]

Even on the heels of a string of Northern victories in the summer of 1863, not every recruiting foray was successful. Early in August, a party of 250 infantry from three Corps d'Afrique regiments, 50 men of the 3d Massachusetts Cavalry, and 2 guns from the 2d Vermont Battery headed north from Port Hudson to seek recruits for the newly formed 12th Corps d'Afrique Infantry. The expedition was not organized well. Not only was the infantry force made up of detachments from three different regiments, but it was commanded by a lieutenant from yet another regiment because he was a few days senior to the other officers present. The entire command was led by 1st Lt. Moore Hanham, formerly of the 6th New York Infantry, who had no connection to any of the regiments represented in the expedition but who had been appointed major in the 12th Corps d'Afrique, which needed to fill its companies before officers and men could muster in and begin drawing pay.[59]

Hanham's force reached the town of Jackson, about fifteen miles north of Port Hudson, on the first day and found fifty likely recruits. The next day, in midafternoon, about five hundred Confederate horsemen appeared unexpectedly. They first captured the expedition's scouts and then attacked the main body, driving it out of the town. During the retreat, one of the Union guides was shot and the entire force lost its way. Taking a route that proved impassable for wheeled transportation, the troops had to abandon their two cannon and several quartermaster's wagons. The expedition reported seventy-eight officers and men killed, wounded, and missing. General Andrews' report mentioned favorably the conduct of the white cavalry and artillery and of a contingent from the 6th Corps d'Afrique Infantry led by its own officer, 1st Lt. Benjamin Y. Royce. Maj. George Bishop, commanding the 6th, reported 2 killed, 6 wounded, and 9 missing of the hundred men his regiment had contributed to the expedition. "From what we can learn," he added, "it was a badly managed affair and the result not unexpected."[60]

Officers assigned to the Corps d'Afrique soon recognized the shortcomings of men caught by urban press gangs and rural raids. Newly assigned officers, many of them brought by General Ullmann from the Army of the Potomac, had not anticipated working with French-speaking recruits who had seldom in their lives

---

[57] Unsigned note, 3 Sep 1863 (Y–14–DG–1863), Entry 1756, pt. 1, RG 393, NA.

[58] Capt H. E. Kimball to Maj Gen N. P. Banks, 7 Aug 1863 (K–291–DG–1863), Entry 1756, pt. 1, RG 393, NA.

[59] *ORVF*, 2: 431, 8: 263.

[60] *OR*, ser. 1, vol. 26, pt. 1, pp. 238–40; Maj G. Bishop to Brig Gen D. Ullmann, 7 Aug 1863 (quotation), Entry 159DD, RG 94, NA.

left their home plantations. The largest plantations—those of five hundred acres or more—occupied 63 percent of the region's cultivated land, and the average sugar plantation was home to more than eighty slaves. Tens of thousands of people lived their entire lives without leaving francophone Louisiana. Work on a sugar plantation was especially hard, and Union officers were appalled at the physical wreckage produced by the unremitting, year-round toil of sugar culture.[61]

In July 1863, two officers of the 1st Regiment, Ullmann's Brigade (mustered in that September as the 6th Corps d'Afrique Infantry but renumbered the next year as the 78th USCI), were concerned enough to write to Maj. George L. Stearns, an abolitionist who had helped to raise the 54th and 55th Massachusetts. By that summer, Stearns had a commission to recruit black soldiers and was in Philadelphia organizing the 3d USCI. Captains Charles B. Gaskill and Delos T. Stiles told him that they had arrived in Louisiana with General Ullmann's contingent of officers in March and four months later had about two thousand former slaves in training at Port Hudson. "They have been drilled sufficiently to develop, somewhat, their capacity to make soldiers," the two captains wrote to Stearns, but:

> These men are far less intelligent than those you are enlisting in the colored regiments at the north. They are brought into camp or to the medical examiner in droves from six to two hundred, hastily past without judgement in regard to their fitness for discipline or soldierly bearing, many of them ungainly, and too degraided to be souldiers, as well as entirely unacquainted with the English language. No exertion on the part of the instructor, can ever make of this class effectual men for an army.

More effective screening of recruits, Gaskill and Stiles believed, would result in "an immense army of comparatively intelligent and active men."[62]

A further solution, the two officers thought, would be to organize regiments at a northern depot with a cadre of one hundred fifty black noncommissioned officers and then ship them south to fill the ranks with former slaves. Gaskill and Stiles offered to undertake the experiment themselves; it was a project that would have removed them from Port Hudson to Philadelphia and raised them at least a grade or two, from captains to field officers. Although the Bureau for Colored Troops failed to act on their proposal, the captains' appraisal of the Corps d'Afrique and its shortcomings typified criticism of Union recruiting methods and results in Louisiana. Gaskill and Stiles, as well as other contemporary observers, seemed barely to suspect that the new soldiers' evident lack of intelligence might have been a display of survival techniques developed in bondage that were being used to deal

---

[61] John C. Rodrigue, *Reconstruction in the Cane Fields: From Slavery to Free Labor in Louisiana's Sugar Parishes, 1862–1880* (Baton Rouge: Louisiana State University Press, 2001), p. 24; Roderick A. McDonald, *The Economy and Material Culture of Slaves: Goods and Chattels on the Sugar Plantations of Jamaica and Louisiana* (Baton Rouge: Louisiana State University Press, 1993), pp. 4–7, 11–15; Hilliard, *Atlas of Antebellum Southern Agriculture*, p. 17.

[62] Capt C. B. Gaskill and Capt D. T. Stiles to Maj G. L. Stearns, 23 Jul 1863, Entry 363, LR by Adj Gen L. Thomas, RG 94, NA. Stiles resigned within weeks of sending the letter; Gaskill finished the war as colonel of the 81st USCI and later served four years as a captain in the all-black 40th and 25th U.S. Infantries.

with a new form of involuntary servitude. As the two captains noted, "They seem in a quandary, whether they have really obtained their long sought liberty or only changed masters."[63]

General Ullmann's occasional missteps did not help in organizing the Corps d'Afrique. Late in the summer, when General Banks had nearly completed his purge of black officers, Ullmann conceived the idea of allowing "free men of color" to elect their own officers, just as white volunteers had done at the beginning of the war. He mentioned this to Adjutant General Thomas, who happened to be in New Orleans. Thomas thought that regiments with elected black officers would be "highly injurious to the organizations already authorized with entirely white officers" and forbade the project. Thomas found Ullmann so troublesome that he asked Banks to bar him from raising "any troops whatever."[64]

While Ullmann's ideas were far in advance of any that Army leaders could adopt at that time, there were other officers in the Corps d'Afrique whose primitive attitudes were even more unwelcome. The appointment of 2d Lt. Augustus W. Benedict of the 75th New York as major of the 4th Native Guards (later the 4th Corps d'Afrique Infantry), for instance, turned out to be a grave mistake. Appointed in March 1863, Benedict became the regiment's lieutenant colonel in a few months. By late autumn, his conduct had managed to anger most of the enlisted men. He had ordered more than one man tied spread-eagle on the ground with molasses smeared on his face to attract flies—the punishment, in one instance, for "stealing some corn to roast." He was also notorious for "kicking and knocking [the men] about." "It was a common thing," Capt. James Miller later told investigators. At Fort Jackson, sixty-five miles downstream from New Orleans, on 9 December 1863, Benedict horsewhipped two of the regiment's drummers, Pvts. Harry Williams and Munroe Miller, for lying to a sentry in order to get out of the garrison. Three other officers witnessed the incident but did not interfere. One of them, Col. Charles W. Drew, "thought it best to delay . . . instead of reprimanding him in the presence of the men." The men's reaction was to seize their weapons, begin firing wildly, and demand Benedict's death. The uprising was spontaneous and leaderless, as far as most of the officers could tell. "I should think that nearly one-half the regiment was engaged in the disturbance, the other half trying to quiet them," Colonel Drew testified.[65]

Led by the colonel, the regiment's officers managed to quell the disturbance in less than three hours. Drew sent Benedict to his quarters, which got him out of the men's sight and beyond their reach. Drew then told the men that he would not talk to them while they were armed; most of them went to their quarters, left their weapons, and came back to hear what the colonel had to say. He called the men

[63] Gaskill and Stiles to Stearns, 23 Jul 1863; Eugene D. Genovese, *Roll, Jordan, Roll: The World the Slaves Made* (New York: Pantheon Books, 1974), pp. 637–38, 646–48; Lawrence W. Levine, *Black Culture and Black Consciousness: Afro-American Folk Thought from Slavery to Freedom* (New York: Oxford University Press, 1977), pp. 121–33.

[64] Col J. S. Clark and Col G. H. Hanks to Col A. B. Botsford, 12 Sep 1863, Entry 159DD, RG 94, NA; Brig Gen L. Thomas to Maj Gen N. P. Banks, 11 Sep 1863 (A–512–DG–1863), Entry 1756, pt. 1, RG 393, NA.

[65] *OR*, ser. 1, vol. 26, pt. 1, pp. 460 ("thought it best," "I should"), 464, 468 ("It was"), 469, 471 ("stealing," "kicking"), 473–74.

Fort Jackson, Louisiana, on the Mississippi River below New Orleans. Here the brutality of Lt. Col. Augustus W. Benedict caused a mutiny in the 76th U.S. Colored Infantry.

around him and assured them that while flogging was wrong, mutiny was a far greater wrong. After assurances that Drew would see their grievances redressed, the men retired for the night. It was the best solution under the circumstances. Captain Miller, the officer of the day, was sure that any show of force would have resulted in the officers' deaths.[66]

The next day, all ten of the regiment's company first sergeants presented a written request for an interview with the colonel "for ther Peace and Satisfaction in Relation to the Conduct of Lieut Conl Benedict." The whipping had "arroused the feeling of the men," but the petitioners hoped that Drew would "certif[y] that the Different Companies did not do any thing aganst him or ther Government." The first sergeants promised Drew that they would "go with him to [the] End if he will look to our Rights." Two days later, Drew assured investigators that since the riotous evening, the men's conduct had been "unexceptionable."[67]

Brig. Gen. William Dwight took command of Fort Jackson on 13 December, four days after the disturbance. A general court-martial convened at the fort and quickly sentenced Benedict to dismissal from the service on the charge of "inflicting cruel and unusual punishment, to the prejudice of good order and military discipline." The court also tried thirteen enlisted men for mutiny, acquitting four, sentencing seven to punishments ranging from dismissal to twenty years' hard labor, and two—including a man who had tried to bayonet

---

[66] Ibid., pp. 460–61, 467.
[67] Ibid., p. 462; Unsigned Ltr, 10 Dec 1863, 76th USCI, Entry 57C, RG 94, NA.

Captain Miller—to be shot. The reviewing authority overturned one conviction because of conflicting evidence and ordered the two condemned men imprisoned "until further orders."[68]

By the end of the month, with Benedict removed, Dwight pronounced the regiment's discipline "excellent." Earlier, he had prepared charges against Drew because the colonel had reasoned with his men rather than ordering them at once to their quarters. In the end, Dwight dropped the charges because, although he thought Drew's methods were "mistaken and unwise," the results could not be faulted. The Department of the Gulf's inspector general likewise thought that Drew's approach was weak—a sign that "the officers are afraid of the men, and . . . the men know it"—but neither the inspector general nor Dwight had been at Fort Jackson on the evening of 9 December. What occurred there was more of a riot than a mutiny. The men had no objective other than Benedict's removal, and most of them readily obeyed orders from an officer who seemed to understand their resentment of Benedict's brutal punishments. Flogging was clearly illegal; Congress had outlawed the practice two years earlier. Black soldiers especially objected to physical punishment, for it reminded them of life in slavery. "These troops view punishment inflicted on their comrades, not as the necessary result of a neglect of duty, but as an abuse of their race and they all feel it," the inspector general concluded.[69]

The men of the 4th Corps d'Afrique Infantry had been dragged off the plantations and "enrolled as fast as found," without even the formality of a physical examination. In September and October 1863, they had received no fresh meat or vegetables and signs of scurvy had begun to appear. Shipping delays were frequent throughout the Army, and scurvy was not uncommon. During those two months, the Department of the Gulf reported 315 cases and the Army as a whole 763. The symptoms disappeared from the 4th Corps d'Afrique Infantry after a shipment of rations reached the regiment, but by December, the men had "been exposed," as General Banks reflected, "to all the trials to which any soldiers can be subjected."[70]

Banks went on to remark that troops were often "unable immediately to comprehend to its full extent the necessity of strict military discipline. . . . A few months' instruction . . . is not sufficient to enable them to comprehend all that is required of citizens or soldiers. . . . It is indispensable that the officers should be men of high character, able to appreciate the capacity as well as the deficiencies of the men placed in their charge." He admitted that in raising the twenty-nine regiments of the Corps d'Afrique quickly, "a large number of officers" had received appointments with only a "very imperfect examination as

[68] *OR*, ser. 1, vol. 26, pt. 1, pp. 476–79.

[69] Lt Col W. S. Abert to Brig Gen C. P. Stone, 14 Dec 1863 ("the officers," "These troops"), and Brig Gen W. Dwight to Brig Gen C. P. Stone, 28 Dec 1863, both in 76th USCI, Entry 57C, RG 94, NA.

[70] *OR*, ser. 1, vol. 26, pt. 1, p. 458; Asst Surgeon J. Homans Jr. to Surgeon R. H. Alexander, 21 Nov 1863, 76th USCI, Entry 57C, RG 94, NA; Fred A. Shannon, *The Organization and Administration of the Union Army, 1861–1865*, 2 vols. (Cleveland: Arthur H. Clark, 1928), 1: 78–80; Bell I. Wiley, *The Life of Billy Yank: The Common Soldier of the Union* (Indianapolis: Bobbs-Merrill, 1952), pp. 225–31; *The Medical and Surgical History of the War of the Rebellion*, 2 vols. in 6 (Washington, D.C.: Government Printing Office, 1870–1888), vol. 1, pt. 1, pp. 396, 452.

to qualifications." Colonels of white regiments had used the Corps d'Afrique as a dumping ground for knaves and incompetents. Men concerned only with promotion found the new organizations a convenient means of jumping a grade or two.[71]

Unfortunately for the 4th Corps d'Afrique Infantry, some of its officers were just the sort of men General Banks deplored. One evening in January 1864, four of them, including the officer of the day and the officer of the guard, set out to inspect the quarters of the company laundresses near Fort Jackson. Every company was entitled to four laundresses, whose rations, quarters, and fuel the Army provided. Their wages came from the washing they did, at rates determined by a council of officers. It was a choice job for an enlisted man's wife, and most laundresses had no trouble finding a husband. On the night in question, the inspecting officers began by making an indecent proposal to one laundress, who flung the contents of a chamber pot in their direction. They left Capt. William H. Knapp at the next woman's cabin, where he had arranged to spend the night. Two of the other officers then threatened women who washed for their companies with loss of employment if they did not acquiesce to the same arrangement Captain Knapp had made with his laundress. One of the women told an investigator "that then 'Charley Goff,' referring to Captain [Charles A.] Goff, got on her bed, while Lt [William H.] Odell held her, and she does not know what would have resulted, had not her vigorous cries caused the inspectors to quit her premises. This they did, stating to her that she was a bitch, whereat she suggested that they must have descended from a similar animal." The investigator also collected testimony from four enlisted men of the 4th Corps d'Afrique Infantry, as well as from the women who washed their clothes, "that scenes similar to this one . . . have been of frequent, almost nightly occurrence for a long time past; that other officers than those arrested have been at other times equally guilty. So that the names of many officers have long been held up to the scandal and contempt of the soldiers of the Regiment." General Dwight recommended immediate dishonorable discharges for the officers in order to avoid the necessity of public testimony by "negro women of more than questionable character" and by enlisted men who knew they would suffer if the officers were acquitted. The men's expectations of the officers' acquittal were justified, for the president revoked the dismissals and they all returned to the regiment, two of them serving with it through the end of the war.[72]

Despite difficulties with the quality of officers and enlisted men, the Corps d'Afrique grew. In late May, Ullmann had brought parts of five regiments numbering 1,400 men to the siege of Port Hudson. By mid-August, seventeen infantry regiments reported a total of 8,107 men. A battery of light artillery and a company of cavalry were organizing. Three companies of heavy artillery

---

[71] OR, ser. 1, vol. 26, pt. 1, p. 458.

[72] Brig Gen W. Dwight to Brig Gen C. P. Stone, 27 Jan 1864 (quotations); AGO, SO 190, 28 May 1864; both in 76th USCI, Entry 57C, RG 94, NA. ORVF, 8: 252; August V. Kautz, Customs of Service for Non-Commissioned Officers and Soldiers (Philadelphia: J. B. Lippincott, 1865), pp. 12–13; Edward M. Coffman, The Old Army: A Portrait of the American Army in Peacetime, 1784–1898 (New York: Oxford University Press, 1986), pp. 112–13.

included about 300 men and two regiments of engineers 1,467. The entire force numbered just over 10,000.[73]

Engineer regiments were unusual in the Union Army: Michigan contributed one, Missouri two, and New York three. None were assigned to the Department of the Gulf, something that Banks' chief engineer noticed soon after his arrival. Deeming engineer regiments essential to future offensive operations, he told Banks that the absence of one had caused "innumerable delays in the movements of our troops, and . . . important failures" in the past. Soon afterward, two corporals in a ninety-day Massachusetts regiment wrote to Banks from Baton Rouge, urging the creation of an engineer regiment to include "the Smartest & most intelligent of the 'Contrabands' at Donaldsonville, Plaquemine & at this place. . . . Many of them are Masons, Blacksmiths & Carpenters." The corporals asked permission to begin organizing such a regiment themselves. This bold attempt to jump from the lower noncommissioned ranks to a major's or colonel's commission may have irked Banks. In any case, he was busy at the time with plans to get rid of black officers in the existing regiments of Native Guards and disapproved the idea of yet another black regiment. A few months later, though, the announcement of Ullmann's impending arrival led him to reconsider, and the 1st Corps d'Afrique Engineers took part in the siege of Port Hudson, although without the presence of the two audacious corporals. By the following year, the Corps d'Afrique included five engineer regiments.[74]

The corporals may have wanted to recruit artisans for their projected regiment, but the recruits who eventually filled the ranks of the Corps d'Afrique engineers were not skilled craftsmen. Throughout the Army, each company kept a descriptive book that listed its members' physical characteristics, age, occupation, birthplace, and place of enlistment. Descriptive books survive for only a few companies in which Corps d'Afrique engineers served. These show that 139 men of the 95th USCI (formerly the 1st Corps d'Afrique Engineers) transferred to the 81st USCI in July 1864. This was one of several consolidations that month, intended to bring some of General Banks' 500-man Corps d'Afrique regiments to full strength. The 139 new men in the 81st included 6 farmers, 1 waiter, 1 teamster, and 1 self-described engineer. The other 130 were listed as "laborer." In the smaller, more meticulous peacetime Army, this would certainly have meant an unskilled pick-and-shovel man. In the enormous wartime volunteer force, it may simply have meant that the same white officers who listed the color of every recruit's complexion, eyes, and hair as "black, black, black" or "dark, dark, dark" may not have bothered to inquire about the men's former livelihoods. "Laborer" and "farmer" often described men who surely must have been slaves. Whatever the recruits' previous status,

---

[73]Lt Col R. B. Irwin to Maj Gen N. P. Banks, 16 Aug 1863 (I–66–DG–1863), and Brig Gen G. L. Andrews to Lt Col R. B. Irwin, 21 Aug 1863 (A–310–DG–1863), both in Entry 1756, pt. 1, RG 393, NA.

[74]Maj D. C. Houston to Maj Gen N. P. Banks, 15 Jan 1863 ("innumerable delays") (H–121–DG–1863), and T. Nugent and T. L. Jewett to Maj Gen N. P. Banks, 19 Feb 1863 ("the Smartest") (N–46–DG–1863), both in Entry 1756, pt. 1, RG 393, NA. Dyer, *Compendium*, p. 39.

*Soldiers from one of the Corps d'Afrique engineer regiments at work along the
Bayou Teche in the fall of 1863*

there seems to have been no effort to enlist artisans for the engineer regiments
of the Corps d'Afrique.[75]

The role of the Corps d'Afrique itself, and of black soldiers in the Union
Army generally, was still uncertain. The post commander at Port Hudson, for
instance, wondered whether the 19th Corps d'Afrique Infantry, "ordered to report . . . for duty in the Quartermaster's Department, [was] to be on such duty
permanently and whether as soldiers or laborers." Early in 1863, Secretary of
War Stanton had sent Adjutant General Thomas west to raise black regiments
in Union-occupied stretches of the Mississippi Valley. Thomas conceived of
the new organizations as garrison troops to man fortified places along the river,
to protect plantations that were being worked by freed slaves, and to "operate effectively against the guerillas. This would be particularly advantageous
on the Mississippi River, as the Negroes, being acquainted with the peculiar
country lining its banks, would know where to act effectively." It is uncertain
whether the adjutant general had seen Col. Thomas W. Higginson's report of
his raid in Florida two months earlier; but the commanding general of the Department of the South had sent it to the War Department on 2 February, and
there was plenty of time for Thomas to have read Higginson's observation that
"black troops . . . know the country, while white troops do not" before he left
Washington in the last week of March.[76]

In the space of two months that spring and summer, battles in Louisiana,
Mississippi, and South Carolina called public attention to black soldiers' met-
tle in both attack and defense. General Andrews, the post commander at Port

---

[75] *OR*, ser. 1, vol. 34, pt. 3, pp. 221–22; vol. 41, pt. 2, p. 118. Returns showed 530,306 officers and
men present for duty, of an aggregate of 847,886, on 30 June 1863. *OR*, ser. 3, 3: 460. Descriptive
books of Companies B, G, H, and I, bound as one, constitute the only surviving volume of the 81st
USCI records. 81st USCI, Regimental Books, RG 94, NA.

[76] *OR*, ser. 1, 14: 194–98 ("black troops," p. 198); Andrews to Irwin, 21 Aug 1863 ("ordered to
report") (A–321–DG–1863); Brig Gen L. Thomas to E. M. Stanton, 1 Apr 1863 ("operate effectively")

Hudson, thought that the quality of arms being issued to new regiments of the Corps d'Afrique was important. "I have no objection to a considerable proportion of smooth-bore muskets *of good quality*," he wrote to department headquarters in August:

> But I prefer and think necessary a larger proportion of rifled muskets. Many of the smooth-bore muskets which have been sent here for issue are old flint-lock muskets altered to percussion, very much out of order. . . . As to the care of these arms, it is certain that colored troops cannot treat them much worse than the white volunteer troops have hitherto done. . . . Anything that has the *appearance* of treating the colored troops as unfit to receive anything but inferior articles of clothing or equipment is promptly felt by both officers and men. . . . I would respectfully recommend that as far as practicable distinctions in arming or equipping the two classes of troops should be avoided for the present at least.

An inspection the next month showed that while the 1st Corps d'Afrique Infantry, the old 1st Native Guards, had .58-caliber Enfield rifles "in excellent order," the 10th, part of Ullmann's Brigade, had .69-caliber Springfield smoothbore flintlocks—altered to accept percussion caps—25 percent of which were "unfit for service."[77]

The question of inferior equipment rankled the U.S. Colored Troops throughout the war. In Louisiana, as in the Department of the South, the reason for such deficiencies lay in long supply lines, slow communications, and haste in raising new black regiments as much as it did in the malice of individual staff officers who had low expectations of black soldiers' abilities and believed that any equipment was good enough for troops who were unlikely ever to meet an enemy. By the summer of 1863, it had become clear that this war had no definite "front" and no reliably safe "rear."

(A–316–DG–1863), Entry 159BB, Generals' Papers and Books (L. Thomas), RG 94, NA.

[77] Andrews to Irwin, 21 Aug 1863 ("I have no") (A–316–DG–1863); Inspection Rpts, 19 Sep 1863, 73d and 82d USCIs, Entry 57C, RG 94, NA.

CHAPTER 5

SOUTHERN LOUISIANA AND THE GULF COAST, 1863–1865

With Port Hudson secured, the Mississippi open to navigation, and regiments of the Corps d'Afrique filling up, Maj. Gen. Nathaniel P. Banks looked around for new objectives. In concert with the Navy, he moved quickly to oust Confederate defenders from the lower Atchafalaya River and wrote to Chief of Staff Maj. Gen. Henry W. Halleck in Washington, D.C., of a possible move against the port of Mobile or against Texas. Banks favored Mobile. Before his letter could reach Washington, though, Halleck told him by telegraph that Texas was the preferable goal "for important reasons." In a subsequent letter, Halleck explained that the impetus behind the telegram was diplomatic rather than military "and resulted from some European complications, or, more properly speaking, was intended to prevent such complications."[1]

While the United States was embroiled in war, the French emperor had landed an army in Mexico and established a puppet monarchy there. A federal move into Texas would cut off a source of Confederate supplies while providing a forceful caution to the French. Therefore, both the president and the secretary of state wanted Union troops in Texas "as soon as possible." Halleck left details of the offensive to Banks but suggested that while coastal operations would merely divide the enemy's force and nibble at the edges of the Confederacy, a move up the Red River would drive a wedge through it. Banks objected that the Red River route was out of the question in August. It was too hot for the survivors of the Port Hudson siege to march across the state, he told Halleck, and water in the river was too low to float transports.[2]

In any case, Banks had already decided on sending a small force to seize the mouth of the Sabine River on the Texas-Louisiana line.[3] The expedition sailed from New Orleans on 4 September 1863, but when it attempted to land on the Texas shore four days later, Confederate batteries disabled two of the gunboats while two other vessels ran aground. The general commanding abandoned the project after failing to get any of his twelve hundred troops ashore. Banks then

---

[1] *The War of the Rebellion: A Compilation of the Official Records of the Union and Confederate Armies*, 70 vols. in 128 (Washington, D.C.: Government Printing Office, 1880–1901), ser. 1, vol. 26, pt. 1, pp. 651, 666, 672 ("for important reasons"), 673 ("and resulted") (hereafter cited as *OR*).

[2] *OR*, ser. 1, vol. 24, pt. 3, p. 584 ("as soon"); vol. 26, pt. 1, p. 696.

[3] *OR*, ser. 1, vol. 26, pt. 1, p. 683.

mounted another expedition that he himself led. It landed near the mouth of the Rio Grande and marched inland to occupy Brownsville, Texas, during the first week of November. The international border was a better site than the Sabine from which to impress the French in Mexico, and an American force there could also threaten the thriving Confederate trade in Southern cotton for European munitions through the Mexican port of Bagdad at the mouth of the river. A division of the XIII Corps, veterans of Vicksburg, made up the bulk of Banks' expedition. The Corps d'Afrique's 1st Engineer and 16th Infantry regiments were attached.

International affairs warmed up within days of Banks' arrival on the Rio Grande. An exiled Mexican general who had been living in Brownsville crossed the river, seized the city of Matamoros, and overthrew the government of the state of Tamaulipas. Banks thought that the general intended to come to terms with the French and deliver to them Tamaulipas and with it control of the right bank of the Rio Grande as far upstream as Laredo. He need not have worried, for within twenty-four hours the general and two members of his staff were seized and shot by another Mexican general, Juan N. Cortina. The governor of Tamaulipas took advantage of the disturbance to flee to Brownsville. Meanwhile, Union troops on the north shore of the river began collecting bales of Confederate cotton. The role of the Corps d'Afrique regiments was to guard the supply depot at Brazos Island.[4]

In mid-November, Banks sailed north with five regiments, about fifteen hundred men, to attack the Texas port of Corpus Christi. With them went the 1st Engineers. The campaign's first step was to subdue Confederate forts on the coastal islands. The 2d Corps d'Afrique Engineers soon arrived from New Orleans to further the siege work. Having seen the troops safely ashore, Banks returned to department headquarters in New Orleans to begin planning the spring campaign of 1864.[5]

Again the question arose: where should federal troops aim their next offensive thrust? Certainly, Richmond, Virginia, would receive attention and the Union force based at Chattanooga would move into Georgia. West of the Mississippi River, Shreveport offered a target attractive to General Halleck. It was the seat of Louisiana's Confederate government, and Halleck was aware of military supplies and cotton to be gathered along the Red River. The parishes that bordered the river from Shreveport to its mouth produced less cotton as did those in the Natchez District, on the Mississippi, but the country in the middle of the state had not been fought over by opposing armies and might be a valuable source of food and forage. The river itself, when sufficient water made it navigable, afforded a highway into northeastern Texas. Defeat of Confederate resistance in Louisiana might free anywhere from five to eight thousand Union troops for campaigns against Atlanta or Mobile. Moreover, the valley of the Red River had a substantial black population, increased in recent

---

[4]Ibid., pp. 399–403, 410, 413–15.

[5]Ibid., pp. 420, 832; Frederick H. Dyer, *A Compendium of the War of the Rebellion* (New York: Thomas Yoseloff, 1959 [1909]), p. 1718; Stephen A. Townsend, *The Yankee Invasion of Texas* (College Station: Texas A&M University Press, 2006), p. 64.

years by thousands of slaves whose owners had sent them out of the way of advancing federal armies. They were expected to furnish many recruits for the Corps d'Afrique. Banks told Halleck that he would be ready to move when the river rose that spring.[6]

The core of Banks' command consisted of some ten thousand men of the XIX Corps, about five thousand in brigades of the XIII Corps that had not been sent to Texas and another ten thousand on loan for thirty days from Maj. Gen. William T. Sherman's Army of the Tennessee. Sherman thought that the Red River Expedition stood a good chance of success if it moved as quickly as his raid on Meridian, Mississippi, had in January. That sortie, he boasted, had accomplished "the most complete destruction of railroads ever beheld." He wanted the borrowed troops returned in time for his spring campaign in Georgia. Completing Banks' force were 721 officers and men of the 3d and 5th Corps d'Afrique Engineers and a brigade consisting of the 1st, 3d, 12th, and 22d Corps d'Afrique Infantry, 1,535 strong. Naval gunboats ascended the Red River to augment the land force. Banks expected another seven thousand Union troops from Arkansas to meet him near Shreveport. He had spent the winter preoccupied with the election of a Unionist state government and delayed leaving New Orleans until 22 March, long enough to attend the new governor's inauguration.[7]

By that time, the troops on loan from Sherman's army had steamed up the Red River and captured a Confederate fort downstream from Alexandria. Acting in concert with naval gunboats, they occupied the town on 16 March. Heavy rains delayed the bulk of Banks' force in its overland march from the southern part of the state, but by 25 March, most of the troops, and the general himself, had reached Alexandria. They set out for Shreveport the next day, with the Corps d'Afrique infantry brigade guarding a train of nine hundred wagons. Stretched out along a single road through the woods, the entire column was about twenty miles long. The Corps d'Afrique engineers moved here and there as needed, making "corduroy roads" by laying logs side by side in otherwise impassable mud and operating a nine-boat pontoon bridge which they laid across deep streams in the army's path and then took up and loaded in wagons when the troops had crossed. After a week of such marching, the expedition

---

[6]*OR*, ser. 1, vol. 34, pt. 2, pp. 56, 133, 497, and pt. 3, p. 191. U.S. Census Bureau, *Agriculture of the United States in 1860* (Washington, D.C. Government Printing Office, 1864), p. 69. Before the war, the Red River parishes were home to more than seventeen thousand black males between the ages of fifteen and fifty. U.S. Census Bureau, *Population of the United States in 1860* (Washington, D.C.: Government Printing Office, 1864), pp. 188–93.

[7]*OR*, ser. 1, vol. 32, pt. 1, p. 173 ("the most"); vol. 34, pt. 1, pp. 167–68, 181, and pt. 2, pp. 494, 497, 542. James G. Hollandsworth Jr., *Pretense of Glory: The Life of General Nathaniel P. Banks* (Baton Rouge: Louisiana State University Press, 1998), pp. 162–71; Gary D. Joiner, *Through the Howling Wilderness: The 1864 Red River Campaign and Union Failure in the West* (Knoxville: University of Tennessee Press, 2006), p. 50. While these regiments of the Corps d'Afrique were in the field, they were renumbered the 73d, 75th, 84th, and 92d United States Colored Infantries (USCIs). The 3d and 5th Engineers became the 97th and 99th USCIs. *OR*, ser. 1, vol. 34, pt. 3, pp. 220–21. For troop strengths, see pt. 1, pp. 167–68. Regiments recalled from Texas augmented the XIII Corps during the campaign. Calculations of troop strength are complicated by the fact that the winter and early spring of 1864 was the season of "veteran furloughs," when men who were near completion of three years' service and had reenlisted for another three went home for a month.

reached Natchitoches, where it rested for four days while the Navy's boats struggled upstream. Despite heavy rains that impeded movement by land, the level of water in the river was falling.[8]

Banks' army left Natchitoches on 6 April and headed for Shreveport. The cavalry division led, followed by its own wagons, then various infantry commands and their wagons. The entire column "stretched out the length of a long day's march on a single narrow road in a dense pine forest" with few clearings where any organized movement off the road was possible. In the rear with the wagon train, the Corps d'Afrique infantry brigade had no part in the encounter at Sabine Crossroads on the second day of the move toward Shreveport. The brigade had just completed an exhausting day's march and made camp when "our army broken & scattered came rushing back into the field where we were lying," wrote Capt. Henry M. Crydenwise of the 1st Corps d'Afrique Infantry. The cavalry in advance of the army, followed closely by the XIII Corps, had met a superior Confederate force and fallen back for about a mile, jamming the narrow road through the woods until cavalry and infantry ran into their own wagon train, which was blocking the road. As one XIII Corps regimental commander reported, "The lines right and left being broken, the regiment was flanked again and driven to the woods." The fleeing troops became a "demoralized mass of retreating cavalry, infantry, artillerymen, and camp followers, crowding together in the midst of wagons and ambulances." It was this mass of panic-stricken soldiers that overran the camp of the Corps d'Afrique infantry brigade. A brigade of the XIX Corps, just arrived, had to force its way through to get to the front and join troops there that had rallied to stem the Confederate advance. After a second day's battle in which more fresh Union troops fought the Confederates to a standstill, Banks' army withdrew toward Grande Ecore on the Red River a few miles from Natchitoches.[9]

Another problem became plain when the retreating federals arrived at Grande Ecore. While they had marched overland, the river had fallen still lower. Supplies came upstream only with difficulty, "through snaggy bends, loggy bayous, shifting rapids, and rapid chutes," as Rear Adm. David D. Porter, commanding the naval gunboats on the river, put it. Porter advised Banks against another attempt on Shreveport during the season of low water. After allowing his army ten days' rest, Banks ordered a further retreat to Alexandria. Along the way, as Confederate Maj. Gen. Richard Taylor complained, the veterans of Sherman's Meridian raid put to the torch "every dwelling-house, every negro cabin, every cotton-gin, every corn-crib, and even chicken-houses." The western troops on loan from Sherman's army would take the blame for most of the destruction, but Banks' New England and New York regiments had been

---

[8]*OR*, ser. 1, vol. 34, pt. 1, pp. 181, 237, 248–49, 304–06; Richard B. Irwin, *History of the Nineteenth Army Corps* (New York: G. P. Putnam's Sons, 1892), p. 296; Ludwell H. Johnson, *The Red River Campaign: Politics and Cotton in the Civil War* (Baltimore: Johns Hopkins University Press, 1958), p. 145.

[9]*OR*, ser. 1, vol. 34, pt. 1, pp. 297 ("The lines"), 429 ("demoralized mass"), 485; H. M. Crydenwise to Dear Parents, n.d. ("our army"), H. M. Crydenwise Letters, Emory University, Atlanta, Ga.; Irwin, *Nineteenth Army Corps*, p. 300 ("stretched out").

The Red River Expedition marches toward Natchitoches, Louisiana, March 1864.

helping themselves to "secesh" property and burning what they could not carry off since the spring of 1862.[10]

Reaching Alexandria after a four-day march, the troops found Porter's boats trapped above the rapids. "The water had fallen so low that I had no hope or expectation of getting the vessels out this season," the admiral reported, "and as the army had made arrangements to evacuate the country I saw nothing before me but the destruction of the best part of the Mississippi Squadron." The possibility of building dams to raise the level of water in the river had occurred to engineer officers as the army marched toward Shreveport; with the expedition's naval component facing abandonment and destruction, they urged the project again. General Banks approved the idea, and the 3d and 5th Corps d'Afrique Engineers went to work at once, the 3d cutting and hauling timbers while the 5th positioned them in the river. Each regiment split into two battalions that worked alternate six-hour shifts around the clock. "Trees were falling with great rapidity, teams were moving in all directions bringing in brick and stone, quarries were opened, flatboats were built to bring stone down from above, and every man seemed to be working with a vigor I have seldom seen equaled," Porter wrote. Details and entire regiments of white troops from the XIII and XIX Corps joined in the work.

---

[10]*OR*, ser. 1, 15: 19–21, 280–89; vol. 34, pt. 1, pp. 205–06, 581 ("every dwelling-house"). *Official Records of the Union and Confederate Navies in the War of the Rebellion*, 30 vols. (Washington, D.C.: Government Printing Office, 1894–1922), ser. 1, 26: 56 ("through snaggy") (hereafter cited as *ORN*).

Maj. Gen. Nathaniel P. Banks' army built the Red River Dam to allow the Union flotilla to escape downstream while his land force retreated. Alexandria was the largest river port in central Louisiana.

The resulting system of dams more than doubled the depth of the river. By 13 May, all ten gunboats were below the rapids and steaming downstream in deep water. Col. George D. Robinson of the 3d Corps d'Afrique Engineers boasted that his regiment and the 5th were "regarded as a complete success by all who have witnessed their operations."[11]

The expedition continued down the Red River, headed for Simmesport on the Atchafalaya. On 17 May, a few miles from there, three hundred Confederate cavalrymen attacked the wagon train and its Corps d'Afrique guard as it passed through some woods. The 22d Corps d'Afrique Infantry stepped out of the road, faced the attackers, and began firing. Company E's 1st Sgt. Antoine Davis got close enough to the enemy to receive a fatal pistol shot in the chest. After an hour and a half of skirmishing, the Confederates withdrew, leaving nine dead on the field. The 22d lost twelve men killed, wounded, and missing. "This was the first time this regiment, as a whole, had been engaged with the enemy," the regiment's commanding officer wrote, "and I must say that their conduct was as good as that of any new troops." He complained that his regiment's .69-caliber smoothbore muskets were "of very inferior and defective quality, many of them becoming useless at the first fire." Despite their faulty weapons, the men of the 22d managed to repel the attack, and the brigade commander praised their "utmost coolness. . . . No one who witnessed their conduct on this occasion can doubt that it is perfectly safe to trust colored troops in action, and depend upon their doing their full share of the fighting."[12]

Later that day, Banks' army began to arrive in Simmesport. His expedition had been a failure, expensive in casualties, time, and opportunities lost in other theaters of operations. In Virginia, the newly promoted Lt. Gen. Ulysses S. Grant, commander of all Union armies, was exasperated. His special emissary to Banks' command, Maj. Gen. David Hunter, described the Department of the Gulf as "one great mass of corruption. Cotton and politics, instead of the war, appear to have engrossed the army," and added that the troops had no confidence in Banks.[13]

On 18 May, Maj. Gen. Edward R. S. Canby reached Simmesport. He headed a specially created geographical command, the Military Division of West Mississippi, which included both the Department of the Gulf and the Department of Arkansas. This was a way Grant and Halleck had devised to remove Banks the hapless general from field operations without alienating Banks the politician, who still had powerful friends in the Lincoln administration. Canby was a West Point graduate with two Mexican War brevets who had jumped from first lieutenant to major when the Army expanded in 1855 and from major to full colonel in one of the new regular infantry regiments in May 1861, becoming the only officer in the Army to receive successive two-grade promotions. He commanded Union troops in New Mexico in 1862, turning back a Confederate attack there, and in New York City after the draft riots the next year. His immediate concern in Louisiana was to resupply the troops and position them advantageously. Banks,

[11]*OR*, ser. 1, vol. 34, pt. 1, pp. 25, 253 ("regarded as"), 256, 402–03; *ORN*, ser. 1, 26: 130 ("The water," "Trees were"), 132.

[12]*OR*, ser. 1, vol. 34, pt. 1, pp. 443 ("utmost coolness"), 444 ("of very," "This was").

[13]*OR*, ser. 1, vol. 34, pt. 1, p. 390.

still titular head of the Department of the Gulf, returned to New Orleans and never commanded troops in the field again.[14]

While Banks and his army were advancing and retreating along the Red River, the troops at Port Hudson were not idle. Hard at work with the 65th United States Colored Infantry (USCI), which had recently come down the Mississippi from St. Louis, 2d Lt. Henry S. Wadsworth wrote home:

> The duty we have to perform here is very arduous both for the officers and men, as the guard detail is so heavy that it brings us on every third day and you know to be without sleep every third night is rather fatiguing and all that are not on guard have to work on the fortifications. . . . There is considerable fears of an attack and . . . all drilling has been stopped for the present and the men kept at work. . . . The garrisons of the posts along the river have been so materially weakened in order to strengthen Gen. Banks force in his wild goose chase up Red River that if the rebels ever intend to make an effort to recover some of their strongholds . . . , the present moment is a very opportune one for them. Should there be an attack it will undoubtedly be repulsed, but if it should not be I think there will not be any of us left to tell about it. We have heard the story of Fort Pillow and every officer . . . has since banished all thoughts of surrender from his mind. The troops here are nearly all colored and they know what to expect in case we are in the enemy's power.

At Fort Pillow, on the Mississippi River north of Memphis, Confederates the month before had killed more than two hundred men of the 6th United States Colored Artillery (USCA) and the 13th Tennessee Cavalry, a regiment of white Unionists. Reports had it that the Union force had surrendered but that Confederates had slaughtered the men rather than take prisoners. An investigation was under way. The incident seemed to confirm the fears that officers and enlisted men alike had entertained ever since the first black regiments were raised. Some resolved to sell their lives dearly, others to take no prisoners. Meanwhile, the men at Port Hudson grubbed stumps and cleared brush that remained from the Confederates' hastily organized defense twelve months earlier. Occasionally, a burning brush pile detonated an unexploded artillery shell below ground, "to the no small amusement of the men, happily no accidents occurred."[15]

Besides the Corps d'Afrique, the garrison consisted of two mounted white regiments totaling fewer than seven hundred officers and men and two batteries of light artillery. Port Hudson's mounted troops were responsible for patrolling the telegraph line between the post and Baton Rouge. On the morning of 7 April, a hundred-man escort and one artillery piece accompanied a repairman south from Port Hudson until they met a superior force of Confederate cavalry about eight miles out. The mounted escort fled, rallied, and broke again when

---

[14]Ibid., pt. 3, pp. 331–32, and pt. 4, pp. 15–17, 73–74. Francis B. Heitman, *Historical Register and Dictionary of the United States Army*, 2 vols. (Washington, D.C.: Government Printing Office, 1903), 1: 279.

[15]H. S. Wadsworth to My Dear Aunt, 5 May 1864, Frederick and Sarah M. Cutler Papers, Southern History Collection, Duke University, Durham, N.C. For more on Fort Pillow, see Chapter 7, pp. 205–09.

the retreat had reached a point about two miles from the Union lines. There, the Confederates surrounded the cannon and captured its crew. Port Hudson's remaining cavalry rode to the rescue, followed by infantry and artillery but too late to save the prisoners and their gun. Brig. Gen. George L. Andrews, commanding the post, reported that "the wonder is that with so small a cavalry force it has been possible to keep open 25 miles of telegraph line on a route so exposed, with the great superiority of the enemy in cavalry, without much more serious disasters."[16]

Camped at Port Hudson that day was the 20th USCI, raised in New York City, which had arrived by sea via New Orleans only two weeks earlier. Company I of the regiment had just buried Pvt. Charles Johnson, dead that day of pneumonia, its first member to die in Louisiana. The regimental band had played a funeral march for the two-mile walk to the cemetery and a livelier tune to bring the troops back through pouring rain. In camp again, 2d Lt. John Habberton had changed into a dry uniform when he heard the order to fall in. "'Fall in!' is a very frequent order here," Habberton wrote in his diary,

> but when I heard the colonel bellowing for his horse it indicated to me, over-coat, and something to eat in the pockets. Went to the cook-house to get some bread, and happening to look toward the works, which surround the place, and which are about a mile from our camp, I saw a neat little skirmish going on. The men . . . turned out *en masse*. Men just off guard fell in, and the sick list deserted the doctor. We have not had such full ranks since they fell in for pay. . . . Off we marched, and half an hour later we were manning a fort near the centre. . . . Here we learned that our pickets had been driven in on the Clinton road, and twelve of them captured. The skirmish had been in front of this fort. The enemy had been repulsed, and the 6th Regt., Corps d'Afrique had gone out to try the strength of the enemy. . . . After standing three hours, and getting wet through, we were ordered back to camp. I only noticed two men in the company who showed signs of fear, and they were roundly laughed at and lightly punched by their more manly comrades. . . . We reached camp at 8 P.M., very wet, muddy, and hungry, and with every private fifty per cent prouder than he ever was before.

Throughout the spring, Union garrisons along the Mississippi River endured raids by small bands of armed men. After the effort of repelling the Red River Expedition, Confederates in Louisiana were too weak to mount a large offensive.[17]

About halfway between Port Hudson and the mouth of the Red River, the little town of Morganza became the site of an army camp with a contingent of Colored Troops that eventually grew even larger than Port Hudson's. The XIX

---

[16] *OR*, ser. 1, vol. 34, pt. 1, pp. 877 (quotation), 879. The cavalry brigade numbered 562 officers and men present in January 1864 and 700 in June. Strength of the entire garrison was 5,079 in January and 5,323 in June. *OR*, ser. 1, vol. 34, pt. 2, p. 193, and pt. 4, p. 610.

[17] *OR*, ser. 1, vol. 34, pt. 1, pp. 933–34; John Habberton Diary, 7 Apr 1864, John Habberton Papers, U.S. Army Military History Institute, Carlisle, Pa.; John D. Winters, *The Civil War in Louisiana* (Baton Rouge: Louisiana State University Press, 1963), pp. 383–84.

Low-lying Morganza was one of the unhealthiest sites in Louisiana or, for that matter, the entire United States.

Corps had arrived at Morganza after the failed spring campaign. Its historian, a staff officer on the expedition, called the site "perhaps the most unfortunate in which the corps was ever encamped."

> The heat was oppressive and daily growing more unbearable. The rude shelters of brush and leaves . . . gave little protection; the levee and the dense undergrowth kept off the breeze; and such was the state of the soil that when it was not a cloud of light and suffocating dust, it was a sea of fat black mud. The sickly season was close at hand, and the deaths were many. The mosquitoes were at their worst.

The brigade of Colored Troops that had accompanied the Red River Expedition became part of Morganza's garrison. By summer, another three regiments, the 62d, 65th, and 67th, had joined it to constitute a division that numbered some twenty-five hundred men in a force of sixty-seven hundred present for duty there.[18]

The force dwindled through the summer as causes arising from the military occupation itself joined with the heat and mosquitoes to sicken the garrison. By August, "the stench of decaying bodies" buried only three feet deep necessitated a search for a new cemetery. The next month, the commissary officer felt obliged to explain that although humidity imparted "a slight musty flavor" to the dried beans, peas, and hominy that the troops received and the heat to which barrels of pickled meat were exposed caused "a *taint* in the brine," cooking the rations removed the unpleasant odor and rendered them fit to eat. "Both officers and men should remember that the Govt. buys for their use the best stores it can procure, & if by reason of the warm climate, the dis-

---

[18] *OR*, ser. 1, vol. 41, pt. 2, p. 327; Irwin, *Nineteenth Army Corps*, p. 349 (quotation).

tance of shipment & unavoidable exposure, they lose some of the original sweetness, yet so long as they *can* be used, they should be, since no better can be provided." The complaint about rations came from a division of the XIX Corps, but heat and humidity attacked the food of black soldiers too. By October, the 62d, 65th, and 67th USCIs, all newly arrived from Missouri, had lost 1,374 dead from an original strength of 3,158 officers and men. An inspection of the 65th revealed that the men "were not examined, or but cursorily" when they entered the service, and that the regiment contained a large number who were "totally unfit for soldiers."[19]

Inadequate physical examinations plagued the Union Army throughout the war. The U.S. Sanitary Commission judged that men in only 9 percent of the two hundred white regiments it studied in 1861 had undergone "a thorough inspection," a situation that left at least one quarter of the troops "not only utterly useless, but a positive encumbrance and embarrassment." Poorly sited latrines in the Colored Troops' camp combined with untidy personal habits "to breed pestilence without limit." Medical officers complained often about careless defecation by white and black troops alike. At Morganza, the soldiers' health had scarcely improved by the end of the summer.[20]

Maintenance of the camp's defenses occupied most of the working day, to the point where Col. Samuel M. Quincy of the 73d USCI protested that "all the fatigue duty on fortifications" fell on the black regiments in violation of a general order prescribing that they should "only . . . take their fair share of fatigue duty with the white troops." From time to time there was an alarm, as in late July, when a cavalry patrol reported that five hundred Confederates had crossed the Atchafalaya. In response, half of the Colored Troops at Morganza received instructions to be "up and under arms daily at 3 a.m. . . . The men will be aroused without beat of drum and with as little noise as possible." The alarm subsided when another patrol, four days later, reported no enemy forces east of the Atchafalaya.[21]

"We have been here about four days now," Capt. Henry M. Crydenwise of the 73d USCI wrote to his family, "We sleep with our clothes on ready to spring up at a moment's notice." He went on:

> They are building fortifications here & straining every energy to complete them. Yesterday I had command of our reg[imen]t at work on the trenches. We worked all day long from day light till dark. . . . About 11 O clock last night the "Long Roll" beat and we turned out expecting to have a fight, but it proved to be our cavalry coming in which had been out on a scout! . . . Just imagine after a hard day's work

---

[19] Maj J. K. Hudson to 1st Lt D. G. Fenno, 11 Aug 1864 ("the stench"); Capt J. E. Howard to Brig Gen G. F. McGinnis, 5 Sep 1864 ("a slight"); Brig Gen D. Ullmann to Lt Col C. T. Christensen, 29 Oct 1864; all in Entry 1976, U.S. Forces at Morganza, Letters Received (LR), pt. 2, Polyonymous Successions of Cmds, Record Group (RG) 393, Rcds of U.S. Army Continental Cmds, National Archives (NA). Lt Col W. H. Thurston to Maj G. P. Drake, 29 Oct 1864 ("were not," "totally unfit"), 65th USCI, Entry 57C, Regimental Papers, RG 94, Rcds of the Adjutant General's Office, NA.

[20] Surgeon C. Allen to 1st Lt D. G. Fenno, 23 Jun 1864 ("to breed"); 1st Lt J. W. Read to 1st Lt A. F. Hunt, 5 Sep 1864; both in Entry 159DD, Generals' Books and Papers (Ullmann), RG 94, NA. Bell I. Wiley, *The Life of Billy Yank: The Common Soldier of the Union* (Indianapolis: Bobbs-Merrill, 1952), pp. 23, 125 ("a thorough," "not only"), 126.

[21] *OR*, ser. 1, vol. 41, pt. 2, pp. 327–28, 353–55 ("up and under," p. 354), 381–82, 415–16, 566 ("only . . . take"); 1st Lt C. S. Sargent to Brig Gen M. K. Lawler, 5 Sep 1864 ("all the fatigue"), Entry 1976, pt. 2, RG 393, NA.

when every thing is hushed and quiet . . . the drums in all the camp begin to beat, slow at first and growing faster, louder & wilder until it is one continuous roll like muttering thunder How quickly the scene is changed. There is no noise or confusion but all through the camp in low smothered voices, you will hear, "*Turn out, Quickly boys Long Roll, the Rebs are coming.*" In a moment the companies are formed and then on *Double Quick* rush to their place in the regimental line. . . . I confess plainly I do not like to fight and Mr. Reb will do me a great kindness by staying away. But should they come we have a large force of colored troops here who will fight to the death and I believe the enemy will pay heavily for the attempt.[22]

Neither the fatigue assignments and sanitary arrangements at Morganza nor the region's security had improved by the end of the summer. On 16 September, a regiment of Confederate cavalry overwhelmed a Union patrol east of the Atchafalaya, killing or capturing thirty-nine men, and Morganza's post commander sent a strong mounted force to intercept the attackers. The 75th and 92d USCIs were among the infantry that moved in support of the Union cavalry. When they reached the river, the black regiments spent two days building gun emplacements to command the ford and "cutting roads in the woods, so [the emplacements] could be approached under cover," Col. Henry N. Frisbie of the 92d reported:

No white troops lifted an ax or a spade while out on that trip . . . yet the colored troops marched as far, did as much guard duty, and . . . while the rest lay in the shade we were hard at work. . . . The work is no objection to either officers or men, but the manner and the circumstances under which it is required. The slur and stigma of inferiority is what displeases so many . . . and makes it so difficult to keep our best officers, for they will not command troops that the Government allows inferiority to become attached to . . . ; but while they bear commissions they want only their fair share of fatigue, but will do any amount of fighting.

Frisbie was also exasperated because his men had been bilked of their beef ration by an officer from another command while they were performing fatigue duty and then had been accused of chicken theft while "white soldiers on the road were catching fowls, and no effort was made to stop them." Personally humiliating was a report by the expedition's commanding officer, which contrasted the "good behavior" of the 75th USCI, led by "an excellent disciplinarian," with that of Frisbie's chicken-stealing 92d. Yet the way in which the report criticized the 92d by comparing it to another nearby all-black regiment typified much official comment on black troops. Inspection reports often used the same basis of comparison. The object was to correct deficiencies in military behavior rather than to vent the writer's racial animus. Responsibility for discipline, or the lack of it, lay with a regiment's white officers.[23]

All through the last twelve months of the war, Union troops in Louisiana—including nineteen regiments of U.S. Colored Troops—acted more as an occupation force than as a field army. About one-third of the black regiments' strength was

---

[22] H. M. Crydenwise to Dear Parents & all, 24 Jul 1864, Crydenwise Letters.

[23] *OR*, ser. 1, vol. 41, pt. 1, pp. 803, 805, 808–10 (quotations). Reports similar to the one about which Colonel Frisbie complained are Col A. J. Edgerton to 1st Lt D. G. Fenno, 31 Aug 1864, 67th

scattered at coastal and river forts between Lake Pontchartrain and the mouth of the Mississippi. Most of it was concentrated at three points along a hundred-mile stretch of the winding river: companies from two or more regiments at Plaquemine, just below Baton Rouge; Port Hudson, headquarters of the Corps d'Afrique in the spring of 1864 but eventually reduced to four regiments of U.S. Colored Troops; and the seven-regiment garrison at Morganza, some thirty miles upstream from Port Hudson. Another two regiments oversaw the coastal sugar parishes from the vantage point of Brashear City, near the mouth of the Atchafalaya. These troop dispositions, and those of the fifty-five regiments of white Union infantry and cavalry and twenty-four batteries of light artillery, were the outgrowth of two years' military occupation of the lower Mississippi Valley and of federal authorities' relations with the region's residents, both black and white.[24]

After Union troops landed in the spring of 1862, they sought to placate as far as possible the anti-secessionist sugar planters who had stayed in residence and wanted assurances that the new regime would respect their right to hold human property. Planters who fled took with them the best field hands among their slaves, mostly men, including heads of families. Those left behind without means of support gravitated to Union camps for food and shelter, as did many who escaped from estates where the master remained in residence. Toward the end of that year, federal authorities issued orders to take over deserted plantations in the La Fourche District and harvest the crops, using the labor of "the negroes who may be found in said district." Able-bodied men could earn ten dollars, less three dollars deducted for clothing, in a work month of twenty-six ten-hour days. Women received less, as did children between the ages of ten and sixteen.[25]

The Emancipation Proclamation, issued on 1 January 1863, exempted by name thirteen Union-occupied parishes. "Officers and soldiers will not encourage or assist slaves to leave their employers," the newly arrived General Banks commented in an order publishing the proclamation, "but they cannot compel or authorize their return by force." During the course of the year and in the winter of 1864, Banks issued further orders regulating agricultural labor, the leasing of abandoned plantations, and the exemption of farmworkers from military service. The combination of military occupation and conscription affected even the planting of crops in Louisiana. Where secessionist plantation owners had fled, northern lessees tended to put in cotton instead of sugar. This was not just because of the "fabulous price" that cotton fetched: fleeing slaveholders and Union press gangs had taken many of the able-bodied men needed to cut and stack the three or four cords of wood required to produce

---

USCI, Entry 57C, RG 94, NA; Lt Col H. C. Merriam to 1st Lt O. A. Rice, 1 Nov 1864, 73d USCI, Entry 57C, RG 94, NA; Capt J. Lovell to Brig Gen D. Ullmann, 17 Jan 1865, Entry 1976, pt. 2, RG 393, NA; also Inspection Rpt, 29 Feb 1864, Entry 323, Dept of Arkansas, Monthly Retained Copies of Inspection Rpts, pt. 1, Geographical Divs and Depts, RG 393, NA.

[24] On 31 October 1864, U.S. Colored Troops regiments in Louisiana numbered sixteen of infantry, two of heavy artillery, and one of cavalry. *OR*, ser. 1, vol. 41, pt. 4, pp. 362–65.

[25] *OR*, ser. 1, 15: 592–95 (quotation, p. 593). Ira Berlin et al., eds., *The Destruction of Slavery* (New York: Cambridge University Press, 1985), pp. 187–99, and *The Wartime Genesis of Free Labor: The Lower South* (New York: Cambridge University Press, 1990), pp. 347–77, contain concise but comprehensive accounts of events in southern Louisiana during the war years.

one hogshead of sugar. In the summer of 1864, one four-parish area yielded more than thirteen hundred conscripts, of whom 35 percent failed a medical examination. Even if all those rejected returned at once to their home plantations, their absence must have caused a considerable disruption of the rural labor force.[26]

Conscription in the cities was no less disruptive. Superintendent of Negro Labor Thomas W. Conway, former chaplain of the 79th USCI, reported "squads of soldiers" in New Orleans "arresting colored men of every description, laborers, printers, and clerks." "The harsh manner in which the thing is done gives offense to very many who declare themselves perfectly willing to fight for the flag if called into the service in any of those forms observed in the case of white men all over the country," he maintained. "I have no doubt the intention is to arrest only those . . . who loiter about spending most of their time in idleness; but . . . in many instances men have been taken from shops, stores and factories, by force." Many of New Orleans' black residents would gladly serve, Conway thought, if subjected to the Union draft instead of press gangs, but "the present harsh and inexorable process of taking them by force will weaken their patriotism to a dangerous extent."[27]

While press gangs riled Louisiana's black residents and interfered with the labor supply, both rural and urban, the federal presence itself was enough to incense Southern whites. At this stage of the war, Union troops often could not distinguish properly enrolled but poorly dressed Confederate soldiers from guerrillas, or guerrillas from common bandits. Neither was it entirely certain whether armed Southerners were pro-Confederate or merely anti-Yankee. Whatever the root of its animus, home-grown opposition, not the main Confederate armies, was the day-to-day worry of Union soldiers in occupied Louisiana during the last year of the war. Colonel Frisbie reported one expedition from Morganza toward the end of 1864 during which the 92d USCI sighted some horsemen thought to be members of "the organized band of guerrilla scouts operating on this side of the Atchafalaya River." "These men continued in sight most of the afternoon and twice fired at the advance guard," Frisbie wrote.

> We camped at the plantation of J. R. Gayle, whose son is a [guerrilla], and . . . who fired at the advance guard and then fled into the swamp on the bayou. A large number of hogs and chickens were here gathered for the purpose of giving our boys a big Christmas, so they were appropriated as contraband of war. . . . In returning we came through the swamp to the residence of Mr. Winston, an outlaw, whose wife now keeps a rendezvous for guerrillas, and . . . she . . . was told that a perseverance in her evil courses would leave her homeless. . . . A small force of

---

[26] *OR*, ser. 1, 15: 666–69 ("Officers and," p. 667); vol. 26, pt. 1, pp. 704, 741–42; vol. 34, pt. 2, pp. 111, 227–31. Capt H. E. Kimball to Maj Gen N. P. Banks, 20 Aug 1864 ("fabulous price") (K–291–DG–1864); Maj S. Hamblin to Maj G. B. Drake, 23 Aug 1864 (H–979–DG–1864); both in Entry 1756, Dept of the Gulf, LR, pt. 1, RG 393, NA.

[27] T. W. Conway to Maj G. B. Drake, 16 Aug 1864 (C–793–DG–1864), Entry 1756, pt. 1, RG 393, NA.

the enemy was in sight all the way down Old River, and their pursuit did not cease until we reached the Mississippi.

The colonel ended by praising his men's "spirit and courage. . . . [W]henever there was any indication of meeting the enemy their conduct pleased me . . . , and their worth I believe is in proportion to the courage, discipline, and efficiency of their officers."[28]

The other adversary in Louisiana was the weather. In mid-January 1865, Lt. Col. Nelson Viall of the 11th USCA reported from the nearly deserted Camp Parapet, near New Orleans, that "the late rains" had collapsed three hundred yards of earthworks and that the troops of his command were too few to undertake repairs while continuing to man the guard posts. At Morganza the next month, the superintendent of levees reported five miles of riverfront "damaged to a very great extent" by the troops themselves constructing gun emplacements and "privy sinks." Unless repairs began at once, he warned, the river would flood the surrounding country. Although details of seventy-five men from each regiment at the post soon set to work, an officer of the 65th USCI reported in mid-March that rising water in the fort threatened three hundred thousand rounds of small-arms ammunition and other stores. At the end of the month, orders went out to "seize every unemployed able-bodied man of color and turn them over to the contractors to be paid however for their labor." During this crucial period, Brig. Gen. Daniel Ullmann, commanding the post, began drinking heavily. His official correspondence had betrayed symptoms of nervousness—"The enemy's cavalry are hovering around all my lines," he had reported the previous November—and on 26 February, word reached regional headquarters that "General Ullmann has not been in condition for several days to give his best attention to the duties devolving upon him." He was relieved from command that day and sent north on 16 March. Meanwhile, the waters continued to rise.[29]

That winter and spring, Union soldiers in Louisiana conducted most of their operations by boat. "I found the roads upon all bayous in good order, but bridges all swept away by high water and the swamps all full," one officer reported in mid-January. "No force can now cross [the] Atchafalaya at any point between Red River and Plaquemine to come to the Mississippi River on account of the water." Men of the 74th USCI operating from Fort Pike and the 93d at Brashear City reported six waterborne expeditions in search of small parties of Confederate irregulars in February and March. The general commanding at Baton Rouge speculated

---

[28] *OR*, ser. 1, vol. 41, pt. 1, pp. 994–95 ("the organized"). On local opposition, see pp. 926–27, 935–37. Donald S. Frazier, "'Out of Stinking Distance': The Guerrilla War in Louisiana," in *Guerrillas, Unionists, and Violence on the Confederate Home Front*, ed. Daniel E. Sutherland (Fayetteville: University of Arkansas Press, 1999), pp. 151–70.

[29] *OR*, ser. 1, vol. 41, pt. 1, p. 935 ("The enemy's"); vol. 48, pt. 1, pp. 984 ("General Ullmann"), 985, 1190–91. "General Ullmann had one of his usual drunks last night," wrote Lt. Col. H. C. Merriam of the 73d USCI. H. C. Merriam Diary typescript, 20 Feb 1865, Historians files, U.S. Army Center of Military History (CMH). See also entry for 30 Jan 1865. Lt Col N. Viall to Capt F. Speed, 13 Jan 1865 ("the late"), Entry 1756, pt. 1, RG 393, NA; G. W. R. Bayley to Col F. A. Starring, 20 Feb 1865 ("damaged"); Capt A. D. Bailie to 1st Lt L. B. Jenks, 1 Mar 1865; 1st Lt W. T. Goodwin to Brig Gen T. J. McKean, 14 Mar 1865; Maj W. H. Clark to Brig Gen T. J. McKean, 30 Mar 1865 ("seize every"); all in Entry 1976, pt. 2, RG 393, NA.

in mid-March that "in a very short time the entire country . . . will be completely abandoned by the rebels, and it is noticeable . . . that there is a strong disposition on the part of almost every one outside our lines to get on good terms with the Federal authorities." Nevertheless, patrols of Union troops that included men of the 75th and 93d USCIs and the 10th and 11th USCAs continued to search the bayous for surviving small bands of Confederates, especially the "gang" led by Capt. William A. Whitaker of the Confederate 7th Louisiana Cavalry. "We know of no horse or mule stealing or any pillaging of any consequence being done in the La Fourche country," the Union general commanding at Thibodeaux wrote in mid-April, "except by the gang controlled by Whitaker, Brown, and King, all of whom claim Confederate authority, and they are the men we wish to rid the country of above all others." By 17 May, Brown, who claimed to be a captain in the Confederate 17th Arkansas Cavalry, had surrendered at Donaldsonville and Whitaker and his followers were withdrawing toward Shreveport: a small instance of the breakup and dispersal of Confederate armies that characterized the end of the war west of the Mississippi River. At the end of the month, the colonel of the 98th USCI reported arriving at New Iberia "with no opposition whatever" aside from "a few threats from rebel soldiers here." The two sides settled down to await confirmation of Confederate surrenders. At Washington and Opelousas, Louisiana, the commanding officer of the 75th USCI arranged a truce until local Confederates could receive instructions. Just before their local truce was to expire on 6 June, the opponents learned that their commanders, General Canby and Confederate Lt. Gen. E. Kirby Smith, had arranged terms on 26 May.[30]

With organized military opposition surrendered or scattered, one more urgent task remained for Union troops in southern Louisiana: the rescue of civilians stranded by high water. For weeks, federal troops south of Donaldsonville had been supplementing cavalry and infantry patrols with small-boat operations against "guerrillas, thieves, and smugglers." On 9 May, the general commanding at Brashear City reported that the flood was destroying an important embankment that provided a rail connection to New Orleans. The next day he issued orders to load the steamer *Cornie*, a light-draft boat often used in antiguerrilla operations, with hardtack and salt to succor destitute families and to remove them and their livestock to higher ground. Troops stationed in exposed positions would move after the civilians had been cared for. Within a week, the rising water threatened the town of Brashear City itself.[31]

Meanwhile, on 12 May, twenty-five men of the 11th USCA boarded the *Cornie* and steamed off to rescue four families—eighteen people in all—and a few of their belongings, as well as a dozen or so pigs and cattle that had scrambled aboard a "raft," or logjam. "About 40 head of cattle, and a large number of hogs, and shoats, were lost, from the impossibility of catching them," 1st Lt. Charles H. Potter reported. "Many would jump from the rafts, and swim to the woods where no boat could

[30] *OR*, ser. 1, vol. 48, pt. 1, pp. 38 ("No force"), 85–86, 108–09, 128 ("in a very"), 146–47, 153–56, 172–78, and pt. 2, pp. 123 ("We know"), 479, 697 ("with no opposition," "a few threats"), 719, 769.

[31] *OR*, ser. 1, vol. 48, pt. 2, pp. 205, 220 (quotation), 364, 382, 393, 437, 446, 465, 477–78.

follow them. . . . We took on board everything we could find, working throughout the night."[32]

The next day, Potter and fifteen artillerymen were off again, rescuing ten people and some ninety head of livestock. Men of the 98th USCI aboard the *Ohio Belle* made five trips later in the month. Ninety-eight black people were among the 153 rescued. "It is the mission of the army now to assist in the restoration of law and order, confidence, and good feeling among the people," Maj. Gen. Francis J. Herron declared while leading Union troops toward Shreveport on 4 June. "In every way, therefore, the utmost care will be taken to teach the inhabitants that we are their friends and not their enemies, and that wherever the authority of the United States exists there is ample security for persons and property." Despite the general's words about "law and order" and "ample security," the fact that black persons rescued were described as "32 Colored Persons" or "16 Contrabands," while white adults appeared by name with the title "Mr." or "Mrs." clearly reflected the attitudes of the reporting officers and augured ill for future relations between the races in the South.[33]

Elsewhere in the Department of the Gulf, black soldiers spent the last year of the war in raids and other coastal operations. On 1 April 1864, about one hundred fifty officers and men of the 20th Corps d'Afrique Infantry boarded a steamer at the eastern end of Lake Pontchartrain and made their way up the western branch of the Pearl River. Finding the channel blocked by driftwood, they landed about three-quarters of their strength and sent the boat downstream while the shore party marched overland in search of the *J. D. Swaim*, a steamer that Confederates had run up the eastern branch two years earlier, at the time Union troops occupied New Orleans. The next day they found the steamer full of water and its engine out of order, but they decided to try to raise it. By the morning of 5 April, they had the *Swaim* afloat, "and the prospects of getting her down the river," wrote the expedition's commander, "were rather favorable than otherwise." They cast off and drifted about three miles downstream, carried by the current, until they ran into "a bed of sunken logs" and were stuck for fifty-six hours. Torrential rain raised the river, and by the morning of the eighth the *Swaim* was able to float free. The next day, farther downstream, they found the boat that had brought them up the western branch. It towed them back to Fort Pike, taking with them sixty-four escaped slaves who had joined the expedition. Fort Pike's garrison used the refurbished *Swaim* in similar raids later in the year.[34]

Farther east along the Gulf Coast, Union soldiers clung to posts at Pensacola and Key West that had not been abandoned to the Confederates in 1861. In the spring of 1864, their garrisons included the 2d USCI at Key West and the 25th, 82d, and 86th USCIs at Fort Barrancas near Pensacola. The 2d had been organized at Arlington, Virginia; the 25th at Philadelphia; the 82d (formerly the 10th

[32] 1st Lt C. H. Potter to 2d Lt W. H. Stillman, 13 May 1865 ("About 40"), filed with Brig Gen R. A. Cameron to Maj W. Hoffman, 16 May 1865 (C–392–DG–1865), Entry 1756, pt. 1, RG 393, NA.

[33] *OR*, ser. 1, vol. 48, pt. 1, pp. 271–72, and pt. 2, pp. 769–70 ("It is the"); Brig Gen R. A. Cameron to Maj W. Hoffman, 29 May 1865 (C–427–DG–1865), Entry 1756, pt. 1, RG 393, NA.

[34] *OR*, ser. 1, vol. 34, pt. 1, pp. 869–70 (quotations); vol. 41, pt. 1, pp. 756–58.

Corps d'Afrique Infantry) at Port Hudson; and the 86th (formerly the 14th Corps d'Afrique) at New Orleans. Southern Florida had few black men to recruit.

Key West, with a population of 2,832, was Florida's second-largest city. It was the seat of Monroe County, which stretched from the tip of the peninsula to Lake Okeechobee. Outside Key West, Monroe County's population amounted to eighty-one people. Dade County, immediately to the east, covered a similar area and boasted eighty-three residents in all. In Manatee County, just north of Monroe, cattle outnumbered the 854 humans by more than thirty-six to one. Free and slave, black residents of the three counties numbered 867, most of whom (611, or 70.4 percent) lived in Key West.[35]

Manatee and neighboring Hillsborough County, around Tampa Bay, grazed more beef cattle than any counties in the Confederacy outside Texas. With shipments from Texas cut off after Union armies gained control of the Mississippi River in the summer of 1863, Confederate commissaries turned increasingly to Florida as a source of beef. As early as January 1864, Brig. Gen. Daniel P. Woodbury, commanding the Union District of Key West and Tortugas, entertained the idea of occupying Tampa "with force sufficient to stop the cattle driving from Middle Florida"; but his plan called for five thousand infantry and cavalry, an impossible number of men for an out-of-the-way operation at a time when Grant and Sherman were trying to gather strength for their spring campaigns. Woodbury had to be content with maintaining a garrison at Fort Myers, a tiny post near the mouth of the Caloosahatchee River in Manatee County. The fort was "too far south for any very effective operations," Woodbury thought, but it was the best site that he could occupy with the few troops at his disposal.[36]

Woodbury's force was an odd assortment: the 2d USCI and some white Floridians known at first as the Florida Rangers and later as the 2d Florida Cavalry. Composed of backwoodsmen who saw the Union Army as the surest refuge from the Confederate draft, the 2d Florida waged the kind of war that erupted whenever white Southerners faced each other on opposing sides. "The colored troops . . . behaved remarkably well," General Woodbury reported after one expedition. "The refugee troops having personal wrongs to redress were not so easily controlled." Conflict between neighbors imparted a special viciousness to the war wherever it occurred.[37]

The 2d USCI had sailed from Virginia to New Orleans in November 1863 and from there to Key West three months later. In the spring, three of its companies took ship for Fort Myers and at once joined the 2d Florida Cavalry in cattle raids. Before long, the white cavalrymen were using their local knowledge to guide parties of black infantrymen who were strangers to the country in scouting the region's waterways—a reversal of the roles that usually obtained when escaped slaves guided Union troops, as they did in South Carolina and northeastern Florida. On one 210-mile foray in May, companies from the two regiments burned a Con-

---

[35] Manatee County had 31,252 cattle apart from "milch cows" and "working oxen" and 854 human residents. Census Bureau, *Population of the United States in 1860*, p. 54, and *Agriculture of the United States in 1860*, p. 18.

[36] *OR*, ser. 1, vol. 35, pt. 1, p. 461 (quotations); Canter Brown Jr., *Florida's Peace River Frontier* (Orlando: University of Central Florida Press, 1991), pp. 156–57.

[37] *OR*, ser. 1, vol. 35, pt. 1, p. 388; Brown, *Florida's Peace River Frontier*, p. 165.

federate barracks and brought back more than a thousand head of cattle, which had to be pastured some twenty miles inland to find sufficient grass. Not all of the raids involved cattle. Joint naval-military expeditions along Florida's Gulf Coast that summer freed 128 slaves and seized or destroyed 523 bales of cotton.[38]

By August, cattle and military livestock had eaten all the grass around Fort Myers and an officer of the 2d USCI had to request grain shipments. "We have lost 17 horses by starvation. . . . The rebels hunt cattle with a force nearly as strong as this garrison, a few miles from where we go for them, which makes it a matter of some hazard. . . . But there are plenty of cattle this side of the Caloosahatchee for the present, though . . . they are extremely wild and require very strong and fleet horses to herd them." For a while, the troops at Fort Myers captured enough livestock to ship to Key West to feed the garrison there, but the cattle raids eventually petered out. By late November, an inspector reported that there was no fresh meat at Fort Myers.[39]

Five hundred miles northwest of Fort Myers, at the western tip of the Florida panhandle, stood the state's largest city, Pensacola. Union troops held Fort Pickens and Fort Barrancas, which guarded the entrance to Pensacola Harbor. They had hung on to Fort Pickens all through 1861 and reoccupied Fort Barrancas when the Confederates evacuated Pensacola in May 1862. In the fall of 1863, the 86th USCI, then numbered the 14th Corps d'Afrique Infantry, arrived at Fort Barrancas. The 82d USCI joined it there in April 1864.[40]

Pensacola was the closest federal base to Mobile, Alabama, one of the Confederacy's last open seaports, which lay some sixty miles to its northwest. It had one rail connection to Mobile and a second that ran the length of the Florida panhandle to Jacksonville on the Atlantic Coast. Brig. Gen. Alexander Asboth, commanding the District of West Florida, had long had his eye on both of these lines as well as on a third that ran one hundred seventy miles from Mobile to Montgomery and connected the seaport with the Confederate interior. Railroads to the east of Montgomery connected it with Atlanta.[41]

While Sherman's army fought its way toward Atlanta, three hundred miles north of Pensacola, General Asboth did what he could to assist. On 9 July, Sherman had dispatched three thousand cavalrymen to cut the railroad east of Montgomery. The raiders might, he told General Canby in New Orleans, find their way to Pensacola, "leave horses there and come back to Tennessee by water." Canby promised to have extra forage and rations ready. On 21 July, Asboth set out to look for the raiders. He took with him the entire 82d USCI, six companies of the 86th, five companies of cavalry, and a pair of light artillery pieces. At a Confederate camp

---

[38]*OR*, ser. 1, vol. 35, pt. 1, p. 406; Col S. Fellows to Capt H. W. Bowers, 19 Apr 1864, 2d USCI, Regimental Books, RG 94, NA. Capt J. W. Childs to Capt H. W. Bowers, 25 Apr 1864; Capt H. W. Bowers to Brig Gen D. P. Woodbury, 8 May 1864; Capt J. W. Childs to Capt H. W. Bowers, 27 May 1864; all in Entry 2269, Dept and Dist of Key West, LR, pt. 1, RG 393, NA.

[39]Capt C. H. Willett to Capt H. W. Bowers, 2 Aug 1864 (quotation); Capt H. A. Crane to Capt H. W. Bowers, 15 Aug 1864; Capt A. A. Fellows to Capt E. B. Tracy, 20 Nov 1864; all in Entry 2269, pt. 1, RG 393, NA.

[40]With a population of 2,876 in 1860, Pensacola had 44 more residents than Key West. Census Bureau, *Population of the United States in 1860*, p. 54.

[41]*OR*, ser. 1, vol. 26, pt. 1, pp. 817–18, 820–21, 833–34; vol. 35, pt. 1, pp. 274, 471, 479–80, and pt. 2, pp. 165–66.

fifteen miles north of Pensacola, the force dispersed three companies of enemy cavalry. Asboth reported having undergone "brisk fire," "repeated skirmishes," and a "determined stand" by the Confederates; but the day's casualties on the Union side totaled one man of the 82d USCI wounded in the arm. Confederate prisoners told Asboth that the raiders he expected to welcome had destroyed twenty-four miles of rail line and then turned back to rejoin Sherman's army instead of continuing on toward the gulf. On 23 July, after burning what captured supplies they could not move, the troops moved north toward Pollard, Alabama, just over the state line. Asboth planned to destroy the railroad there, but heavy rain and reports of massing Confederates brought his expedition to an end halfway to its destination.[42]

On 2 August, just a week after Asboth's return to Pensacola, General Canby launched a strike against two Confederate forts that stood on either side of the main entrance to Mobile Bay. The small expedition included, besides four Midwestern infantry regiments that had formerly belonged to the XIII Corps, the 96th and 97th USCIs (formerly the 2d and 3d Corps d'Afrique Engineers). Despite the regiments' new designations, the nature of their duties was made clear in an exchange between a Department of the Gulf inspector and Maj. Gen. Gordon Granger, commanding the land force. When the inspector complained that black soldiers came in for more than "their fair share of fatigue duty," Granger replied: "Details for fatigue duty have been principally made from the *white* regiments, the colored troops being employed almost exclusively upon engineering service." He may have meant that white troops were unloading supplies while black troops worked on construction projects. Although one nineteenth-century dictionary of military terms included "work on fortifications . . . , in cutting roads, and other constant labor," as forms of "fatigue duty," the final decision as to whether pick-and-shovel work constituted "fatigue duty" or "engineering service" rested with the senior officer present.[43]

Asboth marched most of the Pensacola garrison toward Mobile on 13 August to learn whether any Union troops had come ashore. The first day's march took his force twelve miles "through a marshy country, mostly overflowed in consequence of the frequent heavy rains." The next day, Confederate deserters brought word that five thousand federal soldiers had landed. Satisfied with that, Asboth headed back to Pensacola rather than splash any farther through the swamps.[44]

At this point, despite Canby's promise to supply food and forage to welcome Sherman's raiders, scurvy began to appear in the Pensacola garrison. The commissary's cornmeal was "wormy and sour," so even the arrival of fifty pounds of potatoes was worth reporting. During the first three weeks of September, forty men died in the 25th, 82d, and 86th USCIs. White troops, too, suffered "to a considerable extent." Nevertheless, the black regiments were able to contribute 300 men to a 700-man expedition up the west arm of Pensacola Bay in late October. The general commanding at Pensacola submitted weekly intelligence reports to Gen-

---

[42]*OR*, ser. 1, vol. 35, pt. 1, pp. 416–18 ("brisk fire," p. 417); vol. 38, pt. 5, p. 85 ("leave horses"); vol. 39, pt. 2, p. 183.

[43]Ibid., vol. 41, pt. 2, p. 566 ("their fair"); Endorsement, Maj Gen G. Granger, 15 Sep 1864 ("Details for fatigue"), on Maj G. B. Drake to Maj Gen G. Granger, 30 Aug 1864 (G–36–DG–1864), Entry 1756, pt. 1, RG 393, NA; Henry L. Scott, *Military Dictionary* (New York: D. Van Nostrand, 1864), p. 283.

[44]*OR*, ser. 1, vol. 35, pt. 1, p. 426.

eral Canby in New Orleans but acknowledged that the movements of the Confederate commander, Col. Dabney H. Maury, were "rather mysterious." Maury may have been part of "the whole gang of Confederates" that the Union force hoped to capture when it steamed away from Fort Barrancas on the morning of 25 October, but the record is unclear. The expedition's commander divided his force in two in order to invite an enemy attack, but one of the parties missed its objective by six or seven miles, spoiling the stratagem. On its way back to Pensacola, the expedition stopped at the little town of Bagdad, Florida, and seized about eighty-five thousand feet of lumber.[45]

A seven-company Union garrison at Cedar Key, 115 miles north of the entrance to Tampa Bay, remained quiet until February 1865. Then commanding officer of the 2d Florida Cavalry conceived a plan for a raid on Levy County, the closest point on the mainland to his island base. The object was to capture Confederate prisoners, impound draft animals, free slaves, and "capture the train that arrives at Bronson every Saturday at eleven with supplies." The 2d USCI contributed two hundred men to the expedition. Led by the regiment's Maj. Benjamin C. Lincoln, they reached the Suwannee River on 10 February at a point about ten miles inland, where they routed some Confederate "cow cavalry" (troops charged with rounding up and driving beef cattle destined for the Confederate main armies) and destroyed supplies. By this time, about fifty former slaves had attached themselves to the expedition. Major Lincoln sent a company to escort them to Depot Key, the Florida Railroad's terminus. Finding that the road to the railroad station at Bronson lay "most of the way through swamp," the rest of the expedition turned around, leaving one company of the 2d USCI as a rearguard. On the morning of 13 February, it came under attack by about one hundred twenty Confederate cavalry. Hearing the firing, the main body of troops returned and by noon succeeded in driving off the enemy.[46]

The Union side reported losses amounting to twenty-six killed, wounded, and missing in the five-hour fight, while the Confederates claimed to have inflicted "about seventy" casualties. The Confederate commander admitted that his troops had suffered five wounded, but the Union commander claimed that they left two corpses on the field. Each officer estimated his opponent's numbers at more than double their actual strength.[47]

Meanwhile, recent events in other theaters had changed the shape of the war and troops in the Department of the Gulf were gathering themselves for one last effort. In December 1864, Sherman's army had reached the Atlantic coast at Savannah, Georgia. Far inland, Union troops led by Maj. Gen. George H. Thomas had inflicted a stunning defeat on General John B. Hood's Confederates, killing, wounding, or capturing 6,252 of them at Franklin, Tennessee, on 30 November

---

[45] Ibid., p. 448 ("the whole"), 449, and pt. 2, p. 323 ("rather mysterious"); vol. 52, pt. 1, p. 648. Lt Col F. L. Hitchcock to Lt Col W. S. Abert, 22 Sep 1864 ("wormy and") (H–50–DG–1864), Entry 1756, pt. 1, RG 393, NA.

[46] *OR*, ser. 1, vol. 49, pt. 1, p. 40 ("most of"); Maj E. C. Weeks to Sir [Capt E. B. Tracy], 8 Feb 1865 ("capture the"), Entry 2269, pt. 1, RG 393, NA.

[47] *OR*, ser. 1, vol. 49, pt. 1, p. 43.

and capturing 4,462 men, nearly one-fifth of the remainder, at Nashville two weeks later. What was left of Hood's army retreated into Mississippi.[48]

General Grant, commanding all the armies of the United States while he conducted the siege of Richmond and Petersburg, Virginia, wanted "to see the enemy entirely broken up in the West" while Hood's army was still disorganized. In January 1865, he ordered Thomas and Canby to converge on central Alabama, an almost untouched region that was home to many industries and even to a Confederate navy yard. Thomas would move from the north, Canby from the west and south. They were to aim for the arms factories, foundries, machine shops, and textile mills at Selma and Montgomery, as well as more than two hundred thousand bales of cotton stored here and there throughout the state since the port of Mobile had closed the previous summer. Canby was to take Mobile, if it could be done without holding up the rest of the campaign.[49]

Before the war, the value of Mobile's exports had made it the nation's third-ranking port. It handled half of the cotton grown in the Black Belt, the fertile region drained by tributaries of the Alabama and Tombigbee Rivers, both of which flowed south toward Mobile Bay. By 1865, the Navy's blockade and the capture of two forts at the mouth of the bay had reduced the city's significance. The 11,773 bales of cotton that ran the blockade at Mobile in 1864 before the last ship slipped out in July was barely one-tenth of what came out of Wilmington, North Carolina. Besides lying on a bay with a single easily controlled entrance, Mobile was farther than Wilmington from the blockade runners' favorite ports in the Bahamas, Bermuda, and Cuba. Nevertheless, orders to move into the interior of Alabama that General Canby received in February 1865 left him free to reduce Mobile's remaining defenses if he could do so without a long siege. Canby thought it best to besiege Spanish Fort and Fort Blakely, which commanded the bay from its eastern shore. Failure to capture both forts would prevent Union troops in the central part of the state from receiving supplies by riverboat, the fastest and cheapest means of delivery.[50]

Canby ordered regiments from Morganza and Port Hudson, and as far north as Memphis, to rendezvous at New Orleans and sail for Pensacola. The summons came as a surprise to some. Lt. Col. Henry C. Merriam at Morganza received orders on 21 February to plant vegetable gardens for the 73d USCI. "I suppose this settles us for the summer," he wrote in his diary. The next day came welcome orders for field service. Merriam had visited New Orleans on business the week before and had asked at department headquarters for an active assignment. By the end of the month, his regiment was camped just outside New Orleans. "Great multitudes" thronged Canal Street to see the 73d, which, as the 1st Louisiana Native Guards,

[48]Thomas L. Livermore, *Numbers and Losses in the Civil War in America, 1861–65* (Boston: Houghton Mifflin, 1901), pp. 132–33.

[49]*OR*, ser. 1, vol. 48, pt. 1, p. 580; vol. 49, pt. 1, p. 781 ("to see"). Walter L. Fleming, *Civil War and Reconstruction in Alabama* (Gloucester, Mass.: Peter Smith, 1949 [1905]), pp. 150–51; David G. Surdam, *Northern Naval Superiority and the Economics of the American Civil War* (Columbia: University of South Carolina Press, 2001), p. 172.

[50]*OR*, ser. 1, vol. 48, pt. 1, p. 580; vol. 49, pt. 1, pp. 91–92, 593. Surdam, *Northern Naval Superiority*, pp. 11–12, 169, 171–72; Arthur W. Bergeron Jr., *Confederate Mobile* (Jackson: University Press of Mississippi, 1991), pp. 115–16, 124.

had been one of the earliest black regiments in the Union Army. "I have never seen so much excitement on this great thoroughfare," Merriam wrote. "Hundreds of people have come out from the city to visit friends in the regt." On 1 March, they embarked for Florida, where a force known as the 1st Division, U.S. Colored Troops, was assembling under the command of Brig. Gen. John P. Hawkins.[51]

Not all of the regiments in Hawkins' division reached Florida as speedily as Merriam's. The 68th USCI in Memphis received its orders at the end of January. On 7 February, it landed at New Orleans and was told to begin building a railroad, work much like the "engineer duty" the regiment had performed at Memphis. Twelve days later, the task was done. Lt. Col. Daniel Densmore, the regiment's commander, looked forward to an early departure for Florida. "The force concentrating here is immense," he wrote to his brother. "Troops come from all parts, and are the picked regiments." Densmore wondered why the commanding general at Memphis had chosen the 68th of all the regiments in garrison for the Mobile Expedition. "How mere laborers can so far outstrip old and drilled men, as to carry off the palm for soldiership" challenged his understanding. "We are anxiously awaiting the time when we can be spared for a little drill."[52]

Eleven regiments of U.S. Colored Infantry took part in the campaign on the eastern shore of Mobile Bay. Four of them, the 82d, 86th, 96th, and 97th, had begun existence as Corps d'Afrique infantry or engineers; the 73d and 76th had come into the Union Army as the 1st and 4th Louisiana Native Guards. Four other regiments, the 47th, 48th, 50th, and 51st, had been organized in northern Louisiana's Carroll and Madison Parishes along the Mississippi River by Adjutant General Lorenzo Thomas. The 68th had formed at Benton Barracks, near St. Louis, early in 1864 as the 4th Missouri Colored Infantry.

All of the regiments had taken part in one or more campaigns. The oldest, the 73d, had served in the siege of Port Hudson and in the Red River Expedition. The 76th and 82d had also been at Port Hudson (at that time the 82d was the 10th Corps d'Afrique Infantry, the junior regiment in Ullmann's brigade), and the 97th had been up the Red River as the 3d Corps d'Afrique Engineers. The 48th had fought at Milliken's Bend in June 1863, and the 47th had taken part in the Yazoo Expedition to divert Confederate attention from Sherman's Meridian raid early in 1864. The 96th and 97th had served on the Texas coast before helping to capture the forts at the mouth of Mobile Bay in August 1864. The 86th had been at Pensacola since October 1863 and the 82d since April 1864. Of the eleven regiments, only the 50th, 86th, and 92d had incurred no battle casualties before the Mobile Expedition. West of Virginia and North Carolina, no body of black troops so experienced and so large had ever faced the enemy.[53]

Nevertheless, reports from individual regiments revealed a number of shortcomings that plagued the U.S. Colored Troops. In the 50th USCI, an inspection at Vicksburg revealed that 718 of 842 privates were on guard duty or fatigues every

[51] Merriam Diary, 21 ("I suppose") and 28 ("Great multitudes") Feb 1865.

[52] *OR*, ser. 1, vol. 48, pt. 1, pp. 421, 664; D. Densmore to Dear Brother, 12 Feb 1865, and to Dear Friends at Home, 19 Feb 1865 ("The force"), both in B. Densmore Papers, Minnesota Historical Society (MHS), St. Paul.

[53] Dyer, *Compendium*, pp. 1214–15, 1324, 1344, 1718–19, 1731–32, 1734–37; *Official Army Register of the Volunteer Force of the United States Army*, 8 vols. (Washington, D.C.: Adjutant

day, leaving no time for drill or to keep their uniforms, weapons, and persons clean. At Memphis, an inspector complained, the 68th USCI had been transformed "from a military organization into a gang of laborers," a condition "very destructive to [its] military esprit, drill and general efficiency." As late as January 1865, the 82d USCI at Pensacola carried smoothbore muskets. Meanwhile, the captain commanding the 97th USCI reported that with the regiment's colonel wounded, its lieutenant colonel absent on sick leave, and its major in New Orleans on detached service, there were not enough officers present to assign even one to each company. Such shortages—of adequate arms, of time to drill, and of officers—were always more or less present among black regiments in the Department of the Gulf. To some extent, they were common in the U.S. Colored Troops nationwide.[54]

While General Hawkins' division assembled at Fort Barrancas, a short distance from Pensacola, a strong Union raiding party landed near the mouth of the St. Mark's River some two hundred miles to the east. Its intention was to move inland toward Tallahassee to distract Confederate attention from the march of the Pensacola force toward Mobile. Nearly nine hundred men from companies of the 2d Florida Cavalry and the 2d and 99th USCIs got ashore by the late afternoon of 4 March despite high winds and two of the transports running aground. They camped near their landing place and moved inland the next morning. A small force of Confederates had taken up the planks of the first bridge on the road to Newport and waited on the opposite bank of the river with a cannon. Skirmishers from two companies of the 2d USCI dispersed them with a few shots and filed across the bridge's stringers to the other side. Men of the 99th USCI, formerly the 5th Corps d'Afrique Engineers, undertook repairs and the expedition moved on but not in time to save the next bridge, at Newport, from a fire set by the retreating Confederates.[55]

Seeing the enemy entrenched in a position that commanded the crossing, Brig. Gen. John Newton decided to march north in search of the Natural Bridge. This was not a spectacular geological formation but a sink where the St. Mark's River flowed underground for about a quarter of a mile. Guides assured Newton that this marshy crossing lay only four or five miles to the north, but it proved to be twice that distance, and a local force of Confederates was dug in there. Early in the morning of 6 March, six companies of the 2d USCI set out to probe the enemy's defenses but were stopped by swampy ground. Newton then withdrew his force to a position in a pine forest nearly a quarter of a mile to the rear. The Confederates attacked but were driven off, and the Union troops began an all-night march back to St. Mark's, where they arrived about 4:00 a.m. on 7 March. Newton blamed the brevity of his raid on lack of cooperation from the Navy but claimed nevertheless that the expedition "effected a powerful diversion in favor of [the] column marching from Pensacola." This self-congratulatory assessment was not altogether wrong. Confederate Maj. Gen. Samuel Jones, commanding the District of Florida, called the raid "more formidable" than its predecessors and asked the governor

---

General's Office, 1867), 8: 220–21, 223–24, 241, 246–47, 252, 260, 266, 277–78 (hereafter cited as *ORVF*).

[54] Capt O. J. Wright to Brig Gen L. Thomas, 3 Nov 1864, 50th USCI; Col H. Leib to Capt C. W. Fox, 27 Jan 1865, 68th USCI; Lt Col W. H. Thurston to Capt J. Hibbert, 6 Jan 1865, 82d USCI; Capt M. McDonough to Lt Col G. B. Drake, 21 Dec 1864, 97th USCI; all in Entry 57C, RG 94, NA.

[55] *OR*, ser. 1, vol. 49, pt. 1, pp. 59, 62, 67.

of Georgia what measures state authorities were prepared to take in their own defense.[56]

At Pensacola, after devoting nearly three weeks to the distribution of new weapons and the repair of old ones, to drill and inspections—"to cut down to fighting trim," as Colonel Densmore put it—the 1st Division, U.S. Colored Troops, and two brigades of the all-white XIII Corps headed north through a dense fog on the morning of 20 March. Maj. Gen. Frederick Steele commanded the entire force of twelve thousand men in which the Colored Troops numbered just over five thousand. "After marching three or four miles we came to a spur of Pensacola Bay which runs nearly westward to the main land," as Captain Crydenwise described the 73d USCI's part in the expedition to his parents. "It was about one half a mile in width & 2 1/2 or 3 ft deep. This the whole army had to ford. When we came to it we were ordered to take off Pants, drawers, shoes & stockings. Then fastening our things over our shoulders we crossed very nicely." The soldiers had to wade two arms of the bay, "one of the finest sights I have witnessed in the war," Colonel Densmore thought. "Away in the distance the steady column was disappearing into the mist, the veil beyond which the breakers were roaring angrily." Looking behind him, he could see the men emerge from the fog, wade past him, and then disappear again into the fog ahead. Once across, the troops

> moved up along the beach for a time & then struck inland—wandering through groves of shady pines, or skirting along thickets of live-oak and magnolias. Among the pines there is no underbrush, and the tread of many feet is muffled by the thick coat of dead leaves fallen. . . . On horseback it was a fair march, novelty and beauty on all sides. . . . But on foot the day had a different aspect. Under a knapsack on which a woolen blanket, and a rubber [blanket], and a shelter tent, and a hot sun are bearing, . . . there is less leisure & less spirit, for admiring a country that has fostered only rebels. . . . To heap upon a man a load which he is obliged soon to cast out on the rodeside . . . would not ordinarily seem reasonable. But such is life, especially in the army.

One man of the 50th USCI died on the first day's march. Soldiers who had served long in garrison responded to the heat by strewing their path through the pine forest with discarded belongings.[57]

Rain sprinkled them on and off during the day but began in earnest on the night of 20 March. Col. Hiram Scofield, commanding a brigade of Hawkins' division, reported that "the mud & quicksands are bottomless." "Horses, mules & wagons sink down," he went on, "& an advance [is] impossible except by corduroying," the laborious process of cutting logs and laying them across the roadway to provide a surface. Colonel Merriam and the 73d USCI were in the thick of it. "Labored

---

[56] Ibid., pp. 60–61, 67 (quotation), 1043–44.

[57] Ibid., p. 279; Merriam Diary, 5–13 Mar 1865. Densmore to Dear Brother, 12 Feb 1865 ("to cut down"), and to Dear Friends, 19 Mar 1865 ("one of the"), Densmore Papers. Densmore must have misdated his second letter; Generals Hawkins and Steele both give the date as 20 March. *OR*, ser. 1, vol. 49, pt. 1, pp. 280, 287. H. M. Crydenwise to Dear Parents & All, 22 Mar 1865, Crydenwise Letters; H. Scofield to C. C. Andrews, 1 Apr 1866, C. C. Andrews Papers, MHS.

Col. Hiram Scofield of the 47th U.S. Colored Infantry commanded one of the black brigades in the final assault on Fort Blakely, 9 April 1865.

all day and in the worst mud I ever saw," Merriam recorded in his diary. "In some places . . . mules had to be taken from the wagons and the wagons boosted along for half a mile by the men alone." At nightfall on 22 March, the army had moved just fifteen miles beyond Pensacola.[58]

Early the next afternoon, General Steele reported, the advance found a bridge washed out and had to wait a day and a half while the troops replaced it with a new one three hundred yards long, "built on piles which the men sunk by hand, diving under the water to start them." The army crossed on 25 March, moving through a forest that 1st Lt. John L. Mathews of the 47th USCI considered "the poorest country I ever traveled over." "It is a barren sandy soil covered with pines almost as thick as they can stand," he wrote. "The inhabitants are of the poorest class, and how they manage to exist is more than I can tell; they have an abundance of pale children and yellow dogs, everything else appears scarce." The lieutenant's impression was correct: the four Florida and Alabama counties on the line of march produced less than half as much cotton, on average, as neighboring counties did. Consequently, whites outnumbered black slaves by more than 50 percent.[59]

Along the way, some soldiers were able to kill and eat cattle that ranged in the woods; but heavy rain, deep mud, and short marches upset the expedition's timetable. By 26 March, commissary supplies were running out and the troops were on half rations. Despite the shortage, they marched nine miles on 28 March through "a monstrous swamp." Colonel Merriam was proud of his regiment: "For the first time during the campaign we had two men sick in the ambulance train. . . . It surpasses

---

[58] Merriam Diary, 21 Mar 1865; Scofield to Andrews, 1 Apr 1866.

[59] *OR*, ser. 1, vol. 49, pt. 1, p. 280 ("built on"); Scofield to Andrews, 1 Apr 1866; J. L. Mathews to Dear Father, 5 Apr 1865, John L. Mathews Papers, State Historical Society of Iowa, Iowa City. Statistics for Florida's Escambia and Santa Rosa Counties and Alabama's Baldwin and Conecuh Counties (all on the line of march), as well as neighboring Covington, Mobile, and Monroe Counties (in Alabama) and Walton (in Florida) are in Census Bureau, *Agriculture of the United States in 1860*, pp. 3, 19, and *Population of the United States in 1860*, pp. 8, 54.

anything I ever saw—nine days hard marching on half rations and not a man [so] sick as to fall out of ranks."[60]

The country was "poor & barren of supplies," Colonel Scofield noted the next day. "A few old sheep are all we find to lengthen out our rations now nearly exhausted." The expedition was within thirty miles of Mobile Bay. As Confederate defenders retreated, abandoning their supply depots, local residents moved in and helped themselves. Occasionally, the Union cavalry, riding in advance of the main column, seized a civilian ox team hauling a wagonload of looted goods and made a meal of the oxen, but there was none left over for the infantry. "Ration reduced from one half to one third," Merriam noted. "Nothing foraged today." Not until 30 March did the troops of the two infantry divisions receive a full issue of beef. On the same day, they got a quarter ration of hardtack, the last in their commissary wagons.[61]

For the past six days, the advancing soldiers had heard cannon firing on the eastern shore of Mobile Bay. Spanish Fort, a Confederate post built on a site that had been occupied since the eighteenth century, had come under attack by Union naval vessels on 18 March. A week later, the XVI Corps and two divisions of the XIII Corps began siege operations against it. Its northern neighbor, Fort Blakely, was the objective of the column from Pensacola.[62]

Despite its steamboat landing and county courthouse, the town of Blakely was a tiny place with barely one hundred residents. On the landward side of the village, facing east, two-and-a-half miles of Confederate trenches ran along high ground with swamp at either end. The defenders had slashed the timber and brush for a thousand yards in front of their position and let it lie as an obstruction. Two roads ran inland from the landing at Blakely: one led toward the southeast and Pensacola, the other northeast to Stockton, Alabama. The Union expedition from Pensacola, having marched north as though to threaten Montgomery, halted at Stockton on 31 March to resupply. The next day, it approached Blakely from the northeast.[63]

Hawkins' division was about to make camp for the night after a march of more than fifteen miles, when word came that the cavalry, in advance, had routed a small force of Confederates, taking more than seventy prisoners and driving the rest into the defenses of Blakely. Hawkins' division moved forward to a point about two-and-a-half miles from the Confederate position and bivouacked in line of battle with Brig. Gen. William A. Pile's brigade (73d, 82d, and 86th USCIs) on the left and Col. Charles W. Drew's brigade (48th, 68th, and 76th USCIs) on the right, the north end of the Union line. "Twice while forming line for camp we were again made ready to receive the enemy," wrote Colonel Densmore. "Quiet prevailed at length, . . . and soon with weapon in hand those to whom sleep was permitted were sullenly stretched on the ground making the most of the rest so much needed and which might be broken at any moment." Colonel Scofield's brigade (47th, 50th,

---

[60]Merriam Diary, 26, 27, and 28 ("a monstrous") Mar 1865.

[61]*OR*, ser. 1, vol. 49, pt. 1, pp. 280–81; Merriam Diary, 29 (quotation) and 30 Mar 1865; Scofield to Andrews, 1 Apr 1866.

[62]*OR*, ser. 1, vol. 49, pt. 1, p. 93.

[63]Ibid., pp. 97, 280–83; D. Densmore to C. C. Andrews, 30 Aug 1866, Andrews Papers; Sean M. O'Brien, *Mobile, 1865: Last Stand of the Confederacy* (Westport, Conn.: Praeger, 2001), p. 69.

and 51st USCIs) was in reserve. Scofield noted "some firing on the picket line tonight, & everything indicates the immediate presence of the enemy."[64]

After sunrise the next morning, firing intensified between Drew's and Pile's pickets and the Confederates. Federal troops found themselves facing a continuous line that included nine redoubts, mounting a total of thirty-one guns. In front of the gun emplacements was a line of trenches for the infantry protected by an abatis—a line of sharpened stakes—and in front of that individual rifle pits for the defenders' skirmishers. Late in the morning, as Brig. Gen. Christopher C. Andrews' division of the XIII Corps, which had also made the march from Pensacola, came into line on their left, Pile's and Drew's brigades moved forward. Two companies of each regiment advanced as skirmishers over "thickly wooded and broken country," Colonel Drew reported, their men spaced three paces apart, with the other companies behind them in line of battle. "Notwithstanding the numerous obstacles in the way," he added, "there was scarcely a break in the line the whole distance." To Drew's left, Pile's brigade "soon met the enemy's skirmish line in front of their works, steadily driving them and advancing." When the retreating Confederates scrambled past the abatis, Pile's men halted, took cover, and waited for dark to begin digging their own trenches.[65]

On the extreme right of the Union advance, the 68th USCI found things somewhat more complicated. The lieutenant commanding the regiment's pickets that morning "could discover no rebs on his front," Colonel Densmore recalled, and he moved his men forward to reconnoiter. "They proceeded without interruption for some distance," he wrote:

> and began to think they should find a clear track into the town, when suddenly from a clump of trees (near the edge of the slashing) . . . the Johnnies opened on them with a handsome volley. . . . In a short time the firing became general in that direction. . . . With the advance of our line the enemy fell back, crowded by our skirmishers. . . . In the midst of shot, shell, and bullets we had to cover an abrupt, deep, broken ravine made double difficult by a dense tangle of undergrowth. We expected to come out of it a confused throng. The officers of the Co[mpanie]s emerged, took their respective distance still moving forward, and to our surprise the line quickly filled up, and swept along. . . . Coming at length to a ravine the line was halted, as it was found that . . . the rebels were occupying their rifle pits."[66]

The 68th's skirmishers succeeded in clearing the enemy out of the woods on the high ground that sloped into the swamp and advanced to within one hundred fifty yards of the Confederate defenses. The 48th USCI halted five hundred yards from

---

[64]Densmore to Andrews, 30 Aug 1866; Scofield to Andrews, 1 Apr 1866. Scofield gives the distance marched as fifteen miles, Densmore as seventeen, Hawkins as "eighteen or nineteen." Scofield to Andrews, 1 Apr 1866; Densmore to Andrews, 30 Aug 1866; *OR*, ser. 1, vol. 49, pt. 1, p. 281. Merriam, who detailed a company of the 73d USCI to guard the prisoners, gives the number of prisoners as seventy-three; other sources say seventy-four or seventy-five. Merriam Diary, 1 Apr 1865; *OR*, ser. 1, vol. 49, pt. 1, pp. 95, 281.

[65]*OR*, ser. 1, vol. 49, pt. 1, pp. 215, 288, 295 (quotation), and pt. 2, p. 311.

[66]Densmore to Andrews, 30 Aug 1866.

the Confederates and the 76th six hundred yards. Pile's brigade stopped nine hundred yards short of the enemy trenches. The point at which the opposing lines were closest was the position the 68th held for the rest of the weeklong siege. The Confederates' trenches were better prepared here than elsewhere along the line, and their snipers inflicted greater losses. The one hundred officers and men of the 68th killed and wounded during the siege amounted to more than one-quarter of the casualties in the Colored Troops Division's nine regiments. Densmore, who had been skeptical of his regiment's ability in the field after so many months of fatigue and "engineering" duties in garrison, was reassured. "The style of the negro soldier on that day was certainly most gratifying," he wrote. "More efficiency in drill . . . would have given nicer execution of manouver but the fighting morale, it seemed to me, would satisfy any commander."[67]

That night, all along the line, Union troops dug. Men who still suffered from the "parched-corn diet" they had endured during most of the march from Pensacola worked feverishly to finish the task before daylight exposed them to Confederate snipers. By late morning on 3 April, they had completed a rudimentary system of trenches. Full rations reached them later that day. Divisions from the XIII and XVI Corps moved north to make a continuous Union line around the two besieged forts. Three Confederate gunboats in the river beyond the fort shelled the Union trenches from a range of about one mile. Drew's brigade built an emplacement for four thirty-pounder cannon that drove the boats off on the afternoon of 8 April.[68]

Meanwhile, the Union troops continued to dig. At first, they worked only during the night, but when the trenches and approaches were deep enough to protect the men from sniper fire, they dug in the daytime and rested at night in the many ravines behind the lines. In an unusual role reversal, men of the Colored Troops Division found regiments of the XIII Corps assisting them with digging and construction. By 8 April, when the thirty-pounder battery drove off the Confederate gunboats, the Union trenches lay between five and six hundred yards from the outer defenses of Fort Blakely. Digging, and with it the Union advance, had come to a standstill. "The ground is hard," General Hawkins explained, "and the shovel is a poor instrument without a greater number of picks to assist it." He requested more picks.[69]

On the morning of 9 April, Colonel Scofield, whose brigade had been sharing the trenches with Drew's and Pile's brigades for the past five days, noted success at the southern end of the Union line: "Spanish Fort was taken last night & everyone is jubilant." Rifle fire from the Confederate infantry in Fort Blakely subsided about midday and led to speculation that it was about to be evacuated. Two of Pile's regimental commanders, Colonel Merriam of the 73d USCI and Maj. Lewis P. Mudgett of the 86th, asked permission to send men forward to investigate. A party of ninety-three officers and men from Pile's three regiments routed the enemy's skirmishers and secured their outer line. Pile rushed forward five companies to support his assault party, and Scofield, commanding the brigade on Pile's right, in

---

[67]*OR*, ser. 1, vol. 49, pt. 1, pp. 114 (casualties), 288, 297, 299; Densmore to Andrews, 30 Aug 1866.

[68]*OR*, ser. 1, vol. 49, pt. 1, pp. 283, 321; Densmore to Andrews, 30 Aug 1866; Scofield to Andrews, 1 Apr 1866.

[69]*OR*, ser. 1, vol. 49, pt. 2, pp. 159, 289 ("The ground"), 293, 297; Merriam Diary, 6 and 7 Apr 1865.

the center of the Colored Troops Division's line, brought his skirmishers forward to make a continuous front. The entire movement occurred "without, so far as I can learn, any orders," Scofield reported, "and as the enemy rallied, offering a more stubborn resistance, our skirmishers were strengthened. . . . The order was then given to intrench and hold the ground gained. . . . Just at this time another portion of the line advancing, permission was obtained to move forward and assault the enemy's works."[70]

For seven days, Union besiegers had trouble keeping each regiment's trenches in line with those of its neighbors so as not to expose the flanks to enemy fire. If the lines were not adjusted, one regiment might find itself as much as one hundred seventy yards closer to the Confederate trenches than its neighbor. In the circumstances, the apparently spontaneous advance late on the afternoon of 9 April may well have owed as much to officers' desire to keep their lines straight as to the attackers' enthusiasm. "The skirmishers advanced about 4 p.m., and it seems moved up . . . on account of an advance being made by troops farther on the left," the commander of the 50th USCI, in Scofield's brigade, reported:

> The line advanced . . . , firing their pieces and cheering loudly. . . . I concluded to follow the example of other regiments, as I had no orders, and at any rate I could . . . advance to the support of my own skirmishers and hold the ground they had so gallantly won. The companies were moved out . . . and marched up to the first line of rebel rifle-pits from which our skirmishers had already driven the enemy, and as the line was considerably broken by the heavy firing of the enemy's artillery and the fallen timber, it was halted and reformed. . . . I then sent an officer to the rear to procure 100 spades and picks for the purpose of intrenching. Before they arrived an officer came up and said that . . . we were to advance no farther at present, but hold the ground we then had. About the time the tools arrived, . . . the white troops on the left of the colored division opened fire and commenced cheering, . . . and when they advanced . . . we ceased digging and soon moved forward.[71]

On the right of the Union line, Colonel Drew late in the afternoon ordered his forward regiments, the 68th and 76th USCIs, to advance and clear the enemy's front line. "Before the work was fairly commenced," he wrote, "I heard cheering on my left and saw the skirmishers of [Pile's brigade] advancing. I immediately gave the command forward, and forward the entire command . . . swept with a yell." Officers of the 68th USCI understood that the regiment was to "advance and drive the Johnnies from their rifle pits," Colonel Densmore wrote; but when the men saw the skirmishers advance, "*all* went forward with a cheer. . . . Our boys had not gone more than [twenty-five yards] before the gray backs were on a full skedaddle from their rifle pits." While the skirmishers moved ahead, the rest of the regiment occupied the line of outposts that the Confederates had just

---

[70] *OR*, ser. 1, vol. 49, pt. 1, pp. 289, 291 ("without, so"); Scofield to Andrews, 1 Apr 1866 ("Spanish Fort").

[71] *OR*, ser. 1, vol. 49, pt. 1, pp. 286, 293–94 (quotation); Merriam Diary, 5 Apr 1865.

abandoned. "I had some difficulty in keeping the men down as they wanted to see the fun," Densmore continued,

> when to my great surprise I saw the 76th Regt charging "like mad," and almost immediately my companies on the left broke for the front. I felt a keen chagrin as I saw them go, as I had the utmost confidence in the coolness and obedience of those officers, and I was positive that they fully comprehended the part we had to play. As they charged the trench, however, I saw Col Drew . . . coming along the trench swinging his hat and shouting but in the din I could not hear what he was saying. So I ran toward him, when he cried at me, "Why don't you order your men out" & he shouted "Charge! Charge!" I *could not* comprehend the idea of the order, so entirely different from the plan, & otherwise so inexplicable, so I asked if it was his command that my Regt should charge. He answered "Yes! yes forward on the enemy's works"—and away we went.[72]

The two frontline regiments of Drew's brigade moved along the edge of the high ground at the north end of the Confederate main line, near where a 150-foot bluff dropped off into the swamp. Rifle and artillery fire made men crouch below the edge of the bluff as they moved toward the end of the Confederate line. Felled trees lay thick on the slick, wet clay of the hillside:

> As we continued pushing our way, it became evident that our numbers were being thinned by wounds and exhaustion. . . . While a squad of our men were firing over the brow of the bluff, others were hurried along to take an advance station, while the former squad again would drop down, push along and take a station still further on.

The last bit of cover, when they reached it, lay about fifty yards from the Confederate works. Those in the lead paused to let the others catch up. Densmore counted nineteen officers but only sixty-five enlisted men. "What should we do next? We cheered, fired volleys, cheered again, as if about to charge— we wondered why the reserve did not show itself—fired again, cheered, then listened for any sounds of anybody else battling on our side. Not a shot could we hear." The colonel sent one officer, then another, back to find out what had become of the 48th USCI in brigade reserve. Eventually, an unknown officer appeared in the distance, unseen by the Confederates, and beckoned Densmore and his men to return. They scuttled back across the hillside, picking up their wounded and what dead they could. When they reached the place they had started from, they met the 48th USCI coming up just in time to take part in the last charge on Fort Blakely.[73]

Once again, the movement began on the left, where the men of Pile's brigade had been digging out the old Confederate picket line so that it faced east, the direction of their attack, rather than west, toward the Union lines. They had been digging for about forty minutes, Pile reported, "when cheering on my left notified

---

[72]*OR*, ser. 1, vol. 49, pt. 1, p. 296; Densmore to Andrews, 30 Aug 1866.
[73]Densmore to Andrews, 30 Aug 1866.

me that General Andrews' division was moving forward." Not knowing whether this meant a new attack, or whether the white troops were merely following the advance of his brigade, Pile sent a staff officer to see. He soon received a signal that Andrews' division was assaulting the Confederates' main line of defense. "I lay where I could see it all & never shall forget it," Captain Crydenwise wrote to his parents the next day. "With deafening cheers forward came the Yankee boys," he continued:

> The rebs in their rifle pits to my rear & Left becam[e] frightened & leaving their pits started at full speed for their main work. . . . The original design was only to capture this first line . . . , but the Johnnies were on the full run & the Yankee boys were in hot pursuit & neither could be checked. So on, on they went & quicker than I can tell it the white soldiers on the extreme left were swarming over the main works. . . . The rebs still held that part of the works in our front & continued to fire upon us. . . . At that moment cheer after cheer went up from the line held by the colored troops & . . . we all rushed together for the rebel works & the old 73rd was the first to plant its flag upon that portion of the line captured by the colored troops. . . . Never have I known a company to do as well before under such circumstances. When I got into the fort all my men were with me but one & he got hurt a little while going out.[74]

In the center of the Colored Troops Division's line, 2d Lt. Walter A. Chapman of the 51st USCI took part in the charge. "The rebel line of skirmishers seeing us coming up fell back into their works," he told his parents two days afterward.

> As soon as our niggers caught sight of the retreating . . . rebs the very devil could not hold them. . . . The movement was simultaneous regt after regt and line after line took up the cry and started until the whole field was black with darkeys. The rebs were panic struck[,] . . . threw down their arms and run for their lives over to the white troops on our left to give themselves up, to save being butchered by our niggers. The niggers did not take a prisoner, they killed all they took to a man. . . . I am fully satisfied with them as fighters. I will bet on them every time.[75]

General Pile's brigade was on the Colored Troops Division's left, in line next to General Andrews' two brigades of the XIII Corps. It was to Andrews' troops that the surrendering Confederates ran. As Pile put it, "Many of the enemy . . . threw down their arms and ran toward their right to the white troops to avoid capture by the colored soldiers, fearing violence after surrender." Those who were too far from the white troops to run, Colonel Densmore recalled, "huddled together apparently, & really, in mortal fear of the 'niggers' whom they feared would 'remember Fort Pillow.'" Writing a year later, Densmore blamed "Louisiana regiments," a term that could be stretched to include all of the Colored Troops Division except

---

[74] H. M. Crydenwise to Dear Parents & All, 10 Apr 1865, Crydenwise Letters.
[75] W. A. Chapman to Dear Parents, 11 Apr 1865, W. A. Chapman Papers, Sterling Library, Yale University, New Haven, Conn.

his own Missourians, for attacks on unarmed Confederates. "For a time matters seemed serious. Attempts were made to use bayonets, and shots were fired. Two officers of the 68th Capt. [Frederick W.] Norwood and [2d Lt. Clark] Gleason were severely wounded there while endeavoring to save the prisoners." No one counted the dead prisoners.[76]

All witnesses agreed that the attack of the Colored Troops Division thoroughly broke the Confederates' will to resist. General Hawkins did not mention any killing of prisoners, reporting instead that his division captured two hundred thirty Confederate officers and men. "There would have been more," he explained; "but when the rebels saw it was all up with them many ran over to where the white troops were entering their works." Colonel Scofield, whose brigade was in the center of the division's line and included Lieutenant Chapman's 51st USCI, described a somewhat different scene when he recalled the day's events a year afterward. "When we entered the works the rebels that could not run over & surrender to the white troops crowded together in a little space & lay down upon the ground . . . with the utmost terror depicted in their countenances & many of them begged piteously for their lives," Scofield wrote:

> They were treated as prisoners of war with kindness & courtesy. . . . A happier set of men than the colored soldiers were never seen. They fired their guns in the air & shouted & embraced one another. . . . A few whose joy took a religious turn engaged in prayer. Soon as order could be brought out of disorder the prisoners were conducted to the rear under guard of colored soldiers.[77]

After the surrender, rounding up the prisoners and restoring some order among the victors took time, probably longer than the final assault itself, which lasted only some twenty minutes. Colonel Densmore remembered that it took "less than ten" minutes, while Colonel Merriam wondered "how we whipped them so quickly." With witnesses describing events in different parts of the line, and three of them writing a year and more after the event, it is no wonder that their accounts differ on other points beside the duration of the charge. In the 73d USCI, Captain Crydenwise's soldiers "rushed around me some with their arms around my neck some [took] hold of my hands & it seemed almost that they would shake me in pieces." By 7:00 p.m., with the field entirely dark, Col. Charles A. Gilchrist was able to lead the 50th USCI out of Fort Blakely to find the regiment's wounded and bury the dead. With the 68th USCI on the right flank, Colonel Densmore mused that night:

> the bright burning of fires where a short time before none were permitted, the free & unconcerned going to & fro where for a week we had dodged from cover to cover & so short a time ago the air was thick with death, the deep

---

[76] *OR*, ser. 1, vol. 49, pt. 1, pp. 289–90; Densmore to Andrews, 30 Aug 1866. Lieutenant Gleason died of his wounds nine days later. *ORVF*, 8: 241.

[77] *OR*, ser. 1, vol. 49, pt. 2, p. 306; Scofield to Andrews, 1 Apr 1866.

sleep of the tired ranks, the deep silence of that field of strife, the visits, long apart, of the ambulance coming out there into that deep echoless wood.

His reverie ended some time after midnight, when an order arrived instructing the regiment "to draw five days rations and 60 rounds per man of ammunition & be ready to march at day break."[78]

As it turned out, the Union Army made no immediate move. Instead, before dawn on 11 April, a signal from the opposite shore indicated that the Confederates had evacuated Mobile. Two divisions of the XIII Corps crossed the bay the next morning to occupy the city. On 14 April, the XVI Corps set out for Montgomery by road. The Colored Troops Division followed by riverboat six days later.[79]

The division was still at Blakely when word arrived of the Confederate surrender in Virginia. The capitulation of the South's most successful army raised hopes that the end of the war was at hand. Some officers reflected on their recent service and its meaning, both for themselves and for their men. It was, Lieutenant Chapman wrote to his brother,

> a peace most manfully struggled for but which will amply compensate us for our obstinate perseverance. In this struggle the Nigger has shown himself on the battle-field, to be the equal of the best soldiers that ever stepped. . . . [W]hen we first took our company in I was feeling pretty dubious about them, they went in rather skeary, but after a while when they could distinguish the enemy, they got perfectly reckless, and at night they were anxious to sneak up and [illegible] over some of them. I was delighted with them.

Captain Crydenwise took a larger view. "The bright happy day of peace appears near its dawning. God speed its coming," he told his parents. "The Colored troops in the assault & capture of this place on the 9th done a great thing for the cause & for themselves & have again shown that the men will fight & fight bravely."[80]

April 1865 ended with General Canby's Military Division of West Mississippi still negotiating surrender terms with Confederate commanders. The Colored Troops in the division were scattered along the coast from Key West (two regiments) to Pensacola (one regiment) to Brazos Santiago, near the mouth of the Rio Grande (two regiments). Eighteen regiments garrisoned posts in Louisiana, with nine more just across the Mississippi River at Natchez and Vicksburg. Twelve regiments were in Alabama, at Mobile and Montgomery.[81] They had proven their ability during the war. The era that was about to begin would offer new challenges to the Colored Troops and to black people throughout the South.

---

[78] *OR*, ser. 1, vol. 49, pt. 1, pp. 98, 283, 294, 298 ("less than"); Crydenwise to Dear Parents & All, 10 Apr 1865; Densmore to Andrews, 30 Aug 1866; Merriam Diary, 12 Apr 1865.

[79] *OR*, ser. 1, vol. 49, pt. 1, pp. 99–100, 117, 136.

[80] Merriam Diary, 13 and 17 Apr 1865; W. A. Chapman to Dear Bro, 16 Apr 1865, Chapman Papers; H. M. Crydenwise to Dear Parents & All, 13 Apr 1865, Crydenwise Letters.

[81] *OR*, ser. 1, vol. 48, pt. 2, pp. 248–29, 253–57, 260–61.

CHAPTER 6

THE MISSISSIPPI RIVER AND ITS TRIBUTARIES, 1861–1863

Free navigation of the Mississippi River was of paramount concern to federal authorities from the time the first few states seceded. To achieve that aim, Union armies had to control the river's major tributaries. These drained an enormous territory that stretched from the Appalachian Mountains to the Rockies. Even within a single state, the terrain and climate could be as dissimilar as the Ozark Mountains of northwestern Arkansas were from the malarial lowlands along the state's eastern edge. Forms of agriculture varied just as widely, from the pastures of Kentucky's Bluegrass Region to the cotton fields behind Vicksburg, and with them varied the lives of the people who lived on the land. Among that population were more than three hundred thousand black men of military age—those who were between the ages of fifteen and forty-nine at the time of the 1860 census. The area in contention covered nearly one-quarter of a million square miles and included all or parts of eight states. Although these states shared a drainage basin and a labor system—all except Kansas were slave states—each differed from its neighbors and posed its own problems for Union generals (*see Map 3*).[1]

Kansas attained statehood in January 1861, the same month in which Alabama, Florida, Georgia, Louisiana, and Mississippi seceded. Congress had opened the territory to white settlement in 1854; in the years just after that, "Bleeding Kansas" became a battleground of contending factions that sought its admission to the Union as either a slave state or a free state. Free-state partisans were by no means necessarily pro-black: in Kansas, as in most nonslave states, adult black men could not vote and black children attended segregated schools—if there were any schools for them at all. The 1860 census counted only 627 black residents in the territory among a white population of 106,390, all concentrated along the eastern edge. Soon after the secession movement led to open hostilities, black refugees from nearby slave states began to congregate at Union garrisons: Fort Leavenworth on the Missouri River and Fort Scott in the

---

[1] U.S. Census Bureau, *Population of the United States in 1860* (Washington, D.C.: Government Printing Office, 1864), pp. 4, 6, 14, 16, 174, 178, 266, 268, 280, 282, 460, 464. The total must have been greater than three hundred thousand because the 1860 census included no returns from Sunflower and Washington Counties, Mississippi, in the heart of the Yazoo cotton-growing country. Donald L. Winters, *Tennessee Farming, Tennessee Farmers: Antebellum Agriculture in the Upper South* (Knoxville: University of Tennessee Press, 1994), pp. 135–41, discusses regional and intrastate diversity.

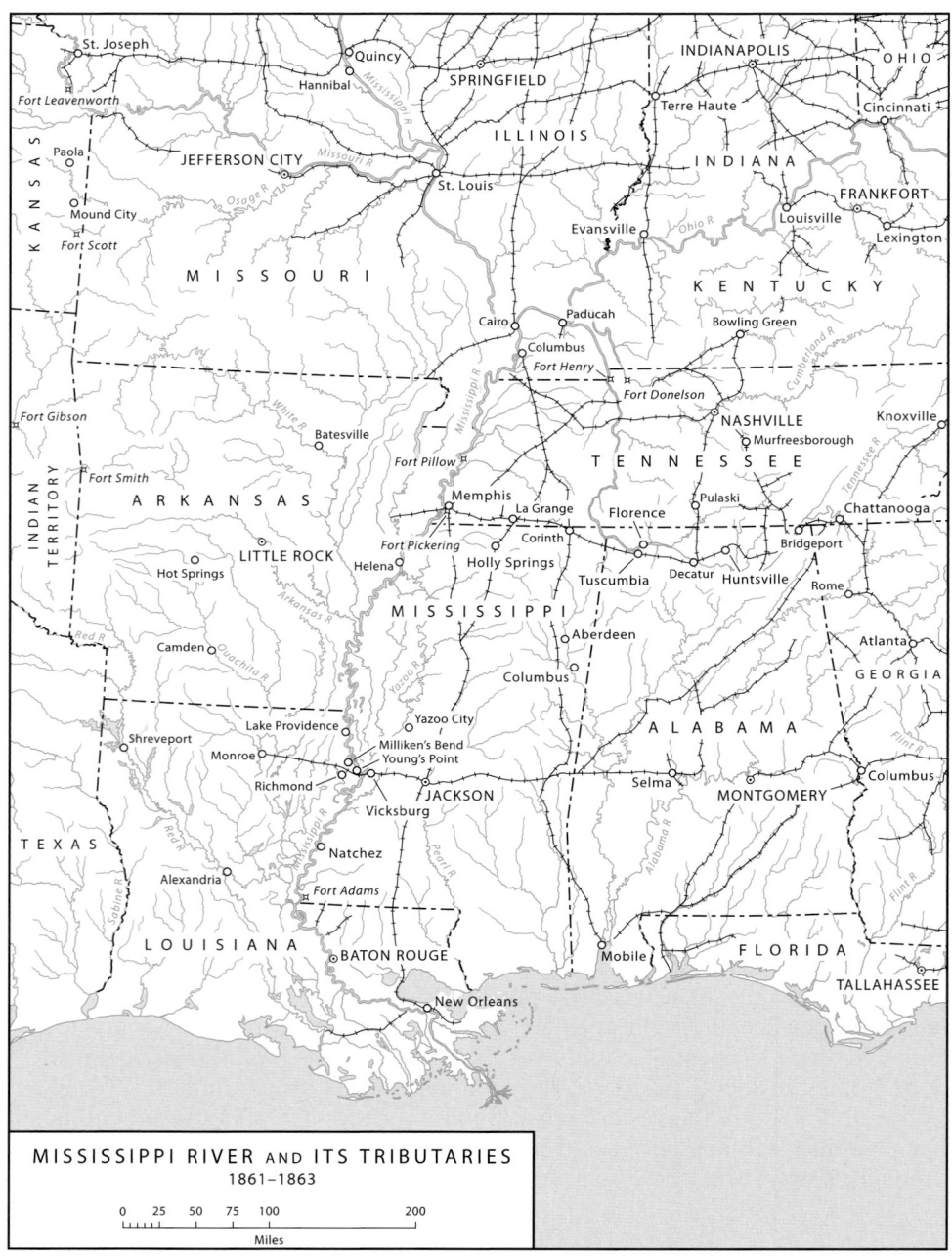

MISSISSIPPI RIVER AND ITS TRIBUTARIES
1861–1863

0 25 50 75 100   200
Miles

Map 3

southeastern part of the state. By July 1862, the city of Leavenworth alone had an estimated fifteen hundred black residents, more than twice the total for the entire territory two years earlier. Most of the state's border with Missouri lay far from a navigable stream, and Union quartermasters had to supply Fort Scott and the posts south of it by slow and expensive wagon trains.[2]

To the east lay Missouri, a slave state that had contributed many agitators to the Kansas controversy during the previous decade. Predominant among its early settlers were Southerners who found the soil in the central part of the state well adapted to corn, hemp, and tobacco—crops that also grew in Kentucky, North Carolina, and Virginia. The Missouri River carried these staples to St. Louis and New Orleans. Slaves tended the crops. In 1860, they accounted for slightly more than 40 percent of the population in the seven-county Little Dixie region of central Missouri, a proportion nearly four times greater than the state-wide average. The total number of slaves in the state was 114,931. Missouri had 3,579 "free colored" residents, of whom a little more than half lived in St. Louis. The nation's eighth largest city was also home to more than fifty thousand native Germans—nearly one-third of its entire population. These immigrants had already formed paramilitary societies before the war, possibly in reaction to nativist animosity but more probably because target-shooting clubs were a popular kind of social association wherever Germans settled in the United States. The St. Louis Germans constituted the largest antislavery bloc in any of the slave states; during the early weeks of the war, they were instrumental in holding the U.S. Arsenal there, and with it the state, for the Union.[3]

No such influential minority existed in Arkansas, which left the Union on 6 May 1861. Most of the state's 111,259 black residents were slaves in the cotton-growing counties along the Mississippi River and its tributaries: the White River, the Arkansas below Little Rock, the Ouachita, and the Red River. The legislature had barred free black adults from living in the state after 1 January 1860; by the time of that year's federal census, only 144 remained. Federal routes of advance through Arkansas lay mostly along the principal waterways and through the best farmland. Agriculture ground to a halt as thousands of black Arkansans gathered at Union Army posts to seek protection and food. Seasonal navigation impeded

---

[2]Nicole Etcheson, *Bleeding Kansas: Contested Liberty in the Civil War Era* (Lawrence: University Press of Kansas, 2004), pp. 43–45, 100–112; Leon F. Litwack, *North of Slavery: The Negro in the Free States, 1790–1860* (Chicago: University of Chicago Press, 1961), pp. 142–50; Richard B. Sheridan, "From Slavery in Missouri to Freedom in Kansas: The Influx of Black Fugitives and Contrabands into Kansas, 1854–1865," *Kansas History* 12 (1989): 28–47, esp. pp. 33–44; "Our Colored Population," *Leavenworth Daily Conservative*, 8 July 1862; Census Bureau, *Population of the United States in 1860*, pp. 598–99.

[3]*The War of the Rebellion: A Compilation of the Official Records of the Union and Confederate Armies*, 70 vols. in 128 (Washington, D.C.: Government Printing Office, 1880–1901), ser. 1, 3: 373 (hereafter cited as *OR*); Ira Berlin et al., eds., *The Wartime Genesis of Free Labor: The Upper South* (New York: Cambridge University Press, 1993), pp. 552–53 (hereafter cited as *WGFL: US*); Census Bureau, *Population of the United States in 1860*, pp. 283, 287, 297, 614; R. Douglas Hurt, *Agriculture and Slavery in Missouri's Little Dixie* (Columbia: University of Missouri Press, 1992), pp. 6, 52, 80. On the St. Louis Germans, see William L. Burton, *Melting Pot Soldiers: The Union's Ethnic Regiments* (New York: Fordham University Press, 1998), pp. 30–32.

efforts to supply most military garrisons and contraband camps. Only in eastern Arkansas did the streams flow year round.[4]

Across the Mississippi River from Arkansas lay the states of Mississippi and Tennessee. Mississippi had followed South Carolina out of the Union on 9 January 1861. Some of its richest farmland, including the Yazoo River country, had belonged to the Choctaw Indians as recently as 1834 and was becoming one of the nation's great cotton-producing regions. The so-called Yazoo Delta really consisted of soil deposited by the Mississippi River during its annual floods, which planters sought to mitigate by building levees. In the Yazoo country, black slaves outnumbered the region's white population by more than four to one. Farther south along the Mississippi in Warren County, of which Vicksburg was the seat, the ratio was smaller, but still more than three to one. As the land rose away from the river, the soil became too poor to support cotton plantations. In the spring of 1862, a Union army entered the state near Corinth, in the northeast corner. Opposing armies marching back and forth quickly devastated Mississippi's food crops, and problems of supply plagued Union operations there throughout the war.[5]

Tennessee was the last state to join the Confederacy, on 8 June 1861. Its agriculture was more varied than that of regions farther south. Cotton plantations and wealth characterized the region around Memphis in the southwest corner of the state; but a dozen counties equally prosperous, with economies based on corn, wheat, and livestock, spanned the middle of the state from north to south. More typically Southern crops in middle Tennessee were tobacco, grown near the Kentucky state line, and cotton, which thrived in the southern tier of counties. The middle and western parts of Tennessee were home to 90 percent of the state's 275,719 slaves. Few of them lived in the mountainous eastern region, although a slightly higher percentage could be found in the valley formed by the upper Tennessee and its tributaries, which connected Chattanooga with Knoxville and Jonesborough in the far northeast corner of the state. Early in 1862, the capture of Forts Henry and Donelson on the lower Tennessee and Cumberland Rivers gave Union armies a precarious entry into the Confederacy's heart that they struggled for more than two years to hold.[6]

Kentucky lay too far north for cotton to grow. In the Bluegrass Region around Lexington, farmers produced corn, wheat, hemp, and livestock. Tobacco growers tended to concentrate in the western part of the state. Most of Kentucky's 225,483 slaves lived in the Bluegrass Region or along the Tennessee line west of Bowling Green. What distinguished Kentucky from

---

[4] Donald P. McNeilly, *The Old South Frontier: Cotton Plantations and the Formation of Arkansas Society, 1819–1861* (Fayetteville: University of Arkansas Press, 2000), pp. 19–20, 62, 112; Carl H. Moneyhon, *The Impact of the Civil War and Reconstruction on Arkansas* (Baton Rouge: Louisiana State University Press, 1994), pp. 14–29; Orville W. Taylor, *Negro Slavery in Arkansas* (Durham, N.C.: Duke University Press, 1958), pp. 257–58.

[5] James C. Cobb, *The Most Southern Place on Earth: The Mississippi Delta and the Roots of Regional Identity* (New York: Oxford University Press, 1992), pp. 3–8, 29–31; Census Bureau, *Population of the United States in 1860*, pp. 270–71.

[6] Stephen V. Ash, *Middle Tennessee Society Transformed, 1860–1870: War and Peace in the Upper South* (Baton Rouge: Louisiana State University Press, 1988), pp. 2–12, 17–18; Winters, *Tennessee Farming*, pp. 135–37; Census Bureau, *Population of the United States in 1860*, pp. 464–67.

Maryland and Missouri, the other slave-holding border states that did not secede, was the number of slaveholders among the white population. Although Kentucky's 919,484 white residents accounted for only 37.2 percent of the total white population in the three states, its 38,645 slaveholders outnumbered those of Maryland and Missouri combined. The sheer number of Kentuckians who owned human property was an important factor in formulating the Lincoln administration's policies, first about emancipation and later about recruiting black soldiers in the state.[7]

In all the slave states west of the Appalachian Mountains, navigable rivers formed an important feature of the land. During the antebellum period, they afforded the cheapest, fastest means of transportation for people and goods. Eighteenth-century settlers had founded Nashville on the Cumberland River. Farther south and east, Chattanooga and Knoxville stood on the upper reaches of the Tennessee. Natchez and Vicksburg, both cotton-shipping ports, were the commercial hubs of Mississippi. Little Rock stood on the south bank of the Arkansas River near the center of the state. Throughout the war, these rivers would provide invasion routes for Union armies headed deep into the Confederacy.[8]

By the first week of September 1861, a squadron of three federal gunboats controlled the Mississippi River from Cairo, Illinois, southward nearly to the Tennessee state line. Until that week, both sides in the war had observed the "neutrality" that Kentucky's state government wished to maintain. Then, within days, a Confederate force occupied the town of Columbus on bluffs above the Mississippi and Brig. Gen. Ulysses S. Grant seized Paducah, where the Tennessee River empties into the Ohio. Five months later, on 6 February 1862, a U.S. Navy flotilla forced the surrender of Fort Henry, which guarded the upper reaches of the Tennessee. Two days after that, Union gunboats touched at Florence, Alabama, 257 miles upstream from Paducah—a foray that took them deep into the Confederacy.[9]

Grant moved next against Fort Donelson, less than ten miles east of Fort Henry on the Cumberland River. The garrison there surrendered on 16 February, and Confederate troops evacuated Nashville a week later. A federal army led by Brig. Gen. Don C. Buell crossed the Cumberland and occupied Tennessee's capital on 25 February, leaving the Confederate General Albert S. Johnston, commanding west of the Appalachians, with a choice of either contesting the occupation of middle Tennessee or defending the Mississippi River. Johnston decided on the western option. As a result, a Union force led by Brig. Gen. Ormsby M. Mitchel was able to march overland from Murfreesborough, Tennessee, to Huntsville, Alabama, which it occupied on 11 April. Later that

    [7]Sam B. Hilliard, *Atlas of Antebellum Southern Agriculture* (Baton Rouge: Louisiana State University Press, 1984), pp. 50, 52, 54, 62, 66–67, 71, 76–77; U.S. Census Bureau, *Agriculture of the United States in 1860* (Washington, D.C.: Government Printing Office, 1864), pp. 229, 231, 234; *Population of the United States in 1860*, pp. 171, 211, 277.

    [8]Richard M. McMurry, *The Fourth Battle of Winchester: Toward a New Civil War Paradigm* (Kent, Ohio: Kent State University Press, 2002), pp. 68, 70.

    [9]*OR*, ser. 1, 4: 180–81, 196–97; 7: 153–56. *Official Records of the Union and Confederate Navies in the War of the Rebellion*, 30 vols. (Washington, D.C.: Government Printing Office, 1894–1922), ser. 1, 22: 299–309 (hereafter cited as *ORN*); J. Haden Alldredge, "A History of Navigation on the Tennessee River System," 75th Cong., 1st sess., H. Doc. 254 (serial 10,119), pp. 7, 84–88.

spring, federal troops took possession of Corinth, Mississippi (30 May), and Memphis (6 June). Thus, by the first week of June, the armies of the North controlled two of Tennessee's major cities and had established garrisons at or near important railroad junctions in neighboring parts of Mississippi and Alabama. A Confederate drive into Kentucky late that summer caused the Union occupiers to abandon Huntsville on 31 August and evacuate much of Middle Tennessee, but they kept their hold on Corinth by defeating a Confederate army there early in October.[10]

Large numbers of black people escaped from bondage and sought refuge near Union Army camps, as they did elsewhere in the South whenever an opportunity offered. "The negroes are our only friends," General Mitchel at Huntsville wrote to Secretary of War Edwin M. Stanton early in May. "I shall very soon have watchful guards among the slaves on the plantations bordering the [Tennessee River] from Bridgeport to Florence, and all who communicate to me valuable information I have promised the protection of my Government." Stanton agreed. "The assistance of slaves is an element of military strength which . . . you are fully justified in employing," he told Mitchel. "Protection to those who furnish information or other assistance is a high duty." Mitchel did try to protect former slaves who aided the Union occupiers, but in July, he was given a new command in South Carolina and could do no more than protest to the War Department at reports that some of his Alabama informants had been returned to their former masters. Union officers in northern Alabama continued to use black laborers to cut timber, build fortifications, and drive teams. With the departure of Huntsville's garrison, many black refugees followed the retreating federals as far north as Kentucky.[11]

As Union troops withdrew across Tennessee in the late summer of 1862, they managed to hold on to Memphis and Nashville. Memphis lay far west of the Confederates' main thrust northward, and a pause to attack Nashville would have interrupted that effort. Even so, the continued federal grip on the two cities certainly owed something to the efforts of the black laborers who had toiled on their defenses. On 1 July, Grant reported "very few negro men" in Memphis, but within two weeks, he had two hundred at work and another ninety-four on the way. By the end of the month, Maj. Gen. William T. Sherman, who succeeded Grant in command of the city, had "about 750 negroes and all soldiers who are under punishment" building Fort Pickering to guard the southern approaches. Toward the end of October, Sherman pronounced the fort "very well advanced, and . . . a good piece of work. We have about 6,000 negroes here, of which 2,000 are men—800 on the fort, 240 in the quartermaster's department, and about 1,000 as cooks, teamsters, and servants in the regiments." Similar efforts were under way at Nashville, where Governor Andrew Johnson had "control of a good many" black refugees who were expected to work on the city's defenses. Johnson believed that a ring of redoubts—earthen gun emplacements like those that surrounded most contested cities—would deter an attack on Nashville. The

---

[10]*OR*, ser. 1, 7: 426–27; vol. 10, pt. 1, p. 642.

[11]*OR*, ser. 1, vol. 10, pt. 2, pp. 162 ("The negroes"), 165 ("The assistance"); vol. 16, pt. 2, pp. 92, 269, 332, 420, 437, 538–85.

idea seemed to have worked, for the advancing Confederates merely feinted in that direction while bypassing the city itself.[12]

West of the Mississippi, control of the lower Missouri River was an important concern of Union strategists. Along with the single line of the Hannibal and St. Joseph Railroad, the lower Missouri formed the eastern end of the overland route to the goldfields of California and Colorado, sources of bullion that funded the Union war effort. For this reason, Lincoln was loath to offend Missouri's slave-holders. When Maj. Gen. John C. Frémont proclaimed martial law throughout Missouri in August 1861 and declared free the slaves of Confederate Missourians, the president was quick to tell him that emancipation would not only "alarm our Southern Union friends and turn them against us," but perhaps also "ruin our rather fair prospects for Kentucky." Within two weeks, Lincoln ordered the abandonment of this part of Frémont's program. The abundance of free white labor in the state and the administration's desire to placate border state slaveholders meant that the need to employ freed slaves and the problems associated with the presence of large numbers of displaced black people were not prominent features of Missouri's Civil War.[13]

Federal military operations in Arkansas began with the Army of the Southwest, led by Brig. Gen Samuel R. Curtis. It drove Confederate troops out of southwestern Missouri and defeated them at Pea Ridge, just over the state line, on 7–8 March 1862. Curtis, an 1831 West Point graduate, Mexican War veteran, and Republican congressman, received a promotion for the victory, which followed within weeks Grant's successes at Forts Henry and Donelson. The defeated Confederates retreated to Van Buren, halfway down the western edge of the state, where they received orders to join the main force east of the Mississippi that was preparing to attack Grant's army. Although the reinforcements from Arkansas arrived too late to take part in the Battle of Shiloh, their departure removed the main body of Confederate troops from the state.

When the new Confederate commander, Maj. Gen. Thomas C. Hindman, reached Little Rock at the end of May, he had to assemble a fresh army. He enforced conscription, which had begun in mid-April, and began forming partisan ranger companies to harass Union communications and supply routes. Partisans, floods, and bad roads prevented Curtis' army from reaching Little Rock in May. It withdrew to Batesville, some ninety miles to the north. Low water the next month kept a Union flotilla laden with supplies from ascending the White River, so Curtis left Batesville and led his troops southeast to Helena on the Mississippi. Living off the land, they arrived there on 12 July 1862. As they neared the river, they found that each county along their route had a greater number and a higher proportion of slaves than the last. The Confederates tried to impede the twelve-day march by having black laborers fell trees and destroy ferries in Curtis' path. The general reacted by issuing certificates of emancipation to any slaves who came his way. By

---

[12] *OR*, ser. 1, vol. 16, pt. 1, pp. 1089–90, and pt. 2, pp. 243 ("control of"), 268, 862–63; vol. 17, pt. 2, pp. 60 ("very few"), 122 ("about 750"), 856. John Y. Simon, ed., *The Papers of Ulysses S. Grant*, 30 vols. to date (Carbondale and Edwardsville: Southern Illinois University Press, 1967–), 5: 199 (hereafter cited as *Grant Papers*).

[13] *OR*, ser. 1, 3: 467, 469 (quotation), 485–86; *WGFL: US*, p. 551.

the time Curtis' army reached Helena, word of his "free papers" had attracted a "general stampede" of escaped slaves.[14]

As the summer wore on, relations between black Arkansans and federal occupiers took many of the same forms that were developing in coastal Georgia and South Carolina and in southern Louisiana. Union scouting parties in northeastern Arkansas "received information through negroes" about enemy movements, troop strength, and morale. Sometimes informants approached furtively, at night. At other times, officers conferred openly with groups of slaves. Soldiers were perplexed by the "immense numbers . . . flocking into our camp daily," of whom "quite a proportion were women and children, who could be of no use to us whatever." "There is a perfect 'Cloud' of negroes being thrown upon me for Sustenance & Support," the quartermaster at Helena complained in late July, just twelve days after his arrival there.

> Out of some 50 for whom I drew rations this morning but twelve were working Stock all the rest being women & children What am I to do with them If this taking them in & feeding them is to be the order of the day would it not be well to have some competent man employed to look after them & Keep their time, draw their Rations & look after their Sanitary Condition &c &c As it is, although it is hard to believe that such things can be, Soldiers & teamsters (white) are according to Common report indulging in intimacy with them which can only be accounted for by the doctrine of total depravity. This question of what shall be done with these people has troubled me not a little & I have commenced my enquiry in this manner hoping that the matter may be systematized.

Despite the quartermaster's concern, black refugees at Helena apparently did not lack for employment. "Every other soldier . . . has a negro servant," the post commander told General Curtis. "While this Continues, it will be impossible to get laborers for the Fort." As happened elsewhere in the occupied South, the Union forces' concern was to care for the refugees and, if possible, to put them to work.[15]

The question of what should be done with "these people" was one that bothered federal commanders on both sides of the Mississippi and indeed wherever Union troops occupied parts of the South. Black refugees were arriving at La Grange in southwestern Tennessee "by wagon loads," Grant told Maj. Gen. Henry W. Halleck in mid-November. Grant put them to work picking the remains of the region's cotton crop and asked for instructions. Halleck had no new ideas: he recommended farm work and employment as quartermasters' teamsters and laborers.

---

[14] *OR*, ser. 1, 13: 28–29, 371, 373, 397–98, 525, 832–33, 875–77; Michael B. Dougan, *Confederate Arkansas: The People and Policies of a Frontier State in Wartime* (University: University of Alabama Press, 1976), p. 91. Independence County (Batesville), where Curtis' march began, had 1,337 black residents (all slaves), who represented 9.3 percent of the total population; Phillips County (Helena) on the Mississippi River was 54 percent black (8,041 slaves and 4 free). Census Bureau, *Population of the United States in 1860*, pp. 15, 17–18.

[15] *OR*, ser. 1, 13: 176 ("received information"), 202, 203 ("immense numbers"), 209–10, 262; Ira Berlin et al., eds., *The Wartime Genesis of Free Labor: The Lower South* (New York: Cambridge University Press, 1990), pp. 659 ("There is"), 660 ("Every other") (hereafter cited as *WGFL: LS*); Earl J. Hess, "Confiscation and the Northern War Effort: The Army of the Southwest at Helena," *Arkansas Historical Quarterly* 44 (1985): 56–75.

Wartime Confederates tried to continue antebellum restrictions on the mobility of slaves, including enforcement of the pass system for black persons absent from their homes. Here, a patrol tries to thwart a suspected escape to Union lines.

Grant should try to keep the cost of feeding the refugees low, he added. "So far as possible, subsist them and your army on the rebel inhabitants of Mississippi." These instructions were in accord with a presidential order issued on 22 July that sanctioned military seizure and use of civilian property in the seceded states and the paid employment of "persons of African descent . . . for military and naval purposes." The order had come five days after Lincoln signed the Second Confiscation Act, which, among its many provisions, authorized the employment of black people in "any military or naval service for which they may be found competent."[16]

Local and regional commanders still faced the dilemma posed by dependents: the very young, the very old, and women of all ages. Even before Grant queried Halleck, he had appointed Chaplain John Eaton of the 27th Ohio to establish a camp for them at La Grange, organize them in work gangs, and set them to "picking, ginning, and baling" cotton. In mid-December, Eaton's authority expanded. He became "General Superintendent of Contrabands" for Grant's Department of the Tennessee, which included the parts of Kentucky and Tennessee west of the Tennessee River as well as Union-occupied northern Mississippi. His office was funded in part by proceeds from the sale of cotton picked on plantations that had been abandoned by their secessionist owners. By the following spring, Eaton had

---

[16]*OR*, ser. 1, vol. 17, pt. 1, pp. 470 ("by wagon loads"), 471 ("So far as"); ser. 3, 2: 281 ("any military"), 397 ("persons of African").

charge of 5,000 black refugees at Cairo, Illinois; 3,900 in and around Memphis; 3,700 at Corinth; 2,400 at Lake Providence, Louisiana; and about 7,000 at other places in the department.[17]

West of the Mississippi River, in the fall of 1862, General Curtis commanded the Department of the Missouri, which included Arkansas, Kansas, Missouri, and the Indian Territory. His opponent, Confederate Maj. Gen. Theophilus H. Holmes, complained to him of reports that Union officers were arming Arkansas slaves, but Curtis was unmoved. "The enemy must be weakened by every honorable means, and he has no right to whine about it," he wrote to the officer commanding at Helena. "The rebellion must be shaken to its foundation, which is slavery, and the idea of saving rebels from the consequences of their rebellion is no part of our business. . . . Free negroes, like other men, will inevitably seek weapons of war, and fearing they may be returned to slavery, they will fight our foes for their own security. That is the inevitable logic of events, not our innovation."[18]

Five hundred miles northwest of Helena, James H. Lane was taking steps to employ former slaves more radical than those taken by any federal official out-side Louisiana and South Carolina. A veteran of both the Mexican War and the Bleeding Kansas struggle, as well as one of the new state's first U.S. senators, Lane had begun to recruit black soldiers at Fort Leavenworth. At the beginning of July 1862, the president had called for two hundred thousand volunteers to strengthen the Union armies. Although the call had been addressed to state governors, Lane received an appointment later in the month as "commissioner of recruiting" to organize at least one brigade of three-year volunteers. The appointment came just five days after passage of the Militia Act, which authorized "persons of African descent" to perform "any military or naval service for which they may be found competent." Lane took the bit in his teeth. "Recruiting opens up beautifully," he told Secretary of War Stanton the day after he began. "Good for four regiments of whites and two of blacks."[19]

Lane's action, like General Hunter's in South Carolina and General Butler's in Louisiana, went beyond what the administration in Washington was willing to accept. General Halleck pointed out that according to the Militia Act only the president could authorize the enlistment of black soldiers and Lane's attempt was therefore void. Yet, the day after Halleck delivered his opinion, a telegram from the Adjutant General's Office seemed to acknowledge the validity of Lane's en-listments by telling the disbursing officer at Fort Leavenworth that recruits "for negro regiments will under no circumstances be paid bounty and premium," the financial incentives that were offered to white volunteers. Meanwhile, the governor of Kansas, like other state governors throughout the North, saw an opportunity to

---

[17] *OR*, ser. 1, vol. 17, pt. 2, p. 278; *Grant Papers*, 6: 316 (quotations); *WGFL: LS*, pp. 626–27, 686.

[18] *OR*, ser. 1, 13: 653, 727, 756 (quotation). The department soon grew to include the territories of Colorado and Nebraska (p. 729). Sickness was widespread among Union soldiers in garrison there, too. Rhonda M. Kohl, "'This Godforsaken Town': Death and Disease at Helena, Arkansas, 1862–63," *Civil War History* 50 (2004): 109–44.

[19] *OR*, ser. 3, 2: 187–88, 281 ("persons of African"), 294 ("Recruiting opens"), 959; Albert E. Castel, *A Frontier State at War: Kansas, 1861–1865* (Ithaca, N.Y.: Cornell University Press, 1958), p. 90.

award military commissions as an extension of his political patronage. When questions arose in August about the governor's power to appoint officers in Lane's new black organizations, Stanton expressed regret "that there is any discord or ill feeling between the Executive of Kansas . . . and General Lane at a time when all men should be united in their efforts against the enemy." Regardless of official displeasure, Lane continued recruiting through the summer, probably with the president's unwritten permission.[20]

In spite of Lane's optimism, it was apparent by October that barely enough black men had enlisted to form one regiment. They had not been mustered in and therefore were ineligible for pay. Then came word that they were to string a telegraph line between their current station, Fort Scott, and Fort Leavenworth, where they had enlisted, some one hundred twenty miles to the north. "These men have been recruited with the promise that they were to fight, not work as common laborers," General Curtis' chief of staff reported, "that they were to be treated in every way as soldiers . . . & that they would have an opportunity to strike a blow for the freedom of their brothers. . . . They are now two months in camp and no one can tell what is to be done with them. . . . They would, I think, commence the construction of this telegraph willingly if they could be *mustered*, in the hope that a time would come when they might fight."[21]

That time came just ten days after the chief of staff's report. On 26 October, Capt. Richard G. Ward led a force of 224 soldiers of the 1st Kansas Colored Infantry, along with six other officers and several white scouts, in search of a force of Confederate irregulars. Two months earlier, the Confederates were said to be "ragged, hungry, and desperate," but by late October, Ward reported that they numbered "some 700 or 800 men, all splendidly mounted." One of his subordinates, 1st Lt. Richard J. Hinton, was more cautious. He thought that there were only 400 of them at first, reinforced to perhaps 600 during the two-day engagement. Meanwhile, one Confederate leader, Jeremiah V. Cockrell, who had been recruiting in western Missouri, claimed to have sworn in 1,500 men.[22]

Ward's party marched through Mound City, Kansas, crossed the state line, and toward the end of the second day's march found the Confederates on an island in the Osage River. The two sides spent 28 October exchanging shots at long range, but the wind was too strong for accurate fire. In the evening, Ward sent runners to the Union garrisons at Fort Scott, at Fort Lincoln on the Little Osage River, and at the town of Paola, asking for mounted reinforcements. The next day, he sent out a party of about fifty men to find food to supplement his force's dwindling ration of beef and dried corn. To distract the Confederates from this foraging party, he dispatched another sixty men led by Capt. Andrew J. Armstrong and 2d Lt. Andrew J. Crew "to engage the attention of the enemy." Armstrong's party met some Confederates about two miles from the Union camp, Ward reported, and "immediately moved forward to the attack and drove the enemy from position to

---

[20] *OR*, ser. 3, 2: 312, 411 ("for negro regiments"), 417, 431, 479 ("that there is"); Castel, *Frontier State at War*, p. 91.

[21] Ira Berlin et al., eds., *The Black Military Experience* (New York: Cambridge University Press, 1982), pp. 71–72.

[22] *OR*, ser. 1, 13: 603 ("ragged"), 733, and 53: 456 ("some 700 or 800"). *New York Tribune*, 11 November 1862. The *Tribune* copied an account in the *Leavenworth Conservative* signed R. J. H.

position until they had been driven some four miles . . . , the enemy shouting to the boys 'come on, you d——d niggers,' and the boys politely requesting them to wait for them, as they were not mounted." Armstrong's patrol killed or wounded seven Confederates, Ward added, "and the boys felt highly elated . . . at their success."[23]

The foragers had returned and the men were eating dinner when Confederate horsemen attacked the camp's pickets. "Suspecting that they were concentrating troops behind the mound south of us," Ward wrote, "we threw out a small party of skirmishers to feel toward them and ascertain their force and retake our picket ground. The boys soon drove the enemy over the hill, and the firing becoming very sharp, I ordered [2d Lt.] Joseph Gardner to take a force of some twenty men and . . . rally the skirmishers and return to camp." Meanwhile, the rest of the 1st Kansas Colored readied itself for a fight. At this point, Ward learned that two of his officers had left the camp without orders and followed Lieutenant Gardner and his party. Ward concealed part of his remaining force, commanded by Captain Armstrong, and went to reconnoiter. He found some of his own men on a mound to his west and some of the enemy occupying a mound to his south. From his men, he learned that Lieutenant Gardner and most of the skirmishers were at a house about half a mile to the south and making ready to fight their way back to camp. Ward told Armstrong to move his men to a position where he could better cover Gardner's return and sent word to the camp guard to prepare to move at once.[24]

While Ward was making these arrangements, the Confederates spied Gardner's skirmishers and "charged with a yell. . . . The boys took the double-quick over the mound in order to gain a small ravine on the north side," but the horsemen overtook them first. "I have witnessed some hard fights," Ward reported, "but I never saw a braver sight than that handful . . . fighting 117 men who were all around and in amongst them. Not one surrendered or gave up his weapon. At this juncture Armstrong came . . . , yelling to his men to follow him, and cursing them for not going faster when they were already on the keen jump." Armstrong's men fired a volley from about one hundred fifty yards while the camp guard, just arrived on the scene, fired from another direction. By this time, a prairie fire had kindled, mingling the smoke of burning grass and gunpowder. The 1st Kansas Colored managed one more volley before the Confederates fled in the smoke. "The men fought like tigers," Lieutenant Hinton observed, "and the main difficulty was to hold them well in hand." Maintaining discipline in the heat of battle was a problem for officers on both sides, in every theater of the war. The Union loss amounted to eight killed, including Lieutenant Crew, one of the officers who had followed the skirmishers without orders, and eleven wounded. Ward did not report the number of Confederate casualties, but Lieutenant Hinton estimated them as fifteen dead and about as many more wounded.[25]

Not many days after the fight at Island Mound, the 1st Kansas Colored returned to Fort Scott, where the commanding officer feared a raid by an enemy force estimated to number eighteen hundred, and worried about $2 million worth of public property in his care. Imminent attack or no, government supplies required

---

[23] *OR*, ser. 1, 53: 456.

[24] Ibid.

[25] Ibid., pp. 457–58 (quotation, p. 457); *New York Tribune*, 11 November 1862.

heavy guards because Americans of every political persuasion, North or South, always stood ready to convert public goods to private use. The men of the regiment assembled to hear the Emancipation Proclamation read on New Year's Day 1863. On 13 January, they were mustered in as a battalion. Still shy of the ten companies required of a regiment, they were at last part of the federal army.[26]

After sporadic local efforts to raise black regiments in Kansas, Louisiana, and South Carolina, the War Department's first initiative came in March 1863, when Secretary of War Stanton dispatched Adjutant General Brig. Gen. Lorenzo Thomas on an inspection tour of the Mississippi Valley in the spring of 1863. The two men disliked each other, so Stanton fulfilled two purposes in sending Thomas west. He not only exiled a bureau chief whose presence irked him; he also had sent an emissary with enough rank to enforce administration policy. Thomas' instructions were to inspect and report on "the condition of that class of population known as contrabands" in government camps scattered from Cairo, Illinois, southward along the Mississippi; to investigate reports of Army officers trafficking in cotton; and to evict any officers who had commandeered steamboats as personal quarters and were in effect using government transports as houseboats.[27]

The most important part of Thomas' instructions, requiring two paragraphs, had to do with "the use of the colored population emancipated by the president's proclamation, and particularly for the organization of their labor and military strength." Thomas was to convince Grant and other generals that efficient use of black labor, both civil and military, was one of the administration's prime interests. Failure to further this cause, whether by unconcern or by outright obstruction, would constitute dereliction of duty. Moreover, Thomas was to set in motion the organization and recruitment of all-black regiments that would be clothed, fed, and outfitted "in the same manner as other troops in the service." Stanton's intention that black troops receive the same uniforms, rations, and equipment as white soldiers suggests that the Lincoln administration conceived a role for the new regiments beyond the purely defensive one that had been announced in the Emancipation Proclamation. Indeed, on the same day that the secretary of war issued Thomas' instructions, he used the phrase "the same as other volunteers" in orders to Maj. Gen. Nathaniel P. Banks about black regiments in the Department of the Gulf.[28]

Thomas reached Cairo before the end of March and filed his first report on 1 April. The southern tip of Illinois was a poor place for a contraband camp, he wrote. There were no abandoned plantations where the freedpeople could live, and it was too far north for them to cultivate crops they were familiar with. The contrabands would be more useful settled farther south. The regiments that

---

[26] *OR*, ser. 1, 13: 790. On nineteenth-century American attitudes toward government property, see William A. Dobak, *Fort Riley and Its Neighbors: Military Money and Economic Growth, 1853–1895* (Norman: University of Oklahoma Press, 1998), pp. 148–54.

[27] *OR*, ser. 3, 3: 100 (quotation); Benjamin P. Thomas and Harold M. Hyman, *Stanton: The Life and Times of Lincoln's Secretary of War* (New York: Knopf, 1962), pp. 163, 379; Michael T. Meier, "Lorenzo Thomas and the Recruitment of Blacks in the Mississippi Valley, 1863–1865," in *Black Soldiers in Blue: African American Troops in the Civil War Era*, ed. John David Smith (Chapel Hill: University of North Carolina Press, 2002), pp. 249–75.

[28] *OR*, ser. 3, 3: 3, 101 (quotations), 102.

Thomas was to organize would play a part in this. "The negro Regiments could give protection to these plantations," he told Stanton, "and also operate effectively against the guerrillas. This would be particularly advantageous on the Mississippi River, as the negroes, being acquainted with the peculiar country lining its banks, would know where to act effectively." Reports of the 1st South Carolina's coastal operations had begun to arrive in Washington in January, and Thomas may have absorbed the lesson that black troops' local knowledge was important to the success of Union military operations. In supposing an active role for these regiments, the adjutant general and the secretary of war seemed for once to have been in agreement.[29]

While Thomas was in Cairo, General Halleck, who remained in Washington, explained the new policy to Grant, who was preparing his campaign against Vicksburg. Emancipation was a military necessity: "So long as the rebels retain and employ their slaves in producing grains, & c.," he told Grant, "they can employ all the whites [as soldiers]. Every slave withdrawn from the enemy is equivalent to a white man put *hors de combat.*" Halleck saw the new black regiments primarily as a defensive force, especially along the Mississippi "during the sickly season," but thought that the Union would eventually use them "to the very best advantage we can." The character of the war had changed during the previous year, Halleck declared, and since there was "no possible hope of reconciliation with the rebels," it became the duty of every officer, whatever his private opinion, "to cheerfully and honestly endeavor to carry out" the administration's policy.[30]

As Halleck's letter made its way to Grant, Adjutant General Thomas steamed down the Mississippi, stopping at Memphis, where he explained the new policy to Maj. Gen. Stephen A. Hurlbut, an Illinois politician who commanded the District of West Tennessee. Hurlbut wanted to raise a regiment of black artillerists to garrison the forts around Memphis, and Thomas authorized him to recruit six companies and select their officers. "The experience of the Navy is that blacks handle heavy guns well," Thomas remarked. The rest of the generals' conversation had to do with administrative matters: the employment of black refugees, who "come here in a state of destitution, especially the women and children"; the cotton trade, licit and illicit; and the problem of smuggling, which resulted partly from the vast quantity of quartermaster's stores warehoused at Memphis.[31]

On 5 April, Thomas boarded a riverboat for Helena, Arkansas. There, he addressed an audience of seven thousand soldiers. His efforts were seconded by speeches from the outgoing and incoming commanders of the District of Eastern Arkansas and the commanding general of the 12th Division, Army of the Tennessee. Thomas' impression was that "the policy respecting arming the blacks

---

[29]Brig Gen L. Thomas to E. M. Stanton, 1 Apr 1863, Entry 159BB, Generals' Papers and Books (L. Thomas), Record Group (RG) 94, Rcds of the Adjutant General's Office (AGO), National Archives (NA). The reports from South Carolina that appear in *OR,* ser. 1, 14: 189–94, arrived at the Adjutant General's Office on 16 January 1863 and 4 February 1863. NA Microfilm Pub M711, Registers of Letters Received, AGO, roll 37. The reports themselves bear no indication of Thomas having read them. Entry 729, RG 94, Union Battle Rpts, NA.

[30]*OR,* ser. 1, vol. 24, pt. 3, pp. 156–57 (quotations).

[31]*OR,* ser. 3, 3: 116.

was most enthusiastically received." The next day, Lt. Col. William F. Wood, 1st Indiana Cavalry, who had been nominated as colonel of the 1st Arkansas (African Descent [AD]), presented his roster of officer candidates: all but two of the thirty-seven names belonged to officers or enlisted men of Indiana regiments in the Helena garrison. Each divisional commander, Thomas explained to one general, was to be responsible for two of the new regiments, appointing a board to examine applicants "without regard for present rank, merit alone being the test. . . . The positions to be filled by whites include all Commissioned [officers] and 1st Sergts; also Non-commissioned Staff." The method worked for the 1st Arkansas (AD). Within a month the regiment was up to strength, "well equipped and in a respectable state of discipline," Thomas told the secretary of war, and ready "to act against the guerrillas."[32]

Thomas' next stop was Lake Providence, Louisiana, where much the same thing happened. On the morning of 9 April, the general addressed four thousand men of the 6th Division and in the afternoon seven thousand men of the 3d Division. He asked for enough nominations from each division to staff two regiments. Within twenty-four hours, the 6th Division presented the names of enough candidates to officer the 8th Louisiana (AD). Five days later, names from the same division filled the officer nominees' roster of the 10th Louisiana (AD). The strain of travel had prostrated the 59-year-old Thomas by 11 April, when he arrived at Milliken's Bend, Louisiana, but his system of accepting officers for the new black regiments along the Mississippi River by nominations from nearby white regiments continued through the spring and early summer. During the next six weeks, he began organizing eight regiments at Helena and other river towns south of it. In telegrams to Stanton, he wrote of organizing "at least" ten regiments. He could enlist twenty thousand men, enough for twenty regiments, "if necessary."[33]

By the time the ailing general reached Milliken's Bend, some thirty miles upstream from Confederate-held Vicksburg, he had conceived a plan for the use of plantations that had been abandoned when their owners fled the federal occupiers. The primary object was to people the plantations with former slaves. Establishing a "loyal population" along the river would secure steamboats on the Mississippi from damage by enemy cannon and snipers concealed ashore and thwart Confederate irregulars. Thomas also hoped "to accomplish much, in demonstrating that the freed negro may be profitably employed by enterprising men." Northern businessmen "of enterprise and capital" would lease and run the plantations, paying an able-bodied black man seven dollars a month, a woman

---

[32] OR, ser. 1, vol. 24, pt. 3, p. 22; ser. 3, 3: 117 ("the policy"), 202 ("well equipped"). Frederick H. Dyer, *A Compendium of the War of the Rebellion* (New York: Thomas Yoseloff, 1959 [1909]), pp. 494–95; Brig Gen L. Thomas to Maj Gen F. Steele, 15 Apr 1863 ("without regard"), Entry 159BB, RG 94, NA; List of Ofcrs, 7 Apr 63, 46th United States Colored Infantry (USCI), Entry 57C, Regimental Papers, RG 94, NA.

[33] OR, ser. 1, vol. 24, pt. 3, p. 29; ser. 3, 3: 121. Brig Gen L. Thomas to Col R. H. Ballinger, 20 May 1863, Entry 159BB; Special Orders (SO) 10, 15 Apr 1863, 48th USCI; List of Ofcrs, 10 Apr 1863, 47th USCI; Capt S. B. Ferguson to Lt Col J. A. Rawlins, 3 Jul 1863, 49th USCI; List of Ofcrs, n.d., 51st USCI; Col G. M. Ziegler to Brig Gen L. Thomas, 5 Aug 1863, 52d USCI; Capt R. H. Ballinger to [Brig Gen J. P. Osterhaus], 19 May 1863, 53d USCI, misfiled with 51st USCI; Dist of Corinth, SO 189, 18 May 1863, 55th USCI; all in Entry 57C, RG 94, NA.

Union troops occupied the Mississippi River landing at Lake Providence, Louisiana, in February 1863, as part of their advance on Vicksburg. It was here three months later that Adjutant General Lorenzo Thomas organized one of the earliest black regiments (the 8th Louisiana, later the 47th U.S. Colored Infantry).

five dollars, and a child between the ages of twelve and fifteen half the wage of an adult. Troops would protect the plantations only if they could be spared from offensive operations. The adjutant general believed that plantation residents, given arms, could defend themselves. He did not mention explicitly that plantation work would help to empty the contraband camps and shift the burden of caring for soldiers' families from the government to "private enterprise"; that was the tendency of federal policy toward "employment and subsistence of negroes" in general.[34] The division of authority that prevailed in South Carolina, between the Treasury and War Departments on the federal side and between charitable organizations and "enterprising men" on the private side, was about to be imposed on the Mississippi Valley.

When Thomas wrote to Stanton again on 22 April, a board he had appointed to lease abandoned plantations had approved eleven lessees and Grant's army was on the move against Vicksburg. Although Thomas continued to address mass meetings of troops whenever he could, resumption of active operations tended to slow the organization of new regiments. "It is important for protection here that the Regiments in course of construction be rapidly filled," he wrote to Grant from Milliken's Bend early in May. One method, he suggested, was to seek po-

---

[34] Draft of order, n.d. [12 or 13 Apr 1863], Entry 159BB, RG 94, NA.

tential black recruits in the camps of white regiments, "where there seem to be so many in excess as waiters and hangers on to those who are not authorized to have them." Putting white soldiers' personal servants in uniform, he told Grant, "will rid you of a good many mouths to feed." Grant assured Halleck that corps commanders in the Army of the Tennessee would "take hold of the new policy of arming the negroes . . . with a will." It was not to be a matter of preference; they would follow orders. Grant added that he intended to further black enlistment "to the best of my ability."[35]

Lower-ranking officers sometimes sought to turn the policy to their own advantage. One brigade commander planned to attach a company of black soldiers to each of his white regiments for fatigue duty. Thomas disapproved the scheme. Late in the summer, one of his own plantation commissioners asked that the 1st Arkansas (AD) return to Helena to protect cotton growers along the river from guerrilla raids. The regiment stayed in Louisiana.[36]

Officers for the new black regiments were close at hand, since they came from white regiments stationed near contraband camps where they would find recruits. Determining their knowledge and abilities, however, sometimes took months. At Helena, a board to examine the colonels of the 2d and 3d Arkansas (AD) and the adjutant of the 3d did not convene till January 1864. One colonel was discharged, and the other resigned within weeks of the examination, but the adjutant held his job until the regiment mustered out in September 1866.[37]

The new officers' abilities varied, but their attitudes toward the men they would lead typified opinion in the vast region from which they came. Regiments in the Army of the Tennessee represented every state from West Virginia to Kansas, from Tennessee to Minnesota. Men from these regiments might accept commissions in the U.S. Colored Troops out of a sense of duty or because they yearned for the higher pay officers received and the better living conditions they enjoyed. Even those of firm antislavery convictions could also view black people as pawns in the sectional struggle, or even as stock minstrel-show characters.

One young nominee, Pvt. Samuel Evans of the 70th Ohio, tried in mid-May to explain to his father his reasons for accepting an appointment in the 1st Tennessee (AD). General Thomas had addressed troops in southwestern Tennessee "day before yesterday and . . . said the aim of the President was to make the Negro self *sustaining*. . . . My doctrine is that a Negro is no better than a white man and will do as well to receive Reble bullets and would be likely to save the life of a white man. . . . I am not much inclined to think they will *fight* as *some* of our white Regts, but men who will stand up to the mark may succeed in making them of some benefit to the Government." Evans' new company already had seventy men. "We have been drilling them some, they learn the school of a

---

[35] *OR*, ser. 1, vol. 24, pt. 1, p. 31 ("take hold"). Brig Gen L. Thomas to E. M. Stanton, 22 Apr 1863, and to Maj Gen U. S. Grant, 9 May 1863 ("It is important"), both in Entry 159BB, RG 94, NA.

[36] Brig Gen L. Thomas to Col W. W. Sanford, 19 May 1863, Entry 159BB, RG 94, NA; S. Sawyer to Brig Gen L. Thomas, 16 Aug 1863, 46th USCI, Entry 57C, RG 94, NA.

[37] Dist of Eastern Arkansas, SO 15, 15 Jan 1864, 56th USCI, Entry 57C, RG 94, NA; *Official Army Register of the Volunteer Force of the United States Army*, 8 vols. (Washington, D.C.: Adjutant General's Office, 1867), 8: 227, 229 (hereafter cited as *ORVF*).

soldier much readier than I anticipated," he wrote, which was not surprising in the light of his low expectations.[38]

Evans' father did not sanction his son's decision. "So far as a sense of duty is concerned I feel perfectly easy," Evans wrote to his brother.

> But I cannot be as well satisfied as if I had his approval. . . . When I was a private in the 70th I . . . was then doing my duty or what I thought was. Now duty calls me . . . to take a place where I could do more good [or] rather make a class of Human beings who were an expense to the Government of an advantage. . . . In the mean time I [would] be pleased if Father were better satisfied. I am sure no one thinks any the less of him because I am where I am. . . . In a logical point of view what is the conclusion we arrive at? That a Negro is no better than a white man and has just as good a right to fight for his freedom and the government. Some body must direct [these] men. Shall I require . . . some one to do what I would not myself condescend to do[?]

After a month of drilling his company, sometimes commanding it while the other officers made recruiting trips through the surrounding country, Evans told his father, "I am pretty well satisfied that Negros can be made to fight."[39]

While Grant's Vicksburg Campaign was in preparation, Sgt. William M. Parkinson of the 11th Illinois complained about the duties his regiment had to perform: "Working on the canal, standing Picket, & making roads. I cannot immagine why they do not have negroes to do it, especially in a Country like this, Where every person is secesh and have plenty of negroes, and why not take them and put them at work[?]" Parkinson thought the Emancipation Proclamation "does the negro neither harm nor good. . . . I am in favor of taking *every* negro, & making him fight." When he accepted an appointment in the 8th Louisiana (AD), he asked his wife and daughter: "Now Sarah what do you think of William M. Parkinson, being Captain of a negro Regt[?] Zetty, what do you say to it, ain't you afraid your pa will get black[?] Sometimes I think I did wrong in offering myself, but I am into it now and if I succeed in raising about seventy darkeys, I will be a Captain." Parkinson got his recruits, became a captain, and after a few days' drill, wrote that the men "learn very fast, faster than any white men I ever saw."[40]

When Sgt. Jacob Bruner of the 68th Ohio wrote to his wife from Mississippi in the first week of January 1863, he was more concerned with whether General Sherman's Chickasaw Bluffs expedition would lead to the fall of Vicksburg and an early Confederate collapse than he was with emancipation. "For my part I do not care whether they are free or not. . . . [I]f general emancipation takes place they will swarm to the north by thousands much to the detriment of poor white laborers. I hold it is the imperative duty of the United States government to send them

---

[38] S. Evans to Dear Father, 17 May 1863, Evans Family Papers, Ohio Historical Society (OHS), Columbus.

[39] S. Evans to Dear Brother, 9 Jun 1863 ("So far as"); S. Evans to Dear Father, 14 Jun 1863 ("I am pretty"); both in Evans Family Papers.

[40] W. M. Parkinson to ——, 11 Feb 1863 ("Working on"); to Sarah Ann, 24 Feb 1863 ("does the negro"); to Dear Sarah, 13 Apr 1863 ("Now Sarah"); to Sarah Ann, 19 Apr 1863 ("learn very"); all in W. M. Parkinson Letters, Emory University, Atlanta.

Vicksburg, viewed from the Mississippi River. On the horizon stands the Warren County Court House, completed in 1860.

out of the country and colonize them." The Chickasaw Bluffs expedition failed, and Bruner was in northeastern Louisiana three months later when he told his wife about General Thomas' visit. "Uncle Abe has at last sensibly concluded to arm the darkey and let him fight," he wrote. After being appointed a lieutenant in the 9th Louisiana (AD), he told her, "My wages will be . . . thirteen hundred and twenty six dollars a year! . . . [N]ow my dear what do you think of it did I meet your approbation in accepting?"[41]

By the time black recruiting got under way in the Mississippi Valley, the previous year's federal advance into northern Alabama, Mississippi, and Arkansas and a subsequent retreat before a Confederate counteroffensive in the fall had caused tens of thousands of black Southerners to leave home and follow the Union Army. Many were men of military age, ready to volunteer or to be coerced into uniform. By the end of May 1863, six new regiments had organized at towns and steamboat landings along the Mississippi River and at the rail junction in Corinth, Mississippi. Two more were recruiting. In June, four more began to form at Columbus, Kentucky, and La Grange and Memphis, Tennessee. The main federal effort that spring was Grant's campaign against Vicksburg. When that Confederate stronghold fell, more extensive efforts to raise black regiments could go forward.

Well to the rear of the Union advance, the enlistment and organization of black soldiers took a different shape. Tennessee, for instance, was exempt from the provisions of the Emancipation Proclamation. Just one day after the secretary of war dispatched Adjutant General Thomas to Cairo and points south, the president wrote to Johnson, the military governor of Tennessee, urging the necessity of "raising a negro military force." Johnson was an East Tennessee Democrat who declared for the Union, the only U.S. senator who did not resign his seat when his state seceded. Soon after Union troops occupied Nashville in February 1862, Lincoln appointed him a brigadier general of volunteers and put him in charge of Tennessee's recon-

---

[41]J. Bruner to Dear Martha, 3 Jan 1863 ("For my part"); to Dear Wife, 9 Apr 1863 ("Uncle Abe"); to Martha, 15 Apr 1863 ("My wages"); all in J. Bruner Papers, OHS.

struction. "The colored population is the great available . . . force for restoring the Union," the president told Johnson in March 1863. "The bare sight of 50,000 armed and drilled black soldiers upon the banks of the Mississippi would end the rebellion at once. And who doubts that we can present that sight if we but take hold in earnest?" There is no record of Johnson's reply, but he was among the least likely of Union officials to implement a policy of arming black people. Two days after the president's note of 26 March, the secretary of war gave Johnson authority to raise twenty regiments of cavalry and infantry and ten batteries of artillery, but apart from those General Thomas organized west of the Tennessee River, the state did not contribute any new regiments to the Union cause until summer. All six of them were white.[42]

In Missouri and Kentucky, which had not seceded and therefore lay outside the scope of the Emancipation Proclamation, efforts to recruit black soldiers barely existed. The question of slavery caused bitter divisions among Missouri's population. Raids and counterraids by pro-Confederate guerrillas and pro-Union (but also largely pro-slavery) state militia characterized the war there. During four years of fighting, the opposing sides met in 1,162 armed clashes, the third largest total of any state. Only Tennessee and Virginia, which suffered campaigns by the main armies of both sides, endured more. As a result, even a staunch Republican like General Samuel Curtis, who commanded the Department of the Missouri in the spring of 1863, moved cautiously. "We must not throw away any of our Union strength," he wrote to a Union sympathizer in St. Joseph. "*Bona fide* Union men must be treasured as friends, although they may be pro-slavery. . . . Slavery exists in Missouri, and it may continue for some time, in spite of all our emancipation friends can do. While it exists we must tolerate it, and we must allow the civil authorities to dispose of the question."[43]

Since Missouri lay north and west of most major military operations, scarce federal resources were stretched to the limit there. Kentucky, on the other hand, lay squarely between the Northern states and the main Union armies invading the central South. In order to secure their supply routes, federal officials tried not to annoy the state's Unionist slaveholders unless it was to draft slave labor for military construction projects. Efforts to enlist black Kentuckians for the Army remained entirely out of the question in the spring of 1863.[44]

In the seceded states along the Mississippi River, recruiting was slow during early spring because much of the country was under water. John L. Mathews, an Iowa infantryman who would accept a lieutenancy in the 8th Louisiana (AD), awoke one March morning to find himself surrounded by the river's overflow. Mathews, like many Union soldiers, was bemused by the southern climate, flora, and fauna and wrote that the Mississippi "had made an island of our little camp and

---

[42] *OR*, ser. 3, 3: 103 (quotations), 105–06; Leroy P. Graf et al., eds., *The Papers of Andrew Johnson*, 16 vols. (Knoxville: University of Tennessee Press, 1967–2000), 3: 195, 213; Peter Maslowski, *Treason Must Be Made Odious: Military Occupation and Wartime Reconstruction in Nashville, Tennessee, 1862–1865* (Millbrook, N.Y.: KTO Press, 1978), pp. 19–26; Dyer, *Compendium*, pp. 1639–41.

[43] *OR*, ser. 1, vol. 22, pt. 2, pp. 134–35 (quotation); Dyer, *Compendium*, p. 582. Virginia was the scene of 2,154 engagements; Tennessee, 1,462. Mississippi (772) and Arkansas (771) were next.

[44] *WGFL: US*, pp. 627–28.

left us as lonesome as an alligator on a sand bank." Brig. Gen. Peter J. Osterhaus called one Union outpost in northeastern Louisiana "perfectly secure, as only the levee is out of water, and [it] cannot be flanked." But while the enemy could not move, neither could recruiters for the new black regiments.[45]

By late April, the water had subsided enough for Grant's main army to cross the Mississippi and begin the campaign against Vicksburg. As the army advanced, officers who had been appointed to the new black regiments began to look for recruits. The 9th Louisiana (AD) at Milliken's Bend numbered about one hundred men at the end of April, enough for two minimum-strength companies. "We drill twice each day," 1st Lt. Jacob Bruner told his wife.

> They learn very fast and I have no doubt they will make as rapid progress as white soldiers. As fast as we get them we clothe them from head to foot in precisely the same uniform that "our boys" wear, give them tents, rations and Blankets and they are highly pleased and hardly know themselves. The company non-commissioned officers will be *colored* except the [First] Serg't. I am happy and think myself fortunate in enjoying so much of the confidence of my country and the President to be able to assist in this new and as I believe successful experiment.[46]

When white officers' exhortations failed to persuade black men to enlist, 1st Lt. David Cornwell of the 9th Louisiana (AD) promoted one of his recruits to sergeant and took him to visit neighboring plantations. Sgt. Jack Jackson was eager to wield authority and acted like a one-man press gang, ordering plantation hands to fall in and join the column, thus securing sixty recruits during a four-day walking tour of the country around Milliken's Bend. The sergeant's approach to his duties grew out of his experience in a world where authority was immediate and personal, but his method of recruiting was common among white Northerners too. When the 11th Louisiana (AD), also headquartered at Milliken's Bend, ordered its officers to "make *every* exertion to procure recruits," the implication was clear.[47]

The result was a body of men whose expectations of the freedom that had come to them so recently hardly matched the realities of military service. "The negroes are a *great deal* of trouble," Capt. William M. Parkinson wrote home from the camp of the 8th Louisiana (AD).

> They are very ignorant, and they expected too much. They thought they would be perfectly free when they became soldiers, and could almost quit soldiering whenever they got tired of it, & could come and go as they pleased. But they find

---

[45] *OR*, ser. 1, vol. 24, pt. 1, p. 490 ("perfectly secure"); J. L. Mathews to Most Ancient and Well-Esteemed Jonadab C., 15 Mar 1863 ("had made"), J. L. Mathews Papers, State Historical Society of Iowa, Iowa City.

[46] J. Bruner to Dear Wife, 28 Apr 1863, Bruner Papers.

[47] John Wearmouth, ed., *The Cornwell Chronicles: Tales of an American Life . . . in the Volunteer Civil War Western Army . . .* (Bowie, Md.: Heritage Books, 1998), pp. 196–99; Anthony E. Kaye, "Slaves, Emancipation, and the Powers of War: Views from the Natchez District of Mississippi," in *The War Was You and Me: Civilians in the American Civil War*, ed. Joan E. Cashin (Princeton, Princeton University Press, 2002): 60–84, esp. pp. 61, 66–67; 11th Louisiana Inf, SO 2, 3 May 1863 (quotation), 49th USCI, Entry 57C, RG 94, NA.

they are very much mistaken. It is very hard to make them understand that they are *bound* to stay and soldier until discharged, and they [still] do not know . . . that it is for three years. But we are gradually letting them know it. We did not force one of them to come into the Regiment. I believe though if we had told them it was for three years, every one of them would [have to have] been forced in.

As the war entered its third year, recruiters for black regiments were not alone in using less-than-honest methods. In 1862, James H. Lane had resorted to "a good deal of humbug" to fill the ranks of his Kansas regiments, black and white alike.[48]

Ruthless recruiting methods filled the ranks of the new black regiments, but officers were often dissatisfied with men who had been confined all their lives to the limits of a large plantation. Captain Parkinson, drilling his company at Lake Providence, Louisiana, thought it "no small job to take charge of eighty or ninety ignorant negroes. It requires all the patience I can muster to get along without cursing them." Still, he reflected, "I believe our negroes will fight as well as white men that have [been] soldiers no longer than they have."[49]

Parkinson managed to control his temper, but his second in command, 1st Lt. Hamilton H. McAleney, did not. The men disliked McAleney, Parkinson told his wife: "He curses them when they do wrong. *I am going to stop it.* I treat them like soldiers, and I make them mind, and if they do not, I put them on extra duty till they are glad to mind me." He thought of getting rid of McAleney somehow, which would offer promotion to 2d Lt. Frederick Smith, "a good drill master, better than I am." The vacant second lieutenancy could then go to 1st Sgt. Silas L. Baltzell, who "does first rate, and gets along with the colored boys very well. His great fault is he is too familiar & good to them." Before Parkinson could act, McAleney received a promotion to captain that created vacancies for the other two men. Parkinson's judgment of his colleagues owed much to the fact that he, McAleney, and Baltzell had all served as enlisted men in the 11th Illinois (Parkinson and Baltzell in the same company). This was a common occurrence in the 8th Louisiana, which was staffed almost entirely from the Army of the Tennessee's 6th Division.[50]

Some officers wondered whether they would be able to control their own troops in the heat of battle. If Union attackers gained the upper hand, Parkinson worried, "I do not believe we can keep the negroes from murdering every thing they come to and I do not think the Rebels will ever take pris[o]ners." One white soldier predicted that the new regiments would be "the greatest terror to the—— rebels. They have old scores to mend, and I assure you there will be no sympathy, or no quarter on either side." General Sherman foresaw increased violence inspired by fear on both sides. "I know well the animus of the Southern soldiery," he told Secretary of War Stanton, "And the truth is they cannot be restrained.

---

[48]Berlin et al., *Black Military Experience*, pp. 410–11, 434–35; W. M. Parkinson to My Wife, 17 May 1863 ("The negroes"), Parkinson Letters; Castel, *Frontier State at War*, p. 90 ("a good deal").

[49]W. M. Parkinson to James, 11 May 1863 ("no small"), and to Lee, 9 May 1863 ("I believe"), both in Parkinson Letters.

[50]Parkinson to Sarah Ann, 24 Feb and 19 Apr 1863; to Lee, 9 May 1863 ("does first"); and to Sarah A., 28 May 1863 ("He curses"), Parkinson Letters. SO 5, Lake Providence, 10 Apr 1863, 47th USCI, Entry 57C, RG 94, NA; *ORVF*, 8: 220.

The effect of course will be to make the negroes desperate, and when in turn they commit horrid acts of retaliation we will be relieved of the responsibility. Thus far negroes have been comparatively well behaved. . . . The Southern army, which is the Southern people, . . . will heed the slaughter that will follow as the natural consequence of their own inhuman acts."[51]

The new black regiments in northeastern Louisiana formed a command known as the African Brigade. Its leader was Brig. Gen. John P. Hawkins, a 33-year-old West Point graduate from Indiana. At the beginning of the war, Hawkins had transferred from a regular infantry regiment to the Subsistence Department; in April 1863, he received promotion from lieutenant colonel to brigadier general in order to lead the African Brigade. It is hard to tell what it was in his background that fitted him for the job of organizing and leading black troops; but Charles A. Dana, the secretary of war's confidential agent with Grant's army, reported that he "[did] not know here an officer who could do the duty half as well as [Hawkins]. . . . [N]one but a man of the very highest qualities can succeed in the work."[52]

A year's service in the lower Mississippi Valley had taken its toll on Hawkins' health; on 11 May, he went on sick leave, relinquishing command of the brigade to Col. Isaac F. Shepard of the 1st Mississippi (AD). Two weeks later, Shepard sent Adjutant General Thomas a long letter in which he reported "good progress" in organizing the regiments. The 1st Arkansas had nearly reached its authorized maximum strength, he said, and the 8th and 10th Louisiana each had seven or eight hundred men. There was some difficulty in the 9th Louisiana, where the commanding officer had distributed arriving recruits evenly among the companies. The result was that the regiment had ten companies, none of which had the statutory minimum number of men necessary to muster into service. The colonel had not realized that pay began only when a company mustered in, not at the time of a man's enlistment or an officer's appointment. The commanding officer of the 11th Louisiana was going about his job correctly, Shepard went on, and his regiment had four full companies mustered in and 361 recruits waiting for medical inspection. Shepard's own regiment had only one company mustered in. His officers had not yet reported, and he did not know whether they were still with their old regiments at the siege of Vicksburg. Still, he was not discouraged, for black recruits were arriving at Milliken's Bend "on the average of at least 75 daily."[53]

Less encouraging was the difficulty Shepard had in feeding and supplying the new regiments. Some of his requisitions were disregarded because they lacked the signature of a general officer. The quartermaster at Young's Point, who had uniforms for three regiments, refused to release them to anyone except a regularly appointed officer of the Quartermaster Department, certainly not to the lieutenant from Shepard's old regiment, the 3d Missouri, whom the colonel had detailed as his new brigade quartermaster. The 10th Louisiana sent its regimental quartermas-

---

[51]*OR*, ser. 1, vol. 32, pt. 3, p. 464 ("I know well"); Parkinson to My Wife, 17 May 1863 ("I do not"); *Janesville* [Wis.] *Daily Gazette*, 26 June 1863 ("the greatest").

[52]*OR*, ser. 1, vol. 24, pt. 1, p. 106 (quotation); on Dana, see Thomas and Hyman, *Stanton*, pp. 267–69.

[53]Col I. F. Shepard to Brig Gen L. Thomas, 24 May 1863, Entry 2014, Dist of Northeast Louisiana, Letters Sent, pt. 2, Polyonymous Successions of Cmds, RG 393, Rcds of U.S. Army Continental Cmds, NA.

ter to Memphis "and drew a full equipment of everything." If the Young's Point quartermaster did not cease quibbling, Shepard told the adjutant general, he would order the other regiments to draw supplies at Memphis as well. Despite these difficulties, he thought that the new soldiers' "progress in instruction [was] truly wonderful. I witnessed an evening parade which would have been no discredit to many old regiments."[54]

Many officers agreed that the recruits adapted well to army life. They were less pleased, though, with the quality of weapons provided for the new troops. Armies on both sides in the war used the Lorenz rifle, with the North alone buying more than 226,000 in various calibers from Austrian manufacturers. The new black regiments along the Mississippi received the .58-caliber model. One colonel called it "an inferior arm, but the best that could be had." Captain Parkinson of the 8th Louisiana (AD) called the weapons "good second class guns." Parkinson's regiment got its rifles the second week in May. The one hundred fifty men of the 1st Mississippi (AD), twenty miles downriver at Milliken's Bend, did not receive theirs until 6 June.[55]

The African Brigade drilled in camps along the Mississippi while Grant's Army of the Tennessee crossed the river south of Vicksburg and marched northeast to Jackson, then west toward Vicksburg, beating the Confederate opposition five times in three weeks. This rapid movement came at the end of four months that the army had spent relatively immobile as it searched for a route that led through the flooded Louisiana countryside to the river south of Vicksburg. While Grant's soldiers negotiated the swamps, the general moved his headquarters to Milliken's Bend, a steamboat landing upstream from the objective, on the opposite bank. The Army of the Tennessee began its campaign at the end of April, leaving the Louisiana side of the river in the care of four thousand recently arrived white troops and the half-dozen new black regiments that were still struggling to organize (*Table 1*).[56]

Throughout May, officers appointed by Adjutant General Thomas to lead the new regiments arrived at landings along the river and began searching the surrounding country for recruits. By early June, the four black regiments that were organizing at Milliken's Bend—the 1st Mississippi (AD) and the 9th, 11th, and 13th Louisiana (AD)—numbered nearly one thousand men. For those among them who had weapons, musketry instruction had begun only in the last week of May.[57]

By then, Grant's army had Vicksburg hemmed in, but the Confederate Maj. Gen. Richard Taylor, commanding the District of West Louisiana, hoped to disrupt the federal supply line and raise the siege. A raid on the main Union supply

---

[54]W. M. Parkinson to Brother James, 28 May 1863, Parkinson Letters. Col I. F. Shepard to Brig Gen L. Thomas, 24 May 1863 ("and drew," "progress"), Entry 2014, pt. 2, RG 393, NA.

[55]Col J. M. Alexander to Lt Col J. H. Wilson, 10 Sep 1863 ("an inferior arm"), 55th USCI, Entry 57C, RG 94, NA. Parkinson to Brother James, 28 May 1863 ("good second"); to James, 11 May 1863. Annual Return of Alterations and Casualties for 1863, 51st USCI, Entry 57, Muster Rolls of Volunteer Organizations: Civil War, RG 94, NA; William B. Edwards, *Civil War Guns: The Complete Story of Federal and Confederate Small Arms* (Gettysburg, Pa.: Thomas Publications, 1997), p. 256.

[56]*OR*, ser. 1, vol. 24, pt. 3, pp. 249, 251.

[57]Ibid., pt. 2, p. 447; Wearmouth, *Cornwell Chronicles*, pp. 204–05, 211, 217.

TABLE 1—BLACK REGIMENTS ORGANIZED BY GENERAL THOMAS, MAY–DECEMBER 1863

Mustered In	Original Designation	Where Organized	USCT No. (1864)
1 May	1st Arkansas Inf (AD)	Arkansas, at large	46th USCI
1 May	9th Louisiana Inf (AD) (renamed 1st Mississippi HA [AD] in September 1864)	Milliken's Bend, La.	5th USCA
5 May	8th Louisiana Inf (AD)	Lake Providence, La.	47th USCI
6 May–8 August	10th Louisiana Inf (AD)	Lake Providence and Goodrich's Landing, La.	48th USCI
16 May	1st Mississippi Inf (AD)	Milliken's Bend, La.	51st USCI
19 May	3d Mississippi Inf (AD)	Warrenton, Miss.	53d USCI
21 May	1st Alabama Inf (AD)	Corinth, Miss.	55th USCI
23 May–22 August	11th Louisiana Inf (AD)	Milliken's Bend, La.	49th USCI
5 June–22 December	1st Tennessee HA (AD)	Memphis, Tenn.	3d USCA
6 June	1st Tennessee Inf (AD)	La Grange, Tenn.	59th USCI
6 June 1863– 19 April 1864	2d Tennessee HA (AD)	Columbus, Ky.	4th USCA
20 June	1st Alabama Siege Arty (AD)	La Grange, Lafayette, Memphis, Tenn.; and Corinth, Miss.	7th USCA
30 June	2d Tennessee Inf (AD)	La Grange, Tenn.	61st USCI
27 July	2d Mississippi Inf (AD)	Vicksburg, Miss.	52d USCI
12 August	3d Arkansas Inf (AD)	St. Louis, Mo.	56th USCI
27 August	6th Mississippi Inf (AD)	Natchez, Miss.	58th USCI
4 September	2d Arkansas Inf (AD)	Arkansas, at large	54th USCI
12 September	2d Mississippi HA (AD)	Natchez, Miss.	6th USCA
26 September	1st Mississippi HA (AD)	Vicksburg, Miss.	5th USCA
9 October	1st Mississippi Cav (AD)	Vicksburg, Miss.	3d USCC
6 November	1st Btry, Louisiana Light Arty (AD)	Hebron's Plantation, Miss.	C/2d USCA
20 November	2d Alabama Inf (AD)	Pulaski, Tenn.	110th USCI
23 November	Memphis Light Btry (AD)	Memphis, Tenn.	F/2d USCA
1 December	7th Louisiana Inf (AD)	Memphis, Tenn.; Holly Springs, Miss.; and Island No. 10, Mo.	64th USCI
1 December	3d Btry, Louisiana Light Arty (AD)	Helena, Ark.	E/2d USCA
7–14 December	1st Missouri Colored Inf	St. Louis, Mo.	62d USCI
11 December	4th Mississippi Inf (AD)	Vicksburg, Miss.	66th USCI
21 December	2d Btry, Louisiana Light Arty (AD)	Black River Bridge, Miss.	D/2d USCA

AD = African Descent; Arty = Artillery; Btry = Battery; Cav = Cavalry; HA = Heavy Artillery; Inf = Infantry; USCA = United States Colored Artillery; USCC = United States Colored Cavalry; USCI = United States Colored Infantry.

Source: Frederick H. Dyer, *A Compendium of the War of the Rebellion* (New York: Thomas Yoseloff, 1959 [1909]), pp. 113, 150, 169, 175, 231–32; *Official Army Register of the Volunteer Force of the United States Army*, 8 vols. (Washington, D.C.: Adjutant General's Office, 1867), 8: 143, 149, 151.

depot in northern Mississippi the previous December had forced a four-month postponement of Grant's offensive, and Taylor thought that an attack at this critical juncture might achieve an even greater effect. In any case, Confederate troops west of the Mississippi were free to menace Union-occupied plantations that grew cotton to finance the Northern war effort and that employed, housed, clothed, and fed thousands of newly freed black people. Thomas had appointed three commissioners to oversee the operations of the plantations' Northern lessees. The commissioners appealed to Grant for protection, but he had no troops to spare from the Vicksburg Campaign.[58]

On 3 June, part of a Confederate cavalry battalion occupied the village of Richmond, Louisiana, about ten miles southwest of Milliken's Bend. The next day, a sixty-man company of the same battalion attacked what General Taylor called "a negro camp on Lake Saint Joseph," some twenty-five miles south of Richmond. From Taylor's brief description of the action, it is impossible to tell whether the camp was a settlement of freedpeople with a white superintendent or a military recruiting party with a white officer. The Confederates reported killing thirteen men, including the officer, and capturing some sixty-five men and sixty women and children. Their scouts found that Union garrisons had abandoned other plantations and landing sites along the river downstream from Milliken's Bend.[59]

At daybreak on 6 June, Col. Herman Leib of the 9th Louisiana (AD) led all ten understrength companies of his regiment out of their camp at Milliken's Bend on a reconnaissance toward Richmond. Two companies of the 10th Illinois Cavalry rode a little ahead of them. Near a railroad depot about three miles from Richmond, the 9th Louisiana scattered the enemy's pickets without much trouble. Soon afterward, a local black resident showed the colonel where a force of enemy cavalry was gathering to attack. Leib reversed his column and began to withdraw. The enemy routed the Illinois cavalrymen, who were now in the 9th Louisiana's rear, but their flight gave the infantry enough warning to form line of battle and discourage the advancing Confederates with one volley. Lieutenant Cornwell called it a "harmless volley" that caused no Confederate casualties because "our men could not hit anything smaller than all out-of-doors." Indeed, it was just as well that the troops did not have to reload and fire a second volley, for they had received less than two weeks' musketry instruction. When the expedition returned to camp, Leib asked Brig. Gen. Elias S. Dennis, commanding the District of Northeast Louisiana, for reinforcements.[60]

While the 9th Louisiana marched to Richmond and back, a new Confederate division was approaching the Mississippi from the west. Led by Maj. Gen. John G. Walker, it was composed entirely of Texas regiments that had been in service

[58] OR, ser. 1, vol. 24, pt. 2, pp. 455–56; Richard Lowe, *Walker's Texas Division C.S.A.: Greyhounds of the Trans-Mississippi* (Baton Rouge: Louisiana State University Press, 2004), pp. 79–81; *Grant Papers*, 8: 355–56.

[59] OR, ser. 1, vol. 24, pt. 2, p. 457.

[60] Ibid., p. 447; Wearmouth, *Cornwell Chronicles*, pp. 207–09 (quotations, p. 209), 216. Published sources spell the colonel's name variously as "Leib" or "Lieb," but his signature reads unmistakably "Leib." NA Microfilm Pub M1818, Compiled Mil Svc Rcds of Volunteer Union Soldiers Who Served with U.S. Colored Troops, roll 94.

for more than a year but had never fought a battle. General Taylor sent it to attack the Union garrisons at Milliken's Bend and at Young's Point, which lay some ten miles downstream, halfway between Milliken's Bend and Vicksburg. Capture of these posts would give the Confederates control of the west bank of the river and allow them to reopen communications with their besieged troops in Vicksburg and possibly to resupply them. General Walker would send one of his brigades to Young's Point and keep another in reserve. The third brigade, led by Brig. Gen. Henry E. McCulloch, cooked two days' rations that afternoon and moved toward Milliken's Bend about 7:00 p.m. Making a night march to avoid the heat, McCulloch planned to attack before broad daylight exposed his men to fire from Union gunboats in the river.[61]

On the afternoon of 6 June, General Dennis ordered the skeletal 23d Iowa, which had suffered heavy losses during Grant's advance on Vicksburg, to reinforce the African Brigade. Dennis also asked Rear Adm. David D. Porter, commanding the U.S. Navy's Mississippi Squadron, for assistance. By nightfall, most of the tiny regiment was ashore at Milliken's Bend and the gunboats USS *Choctaw* and *Lexington* were en route. The Union camp contained more than nine hundred soldiers of the new black regiments and more than one hundred from the 23d Iowa. Just off the boat, the Iowans had not had time to pitch their tents, but the camp of the other regiments occupied about a quarter of a mile of the flood plain. At the water's edge was a natural levee of sediment deposits that rose some fifteen feet above the level of the river. Along the camp's eastern edge ran a manmade levee, between six and ten feet high and broad enough along its crown to accommodate a wagon road. Inland, a farmer had enclosed some pastureland with several rows of hedge trees (bois d'arc or Osage orange). Beyond the pasture lay open fields. Colonel Leib doubled the strength of his pickets along the outer hedge of trees and stationed some mule-mounted infantry about a mile beyond the picket line. McCulloch's fifteen hundred Texans arrived well before dawn the next day.[62]

The Union pickets retreated before the Confederate advance, and Leib ordered his men into a line of rifle pits screened by logs and brush that ran along the crown of the manmade levee where Colonel Shepard of the 1st Mississippi stood. As the sky lightened after 4:30, Shepard saw a body of troops moving toward him. He thought they were his own pickets coming in, but "to my surprize they . . . deliberately halted, came to the front, and marched directly upon us in line of battle, solid, strong and steady." Lieutenant Cornwell watched them form at the far end of the pasture, their line extending "from hedge to hedge, double rank, elbow to elbow. They soon commenced advancing over this smooth open

---

[61] *OR*, ser. 1, vol. 24, pt. 2, pp. 458–59.

[62] Estimates of the strength of the 23d Iowa vary from 105 to 140. *OR*, ser. 1, vol. 24, pt. 2, pp. 463, 467; M. C. Brown to Dear Parents, 12 Jun 1863, M. C. Brown and J. C. Brown Papers, Library of Congress (LC); Wearmouth, *Cornwell Chronicles*, p. 211; Cyrus Sears, *Paper of Cyrus Sears* (Columbus, Ohio: F. J. Heer, 1909), p. 13. The Confederate commander said the Union pickets opened fire about 2:30 a.m.; Colonel Leib reported hearing shots "a few minutes after" 2:53; a Union officer on shore notified Lt. Cdr. F. M. Ramsay aboard the *Choctaw* at 3:15. *OR*, ser. 1, vol. 24, pt. 2, pp. 467–69; Wearmouth, *Cornwell Chronicles*, pp. 207, 216–17; *ORN*, ser. 1, 25: 163.

field, without an obstacle to break their step." He thought that "they had the appearance of a brigade on drill."[63]

The Confederate line crumbled when it came to the hedge of trees at the end of the pasture, where the Union garrison had cut several openings to clear a firing range for target practice. The Confederates had to make their way through these holes "the best they could," General McCulloch reported, "but never fronting more than half a company," perhaps twenty or thirty men in line, before they could resume the advance. Beyond the hedge, they found themselves about twenty-five yards from the levee's base.[64]

The defenders opened fire, but most of their shots "went into the air," Lieutenant Cornwell wrote; before many of the novice soldiers could reload, the Confederates were among them. It was during this five-minute struggle that both sides incurred most of their casualties. Cornwell led about sixty men of the 9th Louisiana (AD) in a counterattack meant to stiffen the Union left, but after a hand-to-hand contest with bayonets and the butts of unloaded rifles, the center of the line gave way and the survivors scrambled for safety on the riverbank.[65]

Until this moment, the crews of the *Choctaw* and *Lexington* in the river below had not been able to see the Union troops on the flood plain, fifteen feet above the water, much less to assist them by firing on their attackers. With the survivors of the fight in plain view on the bank, the boats fired enough shells to keep the Confederates from a further, final advance but only after a few rounds landed among the retreating defenders. "The gun-boat men mistook a body of our men for rebels and made a target of them for several shots before we could signal them off," Lt. Col. Cyrus Sears of the 11th Louisiana (AD) recalled years later. While "our navy did some real execution at Milliken's Bend," he wrote, "I never heard they killed or wounded any of the enemy." The Confederates reckoned their casualties as 184, the vast majority of which must have come during the hand-to-hand struggle on the levee. The Union gunboats did not figure in the Confederate brigade commander's report at all, while the division commander mentioned them only as his reason for breaking off the engagement and withdrawing his troops after several hours' sniping back and forth between the Yankees on the riverbank and his own men, who were firing from the levee they had just captured.[66]

A few days after the fight, 2d Lt. Matthew C. Brown of the 23d Iowa told his parents that his regiment held "until the negroes on our left gave way." Colonel Shepard claimed the opposite, that the 23d Iowa received the Confederate charge

[63]Wearmouth, *Cornwell Chronicles*, pp. 211 ("they had"), 217; Col I. F. Shepard to Brig Gen L. Thomas, 23 Jun 1863 ("to my surprise"), filed with S–13–CT–1863, Entry 360, Colored Troops Div, Letters Received, RG 94, NA.

[64]*OR*, ser. 1, vol. 24, pt. 2, p. 467.

[65]Wearmouth, *Cornwell Chronicles*, pp. 211–13 (quotation, p. 212); Brown to Dear Parents, 12 Jun 1863.

[66]Sears, *Paper*, p. 16 ("The gun-boat"); *OR*, ser. 1, vol. 24, pt. 2, pp. 462–70. The course of that day's events at Milliken's Bend is hard to reconstruct. The volumes of the *Official Records* do not include Colonel Leib's report, only that of the district commander, General Dennis, who was not present. Cornwell, who had a copy of Leib's report, wrote in later years that Dennis framed his report "very nearly in identical language." The near plagiarism led Cornwell to call Dennis' report "a contemptible fraud." Wearmouth, *Cornwell Chronicles*, pp. 215–16. Colonel Sears also had a copy of Leib's report. Both he and Cornwell quoted it at length in their published and unpublished works and used it to attack each other's veracity—Sears in a speech to the Loyal Legion, a veterans'

before it had a chance to form properly and so gave way, taking with it the neighboring black regiments "like the foot of a compass swinging on its center." Whether either officer stood where he could see for more than a few yards in any direction or had more than a few seconds at a time for observation is open to question. According to Leib's report, as quoted by Cornwell and Sears, the regiment to the left of the 23d Iowa was the 13th Louisiana (AD). The monthly post return for Milliken's Bend noted that the 13th had "no legal organization." Apparently, a local commander had begun recruiting without bothering to learn whether Adjutant General Thomas had authorized the regiment. Although a few officers were assigned to it, only some of them reported for duty and it disbanded at the end of July.[67]

More than one Union regiment had a shadowy organization that day. Because of its commanding officer's erroneous ideas about apportioning recruits, of which Colonel Shepard had complained to Thomas, the 9th Louisiana went into action without having been mustered. The regiment's aggressive recruiter, Sergeant Jackson, fought furiously on the levee until he was killed. His name appears at the head of the regiment's roll of men killed in action that year, but because systematic recordkeeping began only when the 9th Louisiana (AD) mustered into federal service that August as the 1st Mississippi Heavy Artillery (AD), nothing more of him survives than what Cornwell's account of the battle tells.[68]

The *Anglo-African*, a weekly newspaper published in New York City, printed a letter about the battle that contained an interesting remark. The writer, who identified himself only as "a soldier of Grant's army," claimed to have been an eyewitness. After the battle, he wrote, he asked Maj. Erastus N. Owen of the 9th Louisiana (AD) why his soldiers had fired so little and fought with clubbed rifles and bayonets. Owen replied that they had received their arms only a day or two earlier, and that many of them had loaded backward, putting the ball in first and making their weapons inoperable. Incidents like this occurred on both sides among troops going into battle for the first time.[69]

In June 1863, the 13th Louisiana had only two officers and an assistant surgeon present to command a force that according to Leib's report included about one hundred enlisted men. The 1st Mississippi was in similar shape, with three officers for one hundred fifty men. With so few officers to manage so many uninstructed recruits, the men of the two regiments can hardly be blamed if they

---

group, in 1908 and Cornwell in a letter to the *National Tribune*, a veterans' weekly, earlier that year (13 February 1908). Cornwell also left a memoir that his grandson published as *The Cornwell Chronicles* in 1998.

[67] Brown to Dear Parents, 12 Jun 1863 ("until the negroes"); Col I. F. Shepard to Brig Gen L. Thomas, 23 Jun 1863 ("like the foot"); Post Returns, Milliken's Bend, Jun 1863 ("no legal organization") and Jul 1863, NA Microfilm Pub M617, Returns from U.S. Mil Posts, 1820–1916, roll 1525. The 13th Louisiana (African Descent) does not appear either in Dyer, *Compendium*, or in *ORVF*. It is listed only once in the *Official Records* among "Union forces operating against Vicksburg." *OR*, ser. 1, vol. 24, pt. 2, p. 158. See also *Grant Papers*, 8: 565–66.

[68] Wearmouth, *Cornwell Chronicles*, p. 212; Annual Return of Alterations and Casualties for 1863, 51st USCI, Entry 57, RG 94, NA.

[69] "At Milliken's Bend," *Anglo-African*, 17 October 1863; Bell I. Wiley, *The Life of Johnny Reb: The Common Soldier of the Confederacy* (Indianapolis: Bobbs-Merrill, 1943), p. 30, and *The Life of Billy Yank: The Common Soldier of the Union* (Indianapolis: Bobbs-Merrill, 1952), pp. 81–82.

broke, as Lieutenant Brown claimed they did. Colonel Leib's report gave the 13th Louisiana's casualties for the day as five wounded and those of the 1st Mississippi as twenty-six but listed none for the 23d Iowa. The 23d, he wrote, "left the field soon after the enemy got possession of the levee . . . and was seen no more." Indeed, the regiment gave way so quickly that the Confederate General McCulloch remarked that the Confederate assault "was resisted by the negro portion of the enemy's force with considerable obstinacy, while the white or true Yankee portion ran like whipped curs almost as soon as the charge was ordered."[70]

Lieutenant Brown told a different story, writing that the 23d Iowa "only fetched 40 men off the field 2/3 of us were killed and wounded." Cornwell agreed years later, calling the casualties "very severe . . . amount[ing] almost to annihilation." Pvt. Silas Shearer of the 23d Iowa, whose tally of the dead in his own company matched the official count, wrote that "about one half of those present were killed and wounded." The *Official Army Register of the Volunteer Force* shows that the 23d Iowa lost 57 officers and men killed, wounded, and missing at Milliken's Bend and a total of 107 in the Vicksburg Campaign during May. Statistical tables in the *Official Records*, though, show the regiment's losses in May as 136. The *Official Records'* statistics were published in 1889; those in the *Register of the Volunteer Force* were hastily compiled and printed in eight volumes between 1865 and 1868. Applying the discrepancy between the two figures for the 23d Iowa's casualties for May 1863 (136, the larger figure, is 127 percent of 107, the smaller) to the 57 casualties the regiment supposedly incurred at Milliken's Bend yields a total of about 72 killed, wounded, and missing. This is much closer to the two-thirds casualty rate Lieutenant Brown mentioned for the eight companies of the 23d that were present at the fight. The entire regiment, Brown told his parents, had been "reduced in the last month from 650 fighting men down to 180."[71]

Colonel Leib's report lists similar casualties for the new black regiments at Milliken's Bend: in his own regiment, the 9th Louisiana (AD), 195 casualties out of about 285 men present; in the 1st Mississippi (AD) 26 out of about 153; and in the 11th Louisiana (AD) 395 casualties out of about 685, including one officer and 242 privates missing. "I can only account for the very large number reported missing . . . by presuming that they were permitted to stray off after the action," Leib commented. It is not strange that the men of the 11th Louisiana were "permitted to stray," for their commanding officer, Col. Edwin W. Chamberlain, rowed out to the *Choctaw* at the first sign of the Confederate attack. He watched the fight from

---

[70] *OR*, ser. 1, vol. 24, pt. 2, p. 467 ("was resisted"); Annual Return of Alterations and Casualties for 1863, 51st USCI, Entry 57, RG 94, NA. Leib's report quoted in Wearmouth, *Cornwell Chronicles*, pp. 217, 219 ("left the field"); Sears, *Paper*, p. 9. On p. 11, Sears denied the existence of the 13th Louisiana, but he was wrong: the recruits and a few officers were present but untrained and barely organized. Leib gave the regiment's strength as 108, of which three were officers. I have not been able to learn whether any of the remaining 105 were white veteran soldiers assigned to the 13th as company first sergeants.

[71] *OR*, ser. 1, vol. 24, pt. 1, p. 584, and pt. 2, p. 130; Brown to Dear Parents, 12 Jun 1863 ("only fetched," "reduced"); David Cornwell, "The Battle of Milliken's Bend," *National Tribune*, 13 Feb 1908, p. 7 ("very severe"); 23d Iowa, Regimental Books, RG 94, NA; Harold D. Brinkman, ed., *Dear Companion: The Civil War Letters of Silas I. Shearer* (Ames, Iowa: Sigler Printing, 1996), p. 50; *ORVF*, 7: 282.

there, his second-in-command alleged, dressed in civilian clothing. When General Dennis heard of Chamberlain's conduct, he called it "very unsoldierlike."[72]

"About that time much chaos prevailed at Milliken's Bend," Colonel Sears reflected years after the war. "Under such circumstances it were strange if the [casualty] counts were not mixed; especially considering the very short acquaintance of the officers with their men." Not all of the missing men made their way back to their regiments after the battle. In the fall of 1865, eight released prisoners of war reported at the Vicksburg headquarters of the 49th United States Colored Infantry (USCI), successor to the 11th Louisiana (AD). Their Confederate captors had taken them to Tyler and other places in east Texas and put them to work on farms, "under guard," the regimental officers who questioned the men stated carefully. Pvt. George Washington of Company A tried to escape but "was caught by dogs and returned to work." Pvt. Nelson Washington of the same company succeeded in escaping only "about the time peace was declared." Pvt. William Hunter of Company B escaped in July 1865, just before the vanguard of Union occupiers reached Texas, and made his way to Shreveport, where federal officers arranged his transportation to Vicksburg. George Washington and the other five men gained their freedom in July, when columns of Union cavalry marched west into Texas on their way to Austin and San Antonio. In March 1866, a board of officers convened to examine the returned prisoners. All had been held "under guard," the board was careful to state, clearing the men of any suspicion of having intended to desert. The board recommended that the former captives "be restored to duty with full pay and allowances"; the eight privates, along with the rest of the 49th USCI, received final payment and discharge a few days later.[73]

The question of how the enemy would dispose of prisoners, enlisted and officer alike, had troubled many soldiers in the new black regiments. What happened at Milliken's Bend was not what anyone had expected. The Confederate General McCulloch reported that a young German-born hospital attendant fetching some water for the wounded "found himself surrounded by a company of armed negroes in full United States uniform, commanded by a Yankee captain, who took him prisoner." The captain asked where the main body of the enemy was, and how his company could rejoin the Union force. The hospital attendant dissembled and led the captain "and his entire company of 49 negroes through small gaps in thick hedges" until they were within reach of a superior Confederate force, which demanded their surrender. "Thus," McCulloch concluded, "by his shrewdness the young Dutchman released himself and threw into our hands 1 Yankee captain and 49 negroes, fully armed and equipped as soldiers, and, if such things are admissible, I think he should have a choice boy from among these fellows to cook and wash for him and his mess during the war, and to work for him as long as the negro lives." McCulloch thought the same when Capt. George T. Marold and his company captured nineteen black soldiers at the farm buildings on the Union right. "These negroes had doubtless been in the possession of the enemy," he wrote, "and would have been a clear loss to their owners but for Captain Marold; and

---

[72]*OR*, ser. 1, vol. 24, pt. 2, p. 158 ("very unsoldierlike"); Wearmouth, *Cornwell Chronicles*, pp. 218–19 (quotation, p. 219); Sears, *Paper*, p. 16. "Quite a number . . . have never been heard from," Leib wrote at the end of the year. Annual Return of Alterations and Casualties for 1863, 51st USCI, Entry 57, RG 94, NA.

[73]Sears, *Paper*, p. 12. Proceedings of a Board of Officers, 14 Mar 1866 (other quotations), and Dept of Mississippi, SO 62, 17 Mar 1866, both in 49th USCI, Entry 57C, RG 94, NA.

should they be forfeited to the Confederate States or returned to their owners, I would regard it nothing but fair to give to Captain Marold one or two of the best of them."[74]

For McCulloch, black people remained property. His superior officer, General Taylor, revealed an even more unpleasant vision when he reported a "very large number of negroes . . . killed and wounded, and, unfortunately, some 50, with 2 of their white officers, captured." Taylor asked higher headquarters for "instructions as to the disposition of these prisoners." Toward the end of the month, he received a letter from General Grant asking about the truth of a report that "a white captain and some negroes, captured at Milliken's Bend, . . . were hanged soon after." Taylor denied indignantly that his troops had perpetrated "acts disgraceful alike to humanity and to the reputation of soldiers" and promised "summary punishment" of anyone found guilty of murdering prisoners. "My orders at all times have been to treat all prisoners with every consideration," he told Grant, adding that orders issued in December 1862 required Confederate officers to deliver "negroes captured in arms" to civil authorities for punishment according to state laws against slave insurrections. Grant professed himself "truly glad" to have Taylor's denial and assured him that there had been no retaliation by federal troops against Confederate prisoners. As for the larger question of the treatment accorded to black prisoners of war, Grant did not feel competent to speak for the federal government; "but having taken the responsibility of declaring slaves free and having authorized the arming of them, I cannot see the justice of permitting one treatment for them, and another for the white soldiers." And there the matter rested, at least so far as the black soldiers captured at Milliken's Bend were concerned.[75]

As early as November 1862, the Confederate government had begun discussing what measures should be taken against black soldiers. The commanding general at Savannah reported four "negroes in federal uniforms with arms (muskets) in their hands" captured on St. Catherine's Island, Georgia. He wanted to inflict a "swift and terrible punishment" to deter slaves in the neighborhood "from following their example." The Confederate secretary of war agreed that "summary execution" was a proper response and ordered the general to "exercise [his] discretion" in punishing the prisoners, as well as "any others hereafter captured in like circumstances."[76]

The status of black prisoners of war never received a satisfactory resolution; neither did the difference between black Union soldiers who had been free before enlistment and those who had joined the army straight from slavery. Some black captives, like those of the 54th Massachusetts who were taken at Fort Wagner and at Olustee, were sent to the same Confederate camps that housed other Union prisoners of war. Southerners among the Colored Troops who had enlisted, served, and been captured not far from their peacetime homes were usually returned to their former masters. Still

[74] OR, ser. 1, vol. 24, pt. 2, pp. 468–69 ("found himself," "These negroes"); W. M. Parkinson to My Dear Wife, 28 May 1863, Parkinson Letters; Joseph T. Glatthaar, *Forged in Battle: The Civil War Alliance of Black Soldiers and White Officers* (New York: Free Press, 1990), pp. 202–04.

[75] OR, ser. 1, vol. 24, pt. 2, p. 459 ("very large"), and pt. 3, pp. 425 ("a white"), 443–44 ("acts disgraceful"). *Grant Papers*, 8: 468 ("but having"). The order is in OR, ser. 2, 5: 795–97.

[76] OR, ser. 2, 4: 945–46 ("negroes in Federal," "swift and terrible"), 954 ("summary execution"). Union reports of the operation, which do not mention any prisoners lost, are in ser. 1, 14: 189–92. The descriptive book of the 33d USCI, which records enlistments in the regiment as far back as October 1862 and whether a soldier died, was discharged, or mustered out with the regiment, does not record any men missing in November 1862, so the identity of the four captives remains unknown. 33d USCI, Regimental Books, RG 94, NA.

others, from North and South alike, were slaughtered on the battlefield by an enemy who after the war would turn lynching into a regional means of social control.[77]

Black prisoners, of course, were not alone in suffering cruel and unusual treatment during the course of the war. In July 1864, when the city of Charleston had been under bombardment for a year, Confederate authorities there sent for fifty captive Union "officers of rank . . . for special use . . . during the siege." They intended to expose the prisoners to federal artillery fire, but the project collapsed when Secretary of War Stanton ordered six hundred captured Confederate officers sent to South Carolina "to be . . . exposed to fire, and treated in the same manner as our officers . . . are treated in Charleston."[78]

In 1863, when the Union Army was enlisting black soldiers for the first time, no one knew what course of action to expect and many feared the worst. Captain Parkinson expected to be killed if he surrendered. "Altho they may get me & hang me, still I would say I died in a good cause," he told his brother. As it turned out, Parkinson died of disease at Milliken's Bend a month after the battle. Capt. Corydon Heath of the 9th Louisiana (AD) and 2d Lt. George L. Conn of the 11th Louisiana (AD) were both captured at Milliken's Bend. Heath's entry in the *Official Army Register of the Volunteer Force* says that he was "taken prisoner June 7, 1863, and murdered by the enemy at or near Monroe, La., June —, 1863." Conn also became a prisoner and was thought to have been "murdered by the rebels August —, 1863," but his fellow prisoner, Pvt. Robert Jones of the same regiment, stated long after the war that Conn drowned in the Ouachita River at Monroe, Louisiana. Jones' account of Conn's death contains no hint of murder. That only two other officers' murders were recorded in nearly two years of conflict indicates that the unbridled savagery of some victorious Confederates resulted from slack discipline in the heat of battle rather than carefully planned, army-wide policy.[79]

Late in June 1863, the same Texas division that had been repulsed at Milliken's Bend undertook an extensive raid against the leased plantations on the west bank of the Mississippi River. "The torch was applied to *every* building: Gin houses, cotton, fences, barns, cabins, residences, and stacks of fodder," a surgeon with the expedition recorded in his diary. "The country . . . has been pretty well rid of Yankees and Negroes." Companies E and G, 1st Arkansas (AD), were stationed at a plantation known as the Mounds and had prepared a fortified position at the top of one of the prehistoric sites. There, they were approached by two Confederate cavalry regiments. "I consider it an unfortunate circumstance that any armed negroes were captured," the Confederate

---

[77]Dudley T. Cornish, *The Sable Arm: Negro Troops in the Union Army, 1861–1865* (New York: Longmans, Green, 1956), pp. 168–70; William Marvel, *Andersonville: The Last Depot* (Chapel Hill: University of North Carolina Press, 1994), pp. 154–55. Some of the evidence of reenslavement is in the pension applications of black Union veterans. See Deposition, William H. Rann, 21 Mar 1913, in Pension File XC2460295, William H. Rann, 110th USCI, Civil War Pension Application Files (CWPAF), RG 15, Rcds of the Veterans Admin, NA.

[78]*OR*, ser. 2, 7: 217 ("officers of rank"), 567 ("to be . . . exposed"); Lonnie R. Speer, *War of Vengeance: Acts of Retaliation Against Civil War POWs* (Mechanicsburg, Pa.: Stackpole Books, 2002), pp. 95–113, summarizes this episode.

[79]Parkinson to Sarah Ann, 19 Apr 1863; Parkinson to Brother James, 28 May 1863 ("Altho"). *ORVF*, 8: 152, 222; Deposition, Robert Jones, 12 Oct 1901, in Pension File C2536702, Robert Jones, 46th USCI, CWPAF, RG 15, NA. Other officers who were captured and then killed were Capt. C. G. Penfield, 44th USCI, near Nashville, Tennessee, on 22 December 1864 and 2d Lt. J. A. Moulton, 67th USCI, at Mount Pleasant Landing, Louisiana, on 15 May 1864. *ORVF*, 8: 217, 240.

General Walker reported; "but . . . Col. [William H.] Parsons . . . encountered a force of 113 negroes and their 3 white officers . . . , and when the officers proposed to surrender upon the condition of being treated as prisoners of war, and the armed negroes unconditionally, Colonel Parsons accepted the terms. The position . . . was of great strength, and would have cost much time and many lives to have captured by assault." The company officers, in other words, assured themselves of treatment according to the laws of war and let their men depend on the Confederates' goodwill.[80]

Surviving regimental records list eighty enlisted men and three officers taken prisoners of war at "the Mound Plantation." Of the enlisted men, 8 escaped and rejoined the regiment during the next twelve months; 8 died while held prisoner; 22 returned to the regiment late in 1865, while it was serving in Texas; and the fate of the rest remained unknown when company officers completed their descriptive books before muster-out in January 1866. A Confederate captain selected Pvt. Samuel Anderson as a personal servant and took him to Hill County, Texas, north of Waco. Like many Southerners, the captain intended to keep black people in a state as close to slavery as possible for as long as possible; and Anderson did not get a chance to escape until 1867. Just as unusual was the case of Pvt. Benjamin Govan of the same company, who was captured at the Mound Plantation before his name was entered in the company books. After his release from captivity in 1865, Govan had to convince an entirely new set of officers that he did in fact belong to the regiment.[81]

"All of the officers in my Co[mpany] were put in prison after we got to Monroe [Louisiana]," Private Anderson told pension examiners thirty years after the war, "and two or three weeks afterwards they were paroled, but I never heard that any of the colored men of my co[mpany] were paroled." Capt. William B. Wallace and 2d Lt. John M. Marshall of Company E and 1st Lt. John East of Company G, the three officers who surrendered, gave their paroles later that year and returned to the regiment. Wallace resigned that November and Marshall in February 1865. East's exact movements are obscure. Company G's descriptive book shows him missing in action, while the regimental descriptive book lists him as exchanged in May 1865 for a Confederate officer of equal rank. The adjutant general's published record shows East still with the regiment at the time of its muster-out in January 1866. But the officers' imprisonment, parole, and exchange are of secondary interest. What the surrender at the Mound Plantation shows is that Confederate troops did not slaughter all black soldiers who fell into their hands as a matter of policy. Black enlisted men stood a good chance of surviving capture if the surrender took place while Confederate officers still had their men under control. Once the opposing sides closed, policy went by the board and frenzied hatred often governed men's actions.[82]

---

[80] *OR*, ser. 1, vol. 24, pt. 2, pp. 450, 466 ("I consider"); Lowe, *Walker's Texas Division*, pp. 107–08 ("The torch").

[81] Deposition, Samuel Anderson, 23 Jun 1896, in Pension File SC959813, Samuel Anderson, 46th USCI, CWPAF, RG 15, NA; Descriptive Books, Companies E and G, 46th USCI, and HQ 46th USCI, SO 65, 2 Dec 1865, both in 46th USCI, Regimental Books, RG 94, NA. On white Southerners' attempts to continue slavery by other means, see Ira Berlin et al., eds., *The Destruction of Slavery* (New York: Cambridge University Press, 1985), pp. 341, 411, 518; *WGFL: LS*, p. 75; Moneyhon, *Impact of the Civil War*, pp. 207–21.

[82] Deposition, Samuel Anderson, 23 Jun 1886; Descriptive Book, Company G, and Regimental Descriptive Book, 46th USCI, Regimental Books, RG 94, NA; *ORVF*, 8: 219.

CHAPTER 7

ALONG THE MISSISSIPPI RIVER
1863–1865

On 4 July 1863, the Confederate garrison of Vicksburg laid down its arms. Some thirty-three thousand Confederates, including those in the hospital, surrendered to a federal army that numbered twice as many men. Half of the Union force, under the eye of Maj. Gen. Ulysses S. Grant, encircled the town while the other half, commanded by Maj. Gen. William T. Sherman, held the country to the east and kept a Confederate relief force at bay. The 2,574 members of the African Brigade remained across the river, camped at Milliken's Bend and Goodrich's Landing on the Louisiana shore. No one bothered to calculate the total number of black civilians employed by Union engineers, quartermasters, and other staff officers during the course of the siege (*see Map 4*).[1]

When Port Hudson surrendered four days later, Northern vessels could navigate the nation's great central highway from Cairo, Illinois, to the mouth of the Mississippi for the first time in more than two years. Being open to navigation did not render the river safe or secure, though. Steamboats on the Mississippi and other waterways were exposed to rifle fire and occasional cannon fire from shore. Even while Grant's army laid siege to Vicksburg in the late spring of 1863, regular and irregular Confederate raiders struck the plantations that lined the banks of the Mississippi, terrorizing black residents and Northern lessees alike. Confederate Maj. Gen. John G. Walker claimed afterward to have "broken up the plantations engaged in raising cotton under federal leases from Milliken's Bend to Lake Providence [more than forty miles of crooked river], capturing some 2,000 negroes, who have been restored to their masters." In July, 1st Lt. John L. Mathews of the 8th Louisiana Infantry (African Descent [AD]) wrote home from Milliken's Bend: "The secesh made another dash on a plantation a few nights since and carried off about one hundred negroes mostly women and children," besides kidnapping the lessee, Lewis Dent, a brother-in-

[1] *The War of the Rebellion: A Compilation of the Official Records of the Union and Confederate Armies*, 70 vols. in 128 (Washington, D.C.: Government Printing Office, 1880–1901), ser. 1, vol. 24, pt. 2, p. 325, and pt. 3, pp. 452–53 (hereafter cited as *OR*).

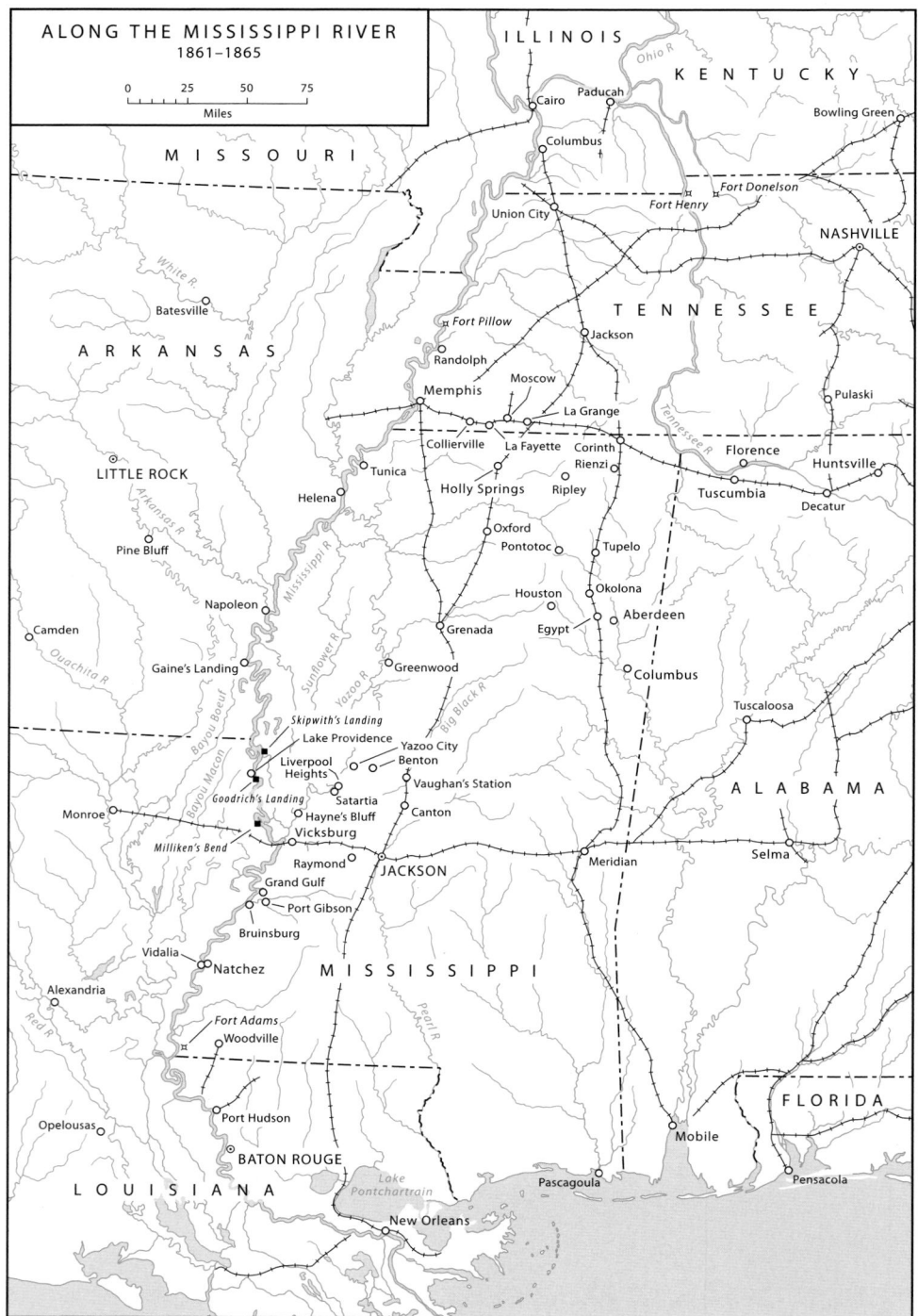

ALONG THE MISSISSIPPI RIVER
1861–1865

0   25   50   75
Miles

ILLINOIS

KENTUCKY

Cairo

Paducah

Bowling Green

MISSOURI

Columbus

Fort Donelson

Union City

Fort Henry

NASHVILLE

TENNESSEE

Batesville

Fort Pillow

Jackson

ARKANSAS

Randolph

Memphis

Moscow

La Grange

Pulaski

Collierville

La Fayette

Corinth

Rienzi

Florence

Huntsville

LITTLE ROCK

Tunica

Holly Springs

Ripley

Tuscumbia

Decatur

Helena

Oxford

Pontotoc

Tupelo

Pine Bluff

Houston

Okolona

Aberdeen

Napoleon

Grenada

Egypt

Camden

Gaine's Landing

Greenwood

Columbus

Tuscaloosa

Skipwith's Landing

Lake Providence

Yazoo City

Benton

Liverpool
Heights

Vaughan's Station

ALABAMA

Monroe

Goodrich's Landing

Satartia

Canton

Hayne's Bluff

Vicksburg

Milliken's Bend

Raymond

JACKSON

Meridian

Selma

Grand Gulf

Port Gibson

Bruinsburg

Vidalia

Natchez

MISSISSIPPI

Alexandria

Fort Adams

Woodville

FLORIDA

Opelousas

Port Hudson

Mobile

BATON ROUGE

Pascagoula

Pensacola

LOUISIANA

Lake
Pontchartrain

New Orleans

Map 4

law of General Grant. "A good many of those . . . were wives of members of our company," Mathews added, "[and] the boys think tis pretty hard."[2]

Union regiments marched into the undefended city of Natchez on 13 July, completing their occupation of population centers along the Mississippi. They captured about twenty Confederate soldiers and the next day seized a herd of five thousand Texas cattle not far from the town. Natchez was an important crossing point for livestock and other Confederate supplies. Its new federal commander voiced a familiar plea for "instructions as to what policy I shall pursue with regard to the negroes. They flock in by thousands (about 1 able bodied man to 6 women and children). I am feeding about 500, and working the able bodied men. . . . I cannot take care of them. What shall I do with them? They are all anxious to go; they do not know where or what for." This call for advice from the commanding officer of an important town came three months after Adjutant General Lorenzo Thomas announced the policy of enlisting black soldiers and eight months after Grant appointed Chaplain John Eaton as general superintendent of contrabands, "to take charge of all fugitive slaves," late in 1862. The plea illustrates clearly the precarious nature of communications and command that bedeviled the efforts of both sides during the war.[3]

Nevertheless, most cities along the Mississippi, from St. Louis southward, became centers for recruiting and organizing black soldiers during the summer and fall of 1863. The first black regiment to be organized in Missouri took shape that August and September in St. Louis. To placate the state's slaveholders, Union authorities named it the 3d Arkansas Volunteer Infantry (AD). Not until December would federal recruiters in the border states feel sure enough of white residents' loyalty to name a black regiment, the 1st Missouri Colored, after the state where it was raised. Similar political considerations caused a regiment organized at Columbus, Kentucky, to be called the 2d Tennessee Heavy Artillery (AD).[4]

Farther south along the Mississippi, organizers of black troops raised a regiment of heavy artillery and a regiment of infantry at Memphis; one regiment each of cavalry and heavy artillery and two of infantry at Vicksburg; and one regiment of heavy artillery and another of infantry at Natchez. All this activity took place in Grant's Department of the Tennessee, which included most of the state of Mississippi, a few posts at steamboat landings in northern Louisiana, and those parts of Kentucky and Tennessee that lay west of the Tennessee River. At the same time,

---

[2] *OR*, ser. 1, vol. 17, pt. 1, p. 720; vol. 24, pt. 2, pp. 466 ("broken up"), 507–08. J. L. Mathews to Dear Sister, 12 Jul 1863, J. L. Mathews Papers, State Historical Society of Iowa, Iowa City. An unofficial Confederate source estimated the number of black captives taken in late spring at fourteen hundred. Richard Lowe, *Walker's Texas Division C.S.A.: Greyhounds of the Trans-Mississippi* (Baton Rouge: Louisiana State University Press, 2004), p. 106. On riverine warfare in Arkansas, see Robert B. Mackey, *The Uncivil War: Irregular Warfare in the Upper South, 1861–1865* (Norman: University of Oklahoma Press, 2004), pp. 29–36.

[3] *OR*, ser. 1, vol. 24, pt. 2, pp. 680–81 (quotation, p. 681); Ira Berlin et al., eds., *The Wartime Genesis of Free Labor: The Lower South* (New York: Cambridge University Press, 1990), pp. 670–71 (quotation, p. 670) (hereafter cited as *WGFL: LS*).

[4] Frederick H. Dyer, *A Compendium of the War of the Rebellion* (New York: Thomas Yoseloff, 1959 [1909]), pp. 1000, 1322, 1642.

federal officials in Arkansas and Kansas managed to organize a second regiment of black infantry in each state.[5]

Since procedures for recruiting troops and appointing officers did not change after the fall of Vicksburg, problems that had dogged these endeavors from the start persisted. The 12th Louisiana Infantry (AD) got off to an especially bad beginning, and the record of its first two months is worth quoting as an example of what could go wrong. "The reg[iment] was made up mostly from 800 recruits from Natchez, Miss., who arrived in camp in a half famished condition," the adjutant recorded on the bimonthly muster roll for July and August. "They were badly clothed without blankets or tents but these things were [soon] supplied; in the meantime we had rainy & bad weather." In mid-August, thirteen sick men died in one day. "Many [recruits] both sick and well became frightened and left without leave. . . . Numbers died, whom we failed to identify by name or the company to which they belonged." Still, the adjutant wrote at the end of the month, "Our hospital arrangements are now good. We are well supplied with . . . clothing & commissary stores and the men are getting pleased with their new mode of life."[6]

Rather than adapt readily to army life, some enlisted men accused recruiters of kidnapping them from their home plantations. Officers denied the charge. Soldiers missed their families, the commanding officer of the 8th Louisiana (AD) wrote, and "will resort to almost any means to get back to see them and . . . this motive went far to cause them to make the declarations they did as to their being forced into the service." Brig. Gen. John P. Hawkins, back from sick leave and again in command of the African Brigade at Goodrich's Landing, Louisiana, reported in October that the 1st Arkansas Infantry (AD) "was raised at Helena [Arkansas] and have left behind them their wives and children and naturally they are very anxious about them. . . . If these husbands can be near their families they will do a great deal towards taking care of them and thus relieve the Government of their support. I think it would be a matter of humanity to let this change be made." The federal army camp at Goodrich's Landing lay south of Lake Providence, more than one hundred fifty miles downriver from Helena. General Hawkins' recommendation echoed that of the plantation commissioner, Samuel Sawyer, who had wanted the 1st Arkansas (AD) returned to Helena two months earlier to guard cotton pickers, but the humanitarian concerns of a general counted for no more than a civilian official's fears for the safety of his workers and their crop. The men of the 1st Arkansas did not see their homes again until February 1866.[7]

New black regiments along the Mississippi, like those on the Atlantic and Gulf Coasts, continued to draw their officers from whatever white regiments happened to be at hand. Thus, all but one of the twenty-seven enlisted men who became

---

[5]Ibid., pp. 1000, 1187, 1214, 1343–44, 1642.

[6]National Archives (NA) Microfilm Pub M594, Compiled Rcds Showing Svc of Mil Units in Volunteer Union Organizations, roll 210, 50th United States Colored Infantry (USCI).

[7]Col H. Scofield to AAG [Assistant Adjutant General] Dist of Northeast Louisiana, 19 Jul 1863 ("will resort") (S–463–B–DT–1863), Entry 4720, Dept of the Tennessee, Letters Received (LR), pt. 1, Rcds of Geographical Divs and Depts, Record Group (RG) 393, Rcds of U.S. Army Continental Cmds, NA; Brig Gen J. P. Hawkins to Brig Gen J. A. Rawlins, 8 Oct 1863 ("was raised") (H–34–17AC–1863), Entry 6300, XVII Corps, Ltrs, Rpts, and Orders Received, pt. 2, Rcds of Polyonymous Cmds, RG 393, NA; S. Sawyer to Brig Gen L. Thomas, 16 Aug 1863, 46th USCI, Entry 57C,

company officers in the 6th Mississippi Infantry (AD) in Natchez came
from white regiments stationed there
in August 1863. So did the colonel,
lieutenant colonel, and major. Of
these thirty officers, seven—including the colonel and the major—suffered dismissal before the end of
the war. In many Colored Troops
regiments, officers received their appointments long before the authorities found time to examine them. At
Milliken's Bend, a captain and three
lieutenants of the 3d Mississippi
(AD) wrote a letter in which they
claimed to be "incompetent to fill
the responsible positions we now occupy" and offered their resignations,
which were accepted.[8]

When Capt. Embury D. Osband
of the 4th Illinois Cavalry received
his appointment as colonel of the 1st
Mississippi Cavalry (AD) in October
1863, he declined to accept a list of
officer candidates that named five
corporals and fifteen privates from
his old regiment to serve as company officers in the new one. Osband
wrote directly to Adjutant General

*Col. Embury D. Osband chose carefully
the officers for his new regiment, the 1st
Mississippi Cavalry (later the 3d U.S.
Colored Cavalry). During the last eighteen
months of the war, the regiment frequently
took part in the long-distance raids that
characterized mounted operations west of
the Appalachian Mountains.*

Thomas protesting the nominations and offering his own slate of officer candidates, who were also all officers and enlisted men of the 4th Illinois Cavalry. The
difference between the two lists was that in the new one no nominee of a grade
lower than sergeant would receive a captain's appointment, and only two privates
would become first lieutenants. It was clear that the new colonel favored men with
some experience of authority. Only five names from the first list appeared on Osband's, three of them in lower grades than had been proposed earlier. By the end
of the war, just one of his nominees had been dismissed—the only case in the regiment. Osband's company of the 4th Illinois Cavalry had served as General Grant's
headquarters escort since November 1861, and Grant spoke highly of it. "It would

Regimental Papers, RG 94, Rcds of the Adjutant General's Office, NA. Further correspondence
about plantation press gangs is in Ira Berlin et al., eds., *The Black Military Experience* (New York:
Cambridge University Press, 1982), pp. 146–49; *WGFL: LS*, pp. 707–09.

[8]Col A. S. Smith to Capt J. H. Munroe, 31 Aug 1863, 58th USCI, Entry 57C, RG 94, NA; Capt
A. D. Beekman et al. to Col R. H. Ballinger, 27 Sep 1863 (quotation), 53d USCI, Entry 57C, RG 94,
NA; Dyer, *Compendium*, pp. 1049–51, 1057, 1059, 1067, 1077, 1087, 1140, 1298, 1678–81; *Official
Army Register of the Volunteer Force of the United States Army*, 8 vols. (Washington, D.C.: Adjutant
General's Office, 1867), 6: 228, 7: 184, 8: 226, 231 (hereafter cited as *ORVF*).

not be overstating the merits of this company," he wrote, "to say that many of them would fill with credit any position in a cavalry regiment." Nearly two years' association with Grant must have helped give Osband the confidence to approach the adjutant general directly.[9]

Training began when a regiment's commander assigned its officers and men to companies and mustered them into service. At Corinth, Mississippi, Col. James N. Alexander's 1st Alabama Infantry (AD) managed only "a few days' drill" in May before the post commander assigned the men to guard duties, picket, and fatigues, "in all of which," Alexander wrote in September, "they have been doing a heavy duty ever since." Otherwise, the colonel had no complaint: "Every facility that could be, has been given us to complete our outfit." As for the excessive fatigue duty, which officers of the U.S. Colored Troops deplored in all parts of the country, Alexander thought that a higher-ranking commanding officer would be better able to look after the troops' interests. "We report to the commander of the Post . . . and when a man gets ahold of us, who does not believe in the Black Man, [the troops] suffer and we have no remedy. For this and other reasons . . . it is of the utmost importance that these troops be Brigaded. My experience is that the more they are kept to themselves the better." A brigade of Colored Troops led by a general officer would fare better, Alexander reasoned, than a lone black regiment in an otherwise white garrison. The higher the commanding officer's rank, the better he could defend his men from onerous details imposed on them because of their race. Regimental officers wanted to drill their men thoroughly rather than to employ them as guards and laborers because the men's eventual behavior in battle would reflect credit or disgrace on those who had trained them.[10]

The quality of the troops' weapons was as important as their proficiency in drill. At Goodrich's Landing, General Hawkins tried for weeks to get the Ordnance Department to replace his brigade's rifles, which he called "third rate," with Springfields. Eleven years' experience in peace and war, as infantry officer, quartermaster, and commissary, had placed him at different times on both the giving and the receiving ends of the Army's supply system. He followed the Ordnance Department's instructions and filed an inspection report on the weapons he wanted replaced. Nothing happened, and at length he complained to Adjutant General Thomas: "A Quartermaster *tries* to distribute the best kind of harness, wagons, and everything else. A Commissary tries to procure the best and most healthy food. The Ordnance Dept. has to be begged. . . . It is hedged around with unbusinesslike restrictions and appears to have no power to accommodate itself to circumstances or to the exercise of any discretion." Knowing that some regiments of his brigade were famous for their backs-to-the-river defense of Milliken's Bend that

[9] *OR*, ser. 1, vol. 24, pt. 1, p. 59 (quotation); Capt E. D. Osband to Brig Gen L. Thomas, 10 Oct 1863 (O–4–AG–1863), Entry 363, LR by Adj Gen L. Thomas, RG 94, NA; *ORVF*, 8: 143.

[10] Col J. M. Alexander to Lt Col J. H. Wilson, 10 Sep 1863 ("a few"), and Col J. M. Alexander to Brig Gen L. Thomas, 17 Oct 1863 ("We report"), both in 55th USCI, Entry 57C, RG 94, NA. Complaints about excessive guard and fatigue duty for Colored Troops arose throughout the war and across the South: at Natchez, Col A. S. Smith et al. to Col W. E. Clark, 18 Dec 1863, 58th USCI; at Little Rock, Col J. E. Cone to 1st Lt L. Harwood, 21 Apr 1864, 54th USCI; at Vicksburg, Capt O. J. Wright to Brig Gen L. Thomas, 3 Nov 1864, 50th USCI; at Memphis, Col H. Leib to Capt F. W. Fox, 27 Jan 1865, 68th USCI; all in Entry 57C, RG 94, NA.

June, Hawkins ended his complaint against the Ordnance Department's procedures: "Should I ever lead my Brigade into battle and get whipped I will at least have the satisfaction of knowing that it was [done] according to rule."[11]

Life in camp revealed many shortcomings in the Army's supply system. Men sometimes ran out of fuel. When this happened, nearby fences became a handy substitute. A monotonous and insufficient diet promoted diarrhea and scurvy. Black soldiers and white suffered from these diseases at about the same rate: 23.1 percent among blacks and 24.5 percent among whites. The search for nourishment led soldiers throughout the Union Army to raid vegetable gardens and hen roosts. From Memphis to Natchez, the story was the same: when supplies ran short, men would forage or, as neighboring civilians thought of it, steal. The need to supplement what little the Army issued led soldiers everywhere in the occupied South to commit acts that

Brig. Gen. John P. Hawkins. His leadership of black soldiers at Mississippi River garrisons and during the Mobile Campaign earned him six brevets.

strained civil-military relations throughout the war and well into the era of Reconstruction. Southern civilians might dismiss pillaging by white soldiers as incidental to the war; when black soldiers did the same, it signaled social upheaval.[12]

Between periods of on-duty ditch digging and off-duty foraging, life in the Mississippi River garrisons did not demand too much of officers and men. Whenever the schedule of guard duty and fatigues allowed, good officers drilled their men and

---

[11] Brig Gen J. P. Hawkins to Lt Col W. T. Clark, 15 Nov 1863 ("third-rate"), and to Brig Gen L. Thomas, 15 Nov 1863 ("A Quartermaster"), both in Entry 2014, Dist of Northeast Louisiana, Letters Sent, pt. 2, RG 393, NA.

[12] Capt O. F. Walker et al. to 1st Lt L. Methudy, 29 Nov 1864 (fuel shortage), 3d United States Colored Artillery (USCA), Entry 57C, RG 94, NA. Officers of Colored Troops received complaints of theft from vegetable gardens around Vicksburg: Lt Col A. L. Mitchell to Col O. C. Risdon, 10 May 1864, 53d USCI; of fences for firewood at Memphis, Col J. E. Bryant to 1st Lt A. F. Avery, 2 Feb 1865, 46th USCI; and theft of livestock at Fort Smith, 1st Lt T. A. Pollock to Lt Col J. N. Craig, 8 Dec 1865, 57th USCI; all in Entry 57C, RG 94, NA. On army-wide foraging practices, see Bell I. Wiley, *The Life of Billy Yank: The Common Soldier of the Union* (Indianapolis: Bobbs-Merrill, 1952), pp. 127–28, 233–36. For disease statistics, see *Medical and*

taught them to how handle their weapons. Good colonels tried to get rid of incompetent or vicious officers. An exasperated commanding officer might resort to bizarre measures. At one point, Colonel Alexander polled officers of the 1st Alabama to determine whether he or Maj. Edgar M. Lowe should resign. The vote was a tie.[13]

As the regiments mustered in, company by company, they began to take part in military operations. In late May, twenty-seven officers and men of the 2d Arkansas (AD), accompanied by detachments from two white regiments, cruised both shores of the Mississippi for recruits, ranging from Helena as far south as the mouth of the Arkansas River and sometimes moving inland six or seven miles to investigate a likely plantation. At one point, the waterborne recruiters exchanged shots with Confederates on shore. "The conduct of the colored soldiers was highly creditable," reported Brig. Gen. Benjamin M. Prentiss, commanding at Helena. "The [plantation] blacks hailed with joy the appearance of the colored soldiers." The expedition returned with 125 recruits.[14]

That fall, the regiments at Goodrich's Landing began to scout the country nearby for cotton and livestock. On 23 September, officers and men of the 10th Louisiana Infantry (AD) found one hundred ten bales on a plantation a day's march from their base. A week later, companies of the 1st Mississippi (AD) returned from a three-day scout with sixty bales. These expeditions were not always bloodless. On 11 November, forty-five men of the 6th Mississippi (AD) left Natchez with a train of four wagons. Only two miles outside the town, about sixty Confederate cavalry attacked. The train's escort drove them off, but at a cost of four men killed and six wounded. "The men behaved well, returning the enemy's fire briskly and finely routing them," the regiment's adjutant reported, even though continual details to work on the town's fortifications had forestalled any attempts at military training.[15]

Before being appointed colonel of the 1st Mississippi Cavalry (AD), Captain Osband had led a battalion of the 4th Illinois Cavalry through the country around Vicksburg rounding up laborers to improve the town's defenses. "You will arrest and bring in . . . all able-bodied negroes who are found floating around doing nothing, and bring them in to be put on the new fortifications to work," Maj. Gen. James B. McPherson ordered. Once recruiting for Osband's new regiment began, his officers had to seek soldiers rather than laborers, but the method remained much the same. On 10 October 1863, the date of Osband's appointment as colonel, General Grant advised that the new regiment should fill its ranks "from the plantations around owned by persons of disloyalty." Soon afterward, Osband led the one organized company of his new regiment and a battalion of the 4th Illinois Cavalry on a raid that went as far as Satartia, a village on the Yazoo River about thirty miles northeast of Vicksburg. By mid-November, he had secured enough men to muster in three companies. A march from the mouth of the Yazoo to Skipwith's Landing, on the Mississippi River in Issaquena County, revealed "a deserted and abandoned country" that had been picked

---

Surgical History of the War of the Rebellion, 2 vols. in 6 (Washington, D.C.: Government Printing Office, 1870–1888), vol. 1, pt. 1, pp. xxxvii, xliii.

[13]Testimony, Capt H. Simmons, Investigation, 17 Mar 1864, and Endorsement, Brig Gen A. L. Chetlain, 1 Apr 1864 (quotation), in A–15–CT–1863, Entry 360, Colored Troops Div, LR, RG 94, NA.

[14]*OR*, ser. 1, vol. 22, pt. 1, pp, 339–40.

[15]NA M594, roll 210, 48th and 51st USCIs, and roll 211, 58th USCI (quotation).

clean by Confederate cavalry before Osband could find any more recruits. For the rest of the month, Osband and his 131 officers and men continued recruiting while watching for unauthorized cotton speculators and "doing good service," as McPherson told General Sherman, "keeping the country west of the Sunflower [River] clear of guerrillas." Their efforts netted six 500-pound bales of cotton for the Treasury Department and sixty recruits for the regiment, enough to start a fourth company.[16]

The Union general commanding at Memphis had declared that "organized warfare is over in Arkansas," but early in December, Osband received orders to move his tiny command across the Mississippi River and deal with "some forty rebel cavalry who were hanging negroes and driving off stock."[17] Besides 125 officers and men from his own four companies, Osband took along seventy-six officers and men of the 4th Illinois Cavalry, some of whom had received appointments as captains and lieutenants in the 1st Mississippi Cavalry (AD) but could not join the new regiment until there were enough recruits to form more companies. These prospective officers hoped to do some recruiting in Arkansas while routing enemy marauders.

A riverboat set the troops on the Louisiana shore. They marched inland through swampy country some fifteen miles to Boeuf River, then followed it north for another mile or two to the Arkansas state line. The troops managed to capture fifteen Confederate scouts who were observing their progress. About dark on 12 December, they camped at the Meriwether Plantation, not far from the state line. The 1st Mississippi Cavalry bivouacked between the slave quarters and the planter's house, where they kept the prisoners under guard, while the 4th Illinois Cavalry took over the cotton-gin house, about one hundred fifty yards off. There was no time for a thorough reconnaissance before nightfall, but Osband posted ten-man pickets on the road in either direction and a ten-man camp guard. The next morning, the men were up before daybreak, had breakfasted, and were waiting with horses saddled for enough light to begin the day's march when a force of more than one hundred Confederates opened fire on the 4th Illinois, stampeding many of the horses. Dismounted troopers splashed across the marshy ground that separated them from the camp of the 1st Mississippi Cavalry. There, the Union defenders exchanged shots with the enemy. The Confederates withdrew before daylight, taking with them thirteen prisoners from the 4th Illinois Cavalry captured during the first minutes of shooting. Osband identified the attackers as members of "Capers' battalion," one of several Partisan Ranger organizations formed in the summer of 1862. These northern Louisiana cavalrymen were probably in the neighborhood to further the last stage of a large arms shipment from Richmond, Virginia, to the Confederate depot at Shreveport and had used their knowledge of local geography to approach the camp through the surrounding swamps, slipping by Osband's pickets on the roads. Union casualties in the hour-long engagement amounted to seven killed and thirty-three wounded; the 1st Mississippi Cavalry lost one killed and fifteen wounded. With nearly one in eight of the survivors needing

---

[16]*OR*, ser. 1, vol. 30, pt. 3, p. 477 ("You will arrest"), and pt. 4, p. 233 ("from the plantations"); vol. 31, pt. 1, p. 566 ("a deserted"), and pt. 3, pp. 237, 293, 309 ("keeping the country"). Col E. D. Osband to Lt Col W. T. Clark, 25 Nov, 27 Nov, 4 Dec 1863, all in 3d United States Colored Cavalry (USCC), Regimental Books, RG 94, NA. Edwin M. Main, *The Story of the Marches, Battles and Incidents of the Third United States Colored Cavalry* (New York: Negro Universities Press, 1970 [1908]), pp. 65–70, 75–78.

[17]*OR*, ser. 1, vol. 31, pt. 3, p. 104 ("organized warfare"); vol. 53, p. 476 ("some forty").

medical attention, Osband withdrew his force to Skipwith's Landing. The expedition had not accomplished what it set out to do, but the new soldiers of the 1st Mississippi Cavalry (AD) had fired back at the Confederates and driven them off.[18]

By the summer of 1863, federal garrisons dotted the banks of the Mississippi from Cairo, Illinois, to the river's mouth, allowing Union generals at last to turn their attention to other matters. The important task of relieving the garrison of Chattanooga and driving the city's Confederate besiegers into Georgia took most of the fall. In late November, as a result, Grant and Sherman could attend to unfinished business before beginning the next year's major campaigns. High on Sherman's list was the rail junction at Meridian, Mississippi. He had intended to destroy it after the capture of Vicksburg that summer, but heat and drought had kept his army from marching any farther east than Jackson. Demolition of the railroads at Meridian, near the Alabama state line, "would paralyze all Mississippi," Sherman told Maj. Gen. Henry W. Halleck, the Army chief of staff.[19]

This project brought Sherman west from Chattanooga and caused him once again to voice his concerns about secure navigation routes. "I propose to send an expedition up the Yazoo," a tributary of the Mississippi, he told Halleck, "to . . . do a certain amount of damage and give general notice that for every boat fired on we will destroy some inland town, and, if need be, fire on houses, even if they have families. . . . [T]here is complicity between guerrillas and the people, and if the latter fire on our boats loaded with women and children, we should retaliate." Sherman did not want to disperse Union armies in scattered garrisons to occupy the country away from the rivers. "I do not believe in holding any part of the interior," he told Halleck. "This requires a vast force, which is rendered harmless to the enemy by its scattered parts. With Columbus, Memphis, Helena, and Vicksburg strongly held, and all other forces prepared to move to any point, we can do something, but in holding . . . inferior points on the Mississippi, and the interior of Louisiana, a large army is wasted in detachments." He intended to order Hawkins' African Brigade to march through northern Louisiana toward the Ouachita River, "and hold that rich district responsible for the safety of the [Mississippi] from the mouth of Red River up to the Arkansas." The purpose was to raid and exact reparations by seizing cotton that was ginned, baled, and ready for market. This was nothing Sherman had not already done: to punish attacks on Union shipping the previous fall, he had first expelled a few Confederate sympathizers from Memphis and later burned the town of Randolph, Tennessee.[20]

In order to concentrate the force required for his strike at Meridian, Sherman had to withdraw white regiments from the Vicksburg garrison and replace them with Colored Troops. In mid-January 1864, General Hawkins received

---

[18]*OR*, ser. 1, vol. 22, pt. 2, p. 1092; vol. 53, p. 476 (quotation). NA M594, roll 204, 3d USCC; Main, *Third United States Colored Cavalry*, pp. 82–87. Main estimates the attacking force at five hundred, or the entire Partisan Ranger battalion, but Osband's official report gives its strength as only one hundred forty. Stewart Sifakis, *Compendium of the Confederate Armies*, 11 vols. (New York: Facts on File, 1995), 8: 54–55, outlines the history of the 13th Louisiana Cavalry Battalion, Partisan Rangers.

[19]*OR*, ser. 1, vol. 31, pt. 3, p. 185 (quotation); vol. 32, pt. 1, p. 173.

[20]*OR*, ser. 1, vol. 17, pt. 1, pp. 144–45, and pt. 2, pp. 235–36, 240, 244, 259–62, 272–74, 285, 288–89; vol. 31, pt. 3, pp. 497–98 (quotations), 527. Stephen V. Ash, *When the Yankees Came: Conflict and Chaos in the Occupied South, 1861–1865* (Chapel Hill: University of North Carolina Press, 1995), pp. 64–67, and Mark Grimsley, *The Hard Hand of War: Union Military Policy Toward*

orders to withdraw the African Brigade from Goodrich's Landing, Louisiana, and move downstream to Haynes' Bluff on the Yazoo River about twenty miles north of Vicksburg. Sherman wanted Hawkins' troops to patrol west of the Big Black River, behind the leased plantations that fronted on the Mississippi, and to stamp out "the bands of guerrillas that now infest that country." Hawkins was to commandeer as many as fifty skiffs, rowboats that could carry five or six men each, so that his force could navigate the bayous in parties two or three hundred strong. All the regiments in the African Brigade had mustered in at river towns and steamboat landings between Memphis and Natchez, and most of the soldiers were used to life along the Mississippi and its tributaries. Local knowledge that the men had gained as civilians would be valuable in antiguerrilla operations, and Sherman intended to use it. "Such expeditions will suit the habits of [Hawkins'] troops," he wrote, "and will effectually prevent the smaller bands of guerrillas from approaching the river plantations. . . . The whole country between the Yazoo and Mississippi Rivers is one labyrinth of creeks connecting each other, making it very favorable to parties in boats, and soon the officers and men will get a knowledge of these that will give them every advantage over parties on horseback."[21]

While Hawkins and his men were to scour the country between the rivers, a small force would strike northeast up the Yazoo "by way of diversion, to threaten Grenada," Sherman explained to Halleck, in order to draw Confederate attention from the main Union force's march toward Meridian. This expedition's commanding officer was to notify plantation owners along the Yazoo that they would be held responsible, under threat of reprisals and confiscation, for any guerrilla incursions in the region. He was to collect one thousand bales of cotton for sale in order to indemnify loyal shipowners and merchants who had suffered from guerrilla raids. As the senior commanding officer present, Col. James H. Coates of the 11th Illinois led the expedition. It included his own regiment as well as the 8th Louisiana Infantry (AD) and Colonel Osband's 1st Mississippi Cavalry (AD).[22]

Many in the 8th Louisiana were glad to go. The regiment had "had every available man working on the fortifications at Vicksburg, and detailed to unload stores for white regiments for nearly the whole of the last three months," according to a muster roll for December 1863. "In consequence of which, in spite of every effort of the officers, [the regiment] is rapidly deteriorating in morale and discipline. . . . General fatigue duty, and the handling of spades, shovels and picks, will certainly prevent us from ever acquitting ourselves creditably as soldiers." Except for an enemy raid on one of its company's outposts the previous May that had inflicted eight casualties and another company's involvement

---

Southern Civilians, 1861–1865 (New York: Cambridge University Press, 1995), pp. 112–19, discuss Union retaliation against Southern communities for their support of guerrillas.

[21] *OR*, ser. 1, vol. 32, pt. 2, pp. 125, 181, 310 (quotation). Col G. M. Zeigler to Brig Gen L. Thomas, 17 Aug 1863, 52d USCI, Entry 57C, RG 94, NA, outlines one commanding officer's difficulties in organizing his regiment.

[22] *OR*, ser. 1, vol. 32, pt. 1, p. 183, and pt. 2, p. 360 (quotation). Coates' appointment dated from 8 July 1863; Osband's, from 10 October 1863. Francis B. Heitman, *Historical Register and Dictionary of the United States Army*, 2 vols. (Washington, D.C.: Government Printing Office, 1903), 1: 312, 761.

Federal shipping where the Yazoo River empties into the Mississippi

in a bloodless skirmish two weeks later, the 8th Louisiana had never been under fire.[23]

Coates' two infantry regiments, 947 officers and men, left Vicksburg by boat on 31 January 1864 and arrived at the mouth of the Yazoo by dark. Turning upriver the next morning, the flotilla of six transports and five gunboats stopped at Haynes' Bluff in the evening to pick up a recruiting detachment of the 1st Mississippi Cavalry (AD), eleven officers and twenty-five men. During the night, the boats tied up and took aboard a two-week supply of wood and steamed on in the morning. They paused long enough at Satartia, some twenty-five miles up the winding river, for the cavalry and five companies of the 11th Illinois to go ashore and chase a few Confederates out of the village. The next morning, 3 February, the expedition arrived at Liverpool Heights, which overlooked the Yazoo.[24]

About 10:00, a pair of Confederate twelve-pounders on shore opened fire on the vessels. Colonel Coates landed about half his force, an equal number of men from both regiments. They found it difficult to maneuver effectively among the hills that lined the river. The Confederate defenders, fewer than five hundred men of a Texas cavalry brigade fighting on foot, held their ground, stopping one Union advance with revolver fire at a range of about twenty-five paces. Meanwhile, Coates had landed the balance of his force and the new arrivals exchanged shots with another Texas regiment that Confederate Brig. Gen. Lawrence S. Ross had sent to his left merely to watch and guard a road; Coates thought the Texans' presence represented a flanking movement. Toward dark, the colonel recalled his troops to the boats and dropped downriver a mile to spend the night and plan the next day's operation. The fight had cost his force 6 killed, 21 wounded, and 8 missing, most of them in the 11th Illinois.[25]

Coates thought it necessary at this point to send a report to the general commanding at Vicksburg. Officers of the 1st Mississippi Cavalry (AD) picked Sgts. Isaac Trendall and Washington Vincent to attempt the sixty-mile journey.

---

[23] NA M594, roll 210, 47th USCI.

[24] *OR*, ser. 1, vol. 32, pt. 1, pp. 320–21; Main, *Third United States Colored Cavalry*, p. 94.

[25] *OR*, ser. 1, vol. 32, pt. 1, pp. 315–17, 388–89; NA M594, roll 204, 3d USCC.

Both men were Mississippians who knew the country between Satartia and Vicksburg. Dressed in the rags of plantation slaves, which they had recently been, the two sergeants walked until they came to a plantation where they were able to steal four horses—enough to provide them with remounts and to deter pursuit by putting the horses' owners on foot. Mounted, Trendall and Vincent covered the distance to Vicksburg in ten hours. After delivering Coates' dispatch, they joined the main body of the 1st Mississippi Cavalry (AD) at Haynes' Bluff, where the regimental quartermaster inspected their horses and branded them U.S.[26]

Up the Yazoo at Liverpool Heights, the effort to stop Coates' advance had depleted the Confederates' artillery ammunition, so General Ross let the federal vessels pass on the morning of 4 February with no resistance but rifle shots from the riverbank. The Union soldiers on board returned fire from behind cotton bales and hardtack boxes stacked on deck. Ross thought that the Confederate volleys "must have done much execution," but Coates reported only five men wounded. The flotilla reached Yazoo City, found Ross' brigade there, and dropped back down the river once again. Coates' two regiments, reinforced by five companies of the 1st Mississippi Cavalry (AD), which had marched overland to join them, did not return to occupy the town until 9 February. By that time, the Confederates had moved east, anticipating orders to oppose Sherman's march to Meridian. In order to learn where Ross' men had gone, General Hawkins at Haynes' Bluff ordered the 3d Arkansas (AD) and the 11th Louisiana (AD) to scout from there east toward the Big Black River. They covered the fifty miles to the river and back in five days without event. The enemy they were looking for was some fifteen miles farther north.[27]

Coates led his force up the Yazoo to Greenwood, which it reached on 14 February. Two days later, he sent Osband and two hundred fifty cavalrymen in the direction of Grenada. The party returned the next day and reported that the Confederate Maj. Gen. Nathan B. Forrest had made that town his headquarters. Coates' expedition then floated and marched back to Yazoo City, arriving there on 28 February with its transports and gunboats bearing 1,729 bales (432 tons) of cotton seized from secessionist planters.[28]

By this time, Sherman's raid on Meridian was over and his returning army had reached Canton, some twenty miles north of Jackson, with five thousand freedpeople and one thousand white refugees in tow. On the Confederate side, Ross' Texas cavalry brigade had received orders to return to Yazoo City. A few miles east of town, the force encountered a scouting party of the 1st Mississippi Cavalry (AD). "I immediately ordered [the 6th and 9th Texas Cavalry], which happened to be nearest at hand, to charge them," Ross reported. "The negroes after the first fire broke in wild disorder, each seeming intent on nothing but making his escape. Being mounted on mules, however, but few of them got away. The

---

[26] Descriptive Book, 3d USCC, Regimental Books, RG 94, NA; Main, *Third United States Colored Cavalry,* pp. 97–99.

[27] *OR,* ser. 1, vol. 32, pt. 1, pp. 317, 389 (quotation), and pt. 2, p. 392; NA M594, roll 210, 46th and 49th USCIs.

[28] *OR,* ser. 1, vol. 32, pt. 1, pp. 320–23.

road all the way to Yazoo City was literally strewed with their bodies." The 1st Mississippi Cavalry (AD) reported eighteen casualties among forty-three officers and men engaged. Two days later, after examining the scene and questioning nearby civilians, Osband concluded that five soldiers left behind when Confederate fire felled their mounts had been "brutally murdered."[29]

Coates ordered his regiments to camp outside Yazoo City on high ground that commanded the town and its steamboat landing. Ross' cavalry feinted and sniped at the Union outposts daily. Coates reinforced his picket line on 4 March when he learned that a cavalry brigade of Confederate Tennesseans led by Brig. Gen. Robert V. Richardson, about five hundred fifty strong, had joined the besiegers.[30]

The next day, the Confederates struck in earnest. By 10:00 a.m., the Tennesseans and Texans had surrounded the position east of Yazoo City held by the 11th Illinois and attacked the north end of the town. Six companies of the 8th Louisiana rushed from south of town to drive the attackers off, but they arrived too late. The Confederates "came up in good style," Lieutenant Mathews of the 8th Louisiana wrote.

> Two regiments against six companies. . . . It was soon evident that our force could not hold out against such odds, and they slowly fell back, keeping up a continuous fire, and the enemy following up. Our boys fell back to the main street, which they hastily barricaded with cotton bales. . . . For four hours this desperate hand to hand fight lasted. The rebels taking shelter in the houses, kept up a deadly fire on our men, who nobly held their ground.

The Confederates soon had control of all but the waterfront, where two Union gunboats discouraged further advance. "About 4 o'clock, the enemy began to retire," Mathews wrote. "The boys gave them a few parting rounds, and they were out of reach." Richardson's men in the town had burned some Union military supplies and had captured cotton. The 11th Illinois had refused Ross' demand that it surrender, and the two Confederate commanders decided against a direct assault on the regiment's position. Their casualties in the day's fighting amounted to 64 killed and wounded. The Union force's were 183, of which 144 were from the 8th Louisiana and 13 from the 1st Mississippi Cavalry (AD).[31]

Orders to abandon Yazoo City reached Colonel Coates on 6 March, and the regiments boarded transports for the return trip to Haynes' Bluff and Vicksburg. General Sherman, who had already returned to Vicksburg from Meridian, delivered one thousand bales of Coates' cotton to Treasury Department agents. "The sooner all the cotton in the Southern States is burned or got away the better," he wrote to Grant. The lure of easy profits had attracted "a class of heartless speculators that would corrupt our officers and men and sell their lives by foolish exposure that they might get out stolen cotton and buy it cheap." Clearly, the Treasury Depart-

---

[29] Ibid., pp. 177, 390 ("I immediately"); NA M594, roll 204, 3d USCC; Col. E. D. Osband to 1st Lt H. H. Dean, 1 Mar 64 ("brutally murdered"), 3d USCC, Regimental Books, RG 94, NA; Main, *Third United States Colored Cavalry*, pp. 112–16.

[30] *OR*, ser. 1, vol. 32, pt. 1, pp. 323, 383.

[31] Ibid., pp. 324–25, 383–89; J. L. Mathews to My dear good friend, 20 Mar 1863 (quotations), J. L. Mathews Letters, University of Iowa; NA M549, roll 204, 3d USCC, and roll 210, 47th USCI.

ment's idea of helping to finance the war by sale of the Confederacy's most valuable crop was foundering on the cupidity and lax ethics of ruthless speculators.[32]

The main Union garrisons along the lower Mississippi—Memphis, Helena, Vicksburg, and Natchez—remained quiet during the first months of 1864. Most organized bodies of Confederates had withdrawn some distance from the river. Confederates east of the Mississippi had to contend with Sherman's raid on Meridian; west of the river, they awaited a Union offensive in the Department of the Gulf aimed at Texas. Across the South, Confederate armies were beginning to feel the pinch of scarce supplies.[33]

Troops available to Maj. Gen. Richard Taylor and other Confederate commanders in the region included some 9,000 men east of the Mississippi River; fewer than 25,000 in Louisiana, with headquarters at Alexandria; and another 5,000 in Arkansas, with headquarters at Camden. This left smaller formations responsible for the business of disrupting the operation of plantations along the river that were leased to Northerners by the U.S. Treasury Department. One such organization was a brigade of dismounted Texas cavalry led by a Frenchman in the Confederate service, Brig. Gen. Camille A. J. M. de Polignac.[34]

Union generals preparing to move against Richmond and Atlanta were willing to risk the security of federal posts along the Mississippi River in favor of offensive operations that would further this grand strategy. Confederate generals kept a close eye on federal troop movements and moved to take advantage of any weakness that resulted. Commanding the Union XVII Corps at Vicksburg, General McPherson reported: "The rebel cavalry are becoming very annoying at some points along the river." He noted that the general commanding at Natchez "has tried several times to get a fight out of them, but they invariably keep out of the way, unless they have [an advantage of] about four to one."[35]

Late in January, Polignac proposed to strike at the country around Vidalia, Louisiana, across the river from Natchez. General Taylor approved the plan but at first saw the raid's primary purpose as keeping horses and mules out of Union hands. Only as an afterthought did he add: "If you come across any plantations . . . leased from the enemy, take the able-bodied negro men" to work for the Confederate army. A week later, Taylor was more explicit. "It is desirable," one of his aides wrote to Polignac, "that all the able-bodied negro men and mules, horses, and transportation . . . in the country . . . exposed to the continual ravages of the enemy, or within his own lines, be secured for our own use. The negro men will be sent here, as in the case of negro troops." This was just eight months after Taylor complained that "unfortunately" some black prisoners had been taken at Milliken's Bend. In the middle of the siege of Vicksburg, General Grant had written to him, asking whether the Confederates had hanged Colored Troops officers captured in that fight. Taylor had denied it. Since then, Confederate troops at Fort Wagner, South Carolina, had made prisoners of other black soldiers, and newspapers North and South had discussed extensively the question of their fate. By February

---

[32] *OR*, ser. 1, vol. 32, pt. 1, p. 178 (quotation).

[33] Bell I. Wiley, *The Life of Johnny Reb: The Common Soldier of the Confederacy* (Indianapolis: Bobbs-Merrill, 1943), pp. 118–21 (clothing), 134–35 (food), 258–60 (medicine).

[34] *OR*, ser. 1, vol. 32, pt. 1, p. 335 (Mississippi); vol. 34, pt. 1, pp. 479 (Louisiana), 532 (Arkansas).

[35] *OR*, ser. 1, vol. 31, pt. 3, p. 471 (quotations); vol. 32, pt. 2, p. 607. Dyer, *Compendium*, pp. 1057, 1140, 1678.

1864, General Taylor seemed willing to put black prisoners of war to work rather than slaughter them.[36]

Most river garrisons, from Paducah and Columbus in Kentucky south to New Orleans and its nearby forts, included an outsized twelve-company regiment called heavy artillery. In peacetime, most companies of the Army's four artillery regiments had served in coastal fortifications; only one or two companies in each regiment had trained as horse-drawn light artillery. Fielding as many as six cannon, these companies were called batteries. During the war, most regular and volunteer artillery accompanied the field armies as light batteries; only with the fortification of Washington, D.C., in the fall of 1861 and the capture of Memphis and New Orleans the next spring did the need for specially trained heavy artillery regiments become apparent. The maximum authorized strength for a heavy artillery regiment was 1,834 officers and men, but none of the Union's black heavy artillery regiments ever enrolled that many.[37]

While white troops moved in and out of the Mississippi River port of Natchez, the 2d Mississippi Heavy Artillery (AD) remained in garrison. The regiment had begun recruiting in mid-September and had filled its twelfth and final company only on 21 January 1864. Most of its officers had come from the 30th Missouri Infantry, which had arrived at Natchez the summer before. Nearly all of the enlisted men in the regiment were from plantations in nearby counties and parishes. Many of them became sick soon after enlisting, for Natchez was a notoriously unhealthy place. The number of residents in a nearby contraband camp dwindled from four thousand to twenty-five hundred that fall, partly because of mortality that on one occasion reached seventy-five deaths in one day. Some of the surviving freedpeople fled in disgust or despair to their home plantations.[38]

By February 1864, Company A of the 2d Mississippi Heavy Artillery (AD) was serving as mounted infantry in the village of Vidalia, across the river on the Louisiana shore, attracting the Confederates' attention by forays inland. The men of Companies I, K, L, and M, the most recently organized, had not yet received rifles and could not practice the infantry drill that soldiers in a heavy artillery regiment were required to master. They conducted artillery drill instead, using large cannon mounted in the earthworks around the city that they and other former slaves had helped to dig. The average number of enlisted men in each company was less than half the 147 authorized by law for artillery.[39]

On Sunday, 7 February, the 2d Mississippi's commander, Col. Bernard G. Farrar, was across the river at the Union outpost in Vidalia. Lt. Col. Hubert A. McCaleb remained in Natchez commanding the regiment. About 2:30 that afternoon,

---

[36] *OR*, ser. 1, vol. 24, pt. 2, p. 459 ("unfortunately"), and pt. 3, pp. 425–26 (Grant), 443–44 (Taylor); vol. 34, pt. 2, pp. 935 ("If you come"), 952 ("It is desirable"). *WGFL: LS*, pp. 642–43; Dudley T. Cornish, *The Sable Arm: Negro Troops in the Union Army, 1861–1865* (New York: Longmans, Green, 1956), pp. 163–70.

[37] *OR*, ser. 3, 2: 519; Dyer, *Compendium*, pp. 1693–1709, 1721–23.

[38] *ORVF*, 8: 154; personnel data from Descriptive Book, 6th USCA, Regimental Books, RG 94, NA; James E. Yeatman, *A Report on the Condition of the Freedmen of the Mississippi* (St. Louis: Western Sanitary Commission, 1864), pp. 13–14.

[39] *OR*, ser. 1, vol. 34, pt. 1, p. 129; Jeff Kinard, *Lafayette of the South: Prince Camille de Polignac and the American Civil War* (College Station: Texas A&M University Press, 2001), p. 121. War Department, General Orders 126, 6 Sep 1862, established the maximum strength of a volunteer artillery company at 152 officers and men. *OR*, ser. 3, 2: 519.

Farrar sent word that Vidalia was under attack by "overwhelming numbers of the enemy." McCaleb was to load every available man on the first boat and make for the opposite shore. After turning over command to "the senior convalescent officer" and posting a guard on the camp and its hospital, McCaleb found himself with 432 men representing seven companies of the regiment.[40]

When the steamer *Diligent* deposited them in Vidalia, McCaleb moved his companies about one hundred fifty yards inland from the levee and placed them on either side of a road where a section of artillery—two guns—had taken position. Soon afterward, he spied a force that he thought numbered between twelve and fifteen hundred Confederates moving out of the trees at the edge of the flood plain, about half a mile away. A row of skirmishers preceded them. Farrar ordered McCaleb to take the four companies on the left of the road and join the regiment's Company A on higher ground. Their fire stopped the skirmishers about a hundred yards short of the new Union position, but not the Confederates' advancing line. "On their main body came in splendid style," McCaleb reported, "carrying their arms at a support, presenting a most formidable front." He gave the order to fire at a range of one hundred fifty or two hundred yards. "This caused the enemy to falter and lie down," he continued. "I immediately ordered the men to load, . . . and with one more well-aimed volley the rebel ranks were broken, and their men, panic-stricken, ran away in great confusion. I ordered my men to load and fire . . . at the fleeing mob, and with difficulty prevented them from breaking ranks to follow the enemy, their anxiety being great to do so." The battalion stayed put until well after dark, when it withdrew to the levee. "Thus a force of 300 colored soldiers put to flight, in great confusion, four or five times their number," McCaleb exulted. He admitted that as far as he could tell the enemy's losses amounted only to one killed, five wounded, and a few prisoners. The 2d Mississippi Heavy Artillery (AD) had suffered no casualties. The Confederates had numbered only five hundred fifty by their own commander's count; nevertheless, the skirmish at Vidalia was an easy victory well calculated to raise the morale of a new regiment.[41]

Farther north on the Mississippi, the 6th United States Colored Artillery (USCA), formerly the 1st Alabama Siege Artillery (AD) and later renumbered the 11th United States Colored Infantry (USCI) (New), manned the defenses of Memphis and its outlying posts. One of these was Fort Pillow, some eighty-five miles above the city by river but as little as thirty-five miles by land. Much of western Tennessee was cotton-growing country, and pro-Confederate sentiment predominated among its white population. "We are very near if not in the enemy's country," 2d Lt. George W. Buswell wrote in his diary soon after his regiment, the 68th USCI, arrived in Memphis from St. Louis. It was not surprising, then, that instructions to Maj. William F. Bradford, who commanded the 13th Tennessee Cavalry, a white Unionist regiment assigned to "hunt up and destroy guerrilla parties" near Fort Pillow, cautioned him in early February to "scout the surrounding country . . . as far [from the river] as you may

---

[40] *OR*, ser. 1, vol. 34, pt. 1, p. 129 (quotation).
[41] Ibid., p. 130 (quotation); Kinard, *Lafayette of the South*, p. 122.

deem it safe to take your command." Prudence was important, for "home-made Yankees" taken captive could expect no more mercy from the Confederates than the Union's black soldiers might—less, perhaps, for white prisoners had no cash value.[42]

Four companies of the 6th USCA, numbering about two hundred seventy officers and men, and one section of Battery D, 2d USCA, with two cannon and thirty-five officers and men, made up the rest of Fort Pillow's garrison in the early spring of 1864. Most of the men of the 6th USCA had enlisted at Corinth, Mississippi, in the summer and fall of 1863, while those of the light artillery had enlisted at Memphis in the fall. In mid-January, the 6th USCA, only five companies strong, had moved from Corinth to Memphis. After further recruiting, the regiment had sent its four senior companies to Fort Pillow at the end of March. Since both the light and heavy artillery gained a few recruits among the black refugees who flocked to army camps, officers of the 13th Tennessee Cavalry hoped that a white regiment's presence would encourage white Unionists in the neighborhood to enlist as well. Black soldiers and white, Fort Pillow's garrison amounted to somewhere between four hundred fifty and five hundred fifty men fit for duty during the second week of April 1864.[43]

The fort itself was a sprawling two-mile line of entrenchments that faced inland on the bluffs above the river, dug to protect gun emplacements that Confederates had built on the riverbank early in 1862 and named after one of their generals, the Tennessee politician and Mexican War veteran Gideon J. Pillow. After Confederates in the region surrendered in June 1862, when a Union landing force occupied Memphis, U.S. Navy crews removed the serviceable ordnance, for the Confederates had no naval force to guard against. In the spring of 1864, Fort Pillow's artillery consisted of Battery D's two field pieces and two more that the 6th USCA battalion had brought with it. Well within the post's outer defenses, close to the river, the garrison had constructed a small fort with six embrasures for artillery surrounded by a ditch six feet deep and twelve wide. The 6th USCA's Maj. Lionel F. Booth supervised its final preparation during the two weeks after his battalion arrived at Fort Pillow at the end of March. In siting the earthworks to protect the battalion's camp, he neglected to enclose some nearby cabins that earlier troops had built to serve as

---

[42] OR, ser. 1, vol. 32, pt. 1, p. 562 ("home-made"), and pt. 2, p. 311 ("hunt up"); G. W. Buswell Jnls, 8 Jun 1864, Huntington Library, San Marino, Calif. The 6th USCA changed its designation twice more during the war, becoming the 7th USCA on 26 April 1864 and the 11th USCI (New) on 23 January 1865. The 2d Mississippi Heavy Artillery, at Natchez, became the 6th USCA on 26 April 1864. ORVF, 8: 154, 182.

[43] Three officers who survived the fight estimated the number of Union soldiers present for duty as 550, 500, and 450. OR, ser. 1, vol. 32, pt. 1, pp. 559, 563, 569; NA M594, roll 206, 11th USCI; ORVF, 8: 166. John Cimprich, Fort Pillow, A Civil War Massacre, and Public Memory (Baton Rouge: Louisiana State University Press, 2005), p. 129, lists the garrison's total strength as between 593 and 611. Cimprich bases his count on personnel records in the National Archives, rather than the figures in Fort Pillow's post return at the end of March (OR, ser. 1, vol. 32, pt. 1, p. 556). The 2d USCA was a collective term for nine independent light batteries that served in six states, from South Carolina to Arkansas. Unlike other black artillery regiments, the 2d USCA had no field officers or noncommissioned staff.

barracks. Ravines that creased the bluff's entire front also exposed the position to attack.[44]

An assault was not long in coming. While Sherman made final preparations for the Union advance into northern Georgia, the Confederate cavalry leader Forrest undertook a raid into Tennessee and Kentucky. He planned to range west of the Tennessee River to round up Confederate deserters and attract new recruits, and to punish horse thieves who helped themselves to stock that otherwise might find its way into the Confederate Army. His force of four brigades, about five thousand men in all, left Columbus, Mississippi, on 16 March and covered the one hundred seventy miles to Jackson, Tennessee, in four days. On 24 March, he was at Union City, sixty miles farther north, where he compelled the surrender of the Union garrison. At Nashville that day, Sherman told the local commander not to sidetrack any troops on their way to his own army in order to deal with the raid. "The more men Forrest has, and the longer he stays . . . , the better for us," he wrote. Meanwhile, the raiders reached the Ohio River, another sixty miles farther north, on 25 March. Federal troops at Paducah, Kentucky, repelled a charge on their fort, and the attackers withdrew when they discovered smallpox cases in the town itself during a search for medical supplies. In Jackson, Tennessee, again on 4 April, Forrest told his department commander: "There is a Federal force of 500 or 600 at Fort Pillow, which I shall attend to in a day or two, as they have horses and supplies which we need."[45]

Not long after 5:00 a.m. on 12 April, two brigades of Forrest's cavalry, perhaps fifteen hundred strong, surprised the Union pickets at Fort Pillow. By 10:00, when Forrest arrived on the scene, the federal troops had withdrawn to their earthworks. The Confederates twice sent forward a flag of truce to demand that the garrison surrender. Each time, the defenders refused. Forrest's men used the intervals of truce to move forward, occupying the cabins near the fort as well as nearby ravines from which they fired into the Union position. Soon after the second truce, Forrest ordered a dismounted charge that captured the fort. Some of the defenders died where they stood; others ran for the river. The Confederates killed all they could. The number of Union soldiers killed outright, according to the most careful reckoning, was between 246 and 264. Another thirty-one died of wounds. Two-thirds of the dead were black artillerymen.[46]

The Confederates held Fort Pillow overnight. The Union gunboat *Silver Cloud* arrived early on the morning of 13 April and took aboard twenty wounded soldiers who had hidden along the riverbank. A Confederate flag of truce proposed admitting sailors to the fort in order to bury the dead and carry off the wounded. The boat's master, William Ferguson, wrote his report the next day. It is the first official record of what occurred, written the day the first newspaper account appeared in

---

[44]*OR*, ser. 1, vol. 32, pt. 1, pp. 556, 621; Cimprich, *Fort Pillow*, pp. 48, 74. The adjutant of the 13th Tennessee Cavalry reported six guns; one of Forrest's brigadiers reported five. *OR*, ser. 1, vol. 32, pt. 1, pp. 559, 621.

[45]*OR*, ser. 1, vol. 32, pt. 1, pp. 509, 511 ("The more men"), 609 ("There is a"), 611–12, and pt. 3, pp. 609, 616–17, 663–65. In a report dated 15 April 1864, Forrest wrote that he reached Jackson on 23 March, but according to a report dated 21 March, he arrived "yesterday morning at 11 o'clock" (pt. 2, p. 663).

[46]*OR*, ser. 1, vol. 32, pt. 1, pp. 559–70, 609–17, 620–22; Cimprich, *Fort Pillow*, p. 129.

Memphis, earlier than the reports of surviving Army officers and well before the furor that swept the North as newspapers across the country picked up the story.[47]

"We found about 70 wounded men in the fort and around it, and buried, I should think, 150 bodies," Ferguson wrote.

> All the buildings around the fort and the tents and huts in the fort had been burned by the rebels, and among the embers the charred remains of numbers of our soldiers who had suffered a terrible death in the flames could be seen. All the wounded who had strength enough to speak agreed that after the fort was taken an indiscriminate slaughter of our troops was carried on by the enemy. . . . Around on every side horrible testimony to the truth of this statement could be seen. Bodies with gaping wounds, . . . some with skulls beaten through, others with hideous wounds as if their bowels had been ripped open with bowie-knives, plainly told that but little quarter was shown. . . . Strewn from the fort to the river bank, in the ravines and hollows, behind logs and under the brush where they had crept for protection from the assassins who pursued them, we found bodies bayonet-ed, beaten, and shot to death, showing how cold-blooded and persistent was the slaughter. . . . Of course, when a work is carried by assault there will always be more or less bloodshed, even when all resistance has ceased; but here there were unmistakable evidences of a massacre carried on long after any resistance could have been offered, with a cold-blooded barbarity and perseverance which nothing can palliate.[48]

An Army officer who visited the fort to help remove the wounded spoke with Brig. Gen. James R. Chalmers, one of Forrest's subordinates:

> One of the gun-boat officers who accompanied us asked General Chalmers if most of the negroes were not killed after they (the enemy) had taken possession. Chalmers replied that he thought they had been, and that the men of General Forrest's command had such a hatred toward the armed negro that they could not be restrained from killing the negroes. . . . He said they were not killed by General Forrest's or his orders, but that both Forrest and he stopped the mas-sacre as soon as they were able to do so. He said it was nothing better than we could expect so long as we persisted in arming the negro.[49]

The steamer *Platte River*, carrying fifty-seven of the wounded, "including seven or eight colored men," arrived at Cairo, Illinois, on the evening of 14 April, and the news from Fort Pillow was soon on the telegraph wires. "Fiendish Slaugh-ter," the *Philadelphia Inquirer* proclaimed in bold sans serif type. The *New York Tribune* promised its readers "Shocking Scenes of Savagery." The next week, a

---

[47]Five survivors reported between 14 and 27 April 1864; one, on 17 January 1864. *OR*, ser. 1, vol. 32, pt. 1, pp. 559–70. The 6th USCA regimental report was written in Memphis and based on survivors' accounts. Lt Col T. J. Jackson to Capt G. B. Halstead, 19 Apr 1864, 11th USCI, Entry 57C, RG 94, NA. On press coverage, see Cimprich, *Fort Pillow*, pp. 89–91, 157.

[48]*OR*, ser. 1, vol. 32, pt. 1, p. 571.

[49]Ibid., p. 558. "It has been asserted again and again that Forrest did not order a massacre. He did not need to." Cornish, *Sable Arm*, p. 175.

joint resolution of Congress directed the Joint Select Committee on the Conduct of the War to "inquire into the truth of the rumored slaughter of the Union troops, after their surrender." The committee reported on 6 May. Another joint resolution ordered the printing of forty thousand extra copies. Fort Pillow was on its way to becoming an emblem of the special viciousness that racial hatred imparted to the sectional conflict.[50]

Newspapers passed from one army to the other, and Confederates were not slow to realize what a propaganda weapon they had handed their opponents. Many Southerners abandoned the matter-of-fact tone in which General Chalmers had discussed the slaughter at Fort Pillow. Forrest himself assumed an indignant posture that June when he wrote to the Union commander in West Tennessee: "It has been reported to me that all the negro troops stationed in Memphis took an oath on their knees, in the presence of General Hurlbut and other officers of your army, to avenge Fort Pillow, and that they would show my troops no quarter." Maj. Gen. Cadwallader C. Washburn replied that black soldiers in Memphis may have taken such an oath, but not at their officers' instigation or in their presence. "From what I can learn," he told Forrest, "this act of theirs was not influenced by any white officer but was the result of their own sense of what was due to themselves and their fellows, who had been mercilessly slaughtered." There does not appear to have been any official Union correspondence on the subject. If the troops at Memphis swore to avenge dead comrades, the oath must have been private, voluntary, and outside the purview of their officers. It would not have been at all out of character, or the first instance of such behavior among black soldiers, whose religious observances in camp sometimes went beyond their officers' control. A sacred vow to avenge their dead, like the one that Forrest supposed the black troops at Memphis swore, prefigured more peaceful communal endeavors that arose after the war as freedpeople founded their own schools and political organizations.[51]

The black soldiers of Memphis soon got a chance to take the field. Sherman's campaign against Atlanta was in full swing by the second week in May. General Washburn in Memphis learned that Forrest was once again in northeastern Mississippi preparing "a big thieving raid" on Tennessee and Kentucky "and to interfere with Sherman's [rail] connections" to Chattanooga, Nashville, and the North. Washburn intended to interfere with Forrest first.[52]

To do this, he fielded 3,300 mounted men: 3,600 white infantry; 22 cannon, including 2 from Battery F, 2d USCA; and the 55th and 59th USCIs, 1,200 strong, all under the command of Brig. Gen. Samuel D. Sturgis. Although Sherman himself had sent the West Point graduate and Mexican War veteran to Memphis "to take command of that cavalry and whip Forrest," Sturgis had recently let Forrest's brigades slip away from him. "My little campaign is over, and I regret to say

---

[50]*Philadelphia Inquirer*, 16 April 1864 (quotation); *New York Tribune*, 16 July 1864; "Fort Pillow Massacre," 38th Cong., 1st sess., H. Rpt. 65 (serial 1,207), p. 1.

[51]*OR*, ser. 1, vol. 32, pt. 1, pp. 586 (Forrest), 588 (Washburn); Berlin et al., *Black Military Experience*, pp. 401–02, 606–10; Joseph T. Glatthaar, *Forged in Battle: The Civil War Alliance of Black Soldiers and White Officers* (New York: Free Press, 1990), pp. 170–76; Keith P. Wilson, *Campfires of Freedom: The Camp Life of Black Soldiers During the Civil War* (Kent, Ohio: Kent State University Press, 2002), pp. 47–58, 133–37, 141–46.

[52]*OR*, ser. 1, vol. 39, pt. 2, p. 41.

Forrest is still at large," he prefaced the report of an unsuccessful mounted operation in early May. On the last day of the month, Washburn ordered him to march
toward Corinth, Mississippi, and destroy whatever supplies the Confederates had
there, then to head for Tupelo, following the line of the Mobile and Ohio Railroad
south from there and tearing up the track. The expedition would continue south
to Columbus, then strike west across country to Grenada, and finally return to
Memphis. It would be an easy twenty-day campaign, Washburn thought. "Take
your time," he told Sturgis. "Subsist on the country when you can. . . . I send with
you two colored regiments. See that they have their proper position in march and
take the advance in marching when it is their turn to do so." Washburn did not send
black soldiers merely to guard the expedition's 248 wagons.[53]

The 55th and 59th USCIs had been stationed in Memphis since January and
had developed the sort of troubled relations with nearby civilians that were common whenever troops stayed in one place for long. Brig. Gen. Augustus L. Chetlain, commanding U.S. Colored Troops in Tennessee, learned that "armed squads
of colored soldiers have been in the habit of leaving their camps at a late hour of
the night and visiting houses of citizens on both sides of the picket line for the purpose of pillaging. Several houses have been visited . . . and the inmates assaulted
and robbed." Chetlain promised punishment for enlisted offenders and lax officers.
With active service in the near future, at least one officer asked the post adjutant
to release a few of his men from the guardhouse in order to bring the company up
to strength.[54]

At the beginning of June, the two regiments moved by rail to Lafayette, Tennessee, a station some twenty-five miles east of Memphis, where the expedition
assembled. It set out before dawn on 3 June. Rain, which had been intermittent the
day before, became heavy and continuous. The main body of infantry struggled
southward eighteen miles on the first day, but the wagon train, with the 55th and
59th USCIs as guard, managed only fourteen miles before going into camp at
11:00 p.m. The train caught up with the main body of infantry about noon on the
second day's march, and that part of the expedition stayed in camp on 5 June while
a force of four hundred cavalry scouted toward Rienzi, Mississippi. The expedition
took two more rainy days to reach Ripley, about forty miles from Lafayette. Scouting parties began to meet small bands of Confederates that retreated without offering much resistance. As the rain continued, Sturgis conferred with his cavalry and
infantry division commanders, Brig. Gen. Benjamin H. Grierson and Col. William
L. McMillen. They agreed that although the prospects of accomplishing anything
were dismal there was no better course open to them than to keep on until they

---

[53]Ibid., vol. 32, pt. 1, p. 698 (Sturgis), and pt. 3, p. 411 (Sherman); vol. 39, pt. 1, pp. 89–90, 217,
218 (Washburn). Robert Cowden, *A Brief Sketch of the Organization and Services of the Fifty-ninth
Regiment of United States Colored Infantry* (Freeport, N.Y.: Books for Libraries Press, 1971 [1883]),
p. 69.

[54]2d Lt R. S. Mason to 1st Lt L. Methudy, 31 May 1864, 55th USCI, Entry 57C, RG 94, NA; HQ
U.S. Colored Troops, GO 14, 13 May 1864 ("armed squads"), 59th USCI, Regimental Books, RG 94,
NA. Capt A. G. Tuther to Brig Gen A. L. Chetlain, 7 Mar 1864, and Lt Col J. M. Irvin to Capt C. W.
Dustan, 12 Mar 1864, both in 55th USCI, Entry 57C, RG 94, NA, mention complaints of nocturnal
marauding by black soldiers. Col E. Bouton to Capt C. W. Dunstan, 3 Feb 1864, 59th USCI, Entry
57C, RG 94, NA, is a commanding officer's complaint against civilians dumping animal carcasses
near the regiment's camp.

met the enemy. On 9 June, the expedition sent four hundred sick and exhausted men—nearly 5 percent of its strength—and forty-one of the wagons back to Memphis, "all the eating and non-fighting portion of the command," Sturgis called them. Rain fell for only two hours that day.[55]

On the morning of 10 June, the expedition moved toward Tupelo, cavalry in the lead. The 55th and 59th USCIs took their turn guarding the wagon train for the fourth time since the expedition's start. They plodded along, the 55th with four men assigned to walk beside each wagon while the 59th USCI and the two guns of Battery F brought up the rear. The battery's horses had been without corn for two days, but that morning the commanding officer, Capt. Carl A. Lamberg, had managed to find a wagonload of fodder that he thought would last for about three days. Marching through a part of Mississippi that had been fought over for the past two years, the cav-

Col. Edward Bouton took care that the brigade of black troops he led was formed properly before going into action at Brice's Crossroads. As a result, the brigade came out of that battle in better shape than the rest of the defeated force and was able to help cover the Union retreat.

alry and the wagon teams were in no better shape than the artillery horses. The rear of the column got under way at about 10:30 and had gone only two miles through swampy bottom land when Col. Edward Bouton, commanding the rearguard, noticed enemy cavalry traveling a road about a mile to his right. Soon afterward, he heard the sound of cannon to his front. It came from batteries supporting the Union cavalry division on the far side of Tishomingo Creek firing on a Confederate charge that hit the dismounted troopers not long after they crossed the creek and took up positions east of it.[56]

The wagons followed a muddy road through thick pinewoods with only occasional fields opening on either side. It was after 2:00 p.m. before the train crossed Tishomingo Creek and found a field large enough to park in, about a quarter-mile from a crossroads that took its name from William Brice, whose house and store stood nearby. By that time, Confederate reinforcements had overcome the Union cavalry. Colonel McMillen rushed an infantry brigade forward to halt the rout, but he soon saw that "everything was going to the devil as fast as it possibly could." The infantry covered the last half-mile "at double-quick . . . , my object being to

[55]*OR*, ser. 1, vol. 39, pt. 1, pp. 88 (quotation), 90–91, 162, 199–200, 207; Cowden, *Brief Sketch*, p. 69.

[56]*OR*, ser. 1, vol. 39, pt. 1, pp. 181, 184, 213.

get through [the] retreating cavalry with as little depression as possible to my own men"; but while the lead brigade was relieving the cavalry that was still on the firing line, another Confederate charge struck the Union left. Exhausted by the Mississippi heat and the rapid march, most of McMillen's men refused to advance again; he decided to withdraw while he still had some control of them.[57]

About that time, the officers in charge of the supply train received orders, before they had finished parking the wagons, to start them on the road again and join the retreat. Colonel Bouton told the 55th USCI to leave the wagons and form companies while the 59th joined them from the rear of the column at the double. No orders had reached Bouton, "but getting a partial view of the field, and seeing our cavalry falling back, soon followed by infantry and artillery," he decided to act. "I immediately gathered two companies from the head of the column . . . and threw them forward into what seemed to be a gap in the First Brigade, near the right and rear of what seemed to be the left battalion." The phrases "a partial view" and "seemed to be" show the tenuous nature of a commander's grasp of facts during a battle; the word "confusion" occurs in General Sturgis' report and in reports of division, brigade, and regimental commanders. Seven more companies of the 55th soon reinforced the first two and covered the retreat of the troops on their right. When the way was clear, the 59th filled the vacant space. Captain Lamberg's two cannon fired exploding shells over the woods through which the Confederates were advancing, with orders to substitute canister shot when the enemy came in view, "which order he obeyed as well as possible until he was forced to retire," Bouton reported, "leaving one caisson on the ground, which he was compelled to do on account of its horses being many of them killed."[58]

It was late afternoon before the Confederates forced Bouton's brigade out of its position. The men retired slowly from field to field for about half a mile and at sunset halted on high ground at the edge of some woods. "Our company was in a skirmish line and we were falling back, for Forrest was crowding us," Pvt. George Jenkins of the 55th USCI recalled when he applied for a pension years later. "I would turn & shoot & then retreat. We were crossing a little opening in a kind of old field 200 or 300 y[ar]ds from some woods, when as I turned a bullet struck me in the right hip & passed clean through & went into the left thigh. I fell like a dead man & fainted away, I reckon." The next day, Confederate troops took Jenkins and other prisoners to Mobile, where a surgeon removed the bullet.[59]

In the failing light, the 59th USCI received one last Confederate charge and chased the attackers back "with bayonets and clubbed muskets," Bouton reported, more than half the distance the regiment had just covered. Then Bouton discovered that while his own men charged, the brigade on his left had continued to retire. By

---

[57] Ibid., pp. 208 ("everything"), 209 ("at double-quick"), 210, 213, 903; George B. Davis et al., eds., *The Official Military Atlas of the Civil War* (New York: Barnes & Noble, 2003 [1891–1895]), p. 167.

[58] *OR*, ser. 1, vol. 39, pt. 1, pp. 94 (Sturgis), 98, 105 (McMillen), 124 (Lt Col G. R. Clarke, 113th Illinois), 125 ("but getting"), 126, 129 (Grierson), 145 (Maj A. R. Pierce, 3d Iowa Cav), 213; Cowden, *Brief Sketch*, p. 93.

[59] Depositions, George Jenkins, 18 Nov 1896 (quotation), and Thomas Kimbrough, 2 Jul 1897, both in Pension File SC811848, George Jenkins, Civil War Pension Application Files (CWPAF), RG 15, Rcds of the Veterans Admin, NA.

this time, the field officers of both black regiments were wounded and out of action, leaving the senior captains in command, insofar as either regiment retained any organization at all. The 55th USCI had about 200 men present of 604 that had gone into action, the 59th about 250 of 607. Bouton decided to retreat. Along the way, the men of the 59th picked up ammunition that had been thrown away by stampeding white troops. By 11:00 p.m., when the remnant of Bouton's brigade caught up with the rest of Sturgis' force, the regiment held an average of twenty-five rounds per man.[60]

This came in handy the next day, for the expedition had lost most of its supplies on the day of the battle. Panic-stricken teamsters deserted their wagons, setting fire to some of them. Burning and abandoned wagons blocked the federal retreat on the narrow, muddy road to Ripley, but once Sturgis' command had struggled past them, they delayed the Confederate pursuit as well. The ammunition wagons fell into the hands of Forrest's cavalry. Men of the 55th USCI felt the loss keenly the next morning, when the Confederates caught up with them near Ripley. "As our ammunition was captured we were unable to stand even a test & made a hasty retreat," the regiment's summary of the expedition recorded at the end of the month. "The enemy came on to us with cavalry & scattered both officers and men all through the woods."[61]

Because of the headlong retreat, casualty lists were largely conjectural. "The fighting was desperate, and many reported then 'missing' were killed on the field," one company commander reported; "but I am unable to tell which ones they were. I think most of them were killed. . . . But we were obliged to leave our dead and wounded. . . . Although about 10 wounded have come in [by 30 June] having hid in the bushes and traveled nights living on berries and bark, and occasionally getting food from colored people in the country. They were annoyed very much by [civilians] with blood hounds." Regimental descriptive books for the 55th and 59th USCIs—volumes that contain each soldier's record and were kept up-to-date until the regiments mustered out after the war—show 7 missing men rejoining within a few days after the battle, 12 rejoining between July and October, and 9 rejoining at an unnamed or illegible date. Pvt. Claiborne Merriweather of the 59th USCI was last seen firing a carbine that he had taken from a Confederate whom he had just beaten to death with the butt of his rifle. Left behind in the retreat, Merriweather did not turn up again for seven weeks. Pvt. Henry Guy had to escape from his captors twice, the first time from the hospital where a Confederate surgeon treated his wounds, before he was able to rejoin the 55th USCI at La Grange, Tennessee, late in August.[62]

At least nineteen of Guy's comrades waited until the war was over to rejoin. These men had been taken prisoner and put in hospitals to recover from their wounds or sent to Mobile to work on the city's fortifications when Union forces occupied its seaward approaches in August. After the forts on the eastern shore of Mobile Bay fell in April 1865, the prisoners moved north to Montgomery, where they stayed until after Confederate troops in the region surrendered the next month. Most of the

---

[60]*OR*, ser. 1, vol. 39, pt. 1, p. 126 (quotation), 904; Cowden, *Brief Sketch*, pp. 98–99.

[61]*OR*, ser. 1, vol. 39, pt. 1, pp. 115, 224; NA M594, roll 211, 55th USCI.

[62]NA M594, roll 211, 55th USCI ("the fighting"); Regimental Books, 55th and 59th USCIs, RG 94, NA; Declaration, Henry Guy, 7 Apr 1885, and Affidavit, Henry Guy, 27 Feb 1886, both in Pension File WC571997, Henry Guy, CWPAF.

prisoners rejoined their regiments in June. At least five men died while prisoners of war. Undoubtedly, many more dead were among the 153 men still listed as missing when the regiments closed their descriptive books. Some of these died in the fighting of June 1864 and were left on the field in the Union forces' rapid retreat, but only Pvt. Balam Fenderson's name bears the notation "shot Death, after Surrender." At least eight of the returned prisoners of war received treatment in Confederate hospitals. As sketchy as the statistics are, they show that the Union defeat in June 1864 was not a massacre of the kind that had occurred two months earlier, even though part of the Confederate force in Mississippi had carried out the slaughter at Fort Pillow.[63]

The rout of Sturgis' force was a triumph for Forrest's aggressive tactics. The Union force included ten white infantry regiments that had been in the field for more than a year and a half. Many of the men were veterans of the previous year's Vicksburg Campaign. These regiments had practically dissolved before the charging Confederates. Officers reported scenes of disorder, with men destroying or throwing away their weapons and hiding in the woods or running to keep up with the retreating cavalry. "The infantry being thus left . . . with no ammunition, exhausted with more than twenty-four hours' constant exertion without rest or food, many of them became an easy prey to the enemy," the commanding officer of the 81st Illinois reported. Official correspondence contains only occasional mentions of resistance by the retreating federals: two companies of the 3d Iowa Cavalry "checked the rebel advance" at one point, and the 113th Illinois reported skirmishing "almost the entire distance" back to Collierville, Tennessee. Colonel McMillen's report praised Colonel Bouton's regiments repeatedly. Their action late in the day at Brice's Crossroads "checked the pursuit and ended the fighting for that evening." At Ripley the next morning, they "fought bravely" before being "overpowered by superior numbers." They "fought with a gallantry that commended them to the favor of their comrades in arms." Unfortunately for them and their white comrades, gallantry was not enough to save the expedition.[64]

At camps around Memphis, Union soldiers watched the expedition's survivors straggle in. Sturgis and his staff appeared on 13 June. The rest of the defeated force began to arrive the next day. "The army is badly demoralized," Lieutenant Buswell wrote. "Some of the boys in order to run with ease . . . threw [their rifles] & cartridge boxes into the swamp. . . . The colored boys were praised by every

---

[63] Affidavit, Henry Guy, 27 Feb 1886, in Pension File WC571997, Guy. Depositions, Sandy Sledge, in Pension File SC172409, Ruben Hogan; George Jenkins, 18 Nov 1896, in Pension File WC811448, George Jenkins; Thomas Kimbrough, 29 Apr 1899, and Jordan Watson, 29 Apr 1899, both in Pension File WC430651, Gus Price. Affidavit, Armstead Rann, 30 Aug 1892, in Pension File SO1119709, Armstead Rann; Declaration, Reuben Stafford, 26 Dec 1895, in Pension File WC930742, Reuben Stafford; all in CWPAF. Descriptive Book ("shot Death"), 59th USCI, Regimental Books, RG 94, NA. George S. Burkhardt, *Confederate Rage, Yankee Wrath: No Quarter in the Civil War* (Carbondale: Southern Illinois University Press, 2007), pp. 152–57, alleges that the Confederates massacred black soldiers at Tishomingo Creek, just as they did at Fort Pillow. Reasons for different Confederate behavior at different times and places must remain speculative to a degree, as in all wars. Simon Sebag-Montefiore, *Dunkirk: Fight to the Last Man* (Cambridge, Mass.: Harvard University Press, 2006), pp. 356–60, tells of a British soldier who was rescued by German medics after being wounded a little while earlier by the *SS* (*Schützstaffel*), who carried out a massacre of prisoners.

[64] *OR*, ser. 1, vol. 39, pt. 1, pp. 106 (McMillen), 112 (3d Iowa Cav, 93d Indiana), 116 (72d Ohio), 120 (113th Illinois), 123 (81st Illinois).

soldier for their valor & bravery. In the fight colored soldiers were taken prisoners and paroled same as others." Two days later, Buswell added: "More of the soldiers from the . . . expedition came in today having dodged around from place to place, their only friends being the blacks, who fed them."[65]

In their haste to get away, Sturgis' troops retreated in two days the same distance they had taken almost a week to cover while advancing. Perhaps the roads of northern Mississippi had dried a little; certainly, the expedition was no longer encumbered by its baggage wagons, which were in Confederate hands. In Memphis, General Washburn received Sturgis' first message of defeat on 12 July. Washburn at once sent a telegram to Secretary of War Edwin M. Stanton. He estimated that Sturgis had lost one-quarter or half of his expedition, but "with troops lately arrived [at Memphis] I am safe here." General McPherson, commanding the Army of the Tennessee, had ordered the expedition, Washburn said; "an officer sent me by General Sherman" had carried it out. He sent a less craven, blame-shifting message to Sherman, asking whether Maj. Gen. Andrew J. Smith's recently arrived divisions should carry out Sherman's idea of an offensive against Mobile.[66]

Sherman replied by telegram from Big Shanty on the railroad north of Marietta, Georgia. Postpone the Mobile Expedition, he advised Washburn, and send Smith's force after Forrest and whatever other Confederates remained in Mississippi. "They should be met and defeated at any and all cost." Smith's men were veterans of the Army of the Tennessee. They had marched to Meridian in January, after which Sherman sent them to augment Maj. Gen. Nathaniel P. Banks' Red River Expedition. With that campaign over, they had just landed at Memphis on their way east to join the attack on Atlanta, but Sherman was willing to spare them a while longer in order to defeat Forrest and thus protect his army's vital rail line to Nashville from Confederate raids.[67]

As Smith prepared to move, General Washburn sent Colonel Bouton and his brigade east to guard the forty-mile stretch of the Memphis and Charleston Railroad that ran as far as La Grange, Tennessee, where the expedition would assemble. When Smith's force had arrived there, Bouton's nineteen hundred men would join it to make a total of about fourteen thousand infantry, cavalry, and artillery. Reorganized after Sturgis' expedition, Bouton's brigade included, besides his own 59th, the 61st and 68th USCIs and Battery I, 2d USCA. Some companies of the 61st had been in action at Moscow, Tennessee, the previous December; the 68th had mustered in only that April.[68]

The troops left Memphis in freight cars. Instructions for the move called for "light marching order." At La Grange, Lieutenant Buswell found "not a tent in the entire command, except a few flies for Hd Qrs . . . and each regiment, and the Commissary Dept. The men rolling up in their rubber blankets and lying upon the ground. . . . It is certainly fighting trim throughout, no luggage of any description, except the men have their haversacks & canteens . . . not even a change of underclothing." General Smith believed in the kind of campaigning that his men

---

[65] Buswell Jnls, 14 and 16 Jun 1864.
[66] OR, ser. 1, vol. 39, pt. 2, p. 106.
[67] Ibid., p. 115.
[68] Ibid., pt. 1, pp. 250, 300.

had carried on for the past two years in Tennessee and Mississippi, and, earlier in 1864, in Louisiana.[69]

On 5 July, the expedition set out. Buswell noticed that the 59th USCI burned deserted houses along the route, claiming that the residents had fired on Union troops during the recent retreat. The 59th "and the Kansas Jay hawkers . . . burned the entire town" of Ripley, Mississippi, he noted on 8 July, "except three buildings, the occupants of which were friendly to our wounded boys" on the retreat. Smith's command continued for the next three days by what Colonel Bouton called "easy marches," short distances made necessary by heat and drought. The expedition halted on 12 July at Pontotoc, while cavalry scouted the roads that led southeast to Okolona and due east to Tupelo, two stations on the Mobile and Ohio Railroad. Finding a Confederate force on the Okolona road, Smith decided to move toward Tupelo.[70]

Drummers beat reveille at 3:00 on the morning of 13 July. Smith's cavalry began moving before dawn, but it was 6:00, an hour after sunrise, before Bouton's brigade took the road at the tail of the column. By turning toward undefended Tupelo, rather than confronting Forrest's force at Okolona, Smith left the expedition's rear exposed to Confederate attack. He protected the wagon train by assigning five regiments of veteran white infantry—perhaps fifteen hundred men, a considerable addition to Bouton's three regiments—to guard it. About four men marched beside each wagon.[71]

The train had been on the road for barely an hour when Forrest's artillery began shelling the wagons. Bouton ordered the 59th USCI, the 61st USCI, and Battery I into line to repel the Confederate cavalry. Farther along the road, he organized several ambushes of about one hundred men each hidden in dense underbrush that allowed the enemy to approach within a dozen or so paces without discovering them. "Fighting in the manner I did," Bouton remarked, "with my men concealed and under cover, I was able to punish the enemy pretty severely and suffer comparatively no loss." Firing continued all day long. Toward nightfall, the two infantry regiments became so tired that Bouton had to send the untried 68th USCI into action. The thickly wooded country through which the road to Tupelo passed gave little room for mounted maneuvers and limited gunners' vision, so the Confederate pursuit was able to do little damage. Bouton's brigade suffered one man killed, seven wounded, and nine missing. The train did not reach Tupelo until 9:00 p.m., well after dark.[72]

Bouton's Confederate opponents admitted that the federal troops that day fought better than they had in June. "At no time had I found the enemy unprepared," the Confederate Brig. Gen. Abraham Buford reported, summing up the day's events. "He marched with his column well closed up, his wagon train well protected, and his flanks covered in an admirable manner, evincing at all times a readiness to meet

---

[69]Buswell Jnls, 2 Jul 1864; Cowden, *Brief Sketch*, p. 126 ("light marching"). On XVI Corps troops in Banks' Red River Campaign, see Chapter 4, above.

[70]*OR*, ser. 1, vol. 39, pt. 1, pp. 250–51; Buswell Jnls, 6 and 8 Jul 1864. Many senior officers, Union and Confederate, complained of the heat and its effect on their men. *OR*, ser. 1, vol. 39, pt. 1, pp. 253, 260, 275, 281, 287, 289, 300 (quotation), 308, 311, 326, 331–32, 336, 338, 340–41, 343, 349, 351.

[71]*OR*, ser. 1, vol. 39, pt. 1, pp. 276, 301; Buswell Jnls, 13 Jul 1864.

[72]*OR*, ser. 1, vol. 39, pt. 1, pp. 302 (quotation), 905–06; Cowden, *Brief Sketch*, pp. 127–28.

any attack, and showing careful generalship." It is not clear whether he referred to General Smith's management of his entire force, or to Bouton's rearguard action.[73]

Smith's cavalry had covered the eighteen miles from Pontotoc to Tupelo by noon on 13 July; by midafternoon, the destruction of the Mobile and Ohio Railroad was well under way. The Union force had now gotten between the Confederates and the railroad. While the cavalry tore up the tracks and burned bridges and trestles for several miles on either side of Tupelo, the two infantry divisions and Bouton's brigade halted a mile or two west of town on either side of the road they had traveled that day. The Confederate department commander, Lt. Gen. Stephen D. Lee, who had joined Forrest a week earlier with a small force of infantry, ordered an assault on the Union position for the next morning, 14 July.[74]

Bouton's brigade occupied high ground on the left of the Union line, two-thirds of a mile south of the road. The position was far from the main thrust of the Confederate advance, but it afforded an excellent view. "About 7 A.M. skirmishing was heard along the line," Lieutenant Buswell recorded in his diary. West of the Union camp stood a stone wall, and beyond it an abandoned cotton field, perhaps one mile by three quarters, and beyond that woods. Six batteries of six guns each took station in the field. "The troops were ordered to keep close down and keep quiet behind the stone wall," Buswell wrote.

> Soon the rebs were seen coming through the timber . . . and the batteries commenced firing. . . . They came out into the clearing 3 divisions, 3 lines deep, dismounted, their leader, who we learned was Chalmers, riding back and forth behind their ranks, on a noble white charger, his hat in one hand and sword swinging in the other, cheering on his men. . . . [T]heir ranks were mown through & through, but they charged and charged, until nearly up to the cannon, when orders were given to our forces to fire, when we arose from behind the wall & fence and met them face to face. It was desperate, they came on with many a cheer and occasionally a rebel yell, their losses were tremendous. . . . [T]hey . . . were finally compelled to give way, and back they fell across the field. . . . The [Union] troops . . . remained in line of battle all day, and orders were rec'd to remain so all night, our coffee & hard tack being brought to us on the line.[75]

Heat may have accounted for as many Confederate casualties as did federal gunfire. "These two causes of depletion left my line [of battle] almost like a line of skirmishers," one of Forrest's brigade commanders complained. Another colonel reported that his regiment suffered 25 percent casualties "through exhaustion and overheat." The oppressive weather likewise kept Smith's men from pursuing the retreating Confederates.[76]

About sunset, Bouton shifted the bulk of his brigade north in order to shorten the Union line. The new campsite was some seven hundred yards closer to the road, at the base of the rise the troops had held throughout the day. The brigade left

---

[73] *OR*, ser. 1, vol. 39, pt. 1, p. 330.
[74] Ibid., pp. 306, 312, 316.
[75] Buswell Jnls, 14 Jul 1864.
[76] *OR*, ser. 1, vol. 39, pt. 1, pp. 252, 338 ("through exhaustion"), 349 ("These two").

"a heavy skirmish line" in its old position. Not more than two hours passed before Forrest led a brigade of mounted Confederates "meandering through the woods" and quietly approached the Union pickets. Lieutenant Buswell was in the camp below. "The enemy not knowing our true position . . . failed to lower the muzzles of their guns sufficiently to do us any special harm," he recorded in his diary,

> Though we were . . . near enough to distinctly hear the commands of their officers. . . . It was a very dark night and the fire from cannon and their lines of musketry . . . was a sight terrible to behold. . . . Up to this time very little damage was done [to] our line, quiet was maintained, not a shot on our side, except from distant batteries while the rebs were advancing down the slope. When they got sufficiently near, so that they could be distinguished . . . , orders were sent along our lines to commence firing rapidly and at the same time to advance. Our lines were quite close and the contest for a time was hot. When the rebs fell back, we following . . . until they went down the hill the other side, into the timber, and ceased firing.[77]

In the darkness, Union soldiers could only conjecture the enemy's loss, but Buswell thought that it must have been "considerable. . . . Our own loss was not very severe." Despite what Forrest himself called "one of the heaviest fires I have heard during the war," Confederate casualties were small. Forrest reported no deaths in his command that evening, "as the enemy overshot us, but he is reported as having suffered much from the fire of my own men, and still more from their own men, who fired into each other in the darkness of the night." Wild overestimates of enemy strength and casualties characterized reports of officers on both sides throughout the war.[78]

On the morning of 15 July, General Smith learned that half of his expedition's hardtack had spoiled before it was loaded on the wagons at Memphis and that only one day's supply remained. Moreover, the artillery had exhausted its reserve ammunition the day before, and the only rounds left were those in each gun's caisson. Smith therefore decided to withdraw without doing Forrest further harm. Seeing the federal retreat, the Confederates followed closely and by midmorning caught up with Bouton's brigade, which was guarding the supply wagons. Along with several regiments from one of the white divisions, men of the brigade repelled this attack in a two-hour skirmish. Late that afternoon, they charged the height from which they had watched the previous day's fight and drove off a Confederate battery that threatened the retreat. From there, the road was clear to La Grange, Tennessee, the expedition's starting point. Foraging desperately along the way, the troops reached there on 21 July and were back in their old camps at Memphis a day or two later.[79]

Despite the need to cut the campaign short for want of rations and ammunition, Union officers were satisfied with its result and with their troops' performance. "Forrest, though he likes a good fight, had got more than he bargained for this

---

[77] Ibid., pp. 303 ("heavy skirmish line"), 323("meandering"); Buswell Jnls, 14 Jul 1864.
[78] *OR*, ser. 1, vol. 39, pt. 1, p. 323 (Forrest); Buswell Jnls, 14 Jul 1864.
[79] *OR*, ser. 1, vol. 39, pt. 1, pp. 252, 303, 323; Buswell Jnls, 15–23 Jul 1864.

time," Lieutenant Buswell recorded in his diary. "Smith gave Forrest the roughest handling he has had for a long time," 1st Lt. Samuel Evans of the 59th USCI told his father. An interesting feature of Confederate accounts of the fighting is that only one report mentions the presence of "negroes" in the Union ranks. The reason cannot have been the effectiveness of Bouton's troops' concealment in their ambushes, for they were in plain sight earlier in the day. They had not been the object of the main attacks on 14 July, which most Confederate reports emphasized. After the battle, the Union force withdrew with its 559 wounded (48 in Bouton's brigade), and only 38 federal soldiers were missing (16 from the 61st USCI), so incidents of killing the wounded and returning prisoners to slavery, or setting them to work on fortifications did not occur and require explanation. Perhaps, too, the Confederate commanders had other matters on their minds after the battle: for instance, the necessity of explaining away their lack of success against a Union force in which one-seventh of the soldiers were black.[80]

No sooner were General Smith's regiments back in Memphis, properly fed and with their stock of ammunition replenished, than General Washburn ordered them after Forrest again. Smith's force, including Bouton's brigade, returned to La Grange by rail and set out for Holly Springs, Mississippi, on 4 August. Sherman's instruction was to "take freely of all food and forage," and the command helped itself to whatever still grew in northern Mississippi after more than two years of warfare: corn, potatoes, and fruit. The troops endured much rain but little fighting. On 22 August, the day Bouton's brigade reached Oxford, Smith learned the reason he had not found many Confederates: Forrest, with two thousand men, had raided Memphis the day before, intending to kill or capture Union commanders there. He did not succeed but left town with more than one hundred other prisoners. Smith's expedition turned north, hoping to block Forrest's retreat. Bouton's brigade was back in Memphis on 1 September, having covered fifty miles in the previous two days—"some tall marching," as Lieutenant Evans told his father.[81]

The Oxford expedition marked the end of major infantry operations in which U.S. Colored Troops from the Mississippi River garrisons took part. In Georgia, Sherman's army occupied Atlanta at the beginning of September. Preparations for the March to the Sea—no one yet knew whether it would end at Mobile, Pensacola, or Savannah—took up the next two months. Confederate raiders, Forrest among them, busied themselves meanwhile in northern Alabama and Mississippi and in Tennessee. Sherman, who had overall direction of Union armies from the Appalachians to the Mississippi, issued instructions at the end of October. "Don't be concerned on the river," he wrote from northern Georgia to Maj. Gen. Napoleon J. T. Dana at Memphis. The enemy "cannot make a lodgment on the Mississippi. . . . He cannot afford to attack forts or men entrenched, for ammunition is scarce with him, and all supplies. . . . He will be dependent on the Mobile and Ohio [Rail] road, which should be threatened on its whole length. . . . Give these ideas to all

[80] *OR*, ser. 1, vol. 39, pt. 1, pp. 255–56, 330; Buswell Jnls, 16 Jul 1864; S. Evans to Dear Father, 24 Jul 1864, Evans Family Papers, Ohio Historical Society, Columbus.
[81] *OR*, ser. 1, vol. 39, pt. 1, p. 471, and pt. 2, pp. 201, 221, 233 ("take freely"); Buswell Jnls, 9–22 Aug 1864; S. Evans to Dear Father, 1 Sep 1864, Evans Family Papers.

your river posts. Don't attempt to hold the interior further than as threatening to [Confederate] lines of supply."[82]

Unlike U.S. Colored Troops infantry and artillery regiments, which stayed close to their river-town garrisons during the last ten months of the war, the only black cavalry regiment in the region, the 3d United States Colored Cavalry (USCC), remained active. During the last half of 1864, it was continually in the field taking part in several expeditions that illustrate clearly the nature of warfare in a military backwater. The intention of most of these expeditions was to assist Union operations in other parts of the South or to impede the enemy's.

During the first week of July, the 3d USCC was part of an otherwise white force of 2,800 infantry and cavalry that marched from Vicksburg to Jackson to destroy a railroad bridge over the Pearl River. General Sherman in northern Georgia had read in an Atlanta newspaper that the bridge was being rebuilt since Union troops had last visited the site and recommended a weekly expedition against some part of the Mississippi Central Railroad, "breaking it all the time, and especially should that bridge at Jackson be destroyed." The expedition reached Jackson and destroyed the bridge, but Confederate opposition inflicted two hundred fifty casualties. The 3d USCC lost eight officers and men killed and ten enlisted men wounded. On 11 July, a few days after reaching the Big Black River and replenishing its supplies, the expedition turned east again and spent the next few days marching to Grand Gulf by way of Raymond and Port Gibson, a move intended to support General Smith's Tupelo Campaign by keeping Confederates in southwest Mississippi from joining Forrest in the northern part of the state. From Grand Gulf, the troops returned to Vicksburg by steamboat on 17 July, by which time Smith's troops had found Forrest, beaten him, and begun their return to Memphis.[83]

The next nine weeks were comparatively quiet around the Mississippi River garrisons, but in the second half of September, the 3d USCC began a period of intense activity that lasted until the end of November. In September, the Confederate General John B. Hood reacted to Sherman's capture of Atlanta, first by attacks in northern Georgia on Sherman's supply line to Chattanooga, then by a withdrawal into Alabama to begin preparing his own move against the Union garrison and shipping point at Nashville, still farther in the Union rear. Hood's subordinate, Forrest, operated meanwhile in support of the larger Confederate force. Once again, events taking place elsewhere determined the shape of affairs along the river.

On 19 September, the Union general in command at Natchez reported that a Confederate force that he had thought might be advancing to attack him "was but a portion of Forrest's command visiting this section for supplies." The 3d USCC conducted one of several raids by federal troops that week to deprive the enemy of food and forage in southwestern Mississippi. A month earlier, Colonel Osband had assumed command of the District of Vicksburg's entire cavalry force: five regiments with a combined strength of perhaps two thousand. He sent three

---

[82]*OR*, ser. 1, vol. 39, pt. 3, pp. 527–28.
[83]Ibid., pt. 1, p. 243, and pt. 2, p. 151 ("breaking it"); Main, *Third United States Colored Cavalry*, p. 177.

hundred thirty men of the 3d USCC under the regiment's new commander, Maj. Jeremiah B. Cook, to march north from Vicksburg and scour the country between the Yazoo and Mississippi Rivers for Confederates and for any supplies that might be seized or destroyed. On 22 September, Cook's troopers found a band of one hundred fifty Confederates and chased it north for fifteen miles across the Sunflower River before burning the plantation where the Confederates had camped. The next day, they came across a herd of three hundred cattle, killing eight of the herders and taking five prisoners. One hundred of the cattle lost themselves in canebrakes before the expedition returned to Vicksburg on 26 September, but the soldiers noted plentiful corn and cotton along the route of march.[84]

Maj. Jeremiah B. Cook took over the 3d U.S. Colored Cavalry when Colonel Osband was promoted to brigade command. On 27 November 1864, he led part of the regiment in a dismounted charge across the railroad trestle over the Big Black River.

On the night of 29 September, Osband boarded a steamer with one thousand cavalrymen from three white regiments and the 3d USCC, as well as a section of artillery (two guns). They landed at Bruinsburg, some thirty miles downstream, the next morning and marched another ten miles inland to Port Gibson, where they dispersed a band of Confederate irregulars. In keeping with the increasingly vicious war that both sides were waging, General Dana instructed the ranking officers on this raid to arrest "any prominent rebels, male or female, whose influence in the community at large would make them valuable to us as hostages" for the safety of "such loyal citizens who have been kidnapped from their plantations by the rebel thieves who surround us." Osband's troopers complied by seizing thirteen of the town's "most prominent and wealthy" residents. On 1 October, the expedition marched back to the river and turned over the hostages and 125 cattle to Col. Charles A. Gilchrist, who commanded a force of five hundred men drawn from the 48th and 50th USCIs that had come downstream from Vicksburg by river. By the fall of 1864, along the lower Mississippi, it had become the role of cavalry to rove the country seeking out the enemy and contraband property while the infantry received and warehoused seized goods at river ports or loaded them aboard steamboats. Osband's force marched southeast from the river and reached Natchez on 3 October. Providing three hundred fifty of the cavalry horses with new shoes

---

[84]*OR*, ser. 1, vol. 39, pt. 1, pp. 567–72, and pt. 2, p. 410 (quotation).

required the efforts of every blacksmith in town, while the expedition's sick, exhausted, or disabled horses and men boarded a boat for Vicksburg.[85]

Just twenty-nine hours after reaching Natchez, Osband put twelve hundred cavalrymen from five regiments, including the 3d USCC, and two sections of artillery (four guns) aboard transports and steamed downstream to seek out a Confederate force that had been firing on riverboats. The flotilla reached Tunica Bend, nearly halfway between Natchez and Baton Rouge, well before daylight the next day. The troopers went ashore and headed at once for Woodville, Mississippi, about twenty miles inland, where Osband expected to find the enemy. Before nightfall on 5 October, they had entered the town. Besides seizing the mail and burning the telegraph office, they took several prisoners and a number of wagons loaded with supplies. That night, a black resident brought news that Confederate cavalry intended to attack the expedition at daybreak. Osband sent the 3d USCC and the 5th Illinois Cavalry with two guns toward the left of the enemy's camp on a plantation a few miles south of Woodville while the rest of the command moved to the right. The man who had brought the news led the 3d USCC to a small bridge on the plantation which the regiment filed across before charging the enemy position. Capturing three cannon, the men of the 3d drove the retreating Confederates into the waiting 5th Illinois Cavalry, which took forty-one prisoners. There were no Union casualties. "The fight occurred near the residence of Judge McGehee, who had breakfast cooked for the rebels," Osband reported. "Our men ate the breakfast without difficulty, and giving Judge McGehee half an hour to move out of his residence, burned it, together with the quarters he had erected for the use of the rebels." Two days later, Osband's expedition was back in Natchez and on 9 October boarded transports for Vicksburg.[86]

At the end of the month, four of Osband's regiments swept through Issaquena and Washington Counties north of Vicksburg, killing only two guerrillas but seizing fifty thousand feet of lumber and twenty thousand bricks and allowing the lessees of government plantations to deliver six hundred bales of cotton. "We captured . . . about 100 horses and mules, 300 sheep, and 50 head of beef-cattle," Osband reported, "besides arresting the prominent rebels through the country to be held as hostages." In a separate letter to General Dana, he complained that hardtack issued to the 3d USCC "was so wormy that they could not eat it and were compelled to throw it away. That is one of the reasons our rations are always short" in the field.[87]

On the night of 6 November, Osband put nine hundred forty men and horses from several regiments and two artillery pieces aboard steamboats and headed upstream. Thirty-six hours later, they arrived at Gaines' Landing in the southeast corner of Arkansas. Osband sent men of the 3d USCC splashing inland five or six miles to Bayou Macon. They "brought in some information but saw no enemy," Osband reported. The information had to do with enemy troop strength

---

[85] OR, ser. 1, vol. 39, pt. 1, pp. 575–76, and pt. 2, p. 529 (quotation).

[86] OR, ser. 1, vol. 39, pt. 1, pp. 831–33 (quotation, p. 832), 569, 576; Main, *Third United States Colored Cavalry*, pp. 183–88, 299–300.

[87] OR, ser. 1, vol. 39, pt. 1, pp. 878–79 ("We captured," p. 878), and pt. 3, p. 476 ("was so wormy").

and movements and Confederate plans to sell about four hundred bales of cotton through an intermediary in federally held Memphis. Surreptitious cotton sales were an important source of revenue for the Confederate government, and cotton brokers in Memphis often played fast and loose. Seeing no opportunity for maneuver because, as Osband wrote, the land was "full of water and knee deep in mud; the bayous were bank full, and if crossed must be swam; the whole country [was] so overflowed that it seemed folly to attempt any movement," he re-embarked the 3d USCC and returned to Vicksburg three days after the expedition set out.[88]

As General Hood marched his Confederate army north toward Nashville in early December, Union cavalry in Mississippi moved to cut supply routes in his rear. One attack aimed at the Mobile and Ohio Railroad, which connected Mobile with Columbus, Kentucky, by way of Meridian and Corinth in eastern Mississippi. The other was intended to cut the Mississippi Central, a line that ran from Jackson, Tennessee, to Jackson, Mississippi, through Holly Springs, Oxford, and Grenada. Troops were to destroy a bridge over the Big Black River near Vaughan's Station, about fifty miles northeast of Vicksburg. The 3d USCC took part in this movement, along with the other four regiments of Osband's cavalry brigade.[89]

The expedition—twenty-two hundred cavalry, eight guns, and a pontoon bridge accompanied by part of the 5th USCA—left Vicksburg at daylight on 23 November. In order to deceive Confederate cavalry, which was scattered throughout the state, Osband first feinted toward Jackson, laying his pontoon bridge across the Big Black River about ten miles due east of Vicksburg. The next day, the 3d USCC and the 2d Wisconsin Cavalry crossed the river, continued east another fifteen miles, and camped for the night, taking care to build many campfires. These they abandoned in the middle of the night and retraced their route to the Big Black, where they rejoined the bulk of the command. On 25 November, leaving the 5th USCA to guard the bridge, the cavalry and field guns headed northeast, up the Big Black. A two-day march took them nearly to Benton without a glimpse of the enemy. They reached Vaughan's Station on 27 November shortly after noon.

About four miles south of the station, the track crossed the river on a trestle twenty-five feet high surrounded by a waist-deep swamp. Osband picked his old regiment, the 3d USCC, to seize it. Major Cook's troopers rode south and dismounted about a mile from the bridge as close as they could approach on horseback. As usual when the troops fought dismounted, every fourth man stayed with the horses. Cook led the rest toward the bridge on foot.

A stockade manned by a dozen local residents defended the bridge's south end. Cook put one company on either side of the railroad embankment, in the swamp, and told them to approach the bridge as quickly and quietly as possible.

---

[88]Ibid., pt. 1, pp. 899–900 (quotation, p. 899). On Memphis cotton dealers' lack of caution, see vol. 48, pt. 1, pp. 420–21.

[89]*OR*, ser. 1, vol. 41, pt. 1, pp. 763–74; Main, *Third United States Colored Cavalry*, pp. 199–200; Robert C. Black III, *The Railroads of the Confederacy* (Chapel Hill: University of North Carolina Press, 1998 [1952]), map.

He and the balance of the regiment moved along the track. The defenders saw the men on the track at some distance and began firing but abandoned their position hastily when the troopers in the swamp opened fire and Cook led a charge across the trestle. The retreating Confederates left three dead behind; the 3d USCC's casualties amounted to three men wounded. Stuffing the trestle with dry underbrush, the victors poured kerosene over it and set it alight. Soon after they left to rejoin the main body of the expedition, Confederate cavalry arrived and put out the blaze.[90]

Osband's expedition made its way to Yazoo City, arriving there on 29 November. While the Union troops marched west, the Confederates who had put out the fire—a small force of Arkansas and Mississippi cavalry and mounted infantry—repaired the bridge across the Big Black and crossed it in pursuit. As the Union troops rested their horses on 30 November, the Confederates drew near Yazoo City. Their willingness to engage the Union pickets that day and the next convinced Osband that he faced a much stronger force than was present. Since his own stock of ammunition was low—the 3d USCC alone had fired ten thousand rounds during its assault on the bridge—he ferried his own troops across the Yazoo River during the night of 1–2 December on a single boat, taking sixteen hours to move a dozen horses and men at a time. The entire expedition returned to Vicksburg by steamer on 4 December.[91]

Despite his raid's end in retreat and disengagement, Osband described it as successful. His troops, he wrote, had destroyed bridges and thirty miles of railroad that earlier in the week had carried three trainloads of infantry north to join Hood's Confederate army on its way to attack Nashville. Union generals did not know that the attack on the bridge had failed to destroy it when they issued congratulatory orders a few days afterward. General Dana in Vicksburg called the charge across the trestle "one of the most dashing and heroic acts of the war," and recommended Major Cook's promotion to lieutenant colonel. At his headquarters in New Orleans, Maj. Gen. Edward R. S. Canby approved the promotion, subject to presidential approval. The most striking aspect of these jubilant reports is that they did not mention the race of the men who captured the bridge, other than to name their regiment. In some parts of the Army, at least, it seemed no longer necessary to exclaim at black soldiers' good performance. It had become a matter of course, to be expected more often than not.[92]

Two days after Osband's expedition returned to Vicksburg, General Halleck ordered General Dana at Memphis to move against the Mobile and Ohio Railroad. General Grant, supervising siege operations in Virginia but responsible besides for Union land operations across the country, had begun pondering the Mobile and Ohio a few weeks after the Confederate withdrawal from Atlanta. Late in the fall, with Hood's army advancing north toward Nashville, Grant wanted to do "as much damage as possible" to the line. Dana sought a delay. He had only a thousand troopers at Memphis, he told Halleck, and their horses were in poor

---

[90] *OR*, ser. 1, vol. 45, pt. 1, pp. 779–82, 785; Main, *Third United States Colored Cavalry*, pp. 200–202.

[91] *OR*, ser. 1, vol. 45, pt. 1, pp. 782, 785–86; Main, *Third United States Colored Cavalry*, p. 203.

[92] *OR*, ser. 1, vol. 45, pt. 1, pp. 777, 779, 782 (quotation, p. 779).

condition; but he expected Osband's brigade to arrive from Vicksburg within a week. He would then mount an expedition to destroy the Mobile and Ohio. Believing that time was of the essence, Halleck told him to do the best he could with the force at hand.[93]

Dana set out to increase his mounted strength. To lead the expedition, he way-laid General Grierson, who was passing through Memphis with his cavalry division. "I think the detention is made in accordance with some orders from Washington," Grierson explained to Maj. Gen. James H. Wilson, who expected him and his division at Nashville. Dana also sent one of his officers as far upriver as Cairo, Illinois, to reroute cavalry regiments that were on their way from Missouri to Nashville. By the time Osband and his brigade, which included the 3d USCC, arrived at Memphis in mid-December, enough mounted troops had assembled to launch the expedition.[94]

Then the rain began. By 21 December, Dana reported, "the weather for ten days has been intolerably rainy, and the whole country is overflowed, the roads knee-deep in mud." That morning, the expedition left its wagons and artillery behind and set out, thirty-five hundred troopers with rations, mainly hardtack and coffee, and extra ammunition carried on about one thousand pack animals. Nine regiments of infantry accompanied Grierson's command east along the line of the Memphis and Charleston Railroad to attempt repairs along the track and confuse enemy attempts to guess the column's direction. Rain and sleet continued. Hundreds of cavalry horses broke down on the march and had to be abandoned, their places taken by animals seized at farms along the route. Despite those difficulties, by Christmas Eve, Grierson's cavalry had covered the eighty miles to Ripley, Mississippi, and was within striking distance of the Mobile and Ohio tracks.[95]

During the next forty-eight hours, Osband's brigade alone destroyed nearly half a mile of bridges and trestles on the line south of Tupelo. In succeeding days, the expedition moved farther along the railroad, destroying a Confederate supply depot that included two hundred wagons captured from Sturgis' expedition the previous spring and several trainloads of Confederate supplies. Meanwhile, Grierson's telegrapher tapped the line that ran along the tracks and learned that the Confederate General Richard Taylor planned to reinforce the railroad's defenders. The raiders met the first serious resistance at Egypt, where the garrison surrendered on 28 December minutes before relief arrived. Grierson's cavalry fought the reinforcements to a standstill and then turned due west, moving through Houston before veering southwest toward Winona. There, the expedition struck the line of the Mississippi Central Railroad. Grierson sent Osband's brigade south and another north to tear up track and burn bridges. The column reunited a few miles east of Yazoo City and reached Vicksburg on 5 January. Grierson estimated the damage to Confederate communications as nearly 4 miles of bridges and trestles burned, another 10 miles of track torn up—ties burned to heat the rails so that they could

---

[93]OR, ser. 1, vol. 41, pt. 4, pp. 782, 799; vol. 45, pt. 2, p. 142. John Y. Simon, ed., *The Papers of Ulysses S. Grant*, 30 vols. to date (Carbondale and Edwardsville: Southern Illinois University Press, 1967–), 12: 289, 385–86 (hereafter cited as *Grant Papers*).

[94]OR, ser. 1, vol. 41, pt. 4, p. 902; vol. 45, pt. 2, pp. 90 (quotation), 106–07.

[95]OR, ser. 1, vol. 41, pt. 4, p. 902 (quotation); vol. 45, pt. 1, pp. 844–45. Main, *Third United States Colored Cavalry*, pp. 219–20.

be bent—and 20 miles of telegraph line destroyed. He brought in six hundred prisoners of war and eight hundred head of captured livestock. About one thousand freedpeople left their homes to join the victorious column. In Virginia, Grant pronounced the raid "most important in its results and most successfully executed."[96]

Even before the expedition set out, the Confederate army that had marched north in the fall had received a crushing defeat at Nashville and was retreating toward Tupelo, where it found only the results of Grierson's recent raid. With the main Confederate force between the Appalachian Mountains and the Mississippi River in thorough disarray, Union armies in the region could turn their attention to suppressing guerrilla bands that threatened their own communications and their occupation of the country. When Osband's brigade returned to Memphis in mid-January, it was only to receive orders that took it back downstream to land on the Arkansas shore.[97]

The intent of this expedition was to drive Confederate irregulars from the west bank of the Mississippi. Whether or not the enemy stood and fought, Union troops were to destroy all forage and other supplies they found. Since every waterway in the region was out of its banks, they could count on building rafts and swimming their horses for much of the distance. After the cavalry division's exertions in the railroad raid during the previous month, General Dana was able to assign Osband detachments from only three brigades, 2,621 men in all. The 3d USCC's contingent, 450 strong, was the largest from any one regiment.[98]

The troops went ashore a few miles above Gaines' Landing in southeastern Arkansas before daybreak on 28 January and moved inland at first light. During the two weeks that followed, they worked their way toward Monroe, Louisiana, destroying a Confederate steamboat, a gristmill, and stores of cotton and corn before stopping at Bastrop and returning to Gaines' Landing. Eight men of the 3d USCC drowned during the raid. Osband called it "the most fatiguing scout of my life."

> To describe the roads, the poverty of the people, or the sufferings of my command during this terrible march would be impossible . . . and it is not exaggeration to say that at one time one-half of a regiment might be seen dismounted, struggling with their horses, every one of which was mired and down. No squad of men, much less an army, can live anywhere we have been. The people have neither seed, corn, nor bread, or the mills to grind the corn in if they had it, as I burned them wherever found.

The regimental historian recalled:

> The weather was cold, snow and sleet falling repeatedly. . . . Bridges were swept away, and crossings made extremely difficult. . . . The horses splashed and floundered through mud and water from knee to belly deep. . . . Not much

---

[96] *OR*, ser. 1, vol. 45, pt. 1, pp. 845–46, 848, 856–57; Main, *Third United States Colored Cavalry*, pp. 220–35; *Grant Papers*, 13: 397 (quotation).

[97] *OR*, ser. 1, vol. 41, pt. 4, p. 901; vol. 48, pt. 1, pp. 421, 544–45. NA M594, roll 204, 3d USCC; Black, *Railroads of the Confederacy*, pp. 266–67.

[98] *OR*, ser. 1, vol. 41, pt. 4, p. 901; vol. 48, pt. 1, pp. 68, 544.

attention was paid to the usual route of travel as regarded roads. After one regiment had passed over the ground it was rendered too boggy for others to follow, so the command scattered, each regiment seeking a new route, thus leaving a wide trail, which could be traced years after the war.

More than four hundred freedpeople joined the column. Most managed to survive the trip to Gaines' Landing, but not all. Osband estimated that as many as twenty may have died of exposure along the route.[99]

The expedition to northeastern Louisiana was the 3d USCC's last major effort of the war. Late in April 1865, detachments of Osband's brigade at Memphis boarded four steamers that took them nearly as far as Fort Pillow before putting them ashore to engage in the kind of operation that had become known as a "guerrilla hunt." They managed to capture one man named in their orders, whom they tried by court-martial and hanged. At the end of the month, the general commanding at Memphis, thinking that Confederate President Jefferson Davis might flee the country through his home state of Mississippi, sent the 3d USCC to Vicksburg by boat. The regiment continued on to Fort Adams, below Natchez, and scouted the country there. Meanwhile, far to the east, Union cavalry captured Davis near Macon, Georgia, on 10 May. Not long afterward, the 3d USCC returned to Memphis.[100]

As Confederate troops surrendered in the spring of 1865, first east of the Mississippi River then west of it, regiments of U.S. Colored Troops garrisoned Union strongholds along the river from Columbus, Kentucky, to Natchez, Mississippi. They constituted a majority at each post, nearly four-fifths of the troops at Memphis and more than 83 percent of those at Vicksburg. These regiments—one of cavalry, thirteen of infantry, four of heavy artillery, and five light batteries—would muster out in twos and threes between September 1865 and September 1866. Until then, they would continue to perform duties they had practiced continually during the war's closing months: guarding government property, securing contraband cotton, pursuing outlaws, and protecting the rights of former slaves, many of whom were their own close relatives. For many of them, the transition from war to peace must have been barely noticeable, for after the Confederate surrender they faced the same challenges in their daily lives, on duty and off, that they had before.[101]

---

[99] *OR*, ser. 1, vol. 48, pt. 1, pp. 69–71, 665, 806 (quotation); Main, *Third United States Colored Cavalry*, p. 246.

[100] *OR*, ser. 1, vol. 48, pt. 1, pp. 184, 254–55; vol. 49, pt. 2, pp. 406, 441–42, 557 (quotation), 640.

[101] *OR*, ser. 1, vol. 48, pt. 2, pp. 257 (Natchez), 267 (Helena); NA Microfilm Pub M617, Returns from U.S. Mil Posts, rolls 232 (Columbus), 769 (Memphis), 917 (Fort Pickering), 1330 (Vicksburg). No returns survive for Helena and Natchez from the spring of 1865.

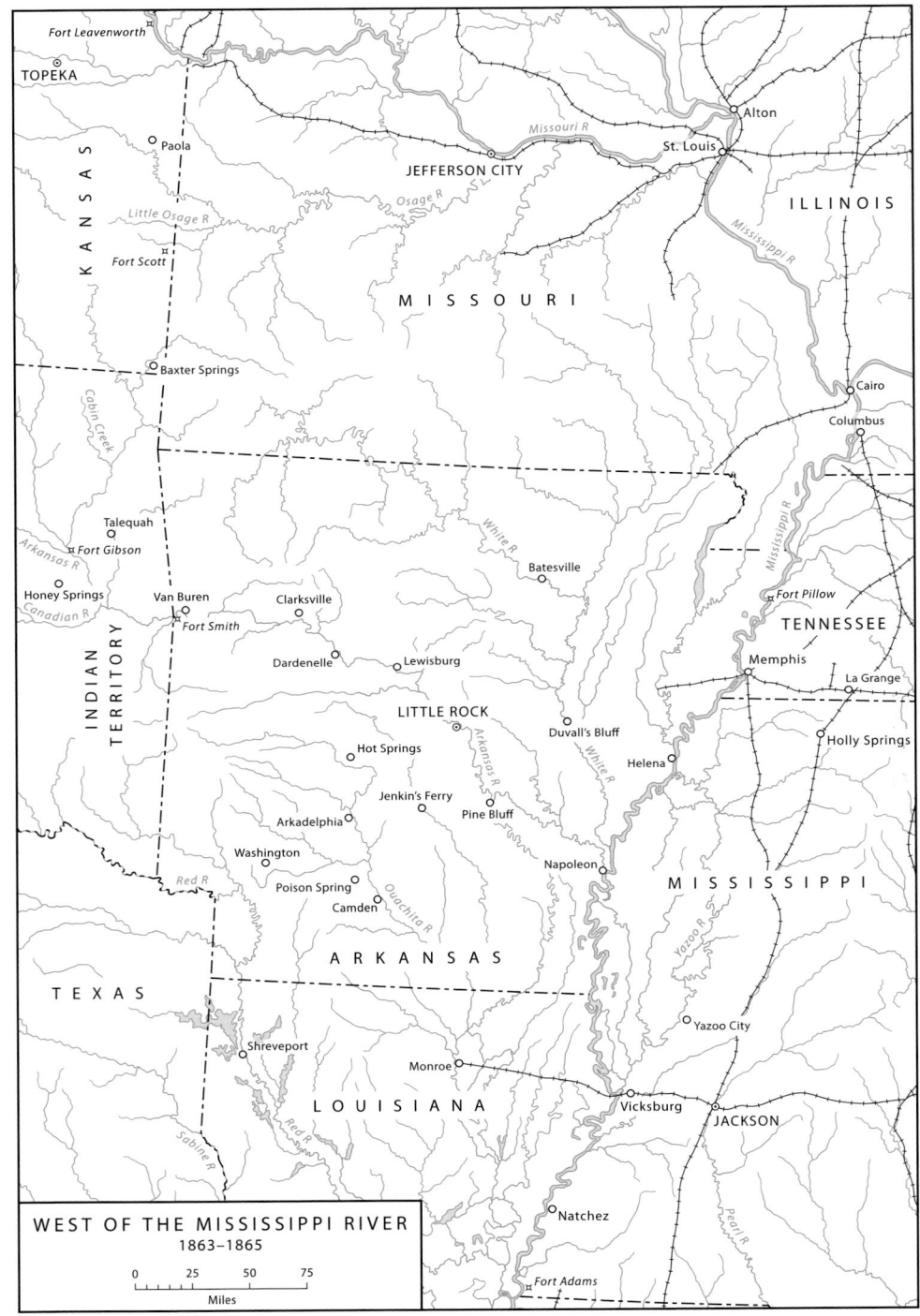

Fort Leavenworth

TOPEKA

K A N S A S

Paola

Little Osage R

Fort Scott

Baxter Springs

Cabin Creek

Talequah

Fort Gibson

Arkansas R

Honey Springs

Canadian R

Van Buren

Fort Smith

I N D I A N   T E R R I T O R Y

Red R

T E X A S

Shreveport

Sabine R

Red R

M I S S O U R I

JEFFERSON CITY

Osage R

Missouri R

St. Louis

Alton

I L L I N O I S

Mississippi R

Cairo

Columbus

White R

Batesville

Clarksville

Dardenelle

Lewisburg

LITTLE ROCK

Arkansas R

Duvall's Bluff

Hot Springs

Jenkin's Ferry

Pine Bluff

Arkadelphia

Washington

Poison Spring

Camden

Ouachita R

A R K A N S A S

White R

Helena

Napoleon

Fort Pillow

Mississippi R

T E N N E S S E E

Memphis

La Grange

Holly Springs

M I S S I S S I P P I

Yazoo R

Yazoo City

Monroe

L O U I S I A N A

Vicksburg

JACKSON

Natchez

Fort Adams

Pearl R

WEST OF THE MISSISSIPPI RIVER
1863–1865

0   25   50   75
Miles

Map 5

CHAPTER 8

ARKANSAS, INDIAN TERRITORY AND KANSAS, 1863–1865

While Maj. Gen. Ulysses S. Grant's army moved against Vicksburg during the spring of 1863, Union garrisons elsewhere along the Mississippi River struggled to hold their own. More than two hundred twenty miles north of Vicksburg by the river's tortuous course lay Helena, Arkansas. Adjutant General Lorenzo Thomas had stopped there early in April to promote the organization of black regiments. The seven thousand white troops he addressed, some of whom would become officers in the new regiments, responded "most enthusiastically," he told Secretary of War Edwin M. Stanton. Men from the nearby contraband camp, Thomas explained to the senior officer there, would fill the ranks. They would be "induced" to join (*see Map 5*).[1]

Maj. Gen. Benjamin M. Prentiss, commanding at Helena, had no trouble raising the 1st Arkansas Infantry (African Descent [AD]). The regiment's new colonel quickly picked thirty-six officers from among the white troops in garrison—thirty-four of them, like himself, from Indiana. There was no dearth of enlisted men. The contraband camp had been full for months, and Prentiss had been shipping freedpeople up the river to St. Louis until Maj. Gen. Samuel R. Curtis, commanding there, threatened to turn the next boatload around and send it back. Curtis had been a three-term Republican congressman from Iowa before the war and knew that white Midwesterners were averse to an influx of former slaves. A month after Thomas' visit, the 1st Arkansas (AD) was complete and traveled downstream to join the Union garrison at Goodrich's Landing, Louisiana.[2]

Organizing the 1st Arkansas (AD) nearly exhausted the supply of able-bodied men in the Helena contraband camp. The 2d Arkansas (AD) took shape much more slowly. Late in May, General Prentiss sent twenty-five men of the regiment, backed by detachments from two white regiments, downstream as far as the mouth of the Ar-

[1] *The War of the Rebellion: A Compilation of the Official Records of the Union and Confederate Armies*, 70 vols. in 128 (Washington, D.C.: Government Printing Office, 1880–1901), ser. 3, 3: 117 (hereafter cited as *OR*); Brig Gen L. Thomas to Brig Gen B. M. Prentiss, 2 Apr 1863, Entry 159BB, Generals' Books and Papers (L. Thomas), Record Group (RG) 94, Rcds of the Adjutant General's Office, National Archives (NA).

[2] *OR*, ser. 1, vol. 22, pt. 2, p. 147; List of Ofcrs, 7 Apr 63, 46th United States Colored Infantry (USCI), Entry 57C, Regimental Papers, RG 94, NA; NA Microfilm Pub M594, Compiled Rcds Showing Svc of Mil Units in Volunteer Union Organizations, roll 210, 46th USCI; Frederick H. Dyer, *A Compendium of the War of the Rebellion* (New York: Thomas Yoseloff, 1959 [1909]), p. 999; Leslie A. Schwalm, *Emancipation Diaspora: Race and Reconstruction in the Upper Midwest* (Chapel Hill: University of North Carolina Press, 2009), pp. 82–97.

kansas River in search of recruits. They scouted the west bank of the Mississippi on the way down and the east bank on their return, sometimes venturing as far as seven miles inland. At one point, a party of Confederates on shore fired on the vessel and the Union troops aboard fired back. Prentiss reported that the men of the detachment "fought with a hearty will and did good service. . . . The regiment is rapidly filling up, and in a few days it is hoped it will be full."[3]

The general was so wrong about the progress of recruiting for the 2d Arkansas (AD) that it calls into question the rest of his remarks about the men of the regiment. Sixteen days after Prentiss' report, 2d Lt. Minos Miller wrote in a private letter that the regiment was "about 300 strong." A month after that, in mid-July, Lt. Col. George W. De Costa, the commanding officer, complained that four hundred recruits at Vicksburg who had been promised to him had been withheld instead and that he would have to go to Memphis in search of others. Late in October, Col. Charles S. Sheley admitted that he still had only four hundred men organized in four-and-a-half companies (enough to entitle the regiment to a full colonel in command). A recruiting party of six officers had rounded up enough men during Maj. Gen. Frederick Steele's advance on Little Rock in August and September to complete the regiment, but Steele refused to send them to Helena. "They are destitute of clothing and suffer much from inclement weather," Sheley told Adjutant General Thomas at the end of October. Sheley tried to send uniforms from Helena for the recruits at Little Rock, but he reported that General Prentiss' successor there "prevents me, stating he would not furnish them clothing until they are placed under his command." The last five companies of the 2d Arkansas (AD) mustered in separately later that fall at Duvall's Bluff, Little Rock, and Pine Bluff, where the men were camped.[4]

Prentiss' report of the regiment's progress in recruiting that spring had been too optimistic by half a year. He had not gone on the expedition that his report described and may merely have been passing on what Colonel De Costa told him. It is possible, too, that he wanted to appear energetic in his pursuit of the new policy of black enlistment, which General Thomas had announced to the troops at Helena only seven weeks earlier. Prentiss had been an Illinois lawyer and local politician in civilian life. In the spring of 1863, his immediate superior was Maj. Gen. John A. McClernand, a five-term Illinois congressman noted for bombast and mendacity but a strong supporter of the Union and of measures for prosecuting the war. Whatever the cause of Prentiss' optimistic forecast for the 2d Arkansas (AD), the report's inaccuracy placed it in the same category as Maj. Gen. Nathaniel P. Banks' description of the Louisiana Native Guard's assault on the Confederate trenches at Port Hudson: fine promotional literature for the new federal policy of enlisting black soldiers but wishful rather than factual.

Besides General Steele's alleged lack of cooperation, there was another reason for the regiment's slow growth. Potential recruits were reluctant to enlist. "We have an order from Prentis[s] to press all able bodied negroes that is

---

[3] *OR*, ser. 1, vol. 22, pt. 1, p. 340.
[4] M. Miller to Dear Mother, 12 Jun 1863, M. Miller Papers, University of Arkansas (UA), Fayetteville; Lt Col G. W. De Costa to Brig Gen L. F. Ross, 19 Jul 1863, and Col C. S. Sheley to Brig Gen L. Thomas, 28 Oct 1863, both in 54th USCI, Entry 57C, RG 94, NA; NA M594, roll 211, 54th USCI.

not employ[e]d as officers['] servents," Lieutenant Miller wrote home, "so they hide from us like chickens from a hawk we search their houses at all hours of the day and night sometimes at midnight sometimes they tell us they wont go but we general[l]y manage to make them last night I had to cock my revolver on one before he would move he toddled in a hurry when he heard it snap." Despite the brutal means recruiters sometimes employed, Lieutenant Miller was optimistic about his regiment's future. "We are drilling every day the negroes learn fast and will fight well," he predicted.[5]

Jackson Brown was one recruit who joined Miller's regiment. "I got free in 1863," when a Union force occupied Pine Bluff on the lower Arkansas River, Brown recalled after the war. He continued to work for his former owner for wages and used the money to buy a pair of mules, intending to go into the hauling business, but a federal quartermaster took the animals. "There was a review that day," a military spectacle that provided a welcome break in the boredom of small-town life:

> Everybody went out to see it, white and black, and when the whole crowd was together, the cavalry made a half moon about us, and the infantry closed up the opening, then they . . . left a guard . . . and the rest of them went through town and gathered up all the horses and mules they could find in the lots and stables . . . , they kept us there two hours, till they had all the stock.

The next time Brown saw his mules, they were pulling a government wagon. With them went his hope of becoming an independent teamster, and he joined a company of the 2d Arkansas (AD) that was recruiting in Pine Bluff. Union quartermasters' requisitioning of livestock cost some black Southerners their jobs and drove more than one of them to enlist.[6]

Men of the 2d Arkansas (AD), like those of some other black regiments in the Mississippi Valley, came under fire before they mustered in. Confederate generals had kept an eye on Helena since a Union force occupied the town in July 1862, and forebodings of a possible federal move against the state capital at Little Rock had spread as far as the government in Richmond. By June 1863, Lt. Gen. Theophilus H. Holmes, commanding the Confederate Department of Arkansas, thought that the time had come to recapture Helena, both to forestall Union operations against the interior of the state and to divert federal troops from the siege of Vicksburg. The assault fell on 4 July—by coincidence, the day Vicksburg surrendered.[7]

At daybreak, more than seventy-six hundred Confederates attacked a line of trenches and gun emplacements around Helena occupied by forty-one hundred Union troops. Rumors of enemy movements had been reaching General Prentiss for ten days, and a dispatch from Memphis on 2 July advised him that an attack might be imminent. He ordered the Helena garrison to stand to arms well before dawn. "On

---

[5]Miller to Dear Mother, 12 Jun 1863.

[6]Deposition, Jackson Brown, Dec 1874, in Case File 10,146, Jackson Brown, Entry 732, Settled Case Files for Claims Approved by the Southern Claims Commission, RG 217, Rcds of the Accounting Ofcrs of the Dept of the Treasury, NA. For a similar case, see Deposition, Luke Turner, Nov 1871, in Case File 7,010, Luke Turner, Entry 732, RG 217, NA.

[7]*OR*, ser. 1, 13: 891–92, 914–15; vol. 22, pt. 1, pp. 408–09.

the morning of the 4th just as our Regt had got formed we heard the pickets commence fireing," Lieutenant Miller wrote, "and we knew the ball had opened."[8]

Companies of the 2d Arkansas (AD) filled a 600-yard gap in the Union line by a levee near the riverbank, half a mile south of town. A section of Battery K, 1st Missouri Light Artillery, stood on either flank. It was a quiet spot, where the greatest danger came from the Missourians' guns firing across the regiment's front at a Confederate attack on the Union trenches west of town. "By the time our regt got posted it was day light and the skirmishing on the right began to get pretty heavy which told us the attack was not going to be made in our regeon so we set down behind the breast works in plain view of the fighting and concluded we would look on," Lieutenant Miller wrote; "but before we had been there 5 minutes the balls began to whistle around us pretty lively and the breast work our part of the leavy was behind run in the rong direction to screen us so we had to content ourselves and trust to providence   I was setting in the line with the men and a ball just passed over my head and wounded two of the men in our Co   I got a handkerchief and tied up one of their wounds while Cap[t. David M. Logan] tied the other." That done, they sat back to watch the battle. "We heard the Rebbels cheering and knew they was chargeing on the batteries" inland from Helena, about one mile northwest of Miller's position.

> In a minute we could see colum[n] after colum[n] pouring over the hills. . . . [A]s soon as they came in sight . . . every batterry that could get range of them let into them with a venge[a]nce . . . and we could see the rebbels . . . falling in all directions. . . . [T]he Rebbels would begin to give way and their officers would Rally them and they would try it again but at last they gave it up. . . . [T]hey retreated down the hill into the gorge and covered themselves behind logs and stumps. . . . [T]hey laid in there about an hour and amused themselves shooting at us."[9]

Fighting lasted until late morning. The defenders inflicted about sixteen hundred casualties (more than 20 percent of the attacking force) before General Holmes recalled his troops. The next day, Lieutenant Miller walked over the battlefield. "Such a sight I never seen before," he recorded. "The Rebbels was laying thick some of them tore all to peices with shell and some shought through with sollid shot   they had laid there 24 hours . . . and began to smell bad." Since the 2d Arkansas (AD) had not yet mustered into federal service, regimental records do not cover the Confederate attack on Helena and no record survives of the regiment's casualties, if there were any. Perhaps they amounted to no more than the three men "hurt" that Miller mentioned in his letter home.[10]

The successful defense of the federal base at Helena allowed General Steele to use the river port as a springboard for his August move into central Arkansas, which resulted in the capture of Little Rock during the last days of summer. While Steele's expedition headed inland, a new black regiment arrived at Helena. The 3d

---

[8] *OR*, ser. 1, vol. 22, pt. 1, p. 388, and pt. 2, pp. 335, 352; M. Miller to Dear Mother, 6 Jun [Jul] 1863, Miller Papers.

[9] *OR*, ser. 1, vol. 22, pt. 1, p. 394; Miller to Dear Mother, 6 Jun [Jul] 1863.

[10] *OR*, ser. 1, vol. 22, pt. 1, pp. 389, 394, 405–06, 410–12; Miller to Dear Mother, 6 Jun [Jul] 1863; NA M594, roll 211, 54th USCI.

Helena, Arkansas, submerged by a flood in 1864—a hint of the mosquitoes and sanitary problems that made it an unhealthy place

Arkansas (AD), organized at St. Louis, included many soldiers who had been born in Arkansas. Some of them had been sent north by General Prentiss in his attempt to clean out the Helena contraband camp late in 1862.[11]

Autumn brought little change to the Helena garrison. Three companies of the 3d Arkansas (AD) scouted the country south of town during October, one company commander recorded on the muster roll, "without any loss or [incident] worthy of record." The regiment's Company D spent November and December on Island No. 63 in the Mississippi River guarding woodcutters at a wood yard that supplied fuel for Union steamboats. The other companies furnished fatigue parties to improve Helena's defenses and guarded warehouses full of government supplies. The men's health suffered, as did that of the garrison's white troops. At the end of October, Company H's commanding officer called the situation "very poor. . . . The quarters of the men have been Shelter Tents, the ground was a steap, bareside hill. The Tents were without floors & during the cold rains the men and the Tents were made drenching wet." Sickness inflicted 649 deaths—about two-thirds of a regiment's authorized strength—before the 3d Arkansas (AD), renumbered the 56th United States Colored Infantry (USCI), mustered out at Helena in September 1866. One inspector called the town "the most deadly place on the river."[12]

As autumn turned to winter, another black regiment, the 1st Iowa Colored Infantry, arrived in Helena. Organized in Keokuk at the southeastern corner of Iowa, the regiment had recruited largely in Missouri, but federal law allowed the state of Iowa

---

[11] *OR*, ser. 1, vol. 22, pt. 1, pp. 474–75, and pt. 2, pp. 402, 432.

[12] *OR*, ser. 1, vol. 41, pt. 3, p. 714 ("the most deadly"); NA M594, roll 211, 56th USCI ("without any loss," "very poor"); Dyer, *Compendium*, p. 1733; Rhonda M. Kohl, "'This Godforsaken Town':

to credit the enlistments against its own draft quota. This accorded with the wishes of Iowa's governor expressed in an official query to the War Department and in a letter to Maj. Gen. Henry W. Halleck that contained one of the most revealing comments on black recruitment by any public official during the war: "When this war is over & we have summed up the entire loss of life it has imposed on the country I shall not have any regrets if it is found that a part of the dead are *niggers* and that *all* are not white men." The officers and men of the 1st Iowa Colored reached Helena on 20 December 1863 and soon took up a round of duties identical to those of the 3d Arkansas (AD).[13]

Three hundred miles west of the Mississippi River, the threat of raids by Confederate irregulars and outright bandits based in Missouri had largely depopulated the eastern tier of Kansas counties during 1862, but Union reinforcements restored some degree of order by the end of the year. At Fort Scott, the 1st Kansas Colored Infantry mustered its existing five companies into federal service on 13 January 1863. Lt. Col. James M. Williams, commanding the incomplete regiment, at once began raising additional companies and gathering in absentees who had strayed during the period of organizational limbo the previous fall. In the meantime, the men continued to labor on the fort's defenses. By the end of April, the regiment was nearly full, but morale and discipline had suffered so much that Williams wrote letters to district and department headquarters asking for a change of duty and a change of station. His men had not received "one cent" of pay since their enlistment, he complained; this, together with endless fatigue assignments, had fostered "a mutinous and insubordinate spirit." To prevent this "from culminating in open anarchy," Williams announced that he was withdrawing the regiment from all fatigue details and intended to concentrate instead on drill. Department headquarters granted his request. Soon after the remaining companies of the regiment mustered in on 2 May 1863 and Williams received a promotion to colonel, the 1st Kansas Colored began its march to another station, fifty miles south of Fort Scott.[14]

The regiment's new headquarters at Baxter Springs lay in the southeastern corner of the state, about five miles from Missouri and even closer to the Indian Territory, the land west of Arkansas that was home to tribes that had moved there from the Southeast a generation earlier. Confederates in the neighborhood were well aware of the presence of what one of their officers called "Colonel Williams' negro regiment." Days after reaching Baxter Springs, two companies of the 1st Kansas Colored helped a cavalry force from Fort Scott rout a band of Confederates and recover about fifty stolen horses and mules. Within the week, Williams issued a challenge to the enemy:

> I came here . . . to put a stop to the Guerrilla or Bushwhacking war which is now being carried on . . . in Jasper and Newton Counties, Mo. It is my desire . . . to follow . . . all the rules applicable to Civilized warfare. I therefore propose that you . . . come to some point and attack me, or give me notice where I can find your

Death and Disease at Helena, Arkansas, 1862–63," *Civil War History* 50 (2004): 109–44.

[13] *OR*, ser. 3, 3: 563, 591; NA M594, roll 212, 60th USCI; Ira Berlin et al., eds., *The Black Military Experience* (New York: Cambridge University Press, 1982), pp. 85 (quotation), 188.

[14] *OR*, ser. 1, 13: 801–05; vol. 22, pt. 1, pp. 825, 837–38. Lt Col J. M. Williams to Capt L. A. Thrasher, 29 Jan 1863, and to Capt H. G. Loring, 21 Apr 1863, both in 79th USCI, Regimental Books, RG 94, NA; *Military History of Kansas Regiments During the War for the Suppression of the Rebellion* (Leavenworth: W. S. Burke, 1870), pp. 407–09.

force and I will fight you on your own grounds. But if you persist in the system of Guerrilla warfare heretofore followed by you and refuse to fight openly like soldiers fighting for a cause I shall feel bound to treat you as thieves and robbers who lurk in secret places fighting only defenceless people and wholly unworthy [of] the fate due to chivalrous soldiers engaged in honourable warfare, and shall take any means within my power to rid the country of your murderous gang.[15]

On 18 May, just one week after Williams issued his challenge, a party of guerrillas surprised a foraging party made up of forty-five men from the regiment and a white artillery battery near Baxter Springs. The Confederates claimed to have chased the federals for about eight miles, capturing five wagons and their six-mule teams. The foraging party lost 16 killed, all from the 1st Kansas Colored Infantry, and 5 prisoners, 2 from the infantry and 3 from the artillery. Later that day, the guerrilla leader Thomas R. Livingston exchanged the artillerymen for three of his own men who had fallen into Union hands. What happened next became the subject of assertion and evasion. Livingston reported: "The prisoners I have subsequently exchanged for Confederate soldiers." The federals alleged that he "refused to exchange the colored prisoners in his possession, and gave as his excuse that he should hold them subject to the orders of the rebel War Department." (Livingston's relation to the Confederate government is unclear. He signed his report, "Major, Commanding Confederate forces." A Union officer called his followers "bushwhackers.") Colonel Williams arrived on the scene and "for the first time beheld the horrible evidence of the demoniac spirit of these rebel fiends in their treatment of our dead and wounded. Men were found with their brains beaten out with clubs, and the bloody weapons left by their sides, and their bodies most horribly mutilated." When Williams heard a report that the Confederates had murdered one of the prisoners, he shot one of the Confederate prisoners he held and the next day burned the town of Sherwood and eleven farms within a few miles of it. According to Livingston, the federals "put 10 of their dead (negroes) that had been left on the battle-ground the day preceding, . . . together with the body of Mr. John Bishop, a citizen prisoner, whom they had murdered, into [one of the houses], and burned the premises." The war of allegations and atrocities was well under way on the western border.[16]

During the week that followed, Livingston and Williams exchanged letters about the fate of the remaining prisoners on either side. Regimental letter books usually recorded only correspondence sent by the commanding officer or adjutant; but Williams must have thought the exchange with Livingston was so interesting that he ordered it copied into the record, so that the Confederate's messages and Williams' replies alternate. (The accuracy of transcription is open to question, for Livingston's first letter was semiliterate; his grammar and spelling improved markedly in the last two.) On 20 May, Livingston announced that he was willing to exchange his white Union prisoners for Williams' captured Confederates, but that "as for the Negrows I cannot Reccognise

---

[15]*OR*, ser. 1, vol. 22, pt. 1, pp. 320, 322 ("Colonel Williams'"); Lt Col J. M. Williams "To Comdg officer of Southern forces in Jasper & Newton Counties Mo," 11 May 1863, 79th USCI, Regimental Books, RG 94, NA.

[16]*OR*, ser. 1, vol. 22, pt. 1, pp. 219 ("bushwhackers"), 322 ("The prisoners," "Major"); *Military History of Kansas Regiments*, pp. 409–10 ("refused to exchange," "for the first time"); *Official Army Register of the Volunteer Force of the United States Army*, 8 vols. (Washington, D.C.: Adjutant General's Office, 1867), 8: 256 (hereafter cited as *ORVF*).

Them as Solgers and In consiquence I will hev to hold Them as contrabands of ware." Williams answered the next day, agreeing to an exchange of white prisoners, but adding:

> In regard to the colored men, prisoners, belonging to my Regiment, . . . it rests with you to treat them as prisoners of war or not but be assured that I shall keep a like number of your men as prisoners untill these colored men are accounted for, and you can safely trust that I shall visit a retributive justice upon them for any injury done them at the hands of the confederate forces. . . . [T]hese men are enlisted and sworn into the service of the United States as soldiers, and I doubt not the Government . . . will take the necessary steps to punish her enemies amply for any such gross violation of all rules of civilized and honorable warfare, and you can rest assured that knowing the justice of the course [cause?], I shall not long wait for orders . . . but will act as I have a right to upon my own judgment, and myself assume the responsibility.[17]

The exchange of white prisoners took place. On 26 May, Williams learned that one of the two men Livingston still held had been murdered in the Confederate camp. Williams demanded that the killer be surrendered to him for execution within two days; if the man did not appear, Williams would pick a substitute from among his own remaining prisoners. Livingston replied that the killer was not a member of his company or subject to his orders and that the man's "whereabouts is to me unknown." There the correspondence, as recorded in Williams' regimental letter book, stopped. It was one of the earliest exchanges between Union and Confederate officers about the rights and proper treatment of black soldiers, and, like later exchanges on the subject between other commanders, began with statements of high principle—"I cannot Recognize them," and "these men are enlisted . . . as soldiers"—and ended with threats of violence and retaliation.[18]

Old free-state/slave-state hostilities between white people along the Kansas-Missouri line were similar to those in the Indian Territory just to the south. Since the 1830s, that land had been home to five tribes that had moved there, under federal compulsion, from Alabama, Florida, Georgia, Mississippi, and Tennessee. The federal policy known as Indian Removal had given rise to intratribal factional disputes that sometimes reached murderous intensity. A generation later, the secession movement caused a new schism that divided those Indians who owned slaves—a custom they had brought with them from their old homelands in the Southern states—and who therefore wished to cooperate with the Confederacy from those who did not own slaves and wished to abide by the terms of tribal treaties with the United States. Confederate tribesmen persecuted many of their opponents, who fled to Kansas and formed Union regiments. In April 1863, federal troops occupied Fort Gibson, a prewar military post some twenty miles above the head of navigation on the Arkansas River and about the same distance west of

---

[17]Maj T. R. Livingston to Col J. M. Williams, 20 May 1863, and Col J. M. Williams to Maj T. R. Livingston, 21 May 1863, both in 79th USCI, Regimental Books, RG 94, NA.

[18]Livingston to Williams, 20 May 1863 ("I cannot"); Williams to Livingston, 21 May 1863 ("these men"). Williams to Livingston, 26 May 1863; Livingston to Col J. M. Phillips, 27 May 1863 ("whereabouts"); both in 79th USCI, Regimental Books, RG 94, NA.

Tahlequah, the capital of the Cherokee Nation. On a hill overlooking the old site, they laid out a fortified position that they named after the district commander, Maj. Gen. James G. Blunt.[19]

Pro-Union refugees flocked to the Union outpost in northeastern Indian Territory, as they did along the Mississippi River. Refugees and troops alike required rations, and federal wagon trains soon began rolling toward Fort Gibson. The closest supply depot was at Fort Scott, Kansas, one hundred sixty miles to the north. On 26 June, the 1st Kansas Colored left Baxter Springs and joined a train headed for Fort Gibson. The regiment was part of a 1,600-man reinforcement that would increase Union strength in the Indian Territory by 65 percent.[20]

The ox teams plodded south, covering the hundred miles between Baxter Springs and Fort Gibson at a rate of ten or twelve miles a day. They neared Cabin Creek, almost halfway to their destination, on 1 July. About noon, the men of the escort found a Confederate force on the opposite bank commanding the ford. Recent heavy rains made the creek too deep to cross, so the train circled its wagons and waited while Colonel Williams consulted with the senior officers of the rest of the escort, which included a battalion of the 3d Indian Home Guards and companies of white soldiers from Colorado, Kansas, and Wisconsin regiments. They decided to move their artillery pieces—three twelve-pounders and two six-pounders—to cover the ford and to try to cross on the following day.[21]

The next morning at 8:00, the guns opened fire on places beyond the creek where the enemy had been seen the day before. When one of the Indian companies tried to cross, small-arms fire erupted from the undergrowth that lined the shore where the Confederates had moved during the night. Colonel Williams saw the Union advance retreat "somewhat confusedly" and ordered artillery fire on the enemy's new position as well as rifle fire from three companies of the 1st Kansas Colored that had been about to wade the creek. Not long after 9:00, the infantry companies were able to cross in chest-deep water, losing three or four men wounded. The Confederates withdrew from the underbrush and formed line of battle some four hundred yards from the creek, but a charge by one company of Union cavalry broke them, as much to Williams' surprise as anyone's, and the entire six companies of federal mounted troops chased them from the field. The wagon train then crossed the creek and arrived at Fort Blunt, some fifty miles to the south, three days later.[22]

General Blunt himself arrived on 11 July and resolved to move against the brigade that Colonel Williams had defeated before the Confederates could reinforce it. Characteristically, each side overestimated the strength of the other; Blunt thought that his opponent, Brig. Gen. Douglas H. Cooper, commanded six thousand men, which another Confederate general reported as "much more than the number which [Cooper] has had together at any time." Cooper reckoned Blunt's

---

[19] OR, ser. 1, vol. 22, pt. 1, p. 349, and pt. 2, pp. 190, 256, 266, 276. Robert W. Frazer, *Forts of the West: Military Forts and Presidios, and Posts Commonly Called Forts, West of the Mississippi River to 1898* (Norman: University of Oklahoma Press, 1965), p. 121.

[20] OR, ser. 1, vol. 22, pt. 1, p. 379, and pt. 2, pp. 283, 300, 337, 342, 416, 478.

[21] Ibid., pt. 1, pp. 380, 382, and pt. 2, p. 478.

[22] Ibid., pt. 1, pp. 380–81 (quotation, p. 380).

strength at forty-five hundred, an overestimate of 50 percent. Nevertheless, Blunt moved across the Arkansas River on 16 July with, as he reported, "less than 3,000 men, mostly Indians and negroes." The next morning, Union cavalry encountered the enemy pickets and drove them to where the Confederate main force was waiting near Honey Springs, some twenty miles south of Fort Gibson.[23]

Blunt halted his men behind a ridge about half a mile from the enemy position and allowed them time to eat while he reconnoitered. Afterward, he formed the force in two columns, the 1st Kansas Colored and a white regiment, the 2d Colorado Infantry, in one brigade under Colonel Williams' command, and the 6th Kansas Cavalry and 3d Indian Home Guards in another brigade. In order to conceal their strength from the Confederates more effectively, the two brigades advanced in column—twenty-five or thirty men wide and about twenty ranks deep—rather than on a broad front. When they had covered about half the distance and were a quarter-mile from the enemy, they moved from column into line of battle. Blunt noticed that their front was at least as long as that of the Confederates.[24]

Williams' two regiments advanced until they were about forty paces from the woods where the enemy waited. So close were the two sides that his command to fire may have been mistaken by the Confederates as coming from one of their own officers. The two volleys came at once. Williams fell, wounded in the face, chest, and hands. The second-in-command, Lt. Col. John Bowles, was at the right of the brigade line and did not learn of Williams' wounding for some time. Meanwhile, the 1st Kansas Colored stood its ground and, when Bowles finally took command, stopped a Confederate charge with three volleys and chased the survivors through a cornfield. Union cavalry continued the pursuit past blazing supply warehouses two miles to the south set alight by the retreating enemy. The federal troops slept on the battlefield that night. The Confederates withdrew south toward the Canadian River.[25]

The 1st Kansas Colored's attack at Honey Springs marked the first time in the war that black soldiers in regimental strength had carried out a successful offensive operation against Confederate troops. The regiment sustained thirty-two casualties, half again as many as the 2d Colorado. General Blunt voiced the same sort of approval, mingled with surprise and relief, that other Union commanders expressed throughout the war. The difference was that Blunt, unlike General Banks at Port Hudson a few weeks earlier, had been present and had seen what he described. The 1st Kansas Colored, he reported, had "particularly distinguished itself; they fought like veterans, and preserved their line unbroken throughout the engagement."[26]

Blunt's victory at Honey Springs allowed his Army of the Frontier to move southeast down the Arkansas River. On 1 September, it occupied Fort Smith, an antebellum military post that had given its name to the westernmost town in Arkansas. Nine days later, General Steele's force, operating from Helena, entered Little Rock. Union armies had gained control of the major towns along the Arkansas River, but Confederates, uniformed and guerrilla, still moved freely through large

---

[23]*OR*, ser. 1, vol. 22, pt. 1, pp. 447 ("less than"), 458, and pt. 2, p. 1078 ("much more").
[24]Ibid., pt. 1, pp. 447–48.
[25]Ibid., pt. 1, pp. 448, 450; NA M594, roll 213, 79th USCI.
[26]*OR*, ser. 1, vol. 22, pt. 1, pp. 448 (quotation), 449.

Artists' representations of static scenes tended to stay closer to the truth than their depictions of battles. Frank Leslie's Illustrated Newspaper *image and photograph show the Union outpost at Fort Smith, Arkansas, in 1865.*

parts of the rest of the state. At Fort Smith, a new regiment numbered the 11th USCI began to organize and Union troops settled in for a hard winter. Soon the water level in the river fell, blocking transportation and putting the garrison on half rations until the spring rise came.[27]

The numeral assigned to the new regiment at Fort Smith represented a nationwide attempt to standardize nomenclature in the black regiments. Early in March, Adjutant General Thomas ordered new federal numbers for the Arkansas, Louisiana, Mississippi, and Tennessee regiments that he had raised as state organizations. The 1st Arkansas (AD) became the 46th USCI, the 2d Arkansas the 54th USCI, the 3d the 56th USCI, and the 4th the 57th USCI. In New Orleans, General Banks adopted consecutive federal numbers for his Corps d'Afrique regiments a few weeks later. The two black Kansas regiments were outside both generals' purview and retained their state designations until December, when the 1st Kansas Colored became the 79th USCI (New) and the 2d the 83d USCI (New).[28]

Those numbers were vacant because the regiments that had originally held them had been the source of many inspectors' complaints in the Department of the Gulf, where they were part of the Corps d'Afrique. Exasperated authorities broke up both regiments in July 1864, along with three others, and sent the enlisted men to fill the ranks of other regiments while ordering the officers to appear before examination boards that would determine their competence. Thirty-five of the officers of the original 79th and 83d resigned or received discharges. Thirteen passed their examinations and transferred to other regiments.[29]

On 17 March 1864, orders came to Fort Smith requiring a division of troops to join General Steele's command at Little Rock. Steele was to march south and join General Banks' Red River Campaign toward Shreveport and eastern Texas. Maj. Gen. William T. Sherman, commanding the Military Division of the Mississippi and in charge of Union operations west of the Appalachians, wanted Steele to move rapidly, but the Frontier Division from Fort Smith showed no sign of arriving, and it was 23 March before Steele set out with his forty-eight hundred men. One hundred recruits of the 4th Arkansas (AD) received axes, picks, and shovels and helped build roads for the thirty-four wagons that carried parts of the expedition's pontoon bridge.[30]

The 4,000-man Frontier Division finally got under way the same week that Steele's column left Little Rock. It moved southeast by way of Hot Springs. "The weather was rainy, cold, and disagreeable, the roads soft and spongy," a former officer of the 2d Kansas Colored recalled anonymously in a newspaper account soon after the war. "We had to travel many hours each day, to make the distance that was necessary. Many places in the road had to be 'corduroyed' to render them passable. The country became mountainous and stony, which, with the mud-holes, used up the mules pretty fast. . . . Often all we had for food was corn meal, ground in hand mills, and the cattle, hogs &c., we killed after camping." Delayed by high water,

---

[27] Ibid., pp. 10–11, 16–17; vol. 34, pt. 2, pp. 24, 51–52, 705, 739.

[28] OR, ser. 3, 4: 164–65, 214–15.

[29] "Broken up" is the term used in Dyer, *Compendium*, pp. 1735–36, and *ORVF*, 8: 255, 261, 269, 271–72, 275, to describe the end of the old 79th, 83d, 88th, 89th, and 90th USCIs.

[30] OR, ser. 1, vol. 34, pt. 1, pp. 657, 660–62, 672, and pt. 2, pp. 638, 647.

bad roads, and short supplies, the Frontier Division did not catch up with Steele's force south of Arkadelphia until 9 April.[31]

By feinting toward the Confederate state capital at Washington, Steele's command drew the enemy garrison out of Camden, on the Ouachita River some ninety miles south of Little Rock. Union troops occupied the undefended town on 15 April. "They had marched the whole distance on half rations of hard bread, quarter rations of bacon, and full rations of coffee and salt," one of Steele's staff officers reported, "and of this short allowance we had very little left." Besides food for the men, the expedition needed forage for the animals that pulled the supply wagons. On the evening of 16 April, Colonel Williams and the 1st Kansas Colored received orders to escort a forage train the next day.[32]

Five hundred officers and men of the regiment, with some 200 cavalry, 2 ten-pounder field guns, and a train of 198 wagons, got under way shortly before dawn. They marched eighteen miles west of Camden before Williams called a halt and broke up the party to search nearby farms for feed. The detachments returned by midnight with nearly one hundred wagons full of corn. The next day, the expedition began its return march to Camden, with scouts and wagons still out to gather any available grain. Not long after starting, Williams' column met reinforcements: more than three hundred fifty men of the 18th Iowa Infantry and eighty cavalry from Camden, along with two twelve-pounder mountain howitzers. These were a welcome addition to the force, for the previous day's exertions, on top of a 24-day march from Fort Smith on reduced rations, had put about one-fifth of the men in the 1st Kansas Colored out of action. With cavalry outriders and many of the wagons still seeking forage and the usual stragglers fallen behind or wandered off, Williams' immediate command had dwindled to barely one thousand men.[33]

For weeks, Confederate horsemen had been retreating, first from Arkadelphia and then from Camden, while they observed the federal advance. When the cavalry division commander, Brig. Gen. John S. Marmaduke, learned that a Union forage train was on the road, he decided to capture or destroy it and perhaps reverse the course of the campaign. Overnight, he assembled a force of some two thousand men from his scattered brigades, along with eight cannon. Marmaduke's scouts had told him about the federal reinforcements, and he believed the Union strength to be about twenty-five hundred (more than twice its actual size). Nevertheless, he placed his available force in a position to block the Union foragers' return route at a place called Poison Spring, fourteen miles west of Camden. The wagons rolled into sight about 10:00 on the morning of 18 April. As the opposing sides began to exchange shots, Marmaduke welcomed the arrival of Brig. Gen. Samuel B. Maxey with twelve hundred Texas and Choctaw cavalry. He put the new arrivals on the

---

[31]"The Camden Expedition," (Lawrence) *Kansas Daily Tribune*, 15 February 1866; *OR*, ser. 1, vol. 34, pt. 1, p. 657. The anonymous former officer who described the campaign for the *Tribune* said that the 2d Kansas Colored broke camp on 23 March; the regimental record says 24 March. The 1st Kansas Colored's record of events lists a departure date of 25 March. NA M594, roll 213, 79th USCI, and roll 214, 83d USCI.

[32]*OR*, ser. 1, vol. 34, pt. 1, pp. 676 (quotation), 680, 682–83, and pt. 3, p. 237.

[33]Ibid., pt. 1, pp. 743–44.

left of his own troops and more or less at right angles to their line, in woods on the south side of the road to Camden.[34]

On the Union side, Colonel Williams halted the wagons and sent for several companies of his own regiment, the 1st Kansas Colored, which had been guarding the rear of the train. Some of the wagons, with cavalry escorts, had dispersed to ransack farms along the way for feed, but the train still stretched well over a mile in length. While he waited at the head of the column, Williams had his cannon fire a few rounds at the Confederates to warn the stray foragers to return and to learn perhaps whether the enemy had any artillery of his own hidden in the thick woods that lined the road. The answer to that question came when Confederate cannon opened fire just as six companies of the 1st Kansas Colored arrived from the tail of the column. After half an hour's bombardment, Marmaduke's and Maxey's cavalry, dismounted, advanced on the forage train. It was then about noon.[35]

The men of the 1st Kansas Colored, supporting the expedition's artillery, were unable to see the enemy in the dense foliage but managed to fire at least two volleys at ranges of less than one hundred yards. By the time they had repelled several Confederate charges, more than one hundred of their number lay dead or wounded and four companies of the regiment were without an officer. When the artillerymen moved their guns, Maj. Richard G. Ward, commanding the 1st Kansas Colored, ordered the men to retire toward the parked wagons. Most had the presence of mind to keep firing as they withdrew, but "a portion retired precipitately," as Ward put it in his report, and left the fight.[36]

The adjutant, 1st Lt. William C. Gibbons, had been on the left of the regiment's front during most of the action. When he saw the troops to his right running away, he "ordered the men to fall back in as good order as possible. . . . [T]he infantry had all passed me and the enemy were bearing down on us with a yell. I need not say I mounted quick and rode away quicker." About one hundred fifty yards off, he found the survivors of two intact companies under command of their own officers and a third officer with some of the regiment's stragglers, about one hundred in all. Gibbons and the three officers got the men to face the Confederates, who were advancing across an open field. "I ordered the men to fire . . . , but this line could not stand longer than to deliver one volley. I saw that the right [of the Union line] was entirely broken and the men pouring past me, and the [enemy] had but to charge across the field, leap the fence, and our retreat was cut off. Then, seeing the train was lost, my first idea was to save the men. So I ordered them to scatter." He watched artillerymen cut their horses loose from the guns, mount them, and make their escape. As Gibbons himself rode off, he saw at a distance victorious Confederates beginning to shoot any wounded Union soldiers who still lay on the field. He "rode slowly on . . . , giving such directions to all our men I met as I thought would insure their safety." Finally, about four miles from the battlefield, he put spurs to his own horse and "rode as fast as the nature of the country would allow

---

[34] Ibid., pp. 818–19, 825; pt. 2, p. 1097; pt. 3, pp. 723–24, 751–52.
[35] Ibid., pt. 1, pp. 744–45, 748, 751–52. On dense woods and undergrowth, see pp. 757, 828, 842; *Report of the Adjutant General . . . of Kansas*, p. 414.
[36] *OR*, ser. 1, vol. 34, pt. 1, pp. 745, 753–54.

for Camden," arriving there about 8:00, an hour after dark. Many of the men took three days, on foot and through swamps, to make the same journey.[37]

The initial casualty count for the entire force was 92 killed, 97 wounded, and 106 missing. Colonel Williams reported that many of his regiment's wounded were left on the field and that eyewitnesses assured him "that they were murdered on the spot. . . . Many of those missing are supposed to be killed." A revised tally showed 204 "killed and missing" and 97 wounded. The 1st Kansas Colored's share was 117 (all noted as "killed") and 65 wounded. Fatalities that amounted to nearly 65 percent of casualties strongly suggested a massacre. Both Major Ward and Adjutant Gibbons reported having seen Confederate soldiers shooting the wounded.[38]

Confederate officers' reports do not mention a massacre; they could not be expected to. From their point of view, the men of the 1st Kansas Colored were escaped slaves, armed and deserving immediate punishment. Moreover, they and their white comrades had been foraging and looting their way through Arkansas. Private letters and journals written by Confederates a few days after the event blamed Maxey's Choctaw cavalry for much of the killing. "The havoc among the negroes had been tremendous," wrote a Texan diarist. "Over a small portion of the field we saw at least 40 dead bodies lying in all conceivable attitudes, some scalped & nearly all stripped by the bloodthirsty Choctaws." The fact that the 1st Kansas Colored was in the thick of the fighting that day—the regiment's sixty-five wounded men who eventually reached Camden amounted to more than two-thirds of the entire expedition's surviving wounded—meant that most of the men who were too badly wounded to be moved from the field were black and likely to die at the hands of vengeful Confederates.[39]

Survivors brought the news of the fight at Poison Spring to the main body of federal troops at Camden. A week later, Confederates captured another supply train and with it some nine hundred men of the all-white infantry escort. Of the "large number of citizens [civilians], cotton speculators, [white] refugees, . . . and also some 300 negroes" who accompanied the train to what they hoped would be security and freedom, many "were inhumanly butchered by the enemy," the escort's commander reported. General Steele, faced with the prospect of starvation and the arrival of Confederate reinforcements after the collapse of Banks' Red River Campaign, decided to turn his force north on 26 April and return to Little Rock. This time, to avoid some bad roads he had encountered along the Ouachita River, he headed somewhat to the east, toward Jenkins' Ferry on the Big Saline. The men were on quarter rations, one-and-a-half pounds of hardtack per man per day; one veteran of the 2d Kansas Colored recalled the men stealing corn from the expedition's mules. About noon on 29 April, a few hours before the expedition reached the ferry, rain began to fall. The pontoon train hurried to the front of the column and managed to span the river in a few hours. Most of the wagons and mounted men crossed before dawn the next day. "I never saw it rain harder than

---

[37] Ibid., pp. 755–56 (quotation); NA M594, roll 213, 79th USCI.

[38] *OR*, ser. 1, vol. 34, pt. 1, p. 754.

[39] Ibid., p. 746; Gregory J. W. Urwin, "'We Cannot Treat Negroes . . . As Prisoners of War': Racial Atrocities and Reprisals in Civil War Arkansas," *Civil War History* 42 (1996): 196–201 (quotation, p. 197).

it did during the night," the expedition's chief engineer reported. The bottom land along the river "soon became a sea of mud, in which wagons settled to the axles and mules floundered about without a resting place for their feet. . . . The rain came down in torrents, putting out many of the fires, the men became exhausted, and both they and the animals sank down in the mud and mire, wherever they were, to seek a few hours' repose."[40]

The infantry began to cross the bridge at daylight, the battered 1st Kansas Colored toward the head of the five-mile column, the 2d Kansas Colored much farther back. By 8:00, the 2d had moved as far as the bridge, hearing all the while the sound of small-arms fire as the Union rearguard exchanged shots with pursuing Confederates. As the firing increased, Col. Samuel J. Crawford, commanding the regiment, turned his men around and marched back toward the fighting. They arrived in time to relieve another regiment that had nearly exhausted its ammunition. Partly concealed by trees and underbrush at the edge of an open field, officers of the 2d Kansas Colored walked back and forth along the line to observe the men's firing and to correct their aim when necessary. "Soon the rebel fire was not so effective as at first," one officer recalled. "The leaves and bark fell from the trees, cut off eight or nine feet high. Their fire gradually slackened—wavered—stopped." Toward noon, Confederate artillerymen struggled through the mud with three cannon and managed to fire a few shots at the Union line. The 2d Kansas Colored and the 29th Iowa charged some two hundred fifty yards across the open field and captured the guns, killing or wounding ten of the gunners and all but two of their horses. Early in the afternoon, word came to retire and join the retreating column. All Union regiments were north of the river by 2:00, but the engineers waited another forty-five minutes for stragglers and walking wounded to catch up before they destroyed the worn-out, sinking pontoon bridge. The column limped into Little Rock three days later.[41]

The 2d Kansas Colored may have been the first black regiment to charge and capture Confederate artillery. It is also possible that the men cheered "Remember Poison Spring!" as they advanced. What seems certain is that they acted in that spirit and took few, if any, Confederate prisoners. The officer who commanded the captured battery reported three of his men "killed by negroes after they had surrendered." Confederate soldiers who wrote to their families soon after the battle mentioned seeing the corpses of wounded men with throats cut and other mutilations. On the Union side, a soldier in the 29th Iowa who had seen the 2d Kansas in action told his brother: "Our white negro officers and the negroes want to kill every wounded reb they come to and will do it if we did not watch them. . . . [O]ne of our boys seen a little negro pounding a wounded reb in the head with the butt of his gun and asked him what he was doing: the negro replied he is not dead yet! . . . [I]t looks hard but the rebs cannot blame the negroes for it when they are guilty of the same trick both to the whites and negroes." Like the U.S.

---

[40] *OR*, ser. 1, vol. 34, pt. 1, pp. 666, 668–69, 677 ("I never"), 692, 712 ("large number"), 715 ("were inhumanly"), 757; pt. 3, p. 267. *Report of the Adjutant General . . . of Kansas*, p. 431; Urwin, "'We Cannot Treat Negroes,'" p. 196.

[41] *OR*, ser. 1, vol. 34, pt. 1, pp. 670, 677, 689, 757–58, 787; *Report of the Adjutant General . . . of Kansas*, pp. 421, 429; "The Camden Expedition," (Lawrence) *Kansas Daily Tribune*, 15 February 1866 (quotation).

Col. Samuel J. Crawford of the 2d Kansas Colored Infantry (later the 83d U.S. Colored Infantry) was awarded the brevet rank of brigadier general at the end of the war.

Colored Troops who captured Fort Blakely, Alabama, black soldiers west of the Mississippi River easily adopted a no-quarter policy of their own.[42]

Steele's attempt to assist Banks' ill-fated Red River Campaign was the Union's last offensive effort in Arkansas. Sherman's Atlanta Campaign demanded all the troops that could be spared from garrisons farther west. The regiments that remained in the Union Department of Arkansas clung to Helena, on the Mississippi River; Little Rock, the state capital; Duvall's Bluff, about fifty miles east of Little Rock on the White River; Pine Bluff, on the Arkansas River some fifty miles downstream from Little Rock; and, far to the west, Fort Smith and Van Buren. The department established and closed a few other garrisons from time to time, as was necessary. Union garrisons also held Fort Gibson in the northeast corner of the Indian Territory and Fort Scott in southeastern Kansas. A department order in September 1864 accurately described "the lines of actual occupation by the military forces of the United States . . . to be within the picket-lines of the posts." Federal authority, in other words, extended only as far as the occupied towns' outermost sentries.[43]

On the west bank of the Mississippi River, Union troops retained only a base at Helena. A census in the summer of 1864 showed 3,308 black residents nearby, of whom 1,045 worked on plantations, 180 were "employed by government," and 486

[42] *OR*, ser. 1, vol. 34, pt. 1, p. 813 ("killed by"); *Report of the Adjutant General . . . of Kansas*, pp. 429, 432; Urwin, "'We Cannot Treat Negroes,'" p. 208; M. P. Chambers to Dear Brother, 7 May 1864 ("Our white"), M. P. Chambers Papers, UA.

[43] *OR*, ser. 1, vol. 41, pt. 3, p. 248 (quotation); vol. 48, pt. 1, p. 959.

were "employed in town"—perhaps by civilian and military officials as domestic servants, or by the contractors who chopped wood on islands in the river. Companies of black soldiers stationed at Helena guarded nearby contraband camps and plantations that provided living quarters and work for freedpeople, as well as islands where woodcutters toiled to provide fuel for steamboats that carried troops and supplies to army garrisons and the plantations' cotton to market. "But for military protection . . . not a bale of cotton would have been raised," the commissioner in charge of plantations assured Adjutant General Thomas, catching in a nutshell the roles of the Army and the freedpeople and the relation between economics, politics, and military operations in the occupied South. Confederate officials were quick to recognize the importance of riverboats to federal operations and undertook not only to fire at passing steamers with cannon and small arms but to destroy the island woodlots that provided the boats' fuel. Attacks on the plantations and contraband camps along the river would deprive thousands of freedpeople of homes and return many of them to slavery. Moreover, federal officials knew that black fugitives from the Confederate interior furnished valuable intelligence as they arrived, day by day, at the plantations and camps. They had good reason, therefore, to keep the freedpeople's new homes safe.[44]

From the winter of 1864 through the end of the war, Helena's garrison included two regiments of black soldiers, the 3d Arkansas (AD) and the 1st Iowa Colored, which were renumbered in March the 56th and 60th USCIs. There were also companies from the 63d and 64th USCIs. These were "invalid" regiments composed of men unfit for field service but sufficiently healthy to stand guard over contraband camps, plantations, warehouses full of government supplies, and wood yards. The Union Army included white invalids, organized as the Veterans Reserve Corps, but these were men who had been wounded in battle. Only the U.S. Colored Troops deliberately signed up men who had been rejected by medical examiners. The 63d and 64th USCIs had companies scattered along the Mississippi from Memphis to Natchez; several companies of the 64th guarded the freedpeople's settlement at Davis Bend, the site of plantations that belonged to Jefferson Davis and his brother Joseph. A few miles upstream from Helena, guard stations included the woodcutters' camps on Island Nos. 60 and 63.[45]

Rather than sit by the river and wait to be attacked, beginning in February 1864 the Helena garrison made repeated forays up the Mississippi and its tributaries in search of Confederates. "I can only keep the guerrillas at bay by constant raids," Brig. Gen. Napoleon B. Buford, the district commander, told General Steele. One such waterborne expedition in February included one hundred mounted men of the 15th Illinois Cavalry with forty men of the 3d Arkansas (AD) to guard the steamer while the cavalry ranged inland. In four days, they captured seven Confederate irregulars and nineteen horses

---

[44]*OR*, ser. 1, vol. 22, pt. 2, pp. 852–53; vol. 26, pt. 1, pp. 739–40; vol. 34, pt. 2, pp. 504–05; vol. 41, pt. 2, pp. 1010–11. Lt Cdr J. M. Pritchett to Maj Gen F. A. Steele, 7 Mar 1864 (P–9–DA–1864), Entry 269, Dept of Arkansas, Letters Received (LR), pt. 1, Geographical Divs and Depts, RG 393, Rcds of U.S. Army Continental Cmds, NA. Census figures in A. R. Gillum to Col J. Eaton, 1 Jul 1864 (G–103–DA–1864), Entry 269, pt. 1, RG 393, NA. S. Sawyer to Brig Gen L. Thomas, 5 Oct 1863 ("But for military") (S–24–AG–1863), Entry 363, LR by Adjutant Gen Thomas, RG 94, NA; Ira Berlin et al., eds., *The Wartime Genesis of Free Labor: The Lower South* (New York: Cambridge University Press, 1990), pp. 630–35; Carl H. Moneyhon, *The Impact of the Civil War and Reconstruction in Arkansas* (Baton Rouge: Louisiana State University Press, 1994), pp. 142–51.

[45]NA M594, roll 211, 56th USCI; roll 212, 60th, 63d, and 64th USCIs.

and mules and seized or destroyed eighteen firearms. The black soldiers gathered six recruits. These operations accomplished little in the long run; at the beginning of April, Buford reported five of the enemy's "midnight raids" on leased plantations during the last two weeks of March. "The lakes, swamps, bayous, and canebrakes make it impossible to guard the district," he complained to Adjutant General Thomas.[46]

Demands imposed by operations elsewhere—Steele's thrust toward Camden early in the spring followed by the necessary reaction to a Confederate recruiting foray north of the Arkansas River as summer began—slowed the tempo of events along the Mississippi for only a few months. On the afternoon of 25 July, General Buford sent inland three hundred sixty men of the 56th and 60th USCIs, with two cannon belonging to Battery E, 2d United States Colored Artillery (USCA), and five days' rations to seize livestock and arrest Confederate sympathizers. Buford warned the expedition's commander to go slowly and carefully, for the raid marked both regiments' first excursion beyond Helena's entrenchments. Instead, Col. William S. Brooks marched his men most of the night, reaching a point some twenty miles southwest of Helena before daybreak on 26 July. They reconnoitered the crossing of a stream called Big Creek, concluded that no enemy was near, and began to water the horses and cook breakfast. "Before the teams were all unhitched," the artillery officer reported, Confederates concealed in dense woods opened fire at one hundred fifty yards' range. They closed to within fifty yards and exchanged shots with the federals for more than three hours, inflicting sixty-two casualties. About 10:00, a nearby column of one hundred fifty troopers of the 15th Illinois Cavalry, also part of the Helena garrison, picked its way through the timber to join the fight. This additional force afforded the infantrymen time to pick up most of their wounded and begin the march back to Helena. They also brought with them the bodies of four slain commissioned officers, among them that of Colonel Brooks.[47]

The Confederate troops at Big Creek were on their way to raid leased plantations near Helena. It was a move that the Confederate cavalry leader, Brig. Gen. Joseph O. Shelby, had been discussing with his regimental commanders for the previous month. Shelby's men struck during the first week in August and, General Steele reported, "swept the plantations below Helena of stock, negroes, and everything else that could be taken away." For weeks afterward, one lessee wrote, it was "impossible to get the colored people to work on the farms outside of the military lines without protection." The raids stopped suddenly a few days later, when higher headquarters ordered the raiders to rejoin the main body of Confederates south of the Arkansas River.[48]

The August raids posed the last serious military threat to the leased plantations and their residents, but problems of administration and health continued. During the final ten months of the war, troops at Helena limited their activities to small patrols that went out from time to time to seize livestock and to arrest Union deserters, Confederate soldiers visiting their homes on furlough, and traders in

---

[46]*OR*, ser. 1, vol. 34, pt. 1, pp. 8–9 ("midnight raids"), 126–27, and pt. 2, pp. 239–41 ("I can only," p. 239).

[47]*OR*, ser. 1, vol. 41, pt. 1, pp. 19–23 (quotation, p. 22), and pt. 3, p. 384.

[48]Ibid., pt. 3, pp. 601 ("swept the plantations"), 994, 1010–11, 1034–35, 1050–51. J. T. Smith to Brig Gen N. B. Buford, 31 Jan 1865 ("impossible to get"), in General Court Martial file, Capt A. L. Thayer (OO–895), Entry 15, General Court Martial Case Files, RG 153, Rcds of the Judge Advocate General's Office, NA.

contraband cotton. Soldiers in one of the Union Army's most disease-ridden garrisons had long been accustomed to performing duties that lay somewhere between combat and commerce. General Buford himself took sick leave, bidding farewell to Helena in February 1865: "At this post," he wrote, "I have watched the guerrilla parties on both sides of the river, the smugglers . . . , and the lessees of plantations, some of whom are as bad as the enemy. The freedmen's department, numbering 5,000, I have endeavored to make self-supporting, but have been defeated . . . by dishonest men, one of whom is now on trial." He was referring to Capt. Albert L. Thayer of the 63d USCI, cashiered by a general court-martial for trading in cotton and contraband goods. In addition, the captain had charged freedmen fees as high as $150 for services that an officer should have performed gratis. A witness had overheard the captain say that he intended to use the superintendency to recoup his losses in cotton speculation; and if he could get the job "during the Cotton season, . . . the Authorities might then muster him out of the service, and be damned."[49]

While General Buford tried to defend the cotton plantations around Helena and to punish corrupt dealings in the crop, he also questioned the pattern of federal troop dispositions throughout the state. "Why do we continue to occupy the interior of Arkansas?" he had asked Maj. Gen. Cadwallader C. Washburn at Memphis in the summer of 1864, after the failure of Steele's Camden expedition.

> What good has arisen from the occupation? . . . Has not the cost of maintaining an army in the interior been vastly beyond what it would have been on the banks of the Mississippi River? . . . Would not the maintenance of four fortified positions on the river and a strict blockade, preventing the enemy from getting supplies, have accomplished much greater results with almost one-fourth the expenditure of men and means?

He cited several sunk or damaged naval and civilian vessels on the Arkansas River, as well as the loss of troops, 700 hundred wagons, 6,000 draft animals and cavalry horses, and 6 cannon in Steele's failed campaign. Nevertheless, the Union high command continued to insist on holding the string of posts that ran up the Arkansas River and included at the western end places where the only reliable year-round means of supply was by wagon from Kansas.[50]

The Army's reason for holding this line—from Pine Bluff through Little Rock to Fort Smith and Fort Gibson in the Indian Territory—was to deter a possible Confederate thrust north into Missouri, a state which, like Arkansas, had been stripped of troops to augment Sherman's offensive in Georgia. Deterrence was a vain hope. Confederates, military and civil, regular and irregular, had always ranged through Arkansas, collecting taxes and enforcing conscription beyond the reach of Union soldiers. Ensuring a continual flow of men and money

---

[49] *OR*, ser. 1, vol. 41, pt. 1, pp. 241–42, 302–03, 759, 816–17, 851; vol. 48, pt. 1, pp. 34–35, 126, 856–57 ("At this post"). Trial transcript, Capt A. L. Thayer (OO–895) ("during the Cotton"), Entry 15, RG 153, NA. Dist of Eastern Arkansas, Special Order 39, 7 Mar 1865, 56th USCI, Entry 57C, RG 94, NA. "Cashiering" meant conviction of "scandalous and infamous conduct." The sentence meant not merely dismissal from the service but a bar to future military employment. Edward S. Farrow, *Farrow's Military Encyclopedia*, 3 vols. (New York: privately printed, 1885), 1: 301.

[50] *OR*, ser. 1, vol. 41, pt. 1, pp. 69–70.

for the secessionist cause had been a chief concern of Lt. Gen. E. Kirby Smith when he came to the Trans-Mississippi Department in the spring of 1863. According to Confederate law, farmers were liable to pay taxes in kind. Army quartermasters would act as tax collectors, using edible crops to sustain the troops and turning over cotton and tobacco to Confederate treasury agents for eventual sale. Within six weeks, the quartermaster general in Richmond had drawn up a list of twenty-four Arkansas counties where it would be worthwhile to collect taxes in kind. All lay in the east and south of the state in the fertile bottomlands along the Arkansas, Ouachita, and White Rivers. Rich soil meant that in most of them, as in similar regions throughout the South, black slaves made up more than 20 percent of the population. The rest of the state was too poor in soil and too Unionist in sentiment to be worth the tax collectors' efforts.[51]

Confederate officers in search of conscripts to swell their army's dwindling ranks did not face the limits that soil, crops, and wealth imposed on tax collectors; by February 1864, most able-bodied white Southern men between the ages of seventeen and fifty were liable to the draft. When General Shelby's cavalry ranged north of the Arkansas River that spring, his recruiters sought men as young as sixteen. Union occupiers were still recovering from the setback of Steele's failed campaign, and Shelby sent his reports from such recently abandoned federal garrison towns as Batesville and Dardanelle. Shelby was "conscripting all around," the federal commander at Duvall's Bluff reported in mid-July, and sending small parties to raid the railroad.[52]

Slipping through the porous Union line along the Arkansas River, Shelby succeeded in drafting about five thousand men between May and July. Not only did the federal defensive line fail to keep out Confederates, but its static nature also hindered the U.S. Colored Troops' efforts to find recruits. At Fort Smith, a mustering-in officer accepted the first four companies of the 11th USCI in December 1863 and a fifth company the following March. Then enlistment stalled. The 11th never grew large enough to allow the appointment of a colonel and a major; and a lieutenant colonel commanded the incomplete regiment until April 1865, when it consolidated with the 112th and 113th USCIs. The two junior regiments had the same trouble at Little Rock, with the 112th organizing only four companies during the spring of 1864 and the 113th seven. Officers at all levels of command recognized the problem. "I had hoped that before now we would have been in Texas and been re-enforced by 10,000 colored troops at least," Brig. Gen. Christopher C. Andrews wrote to President Lincoln that summer from his post on the railroad at Duvall's Bluff. "There are thousands of negroes in that State," he went on, "and if commanders go there who have any zeal in bringing them into the service they will be procured. I am sorry I cannot predict anything promising in [Arkansas]." Recruiting for the 113th USCI at Little Rock that July,

---

[51] Ibid., vol. 22, pt. 2, p. 872; vol. 48, pt. 1, p. 103; ser. 4, 2: 521–23, 576.

[52] *OR*, ser. 1, vol. 34, pt. 3, pp. 829; vol. 41, pt. 2, pp. 232, 234 ("conscripting"), 454, 1027, 1054; ser. 4, 3: 178. On irregular operations during the Civil War, see Daniel E. Sutherland, "Sideshow No Longer: A Historiographical Review of the Guerrilla War," *Civil War History* 46 (2000): 5–23; Robert R. Mackey, *The Uncivil War: Irregular Warfare in the Upper South, 1861–1865* (Norman: University of Oklahoma Press, 2004), pp. 24–71.

Capt. James M. Bowler told his wife that "little can be done until the army moves again." He hoped for an advance "Texasward" at some future date, in September, he thought at first; but as the months dragged on, he began to suppose that it might come in February or March. By February 1865, he had given up trying to predict a date. When the seven companies of the 113th merged with the nine companies of the 11th and 112th that April to make one full-strength regiment, Bowler became its major.[53]

Despite the Union Army's static posture along the Arkansas River, some men from outlying counties managed the trip to the closest federal garrison and enlisted. In March 1864, Henry Powers learned that his master planned to move with his slaves from Lawrence County in northeastern Arkansas to Texas, where many slaveholders sought to safeguard their human property. Powers and four companions took mules and horses and rode fifty miles overnight to Batesville, hoping to enlist. "We would have been killed if we had been caught," he said. "The rebels accused me of conspiring with the colored people of our section to escape & go to the federals. My brother and me was about the only colored people in our part that could read any, and they looked upon us as troublesome." Union officers at Batesville allowed Powers and his companions to enlist in the 113th USCI, but not before impounding their mounts.[54]

At Dardanelle in 1863, a slave named John Aiken "had been quietly organizing about 60 of the most reliable colored men," intending to join the Union Army at the first opportunity. That fall, Confederate officers heard of his activities and he had to move quickly. His owner, who was also his aunt (her brother was Aiken's father), warned him to escape. He spoke to her briefly before he left. Jackson Lewis, another slave who left with Aiken, was present. "I . . . heard her ask him if he was going off with the nasty stinking Yankees instead of going to Texas. [H]e said he was." Besides two of his brothers and Lewis, Aiken eventually persuaded more than one hundred twenty men from Yell County to follow him into the 11th USCI. He became a company first sergeant before the war ended.[55]

Federal posts along the Arkansas River required supplies, and these had to travel for hundreds of miles. By the summer of 1864, Arkansas had been ravaged for three years by the marches and countermarches of opposing armies; agriculture was at a standstill. The only railroad still operating in the state was the forty-nine miles of track that connected Duvall's Bluff on the White River with Little Rock on the Arkansas. Rivers afforded the cheapest way to move supplies, but navigation throughout most of the state was seasonal. Steamboats could go as far west as Fort Smith for only a few months of the year. Early in August, a boat might ascend the Arkansas River "nearly" to the fort, Brig. Gen. John M. Thayer reported. Six weeks later, the water had sunk too low for supplies to be

---

[53] *OR*, ser. 1, vol. 41, pt. 3, p. 163 ("I had hoped"); NA M594, roll 206, 11th USCI, and roll 216, 112th and 113th USCIs; *ORVF*, 8: 181, 292–94; J. M. Bowler to Dear Lizzie, 10 Jul 1864 ("little can") and 11 Dec 1864, both in J. M. Bowler Papers, Minnesota Historical Society, St. Paul.

[54] Testimony, Henry H. Powers, Dec 1872, in Case File 15,480, Henry H. Powers, Entry 732, RG 217, NA.

[55] Depositions, John Aiken, Nov 1871 ("had been"), and Jackson Lewis, May 1874 ("I . . . heard"), both in Case File 9,877, John Aiken, Entry 732, RG 217, NA.

sure of reaching even Pine Bluff, forty miles downstream from Little Rock. Although the river rose again in late autumn, steamboats still could not get above Dardanelle, ninety miles below Fort Smith, by mid-December.[56]

Overland supply of Forts Smith and Gibson posed its own problems. Wagon trains had to originate in General Curtis' Department of Kansas, an entirely different command. Fort Leavenworth on the Missouri River was the supply depot. From there, mules or oxen pulled loaded wagons south some one hundred twenty miles to Fort Scott, headquarters of the District of South Kansas, then another one hundred sixty miles to Fort Gibson and yet another fifty to Fort Smith. At a wagon train's rate of travel, twelve to fifteen miles a day with oxen, fifteen to twenty with mules, the entire one-way journey could take as long as four weeks. A train spent only seven or eight hours of the day traveling, pausing for about four hours at midday to allow the animals to graze so that they would rest properly that night. As trains left Kansas, they entered the Indian Territory and General Thayer's District of the Frontier, part of the Department of Arkansas. In Thayer's command, four black infantry regiments—the 1st and 2d Kansas Colored, the partially formed 11th USCI, and the 54th (formerly the 2d Arkansas [AD])—made up about one-quarter of the force.[57]

By mid-September, as two steamboats lay grounded thirty-five miles upstream from Little Rock—not even one-fifth of the way to Fort Smith—General Thayer realized that his troops' rations for subsistence all came by wagon trains from Fort Scott. The 1st Kansas Colored had moved a month earlier from Fort Smith to Fort Gibson, where its companies stood guard over hay cutters busily laying up forage for the draft animals that hauled the garrison's supplies. The rest of Colonel Williams' all-black brigade remained closer to Fort Smith. The 2d Kansas Colored worked on the town's defenses, contributing what the regiment's bimonthly record of events called "heavy fatigue parties." The 54th USCI furnished guards for government livestock and wagon trains. The 11th USCI's five companies were on Big Sallisaw Creek, some forty miles northwest of Fort Smith, guarding hay cutters.[58]

General Thayer sent all his available transportation to Fort Scott for supplies. The train's 205 empty wagons arrived there, received their loads, and set out for Fort Smith on 12 September joined by ninety-one sutlers' wagons carrying privately owned goods for sale to troops. The escort consisted of two hundred sixty men, only one hundred twenty of them mounted, detailed from three white Kansas cavalry regiments. Worried about his supply line, Thayer sent Colonel Williams with the 11th and 54th USCIs toward Fort Gibson on 14 September with discretion to march there directly or to stop and observe the fords on the

---

[56] *OR*, ser. 1, vol. 41, pt. 2, p. 539 ("nearly"); pt. 3, pp. 213, 474; pt. 4, pp. 617, 780. *Report of the Secretary of War for 1865*, 38th Cong., 1st sess., H. Ex. Doc. 1, vol. 3, pt. 1, no. 1 (serial 1,249), p. 209.

[57] *OR*, ser. 1, vol. 42, pt. 2, pp. 980–84; Henry P. Walker, *The Wagonmasters: High Plains Freighting from the Earliest Days of the Santa Fe Trail to 1880* (Norman: University of Oklahoma Press, 1966), pp. 121–23, 125.

[58] *OR*, ser. 1, vol. 41, pt. 3, pp. 138–39. NA M594, roll 206, 11th USCI (Old); roll 211, 54th USCI; roll 213, 79th USCI; roll 214, 83d USCI ("heavy fatigue").

Arkansas River for signs of Confederate movement. He also urged Fort Gibson's commanding officer to hurry forward additional escorts.[59]

Meanwhile, Confederates in the Indian Territory were not idle. Despite imperfect communications, General Cooper, commanding the Indian Cavalry Division, had word that Maj. Gen. Sterling Price, with the main body of Confederates in Arkansas, was on his way north to invade Missouri. Cooper resolved to be active in his support. He ordered Brig. Gen. Stand Watie's Cherokee-Creek brigade and Brig. Gen. Richard M. Gano's Texas cavalry brigade to "sweep around" north of the Arkansas River above Fort Gibson to raid a large Union hay camp. While doing so, the brigade might "perhaps run into a train now expected from Fort Scott." On the afternoon of 16 September, Watie's and Gano's men found the hay camp twelve or fifteen miles north of Fort Gibson. The guard consisted of Company K of the 1st Kansas Colored and detachments from three companies of the 2d Kansas Cavalry, 125 men in all. The Confederates, who numbered some two thousand, approached the hay camp cautiously from two directions and opened fire on the federal troops, most of whom took shelter in a creek bed nearby. The Union commanding officer and a few mounted men managed to escape after a running fight with the enemy cavalry. Gano then demanded the surrender of the Union soldiers who remained in the creek bed; when they fired on his flag of truce, he reported, "then commenced the work of death in earnest." Company K of the 1st Kansas Colored lost fifteen men killed. Only nine of the company escaped. The white soldiers and civilian hay cutters were more fortunate; the Confederates captured eighty-five of them while losing only three of their own men wounded.[60]

The prisoners said that they expected the Fort Scott supply train to arrive soon, and Gano and Watie moved north separately the next day to find it. On the morning of 18 September, Gano's men discovered the train at the crossing of Cabin Creek, some sixty miles north of Fort Gibson, and watched it while a courier summoned Watie's command. More than three hundred fifty Unionist Cherokees had joined the train's escort since it left Kansas. Its commander had received a message from Fort Scott that warned him of enemy troops operating nearby and had asked the commanding officer at Fort Gibson to forward any reinforcements he could spare. A reply assured him that six companies were on the way. A quick reconnaissance revealed a Confederate force three miles south of the ford but was unable to tell its strength. The escort's commander ordered the wagons corralled, posted sentries, and settled down for the night.[61]

Watie's brigade joined Gano's about midnight. The two generals decided to risk an attack by the light of the moon, which was only three days past full, and pressed their troops forward. As the Confederate skirmishers engaged the federal pickets and

---

[59]*OR*, ser. 1, vol. 41, pt. 1, p. 769, and pt. 3, pp. 106, 187–88, 238, 248–49.

[60]Ibid., pt. 1, pp. 771–72, 781 ("sweep around," "perhaps run"), 785, 789 ("then commenced"), and pt. 3, pp. 930–31; NA M594, roll 213, 79th USCI. General Gano reported 73 Union dead and 85 prisoners; the Union commander, 40 dead and 66 prisoners. Gano's totals may have included civilian hay cutters. The regiment's Record of Events for September 1864 lists Company K's dead as 36; *ORVF*, 8: 256, gives the same figure. The Kansas Adjutant General's report lists the dead at 22. *Report of the Adjutant General . . . of Kansas*, p. 422. The regimental descriptive book names 1 sergeant, 2 corporals, and 27 privates killed, the figures used in the text. 79th USCI, Regimental Books, RG 94, NA.

[61]*OR*, ser. 1, vol. 41, pt. 1, pp. 767, 770, 773, 786, 789. The commanding officer had difficulty keeping track of his Indian reinforcements, reporting them on 22 September 1864 as numbering 410 and three days later as 360 (pp. 767, 770).

their six cannon joined in, most of the Union teamsters and wagon masters mounted mules and made off toward Fort Scott. This left the wagon train with incomplete teams and made it hard for the defenders to change position. At daybreak, the Confederates brought their cannon within one hundred yards of the Union line. "Soon the confusion became great in his ranks," General Watie reported, "and a general stampede ensued." The federal commander admitted that his men "were compelled to fall back in disorder." They did not stop soon. Two days later, the officer commanding the Union outpost at the Osage Catholic Mission in Kansas, more than eighty miles north of Cabin Creek, reported the fugitives' account of the fight: "The entire train . . . has been captured and all the escort killed, as they took no prisoners." Later in the day, he counted eleven officers of the escort who had made their way to safety accompanied by small numbers of enlisted men. There had been no general massacre, it turned out, but the supply train was firmly in the Confederates' grasp. They shot the wounded mules and used the remaining seven hundred forty to haul away one hundred thirty wagons that were still sufficiently sound to move. The rest they burned.[62]

Meanwhile, the scattered regiments of Colonel Williams' brigade had been hurrying to meet the train. On 14 September, companies of the 11th USCI left the hayfields they had been guarding north of Fort Smith and marched thirty-five miles to Fort Gibson in two days. From there, they set out again on 17 September, heading north on the road to Fort Scott. They made forty miles to the crossing of Pryor's Creek before meeting Williams late in the morning of the second day's march. With Williams was a collection of companies from the 54th USCI and the 1st Kansas Colored Infantry. Some of the men had been stationed near Van Buren, Arkansas, others near Fort Gibson; those who came from Arkansas had marched nearly eighty miles in a little more than two days. When the Confederates appeared early that afternoon, traveling at a great rate—they had covered twenty miles, a good day's journey, since they captured the train that morning— the two sides exchanged shots all afternoon in an inconclusive engagement that both claimed to have won. Williams' men stopped the Confederates' march for a few hours but were too tired to recapture the train. Gano's and Watie's cavalry slipped around them in the night and continued south with the wagons. On 20 September, Williams' brigade turned around and headed back to Fort Gibson.[63]

The second fight at Cabin Creek was the last engagement in which black soldiers faced Confederates in the Indian Territory, and very nearly the end of their service there. Although they continued to escort supply trains during the autumn of 1864 and the early winter of 1865, their presence at Forts Smith and Gibson was about to end. Maj. Gen. Edward R. S. Canby, in charge of Union armies west of the Mississippi River since the disastrous Red River Campaign that spring, was dissatisfied with General Steele's recent attempts to supply the garrison at Fort Smith. Two courses of action occurred to Canby: to relieve Steele as commander of the Department of Arkansas and to abandon the post. He accomplished the first on 25 November, replacing Steele with Maj. Gen. Joseph J. Reynolds, and

---

[62]*OR*, ser. 1, vol. 41, pt. 1, pp. 768 ("were compelled"), 770, 774–75 ("The entire train," p. 774), 787 ("Soon the confusion"), 789–90.
    [63]Ibid., pt. 1, pp. 765, 787, 791, and pt. 3, p. 609; NA M594, roll 206, 11th USCI; roll 211, 54th USCI; roll 213, 79th USCI.

issued orders in mid-December to evacuate Fort Smith. When General Grant, at his headquarters in Virginia, heard of Canby's order to abandon the post, he countermanded it; but by the time the order reached Arkansas, most of the Fort Smith garrison was already on the road. Since a rise in the river made it possible for boats to reach the post, the Union command hurried supplies upriver. A few of the recently departed troops returned to Fort Smith, but the brigade of Colored Troops continued its march to Little Rock.[64]

Regardless of the level of the river, the troops had to be fed. When the Arkansas River was too low for steam navigation, the overland route from Kansas by way of Fort Gibson was still the most reliable way to reach Fort Smith. General Thayer, commanding there, ordered 40 tons of hardtack, 22 tons of flour, 9 tons of sugar, 5 tons of green coffee beans, and other supplies for the garrison. The 54th USCI left Fort Smith on 7 December and marched north to meet the train: "Crossed Ark[ansas] River by ferrying & wading," an officer in Company C wrote. "Very little transportation, no tents, ponchos; blankets very poor. A great many men [were] unfit for the march for the want of large shoes. Marched 30 m[iles] first day. Weather cold." Two weeks later, he recorded: "Quite a number of men with frozen feet. Waded River; quite cold, water deep." Officers in other companies recorded similar complaints. On 20 December, the regiment met the train at Shawnee Creek, Kansas, some thirty-five miles south of Fort Scott, and began the march back.[65]

The wagons rolled into Fort Gibson on 31 December. There, the train and escort rested for five days before setting out again on the last leg of their journey. Bad weather and muddy roads often restricted their rate of travel to no more than three miles a day. "We are out of forage, and the mules are much worn," the commanding officer of the 54th USCI reported after five days on the road, "the Salliseau [Sallisaw Creek] impassable and the rain falling. I will be unable to make much progress unless forage be sent for the animals." The train was scattered along the road for three miles, he told General Thayer; while he could not move forward, he would put the men to work repairing the road so the rest of the wagons could catch up. The regiment and the train it guarded did not reach Fort Smith until 14 January. The seventy-mile trip had taken ten days.[66]

After four days' rest, the 54th USCI, along with the 79th and 83d, made ready to leave Fort Smith and begin the march to Little Rock. Men who were too weak to walk after the previous month's exertions boarded the steamer *Lotus* for the trip downstream. Since General Thayer was still following orders to abandon the town, three other boats, buoyed by a sudden rise in the Arkansas River, carried several hundred Unionist refugees intent on leaving Fort Smith with the federal garrison. The flotilla cast off on 17 January 1865 and steered for Little Rock, the *Lotus* in line behind the *Chippewa* and the *Annie Jacobs*. Col. Thomas M. Bowen of the 13th Kansas Infantry, the ranking Army officer, rode in the *Annie Jacobs*. The boats steamed downstream, keeping considerable distances between themselves so

[64]*OR*, ser. 1, vol. 41, pt. 4, pp. 272, 606, 624, 706, 754, 795, 848–49, 946, 962; vol. 48, pt. 1, pp. 466–67, 473, 497, 515–16.

[65]NA M594, roll 211, 54th USCI.

[66]*OR*, ser. 1, vol. 48, pt. 1, pp. 404, 413; Lt Col C. Fair to Brig Gen J. M. Thayer, 9 Jan 1865, 54th USCI, Regimental Books, RG 94, NA; NA M594, roll 211, 54th USCI.

as not to present a concentrated target for enemies ashore. That afternoon, eighteen miles above Clarksville, watchers on the *Annie Jacobs* spied the *Chippewa* a mile ahead, aground on the south bank. By the time Bowen was close enough to see that enemy fire had set the *Chippewa*'s main deck ablaze and ordered his own pilot to reverse course, the *Annie Jacobs* too was within range of the Confederates and their sole cannon.[67]

Running with the current, the boats had not kept up a full head of steam. While the *Annie Jacobs* struggled to turn upstream and escape, fifteen solid shot struck, several hitting the machinery and two near the waterline. Bowen ordered the boat run ashore. He had no time to signal the *Lotus*, which by this time had floated within range of the Confederates. As a result, its pilot had little choice but to join the *Annie Jacobs* on the north bank. Soldiers, able bodied and invalid, black and white, disembarked from the boats and took up defensive positions while Bowen wrote a dispatch to General Thayer and a warning to the fourth transport not to come any farther. Learning of a nearby wagon train with a hundred-man escort, he requested their aid. The arrival of the train and its escort in the middle of the night must have alarmed the Confederates, for by daybreak they were nowhere to be found.

Bowen's message to Thayer reached Fort Smith late on 18 January. The 54th, 79th, and 83d USCIs struck their tents at midnight and were on the road in an hour and a half. The brigade arrived at the scene of the attack on the afternoon of 20 January. The *Lotus* could still float, but the *Chippewa* was a burned wreck and the *Annie Jacobs* was fast aground. Filling the *Lotus* and the other remaining boat with sick soldiers and the refugees' women and children, Bowen left a guard on the *Annie Jacobs* and moved downriver, the troops on shore searching for any sign of Confederates. The boats reached Little Rock on 24 January; the force on land, not until the last day of the month.[68]

Once assembled at Little Rock, the three thousand men of Colonel Williams' brigade—nearly all of the U.S. Colored Troops in the state and more than one-quarter of the entire Union force—settled down to life in garrison. An officer in the veteran 54th USCI recorded that "Picket, Escort, . . . Guard and Fatigue Duty" occupied most of his company's time and left "no opportunity for drill." For the 112th USCI, "handling freight, hauling Wood for Post quartermaster, digging sinks [latrines], and Policing at General Hospital" constituted the daily round, one officer complained. "These duties, [along] with . . . building quarters and keeping the Camp in order, has kept the men working continually and [they] have had no opportunity for drill[:] consequently all the instruction received three months ago is forgotten." Thus the garrison of Little Rock passed the time during the last few months of the war.[69]

Union post commanders throughout the state continued to worry about Confederate opposition, whether it was a desperate final offensive by an organized military force, tax collection and enforcement of conscription by civilian gov-

---

[67]*OR*, ser. 1, vol. 48, pt. 1, pp. 13–17, 466, 496; NA M594, roll 214, 83d USCI.

[68]*OR*, ser. 1, vol. 48, pt. 1, pp. 14–16; NA M594, roll 213, 79th USCI.

[69]Colonel Williams' brigade accounted for 3,065 officers and men present for duty, or 26.5 percent of the 11,566 Union troops in the department. *OR*, ser. 1, vol. 48, pt. 1, p. 796; NA M594, roll 211, 54th USCI (quotation), and roll 216, 112th USCI (quotation).

ernment officials, or threats to life and property by "bushwhackers and horse thieves" with secessionist leanings. News of the surrender of the Army of Northern Virginia on 9 April reached General Reynolds at Little Rock by telegraph; two days later, the War Department ordered him to publish the terms that Grant had offered Lee and to begin negotiating the Confederate surrender in Arkansas. Both Maj. Gen. James F. Fagan at Camden and Brig. Gen. M. Jeff Thompson in the northeastern part of the state flatly rejected Reynolds' suggestion at first, but Thompson had second thoughts and on 11 May surrendered his 7,454 officers and men to a Union officer from the adjoining Department of the Missouri.[70]

With that, the Confederate collapse came quickly. The fact that Thompson's command included 157 companies that averaged fewer than 50 men each illustrates one problem that had faced Union occupiers in Arkansas. These companies had operated independently for the most part and indeed without deference to any outside authority. Federal officers saw an instance of this when two Confederate companies rode into Pine Bluff to surrender on 14 May and the leader of one group killed the leader of the other "in a personal altercation." Men like these did not fear federal troops as much as they did their own Unionist neighbors, who fought them with stealth and ferocity that matched their own. One Confederate leader told General Reynolds that his men would not agree to lay down their arms "until they have some assurance from the U.S. authorities that those independent companies and squads claiming protection under the Federal Government are immediately disarmed." The Unionists were responsible for "many murderous crimes and outrageous depredations," he complained. It was the middle of June before the business of paroling the last surrendered Confederates in Arkansas got under way.[71]

By that time, Union generals had been planning the occupation of the state for weeks and pondering a move into Texas. But federal troops in Arkansas made no move in that direction. Instead, the 56th USCI stayed at Helena guarding plantations along the Mississippi River. Colonel Williams' brigade remained in Little Rock. The 57th USCI, formerly the 4th Arkansas (AD), garrisoned Lewisburg and Dardanelle, farther west. Companies of a Louisiana regiment, the 84th USCI, steamed up the Ouachita River to occupy Camden, for a navigable stream was still the quickest route in many parts of the South. Along the Arkansas River and elsewhere in the state, white regiments guarded Fort Smith, Pine Bluff, and a few smaller places. After four years of warfare, the state's roads and bridges could not support a large troop movement, the department's chief engineer reported. They had received no repairs "since the rebellion," and the population was in no better shape. "An army cannot get through Arkansas now," the officer commanding at Fort Smith asserted. "There are no supplies in the country; the people who are left are in a starving condition." Instead of

---

[70] *OR*, ser. 1, vol. 48, pt. 1, pp. 103, 235, 237, and pt. 2, pp. 6 ("bushwhackers"), 7, 40, 68–70, 190, 249.

[71] Ibid., pt. 1, p. 237, and pt. 2, pp. 69, 76, 467 ("in a personal"), 495 ("until they," "many murderous"), 893.

moving through Arkansas, Union troops advanced into Texas overland through Louisiana and by sea.[72]

Regiments in Arkansas remained at their posts awaiting muster-out and discharge. Most white soldiers saw home before the end of the year, as did the men of the 60th, 79th, and 83d USCIs, free-state regiments from Iowa and Kansas. Those from Arkansas, Mississippi, and Missouri who had enlisted later in the war—men of the 54th, 56th, 57th, 66th, and 113th USCIs and a few companies of the 2d USCA and 63d USCI—stayed on for twelve months and more to take part in the difficult business of reviving the state's economy and in the painful postwar adjustment of social relations between Arkansans black and white.

---

[72]Ibid., pt. 1, pp. 756–58, 1024–26, and pt. 2, pp. 97 ("since the rebellion"), 107 ("An army"); NA M594, roll 211, 57th USCI.

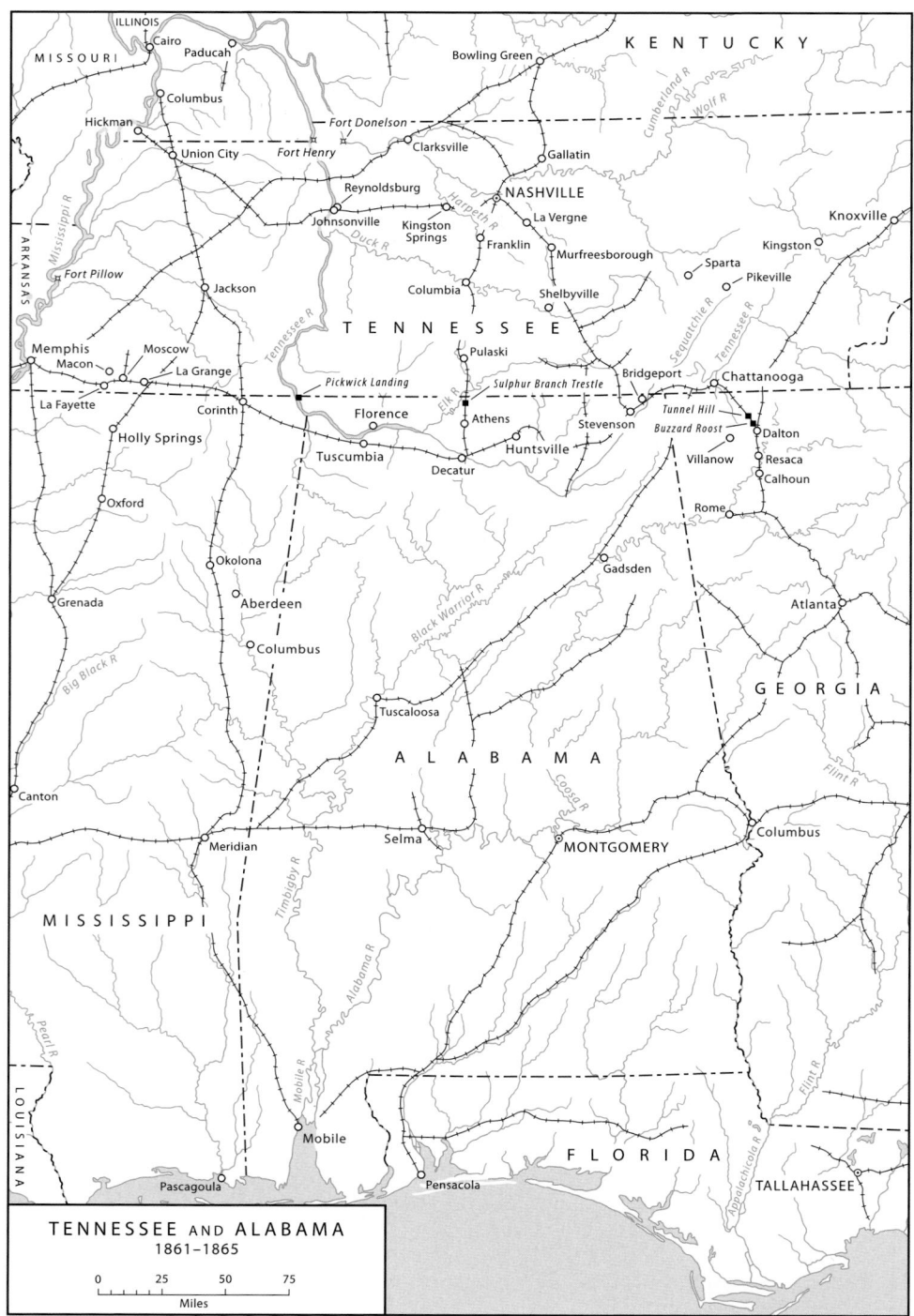

ILLINOIS
MISSOURI
Cairo
Paducah
Columbus
Hickman
Union City
Fort Henry
Fort Donelson
Clarksville
Bowling Green
KENTUCKY
Cumberland R
Wolf R
Reynoldsburg
Gallatin
NASHVILLE
La Vergne
Knoxville
ARKANSAS
Mississippi R
Johnsonville
Kingston Springs
Franklin
Murfreesborough
Kingston
Fort Pillow
Jackson
Harpeth R
Duck R
Columbia
Shelbyville
Sparta
Pikeville
TENNESSEE
Memphis
Macon
Moscow
La Grange
Tennessee R
Pulaski
Bridgeport
Chattanooga
La Fayette
Corinth
Pickwick Landing
Sulphur Branch Trestle
Sequatchie R
Tennessee R
Holly Springs
Florence
Elk R
Athens
Stevenson
Tunnel Hill
Buzzard Roost
Dalton
Tuscumbia
Huntsville
Villanow
Resaca
Oxford
Decatur
Calhoun
Okolona
Rome
Grenada
Aberdeen
Gadsden
Atlanta
Columbus
Black Warrior R
GEORGIA
Tuscaloosa
Flint R
ALABAMA
Canton
Coosa R
Meridian
Selma
MONTGOMERY
Columbus
MISSISSIPPI
Tombigby R
Alabama R
Pearl R
Mobile R
LOUISIANA
Mobile
Pascagoula
Pensacola
FLORIDA
TALLAHASSEE
Appalachicola R
Flint R

TENNESSEE AND ALABAMA
1861–1865

0   25   50   75
Miles

Map 6

CHAPTER 9

MIDDLE TENNESSEE, ALABAMA
AND GEORGIA, 1863–1865

While Union troops along the Mississippi River struggled toward Vicksburg in the spring of 1863, Maj. Gen. William S. Rosecrans' Army of the Cumberland faced a major Confederate force in central Tennessee. Rosecrans' troops had fought their opponents to a standstill near Murfreesborough at the beginning of January and in late June began to push them southeast toward Chattanooga. The federal base of supplies for this advance would be Nashville, on the Cumberland River in the north-central part of the state. The Cumberland was an uncertain and seasonal route for freight, open only from early February to late May, with 40 percent of shipments arriving in March. Neither was the Louisville and Nashville Railroad entirely reliable. Confederate cavalry ranging through Kentucky's Bluegrass Region had attacked the line several times in 1862 and 1863 while the main armies contended in Tennessee, far to the south.[1]

The way out of this dilemma was to open a second railroad to connect Nashville with the Tennessee River, seventy-eight miles to the west. There were no obstacles to navigation on the lower Tennessee, which flowed north through the state from Pickwick Landing near the Alabama line, crossed into Kentucky, and emptied into the Ohio River above Paducah. A partly completed rail line already stretched twenty miles west of Nashville. Begun in 1859 by laying track west from the city and east from Hickman, Kentucky, on the Mississippi River, the Nashville and Northwestern Railroad was only half finished when Tennessee seceded. When the eastern half of the line reached the Tennessee River port of Reynoldsburg, steamboats could unload cargo there for shipment through Nashville to the Union's field armies (*see Map 6*).[2]

Completion of the railroad as far as the Tennessee River would depend largely on the men of two new black regiments raised by the military governor, Andrew Johnson. In April 1863, Secretary of War Edwin M. Stanton issued instructions

---

[1] *The War of the Rebellion: A Compilation of the Official Records of the Union and Confederate Armies*, 70 vols. in 128 (Washington, D.C.: Government Printing Office, 1880–1901), ser. 1, vol. 16, pt. 1, pp. 871–82, 884–87, 892–900, 906–52, 959–89, 1016–18, 1021–1162; vol. 20, p. 980; vol. 23, pt. 1, pp. 50–59, 165–75, 215–21, 381–84, 632–818, 828–43; vol. 52, pt. 1, p. 681 (hereafter cited as *OR*). *Report of the Secretary of War for 1865*, 38th Cong., 1st sess., H. Ex. Doc. 1, vol. 3, pt. 1, no. 1 (serial 1,249), pp. 218, 595; Maury Klein, *History of the Louisville & Nashville Railroad* (New York: Macmillan, 1972), pp. 30–36.

[2] J. Haden Alldredge, "A History of Navigation on the Tennessee River System," 75th Cong., 1st sess., H. Doc. 254 (serial 10,119), pp. 4–7.

Besides being the capital of Tennessee, Nashville was a rail center essential to Union advances farther south.

that made Johnson responsible for "all abandoned slaves or colored persons who have been held in bondage, and whose masters have been, or are now, engaged in rebellion." The governor was to put the able-bodied males to work on public projects. This letter, which Stanton sent just as Adjutant General Lorenzo Thomas was beginning to organize Colored Troops along the Mississippi River, did not mention recruiting black soldiers at all. The reason for this omission is not clear.[3]

Two months earlier, Johnson had visited Washington for policy discussions with both Lincoln and Stanton and probably made clear to them his views about black people and their place in American society. Johnson came from the mountains of eastern Tennessee and had an aversion to black people that was common among white Tennesseans, even those enrolled in Union regiments. Like many whites, North and South, he was more willing to put a shovel than a rifle into a black man's hand. Thus, when Stanton's instructions failed to mention black enlistment, the governor took advantage of the loophole. After receiving letters from Lincoln and Stanton, he began raising one black infantry regiment and later a second, but did not implement the policy of black recruiting with anything like the zeal displayed by Maj. Gen. Nathaniel P. Banks in Louisiana or the adjutant general in the Mississippi Valley. Besides, Johnson clearly understood the importance of the Nashville and Northwestern Railroad. Perhaps because of his insistence on putting his only two black regiments to

---

[3] *OR*, ser. 3, 3: 123 (quotation).

work on the road, progress in laying track far outstripped progress in recruiting black soldiers. While black laborers earned no more than black soldiers, many former slaves in Tennessee and throughout the South still found civilian labor more attractive than submission to military discipline.[4]

On 13 August 1863, the secretary of war dispatched Maj. George L. Stearns to Nashville "to assist in recruiting and organizing colored troops." Stearns was a New England abolitionist, a financial backer of John Brown who had helped to organize the shipment of rifles to Kansas during the 1850s, and a friend of Massachusetts Governor John A. Andrew. When it came time to raise the 54th and 55th Massachusetts in the spring of 1863, Stearns canvassed the states outside New England so effectively that Secretary of War Stanton appointed him a major and assigned him to begin black recruiting in and around Philadelphia. By the end of the war, eleven regiments of U.S. Colored Troops had left Philadelphia for the front, but the second of these was still only half organized in August 1863 when Stearns received further orders from Stanton, this time to report to Nashville.[5]

Before Stearns left Philadelphia, he sent Stanton a long letter in which he asserted "that my [recruiting] agents to be effective must be as heretofore entirely under my control." Stearns intended to operate in Tennessee as he had in Pennsylvania, paying civilian agents with funds raised by a group of New England philanthropists. Arriving in Nashville on 8 September with twenty thousand dollars, he reported at once to General Rosecrans, who ordered him to "take charge of the organization of colored troops in this department." Although Rosecrans' order to "take charge" contradicted both the language and the sense of Stanton's instructions "to assist," Stearns thus gained the full authority that he craved. Only nine days passed before Governor Johnson complained to the secretary of war about the new recruiter's activities. "We need more laborers now than can be obtained . . . to sustain the rear of General Rosecrans' army," Johnson wrote. "Major Stearns proposes to organize and place them in [a military] camp, where they, in fact, remain idle. . . . All the negroes will quit work when they can go into camp and do nothing. We must control them for both purposes." Johnson's concern about controlling the labor of newly freed black people, based on the mistaken idea that they preferred idleness to work, was common among federal authorities in all parts of the South. The state's Unionist government was just establishing itself, the governor continued. "It is exceedingly important for this . . . to be handled in such a

---

[4]Hans L. Trefousse, *Andrew Johnson: A Biography* (New York: W. W. Norton, 1989), pp. 166–68. See, for instance, Col H. R. Mizner to A. Johnson, 3 Sep 1863, in *The Papers of Andrew Johnson*, ed. Leroy P. Graf et al., 16 vols. (Knoxville: University of Tennessee Press, 1967–2000), 6: 343, 353–54, 377, 417 (hereafter cited as *Johnson Papers*). Officers organizing black regiments at Nashville and Gallatin reported violence directed against their recruits by white soldiers from Kentucky and Tennessee. Capt R. D. Mussey to 1st Lt G. Mason, 14 Mar and 4 Apr 1864; to Capt G. B. Halstead, 23 May 1864; to D. K. Carlton, 26 Jun 1864; all in Entry 1141, Dept of the Cumberland, Org of Colored Troops, Letters Sent (LS), pt. 1, Geographical Divs and Depts, Record Group (RG) 393, Rcds of U.S. Army Continental Cmds, National Archives (NA).

[5]*OR*, ser. 3, 3: 676–77 (quotation, p. 676), 682–83.

way as will do the least injury." In other words, Johnson wanted no New England abolitionists recruiting in his state.[6]

Stanton reacted as Johnson had hoped. Telegrams from Washington to the governor and the recruiter arrived in Nashville the next day, reaffirming that Stearns' assignment was "to aid in the organization of colored troops under [Johnson's] directions and the directions of General Rosecrans." If Stearns could not conform to these instructions, Stanton added, he "had better leave Nashville and proceed to Cairo to await orders." This would remove him entirely from the Department of the Cumberland. Stearns seemed to take the admonition in good part. On 24 September, he reported that recruiting had begun "with good success." Only twelve days passed, though, before Johnson complained that Stearns' recruiters had raided "the rendezvous of colored laborers and [taken] away some three hundred hands" who had come to work expecting to lay track on the Nashville and Northwestern. The conflict between Stearns and Johnson eventually required an order from Stanton that settled matters in the governor's favor. Stearns left Nashville that fall, replaced by his assistant, Capt. Reuben D. Mussey. Once again the federal government established rival and conflicting authorities to organize Colored Troops, as it had done elsewhere in the occupied South, forcing recruiters to compete with the Army's staff departments—engineers, quartermasters, and commissaries of subsistence—for the services of black workers.[7]

Stearns himself had been opposed to the press-gang approach in recruiting black soldiers. Impressment caused the unwilling to "run to the woods," he told Stanton, "imparting their fears to the Slaves thus keeping them out of our lines, and we get only those who are too ignorant or indolent to take care of themselves." Nevertheless, impressment was common in the Department of the Cumberland, as it was elsewhere in the occupied South. In October, Stearns' agent at Gallatin reported that "every Negro who comes in from the Country is brought by the picket parties . . . to this office"—in other words, outpost guards brought men to the recruiter at gunpoint. In February 1864, a "conscripting party" seized "nearly all the negro force" working on the Tennessee and Alabama Railroad near Columbia. That fall, Captain Mussey's annual report stated that in the search for black recruits "none were pressed," but the unpublished correspondence of his own office told a different story.[8]

Evidence of further confusion in federal recruiting efforts was the numbering system used for the new organizations. Authorities in Nashville called the first two the 1st and 2d U.S. Colored Infantry regiments. Their men came from the Depart-

---

[6]Ibid., pp. 683 ("that my"), 786 ("take charge"), 820 ("We need"); Maj G. L. Stearns to Capt C. W. Foster, 5 Aug 1863 (S–94–CT–1863), and to E. M. Stanton, 17 Aug 1863 (S–114–CT–1863), both filed with (f/w) S–18–CT–1863, Entry 360, Colored Troops Div, Letters Received (LR), RG 94, Rcds of the Adjutant General's Office, NA.

[7]*OR*, ser. 3, 3: 823 ("had better"), 876; Maj G. L. Stearns to Maj C. W. Foster, 24 Sep 1863 ("with good") (S–176–CT–1863, f/w S–18–CT–1863), Entry 360, RG 94, NA; A. Johnson to Maj G. L. Stearns, 6 Oct 1863 ("the rendezvous"), Entry 1149, Rcds of Capt R. D. Mussey, pt. 1, RG 393, NA; Dudley T. Cornish, *The Sable Arm: Negro Troops in the Union Army, 1861–1865* (New York: Longmans, Green, 1956), pp. 326–28; Peter Maslowski, *Treason Must Be Made Odious: Military Occupation and Wartime Reconstruction in Nashville, Tennessee, 1862–65* (Millwood, N.Y.: KTO Press, 1978), pp. 102–07.

[8]*OR*, ser. 3, 4: 476 ("none were"); Maj G. L. Stearns to E. M. Stanton, 17 Aug 1863 ("run to") (S–114–CT–1863, f/w S–18–CT–1863), Entry 360, RG 94, NA; J. N. Holmes to Maj G. L. Stearns,

ment of the Cumberland, east of the Tennessee River. West of the river lay Maj. Gen. Ulysses S. Grant's Department of the Tennessee, which also included most of the state of Mississippi and adjoining parts of Arkansas and Louisiana. The plantation country of West Tennessee was home to more than 36 percent of the state's black residents; recruiting there was the responsibility of Adjutant General Thomas. The two black infantry regiments organized at La Grange were called the 1st and 2d Tennessee (African Descent [AD]). While the ranks of all these regiments filled, between June and November 1863, recruiters in and around Washington, D.C., were raising two other regiments known as the 1st and 2d United States Colored Infantries (USCIs). Not until October did a monthly return from the Department of the Cumberland reach the Adjutant General's Office in Washington and alert administrators to the problem. The two eastern infantry regiments kept their designations; and since nine others raised in Arkansas, Maryland, Ohio, Pennsylvania, and Virginia had already received consecutive numbers, the two regiments from the Department of the Cumberland became the 12th and 13th USCIs.[9]

The 12th filled the last of its ten companies in August 1863. By the end of September, more than three hundred of its officers and men were guarding Elk River Bridge, halfway between Nashville and Chattanooga on the rail line that supplied Union troops in southeastern Tennessee. The Army of the Cumberland, after a stunning defeat at Chickamauga Creek in Georgia in mid-September, retreated to its base at Chattanooga, where victorious Confederates occupied the heights around the city. As the XI and XII Corps arrived in Tennessee from the Army of the Potomac to help relieve the besieged garrison, the 12th USCI left Elk River and moved north. Toward the end of October, the regiment took station near the Nashville and Northwestern end-of-track about thirty miles west of the state capital. The few companies of the 13th USCI that had enough men to be mustered into service were already there. Their first tasks had been to entrench their position, to provide guards for railroad surveyors operating miles in advance of construction gangs, and to send foraging parties through the surrounding country to secure feed for the horses and mules. The 13th had no men to spare, Lt. Col. Theodore Trauernicht complained, either for its planned labor on the railroad or to protect nearby Unionist civilians, who were "kept continually in a state of terror by small bands of guerrillas and horse-thieves." The regiment needed more recruits. "Give me a full regiment," he wrote, "and we can do much good . . . ; as we are, I fear we can only be an expense to the Government."[10]

Four days later, Trauernicht was in a better mood. "The command is doing well," he reported, "indeed under the circumstances much better than I expected." The work of fortifying the camp was done, and the troops felt "comparatively safe now. We

12 Oct 1863 ("every Negro"), and J. M. Nash to A. Anderson, 23 Feb 1864 ("conscripting"), both in Entry 1149, pt. 1, RG 393, NA; Maslowski, *Treason Must Be Made Odious*, pp. 100–101.

[9]Maj C. W. Foster to Maj G. L. Stearns, 17 Oct 1863 (S–335–CT–1863, f/w S–18–CT–1863), Entry 360, RG 94, NA. The 1st and 2d Tennessee (African Descent) became the 59th and 61st United States Colored Infantries (USCIs) in March 1864. The future 14th, 15th, and 16th USCIs began their existence as Major Stearns' 3d, 4th, and 5th regiments. Maj T. J. Morgan to Maj G. L. Stearns, 30 Oct 1863, and Lt Col M. L. Courtney to Maj G. L. Stearns, 16 Nov 1863, both in Entry 1149, pt. 1, RG 393, NA; U.S. Census Bureau, *Population of the United States in 1860* (Washington, D.C.: Government Printing Office, 1864), pp. 466–67.

[10]*OR*, ser. 1, vol. 30, pt. 1, p. 170, and pt. 4, pp. 482 ("kept continually"), 483 ("Give me").

Railroad bridge over Elk River, between Nashville and Chattanooga, where the 12th U.S. Colored Infantry stood guard in September 1863

have alarms every night and the greatest vigilance is necessary on our part of prevent our men being picked off by rebels who prowl around our lines after dark and seem to have a great animosity towards the colored soldier." Despite the lack of opportunity for drill and instruction, the men seemed to be adapting to military life and "do their duty *well*."[11]

By late November, the 13th USCI had moved its camp to Section 49, "the most advanced post" on the Nashville and Northwestern, Col. John A. Hottenstein reported. The end-of-track stood nineteen miles west of where it had been on 19 October. Construction gangs had managed to lay only half a mile of track a day for thirty-eight days, even though the 13th USCI finally had enough men to help in the work. On 27 November, Hottenstein asked for the last one hundred recruits needed to fill the regiment, explaining, "I have to work the men very hard. . . . It is impossible to recruit here and the country is full of the enemy." Local whites were likely to kill any potential recruits who tried to reach the regiment's camp on their own. Despite the colonel's complaints, the regimental adjutant was optimistic, even cheerful, nine days later when he reported, "Everything 'goes bravely on' [one half of the regiment] is detailed to work on R.R. for the ensuing week, the other does guard, foraging and other duties. No enemy of any consequence in the vicinity."[12]

Harassment from Confederates was not the only impediment that track crews faced. Early in January 1864, Col. Charles R. Thompson of the 12th USCI reported that about one hundred of his men lacked shoes. "If there is any prospect of our get-

[11]Lt Col T. Trauernicht to Capt R. D. Mussey, 23 Oct 1863 (misfiled with 2d USCI), Entry 57C, Regimental Papers, RG 94, NA.

[12]Col J. A. Hottenstein to Maj G. L. Stearns, 27 Nov 1863 ("the most"), Entry 1149, pt. 1, RG 393, NA; 1st Lt J. D. Reilly to Capt R. D. Mussey, 6 Dec 1863 ("Everything"), 13th USCI, Entry 57C, RG 94, NA.

ting a supply of shoes we can help on the work here materially," he told Brig. Gen. Alvan C. Gillem, who commanded all troops on the Nashville and Northwestern Railroad. Thompson had to threaten to relieve his regimental quartermaster, but the men got their shoes. By the end of January, thirty-four miles of track had been laid, and by late March, the chief quartermaster in Nashville was ordering construction of storehouses and a levee at Reynoldsburg, at the other end of the line. The Nashville and Northwestern track was completed to the Tennessee River well before shallow water barred steamboats from the Cumberland.[13]

Although the ranks of both regiments finally filled, recruiting of Colored Troops in the Department of the Cumberland lagged. In October 1863, one of Stearns' civilian agents wrote from Clarksville, about forty-five miles northwest of Nashville, that previous commanders of the Union garrison had always turned away escaped slaves who sought refuge there. Since the new colonel approved of attempts to recruit black soldiers, the agent said, "There is now here about one hundred thirty [who] are anxious to enlist. . . . I think they will come in now fast." At Gallatin, the same distance northeast of Nashville, 203 recruits were waiting for tents and overcoats. Besides shelter and clothing, the agent there requested blank forms for certificates of enlistment that the former slaves could leave with their wives. The documents would entitle soldiers' families to federal protection "if their masters abuse them." A third agent wrote from a federal garrison twenty-five miles south of Murfreesborough that "no men can be got outside [the Union lines] without a military escort for protection." The parlous state of the post's defenses had not stopped him from signing up "as many as . . . possible" of the twenty or thirty black civilians laboring on the earthworks.[14]

The Union Army would need all the labor it could hire to sustain the coming year's advance into the heart of the Confederacy. In the fall of 1863, federal divisions from places as distant as Maryland and Mississippi had converged on Chattanooga by rail to raise the siege and turn the Confederates back into northern Georgia. Rosecrans was gone as commander of the Department of the Cumberland and its field army; in his place was Maj. Gen. George H. Thomas, a Unionist Virginian who had grown up in a slave-holding family. Grant, who had organized the relief of Chattanooga, went east in March 1864 to assume command of all the Union armies. His successor in the region between the Appalachians and the Mississippi, Maj. Gen. William T. Sherman, commanded the Military Division of the Mississippi, which included the Armies of the Cumberland, the Ohio, and the Tennessee. Each army represented a geographical department of the same name; taken together, their troop strengths amounted to more than 296,000 men present. Nearly two-thirds of those served in garrisons or in guard outposts along the region's railroads. "If I can put in motion 100,000 [men] it will make as large an army as we can possibly supply," Sherman told Grant. Sherman's staff calculated that the spring campaign against Atlanta would require one hundred thirty carloads of freight a day to keep the armies

---

[13] *OR*, ser. 1, vol. 32, pt. 2, p. 269, and pt. 3, p. 155; *Johnson Papers*, 6: 701; Col C. R. Thompson to Brig Gen A. C. Gillem, 8 Jan 1864 (quotation), 12th USCI, Regimental Books, RG 94, NA.

[14] C. B. Morse to Maj G. L. Stearns, 22 Oct 1863 ("There is"); J. H. Holmes to Maj G. L. Stearns, 8 Oct 1863 ("if their"); W. F. Wheeler to Maj G. L. Stearns, 4 Oct 1863 ("no men"); all in Entry 1149, pt. 1, RG 393, NA.

in the field. One thousand freight cars and one hundred locomotives would be necessary to handle this volume of traffic.[15]

The need for railroad track layers, for teamsters to haul goods beyond the rail line, and for full crews to maintain roads over which the teamsters' wagons rolled was apparent to Union generals west of the Appalachians. Late in November 1863, as Grant prepared to drive the Confederates from the heights around Chattanooga, he took time to order Brig. Gen. Grenville M. Dodge to "impress negroes for all the work you want from them" to repair the railroad near Pulaski, Tennessee. Early the next month, Dodge reported that he had enough men to repair bridges and right of way, but that he faced stiff competition from recruiters. "The . . . officers of colored troops claim the right to open recruiting offices along my line; if this is done I lose my negroes. . . . So far I have refused to allow them to recruit. They have now received positive orders . . . to come here and recruit. I don't want any trouble with them, and have assured them that when we were through with the negroes I would see that they go into the service. . . . Please advise me." Grant at once told Dodge to arrest any recruiters who interfered with his track crews. Generals in the field thought that preparation for the coming year's operations was more important than the War Department's policy of putting black men in uniform. An advance into mountainous northern Georgia, where the Confederate General Braxton Bragg's Army of Tennessee had retreated after its defeat at Chattanooga, would take Union troops beyond navigable rivers and force them to rely more than ever on wheeled transportation.[16]

Confederate leaders knew this well. All through the fall of 1863, while Grant and Sherman moved to relieve the beleaguered Union garrison at Chattanooga, Bragg and General Joseph E. Johnston, who between them had charge of all Confederate troops between the Appalachians and the Mississippi, urged their cavalry commanders to strike "the advancing columns of the enemy, . . . breaking his communications, and if possible throwing a force north of the Tennessee to strike at the enemy's rear." The result was a series of raids on the Memphis and Charleston Railroad, one of the Confederacy's longest.[17]

The track operated by the Memphis and Charleston ran east from Memphis through the southern tier of Tennessee counties and dipped down to Corinth, Mississippi. It crossed the Tennessee River at Decatur, Alabama, met the track of the Tennessee and Alabama just beyond the river, and ran on through Huntsville to end at Stevenson. From there, the Nashville and Chattanooga and a series of shorter lines offered connections eastward to Atlanta, Savannah, and Charleston. In late October, Confederate Maj. Gen. Stephen D. Lee's cavalry struck the Memphis and Charleston at Tuscumbia, forty miles west of Decatur, and several other points along the line in northern Alabama. A week later, Brig. Gen. James R. Chalmers' command, two

---

[15]*OR*, ser. 1, vol. 32, pt. 3, pp. 469 (quotation), 550, 561, 569; Christopher J. Einolf, *George Thomas: Virginian for the Union* (Norman: University of Oklahoma Press, 2001), pp. 13, 15, 18–21, 74; William T. Sherman, *Memoirs of General William T. Sherman*, 2 vols. (New York: D. Appleton, 1875), 2: 9–12.

[16]*OR*, ser. 1, vol. 31, pt. 3, pp. 220 ("Impress negroes"), 367 ("The . . . officers"). The Tennessee and Alabama was also known as the Central Alabama and the Nashville and Decatur.

[17]*OR*, ser. 1, vol. 30, pt. 4, p. 763 (quotation); vol. 31, pt. 3, pp. 594, 610. Peter Cozzens, *The Shipwreck of Their Hopes: The Battles for Chattanooga* (Urbana: University of Illinois Press, 1994), pp. 34–35.

small brigades amounting to some seventeen hundred men, attacked three stations within forty miles of Memphis. Neither raid did any lasting damage.[18]

In mid-November, Confederate mounted troops throughout the region readied themselves for another assault on the Union lines of communications. By the time preparations were complete, Grant's armies had broken the siege of Chattanooga and driven Bragg's troops into northern Georgia. Swollen rivers impeded the progress of the Confederate cavalry, but the expedition was under way by the end of the month. General Chalmers led three small brigades out of Oxford, Mississippi, and on 4 December reached Moscow, Tennessee, on the Memphis and Charleston. Chalmers told Col. Lawrence S. Ross and his Texans to burn the railroad bridge that spanned the Wolf River.[19]

The bridge guard at Moscow was the 2d Tennessee (AD), camped west of town near where the railroad and a wagon road crossed the river. The regiment had mustered in its last four companies as recently as late August, after an expedition returned with two hundred ten recruits, but it had not been idle since. A bridge guard did not lead a passive existence. It was responsible for detecting and suppressing enemy activity, intercepting Confederate mail service, and capturing furloughed soldiers during their visits home. Company G's Record of Events, entered on the bimonthly muster roll, described one capture tersely:

> November 25 1863 Capt [Henry] Sturgis with 40 men from the company marched to Macon Tenn, starting from camp at 6 o'clock P.M. Captured Lt [Joseph L.] Newborn, 13" Tenn Infty (Rebel) one Colts Navy Revolver, one Mule saddle & equipments. Returned to camp at 4 o'clock A.M. November 26. Slight skirmishing while returning. No loss. Distance marched twenty miles.[20]

Just a week after Company G's night march, a few Confederate cavalry appeared in midafternoon, "dashing up on the gallop even to the bridge, and firing on the pickets stationed there," Col. Frank A. Kendrick reported. A local Unionist had told Kendrick four days earlier that mounted Confederates were on the move. Since then, the men of the regiment had been especially wary, removing the planks of the wagon bridge and replacing them only when the guard allowed traffic to approach. Unable to cross the dismantled bridge, the Confederates rode off.[21]

The next day, 4 December, heavy smoke appeared on the western horizon not long after noon. Kendrick conferred with officers of the 6th Illinois Cavalry, who arrived about that time in advance of a column moving to intercept the Confederate force. They decided that the enemy must have avoided Moscow and gone on toward La Fayette, some eight miles to the west. When the

---

[18]*OR*, ser. 1, vol. 31, pt. 1, pp. 25–31, 242–54, and pt. 3, pp. 746–47; Robert C. Black III, *The Railroads of the Confederacy* (Chapel Hill: University of North Carolina Press, 1998 [1952]), pp. 5–6.

[19]*OR*, ser. 1, vol. 31, pt. 1, pp. 589–90, and pt. 3, pp. 704–05, 865.

[20]Ibid., pt. 3, p. 190; Maj E. R. Wiley Jr. to "Captain," 24 Aug 1863, 61st USCI, Entry 57C, RG 94, NA; NA Microfilm Pub M594, Compiled Rcds Showing Svc of Mil Units in Volunteer Union Organizations, roll 212, 61st USCI (quotation).

[21]*OR*, ser. 1, vol. 31, pt. 1, p. 583 ("dashing up"), and pt. 3, p. 276.

planks on the wagon bridge were laid in place, the 6th Illinois Cavalry moved on in pursuit, followed closely by another cavalry regiment and the column's artillery. Soon afterward, the men of the 2d Tennessee (AD) heard firing and the 6th Illinois Cavalry reappeared "in much disorder," as Kendrick described the scene. "The bridge soon became obstructed with artillery, caissons, and wagons from the train which had got over, and great numbers of the retreating cavalry plunged headlong into the river, which, though narrow, is deep and rapid, and many men and horses were thus lost."[22]

The officer commanding the 7th Illinois Cavalry, the third regiment in the column, agreed with Kendrick:

> When we got to the bridge it was so clogged with horses, ambulances, wagons, and artillery that it was almost impossible to get a man across it. Several of the horses had broken through the bridge and were [stuck] fast, and the bridge was so torn up that it was impossible to clear it. I ordered my men across, and succeeded by jumping our horses, crawling under wagons and ambulances, &c., in getting about 50 men across. . . . Several were knocked off the bridge into the river. I found it impossible to get any more men across without their swimming, which so injured their ammunition as to nearly render it useless.

By this time, Kendrick had reinforced the guard on the wagon bridge and stationed two companies at the railroad bridge, some three hundred yards away. The balance of the regiment, with a few cannon, occupied an earthwork that commanded both bridges. Confederate cavalry appeared, first at the wagon bridge and soon afterward at the railroad bridge. The 2d Tennessee (AD) defended both, while the 7th Illinois Cavalry struggled to rescue the artillery that had crossed the wagon bridge. After an hour of fighting, sometimes hand to hand, the cavalrymen managed to retrieve the cannon, and the entire Union force was once more on the east side of the river. All the while, men of the 2d Tennessee (AD) who had been detailed to serve the cannon directed fire from their fort at the attacks on both bridges. As cavalry on both sides usually did, the Confederates had left their horses in the care of every fourth trooper while the remaining three men advanced to fight on foot. After several artillery rounds landed among the horses, the Confederate force withdrew.[23]

Such raids by organized bodies of Confederates rarely troubled construction crews along the Nashville and Northwestern track, which lay more than one hundred miles northeast of the Memphis and Charleston, but sporadic attacks by enemy irregulars required vigilance. "We have alarms every night," Colonel Trauernicht reported from a camp of the 13th USCI. During one of several attacks in November, a shot fired by "guerrillas" wounded Sgt. Joshua Hancock of the 12th USCI while he commanded an outpost on the railroad thirty-eight miles west of Nashville. Both regiments spent that fall and winter guarding the railroad and sometimes furnishing crews to lay track while other

---

[22]Ibid., pt. 1, p. 584.
[23]Ibid., p. 586.

black regiments in the Department of the Cumberland continued to struggle to fill their ranks.[24]

Since the Emancipation Proclamation exempted Tennessee from its provisions, the effort to enlist black soldiers there was a more complicated matter than it was farther south. Recruiting parties went out with instructions to "impress all able bodied negroes under 35 years of age," but local slaveholders proclaimed their personal loyalty to the Union in hopes of saving their human property. "I am likely to get myself into *hot water* in this business of impressment," Lt. Col. Charles H. Pickering of the 17th USCI admitted. White troops at La Vergne, between Nashville and Murfreesborough, had recently arrested an entire company from Pickering's regiment and released six black recruits "gathered up" in the neighborhood, as well as a white man the company commander had arrested "for having, with violence, opposed the detachment sent to take his slaves." The company commander had left Pickering's written instructions in camp and could show no authority for seizing the slaves, so the white troops returned them to their master. Union officers elsewhere in the Department of the Cumberland also interfered with attempts to gather black recruits by force.[25]

Impressment was not a selective way to get men. At Gallatin, Col. Thomas J. Morgan found that "not one" of the recruits for the 14th USCI had undergone medical examination. "In view of the informal and unsatisfactory manner in which the entire work has been performed," he wrote, "I propose to commence at the beginning, subject every man to a rigid examination, and take none who are fit only for the filling of hospitals." Captain Mussey, in charge of black recruiting in the Department of the Cumberland since Major Stearns' falling out with Governor Johnson, planned to use the 42d and 101st USCIs as "invalid or laboring regiments, composed of men unfit for field duty but fit for ordinary garrison duty," similar to the 63d and 64th USCIs on the lower Mississippi. As mortality rates throughout the U.S. Colored Troops attested, not all commanders were so scrupulous. Unfit men appeared in the ranks of all regiments, black and white, throughout the war.[26]

The U.S. Sanitary Commission, an investigative and advisory body composed mostly of physicians, had surveyed two hundred of the new volunteer regiments in the fall of 1861. Only eighty-four (42 percent) had offered recruits what commissioners called "a thorough inspection" at the time of enlistment, and only eighteen of those had backed up the initial examination with another at the time of mustering in. (Normal peacetime procedure subjected recruits to

---

[24]Trauernicht to Mussey, 23 Oct 1863 ("We have"); Lt Col E. C. Brott to Col A. A. Smith, 8 Jan 1864, 15th USCI; Lt Col M. L. Courtney to Capt R. D. Mussey, 24 Dec 1863 and 16 Jan 1864, 16th USCI; Col W. R. Shafter to Capt R. D. Mussey, 28 Dec 1863, 17th USCI; all in Entry 57C, RG 94, NA. NA M594, roll 207, 12th USCI ("Guerrillas").

[25]Ira Berlin et al., eds. *The Black Military Experience* (New York: Cambridge University Press, 1982), pp. 122–26. Col W. B. Gaw to Capt W. Brunt, 9 Feb 1864 ("impress all"), 16th USCI; Lt Col C. H. Pickering to Capt R. D. Mussey, 13 Feb 1864 ("I am likely"), 17th USCI; Col W. B. Gaw to Capt R. D. Mussey, 17 Feb 1864, 16th USCI; all in Entry 57C, RG 94, NA. Col T. J. Downey to Capt R. D. Mussey, 24 Feb 1864, Entry 1149, pt. 1, RG 393, NA.

[26]*OR*, ser. 3, 4: 765 ("invalid"); Col T. J. Morgan to Maj G. L. Stearns, 2 Nov 1863 ("not one"), misfiled with 3d USCI, Entry 57C, RG 94, NA. For the 63d and 64th USCIs, see Chapter 6, above.

examination at the place of enlistment, usually by a civilian doctor on contract, and a second examination by the regimental surgeon before assignment to a company.) The Sanitary Commission learned that the Army of the Potomac alone had discharged more than eight hundred fifty men within a few weeks' time "on account of disabilities that existed at and before their enlistment, and which any intelligent surgeon ought to have discovered on their inspection as recruits."[27]

Although examiners in 1863 rejected nearly one-third of drafted men, black and white, and more than one-quarter the next year, pressure to enlist black Southerners to help fill Northern states' draft quotas continued to ensure a high number of unfit recruits in the U.S. Colored Troops. As late as January 1865, the 17th USCI transferred twenty-five men to the 101st for a variety of causes, including both youth and old age, as well as cases of rheumatism, hernia, back injury, "heart disease," and hemorrhoids. In May, the same regiment sent thirty men to the 42d USCI, more than half of them complaining of rheumatism.[28]

However perfunctory the physical examinations were, it was important to organize the men and muster in the companies so that the quartermaster could provide clothing and shelter in the middle of winter. "In their present condition they cannot live decently," Lt. Col. Michael L. Courtney of the 16th USCI reported from Clarksville, "nor are they learning to drill as they would if they were provided with their arms, and at the present time, three companies have to do all the guard duty." Drill was important to officers because they wanted to lead troops in the field rather than spend time supervising quartermaster's details digging ditches or shifting freight. Colonel Morgan spoke for most officers when he announced his intention "to put this Reg[imen]t . . . upon a *War footing*." His success at that became evident four months later when the department commander, who had earlier expressed doubts about black men's aptitude for military service, appeared to be "exceedingly pleased with the 14th," as an officer in Nashville reported, "and [said] he [wished] he had a Brigade of U.S.C.T." Nor was Morgan's the only new black regiment to receive compliments about its appearance and discipline. When the 15th USCI marched from Columbia to Shelbyville that December, civilians along the forty-mile route commented on the troops' avoidance of straggling and looting.[29]

Despite all the difficulties of raising fresh regiments—examining the recruits, then clothing, housing, feeding, arming, and drilling them—the ranks of the new black organizations filled during the winter. By spring 1864, the

---

[27]U.S. Sanitary Commission, *A Report to the Secretary of War of the Operations of the Sanitary Commission, and upon the Sanitary Condition of the Volunteer Army . . .* (Washington, D.C.: McGill & Witherow, 1861), pp. 12, 14 ("a thorough"), 15 ("on account").

[28]Leonard L. Lerwill, *The Personnel Replacement System in the United States Army* (Washington, D.C.: Department of the Army, 1954), pp. 47–49; *Report of the Secretary of War, 1863,* 38th Cong., 1st sess., H. Ex. Doc. 1 (serial 1,184), p. 123; *Report of the Secretary of War, 1864,* 38th Cong., 2d sess., H. Ex. Doc 83 (serial 1,230), p. 64; Special Order 4, 12 Jan 1865 ("heart disease"), and Special Order 30, 4 May 1865, both in 17th USCI, Entry 57C, RG 94, NA. Berlin et al., *Black Military Experience*, pp. 76–78, outlines the shortcomings of the Union program of filling Northern states' draft quotas with Southern recruits.

[29]Courtney to Mussey, 16 Jan 1864 ("In their"). Capt R. D. Mussey to Col W. B. Gaw, 29 Feb 1864 ("exceedingly pleased"), 16th USCI; Col T. J. Morgan to Capt R. D. Mussey, 6 Dec 1863, 14th USCI; Col T. J. Downey to Capt R. D. Mussey, 23 Dec 1863 and 8 Feb 1864, 15th USCI; all in Entry 57C, RG 94, NA.

Black recruits in Tennessee. All in this picture have shoes and seem to be better clad than many who joined the Union Army.

regiments had arrived at the stations where they would spend most of the year. The 12th and 13th USCIs continued to guard the line of the Nashville and Northwestern. The 14th and 16th went to Chattanooga. The 15th remained at Nashville and the 17th at Murfreesborough. During the spring and summer, other regiments would join them: the 40th and 101st from Tennessee and the 100th from Kentucky at posts along the Louisville and Nashville Railroad; the 42d and 44th at Chattanooga; the 1st U.S. Colored Artillery at Knoxville; and the 2d and 3d Alabama (AD), renumbered the 110th and 111th USCIs in June, at Pulaski, Tennessee, and Athens, Alabama. Besides searching constantly for new recruits to fill their own ranks, these regiments guarded major rail lines that supplied Sherman's campaign in northern Georgia.[30]

The men of these regiments served sometimes as laborers. The chief quartermaster of the department, Col. James L. Donaldson, explained his predicament that fall, after Atlanta had fallen and the crisis had passed. Early in 1864, his workforce had expanded from six or eight thousand employees to more than fifteen thousand (4,510 of them working on the railroads), yet he still lacked workmen. The press of business had forced him to ask for the

---

[30] *OR*, ser. 1, vol. 32, pt. 3, p. 48; Frederick H. Dyer, *A Compendium of the War of the Rebellion* (New York: Thomas Yoseloff, 1959 [1908]), pp. 997, 1721, 1726, 1730–31, 1737–39.

detail of Colored Troops to supplement civilian laborers. "I did not want to do this," he explained later to the recently promoted Col. Reuben D. Mussey, "for I believe in Colored Troops and think they should take the Field and fight the same as White ones, but I knew there were Colored Regts. in the Dept. not yet fit for the Field and that, for obvious reasons, they had more work in them than I could get out of any other troops."[31]

When enough supplies had been unloaded from boats and trains at Nashville to ensure a steady flow to Sherman's campaign, Donaldson excused the men of the 15th and 17th regiments from stevedore tasks and assigned them to the more military duty of guarding rail lines and quartermaster depots. The 15th USCI stretched out along the Edgefield and Kentucky Railroad, guarding bridges and trestles from the north bank of the Cumberland River opposite Nashville forty miles northwest to the state line; the 17th concentrated at Nashville, with companies stationed up and down the river at sawmills and wood yards, and sometimes provided armed guards for riverboats. Donaldson praised both regiments and told Mussey that he looked forward to the day when they could take part in active military operations.[32]

In the southeastern corner of the state, Colonel Morgan of the 14th USCI arrived at Chattanooga with three thousand blank enlistment forms in February 1864. That part of Tennessee was untapped territory for Union recruiters, who hoped to raise two more regiments of Colored Troops there. By the middle of the next month, Morgan's regiment was on the march, scouring the country for recruits along a 150-mile route that took them up the Sequatchie River and over the Cumberland Mountains to Sparta before turning east to Kingston on the Tennessee River. "The men manifested the most commendable endurance, cheerfulness, and courage," Capt. James H. Meteer noted on his company muster roll at the end of the month, "often marching 20 miles per day over these m[oun]t[ain]s, carrying knapsacks and several days rations."[33]

The trip was an eye-opener for Meteer, who had referred to his new regiment as the "14th 'Unwashed Americans'" when he joined it in January. "We fully expected to meet reb Col Hughes of Bushwhacking notoriety, for he had been severely punishing [the 5th] Ten[nessee] Cavalry for some time and [his] robbing crew of hangers on had been committing some of the most fiendish deeds ever recorded" on Unionist civilians. John M. Hughs was more than a bushwhacker. Colonel of the Confederate 25th Tennessee Infantry, he operated in the middle part of the state, apart from his regiment. Authorized to round up deserters and to enforce conscription, he also led a band of about one hundred guerrillas. During the winter, Hughs and his men had clashed several times with the Union 5th Tennessee Cavalry, but they left the 14th

---

[31] *OR*, ser. 1, vol. 52, pt. 1, p. 684; Col J. L. Donaldson to Col R. D. Mussey, 9 Oct 1864 (f/w M–750–CT–1864), Entry 360, RG 94, NA.

[32] Donaldson to Mussey, 9 Oct 1864; NA M594, roll 207, 15th and 17th USCIs.

[33] Col T. J. Morgan to Capt R. D. Mussey, 3 Feb 1864, Entry 1149, pt. 1, RG 393, NA; NA M594, roll 207, 14th USCI. The entry in Company K's Record of Events is anonymous, but the wording is almost identical to that in a private letter Meteer wrote after the expedition. J. H. Meteer to C. Mills, 18 Apr 1864, Caleb Mills Papers, Indiana Historical Society, Indianapolis.

Part of the country in east-central Tennessee through which Capt. James H. Meteer and the 14th U.S. Colored Infantry marched in the early spring of 1864, seeking recruits

USCI alone on its march, sending only two or three shots into the regiment's camps throughout the entire expedition.[34]

Captain Meteer thrived on the rigors of mountain campaigning, but his first sight of slavery in practice shocked him. "Among the 120 recruits we brought back," he wrote,

> There are not 20 genuine Africans and as many as 10 of them could have enlisted in a *white regt* without . . . being discovered. At Pikeville a wealthy man who glories in the title of *Colonel Bridgeman* came and offered his darky [for enlistment] and claimed his 300 dollars [bounty due to a slaveholder who allowed a slave to enlist]. Before the termination of his interview . . . a black woman came and declared that the 'boy' was her son and *Col Bridgeman was his father*—that he had slept with her about two years, and after the birth of the boy she was exchanged for a more enticing bed-fellow. Want had driven [Bridgeman] to come and offer the fruit of his illegitimate dalliance with his *chattel* for sale. . . . *[T]here is no crime . . . too hellish for an upholder of African slavery to do.*

Traffic in human beings shocked the young man who had only recently called his black soldiers Unwashed Americans, but who declared after a few weeks in the field with them that he was ready "to fight 30 years for their freedom if necessary." "We expect

---

[34] *OR*, ser. 1, vol. 32, pt. 2, p. 268; J. H. Meteer to Dear Prof, 26 Jan 1864 ("14th 'Unwashed'"), and to Dear Sir, 18 Apr 1864 ("We fully"), both in Mills Papers; Sean M. O'Brien, *Mountain Partisans: Guerrilla Warfare in the Southern Appalachians, 1861–1865* (Westport, Conn.: Praeger, 1999), pp. 64–67.

soon to meet the enemy," he added, "and with . . . Ft. Pillow . . . fresh in our memory woe be unto us if we don't fight desperately."[35]

By the end of July, Sherman's troops had driven Confederate General John B. Hood's army into trenches around Atlanta and were probing toward a railroad line south of the city that was the garrison's only source of supplies. Deciding to counter this move with a cavalry raid on the federal rear, Hood sent Maj. Gen. Joseph Wheeler with four thousand troopers to cut the Western and Atlantic Railroad between Atlanta and Chattanooga. On 13 August, Wheeler's men reached Calhoun, seventy miles to the north, where they tore up track and captured more than one thousand head of cattle. The next day they rode into Dalton, twenty miles farther on, but could not overcome the Union garrison, a mixed crowd of nearly five hundred infantry, cavalry, convalescents, teamsters, and civilian scouts.[36]

Word of Wheeler's movements and the resistance he met at Dalton reached Chattanooga, thirty rail miles to the north, by midafternoon on 14 August. The federal commander there had a relief expedition loaded in freight cars by 6:00 p.m., with Colonel Morgan's 14th USCI making up about half of the 1,200-man force. By midnight, the train reached Tunnel Hill, about eight miles north of Dalton by rail. The hill took its name from a 1,400-foot railroad tunnel that ran through it. If Wheeler's raiders managed to damage the tunnel severely enough to stop traffic, repairs could take months, slowing the pace of Sherman's campaign if not ending it entirely. The troops from Chattanooga detrained at the north end of the tunnel and began walking across the hill toward Dalton.[37]

Two local residents guided them as far as Buzzard Roost, halfway to Dalton, where they stopped about 2:00 a.m. to wait for daylight. An hour later, two depleted veteran white regiments, three hundred eighty men with two cannon, caught up with them. The entire force, some sixteen hundred strong, advanced not long after daybreak. Half a mile farther on, the Confederate advance guard appeared, moving toward Tunnel Hill. The Union force formed line of battle with the 14th USCI in the center flanked by three white regiments on the right and two on the left. When the line moved forward, the Confederates, weakened by the absence of a large detachment sent to guard their captured cattle, fell back through Dalton and beyond. "This was the first fight for the Regt, and had been anticipated with much concern—but the men behaved so gallantly that we [officers] feel truly proud of them," Chaplain William Elgin recorded in his journal. Colonel Morgan was also pleased with the men's behavior. The skirmishers "pushed forward boldly and steadily," he reported. "The conduct of the entire regiment was good." The relieving force suffered twenty-three casualties. The Confederates left ninety dead and wounded on the field, 60 per-

[35] Meteer to Dear Sir, 18 Apr 1864.

[36] OR, ser. 1, vol. 38, pt. 1, pp. 324, 619–20; pt. 3, p. 957; pt. 5, pp. 260, 271, 930, 967.

[37] OR, ser. 1, vol. 38, pt. 2, pp. 495, 508–09. White troops in the relief force numbered 627; total strength of the 14th USCI was 651. OR, ser. 1, vol. 38, pt. 1, p. 619, and pt. 5, p. 635. Stephen Davis, *Atlanta Will Fall: Sherman, Joe Johnston, and the Yankee Heavy Battalions* (Wilmington, Del.: Scholarly Resources, 2001), p. 168.

cent of their casualties in the entire raid. The Western and Atlantic Railroad, its damaged stretches soon repaired, was safe for the time being.[38]

Meanwhile, Sherman's armies continued to menace Atlanta. They seized the city's remaining rail outlet and cut the last telegraph wire on 31 August, causing Hood's force to withdraw to the south the next day. Still, Hood sought to disrupt the federal supply line and force Sherman out of northern Georgia. On 11 September, he sent a telegram to Lt. Gen. Richard Taylor, recently appointed to command Confederate troops in Alabama and Mississippi: "Hasten [Maj. Gen. Nathan B.] Forrest and get him operating upon Sherman's communications. It is all-important." Two days later, Taylor replied that Forrest had his orders and would move north soon.[39]

The 14th USCI had been patrolling the railroads that ran into Chattanooga from the west and north as part of a 3,500-man force sent to protect the railroads from Wheeler's cavalry. On 1 September, the men clambered into boxcars for the 130-mile ride to Murfreesborough, which they reached at midnight. They did not see Chattanooga again for twelve days, by which time they had traveled though the country around Pulaski, Tennessee, and Athens, Alabama, "a scout of . . . over 500 miles travelling by rail and foot," Chaplain Elgin wrote. "And in all this time my Regt. did not fire a shot. . . . The expedition results in forcing Wheeler to leave our communications and retreat south of the Ten[nessee River]. In all other respects dull and fruitless." Uneventful as it may have been, the expedition had achieved its purpose.[40]

Union generals were fully aware of the importance of railroads and were as keen to protect their own supply lines as they were to destroy those of the enemy. Earthworks and blockhouses with garrisons of various sizes dotted rail lines, especially at points where Confederate raiders might burn one of the trestles that spanned waterways and valleys. Staff officers in the Department of the Cumberland included a major whose title was inspector of fortifications and two lieutenants who served as assistant inspectors of blockhouses and railroad defenses. In mid-September 1864, the garrisons on the Tennessee and Alabama Railroad at Athens, Alabama, and Sulphur Branch Trestle, ten miles to the north, consisted of about twelve hundred officers and men. Eight hundred of them belonged to companies drawn from three USCI regiments: the 106th, 110th, and 111th.[41]

Forrest's Confederates numbered about forty-five hundred. Four hundred of them marched on foot, expecting to get mounts as soon as they were able to rout a large enough body of federal cavalry. The column drew near Athens late in the afternoon of 23 September. As the troopers exchanged shots with Union pickets, the garrison commander, Col. Wallace Campbell, arrived by rail with a party of one hun-

---

[38]OR, ser. 1, vol. 38, pt. 1, pp. 619–20; pt. 2, pp. 506 (quotation), 508–09; pt. 3, pp. 957, 961. W. Elgin Jnl, 18 Aug 1864 ("This was"), W. L. Clements Library, University of Michigan, Ann Arbor; Edward G. Longacre, *A Soldier to the Last: Maj. Gen. Joseph Wheeler in Blue and Gray* (Washington, D.C.: Potomac Books, 2007), p. 170; Richard M. McMurry, *Atlanta 1864: Last Chance for the Confederacy* (Lincoln: University of Nebraska Press, 2000), p. 165.

[39]OR, ser. 1, vol. 39, pt. 2, pp. 778, 831 ("Hasten Forrest"); Anne J. Bailey, *The Chessboard of War: Sherman and Hood in the Autumn Campaigns of 1864* (Lincoln: University of Nebraska Press, 2000), pp. 19–20; Thomas E. Connelly, *Autumn of Glory: The Army of Tennessee, 1862–1865* (Baton Rouge: Louisiana State University Press, 1971), pp. 456, 464–65.

[40]OR, ser. 1, vol. 38, pt. 2, p. 497; NA M594, roll 207, 14th USCI; Elgin Jnl, 1 and 12 Sep 1864 (quotation).

[41]OR, ser. 1, vol. 39, pt. 1, pp. 508, 520, 523, 535; NA M594, roll 216, 110th and 111th USCIs.

A typical federal blockhouse on the Nashville and Chattanooga Railroad

dred men that had gone out earlier in the day to drive off Confederates who had been tearing up the track south of town. Campbell's little force barely changed the odds in the fight; by nightfall, the Union garrison had withdrawn inside its earthworks. When the Confederates occupied the town, where the quartermaster and commissary depots were, Campbell led thirty white cavalry and twenty black infantry on a raid that set fire to the warehouses. They also captured two prisoners, one of whom told them that Forrest's strength was ten or twelve thousand men with nine cannon.[42]

Although the reported Confederate troop strength was a gross exaggeration, the prisoners were more accurate about the artillery. By dawn the next day, Forrest's two batteries had their guns trained on the Union fort. They began firing soon after 7:00, and about one-third of the Confederates began to advance. Forrest then halted the attack and demanded the surrender of the fort. When Campbell refused, Forrest requested a personal meeting and the federal commander rode out to meet him. "He accompanied me along my lines," Forrest reported, "and after witnessing the strength and enthusiasm of my troops he surrendered the fort with its entire garrison."[43]

The tone of Forrest's official account of his meeting with Campbell was almost offhand, but he related a different version of the day's events to his earliest biographers a few years after the war. According to his reminiscence, he took Campbell on a tour of

---

[42] *OR*, ser. 1, vol. 39, pt. 1, pp. 521, 542.
[43] Ibid., pp. 521–23, 543–44 (quotation, p. 543).

the Confederate position and pointed out the four hundred troopers without horses as the vanguard of a nonexistent infantry force. He arranged the horses of other cavalrymen who were then in the firing line, fighting on foot, to suggest the presence of another four thousand horsemen beside those he had already committed to battle. While Campbell was viewing the horses, Forrest's two batteries changed ground, convincing the federal commander that he confronted a force nearly as large and with even more artillery as the one his prisoner had spoken of the night before. After viewing Forrest's display, Campbell concluded that he faced an enemy force of at least eight thousand men and told his officers, according to their account, "The jig is up; pull down the flag." While the estimate was double Forrest's actual strength, it was similar to figures offered that week by other federal commanders, who reported anywhere from six thousand to eight thousand Confederate raiders in northern Alabama. At 11:00, Campbell surrendered the fort and its garrison of 571, including twenty-nine officers and 418 enlisted men of the 106th, 110th, and 111th USCIs. "It is reported that the captured Colored Troops were marched South to be given back to their owners," Colonel Mussey wrote a week later, when the news reached Nashville. "I do not think they were butchered by Forrest."[44]

Mussey was partly right. There was no massacre of the surrendered troops. After the surrender, the Confederates separated captive officers from enlisted men. The officers headed west toward Memphis, parole, and eventual exchange. The men marched south. Rather than languish in one of the South's notorious prison camps, they traveled to Mobile, where most of them labored on the city's fortifications. Some worked as blacksmiths, like Pvt. Dick Brown of the 110th USCI, or hospital nurses, like Pvt. Simon Rhodes of the 111th. Others, sick or injured, spent time in Confederate hospitals, as did Sgt. Anthony Redus and Cpl. William Redus, both of the 110th.[45]

Most of the captured enlisted men remained with the Confederates until the spring of 1865, but some escaped. Pvt. John Young of the 111th, who had been hit in the head by a shell fragment, noticed that there was no guard on the wounded prisoners and simply walked away while en route to Mobile. He rejoined the remains of his regiment by mid-October. The men who filled the ranks of the 106th, 110th, and 111th came mostly from the country between Decatur, Alabama, and Pulaski, Tennessee. Their knowledge of local geography must have helped a number of them to escape.[46]

Local connections could help in other ways, too. William Rann had left home when Union occupiers withdrew from northern Alabama late in 1862 and had worked as an officer's servant before joining the 110th USCI. As the prisoners moved through Tuscumbia, some forty miles west of Athens, "my old master

---

[44] Ibid., pp. 505–06, 523–24 ("The jig is up," p. 524); Capt R. D. Mussey to 1st Lt C. P. Brown, 3 Oct 1864 ("It is reported"), 110th USCI, Entry 57C, RG 94, NA; Thomas Jordan and J[ohn] P. Pryor, *The Campaigns of Lieut.-Gen. N. B. Forrest, and of Forrest's Cavalry* (New York: Da Capo Press, 1996 [1868]), pp. 562–63. In the preface (p. xiv), the biographers quote a letter in which Forrest said that he provided them with "all the facts and papers in my possession or available to me. . . . For the greater part of the statements of the narrative I am responsible."

[45] Deposition, William Redus, 19 Mar 1891, in Pension File SC569893, Dick Brown; Deposition, Simon Rhodes, 12 May 1888, in Pension File SC404448, Henry Everly; Deposition, Anthony Redus, 3 Sep 1883, in Pension File SC253310, Anthony Redus; Deposition, William Redus, 12 Mar 1903, in Pension File WC905951, William Redus; all in Civil War Pension Application Files (CWPAF), RG 15, Rcds of the Dept of Veterans Affairs, NA.

[46] Proof of Incurrence of Disability, 20 Nov 1900, in Pension File SC615667, John Young, CWPAF; Deposition, Jesse Phillips, 12 May 1888, in Pension File SC404448, Everly.

found me and took me away from the soldiers and took me home and kept me there. Whenever soldiers would come there they would run me out into the mountains. They kept me at home till the surrender." Rann's remarks do not mention any punishment for his having run away two years earlier or what chores he had to do while he stayed with his former owner until the end of the war. In the spring of 1865, Rann reported to the officer commanding the Union garrison at Florence, across the Tennessee River from Tuscumbia. From there he returned to his regiment, which by that time was stationed on the railroad west of Nashville.[47]

The surrendered officers of the 110th USCI headed first for Meridian, Mississippi, en route to the Union lines at Memphis. Their parole (a pledge not to fight against the Confederacy) served to release them pending formal exchange for Confederate officers held prisoner in northern camps. Before returning to Union lines, every one of them signed a statement that roundly condemned Campbell's surrender of "the best fortification on the line of the Nashville and Decatur Railroad." "We also feel it our duty to make mention of the bearing and disposition of the soldiers in the fort, both white and black," the statement continued.

> It was everything that any officer could wish of any set of men. So far from there being any disposition on the part of the men to surrender or to avoid a fight, it was just the reverse. . . . The soldiers were anxious to try conclusions with General Forrest, believing that in such a [fort] they could not be taken by ten times their number. When told that the fort had been surrendered and that they were prisoners, they could scarcely believe themselves, but with tears demanded that the fight should go on, preferring to die in the fort they had made to being transferred to the tender mercies of General Forrest and his men.

The district commander announced officially that Campbell's decision to surrender "is disapproved by every one, and disgraceful in the extreme." In a letter to General Sherman, he called Campbell "a damned coward." All the officers who had been at Athens demanded a court of inquiry; but Campbell's next assignment after the prisoner exchange took him to another department, and by the time hostilities ended he had submitted his resignation and left the service.[48]

Forrest's men moved north along the railroad on 25 September, the day after they seized Athens, capturing four more federal strongpoints. At Sulphur Branch Trestle, 227 officers and men of the 111th USCI and some five hundred white cavalry offered the sole resistance. They surrendered only after a two-hour bombardment and the death of their senior officer. Two days of fighting on the Tennessee and Alabama

---

[47]Deposition, William H. Rann, 21 Mar 1913, in Pension File XC2460295, William H. Rann, CWPAF.

[48]OR, ser. 1, vol. 39, pt. 1, pp. 523–26 ("the best," p. 524), 528 ("is disapproved"), and pt. 2, p. 521 ("a damned coward").

Railroad had cost the 106th USCI two of its four companies captured; the 110th lost all five companies that were present; and the 111th, seven out of ten.[49]

Forrest attributed the ease of his sweep along the rail line to the poor quality of officers in black regiments. He told his biographers after the war that the only reason the garrison at Sulphur Branch Trestle had held out for two hours was that the officers were too terrified to wave a white flag; black soldiers by themselves, he believed, were not capable of sustained resistance. Forrest alleged that the commander of one surrendered blockhouse accompanied his force and helped to arrange the surrender of others. More than a year afterward, the commanding officer of the 110th USCI admitted his own regiment's deficiencies, blaming them on the scattered stations of the companies—half of which were absent, marching to the sea as a pioneer battalion in Sherman's army—and lack of opportunities for drill and instruction.[50]

Early in October, with Union reinforcements arriving in northern Alabama by rail from as far away as Atlanta, Forrest turned south again. "The severe engagements . . . had exhausted nearly all my artillery ammunition," he explained. While Forrest's cavalry withdrew from Tennessee, the main Confederate army began a move to cut Sherman's supply line north of Atlanta, where General Hood had decided to direct his entire force against the Western and Atlantic Railroad. Confederate troops worked their way around the city and during the first week of October took part in a dozen small clashes at stations and water tanks along the line.[51]

At Dalton, where two months earlier the 14th USCI had gone into battle for the first time, the 44th USCI guarded the railroad. Organized at Chattanooga that spring, the regiment had come to Dalton on 14 September and had begun to fortify the place. On 2 October, when the earthworks were nearly finished, a Confederate force led by General Wheeler rode up and demanded the garrison's surrender. The commanding officer, Col. Lewis Johnson of the 44th USCI, refused. The raiders, who numbered four or five thousand by Johnson's calculation, withdrew during the night.[52]

A week later, Johnson reported "rebel cavalry in small squads" near his position, and civilian rumors of a "strong force of rebels" to the southwest. On 12 October, word reached him of fighting at Resaca, some fifteen miles south of Dalton; and he asked Maj. Gen. James B. Steedman, commanding at Chattanooga, to send seventy-five thousand rounds of rifle ammunition. The next morning, Johnson's cavalry scouts came racing into town, unable even to tell whether their pursuers were cavalry or infantry. Only at noon, when the Confederates arrived and began to exchange shots with the garrison, did Johnson realize that he faced a large part of Hood's army.[53]

Hood sent a demand for surrender that included the warning: "If the place is carried by assault, no prisoners will be taken." The captain commanding the garrison's company of white cavalry told Johnson that a reconnaissance indicated that the Confederates "had men enough to eat us up." Johnson sent the cavalry captain

[49] Ibid., pt. 1, pp. 533–35, 544. NA M594, roll 215, 106th USCI; roll 216, 110th and 111th USCIs.

[50] Lt Col D. F. Tiedemann to Maj A. R. Nininger, 22 Nov 1865, Regimental Books, 110th USCI, RG 94, NA; NA M594, roll 216, 110th USCI; Jordan and Pryor, *Campaigns of . . . Forrest*, pp. 566, 569–70.

[51] *OR*, ser. 1, vol. 39, pt. 1, pp. 546 (quotation), 576, 806–07, 809; Bailey, *Chessboard of War*, pp. 26–27.

[52] *OR*, ser. 1, vol. 39, pt. 3, pp. 31, 57, 784; NA M594, roll 209, 44th USCI.

[53] *OR*, ser. 1, vol. 39, pt. 1, p. 718, and pt. 3, pp. 190 (quotations), 233–34.

The country around Dalton, Georgia, drawn by Alfred R. Waud in October 1864

and two of his own officers with a flag of truce to get a more accurate idea of the enemy's strength; they reported that two infantry corps of the three that made up Hood's army were in the immediate vicinity and that the third was not far off.[54]

While Johnson's officers were talking to Hood's, the Confederates continued to advance their artillery until Johnson was able to see twenty pieces on a height overlooking his fort, about five hundred yards to the southeast. Toward 3:00, Hood asked to speak with the federal commander. When he appeared, Hood told him to "decide at once; that I already had occupied too much of his time," Johnson reported, "and when I protested against the barbarous measures which he threatened . . . he said that he could not restrain his men, and would not if he could; that I could choose between surrender and death." Although Johnson overestimated the size of Hood's force by 25 percent, it was still several times larger than Wheeler's had been ten days earlier, and better armed. After consulting with his officers, Johnson decided to surrender.[55]

By 4:00 that afternoon, the Union soldiers had stacked arms and black infantry stood separate from their white officers and the enlisted cavalrymen, who were to be paroled and exchanged. Black soldiers lined up for inspection by slaveholders in the Confederate ranks who wanted to identify escaped property. Hood's force at Dalton included thirty-seven Tennessee infantry regiments, so there was some possibility that a Confederate soldier might recognize one of his former slaves among

---

[54] Ibid., pt. 1, p. 718 (quotations), and pt. 3, p. 257.
[55] Ibid., pt. 1, p. 719 (quotation), and pt. 2, pp. 850–51.

the Union prisoners and reclaim him. In any case, black soldiers lost their shoes to barefoot Confederates. Many would endure the winter barefoot, suffering frostbite while working on fortifications at Corinth and other sites in Mississippi.[56]

Not all of the captured soldiers lived to endure the winter's labor. Their first assigned task, before leaving Dalton, was to tear up two miles of railroad track. When one soldier of the 44th refused to do the work, a Confederate shot him. Five or more men who had just left the hospital were shot, some of them before the prisoners set out for Villanow, a day's march to the southwest; others, when they fell out along the route. "From the treatment I received," Colonel Johnson reported, "I am sure that not a man would have been spared had I not surrendered when I did, and several times on the march soldiers made a rush upon the guards to massacre the colored soldiers and their officers. . . . [W]e were only saved from massacre by our guards' greatest efforts."[57]

Hood "could not restrain his men, and would not if he could," as Johnson recalled just four days after the surrender. The Confederate general did not file his report until four months later and passed over the incident in one sentence; but his remark to Johnson echoed some thoughts that General Forrest committed to paper in his report of the Union surrender at Athens, Alabama, just as Hood was threatening the Union commander at Dalton, Georgia. Forrest wanted "to prevent the effusion of blood that I knew would follow a successful assault," he told Lt. Gen. Stephen D. Lee; the surrender would "spare my men and the massacre of the garrison." Like Hood, Forrest knew that he could not control his men in the fury of an attack. Generals on both sides were aware of this: orders for Sherman's army marching through Georgia repeatedly reminded officers to exercise "proper control of their men" and "keep them well in hand." The disciplinary problems of an army on the march were exacerbated by the excitement of battle and complicated still further by racial hatred. Even Unionist Southerners had no use for black soldiers; recruiters for the U.S. Colored Troops in Tennessee found "bitter feeling . . . still existing . . . particularly in the Tennessee (*White*) Regiments." In Gallatin, where white Tennessee Unionists formed the garrison, "no negro dares to walk the streets." White soldiers there "recently burned the building . . . in which the Colored people had their school—out of pure wantonness." Even before the fighting ended, white Southerners on both sides exhibited the kind of behavior that would later manifest itself in arson, lynching, and other forms of terror as social control.[58]

After the surrender at Dalton, all of the officers of the 44th USCI had asked to go south with their men rather than north to parole and exchange, but Hood refused. "As no guards were placed between officers and men that night," Johnson

---

[56]Ibid., pt. 1, pp. 719–20, 807, and pt. 2, pp. 851–55; Deposition, William McColley, 7 Nov 1899, in Pension File SC821866, William McColley, CWPAF; James L. McDonough, *Nashville: The Western Confederacy's Final Gamble* (Knoxville: University of Tennessee Press, 2004), p. 37.

[57]*OR*, ser. 1, vol. 39, pt. 1, pp. 720–21, 723 (quotation, p. 721). General Thomas approved Johnson's decision to surrender (pp. 723–24). Company and regimental descriptive books of the 44th USCI list at least thirty-nine men who died while prisoners of war. It is hard to tell which were captured at Dalton on 13 October and which near Nashville on 2 December and impossible to identify the man who was shot for refusing to tear up the track. Regimental Books, 44th USCI, RG 94, NA.

[58]*OR*, ser. 1, vol. 39, pt. 1, pp. 543 ("to prevent," "spare"), 719 ("could not"), 801–03; 44: 458 ("keep them"), 463, 489, 544, 579, 594, 641 ("proper control"). Capt R. D. Mussey to Capt G. B.

reported, "and we expected to be separated from them on the next day, they were instructed how to proceed to make their escape." The men might have needed to be told where to report when they rejoined the Union army, but the officers were talking to the heirs of a long and persistent tradition of escape who needed little instruction or encouragement to get away from their captors. The prisoners began to leave at once. Pvt. David Steele, a pension applicant in 1907, testified: "I made my escape immediately and went back to Chattanooga and staid there until the officers were paroled and came there and recruited up the regiment." Pvt. William McColley also "had a chance to get away and took to the woods," finding his way to regimental headquarters. "The men are escaping daily and reporting to Camp," an officer recorded at the end of the month.[59]

Other enlisted men escaped but did not report. By the second week in November, five of the regiment's paroled officers had to visit stations along the railroad between Chattanooga and Atlanta to collect soldiers who had found their way there. "Quite a number of men are at these different points and some are yet coming in daily," Johnson told the department's adjutant general. Still others did not return at all and six months later turned up as teamsters and officers' servants in Sherman's army, which by that time had marched through Georgia and the Carolinas. Clearly, not all of the former slaves in the 44th USCI saw military service as a necessary way station on the road to freedom, but enough men escaped from captivity to reconstitute a skeleton force by late November. One company numbered only thirty-five men.[60]

Small numbers of Union officers, like those from the 44th USCI, were able to move freely along the Western and Atlantic Railroad a month after the capture of Dalton because Sherman acted aggressively after Hood's raid, forcing the Confederates out of northern Georgia, where the opposing armies had nearly stripped the country of food and forage, and west into Alabama. Hood's army reached Gadsden, Alabama, on 20 October and turned northwest toward the Tennessee River. This movement marked the beginning of the last Confederate offensive of the war. Its destination was Tuscumbia, where Hood's quartermasters were gathering supplies for a march north into Tennessee.[61]

The Confederate army struck the Tennessee River at Decatur, Alabama, some seventy miles northwest of Gadsden, on 26 October. Decatur stood on the south bank where the Memphis and Charleston tracks crossed the river, a mile or two southwest of that line's junction with the Tennessee and Alabama Railroad, which

---

Halsted, 23 May 1864 ("bitter," "no negro," "recently") (M410–CT–1864), Entry 360, RG 94, NA. For other incidents involving white Tennessee Unionists, see Capt R. D. Mussey to 1st Lt G. Mason, 14 Mar 1864 (M–223–CT–1864), Entry 360, RG 94, NA; Capt R. D. Mussey to 1st Lt G. Mason, 18 Apr 1864 (M–26–AG–1864), Entry 363, LR by Adj Gen L. Thomas, RG 94, NA.

[59] OR, ser. 1, vol. 39, pt. 1, pp. 719–23 ("As no guards," p. 723); Deposition, David Steele, 3 Sep 1907 ("I made"), in Pension File SC189837, David Steele, CWPAF; Depositions, William McColley, 7 Nov 1899 ("had a chance") and James Taylor, 13 Nov 1899, both in Pension File SC821866, McColley; NA M594, roll 210, 44th USCI ("The men").

[60] OR, ser. 1, vol. 39, pt. 1, p. 720; Col L. Johnson to Brig Gen W. D. Whipple, 8 Nov 64 ("Quite a number"), and to Col C. W. Foster, 3 May 65, both in 44th USCI, Entry 57C, RG 94, NA; NA M594, roll 210, 44th USCI.

[61] OR, ser. 1, vol. 39, pt. 1, pp. 799, 806, 811, and pt. 3, pp. 823, 845–46, 853; Bailey, *Chessboard of War*, p. 39.

ran north through Athens to Nashville. Union Brig. Gen. Robert S. Granger, commanding the District of Northern Alabama, understood that Decatur, the bridge, and the rail junction were critical to the federal position in that region. He summoned all the reinforcements he could, doubling the garrison's size in twenty-four hours to about three thousand troops. Among the reinforcements were some five hundred officers and men of the 14th USCI.[62]

Earlier that month, the regiment had been in Lincoln County, Tennessee, just across the state line. Reports of Confederates recruiting there had reached the general commanding troops on the Nashville and Chattanooga Railroad, and he asked for "one of the colored regiments . . . to clear out that county." Whether or not patrols of the 14th USCI served to deter enemy recruiters, General Hood's offensive soon demanded the regiment's presence elsewhere on the railroad. The 14th reached Decatur late in the afternoon of 27 October. Eight of its companies took positions in the sixteen hundred yards of earthworks that guarded the town. The remaining two went north of the river to protect a pair of cannon that covered the Confederate trenches and an artillery battery on the south bank. Throughout the night, the men of those two companies toiled alongside white artillerymen and infantrymen to prepare emplacements for the guns. At daybreak, they put down their shovels, picked up their rifles, and went down to the riverbank while the cannon opened fire on the enemy battery.[63]

The riflemen of the two companies spent most of the morning shooting at the Confederate gunners across the river. About noon, the rest of the 14th USCI, still on the south bank, received an order to charge the artillery position on the Confederate right, which had been under fire since dawn. Eight companies of the regiment, nearly four hundred men, formed line with skirmishers in advance and crossed six hundred yards of open field to drive the Confederates out of their position. They took a few prisoners and spiked the cannon with rattail files. Almost at once came an order to retire. "The enemy recovered from his fright," Colonel Morgan reported, "and while I occupied his works . . . moved for my rear, and rendered my position very hazardous. A fleet foot saved the regiment." The hasty retreat led one observer to remark that the Confederates "drove the Fourteenth back," but the brigade commander and General Granger complimented Morgan and his men on the charge. When their reports reached department headquarters in Nashville, General Thomas wrote that he was "glad to hear of the success of the colored regiment." Casualties in the 14th USCI amounted to fifty-five officers and men dead, wounded, and missing.[64]

In the end, artillery fire saved the Union position at Decatur. The battery north of the river, guarded by the two companies of the 14th USCI, along with two federal gunboats, shelled the Confederate position heavily during the late afternoon of 28 October. The next morning, Colonel Morgan and his men moved toward the enemy trenches and found them occupied by a rear guard that was still strong enough

---

[62] *OR*, ser. 1, vol. 39, pt. 1, pp. 695–96.

[63] Ibid., pp. 695, 697, 706, 714–16, and pt. 3, pp. 172, 237–38, 704 (artillery), 709 (68th Indiana), 710 (73d Indiana), 713 (29th Michigan).

[64] Ibid., pt. 1, pp. 698, 703, 709 ("drove the Fourteenth"), 714–17 ("The enemy," p. 715), and pt. 3, p. 488 ("glad to hear").

to hold the Union force at bay until nearly dark. Hood and the rest of his army, some thirty-five thousand men, marched west to Tuscumbia and Florence, where they remained for three weeks, checked by foul weather and lack of supplies.[65]

While Hood's army waited, Forrest ranged through western Tennessee on the lookout for supplies and recruits with a force about one-tenth the strength of Hood's. On 29 October, his cavalry was on the Tennessee River in the northern part of the state, not far from the Kentucky line. His artillery shelled a steamer carrying seven hundred tons of freight and drove it to shore, where the crew abandoned it. The next day, the guns damaged four more boats and two barges. Forrest ordered his troops south toward the river port of Johnsonville on 1 November. Two days later, they arrived opposite the western terminus of the Nashville and Northwestern Railroad.[66]

Having helped to build the railroad, the men of three black infantry regiments now stood watch over it. The 13th USCI covered the western stretch, with its regimental headquarters and four companies at Waverly, the county seat, about twenty miles east of Johnsonville. The 12th concentrated at the eastern end, although one of its companies furnished the provost guard at Johnsonville, where Colonel Thompson, in general command of troops along the railroad, made his headquarters. Companies of the 100th guarded bridges and trestles in the central part of the line. Thompson's entire command amounted to some nineteen hundred men posted at twenty-two sites along seventy-eight miles of track; but their presence was not sufficient to prevent incursions by Confederate irregulars, whose methods ranged from train wrecking to arson to armed robbery. That summer, one company of the 100th USCI had reported "frequent exchange of shots with the Guerrillas" in Section 57 of the road, fifty-seven miles west of Nashville. On the morning of 22 August, the company's report went on, "all the pickets East and South of the long trestle were attacked simultaneously, but held their ground . . . until reinforced by the guard[,] when the guerrilla gang was driven to the forest." The defenses of the port of Johnsonville itself included twelve cannon ashore, two of them forming a section of Battery A, 2d U.S. Colored Artillery (USCA). There was also a regiment of white infantry, some seven hundred strong, and eight hundred armed civilian employees of the Quartermaster's Department. Three Navy gunboats patrolled the Tennessee River. On 31 October, when Thompson got word of Forrest's presence along the river, he summoned nearby companies of the 13th and 100th. This increased the strength of the garrison by five hundred men.[67]

The new town, named for the state's military governor, had become a thriving supply depot for the Union army. Brig. Gen. James E. Chalmers, commanding one of Forrest's divisions, reported seeing at least eight transports and twelve barges tied up along the waterfront near a large warehouse that had enough supplies

[65] Ibid., pt. 1, pp. 698–99, 702, 715, 808–09, and pt. 3, pp. 888–89, 893, 903–05, 913; Richard M. McMurry, *John Bell Hood and the War for Southern Independence* (Lexington: University Press of Kentucky, 1982), pp. 152–82.

[66] *OR*, ser. 1, vol. 39, pt. 1, pp. 860–61, 863, 868–71, and pt. 3, pp. 810, 816.

[67] Ibid., pt. 1, pp. 861, 877–78, and pt. 3, p. 553; *Official Records of the Union and Confederate Navies in the War of the Rebellion,* 30 vols. (Washington, D.C.: Government Printing Office, 1894–1922), ser. 1, 26: 621 (hereafter cited as *ORN*); NA M594, roll 207, 12th and 13th USCIs, and roll 215, 100th USCI (quotation).

stacked outside it to cover an acre of ground. During the night, the Confederates placed ten cannon to cover both the port across the river and the main channel, which ran close to their own position on the west bank. The next day, 4 November, they opened fire and managed to disable the Union gunboats in half an hour. Colonel Thompson, fearing a cross-river assault by an enemy whose strength he imagined as numbering five thousand, ordered the depot quartermaster to burn the craft tied up at the wharf. Flames quickly spread to the supplies piled outside the warehouse and then to the warehouse itself. Troops and civilian workers alike refused to expose themselves to Confederate snipers in order to fight the blaze. "By night the wharf for nearly one mile up and down the river presented one solid sheet of flame," Forrest exulted. The next morning, he and his men began a slow and tedious march by muddy roads back to Mississippi.[68]

By the time the first reinforcements arrived the next afternoon, $1.5 million worth of boats, buildings, and supplies lay in ashes. The attack on Johnsonville had been a reversal for the Union, but Colonel Mussey was pleased with the black soldiers' behavior. Mussey was titular head of the 100th USCI, although his duties as commissioner of Colored Troops kept him in Nashville. There, favorable reports reached him about black artillerymen's coolness under fire and about the deadly aim of 13th USCI sharpshooters. "The affair was slight," he concluded (Union casualties amounted to eight killed and wounded), "but it has gained great credit for the colored troops."[69]

While black soldiers at the western end of the railroad battled organized bodies of Confederates, those farther east contended with guerrilla bands of the kind that operated everywhere in the occupied South. Ten days after Forrest's men withdrew from Johnsonville, a company commander in the 12th USCI reported an encounter with irregulars thirty miles outside Nashville. "We caught three bushwhackers . . . who were shot in attempting to escape in the brush. Beard's distillery being a regular rendezvous for guerrillas we burnt it with several other buildings used for secreting plunder." Both incidents were typical of the war at this stage, as conducted outside the lines of the main contending armies. "There is a new company of guerrillas in process of organization," the captain went on. "Many young men who have hitherto held themselves aloof from the bushwhackers have been emboldened to unite themselves with this company, owing no doubt to the proximity of Hood's Army. There are numerous squads of Confederate soldiers in the Duck river country recruiting and conscripting for the rebel army."[70]

The captain's report anticipated Hood's move by nearly a week. The Confederate Army of Tennessee did not leave Florence, Alabama, until 20 November. Three days after that, General Thomas told Colonel Thompson to prepare for the evacuation of Johnsonville if the enemy should appear in overwhelming force, even though reports of Hood's movements indicated that his path lay more to the east,

---

[68] *OR*, ser. 1, vol. 39, pt. 1, pp. 862, 871 ("By night"), 875, and pt. 3, p. 608; *ORN*, ser. 1, 26: 622–23 and map opposite 26: 630.

[69] An inspector estimated the total value of property destroyed at several places along the river during Forrest's raid as $2.2 million. *OR*, ser. 1, vol. 39, pt. 1, pp. 862, 868 ("The affair"). Seven months later, the chief quartermaster of the Department of the Cumberland reported the loss at Johnsonville as $1.5 million (vol. 52, pt. 1, p. 683).

[70] Capt G. M. Everett to Lt Col W. R. Sellon, 15 Nov 1864, 12th USCI, Entry 57C, RG 94, NA.

where Union generals thought he would threaten the Nashville and Chattanooga Railroad. On 25 November, with the northward direction of Hood's army more clear, Thompson received orders to send Battery A, 2d USCA, to reinforce the garrison of Nashville. Mounted men of the 12th and 13th USCIs patrolled the north bank of the Duck River. They saw no organized groups of Confederates, although Thompson reported guerrillas "very thick" south of the river. Incessant rains earlier in the month had increased the flow of the river and prevented the guerrillas from crossing.[71]

As Hood drew closer to Nashville, General Thomas received word that four Confederate cavalry regiments had somehow crossed the Duck River. On 29 November, he ordered the evacuation of Johnsonville. The first telegrams arrived soon after sunrise and were indefinite, with phrases like "as the case may be" and "unless it should become actually necessary to move hastily, of which there is no prospect now." By noon, with Hood's army approaching Franklin, twenty miles south of Nashville, the language became more definite: Thomas ordered forty freight cars to Johnsonville to carry off government property; Colonel Thompson was to dismantle any cannon that could not move, throw the gun carriages into the river, and "move promptly" to Clarksville, some sixty miles to the northeast. In midafternoon, the telegraph line went dead between Johnsonville and 12th USCI headquarters at Kingston Springs, twenty miles west of Nashville.[72]

Mounted companies of the 12th USCI had been on a scout for three days. While waiting for their return, Lt. Col. William R. Sellon received orders to withdraw the 12th and 100th to Nashville along the line of the railroad as soon as the last train from Johnsonville passed. As Sellon prepared to evacuate Kingston Springs on 30 November, the mounted patrol returned with the news that no Confederates had crossed Duck River since the four cavalry regiments had moved north earlier that week. After dark, a telegram from Maj. Gen. John M. Schofield reached General Thomas, announcing that Hood's army had attacked the Union earthworks at Franklin that day "with very heavy loss, probably 5,000 or 6,000 men. Our loss is probably not more than one-tenth that number." Schofield's estimate was close to the total number of Confederate casualties (more than six thousand two hundred fifty), but the defenders had suffered more than twenty-three hundred and Hood's force still outnumbered his own by three to one. The victorious Union troops abandoned their hastily dug position and withdrew north toward Nashville ahead of the battered Confederates.[73]

Sellon's command was not the only one moving to reinforce Nashville. At Chattanooga, General Steedman readied five thousand men—convalescents and conscripts belonging to Sherman's army but who had arrived too late to join it on the March to the Sea, and six infantry regiments, including the 14th, 16th, and 44th USCIs—on 25 November. Five days later, word came from General Thomas:

---

[71]*OR*, ser. 1, vol. 45, pt. 1, pp. 669, 995, 1049–50, 1100, 1128; Lt Col W. R. Sellon to 1st Lt T. L. Sexton, 23 Oct 1864; Col J. A. Hottenstein to Col C. R. Thompson, 26 Nov 1864; Lt Col W. R. Sellon to Col C. R. Thompson, 28 Nov 1864; all in 13th USCI, Entry 57C, RG 94, NA.

[72]*OR*, ser. 1, vol. 45, pt. 1, pp. 1138, 1161 ("as the case"), 1162 ("move promptly"), 1163.

[73]*OR*, ser. 1, vol. 45, pt. 1, pp. 1171 ("with very"), 1194–95; Thomas L. Livermore, *Numbers and Losses in the Civil War in America, 1861–65* (Boston: Houghton Mifflin, 1909), pp. 131–32.

"Embark your troops immediately on the cars and come to Nashville as soon as possible."[74]

Most of Steedman's force arrived there on 1 December, but the next to last of the troop trains derailed seven miles north of Murfreesborough. Crews worked through the night to remove the wreck, and the train that had been last in line stayed in Murfreesborough until the next day. On board were 307 officers and men belonging to Colonel Johnson's reorganized 44th USCI and two companies of the 14th, as well as twenty-five white soldiers of the 115th Ohio. Their train left Murfreesborough at 8:00 the next morning and crawled northwest, averaging about seven miles per hour. It reached Mill Creek Bridge and its nearby blockhouse, five miles outside Nashville, late in the morning. Forrest's cavalry was there already.[75]

"You will have to be careful how you use the railroad now or the enemy will get your trains," General Thomas had warned Steedman, but there was little that Colonel Johnson, the highest ranking officer on the train, could do. Hood's army had left Franklin the day before and moved straight north toward Nashville. By 2 December, it was taking positions about four miles south of the city. Forrest's troopers guarded the Confederate flanks, with one of the divisions and its artillery battery menacing federal communications on the Nashville and Chattanooga Railroad. One of the same three-inch guns that had sunk Union transports at Johnsonville four weeks earlier fired a shot that disabled the locomotive pulling Johnson's troops toward Nashville.[76]

The men scrambled out of the boxcars and headed for the blockhouse, which they found already occupied by a lieutenant's command from the 115th Ohio assigned to guard the bridge. Under fire from Forrest's artillery and dismounted troopers, Johnson's men took what cover they could behind stumps and tree trunks that had been felled to clear ground near the blockhouse. By nightfall, they had fired nearly all of the forty rounds each man carried in his cartridge box and had received another two thousand—about six cartridges per man—from the blockhouse garrison. "The rebels had enough men to just eat us up," Pvt. John Milton recalled. Twelve black soldiers lay dead; forty-six were wounded; and nearly as many were missing. With more than one-third of his command out of action, Johnson left the surgeon and chaplain of the 44th USCI in charge of the wounded and led the rest of his men quietly through the Confederate position "without much trouble," he reported. They reached Nashville "about daylight" the next day.[77]

Confederates captured the regiment's wounded, along with the surgeon and chaplain who had stayed to care for them. Sgt. Jacob Strawder and Pvt. Granville Scales both fell into Confederate hands. Scales' arm was shot "all to pieces," he told the Bureau of Pensions after the war. A Confederate surgeon "cut it off fer him near the Shoulder & cared for him as kindly as if he were white & of his own command." Left behind by the Confederates a few days later, Scales was soon back

---

[74] OR, ser. 1, vol. 45, pt. 1, pp. 502–03, 880–82, 1050, 1072, 1190 (quotation).

[75] Ibid., pp. 503, 535, 540–51, 754.

[76] Ibid., pp. 675, 754. Forrest's report identifies the Confederate cannon as belonging to the battery commanded by Capt J. W. Morton (p. 754). The battery's armament consisted of four "3-inch rifles" (vol. 39, pt. 2, p. 610).

[77] OR, ser. 1, vol. 45, pp. 540–41 ("without," "about," p. 541), 631–32; Affidavit, John Milton, 18 Nov 1905 ("The rebels"), in Pension File C2513010, Alex Prier, CWPAF.

Union troops aboard a train in northern Georgia in 1864

within Union lines and in a hospital at Nashville along with other wounded prisoners from the 44th. Pvt. Martin Buck and Pvt. Wiley Hunt both died there weeks later, Buck of typhoid fever and Hunt of pneumonia. The Confederates, many of whom lacked shoes, took Strawder's and marched him barefoot with the other unwounded captives to Franklin. There, Pvt. Henry Walker and other men with frostbitten feet joined the wounded in a Confederate hospital. They returned to the Union Army at Nashville by the end of the month. Those well enough to march continued south. "They . . . put 33 of us in jail without food left us there two days & marched us to Meridian Miss," Pvt. Owen Gideon recalled, "& on the way . . . it snowed and I stole a blanket from a rebel captain & slept." The survivors remained prisoners until the following spring.[78]

When the ranking officers of the 14th and 44th USCIs reported the names of the day's casualties, they listed 26 enlisted men wounded, 48 missing, and 12 taken prisoner. In all, nearly half of the eighty-six soldiers in the casualty list survived the war to file their own pension claims and at least one other testified on behalf of a comrade's application without filing his own. By the time the two regiments mustered out of service in the spring of 1866, only seven of the men named in the two casualty lists still appeared on the rolls as "missing in action." Confederates

---

[78] Asst Surgeon C. W. Oleson to 1st Lt F. McNeil, 9 Dec 1864, 14th USCI, and Col L. Johnson to Adj Gen, 2 Jan 1865, 44th USCI, both in Entry 57C, RG 94, NA. Deposition, Granville Scales, 18 Dec 1878 (quotation), in Pension File WC969411, Granville Scales; Pension File MO317804, Martin Buck; Pension File SC805183, Joseph Cloudis; Pension File MC254302, Wiley Hunt; Pension File SC486807, Jacob Strawder; Pension File WC512598, Henry Walker; Deposition, Owen Gideon, 23 Feb 1897 ("They . . . put"), in Pension File WC599132, Owen Gideon; all in CWPAF. For other soldiers of the 44th USCI who received medical attention in Confederate hospitals, see Pension Files SC189837, David Steele, CWPAF, and C2513010, Prier.

did not kill all, or even most, of the prisoners on the Nashville and Chattanooga Railroad that day.[79]

Still, rumors and reports of murdered prisoners continued to reach the regiments as soldiers escaped and made their way back to Union garrisons. "I have learned of the death of some more of my boys," 2d Lt. Morris S. Hall of the 44th USCI told his sister late in the winter. "I think some twelve have already died. . . . Oh how terribly some of those men have suffered and without cause. One the last I heard from him escaped, was recaptured, and then shot down in cold blood. . . . I can not but feel sad when I think of it. Will not a just God avenge their wrongs[?]" Hall decided to withdraw the resignation he had submitted after being passed over for promotion. "I have become attached to my men and the feeling that I was in the path of duty has always actuated me," he explained.[80]

By the time Colonel Thompson's brigade of U.S. Colored Troops reached Nashville, Steedman's regiments were already there. Thompson's force, which had been guarding the Nashville and Northwestern Railroad, did not arrive until 7 December. While Johnson's trainload of men came under attack by Forrest's cavalry southeast of Nashville on 2 December, Thompson's two thousand troops found their approach to the city blocked by part of Hood's army and had to make a thirty-mile detour by way of Clarksville. "They did some heavy marching but left no stragglers," Colonel Mussey noted when they reached Nashville. Thompson reported to Steedman, and his three regiments joined the rest of the general's command on the southeast outskirts of the city.[81]

For the next few days, they dug. Their trenches became part of the federal army's two lines of defense outside Nashville. The inner line lay on the south and west, just outside the city itself. The outer, about a mile beyond, extended across the peninsula formed by a bend in the Cumberland River on which Nashville stood. Both lines ran along the hills that ringed the city and faced the Confederate works, which lay a mile and more beyond the Union outer line. In the section held by Steedman's command, the defenses consisted of "a breast-work of rails and earth with a light palisade in front," as one regimental commander described them. The troops worked unceasingly to improve the position. "This has been a clear, warm day," Chaplain Elgin of the 14th USCI recorded on Sunday, 4 December, "but its sacred hours have all been spent in building defenses, thus preventing any services."[82]

Besides digging, Steedman's troops carried out small offensive operations against the nearest Confederates. On 5 December, Colonel Morgan's brigade—the 14th, 16th, 17th, and 44th USCIs and three companies of the 18th USCI—and two understrength white regiments moved against the enemy opposite their position,

[79] Asst Surgeon C. W. Oleson to 1st Lt F. McNeil, 9 Dec 1864, 14th USCI, Entry 57C, RG 94, NA; Johnson to Adj Gen USA, 2 Jan 1865; 14th and 44th USCIs, Regimental Books, RG 94, NA.

[80] M. S. Hall to Dear Sister Emma, 16 Mar 1865, M. S. Hall Papers, Bentley Library, University of Michigan, Ann Arbor.

[81] OR, ser. 1, vol. 45, pt. 1, p. 503, and pt. 2, p. 164; Col R. D. Mussey to Capt C. P. Brown, 12 Dec 64 (quotation), Entry 1141, pt. 1, RG 393, NA; NA M594, roll 215, 100th USCI.

[82] OR, ser. 1, vol. 45, pt. 1, pp. 535 ("a breast-work"), 548, and pt. 2, pp. 32–33; Elgin Jnl, 4 Dec 1864 ("This has been"); Jacob D. Cox, The March to the Sea: Franklin and Nashville (New York: Charles Scribner's Sons, 1882), p. 109, map.

taking some prisoners and running off the rest. Two days later, after the Confederates returned, Morgan's troops drove them off again, this time at the cost of some half-dozen wounded. "In this, as in the other affair," Elgin recorded, "the Colored Troops did as well as any Troops could do. The movement was witnessed by a great many soldiers and citizens all of whom speak in the highest praise of the conduct of the Col[ored] Troops. For our part we feel proud of the command."[83]

General Grant, from his headquarters in Virginia, had been urging Thomas to attack the Confederates since 2 December, the day Hood's army arrived outside Nashville. Thomas delayed, claiming that he required fifty-five hundred additional horses to mount all of his twelve thousand five hundred cavalrymen in order for them to act effectively in pursuit after Hood's prospective defeat. On 6 December, Grant issued a direct order: "Attack Hood at once, and wait no longer for a remount of your cavalry." While Thomas continued to demur and Grant and Stanton discussed relieving him of command, a storm on 9 December covered the hills around Nashville with a sheet of ice that immobilized both armies.[84]

Disgusted at Thomas' inaction, Grant dispatched Maj. Gen. John A. Logan, a former corps commander in Sherman's army, to relieve him. On 13 December, as the Adjutant General's Office in Washington issued Logan's orders, Thomas noted "indications of a favorable change in the weather" at Nashville. "As soon as there is I shall . . . assume the offensive," he wrote to Halleck.[85]

Thomas called a conference of his senior generals on the afternoon of 14 December. On the right of the federal line, Maj. Gen. Andrew J. Smith would lead two divisions, veterans of the Red River Campaign and the Tupelo expedition earlier that year, to deliver "a vigorous assault" on the Confederate position. Elsewhere along the line, the IV and XXIII Corps would play supporting and subsidiary roles. Steedman's force, which included eight U.S. Colored Infantry regiments, numbered more than nine thousand officers and men present for duty—12 percent of the available infantry. Stationed on the extreme left of the Union line, on the southeastern edge of Nashville, it had orders to hold its position and to "act according to the exigencies which may arise during these operations." Its real role on the first day was to create a diversion and cause the Confederates to reinforce their right and weaken their left, where Smith's troops would deliver the main attack. That evening, orders took the 16th USCI to the rear to guard the army's pontoon train, which stood ready to bridge rivers during the anticipated pursuit of a defeated Confederate army. A brigade of white troops took the place of the 16th.[86]

The next morning, fog "lay like a winding sheet over the two armies," Colonel Morgan reported. About 7:00, as it lifted, the 14th USCI moved forward deployed as skirmishers, followed by the 17th and 44th in line of battle. When rifle fire

---

[83]Colonel Morgan's report gave the number of prisoners as eight; Chaplain Elgin gave the number as seventeen. *OR*, ser. 1, vol. 45, pt. 1, p. 535; Elgin Jnl, 5 Dec 1864. Regimental records show five wounded on 7 December; Elgin said there were five in the 14th USCI alone. NA M594, roll 207, 14th and 18th USCIs; Elgin Jnl, 7 Dec 1864 ("In this").

[84]*OR*, ser. 1, vol. 45, pt. 1, pp. 37, 127, 153–54, 359, 747, and pt. 2, pp. 17, 29, 70 (quotation), 84, 96, 118–19, 132–33, 143. The figures are from the report of Thomas' cavalry commander, Maj. Gen. J. H. Wilson (pt. 1, p. 551).

[85]Ibid., pt. 2, pp. 169 (quotation), 171, 230, 265; Brooks D. Simpson, *Ulysses S. Grant: Triumph over Adversity, 1822–1865* (Boston: Houghton Mifflin, 2000), pp. 393–98.

[86]*OR*, ser. 1, vol. 45, pt. 1, pp. 37 (quotation), 54–55, 94, 526–27, 535.

stopped the skirmishers, the 17th and 44th rushed the Confederate trenches and captured them. They then pushed on as far as the Nashville and Chattanooga Railroad tracks, where artillery fire stopped them. While these regiments were pressing forward, Morgan ordered two white battalions to attack the trenches just west of those that his own troops had just taken. One battalion, made up of veterans from five Ohio regiments, succeeded; but the other, "mostly new conscripts, convalescents, and bounty jumpers," according to its brigade commander, ran headlong to the rear. Morgan found that he had misjudged Confederate strength and withdrew his regiments to a less-exposed position from which they sniped at the enemy until dusk. Smith's attack on the Confederate left began about three hours after Morgan's and continued through the day, advancing more than a mile and capturing 36 cannon and 5,123 prisoners. During the night, the survivors of Hood's army retired to another line a mile or two south of their position that morning. "The enemy had been deceived," Morgan reported, "and, in expectation of a real advance upon his right, had detained his troops there, while his left was being disastrously driven back."[87]

Soon after daybreak on 16 December, skirmishers of the 13th USCI moved forward past the previous day's corpses "all stripped of their clothing and left upon the open field," as one officer reported. They found the Confederate trenches empty. The rest of Colonel Thompson's brigade followed, moving almost due south for two miles, ahead of the rest of Steedman's command. By early afternoon, Steedman, at the east end of the Union line, was in touch with the headquarters of IV Corps, on his right, and preparing to support the main attack on the new Confederate position. Thompson's brigade would lead, along with a brigade of white troops that included the battalion that had "stampeded" the day before. The 18th USCI had reinforced that brigade since the previous day's attack.[88]

Steedman's line started forward about 3:00 p.m. On the left, the 12th USCI had to move in column to get past some dense undergrowth. When it passed the thicket and opened from column into line, its rapid movement led officers of the 13th and 100th to think that Colonel Thompson had ordered a charge and those regiments began to advance at a run. "Being under a heavy fire at the time," Thompson reported, "I thought it would cause much confusion to rectify this, so I ordered the whole line to charge." Felled trees and the angle of the Confederate works split the 12th and half of the 100th from the other half of the 100th. Confederate fire tore into both bodies of men. Colonel Hottenstein, some distance behind with the 13th USCI, saw that "the troops in our front began to lie down and skulk to the rear, which, of course, was not calculated to give much courage to men [of the 13th] who never before had undergone an ordeal by fire." On their left, the battalion of "conscripts, convalescents, and bounty jumpers" ran away again and its brigade commander "saw it no more during the campaign." The rest of the brigade—the 18th USCI and two veteran white battalions—pressed forward but failed to hold a position close to the Confederate line. The 13th USCI finally pushed through the disordered 12th and 100th and reached the enemy defenses; but it soon retreated,

    [87]OR, ser. 1, vol. 45, pt. 1, pp. 433, 436, 527 ("mostly new"), 531, 536 ("lay like"), 539; Dyer, Compendium, p. 1505; McMurry, John Bell Hood, p. 179.
    [88]OR, ser. 1, vol. 45, pt. 1, pp. 527 ("stampeded"), 528 ("all stripped"), 543, 548.

joining the survivors of the brigade near where the afternoon's attack had begun. Thompson's brigade had lost 80 officers and men killed and 388 wounded in less than half an hour, by far the highest loss in any Union brigade that day.[89]

By the time Thompson had withdrawn his men from the east end of the Confederate line, General Smith's brigades were attacking the other end, as they had the day before. Their assault succeeded, and the Confederate division that had just defeated Steedman's regiments and "was thus in the highest state of enthusiasm," its commander reported, soon "saw the troops on [its] left flying in disorder" and had to join the retreat. "Rebs were seen running in every direction a perfect rout," Lieutenant Hall of the 44th USCI wrote to his mother. Steedman's troops and those of the IV Corps, which had also failed to take its objective that afternoon, collected themselves and followed the enemy south on the road toward Franklin. "Began raining in the afternoon & continued all evening," 2d Lt. Henry Campbell of the 101st USCI entered in his journal. "Troops too tired to follow the rebels far."[90]

Night fell as Steedman's two brigades of U.S. Colored Troops, along with the IV Corps, pursued the Confederates. They bivouacked about eight miles south of Nashville and continued the pursuit the next day, reaching Franklin in the early afternoon. There they found that the retreating Confederates had burned the bridges across the Harpeth River. Since their rapid advance had left the pontoon train far behind, they had to wait while a regiment of the IV Corps built a new bridge. Rain began to fall again on 18 December, making it impossible for troops to advance through the fields on either side of the highway. Steedman's two brigades, about three miles beyond Franklin and headed south, received orders that morning to turn around and march to the Nashville and Chattanooga Railroad at Murfreesborough, thirty miles east of Franklin. They arrived on 20 December. From there, trains took them southeast to Stevenson, Alabama, then west toward Decatur, where some of the men had begun the campaign two months earlier. The object of their movement was to secure the Tennessee River crossing before the remains of Hood's army could reach it. The rest of General Thomas' army followed the retreating Confederates by a more direct but slower route along muddy roads through Columbia and Pulaski, having to wait twice for the pontoon train to bridge swollen rivers.[91]

Late in the afternoon of 26 December, Steedman's troop trains stopped where the tracks of the Memphis and Charleston Railroad crossed Limestone Creek, about eight miles east of Decatur. The bridge was out, so the men got off the train and followed the creek downstream to the Tennessee River. There they met a fleet of ten gunboats and transports with food and forage, which General Thomas had sent to help intercept the Confederate retreat. The boats ferried Steedman's force across the river. Once ashore, the troops had "to wade a deep bayou, deploy as skirmishers, and protect [the] landing," an officer of the 12th USCI recorded. "In wading bayou some men got out of their depth, none lost—slight skirmish." A few shots were enough to oust a weak Confederate cavalry regiment that guarded De-

---

[89] Ibid., pp. 527 ("conscripts"), 528 ("saw it"), 543 ("Being under"), 544, 546, 548 ("the troops"), 698.

[90] Ibid., pp. 290–91, 505, 698 ("was thus," "saw the troops "); M. S. Hall to Dear Mother, 17 Jan 1865 ("Rebs"), Hall Papers; H. Campbell Jnl, 18 Dec 1864, Wabash College, Crawfordsville, Ind.

[91] *OR*, ser. 1, vol. 45, pt. 1, pp. 135, 159–64, 291, 505, 549, and pt. 2, pp. 260, 325–26.

Part of the Nashville battlefield, taken as victorious Union troops pursued retreating Confederates south of the city

catur. By 7:00 that evening, Union troops controlled the town. Two days later, they learned that Hood's army had found another crossing some forty miles downstream and was already south of the Tennessee River on its way to Corinth, Mississippi.[92]

When that news arrived, Steedman's men were marching west toward the site of Hood's crossing. Detachments of white Union cavalry that accompanied them routed the fleeing Confederates near a town called Courtland, some twenty miles west of Decatur, allowing the infantry to reach there without further trouble. On 30 December, a company commander in the 12th USCI noted that "want of . . . blankets & tents, cold & wet weather, the passage of numerous streams & the usual hardships of a winter campaign have seriously lessened our numbers & impaired the efficiency of those present. The men . . . are deficient in energy on the march." Fortunately for the troops, this phase of the campaign was nearing an end. On New Year's Day, General Thomas ordered Steedman to break up his division and return to Chattanooga with Morgan's brigade, sending Thompson's brigade to Nashville.[93]

Regimental officers saw the lull in active operations as an opportunity to bring their commands up to strength and devote some attention to discipline and drill. Lt. Col. Henry Stone, ordered back to the Nashville and Northwestern Railroad,

[92]Ibid., pt. 1, p. 506, and pt. 2, pp. 384, 400–403, 698; *ORN*, 26: 671–82; NA M594, roll 207, 12th USCI (quotation).

[93]*OR*, ser. 1, vol. 45, pt. 2, pp. 401, 480, 493; NA M594, roll 207, 12th USCI (quotation).

asked that all the companies of the 100th USCI be stationed together for the first time. The regiments at Chattanooga, he pointed out, "have had the good fortune to be placed in such positions as have given them the facilities" for instruction, and he asked the same advantages for his own regiment and the others in Thompson's brigade. Colonel Thompson agreed with Stone; but General Thomas, who retained his command because of his victory over Hood, decided that drill was less important than guarding the Nashville and Northwestern, which was still a major supply artery for his army.[94]

Guard duty did not mean inactivity. Even in the last months of the war, Confederate guerrillas operated widely throughout the Department of the Cumberland. Field operations began as soon as the troops reached their new stations. The commanding officer of Company C, 18th USCI, noted "frequent night scouts" near Bridgeport, Alabama, in late January "to look for guerrillas, who commit depredations on the citizens." For the 42d USCI, an "invalid" regiment that General Steedman left in Chattanooga during the Nashville Campaign, antiguerrilla duty had never stopped. One company of the regiment covered an estimated seventy-two miles in four days during a "short but severe campaign" in early January against Confederate irregulars who had fired on a party of federal soldiers guarding a cattle herd. "My men is very mutch exposed & very badly quartered, besides quite a number of them sick," one company commander complained as winter ended. "They have had no less than five fights since the first day of this month." On 18 March, "the rebel Colonel" Lemuel G. Mead, who had recruited a force known as Mead's Confederate Partisan Rangers in Union-occupied Tennessee, attacked an outpost of the 101st USCI at Boyd's Station, Alabama, on the Memphis and Charleston Railroad, killing five men of Company E. A few weeks later, as the Confederacy collapsed, Union troops accepted the surrender of Mead's men, although one federal officer characterized them as "ragamuffins, bushwhackers, . . . horse-thieves, and murderers."[95]

With the close of hostilities, regiments of U.S. Colored Troops in the Department of the Cumberland began issuing furloughs to enlisted men for home visits. Black soldiers in central Tennessee and northern Alabama found themselves closer to home at the end of the war than did those in most other parts of the conquered South. For men in the northern and Kentucky regiments of U.S. Colored Troops who served in Virginia during the war and took ship for Texas soon afterward, distance prohibited furloughs, as it did for those serving in Florida and around Mobile. During the war, Memphis and other Mississippi River towns had attracted black refugees from plantations in the surrounding counties, including the families of many soldiers in garrison, so that furloughs for troops in garrison there were not as necessary. Only in the Department of the Cumberland and along the lower

---

[94]Lt Col H. Stone to Brig Gen W. D. Whipple, 16 Jan 1865, f/w 12th USCI, Entry 57C, RG 94, NA.

[95]*OR*, ser. 1, vol. 49, pt. 1, pp. 86 ("the rebel"), 559 ("ragamuffins"), 1023; Capt J. H. Hull to 1st Lt A. Caskey, 24 Mar 1865 ("My men"), 101st USCI, Entry 57C, RG 94, NA. NA M594, roll 207, 18th USCI ("frequent night"); roll 209, 42d USCI ("short but"); roll 215, 101st USCI. Mead's Confederate Partisan Rangers had a short official existence, from March 1865 to the Confederate surrender. Stewart Sifakis, *Compendium of the Confederate Armies,* 11 vols. (New York: Facts on File, 1992–1995), 3: 77.

Mississippi did large numbers of U.S. Colored Troops finish the war reasonably near the places where they had enlisted, but still at some distance from their families. During their service, most of the Tennesseans had covered the country from Dalton, Georgia, in the east to Decatur, Alabama, in the west and as far north as the Kentucky state line. They had left their families behind and felt a strong desire to see them again.[96]

Company commanders would specify the number of men who could request furloughs, the term of the furloughs (usually ten or twenty days), and the purpose: "their families are residing with their former masters, and these men desire to visit them to provide for them untill their term of service expires," was the formula in Company B of the 110th USCI. Commanding officers had authority to extend a furlough because of sickness, whether of the enlisted man or of one of his relatives.[97]

Black soldiers who received furloughs to visit their families often found them living with their former masters or in the contraband camps established by Union occupiers at several sites: Nashville, Clarksville, and Gallatin, Tennessee, and Huntsville, Alabama. Living conditions in the camps had attracted the attention of War Department investigators as early as the spring of 1864. While touring the region, inspecting camps and collecting testimony, they learned that residents' welfare depended almost entirely on the energy and dedication of a camp's commander. The general at Nashville was "culpably negligent," they reported, while the chaplain in charge at Huntsville "was wholly devoted to the care of its inmates."[98]

The camp at Clarksville had provided 136 soldiers for the Union Army; the one at Gallatin, "several hundred." The investigators' report made clear the government's responsibility toward them. "If we take colored soldiers into our armies, . . . we must take them under the obligation to take care of the families that would be otherwise left in want. When the enlisting colored soldiers are assured that the care of their families shall be the care of the government, that assurance must be made good. If we exact good faith from them, we must keep good faith with them." Further, the investigators recommended establishment of a federal office "nominally military, under the general authority and supervision of the War Department, . . . for this distinct service." The U.S. Senate published its report on 27 February 1865.[99]

Four days later, Congress passed a law it had been tailoring for more than fourteen months to "establish a bureau for the Relief of Freedmen and Refugees." The term *refugees* applied usually to white Unionists displaced by the fighting; *freedmen* generally referred to black Southerners of any age and both sexes, including those who had been free before the war. Even these latter saw changes in their legal status as the coming of emancipation and the war's end swept away many antebellum statutes. An agency of the War Department called the Bureau of Refugees,

---

[96]On the situation in the Department of the Cumberland, see Ira Berlin et al., eds., *The Destruction of Slavery* (New York: Cambridge University Press, 1985), p. 265, and *The Wartime Genesis of Free Labor: The Upper South* (New York: Cambridge University Press, 1993), pp. 376–85. Documentation is missing for most Louisiana-raised U.S. Colored Troops regiments that were still stationed there at the end of the war.

[97]Abstracts 81 and 110 ("their families") in Letterbook, 110th USCI, Regimental Books, RG 94, NA.

[98]"Condition and Treatment of Colored Refugees," 38th Cong., 2d sess., S. Ex. Doc. 28 (serial 1,209), pp. 9 ("culpably"), 12 ("was wholly").

[99]Ibid., pp. 9, 11 ("several"), 20 ("If we take"), 22 ("nominally").

Sgt. Henry J. Maxwell,
2d U.S. Colored Artillery

Freedmen, and Abandoned Lands would assume "control of all subjects relating to refugees and freedmen from rebel states, or from any district of country within the territory embraced in the operations of the army." Its first concern was the welfare of "destitute and suffering refugees and freedmen and their wives and children." As the year wore on, the Bureau's agents would supervise labor contracts between former slaves and white planters, who were no longer slaveholders but still owned most of the best farmland.[100]

In July 1865, the 14th USCI had six men on furlough and nine applications pending when the regimental commander asked permission for three of his soldiers to attend "the Convention of Colored People of this State" at Nashville the next month. Garrison and district headquarters approved the soldiers' request. Many black Southerners were aware of impending political changes that would affect their future and sought to influence the results by exercising their new rights to petition and to assemble peaceably.[101]

The convention met on 7 August at a chapel of the African Methodist Episcopal Church. Twenty of the 116 delegates were soldiers in Tennessee regiments of the U.S. Colored Troops. Sgt. Henry J. Maxwell of Battery A, 2d USCA, addressed them on the first day. "We want the rights guaranteed by the Infinite Architect," he told them. "We have gained one—

---

[100] *U.S. Statutes at Large*, 13: 507–08; Ira Berlin et al., eds., *The Wartime Genesis of Free Labor: The Lower South* (New York: Cambridge University Press, 1990), pp. 373–74. H. R. 51, introduced on 14 December 1863, originally called for a "Bureau of Emancipation." *Congressional Globe*, 38th Cong., 1st sess., 134: 19.

[101] Lt Col H. C. Corbin to Brig Gen A. J. Alexander, 19 Jul 1865 ("the Convention"), 14th USCI, Entry 57C, RG 94, NA. See also "Petition of the Colored Citizens of Nashville," 9 Jan 1865, in Berlin et al., *Black Military Experience*, pp. 811–16.

the uniform is its badge. We want two more boxes, beside the cartridge box—the ballot box and the jury box." The convention adjourned four days later, resolving to work closely with agents of the Freedmen's Bureau and to attempt a census of "our people" in the state. The soldiers returned to their regiments. For the next two years, helping to enforce the edicts of the Freedmen's Bureau and assisting its agents would take up most of the time of U.S. Colored Troops in Tennessee and other parts of the occupied South.[102]

---

[102] *Colored Tennessean* (Nashville), 12 August 1865.

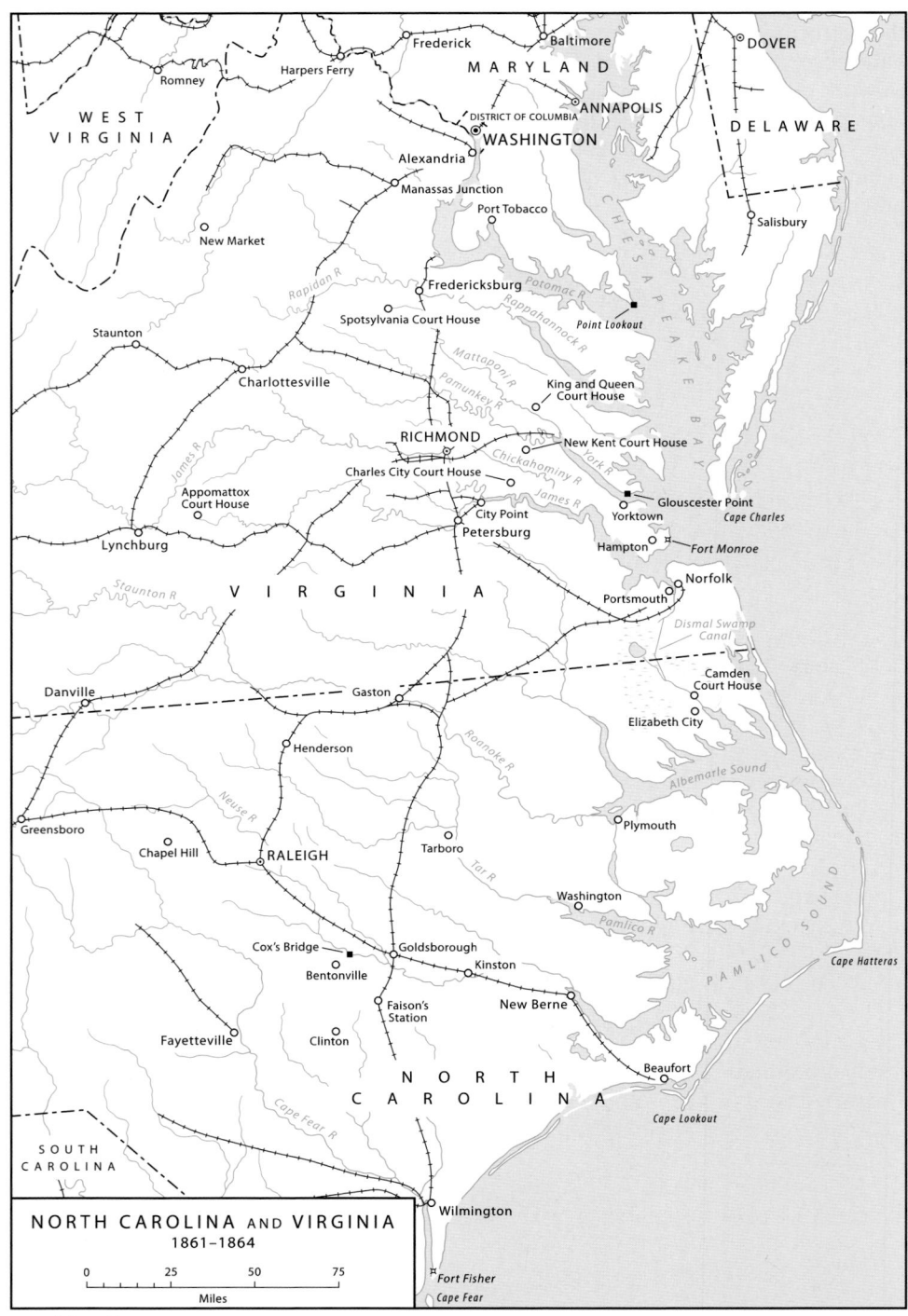

Romney
Frederick
Baltimore
DOVER
Harpers Ferry
MARYLAND

WEST
VIRGINIA
DISTRICT OF COLUMBIA
ANNAPOLIS
DELAWARE
WASHINGTON

Alexandria
Salisbury

Manassas Junction
Port Tobacco

New Market
Rapidan R

Fredericksburg
Potomac R

Spotsylvania Court House
Rappahannock R
Point Lookout

Staunton
Mattapony R

Charlottesville
Pamunkey R
King and Queen
Court House

James R
RICHMOND
New Kent Court House

Charles City Court House
Chickahominy R
York R

Appomattox
Court House
City Point
James R
Glouscester Point

Lynchburg
Petersburg
Yorktown
Cape Charles

V I R G I N I A
Hampton
Fort Monroe

Staunton R
Norfolk

Portsmouth

Danville
Gaston
Dismal Swamp
Canal

Camden
Court House

Henderson
Elizabeth City

Roanoke R

Neuse R
Albemarle Sound

Greensboro

Chapel Hill
RALEIGH
Tarboro
Plymouth

Tar R

Washington
P A M L I C O   S O U N D

Pamlico R

Cape Hatteras

Cox's Bridge
Goldsborough

Bentonville
Kinston

Faison's
Station
New Berne

Fayetteville
Clinton

N O R T H
Beaufort

C A R O L I N A
Cape Lookout

SOUTH
CAROLINA
Cape Fear R

Wilmington

NORTH CAROLINA AND VIRGINIA
1861–1864

0   25   50   75
Miles

Fort Fisher
Cape Fear

Map 7

CHAPTER 10

NORTH CAROLINA AND VIRGINIA
1861–1864

When the Confederate Congress, meeting in Montgomery, Alabama, voted on 20 May 1861 to move the seat of government east to Richmond, Virginia, it altered drastically the shape of the impending conflict. Suddenly, the capitals of the contending governments lay only a few days' march apart. Both sides massed their principal armies in this comparatively small space, where they struggled back and forth across the same terrain for four years. The concentrated drama and violence of this contest, conducted close to major communications centers and millions of newspaper readers, often overshadowed events in other parts of the country. Nevertheless, Union armies in the Mississippi Valley and in scattered coastal enclaves continued to follow the broad outlines of the scheme set forth by Lt. Gen. Winfield Scott during the first spring of the war (*see Map 7*).[1]

Learning of the secessionists' plan to move their capital and unsatisfied with the slow progress that Scott's "Anaconda" promised, Northern editors at once began urging the federal government to capture Richmond before the Confederate Congress convened there in July. A headline in Horace Greeley's *New York Tribune* exhorted: "To Richmond! To Richmond! Onward!" Military authorities at Washington took a much more cautious view, but they wanted to get some use out of the regiments that had responded to the president's summons, for the militia's three-month term of service would expire in mid-July. To this end, they organized a three-pronged sweep intended to drive Confederate troops from the Virginia counties along the Potomac River, where they threatened the federal capital and its link to the West, the Baltimore and Ohio Railroad. The Northern press misinterpreted this operation as the long-awaited offensive. "The Army is in motion, . . . advancing upon Richmond . . . that centre of rebellion," the *New York Times* reported. The movement ended in disaster on 21 July at Manassas, just thirty-five miles—a day's brisk retreat, as it turned out—from Washington. The Union Army returned to the capital; the militia regiments went home; and volunteers, enlisted for three years' service, began arriving to take their place.[2]

The defense of Washington was uppermost in the mind of Maj. Gen. George B. McClellan when he arrived later that summer to take charge of the volunteer regiments that were gathering there. He formed them into brigades and divisions

---

[1] *Journal of the Congress of the Confederate States of America, 1861–1865*, 58th Cong., 2d sess., S. Doc. 234, 7 vols., serials 4,610–4,616, 1: 254–55.

[2] *The War of the Rebellion: A Compilation of the Official Records of the Union and Confederate Armies*, 70 vols. in 128 (Washington, D.C.: Government Printing Office, 1880–1901), ser. 1, 2: 709,

and called his new command the Army of the Potomac. Country roads outside the city were so bad that the troops received supplies, whenever possible, by boat. "Not less than twenty of my teams are on the road struggling to work their way through the mud," Brig. Gen. Joseph Hooker reported from southern Maryland in early November. "If this should be continued, I shall not have a serviceable team in my train, nor will the depot quartermaster in Washington if he permits his teams to be put on the road." Hooker thought of withdrawing his troops from southern Maryland—a tobacco-growing region full of slaveholders and Confederate sympathizers—to a point closer to the federal supply railhead in Washington. Since each side tried to use artillery fire to interdict the other's shipping, control of the shoreline was clearly necessary to secure the defenses of the capital.[3]

While the garrison of Washington reorganized and gathered strength, ships of the U.S. Navy patrolled Chesapeake Bay and the rivers emptying into it. Slaves from the Tidewater counties of Virginia, sometimes entire families of them, took to boats and made their way to these vessels, which put them ashore at Washington or Fort Monroe. There, those who were able to work found employment with Army quartermasters. Confederate authorities, of course, took a different view of the matter. At Yorktown, one Virginia general complained in mid-August that "from $5,000 to $8,000 worth of negroes [were] decoyed off" each week.[4]

Some of the more enterprising and politically connected Union generals sought independent commands that summer, rather than spend the rest of the year camped near Washington, helping to train McClellan's army. Maj. Gen. Benjamin F. Butler, who took charge of the maritime expedition that captured New Orleans the following spring, was one; another was Brig. Gen. Ambrose E. Burnside, a Rhode Islander who had graduated from West Point in 1847, one year after McClellan. Burnside proposed raising a marine division of ten New England regiments with shallow-draft boats to secure the Potomac estuary and Chesapeake Bay. The War Department approved the plan, but by January 1862, when Burnside was able to gather the troops, McClellan had been appointed to the command of all Union armies and used his new authority to order Burnside's force to North Carolina. The object of the expedition was to land on the coast, to penetrate inland as far as Goldsborough, and there to cut an important rail line that ran from the deepwater port of Wilmington, in the southeastern corner of the state, north to Richmond, carrying supplies to the Confederate army that threatened Washington. The line was especially useful because it was of uniform gauge, a rarity in the South, and was thus able to move material rapidly along its entire 170-mile length.[5]

More than 160,000 people lived in the seventeen counties that lined the serrated coastline behind the Outer Banks. The region was home to 68,519 slaves (42.7 percent of the population) and 8,049 free blacks (5 percent). Of the black

711, 718–21 (hereafter cited as *OR*); *New York Tribune*, 30 May 1861; *New York Times*, 18 July 1861.
    [3]*OR*, ser. 1, 5: 372–77, 407–11, 421–24, 643 (quotation).
    [4]*OR*, ser. 1, 4: 614, 634 (quotation). *Official Records of the Union and Confederate Navies in the War of the Rebellion*, 30 vols. (Washington, D.C.: Government Printing Office, 1894–1922), ser. 1, 4: 508, 583, 598, 681–82, 748; 6: 80–81, 107, 113, 363 (hereafter cited as *ORN*).
    [5]*OR*, ser. 1, 5: 36; Robert M. Browning Jr., *From Cape Charles to Cape Fear: The North Atlantic Blockading Squadron During the Civil War* (Tuscaloosa: University of Alabama Press,

population, free and slave, 14,870 were men of military age. Burnside, like many Union officers, did not know what to do with them at first. "They are now a source of very great anxiety to us," he wrote in March 1862, one week after his force had seized New Berne. "The city is being overrun with fugitives from the surrounding towns and plantations. . . . It would be utterly impossible, if we were so disposed, to keep them outside of our lines, as they find their way to us through woods and swamps from every side."[6]

New Berne had a population of 5,432 that made it the state's second largest town and its second-ranking seaport. Most of the seven sites in North Carolina defined as ports in a Treasury Department report issued just before the war were small places, handling fewer than two dozen vessels a year. Their trade consisted of shipping turpentine, barrel staves, and lumber, mostly to the West Indies. Barrel staves were necessary for what the West Indies sent in return: molasses and sugar. The combined trade of the state's six smaller ports amounted to less than one-fifth that of Wilmington, the state's largest city, which remained in Confederate hands for most of the war. Wilmington, in turn, handled only a fraction of the number of ships that called at Baltimore and Charleston, the two closest seaports of any size. Although North Carolina's tiny ports shipped chiefly forest products, they offered attractive anchorages both to Confederate blockade runners and to any force trying to secure a beachhead.[7]

Many escaped slaves from inland relied on black residents along the coast to guide them to Union lines. Just as often, black mariners helped federal vessels negotiate the tricky shoals and tidal creeks that lined the shore. In coastal North Carolina, as elsewhere in the occupied Confederacy, black Southerners and federal troops helped each other even as they caused problems for each other. While black residents put their local knowledge to work for the Union Army, those who found sanctuary at federal garrisons—tens of thousands of them throughout the South—represented mouths to feed. The troops' presence guaranteed the safety of escaped slaves, but in return quartermasters and other officers exacted compulsory labor for wages that were more often promised than paid.[8]

Burnside soon discovered, as General Butler had at Fort Monroe, that the solution to his problem was to put the newcomers to work. "The negroes continue to come in," he reported nearly two weeks after landing at New Berne, "and I am employing . . . them on some earth fortifications in the rear of the

---

1993), pp. 19–21; *Report of the Joint Committee on the Conduct of the War,* 9 vols. (Wilmington, N.C.: Broadfoot, 1998 [1863–1865]), 3: 333; Robert C. Black III, *The Railroads of the Confederacy* (Chapel Hill: University of North Carolina Press, 1998 [1952]), p. xxv; Richard M. McMurry, *Two Great Rebel Armies: An Essay in Confederate Military History* (Chapel Hill: University of North Carolina Press, 1989), pp. 24–28.

[6]*OR,* ser. 1, 9: 199 (quotation); U.S. Census Bureau, *Population of the United States in 1860* (Washington, D.C.: Government Printing Office, 1864), pp. 350, 352, 354, 356, 358–59.

[7]Census Bureau, *Population of the United States in 1860,* p. 359. "Commerce and Navigation of the United States in 1860," 36th Cong., 2d sess., H. Ex. Doc. unnumbered (serial 1,102), pp. 311, 322, 339, 341, 345, 350, 475, 499, 557, 561.

[8]David S. Cecelski, *The Waterman's Song: Slavery and Freedom in Maritime North Carolina* (Chapel Hill: University of North Carolina Press, 2001), pp. 153–66; Barbara B. Tomblin, *Bluejackets and Contrabands: African Americans and the Union Navy* (Lexington: University Press of Kentucky, 2009), pp. 31–33, 99–105 (Potomac-Chesapeake), 50–52 (North Carolina), 173–75, 181–82 (pilots).

city, which will enable us to hold it with a small force when it becomes necessary to move the main body." By mid-May, there was a definite procedure: admit all escaped slaves; enroll them; "give them employment as far as possible, and . . . exercise toward old and young a judicious charity." Yet the moment to move against the railroad at Goldsborough never came. Although his troops managed to occupy Beaufort and ran up the United States flag at Washington, disease exacted a stiff price—nearly three thousand on the sick list, more than one-fifth of the expedition. Matters did not improve before Burnside and half of the federal troops in North Carolina were recalled to Virginia at the end of June to support McClellan's faltering campaign against Richmond. By that time, the number of black residents at New Berne had increased by seventy-five hundred—more than the entire population of the town two years earlier—and twenty-five hundred more escaped slaves were living at Beaufort and other sites along the coast.[9]

Burnside's successor, Maj. Gen. John G. Foster, hung on to the Union beachheads with the ten regiments that remained in North Carolina, a force of nearly eight thousand men. For the rest of the year, his troops sparred with nearby Confederates. On 10 December, the Union enclave at Plymouth, where the Roanoke River emptied into Albemarle Sound, suffered a raid. Four days later, Foster's men captured the town of Kinston, a county seat and Confederate brigade headquarters some thirty-five miles inland from New Berne. Such back-and-forth activity encouraged many more slaves to leave their homes and seek refuge at federal garrisons. "Negroes are escaping rapidly," a Confederate general lamented, "probably a million of dollars' worth weekly in all . . . , and gentlemen complain, with some reason, that [the eastern] section of the State is in danger of being ruined if these things continue." Union strength in the department gradually increased to thirty-two regiments (nearly twenty-two thousand men) by the end of the year. Then it plunged in January, when strategists at the War Department decided to mount an offensive against Charleston in 1863 and Foster led some ten thousand of his troops off to South Carolina. The incessant shuttling of scarce manpower between backwater departments hindered the success of Union coastal operations throughout the war.[10]

During 1862, great changes occurred farther north, along the Potomac River and lower Chesapeake Bay. The District of Columbia and neighboring Alexandria, Virginia, attracted thousands of black people escaping from bondage on both sides of the river. At the beginning of the war, although it was relatively easy for an escaped Maryland slave in a strange city—Washington or Alexandria—to pretend to have escaped from a disloyal owner in Virginia, slaveholders of all political opinions in Maryland had been able to call on the assistance of federal officers, civil and military, to retrieve their human property. Then, in March 1862, Congress passed an additional Article of War that forbade Army officers

---

[9] *OR*, ser. 1, 9: 271, 273, 373 ("The negroes"), 376–77, 381, 385, 390 ("give them"), 404, 406, 408; Vincent Colyer, *Report of the Services Rendered by the Freed People to the United States Army, in North Carolina* . . . (New York: by the author, 1864), p. 6; Browning, *From Cape Charles to Cape Fear*, pp. 83–86.

[10] *OR*, ser. 1, 9: 344–51, 411–15, 477 (quotation); 18: 45–49, 52–60, 500–501.

New Berne headquarters of the Superintendent of the Poor, where residents received clothing in the spring of 1862. One man in the foreground seems to be wearing a Union army uniform, although recruiting of black troops in North Carolina would not begin for another year.

from assisting slave catchers. The month after that, another act of Congress freed the nearly thirty-two hundred slave residents of the District of Columbia, promising to compensate their former owners. Meanwhile, General McClellan moved the Army of the Potomac by water from Washington to the Virginia peninsula between the York and James Rivers. As that army advanced slowly toward Richmond, a much smaller expedition from Fort Monroe, at the tip of the peninsula, crossed the James estuary to occupy the port of Norfolk. By summer, Union occupiers had a firm hold on both shores of the estuary. Although McClellan failed in his attempt to take Richmond, the Norfolk garrison began to attract thousands of escaped slaves.[11]

The president meanwhile began preparing an Emancipation Proclamation, but refrained from a public announcement until September, a few days after McClellan's army turned back a Confederate invasion of Maryland at Antietam. When the proclamation took effect on New Year's Day 1863, it applied only to slaves held in parts of the seceded states that were not yet under federal control.

[11]*OR*, ser. 2, 1: 810; Census Bureau, *Population of the United States in 1860*, p. 587; Ira Berlin et al., eds., *The Destruction of Slavery* (New York: Cambridge University Press, 1985), pp. 159–67, and *The Wartime Genesis of Free Labor: The Upper South* (New York: Cambridge University Press, 1993), pp. 90–92, 245–49; Browning, *From Cape Charles to Cape Fear*, pp. 40–41; Louis S. Gerteis, *From Contraband to Freedman: Federal Policy Toward Southern Blacks, 1861–1865* (Westport, Conn.: Greenwood Press, 1973), p. 22.

Despite its limited scope though, the Proclamation was no empty gesture. In February 1862, a Union force had entered and occupied Nashville; in April, New Orleans; in May, Memphis. In October, a few weeks after defeated Confederates retired from Maryland, a federal army in Kentucky turned back another invasion attempt at Perryville. Despite Union reversals that December in both Mississippi and Virginia, the zone of federal dominance was growing steadily, and with it the zone of freedom. There was every reason to expect further growth in the coming year. Moreover, the Proclamation finally admitted black men "into the armed service of the United States to garrison forts . . . and other places, and to man vessels of all sorts in said service." It had been nearly forty-three years since a War Department order, issued during John C. Calhoun's tenure as secretary of war, banned black enlistments in the Army entirely.[12]

Up and down the Atlantic Coast, from Boston and New York to Hampton and Norfolk, in the free states and wherever Union troops occupied a southern town, black people celebrated emancipation on New Year's Day 1863. They heard the Proclamation read; they attended prayer meetings; in some places, they marched in processions. "Some thousands of people" attended a barbecue and "Freedom Jubilee" at Beaufort, South Carolina, where Col. Thomas W. Higginson was organizing a regiment of former slaves. At Norfolk, Virginia, four thousand people followed a band through the streets. Union army bayonets backed public celebrations like these. Residents of Philadelphia, a city that had endured three anti-black riots a generation earlier, gave thanks behind closed doors, in churches and private homes. In Brooklyn, an audience of blacks and whites gathered at a Methodist church to hear three white speakers and the black author and lecturer William Wells Brown. "Rejoicing meetings were advertised . . . in nearly every city and large town," Brown wrote, recalling the occasion not long after the war.[13]

The idea of black men donning military uniforms gained public support after the summer of 1862. In April of that year, the Confederacy had begun conscription, and the necessity for a draft in the North became plain when states took months to answer the president's call in July for three hundred thousand more volunteers. "Recruiting for [three-year enlistments] is terribly hard," the governor of Maine complained. He and other Northern governors praised Lincoln's September announcement of Emancipation in the coming year and emphasized the direct connection to military manpower needs. To have delayed Emancipation, twelve of the governors said in a letter to the president, "would have discriminated against the wife who is compelled to surrender

---

[12] *OR*, ser. 3, 3: 3. See also Richard M. McMurry, *The Fourth Battle of Winchester: Toward a New Civil War Paradigm* (Kent, Ohio: Kent State University Press, 2002), pp. 50–51.

[13] *New York Times*, 3 January 1863; *Baltimore Sun*, 3 January 1863; William W. Brown, *The Negro in the American Rebellion: His Heroism and His Fidelity* (Athens: Ohio University Press, 2003 [1867]), p. 62 ("Rejoicing"); William Dusinberre, *Civil War Issues in Philadelphia, 1856–1865* (Philadelphia: University of Pennsylvania Press, 1965), pp. 152–53; Robert F. Engs, *Freedom's First Generation: Black Hampton, Virginia, 1861–1890* (Philadelphia: University of Pennsylvania Press, 1979), p. 36; Christopher Looby, ed., *The Complete Civil War Journal and Selected Letters of Thomas Wentworth Higginson* (Chicago: University of Chicago Press, 2000), p. 255 ("Some thousands").

her husband, against the parent who is to surrender his child to the hardship of the camp and the perils of battle, in favor of rebel masters permitted to retain their slaves."[14]

While the state of Massachusetts was filling one black regiment and preparing to organize another, Secretary of War Edwin M. Stanton in Washington was setting in motion the bureaucratic machinery to produce many more nationwide. Early in the spring of 1863, with recruiting for the 54th Massachusetts progressing, Governor John A. Andrew suggested to Stanton that "some brave, able, tried and believing man" raise a brigade of black soldiers in the Union enclaves of North Carolina. Andrew knew several such men among the colonels of his own state's regiments, he told Stanton. Since twelve of the twenty-seven Union regiments then serving in North Carolina were from Massachusetts, the governor took a keen interest in the progress of the war there.[15]

The man whose name Andrew put forward was Edward A. Wild, who had begun his military experience eight years earlier as a medical volunteer with the Turkish Army during the Crimean War. A native of Massachusetts, Wild organized a company of the 1st Massachusetts in the spring of 1861 and led it through the Peninsula Campaign a year later. The governor appointed him colonel of one of the state's new regiments in the summer of 1862. Within a month of taking command, Wild suffered a wound that necessitated amputation of his left arm. He spent the next six months in Boston, gaining strength while helping Andrew decide on officer appointments in the state's new black infantry regiments. A man of strong abolitionist beliefs, Wild was equipped with a list of Massachusetts soldiers who had volunteered to serve with black troops; he was just the man, the governor thought, to raise new regiments among the black population of coastal North Carolina. Stanton agreed, and announced Wild's appointment on 13 April.[16]

En route from Boston to North Carolina, Wild stopped in Washington to deliver a roster of officers for the first of his new regiments. The list clearly showed his method of selection. Of thirty-six nominees, thirty-two had previous military experience, thirty of them in Massachusetts regiments. Six were from Wild's first command, Company A of the 1st Massachusetts. When the War Department proposed that his nominees undergo an examination, as officer candidates elsewhere did, Wild pleaded for exemption. "Examining Boards must, by natural tendency, fall into the error of accepting the book-men, and rejecting the men of practical experience," he wrote.

> Many a man can take the best care of his company, can direct the drill, and go through his part in the evolutions on the field without a mistake—can conduct his men admirably in the fight, who yet, when summoned formally before a Commission, would utterly fail of expressing his ideas on subjects of daily familiarity. I would far rather select a man for what he *has* done in camp

---

[14] *OR*, ser. 3, 2: 201 ("Recruiting"), 583 ("would have"); Ira Berlin et al., eds., *The Black Military Experience* (New York: Cambridge University Press, 1982), pp. 10–11.

[15] *OR*, ser. 1, 18: 547–49; ser. 3, 3: 14, 100–101, 109–10 (quotation), 212, 214.

[16] *OR*, ser. 1, 18: 122; ser. 3, 3: 117. Richard Reid, "Raising the African Brigade: Early Black Recruitment in Civil War North Carolina," *North Carolina Historical Review* 70 (1993): 274–75.

A surgeon before he became a soldier, Brig. Gen. Edward A. Wild early in the war received wounds that mangled his right hand (gloved in this photograph) and caused amputation of his left arm. Being deprived of his prewar livelihood did nothing to mitigate the hatred Wild felt for slaveholders.

and field, than for any feats he may have performed before an Examining Board.

The Adjutant General's Office acquiesced. The roster for Wild's second new regiment included five officers who had served in the Massachusetts regiment he had commanded as a colonel. Ten men from the company he had led at the beginning of the war became officers in his third North Carolina regiment. In an era of rudimentary or nonexistent personnel systems, the new general had to rely on the same principle that Col. Embury D. Osband used in organizing the 1st Mississippi Cavalry (African Descent): first-hand knowledge of a candidate's abilities.[17]

Wild landed at New Berne on 18 May. The next day, General Foster's headquarters announced his arrival and the purpose of his visit, adjuring all Union troops "to afford [him] every facility and aid. . . . The commanding general expects that this order will be sufficient to insure the prompt obedience (the first duty of a soldier) of all . . . to the orders of the War Department." The order was necessary because in the spring of 1863, many white soldiers, even those from Massachusetts, still opposed the idea of black enlistment. The most prominent among them was Brig. Gen Thomas G. Stevenson, former colonel of the 24th Massachusetts, a regiment that had landed a year earlier with Burnside's expedition. Stevenson

---

[17]Brig Gen E. A. Wild to Maj T. M. Vincent, 27 Apr 1863 (W–9–CT–1863); 25 Jun 1863 (W–38–CT–1863, filed with [f/w] W–9–CT–1863); 4 Sep 1863 (W–158–CT–1863, f/w W–9–CT–1863); 4 Sep 1863 (W–159–CT–1863) (quotation); all in Entry 360, Colored Troops Div, Letters Received (LR), Record Group (RG) 94, Rcds of the Adjutant General's Office, National Archives (NA). Maj T. M. Vincent to Brig Gen E. A. Wild, 2 Oct 1863, E. A. Wild Papers, U.S. Army Military History Institute (MHI), Carlisle, Pa. Other works consulted in determining the number of soldiers from Wild's previous commands who were appointed to the new North Carolina regiments include: NA Microfilm Pub T289, Organization Index to Pension Files of Veterans Who Served Between 1861 and 1900, roll 550, 35th United States Colored Infantry (USCI); *Official Army Register of the Volunteer Force of the United States Army*, 8 vols. (Washington, D.C.: Adjutant General's Office, 1867), 8: 206–10 (hereafter cited as *ORVF*); *Massachusetts Soldiers, Sailors, and Marines in the Civil War*, 8 vols. (various places and publishers, 1931–1937).

suffered a few days' suspension from duty for declaring at a private gathering in February 1863 that he would rather lose the war than fight alongside black troops. Although Wild, when he heard of the remark, called it "treasonable language," the authorities decided not to institute formal proceedings and restored Stevenson to duty. At Plymouth, three white members of the garrison assaulted three of Wild's recruiters, black men themselves, including Assistant Surgeon John V. DeGrasse and Chaplain William A. Green. Regardless of impediments, recruiting went on.[18]

As a Massachusetts abolitionist, Wild was able to call on extra help in securing men for the new regiments. One of his most important associates was Abraham H. Galloway, a North Carolina native. Galloway escaped from slavery by sailing from Wilmington to Philadelphia with a cargo of turpentine in 1857, when he was twenty years old. He returned to North Carolina early in the war and put his local knowledge to work gathering intelligence for the Union occupiers. His contacts were so extensive by 1863 that he could engineer his mother's escape from slavery in Confederate-held Wilmington, bring her within Union lines, and then enlist the aid of high-ranking officers to ship her farther north. With the understanding that federal authorities would guarantee support for black soldiers' families and provide schooling for their children, Galloway went to work for Wild. Recruiters ranged through every coastal enclave held by Union occupiers. "I send you a party of well drilled men," Wild wrote to one of his officers who planned to attend a two-day religious meeting at Beaufort. "By thus making an exhibition of a specimen of our forces, you will prove to the colored people of that vicinity that we are in earnest, and you will greatly encourage recruiting." Wild himself visited Hatteras Island and returned with one hundred fifty recruits. The 1st North Carolina Colored Infantry was full by late June.[19]

While recruiting for Wild's second regiment got under way during the first week of July, twenty men of the 1st North Carolina took part in a raid inland by more than six hundred cavalry. The objective was the Wilmington and Weldon Railroad, the same line that Burnside's expedition had aimed at eighteen months earlier. The black soldiers acted as pioneers, building bridges and repairing roads for the advancing cavalry. When the raiders reached the railroad, though, the white troopers were slow to organize dismounted crews to tear up the track. In their haste, they left the work of destruction only half done, allowing trains to begin running again soon after their departure. As usually happened when federal troops visited parts of the South where they had not been before, several hundred slaves

---

[18]*OR*, ser. 1, 9: 358; 18: 723 ("to afford"). Maj G. O. Barstow to Maj Gen D. Hunter, 16 Feb 1863 (f/w S–1562–AGO), NA Microfilm Pub M619, LR by the Adjutant General's Office, 1861–1870, roll 219; Brig Gen E. A. Wild to Brig Gen H. W. Wessells, 12 Jul 1863 ("treasonable language"), Wild Papers; Reid, "Raising the African Brigade," p. 278.

[19]Brig Gen E. A. Wild to Capt J. C. White, 17 Jun 1863 (quotation), and Maj G. L. Stearns to Brig Gen E. A. Wild, 26 Jun 1863, both in Wild Papers; E. A. Wild to My Dear Kinsley, 30 Nov 1863, E. A. Kinsley Papers, Duke University (DU), Durham, N.C.; Reid, "Raising the African Brigade," pp. 280–83; Cecelski, *Waterman's Song*, pp. 182–87.

managed to join the expedition and accompanied it back to Union lines. As many as one hundred of them may have been potential recruits.[20]

Wild had hoped to continue recruiting in North Carolina, but, as happened often during the war, events in other parts of the country dictated a change of plans. At Charleston, South Carolina, Maj. Gen. Quincy A. Gillmore pursued land operations that summer in support of a naval attack on the city. After his attempt to storm Fort Wagner failed on 17 July, Gillmore complained to Maj. Gen. Henry W. Halleck, the Army chief of staff, that disease and battle casualties had sapped his troop strength, and asked "urgently . . . for 8,000 or 10,000 [veteran] troops." The closest reinforcements who could be spared were the men of the 1st North Carolina Colored. The regiment boarded transports just one week after receiving its colors and only returned to North Carolina for discharge in the spring of 1866.[21]

General Foster had already left New Berne and gone north to Fort Monroe, where he took command of the new Department of Virginia and North Carolina on 18 July. General Halleck anticipated that the Confederates would draw troops from their coastal defenses to support the Army of Northern Virginia during the weeks after Gettysburg and hoped that Foster would "do the rebels much injury." Just six weeks after moving to Fort Monroe, Foster ordered the 2d North Carolina Colored Infantry and the other black regiments in his old department—the 3d North Carolina Colored Infantry, still recruiting, and the 1st United States Colored Infantry (USCI), recently arrived from Washington, D.C.—to take station at Portsmouth, Virginia.[22]

The advent of the 1st USCI in North Carolina and of the 3d USCI at Charleston later in the summer marked an epoch in black soldiers' role in the war. Of the regiments raised in the North by the War Department, these were the first to take the field and among the first to receive consecutive numbers as federal rather than state volunteers. The new system of designation began that spring, while Governor Andrew was raising the 54th Massachusetts and Adjutant General Lorenzo Thomas along the Mississippi River, Maj. Gen. Nathaniel P. Banks and Brig. Gen. Daniel Ullmann in Louisiana, and Col. James Montgomery in South Carolina were also organizing regiments.

On 22 May, Secretary of War Stanton issued an order that established a bureau of the Adjutant General's Office in Washington to deal with "all matters relating to the organization of colored troops" and provided for examining boards to test the ability of prospective officers. As Adjutant General Thomas organized regiments along the river that spring, he appointed the officers on his own authority from among the white troops at towns and steamboat landings where he stopped. Boards of officers from the river garrisons, rather than boards convened by the War De-

---

[20]*OR*, ser. 1, vol. 27, pt. 2, pp. 859–67. General Foster estimated the number of escaping slaves as four hundred (p. 860); Reid, "Raising the African Brigade," p. 288, quotes a newspaper estimate of two hundred. The raid's effect was so slight that John G. Barrett, *The Civil War in North Carolina* (Chapel Hill: University of North Carolina Press, 1963), ignores it entirely, while noting that railroad officials "kept a large labor force on duty to repair any damage done to the line by raids . . . , and the road was in operation again by August 1," after another raid later in the month (p. 166).

[21]*OR*, ser. 1, vol. 28, pt. 2, pp. 23 (quotation), 30.

[22]Ibid., vol. 27, pt. 3, pp. 553 (quotation), 723; Capt J. A. Judson to Col A. G. Draper, 29 Aug 1863, 36th USCI, Entry 57C, Regimental Papers, RG 94, NA.

partment, examined Thomas' candidates. For most of the next two years, Thomas, west of the Appalachians, continued to correspond directly with Stanton rather than with the new Bureau for Colored Troops in his own Washington office. Such vague areas of responsibility and ill-defined chains of command characterized the Union's effort to enlist black soldiers throughout the last two years of the war.[23]

During the rest of 1863, one Northern governor after another adopted the program of black recruitment. The wholesale organization of new state regiments that had occurred during the first two summers of the war was over. Henceforth, white men who enlisted or were drafted would go to fill the ranks of existing regiments. Helping to organize U.S. Colored Troops therefore gave state governors a last chance to distribute patronage by naming the thirty-nine officers required to field an infantry regiment. The governor of Ohio was one of the first to express an interest. Maj. Charles W. Foster, chief of the Bureau for Colored Troops, sent him a copy of the War Department order that stipulated the number of officers and men necessary to make up a regiment, adding: "To facilitate the appointment of the officers, it . . . would be well to forward to the War Department as early as practicable the names of such persons as you wish to have examined for appointments." The same sentence appeared that summer and fall in letters to the governors of Rhode Island, Michigan, and Illinois. Each of those states raised a black regiment, as did Connecticut and Indiana. Ohio managed to raise two.[24]

In New York City, a private organization seized the recruiting initiative from the state's reluctant Democratic governor. Early in December 1863, after the governor told the recruiting committee of the Union League Club that "the organization of negro regiments . . . rests entirely with the War Department in Washington," committee members wrote directly to Secretary of War Stanton. Describing their organization as "composed of over 500 of the wealthiest and most respectable citizens," the writers offered their money and energy in the cause of black enlistment. Major Foster quickly conveyed Stanton's acceptance of the proposal, and local recruiters went to work. Even though private citizens rather than elected officials took charge of the project, they made sure that the list of officer candidates was heavy with veterans of New York regiments.[25]

The first of the New York Union League's regiments, numbered the 20th USCI, took ship for New Orleans early in March 1864. Presentation of colors in Union Square and the regiment's march down Broadway attracted tens of thousands of spectators. Among daily newspapers, the Republican *Times* allotted two-and-a-

---

[23] *OR*, ser. 3, 3: 100–101, 215–16 (quotation, p. 215). Brig Gen L. Thomas to Col E. D. Townsend, 14 Apr 1863; to Maj Gen J. A. McClernand, 8 May 1863; to Col E. D. Townsend, 20 May 1863; all in Entry 159BB, Generals' Books and Papers (L. Thomas), RG 94, NA. Michael T. Meier, "Lorenzo Thomas and the Recruitment of Blacks in the Mississippi Valley, 1863–1865," in *Black Soldiers in Blue: African American Troops in the Civil War Era*, ed. John David Smith (Chapel Hill: University of North Carolina Press, 2002), pp. 249–75.

[24] *OR*, ser. 3, 3: 380 (quotation), 383, 572, 838. The War Department order that fixed the personnel limits of regiments is on pp. 175–76.

[25] *OR*, ser. 3, 3: 1106–07 (quotations, p. 1107), 1117–18; 4: 4, 10–11, 55. Maj C. W. Foster to G. Bliss, 28 and 29 Dec 1863, 14 Jan 1864, all in Entry 352, Colored Troops Div, Letters Sent (LS), RG 94, NA. Melinda Lawson, *Patriot Fires: Forging a New American Nationalism in the Civil War North* (Lawrence: University Press of Kansas, 2002), pp. 88–90, 98–120.

half columns to the story, followed by an editorial the next day. The news story began: "The scene of yesterday was one which marks an era of progress in the political and social history of New-York." The Democratic *Herald* disagreed, giving the story slightly more than one column and printing no editorial. Its account began: "There was an enthusiastic time yesterday among the colored population of the city." Several other newspapers, some politicians, and the city's white militia viewed the event unfavorably. Plainly, not all Northern whites were reconciled to the spectacle of black soldiers on parade.[26]

Leading an advance party of the 20th USCI to clear crowds from the pier was 2d Lt. John Habberton, a veteran of operations in North Carolina and around Norfolk. He and his men watched the regiment embark. "First came a platoon of Police," Habberton wrote in his diary. "Behind them marched a hundred of the Union League Committee. . . . Then came the garrison band of Governor's Island, playing 'John Brown.' As the band reached the head of the dock, the Union League chaps sang to the music." Meanwhile, Habberton and his men arrested a vendor, whom they caught "selling big pies with bottles of whiskey inside," and turned him over to the city police. At last, the regiment came in sight. "The head of the column reaching the vessel's side, the band halted, commenced playing 'Kingdom Coming' and the companies marched aboard as fast as possible," Habberton continued.

> The band continued to play popular airs until all the men were on board, the police took a last look through the ship, the jolly Union Leaguers said "goodbye" "give 'em fits" "stick to the flag" and all the rest of the regulation remarks for such occasions, the . . . guard marched aboard, the cables were slipped, and by Dark the vessel lay in the stream, and the officers and men were walking into supper. As soon as possible . . . all went to bed, pretty tired with their day's work.

Two other black regiments, the 26th and 31st USCIs, left New York City for South Carolina and Maryland in the spring.[27]

Philadelphia was another city where private philanthropists helped to remove black enlistment from the hands of the state's governor. Despite the virulent prejudice of many white residents, the city had a well-established black community in 1860 that numbered some twenty-two thousand in an entire population of more than half a million. Among them were about forty-two hundred black men of military age, nearly 40 percent of the state's total. In mid-June 1863, the War Department allowed the Supervising Committee for Recruiting Colored Troops to begin enlisting black soldiers. The committee itself was presumably all white, for although the constitution of its parent organization, the Union League of Philadelphia, did not forbid

---

[26]*New York Times*, 6 (quotation) and 7 March 1864; *New York Herald*, 6 March 1864. Dudley T. Cornish uses the embarkation of the 20th USCI as a liminal incident with which to begin the preface of *The Sable Arm* and refers to it again later in the book. His account relies on one *New York Times* editorial and a pamphlet published by the New York Association for Colored Volunteers. *The Sable Arm: Negro Troops in the Union Army, 1861–1865* (New York: Longmans Green, 1956), pp. xi–xii, 253–54; Ernest A. McKay, *The Civil War and New York City* (Syracuse: Syracuse University Press, 1990), p. 240.

[27]J. Habberton Diary, 5 Mar 1864 (quotation), MHI.

The 20th U.S. Colored Infantry receives its regimental colors, 5 March 1864.

black membership, the club's three hundred-dollar entry fee and sixty-dollar annual dues had that effect.[28]

Leaders of the city's black community, some of whom had begun urging enlistment in 1861, joined in enthusiastically. Fifty-four of them lent their names to a recruiting poster that urged "Men of Color, To Arms! To Arms!" They organized a mass meeting on 24 June, and another one twelve days later at which Frederick Douglass appeared among the speakers who urged enlistment. The chief federal official present was Maj. George L. Stearns, who had been recently appointed recruiting commissioner for U.S. Colored Troops after several months spent working closely with Governor Andrew to raise the two black infantry regiments from Massachusetts. Companies of recruits formed in Philadelphia as the men arrived there; when each company reached the required strength, it reported to Camp William Penn, eight miles outside the city. There, a Regular Army officer who represented the Provost Marshal General's Office mustered it into federal service and the company became part of a regiment. Between recruits' arrival and muster-in, the committee of civilian philanthropists took

[28] *OR*, ser. 3: 376, 404–05; Census Bureau, *Population of the United States in 1860*, p. 410; W. E. B. Du Bois, *The Philadelphia Negro: A Social Study* (New York: Schocken Books, 1967 [1899]), pp. 17–24, 27–30; Roger Lane, *Roots of Violence in Black Philadelphia, 1860–1900* (Cambridge: Harvard University Press, 1986), pp. 16–20; *Chronicle of the Union League of Philadelphia, 1862–1902* (Philadelphia: Union League, 1902), p. 445.

responsibility for feeding and sheltering them, a function that committees of neighbors had performed when towns and counties across the North raised regiments of white volunteers in 1861 and 1862.[29]

By August 1863, the first of Philadelphia's black regiments, the 3d USCI, was ready to embark for South Carolina. Two more, the 6th and 8th, were complete by fall. Through the winter, Camp William Penn turned out black infantry regiments at the rate of one a month. Eleven in all left Philadelphia by the end of summer 1864, most of them destined for Virginia and operations against Richmond and Petersburg. Nearly one in ten of all the Union's black infantry regiments entered service at Camp William Penn or in the city itself.[30]

In other Northern states, governors kept greater control of recruiting and retained the power to nominate officers. Nearly all of the officers of the 5th and 27th USCIs (Ohio), the 28th (Indiana), the 29th (Illinois), and the 102d (Michigan) had served in one of their state's volunteer regiments or was at least a resident of that state. Besides soldiers from his own state, the governor of Ohio named several civilians from Oberlin College, an abolitionist stronghold that had begun admitting black students more than twenty years earlier. Although only white men officered the Ohio regiments, the governor took advice on nominees from John M. Langston, a black Oberlin alumnus of 1849, and Langston's brother-in-law, Ordinatus S. B. Wall. Both men had recruited black Ohioans for the 54th and 55th Massachusetts and took an active part in raising the 5th and 27th USCIs.[31]

Although the city of Washington, D.C., lacked powerful elected officials to promote black enlistment, it was nevertheless a good recruiting ground for a place its size. Smaller than Albany, New York, in 1860, Washington had a black population that more than tripled during the next ten years, from 10,983 (9,209 free, 1,774 slave) to 35,454. Former slaves who fled to Washington from nearby rural counties in Maryland and Virginia increased the number of dwellers in the city's crowded, unhealthy alleys tenfold. Reflecting the residents' rural backgrounds, the source of income in more than half of these alley households was unskilled labor. Wartime Washington was a boom town, but few economic benefits trickled down to its black residents. Between the spring of

---

[29]OR, ser. 3, 3: 374, 381, 682–83; James M. Paradis, *Strike the Blow for Freedom: The 6th United States Colored Infantry in the Civil War* (Shippensburg, Pa.: White Mane Press, 1998), pp. 9–11; J. Matthew Gallman, *Mastering Wartime: A Social History of Philadelphia During the Civil War* (New York: Cambridge University Press, 1990), pp. 45, 47–48; James W. Geary, *We Need Men: The Union Draft in the Civil War* (DeKalb: Northern Illinois University Press, 1991), p. 9; Russell L. Johnson, *Warriors into Workers: The Civil War and the Formation of Urban-Industrial Society in a Northern City* (New York: Fordham University Press, 2003), pp. 245–47, 250–51, 267–72; Thomas R. Kemp, "Community and War: The Civil War Experience of Two New Hampshire Towns," in *Toward a Social History of the American Civil War: Exploratory Essays,* ed. Maris A. Vinovskis (New York: Cambridge University Press, 1990), pp. 38–39; Emma L. Thornbrough, *Indiana in the Civil War Era, 1850–1880* (Indianapolis: Indiana Historical Society, 1965), pp. 177–79.

[30]OR, ser. 3, 3: 1085–86; 4: 789. Lt Col L. Wagner to Maj C. W. Foster, 6 Jan 1864 (W–29–CT–1864); 18 Feb 1864 (W–154–CT–1864); 9 Mar 1864 (W–244–CT–1864); all in Entry 360, RG 94, NA.

[31]Edward A. Miller, *Black Civil War Soldiers of Illinois: The Story of the Twenty-ninth U.S. Colored Infantry* (Columbia: University of South Carolina Press, 1998), pp. 12–28; Versalle F. Washington, *Eagles on Their Buttons: A Black Infantry Regiment in the Civil War* (Columbia: University of Missouri Press, 1990), pp. 12–13, 18–26.

*A range of emotions from uncertainty to truculence plays on the faces of these
Philadelphia recruits in early 1864. Their regiment, the 25th U.S. Colored Infantry,
sailed soon afterward for the Gulf of Mexico, where it formed part of the garrison of New
Orleans, and later of Pensacola.*

1863 and the end of the war, black Washingtonians provided the Union Army with 3,269 soldiers.[32]

In a city where federal authorities had arrested the mayor as a Confederate sympathizer during the early months of the war, other civic leaders had to assume the burden of launching a movement for black enlistment. In April 1863, two white military chaplains assigned to hospitals in Washington suggested in letters to President Lincoln that they could raise a black regiment in the city and lead it themselves; but not until a 29-year-old minister of the African Methodist Episcopal Church, Henry McNeal Turner, sponsored several mass meetings in May did the project gather momentum. As recruits joined, companies of the 1st USCI mustered in during May and June. That fall, when the regiment was serving in Virginia, Turner became its chaplain.[33]

Since Washington was a loyal city with a majority of free people in its black population, recruiters for the 1st USCI could not use the press-gang methods that characterized Union recruiting in the Mississippi Valley and elsewhere in the occupied South.

[32]U.S. Census Bureau, *Statistics of the Population of the United States* (Washington, D.C.: Government Printing Office, 1872), p. 97; Frederick H. Dyer, *A Compendium of the War of the Rebellion* (New York: Thomas Yoseloff, 1959 [1909]), p. 11; Constance M. Green, *The Secret City: A History of Race Relations in the Nation's Capital* (Princeton: Princeton University Press, 1967), pp. 61–64, 81–84; James Borchert, *Alley Life in Washington: Family, Community, Religion, and Folklore in the City, 1850–1970* (Urbana: University of Illinois Press, 1980), pp. 40–41.

[33]*OR*, ser. 2, 2: 229, 596–99; C[arroll] R. Gibbs, *Black, Copper, and Bright: The District of Columbia's Black Civil War Regiment* (Silver Spring, Md.: Three Dimensional Publishing, 2002), pp. 32–39.

The regiment took nearly two months to fill its ranks, but this was no longer than the time needed to recruit the first black regiments in other Northern and border-state cities during the summer of 1863. Despite antagonism from many white residents in places like Baltimore, Philadelphia, and Washington, black regiments during the third summer of the war were able to organize as quickly as many white volunteer regiments had done in 1861 and 1862, when enthusiasm for the war was high.[34]

The streets of Washington provided a setting for the kind of rowdiness and violence that typify boom towns. In July 1863 alone, city police arrested 1,647 soldiers, nearly all of them white, mostly for absence without leave, drunkenness, and disorderly behavior. Many white civilian residents were new arrivals who worked for the Army or Navy and competed directly for jobs as laborers and teamsters with black Washingtonians and escaped slaves. These white workers displayed a hostility toward black recruiting that often took physical, even brutal, forms. The murder and arson that characterized the New York Draft Riots in July were only extreme examples of the hatred directed at black people that flourished in American cities at the middle of the nineteenth century. In Washington, an act of Congress had abolished slavery eight months before the Emancipation Proclamation. With that, black people lost their cash value and their lives became worth nothing in the eyes of many white ruffians. Racially inspired assaults among civilians occurred several times a week during the summer of 1863, and individual black soldiers in town also suffered insults and beatings. As companies of the 1st USCI mustered in, military authorities withdrew them to Analostan Island (since renamed Theodore Roosevelt Island), less than two miles due west of the White House and just south of Georgetown.[35]

An urgent call for protection from the chaplain who commanded one of the Washington contraband camps brought two companies of the regiment back to the mainland. At the beginning of June, the camp had suffered an attack by rioters whom the *Evening Star* described as "a disorderly gang." White troops from the city's garrison went to New York in mid-July to help suppress the Draft Riots, leaving the camp without an armed guard. The camp chaplain heard remarks "freely uttered by the rowdy class" that "threatened outbreaks of popular violence here similar to those so recently occurring in New York," and asked for a guard from "the colored regiment" and 150 muskets to arm able-bodied male residents of the camp. Two companies arrived within a few days, and stood guard over the camp while the regiment received its last recruits. The 1st USCI sailed for North Carolina at the beginning of August, after a review by Maj. Gen. Silas Casey, a veteran of the Mexican War and Indian campaigns on the Pacific Coast who chaired the examining board that met in Washington to evaluate officer applicants for the U.S. Colored Troops. The old soldier observed cautiously that the new regiment looked

---

[34]NA Microfilm Pub M594, Compiled Rcds Showing Svc of Mil Units in Volunteer Union Organizations, roll 205, 1st USCI; (Washington) *Evening Star*, 5 May 1863; Edward G. Longacre, *A Regiment of Slaves: The 4th United States Colored Infantry, 1863–1866* (Mechanicsburg, Pa.: Stackpole Books, 2003), pp. 13, 19, 28; Paradis, *Strike the Blow for Freedom*, pp. 5, 9, 11, 22–23, 29–31; Washington, *Eagles on Their Buttons*, p. 12.

[35]Arrest statistic is in (Washington) *Evening Star*, 3 August 1863. Incidents of insult and assault offered to black soldiers are issues for 22 May and 5, 12, and 23 June 1863. Iver Bernstein, *The New York City Draft Riots: Their Significance for American Society and Politics in the Age of the Civil War* (New York: Oxford University Press, 1990), pp. 27–31.

as well as any body of white troops who had been in the service for the same length of time.[36]

The District of Columbia lay between two slave states. Maryland had never seceded, and federal troops had occupied the Virginia shore of the Potomac during the first weeks of the war. Both sides of the river were thus under Union occupation and exempt from the provisions of the Emancipation Proclamation. Since the federal capital's rail links north and west ran through Maryland, the Lincoln administration tried carefully to avoid measures that would increase the influence of the state's secessionist minority, a group that the mustering officer for U.S. Colored Troops in Baltimore called "vindictive and dangerous." Not until early October 1863 did the Adjutant General's Office issue confidential orders to govern black enlistments in Maryland, Missouri, and Tennessee. (At this point in the war, the federal government was still too cautious to attempt raising black troops in Kentucky.)[37]

The first black regiment raised in Maryland mustered in at Baltimore, becoming the 4th USCI. Its colonel was Samuel A. Duncan, formerly an officer of the 14th New Hampshire. Entering the Army in the summer of 1862, Duncan was disappointed to spend his first year in garrison duty at Washington and hoped for active service with the U.S. Colored Troops. His new regiment's march through Baltimore in September 1863 "did much . . . to soften the prejudice against col[ore]d troops—nowhere stronger, perhaps, than here," he told his mother.

> I have certainly no desire to return to my old regt. I am, in fact, almost convinced that a negro regt. is preferable to a white one—you are under no obligations to associate with the men—are an entire stranger to them, and of course they expect to know their Col. as an officer only—in consequence of which a much better discipline is possible among them than if you were obliged to humor your men on the score of old acquaintance.

Duncan thought that discipline suffered in white volunteer regiments, where most of the officers and men in any company came from the same town or county.[38]

The three most eligible kinds of recruit for black regiments in Maryland were free men; slaves who could show written consent from a loyal master; and slaves of disloyal masters, who could enlist without permission. Only when these categories failed to provide enough men did the rules allow recruiters to accept slaves of loyal masters without permission or to employ the harsh methods that they used commonly in the occupied South.

Since slaves would gain their freedom when they entered the Army, each one, whether enlisting with or without consent, would bring a loyal master three hundred dollars' compensation from the federal government. This was a bargain for

---

[36]Chaplain J. I. Ferree to Brig Gen J. H. Martindale, 20 Jul 1863 ("freely uttered"), and to Capt J. E. Montgomery, 22 Jul 1863 ("threatened"), both in Entry 646, Military District of Washington (MDW), LR, pt. 2, Polyonymous Successions of Cmds, RG 393, Rcds of U.S. Army Continental Cmds, NA; MDW, Special Order 172, 24 Jul 1863, Entry 649, MDW, Special Orders, pt. 2, RG 393, NA; (Washington) *Evening Star*, 2 June 1863; *New York Tribune*, 23 July 1863.

[37]*OR*, ser. 3, 3: 860–61, 882 (quotation).

[38]S. A. Duncan to My Dear Mother, 21 Sep 1863, Duncan-Jones Family Papers, New Hampshire Historical Society, Concord.

Maryland slaveholders, for human beings had declined sharply in value after the Emancipation Proclamation. At an estate sale in Rockville that May, the *Evening Star* noted, "negroes sold at remarkably low prices." Thirteen of them, "for the most part likely young boys," fetched a sum "less than one thousand dollars." Two months later, after Union victories at Gettysburg, Vicksburg, and Port Hudson, seven "likely, full-grown young negroes brought in all *one hundred and twenty-six dollars*, an average of only eighteen dollars a head," according to a report that appeared in several Northern newspapers. Toward the end of the year, a slaveholder in Charleston, West Virginia, offered to sell the Army five "stout active fine looking men. . . . I will take less than *one half* of . . . what they would have sold for previous to this rebellion." With federal armies moving forward all across the South, human property was becoming a poor financial risk and the Army was likely to offer owners the best bargain.[39]

Despite the War Department's attempt to impose order on black enlistments in the border states, voluntary enlistments soon declined. By that fall, as a result, recruiting in Maryland had become as rough and tumble a business as it was anywhere else in the South. Boarding oyster boats in Chesapeake Bay, 2d Lt. Joseph M. Califf and a squad of men from the 7th USCI "knocked at the cabin door— 'Captain—turn out your crew'—As soon as they came on deck, asked each one— '*Are you a slave*'—'*Yes sir*'—'Get into that boat.' . . . There was a fine fellow on board who said he was free," Califf wrote in his dairy.

> I left him, but when I had pushed off, one of the recruits told me he was a slave—I returned, but he still persisted and the Captain said he would take his oath, he was free. I left again, but the boys still said he was lying to me and told me his Master's name. I returned a second time, . . . jumped down into the hold, and heard something rattling among the oyster shells. I called for a light, when I found the fellow, crawled back on the oysters. I had him into my boat in short order. . . . During the day we got over 80 men.

Energetic recruiters brought in 1,372 men during November, filling Maryland's second and third black regiments, numbered the 7th and 9th USCIs.[40]

Enough opposition to black enlistment existed to make it a risky business for both officers and recruits. When free black farmers signed on, white neighbors sometimes removed the fence rails that surrounded their cornfields, allowing livestock to ravage the crops. The arrest of a civilian recruiting agent in Frederick was complicated by his lack of military status, which made it more difficult for military authorities to work for his release. Other agents faced threats of legal action and physical harm. Far more serious was the death in tobacco-producing Charles County of 2d Lt. Eben White, 7th USCI, at the hands of two slavehold-

---

[39] *OR*, ser. 3, 3: 861; (Washington) *Evening Star*, 12 May 1863 ("negroes sold"). The Associated Press story appeared in the *New York Times* and *Philadelphia Inquirer* on 31 July 1863 and the *New York Tribune* on 4 August 1863. J. T. Caldwell to Secretary of War, 10 Nov 1863 ("stout active") (C–339–CT–1863), Entry 360, RG 94, NA.

[40] J. M. Califf Diary typescript, 29 Nov 1863 (quotation), Historians files, U.S. Army Center of Military History; Rpt, Col W. Birney, 3 Dec 1863 (B–648–CT–1863, f/w B–40–CT–1863), Entry 360, RG 94, NA.

ers, father and son. The father called White a "Damned Nigger-stealing son of a bitch," and the son spat in his face; each fired at him, the father with a shotgun, the son with a revolver. Another shotgun blast took off the hat of Pvt. John W. Bantum, who accompanied White, and lodged a few birdshot pellets in his scalp. Bantum ran for his life and took news of White's death to his captain. The killers escaped to Virginia. When another officer of the recruiting detail rode forty miles to the Union garrison at Point Lookout to report the murder, the commanding officer's response expressed a frustration common to officers attempting to keep order in an occupied but hostile country: "Jesus Christ, we have fivety miles to Gaurd [*sic*] and but Three Hundred men to do it with."[41]

By the late fall of 1863, black regiments raised in Maryland and the North were serving either along the coast of Florida and South Carolina in the Department of the South or around the mouth of the James River in Virginia. Anticipating a Confederate move in Virginia, General Foster had withdrawn troops from his North Carolina garrisons in August to reinforce the federal military and naval bases at Norfolk and Portsmouth. On the north bank of the James, forays by enemy cavalry trying to gather conscripts for the Confederate Army could cause what the local Union commander called "a general skedaddle" among white residents of the peninsula between the James and the York. Such raids had to be deterred, if not stopped entirely. By the third week of November, the 4th USCI, the first of Maryland's black regiments, and the 6th USCI, the second black regiment organized at Philadelphia, were camped near Yorktown on the peninsula. At Portsmouth and Norfolk were the 1st USCI, which had arrived in September after a brief posting to North Carolina; the 5th, from Ohio; and the 10th, organized in Virginia. There, too, were the 2d and 3d North Carolina Colored, both regiments still striving to fill their companies. Wild's three North Carolina regiments would receive new designations—the 35th, 36th, and 37th USCIs—in the coming spring. Meanwhile, attempts to enlist black civilians who were already working for the Army brought officers of these regiments into conflict with local quartermasters and other staff officers, and they began to look outside Union lines for recruits.[42]

November brought another change to the Department of Virginia and North Carolina: Maj. Gen Benjamin F. Butler returned to Fort Monroe, where he had spent much of the first spring and summer of the war. He had been without an assignment since December 1862, when he left the Department of the Gulf. One of the most prominent pro-war Democrats and a possible vice-presidential or presidential nominee in the 1864 election, Butler was a man for whom the Lincoln administration had to find a place. He took command at Fort Monroe

---

[41] Col W. Birney to Adjutant General of the Army, 20 Aug 1863 (B–128–CT–1863, f/w B–40–CT–1863), and to Lt Col W. H. Chesebrough, 26 Aug 1863 (B–134–CT–1863, f/w B–40–CT–1863); W. T. Chambers to Col W. Birney, 22 Aug 1863 (C–134–CT–1863); Capt L. L. Weld to Col W. Birney, 23 Nov 1863 ("Damned") (B–505–CT–1863, f/w W–151–CT–1863); 1st Lt E. S. Edgerton to Col W. Birney, 25 Nov 1863 ("Jesus") (E–51–CT–1863, f/w W–151–CT–1863); all in Entry 360, RG 94, NA.

[42] *OR*, ser. 1, vol. 29, pt. 2, pp. 99, 104 (quotation). Capt H. F. H. Miller to Col A. G. Draper, 11 Sep 1863; 2d Lt J. N. North to Col A. G. Draper, 16 Sep 1863; both in 36th USCI, Regimental Books, RG 94, NA; NA M594, roll 205, 1st USCI, and roll 206, 4th, 5th, 6th, and 10th USCIs; Richard M. Reid, *Freedom for Themselves: North Carolina's Black Soldiers in the Civil War Era* (Chapel Hill: University of North Carolina Press, 2008), pp. 76, 123, 153.

on 11 November, and General Foster moved five days later to the Department of the Ohio, where he replaced General Burnside, whose irresolute leadership in eastern Tennessee was complicating Grant's effort to raise the Confederate siege of Chattanooga. Throughout the war, political considerations served to prolong the careers of generals who had small military ability but great influence in Washington.[43]

General Wild had managed by this time to return from South Carolina and was at Norfolk in charge of Colored Troops in the Department of Virginia and North Carolina. His command was still known as the African Brigade, although it had become a mixture of USCI (the 1st, 5th, and 10th) and North Carolina regiments and even included a detachment from the 55th Massachusetts. Uppermost in Wild's mind was the job of filling the ranks of his own incomplete North Carolina regiments. On 17 November, he ordered Col. Alonzo G. Draper and two companies of the 2d North Carolina Colored on a recruiting expedition. Each man was to carry forty rounds of ammunition and three days' rations. "All Africans, including men, women, and children, who may quit the plantations, and join your train . . . are to be protected," Wild ordered. "Should they bring any of their master's property with them, you are to protect that also, . . . for you are not bound to restore any such property. . . . When you return, march slowly, so as to allow the fugitives to keep up with you." White civilians found with firearms were to be arrested. "Should you be fired upon," Wild went on, "you will *at once* hang the man who fired. Should it be from a house, you will also *burn* the house immediately. . . . Guerrillas are not to be taken alive." Wild enjoined "strict discipline throughout. March in perfect order so as to make a good impression, and attract recruits."[44]

Draper set out that afternoon with 6 officers and 112 men—about two-fifths of the entire strength of the skeletal regiment—toward Princess Anne County, between Norfolk and the ocean. They marched southeast about ten miles and camped for the night. The next day, they began recruiting, "collecting at the same time, such colored men, women, and children, as chose to join our party." The expedition managed to move another nine miles along the road, but side trips to visit every crossroads settlement and plantation along the way equaled a march of more than twice that distance, Draper calculated. On the fourth day out, hearing that guerrillas were massing in the southern part of the county, the recruiting party made for the farm of one of their leaders, who was not at home. "Our rations being nearly exhausted, we . . . supplied ourselves liberally with fresh pork, poultry, and corn" in the guerrilla's absence, Draper reported, "taking his two teams for transportation, and also his servants, who desired to go, and who informed us that [he] and

---

[43]*OR*, ser. 1, vol. 29, pt. 2, p. 447; vol. 31, pt. 3, pp. 145–46, 163, 166. Benjamin F. Butler, *Autobiography and Personal Reminiscences of Major-General Benj. F. Butler* (Boston: A. M. Thayer, 1892), pp. 631–35, and *Private and Official Correspondence of Gen. Benjamin F. Butler During the Period of the Civil War*, 5 vols. ([Norwood, Mass.: Plimpton Press], 1917), 3: 348–49 (hereafter cited as *Butler Correspondence*). Chester G. Hearn, *When the Devil Came Down to Dixie: Ben Butler in New Orleans* (Baton Rouge: Louisiana State University Press, 1997), pp. 226–30.

[44]*OR*, ser. 1, vol. 29, pt. 2, pp. 290, 412, 619; 1st Lt H. W. Allen to Col A. G. Draper, 17 Nov 1863 (quotations), 36th USCI, Regimental Books, RG 94, NA. Wild's pleas for reassignment are in Col E. A. Wild to Maj T. M. Vincent, 4 Sep 1863 (W–159–CT–1863, f/w W–9–CT–1863), Entry 360, RG 94, NA, and Col E. A. Wild to Maj T. M. Vincent, 30 Sep 1863, Wild Papers.

forty men had that morning taken breakfast there and started off with the avowed purpose 'of giving the black soldiers hell.'"[45]

Draper's men marched warily, always with an advance guard and flankers in the woods that lined the road. Their practice had been to prepare supper late in the afternoon and move on to another site before camping for the night. To ward off a retaliatory attack after their raid on the guerrilla's farm, they surrounded the camp that night with a four-foot enclosure of fence rails (destroying several hundred yards of farmers' fences). The next morning, they moved on, repairing a bridge the guerrillas had destroyed and spending the night at a plantation, which they fortified with the expedition's wagon train. The women and children in the party took shelter from a heavy rainstorm in the slave quarters while the men slept in barns and sheds.

On 22 November, Draper decided to capture another notorious guerrilla leader who was supposed to be nearby and might pay a visit to his family. Leaving the wagons and the black civilians in care of an officer and twenty-five men, Draper took the remaining ninety-two by a circuitous route that brought them, soon after sunset, close to the guerrilla's house. A black resident of the neighborhood led them to a ford where they found a flatboat that allowed them to make part of the final approach by water. The guerrilla leader did not appear until noon the next day, and he surrendered only after the men of the 2d North Carolina Colored shot the hull of his boat full of holes. Also arrested in the course of the expedition were three Confederate soldiers on furlough and six civilians who were found with weapons. One of them was reputed to have murdered a Union soldier; another ran a Confederate post office. "Nineteen twentieths of all the citizens of Princess Anne appear to be the friends and allies of the guerrillas," Draper reported. "The blacks are the friends of the Union." About 475 of them accompanied the Union troops, "besides many who came in separately." The expedition returned to Norfolk on 26 November, having covered more than two hundred fifty miles in nine days.

Not all Union officers in southeastern Virginia approved of Draper's expedition, although it is not clear whether they opposed the enlistment of black soldiers in principle or were merely alienated by General Wild's prickly personality. For whatever reason, the colonel commanding the 98th New York, stationed at an outpost along the recruiters' route, sent a subordinate to interview farmers in the wake of what the colonel termed Draper's "marauding & plundering expedition." While the colonel's cover letter spoke of the recruiting party "having committed the grossest outrages, taking the last morsel of food from destitute families, grossly insulting defenceless women, . . . stealing horses & otherwise disgracing their colors & cause," the captain's report identified forty-eight farms that he visited along Draper's route. Twenty-three householders—nearly half of those queried—reported having lost no property

---

[45]Information in this and the following paragraphs is from Col A. G. Draper to Capt G. H. Johnston, 27 Nov 1863, 36th USCI, Regimental Books, RG 94, NA. Draper estimated his regiment's strength as "about three hundred officers and men." Col A. G. Draper to Maj R. S. Davis, 14 Nov 1863, 36th USCI, Entry 57C, RG 94, NA. The enemy force that Draper sought was one that even Confederate authorities referred to as guerrillas. *OR*, ser. 1, vol. 29, pt. 2, p. 818.

and suffered no insults from the troops. Only five complained of the recruiters' offensive language or threatening behavior.[46]

When the report reached Draper, he questioned the officers who had accompanied his expedition and received convincing accounts that exonerated them and their men. In replying to the accusations, Draper admitted that he had found one group of soldiers looting and had them tied up by the thumbs. He had met the colonel who complained of the recruiters' conduct only once, Draper said. That was while he had been questioning some white soldiers whom he found slaughtering poultry in a farmyard. They explained that the farmer's wife had refused to sell to Yankees; moreover, these soldiers belonged to the 98th New York, the accusing colonel's own regiment. Draper must have relished including that detail, for he saved it until the end of his letter and used it as the climax of the story. Whatever troops were responsible for the dead chickens, the fact that his own men had managed to remove food, draft animals, and wagons from barely half of the farms along their route should have disposed of the complaint that he had run a "marauding & plundering expedition." Draper's account of the expedition did not mention how many recruits it secured, but they probably numbered fewer than one hundred. While General Wild's order directed that the "able-bodied men" would go into the Army, adult males accounted for less than one-fifth of the 475 slaves who escaped and joined the column.[47]

Soon after Draper's return, Wild began organizing another expedition. "Our navigation on the Dismal Swamp Canal had been interrupted," cutting off federal bases in Virginia from those in North Carolina, "and the Union inhabitants [of coastal North Carolina have been] plundered by guerrillas," General Butler explained to Secretary of War Stanton. On 5 December, eleven hundred men of the 1st USCI and the 2d North Carolina Colored marched out of Portsmouth, heading south by way of the canal. At the same time, 530 men of the 5th USCI left Norfolk, along with another hundred from detachments of the 1st North Carolina Colored and the 55th Massachusetts. The two columns met at Camden Court House, North Carolina, and continued on to Elizabeth City, where two steamboats delivered supplies. "The guerrillas pestered us," reported Wild, who hanged the only one his troops caught alive. During the expedition, Union troops frequently exchanged shots with Confederate irregulars, killing or wounding at least thirteen of them while suffering twenty-two casualties of their own. Besides that, "many [were] taken sick by fatigue and exposure, 9 with small-pox, many with mumps." The nineteen-day expedition may have released as many as 2,500 slaves, but few recruits were among them. As Wild wrote, "the able-bodied negroes have had ample opportunities for escape heretofore, or have been run over into Dixie" to labor far beyond the reach of Union raiders. Butler praised the energy of Wild and his men but admitted that Wild may have "done his work . . . with too much stringency." He felt

---

[46]Lt Col F. F. Wead to Capt H. Stevens, 27 Nov 1863 (quotations); Capt J. Ebbs to Lt Col F. F. Wead, 24 Nov 1863; both in 36th USCI, Regimental Books, RG 94, NA. For Wild's disagreements with the commander of the Portsmouth garrison, see *OR*, ser. 1, vol. 29, pt. 2, pp. 542–43, 562.

[47]Col A. G. Draper to Maj R. S. Davis, 4 Jan 1864; 1st Lt H. W. Allen to Col A. G. Draper, 17 Nov 1863 ("able-bodied"); and Capt J. Ebbs to Lt Col F. F. Wead, 24 Nov 1863; all in 36th USCI, Regimental Books, RG 94, NA; Ebbs to Wead, 24 Nov 1863.

*In December 1863, Brig. Gen. Edward A. Wild led more than seventeen hundred men from five black regiments through northeastern North Carolina, freeing slaves, hunting Confederate guerrillas, and enlisting black soldiers. The greeting exchanged between a soldier and civilian (*right foreground*) indicates that two of Wild's regiments had been raised in North Carolina and knew the country and the people they were operating among.*

"much indebted to General Wild and his negro troops for what they have done, and . . . while some complaints are made of the action authorized by General Wild against the inhabitants and their property, yet all . . . agree that the negro soldiers made no unauthorized interferences with property or persons, and conducted themselves with propriety."[48]

Just a month after Wild's expedition returned, one of the participants wrote a letter that showed how different the war in Virginia had been during its first three years from the one waged elsewhere in the South. The nature of Virginia's agriculture—which concentrated on corn, wheat, tobacco, and livestock—meant that although slaves constituted more than one-third of the population in the Tidewater and Piedmont regions of the state, most of them lived in two- and three-family groups, rather than on extensive plantations. The contending armies moved repeat-

[48] *OR*, ser. 1, vol. 29, pt. 1, pp. 910–18 ("The guerrillas," p. 912; "many," p. 914; "the able-bodied," p. 913), and pt. 2, p. 596 ("Our navigation," "done his work"). Browning, *From Cape Charles to Cape Fear*, pp. 124–28; Wayne K. Durrill, *War of Another Kind: A Southern Community in the Great Rebellion* (New York: Oxford University Press, 1990), pp. 145–53.

edly back and forth across the same narrow stretch of country, concentrating on each other's movements rather than on sweeping raids that made it possible for hundreds of slaves to escape bondage. Each army usually operated within a few days' march of its base of supply and did not rely on foraging as often or as completely as did the western armies.[49]

The attitudes of 1st Lt. Elliott F. Grabill of the 5th USCI had been shaped by two years of such warfare. Grabill joined the Oberlin company of the 7th Ohio in June 1861 and served with it in the Shenandoah Valley Campaign the following spring and in all the campaigns of the Army of the Potomac through the summer of 1863, ending with the occupation of New York City after the Draft Riots. Appointed to the 5th USCI, he became the adjutant; Lt. Col. Giles W. Shurtleff, who had been his company commander in the 7th Ohio, became the regiment's second-in-command. Grabill came from one of the most fervently abolitionist towns in Ohio, and having served in the Army of the Potomac, he did not like what he saw during Wild's foray into North Carolina. When the 5th USCI moved across the James River and camped near Yorktown, Grabill condemned the "contraband stealing expedition" in a letter to his fiancée, calling it "a most disgraceful affair."

> In all my experience . . . of army life I have never before seen or taken part in an expedition of which I was so heartily disgusted. It was a grand thieving expedition. Our Colonel used every effort to prevent his command from indulging in this unsoldierly conduct; but when the other troops of the brigade were permitted almost unbridled license and the General himself gave the encouragement of example and even on several occasions gave directions to further . . . such robbery, it was difficult to promote the best of discipline in our regiment. . . . We were not organized into an armed force for this little petty stealing. It is subversive of military discipline and makes an army a mob with all its elements of evil. . . . In Gen. Wilds Brigade we were with N.C. Colored Vol[unteer]s—contrabands picked up . . . on the plantations not remarkable for intelligence or quickness of discernment and skilful performance of military duty. Nor were their officers of that culture and general knowledge which the Military Boards of Examination pass. They were appointed on the mere recommendation of Gen. Wild. *We* are appointed because we are proven worthy of appointment by our examination. *They* are *N.C.* Volunteers; *we* are *United States* Colored Troops.

Grabill and Col. Robert G. Shaw of the 54th Massachusetts were the same age (both born in 1837), shared abolitionist convictions, and had served for two years in Virginia in the body of troops that became the XII Corps of the Army of the Potomac, Grabill with the 7th Ohio, Shaw with the 2d Massachusetts. A ferocious

---

[49]Mark Grimsley, *The Hard Hand of War: Union Military Policy Toward Southern Civilians, 1861–1865* (New York: Cambridge University Press, 1995), pp. 105–11; Sam B. Hilliard, *Atlas of Antebellum Southern Agriculture* (Baton Rouge: Louisiana State University Press, 1984), pp. 34, 36, 49–56, 61–62, 66–67, 76; Lynda J. Morgan, *Emancipation in Virginia's Tobacco Belt, 1850–1870* (Athens: University of Georgia Press, 1992), pp. 19–22, 26–27, 36–43, 105–06, 111–13.

fighter like Wild caused the same revulsion in Grabill that Col. James Montgomery of the 2d South Carolina Colored had inspired earlier that year in Shaw.[50]

Grabill wrote his letter of complaint on the peninsula north of the James River. The 5th USCI had left Norfolk on 20 January and sailed to Yorktown, on the north side of the peninsula, where it reinforced the 4th and 6th. Those two regiments had arrived from Baltimore and Philadelphia in early October. Within a week of its arrival on the peninsula, the 4th USCI took part in a raid across the York River. Ten gunboats accompanied a transport that bore 744 officers and men of the regiment, 500 white cavalrymen and their horses, and 4 artillery pieces to Mathews County, on Chesapeake Bay. During the next four days, the expedition destroyed about one hundred fifty small craft that the raiders believed might be of use to Confederate irregulars and captured a herd of eighty cattle. The general commanding at Yorktown, who had not seen black soldiers before, reported favorably: "The negro infantry . . . marched 30 miles a day without a straggler or a complaint. . . . Not a fence rail was burned or a chicken stolen by them. They seem to be well controlled and their discipline, obedience, and cheerfulness, for new troops, is surprising, and has dispelled many of my prejudices."[51]

Colonel Duncan was pleased with his regiment, the 4th USCI. "The endurance, and the *patience* of the men, uttering no complaints, was remarkable," he told his mother. "On the homeward trip, which was severer than marching out, the men were shouting and singing most of the way, and upon reaching camp they fell to dancing jigs." Duncan thought well of his officers, too, "fine, accomplished gentlemen," and of the regimental chaplain, a minister of the African Methodist Episcopal Church, "Mr. [William H.] Hunter—an able and agreeable and hard working man—as black as the ace of spades." Constant fatigues left no time for drill, for the campsite at Yorktown was filthy after more than two years of occupation, first by Confederate and then by Union troops. The arrival of the 6th USCI spared Duncan's regiment some of that work. Among the officers of the 6th the colonel recognized two acquaintances from the 14th New Hampshire and soon developed a close working relationship with their regiment. A month later, after taking part in another expedition, Duncan's confidence was undiminished. "The colored soldiers develop remarkable qualities for marching, and I think will be equally brave in battle. . . . I am perfectly willing to risk my reputation with the negro soldiers."[52]

One of these was Sgt. Maj. Christian A. Fleetwood, a free-born, literate Baltimorean who had been among the first to show an interest in the new regiment that summer. After putting his affairs in order, the 23-year-old signed his enlistment papers on 11 August. Eight days later, the commanding officer appointed him the senior noncommissioned officer of the regiment. A neat appearance,

---

[50] E. F. Grabill to Dear Anna, 23 Jan 1864, E. F. Grabill Papers, Oberlin College (OC), Oberlin, Ohio; Gerald F. Linderman, *Embattled Courage: The Experience of Combat in the American Civil War* (New York: Free Press, 1987), pp. 180–85, 191–201, 211–15; James M. McPherson, *For Cause and Comrades: Why Men Fought in the Civil War* (New York: Oxford University Press, 1997), pp. 168–76; Charles F. Royster, *The Destructive War: William Tecumseh Sherman, Stonewall Jackson, and the Americans* (New York: Knopf, 1991), pp. 361–63.

[51] *OR*, ser. 1, vol. 29, pt. 1, pp. 205–07 ("The negro," p. 207); NA M594, roll 206, 4th, 5th, and 6th USCIs.

[52] S. A. Duncan to My Dear Mother, 18 Oct 1863 ("The endurance"), and to My Dear Friend, 20 Nov 1863 ("The colored"), both in Duncan-Jones Papers.

good manners, and legible handwriting were among the chief qualifications for a sergeant major. Fleetwood kept a diary, but the entries were always laconic. Of the raid to Mathews County, he recorded only "weather fine for marching." He and the other senior noncommissioned officers of the 4th USCI quickly established social relations with the noncommissioned staff of the 6th when that regiment reached Yorktown on 18 October. "Singing[,] dominoes & c.," Fleetwood wrote the next day, and eleven days later: "N.C.S. [Non Commissioned Staff] of 6th over to our social. Bully time." Close, informal acquaintance between senior noncommissioned officers within a brigade could foster cooperation in camp and in the field.[53]

Morale was high among the new arrivals. "There has sprung up quite a rivalry between this regiment & the fourth," 2d Lt. Robert N. Verplanck wrote to his sister from the 6th USCI camp,

> each one trying to outdo the other in drill, guard-mounting and sentinel duty; it will have very good effect on both, but we are somewhat ahead of the fourth at present on drill & can not learn a great deal from them. The men of our regiment are composed of [a] more intelligent class of men & learn quicker. They don't seem to mind working on the forts at all but rather to enjoy it for as they work they are in a continual gale of merriment & do twice as much as white troops.

Despite their skylarking, the men were incensed at the thoughtlessness of Congress in affording them only the same ten dollars a month, less a three-dollar deduction for clothing, that the government paid unskilled black laborers. When a paymaster arrived, the men refused to accept the money. "It does certainly seem hard that they should not get full pay when they were promised it by the men that enlisted them," Verplanck remarked in a letter to his mother,

> and for a drafted man it is certainly harder yet. The men are all hard up enough for money but they consider it a matter of pride and are willing to let the money go. One of our men said that if he was not to be put on an equality with white troops he was willing to serve the government for nothing. . . . I am sorry that they will not take the seven dollars as they will be without a good many little comforts which they would otherwise have, but at the same time I must say that I admire their spirit.[54]

In December, the 6th USCI took part in a raid, this one overland, forty miles from Yorktown to a Confederate cavalry camp at Charles City Court House, halfway to Richmond. The regiment, guarding ambulances and rations, stopped some miles short of the objective while the white cavalry pushed on through "a severe storm of wind and rain" and routed the enemy, capturing ninety men and fifty-five horses,

---

[53] Compiled Military Service Record (CMSR), Christian A. Fleetwood, NA Microfilm Pub M1820, CMSRs of Volunteer Union Soldiers Who Served in the U.S. Colored Troops, roll 36; C. A. Fleetwood Diary, 5 Oct 1863 ("weather"), 19 Oct 1863 ("Singing"), 27 Oct ("N.C.S."), C. A. Fleetwood Papers, Library of Congress; Longacre, *Regiment of Slaves*, pp. 13–14.

[54] R. N. Verplanck to Dear Jenny, 24 Oct 1863, and to Dear Mother, 26 Nov 1863, both in R. N. Verplanck Letters typescript, Poughkeepsie [N.Y.] Public Library.

Charles City Court House, on the road between Williamsburg and Richmond, in the spring of 1864

reported Brig. Gen. Isaac J. Wistar, commanding at Yorktown. The attackers suffered five wounded, whom they brought back to the place where the 6th USCI guarded the wagons. Again, Wistar wrote that the "colored infantry did what was required of them, . . . very severe duty (weather and roads considered). . . . Their position . . . , in readiness to receive and guard prisoners and horses, issue rations, attend to wounded, and do picket duty, on the return of the other exhausted troops, was found [to be] of extreme advantage." The gradual introduction to active service that the 4th and 6th USCIs received was more effective and cost fewer casualties than the abrupt and catastrophic immersion suffered earlier that year by other new black regiments in the fights at Fort Wagner and Milliken's Bend.[55]

The next operation undertaken by black soldiers stationed on the peninsula grew out of General Butler's other responsibility, besides commanding the department: acting as special agent for the exchange of prisoners of war. The agreement for paroling and exchanging prisoners that had operated during the first two years of the war entailed release of prisoners within weeks, or at least months, of capture, with the understanding that they would not return to the fighting until formal exchange for prisoners of equal rank held by the other side. This understanding broke down when the Confederate government refused to acknowledge the legitimacy of the Union's black soldiers and announced its intention to punish them under state laws that governed slave rebellions and their white officers under laws that punished inciting rebellions. In each case, the penalty was death.

---

[55] *OR*, ser. 1, vol. 29, pt. 1, pp. 974–77 ("a severe," p. 975; "colored infantry," p. 976).

Even when men and officers of the U.S. Colored Troops reached Confederate prisons, their captors refused to release them on the same terms that governed other soldiers. "This is the point on which the whole matter hinges," Stanton explained to Butler. "Exchanging man for man and officer for officer, with the exception the rebels make, is a substantial abandonment of the colored troops and their officers to their fate, and would be a shameful dishonor to the Government bound to protect them."[56]

Butler's Department of Virginia and North Carolina included the Union prisoner of war camp at Point Lookout, Maryland. In the fall of 1863, it housed more than 8,700 captive Confederates. A few days' march up the peninsula from Fort Monroe, the Confederacy's capital held more than 11,000 Union prisoners. About 6,300 of them lived on Belle Isle, an island in the James River a few hundred yards upstream from the city's waterfront. Tobacco warehouses held 5,350 others, including 1,044 officers in the notorious Libby Prison. On the day Butler took command at Fort Monroe, both sides agreed to release all medical officers they held prisoner. Until that spring, chaplains and medical officers had been exempt from imprisonment; but when Confederate authorities insisted on holding a federal surgeon for trial on criminal charges, the system froze, with hostage-taking on both sides quickly followed by retention of all captive medical personnel. When the first Union surgeons to be released arrived in Washington at the end of November, they reported that the number of deaths in all the Richmond prisons averaged fifty a day, or fifteen hundred a month. Inmates, they said, ate meat only every fourth day. The more usual daily ration was one pound of cornbread and a sweet potato.[57]

Northerners received this news with horror. "The only prospect now of relief to our prisoners is by our authorities acceding to the rebel terms for exchange," thus excluding black soldiers from the agreement, a *New York Times* editorialist wrote, "or by Gen. Meade's pushing on his victorious columns. If we do not speedily operate in one of these ways, Death must in a few brief months relieve the last of the . . . Union prisoners." Butler heard of the possibility of a raid on the Richmond prisons just days after he arrived at Fort Monroe. Almost simultaneously with the surgeons' release, General Wistar, commanding at Yorktown, sent Butler a proposal for a raid to free the prisoners, but two months passed before circumstances favored such a move.[58]

When the Confederate Army of Northern Virginia went into winter quarters, General Robert E. Lee turned his attention to the reduced Union garrisons in North Carolina. On 20 January 1864, he ordered Maj. Gen. George E. Pickett to move against New Berne with five infantry brigades drawn from Lee's army and the garrison at Petersburg, Virginia. This shift of about nine thousand men

---

[56] *OR*, ser. 2, 6: 528 (quotation), 711–12; Charles W. Sanders Jr., *In the Hands of the Enemy: Military Prisons of the Civil War* (Baton Rouge: Louisiana State University Press, 2005), pp. 146–47, 151–52.

[57] *OR*, ser. 2, 6: 501, 544, 566–75, 742; *New York Times*, 28 November 1863; *New York Tribune*, 1 December 1863. See *OR*, ser. 2, 6: 26–27, 35–36, 88–89, 109–10, 208–09, 381–82, 473–74, for an outline of the breakdown of the system for exchanging medical officers.

[58] *OR*, ser. 1, vol. 51, pt. 1, pp. 1282–84; *New York Times*, 28 November 1863 (quotation); *Butler Correspondence*, 3: 143–44.

Libby Prison in Richmond housed captured Union officers.

to North Carolina would leave a force of barely thirty-five hundred to defend the Confederate capital. Five days after Pickett received Lee's order and began gathering his brigades, a Union secret agent in Richmond sent Butler word that the Confederates intended to move the Union prisoners of war there to other sites. The agent urged an attack on the city by a force of at least forty thousand federal troops. Butler, with fewer than half that number scattered in five garrisons between Norfolk and Yorktown, decided to act anyway. "Now, or never, is the time to strike," he told Stanton.[59]

General Wistar's sixty-five hundred troops at Yorktown would carry out the raid. Butler began to beg for cavalry reinforcements the day after he heard from the agent in Richmond. While he waited for them, he sought to protect the secrecy of the operation by sending a coded message to an officer in Baltimore, asking him to buy a map of Richmond. "My sending to buy one would cause remark," he explained. Secrecy was important to Butler, for the proposed expedition had acquired more objectives since late November. Besides freeing the prisoners, the raiders intended to torch "public buildings, arsenals, Tredegar Iron Works, depots, railroad equipage, and commissary stores of the rebels," and, if possible, capture Jefferson Davis and members of his cabinet. Wistar did not share Butler's hopes for secrecy. "It will be impossible to disguise the significance of the subject of your telegram any longer," he wrote on 27 January when Butler

---

[59] *OR*, ser. 1, 33: 482, 519–20 ("Now, or never," p. 519), 1076, 1102–03. The estimate of the strength of Pickett's force is derived from statistics on pp. 1165, 1201, 1207, and 1247. *Butler Correspondence*, 3: 228–29, 319, 331–32, 381–83, 564.

told him of the impending arrival of more cavalry. In the end, the reinforcement amounted to only 281 men.[60]

As the plan stood on the eve of its execution, Wistar would move against Richmond with two brigades of infantry, about four thousand men, and one of cavalry, about twenty-two hundred, accompanied by two light batteries. One of the infantry brigades, commanded by Colonel Duncan, included the 4th, 5th, and 6th USCIs; the other, three white regiments. Companies from five cavalry regiments constituted the mounted brigade. The force was to move toward Richmond, the infantry securing a bridge across the Chickahominy River while the cavalry dashed the last twelve miles into the city. There, the raiders would divide into bands of between two hundred fifty and three hundred fifty men. The first of these was to attack the Confederate navy yard on the James River; the second group was to empty Libby Prison and, crossing the bridge to Belle Isle, free the prisoners there. This party would also cut telegraph lines out of the city and destroy several rail bridges and depots. The objective of the third party was Jefferson Davis' residence, where it was to arrest him. The fourth group, after cooperating with the second in freeing the prisoners, was to destroy the Confederacy's leading producer of heavy ordnance, the Tredegar Iron Works. The rest of the cavalry would act as a reserve, waiting in Capitol Square for the other groups to join it after they had done their work. They were to complete the entire project within three hours, before Confederate troops could arrive from their camp on the James River, about eight miles below the city.[61]

The black regiments left their camp near Yorktown about 2:00 p.m. on Friday, 5 February, and reached Williamsburg, a twelve-mile march, after dark. The men carried seventy rounds and six days' rations. "Very tired and footsore from new shoes," Sergeant Major Fleetwood wrote. "Slept by a bush." The next morning, an impromptu tour of the 1862 battlefield by some of the officers delayed the expedition's start. "Fooling and fizzling," Fleetwood complained in his diary, but he used the time to swap shoes with another soldier. The men were still in high spirits, as they had been since the day before, when they learned of the raid they were to carry out. The brigade moved forward late in the morning and did not stop at sunset. It was the night before the new moon and "very dark," Lieutenant Grabill told his fiancée. "Once when Colonel [James W.] Conine sent me forward with a message . . . I rode past the whole brigade and was quite advanced in another brigade before I learned my mistake. . . . I lay down a moment to wait for the column to get past some obstruction. When I woke up I was alone in the silent darkness, and it was some time before I caught up." It was hours past midnight when the brigade finally ended its thirty-mile march at New Kent Court House. "Completely broken down," Fleetwood wrote.[62]

While the infantry made camp, Wistar's cavalry pressed on through the moonless night. At the Chickahominy, they found the planks of the bridge removed. Daylight revealed a Confederate force waiting on the opposite shore and blocking nearby

---

[60]*OR*, ser. 1, 33: 429, 448, 482; vol. 51, pt. 1, p. 1285 ("public buildings"). *Butler Correspondence*, 3: 340 ("It will be"), 351 ("My sending"), 360. Butler gave the strength of the cavalry reinforcement as 380 in *OR*, ser. 1, 33: 439, but as 281 in two different messages in *Butler Correspondence*, 3: 345–46; the latter figure seems more likely.

[61]*OR*, ser. 1, 33: 146, 521–22.

[62]Ibid., pp. 146; NA M594, roll 206, 4th, 5th, and 6th USCIs; Fleetwood Diary, 5 ("Very tired") and 6 ("Fooling," "Completely") Feb 1864; E. F. Grabill to Friend Anna, 11 Feb 1864, Grabill Papers.

fords. With the element of surprise gone and the dash on Richmond forestalled, Wistar thought that an attempt to force a crossing would be pointless and began a return march. Duncan's command was back at Yorktown by Tuesday, 9 February, "entirely disgusted," Fleetwood recorded. The brigade had marched well over one hundred miles—one officer reckoned 125 miles—in less than five days. Several officers found the men's endurance noteworthy. "We performed the hardest marching that I have ever known a regiment to perform," wrote Colonel Shurtleff, who had campaigned in the mountains of West Virginia. "During the long march on Sat[urday] our regiment did not lose a straggler, while the white brigade left five hundred. Some of our boys threw away knapsacks, clothing and all, but they would not fall out."[63]

Butler learned quickly that the Confederates had known about the plan for days. A soldier in one of Wistar's mounted regiments, imprisoned on a murder charge, had escaped and fled to the nearest Confederate outpost, which passed him on to higher authorities. By 4 February, Jefferson Davis felt secure enough in his preparations for the raid to tell General Lee that he saw "no present necessity for your sending troops here." Even though the entire strength of the Richmond garrison was less than that of Wistar's force, all that was necessary to stop the expedition was to dismantle the bridge over the Chickahominy and let the raiders know that they were expected. More successful in freeing the prisoners was a tunnel dug by the inmates at Libby Prison, by which 109 of them were able to escape on 9 February, the day Wistar's force returned to Yorktown. Fifty-nine eventually reached Union lines.[64]

Late that month, Union troops mounted another raid on the Richmond prisons, this one led by a division commander in the Army of the Potomac, Brig. Gen. Judson Kilpatrick. By this time, Duncan's brigade had acquired a fourth regiment, one that Duncan and Col. John W. Ames of the 6th USCI had asked for. The 22d USCI was organizing at Camp William Penn under the command of Col. Joseph B. Kiddoo, former major of the 6th, "an officer of great merit and wide experience, and one whom we would be proud to have . . . with us in the Brigade," Ames and Duncan told General Butler. Kiddoo himself was eager to come to Butler's department, the two colonels said; he felt "that in no other Dept . . . will the experiment of colored troops be carried out on so grand a scale." There was a large element of truth in this flattery, for at this point in the war Butler had thrown himself wholeheartedly into the U.S. Colored Troops project. General Wistar approved the colonels' request, and the 22d USCI reached Yorktown on 13 February.[65]

The new regiment took up the routine of guard duty and fatigues at once, before the men had time to build adequate quarters. "Have lost five men here," Assistant Surgeon Charles G. G. Merrill told his father. "It has been very cold &

Grabill's letter attests to the men's morale, as does a letter signed "Hard Cracker" that appeared in the *Anglo-African*, 20 February 1864, quoted in Noah A. Trudeau, *Like Men of War: Black Troops in the Civil War, 1862–1865* (Boston: Little, Brown, 1998), p. 203. "Hard Cracker" wrote that the column reached New Kent Court House at 1:30 a.m.; Fleetwood, at 2:30; Grabill, at 3:30.

[63]*OR*, ser. 1, 33: 145–48; NA M594, roll 206, 6th USCI; Fleetwood Diary, 7 Feb 1864 ("entirely disgusted"); G. W. Shurtleff to My dear little girl, 11 Feb 1864 ("We performed"), G. W. Shurtleff Papers, OC.

[64]*OR*, ser. 1, 33: 144, 1076, 1148, 1157–58; vol. 51, pt. 2, p. 818 ("no present"). Frank E. Moran, "Colonel Rose's Tunnel at Libby Prison," *Century Magazine* 35 (1888): 770–90.

[65]*OR*, ser. 1, 33: 170–74; Col S. A. Duncan et al. to Maj Gen B. F. Butler, 3 Feb 1864, 22d USCI, Entry 57C, RG 94, NA; NA M594, roll 208, 22d USCI; William G. Robertson, "From the Crater to

rainy, . . . & the men on guard had to stay out all night in the pelting storms—then they would be taken sick, come to the hospital, lie down on the ground, (before we had our bunks built) and die from pure debility & exhaustion." On 26 February, the 22d USCI moved from Yorktown twelve miles up the peninsula to Williamsburg.[66]

Kilpatrick's force, more than thirty-five hundred horsemen, was to enter Richmond from the north, free the prisoners, and head east for the Union garrison at Williamsburg. When Butler heard of the raid, he sent a mixed force of infantry and cavalry forward to New Kent Court House, a small crossroads settlement of the type that was common in Virginia counties, "to aid in case of disaster, to receive prisoners, or to cover retreat," as he told General Halleck on 29 February. Duncan's brigade began its march the next afternoon. About dark, rain began to fall and continued, mixed with snow, through the night. "Slipping, stumbling, falling," Fleetwood recorded in his diary. "Nothing but mud and slush." At midnight, when the column halted for a few hours' rest, "the men with nothing but a blanket bivouacked on the cold damp ground," Surgeon James O. Moore of the 22d USCI wrote. They moved on at 3:30, stopping about dawn for a breakfast of coffee and hardtack. By the time they made camp west of the courthouse that afternoon, they had covered more than forty miles in less than twenty-four hours.[67]

The march took them through country where the white residents seemed terrified of black soldiers. As the column splashed through Williamsburg, 2d Lt. Joseph J. Scroggs of the 5th USCI saw no one in the streets. "Afraid of the 'nigger' I suppose," he noted in his diary. "I went up to a house," Assistant Surgeon Merrill wrote home, "& got a good breakfast of corn bread and milk. They were glad to be protected. The way cows, pigs & hens suffered was a caution." Surgeon Moore agreed with his assistant about the troops' foraging but added that freeing "about twenty" slaves who joined the column was more important than supplementing the troops' rations or punishing disloyal Virginians.[68]

On the morning of 3 March, six miles west of New Kent Court House, Butler's force met Kilpatrick's raiders, who had turned away from Richmond without entering the city. About five hundred men from the city's Confederate garrison and some 750 cavalry and artillery from the Army of Northern Virginia had managed to inflict 340 casualties on the Union force—nearly 10 percent of its total strength. All that remained for Duncan's brigade to do was to cover the horsemen's retreat. "Gen. Wistar has found out that these men can march well & carry anything that is put on them," Lieutenant Verplanck wrote, "so he keeps us following after cavalry

New Market Heights: A Tale of Two Divisions," in *Black Soldiers in Blue*, ed. Smith, pp. 169–99, esp. pp. 169–71, 194–95.

[66] NA M594, roll 208, 22d USCI; C. G. G. Merrill to Dear Father, 28 Feb 1864, C. G. G. Merrill Papers typescript, Sterling Library, Yale University, New Haven, Conn.

[67] *OR*, ser. 1, 33: 183, 193, 198, 615, 618 ("to aid"); Fleetwood Diary, 1 Mar 1864; J. O. Moore to My Dearest Lizzie, 5 Mar 1864, J. O. Moore Papers, DU. Estimates of the distance marched vary from forty-two to forty-five miles. *OR*, ser. 1, 33: 198; NA M594, roll 208, 4th, 5th, and 6th USCIs; J. O. Scroggs Diary typescript, 2 Mar 1864, MHI; R. N. Verplanck to Dear Mother, 13 Mar 1864, Verplanck Letters.

[68] C. G. G. Merrill to My dear Father, 5 Mar 1864, Merrill Papers; Moore to My Dearest Lizzie, 5 Mar 1864; Scroggs Diary, 1 (quotation), 2, and 3 Mar 1864.

& keeping up with them in their raids which I begin to think are of very little account . . . as far as ending the war is concerned."[69]

Throughout the rest of March, Verplanck must have found Union operations in Tidewater Virginia equally unsatisfactory. The day after Duncan's brigade returned to Yorktown, the 4th, 5th, and 6th USCIs boarded transports and crossed the James estuary to Portsmouth. From there, passenger cars took the 5th eight miles south toward the Great Dismal Swamp to guard the railroad against an expected raid by Confederate cavalry. "The products of this region are pine, peanuts & sweet potatoes," wrote Lieutenant Scroggs, who had farmed in Ohio before the war and found little to admire in the South. "No doubt a favorite resort of musquitoes in their season. Truly a delectable country." The threat of a raid seemed to evaporate once the troops arrived. On 9 March, railroad cars and transport ships bore them back to Yorktown.[70]

There, they did not disembark. Instead, the 22d USCI joined them on the transports and all went up the York River to land at a tobacco warehouse on the opposite shore, just above where the Mattaponi River joins the Pamunkey to form the York. The point of the expedition was to punish Confederate sympathizers in the region, who, General Kilpatrick claimed, had ambushed part of his cavalry during the failed raid on Richmond ten days earlier. General Butler called it a matter of "clearing out land pirates and other guerrillas." Kilpatrick was to lead about eleven hundred mounted men and six guns from Gloucester Point along the north shore of the York River, driving before them two regiments of Confederate cavalry that were supposed to be in the neighborhood, along with any irregulars. The infantry from Yorktown, landing upriver, was to block the Confederate retreat.[71]

The transports steamed up the York, sometimes running aground, and did not reach the landing until well after dark. When they finally arrived, the infantry saw "the whole horizon . . . ablaze with the camp fires of men, who at that time ought to have been twenty-five miles below," Assistant Surgeon Merrill wrote. Kilpatrick's men had moved forward before the troops from Yorktown had even arrived. Poor communications between Kilpatrick and Wistar plagued the expedition during the next three days, until rain and rising streams brought operations to a halt. The cavalry managed to burn public buildings and warehouses at King and Queen Court House and took some fifty prisoners, most of them civilians.[72]

More serious than the failure of the expedition was the relaxation of discipline that some officers saw in their men as they moved around the country in small groups. "Kilpatrick's men are in no sort of discipline & leave desolation wherever they go, robbing defenseless men & women & in general are as lawless a set of devils as they could well be," Lieutenant Verplanck complained. In the 22d USCI, Merrill wrote, Colonel Kiddoo "told the boys not to steal hens, chickens, turkeys, geese or anything of the sort, but if any of the above-mentioned called them 'damned niggers' to knock 'em right over the head. Pretty soon up runs a

---

[69]*OR*, ser. 1, 33: 170–71, 183–88, 202, 205, 207, 210, 213; Verplanck to Dear Mother, 13 Mar 1864.

[70]NA M594, roll 206, 4th and 6th USCIs; Scroggs Diary, 6 (quotation), 7, and 9 Mar 1864.

[71]*OR*, ser. 1, 33: 240–41, 662, 671 (quotation).

[72]Ibid., pp. 243–44; C. G. G. Merrill to Dear Father, 13 Mar 1864, Merrill Papers.

drummer boy with a dead goose: the Colonel asks him if he called him a 'damned nigger'; the boy says no, but that he hissed at him & so he hit him with his sword." Stories like this were common all over the occupied South; if the incident actually occurred, the men of the 22d USCI were learning fast. "Disloyal" livestock was fair game wherever Union armies went.[73]

Officers of Duncan's brigade seemed to think that their men's foraging went beyond acceptable bounds. Merrill saw an incident that revealed why the men may have yielded to their emotions: "I found some of our boys hacking away at a sort of cross T set up in the ground, with two pegs projecting from the upper crossbeams," he told his father:

> It was a whipping post & they were in a perfect fury as they cut it down. It seemed as though they were cutting at an animate enemy & revenging upon him the accumulated wrongs of two centuries. As fast as one tired, another took the axe & soon the infernal machine . . . came to the ground—never again to be used for such a purpose—it was burned on the spot where it fell—I send you a piece of it.

Despite the men's legitimate grievances, officers began to grow tired of the season of small expeditions and looked forward to a major campaign. Lieutenant Verplanck thought that raiding was "work unworthy of the true soldier." During a march through Mathews County later in the month, one officer of the 4th USCI found it necessary to order one of his men to shoot another to interrupt his looting. Lt. Col. George Rogers of that regiment reported that "one of the effects of such an expedition [is] to destroy in a week that discipline which it is the work of months to establish." Curiously, no commanding officer in the brigade seems to have issued a regimental order on the subject, which was also of continual concern to officers of veteran white troops.[74]

Elsewhere around the Chesapeake, great changes were under way. Ulysses S. Grant, promoted to lieutenant general in early March, had come east to take charge of all federal armies. "Now if he will . . . not become contaminated by his nearness to Washington all will yet go well with us & we can look to the overthrow of the rebellion before winter," Lieutenant Verplanck wrote. General Burnside had also come east, relieved from command of the Army of the Ohio but still leading the IX Corps. He reported directly to Grant, since he was senior to Maj. Gen. George G. Meade, who commanded the Army of the Potomac. (Burnside, one of that army's unfortunate former commanders, had marched it to disaster at Fredericksburg in December 1862.) An all-black division was building in the IX Corps, as six recently organized regiments—the 19th, 30th, and 39th USCIs, all from Maryland; the

---

[73] Verplanck to Dear Mother, 13 Mar 1864; Merrill to Dear Father, 13 Mar 1864; Bell I. Wiley, *The Life of Billy Yank: The Common Soldier of the Union* (Indianapolis: Bobbs-Merrill, 1952), p. 236.

[74] *OR*, ser. 1, 33: 256 ("one of"); Merrill to Dear Father, 13 Mar 1864; R. N. Verplanck to Dear Mother, 2 Apr 1864, Verplanck Letters. On white troops, see orders to keep the men "well in hand" during Sherman's march through Georgia in *OR*, ser. 1, 44: 452–63, 480–85, 489–90, 498, 504–05, 513 (quotation). Books of the regiments in Duncan's brigade contain no orders about discipline dating from the spring of 1864. 4th, 5th, and 6th USCIs, Regimental Books, RG 94, NA.

27th, from Ohio; the 43d, from Pennsylvania; and the 30th Connecticut—reported to corps headquarters at Annapolis, then moved through Washington to camp near Manassas, Virginia. Regiments from Illinois, Indiana, and New York were en route to join them.[75]

Late in April, after months of debate, the U.S. Senate approved an Army appropriation for the coming fiscal year. The act included a section that awarded black soldiers military pay, rather than an unskilled laborer's wage. It did not move forward to House approval and presidential signature until 15 June, but soldiers felt relieved in late April that it had gotten through the Senate. In the 5th USCI, Lieutenant Scroggs had thought about resigning if an "inexcusably dilatory" Congress did not provide for equal pay. He noted the news with satisfaction. Lieutenant Verplanck was also elated. "The Government has at last determined to give us our rights," he wrote home, "and I am as happy as a clam at high water."[76]

On 22 April, Brig. Gen. Edward A. Hinks arrived at Fort Monroe to take command of the newly formed 3d Division, XVIII Corps, which was to include the black regiments in Butler's command. Duncan's brigade at Yorktown struck its tents and moved down the peninsula in what Lieutenant Scroggs called, after the constant activity of previous months, "an easy march of twenty miles." Besides the 4th, 5th, and 6th USCIs, Hinks' division included the 1st, 10th, and 22d in a brigade commanded by General Wild, as well as Battery B, 2d U.S. Colored Artillery. All busied themselves in preparation for the spring campaign. For Assistant Surgeon Merrill, this meant combing out the unfit men. "There are plenty of them in this regiment," he told his father, "men who ought not to have been enlisted and who will have to be discharged, after . . . helping fill the [draft] quotas of towns & cities in Penn[sylvani]a." Merrill was not the only surgeon to complain about recruits who joined their regiments without having undergone a physical examination at their place of enlistment.[77]

Word of the Union defeat at Fort Pillow and the massacre of black soldiers there reached Fort Monroe four days before General Hinks took command of his new division on 22 April. Newspapers were still detailing those events the next week, when reports arrived that black soldiers and white Unionists had been "taken out and shot" after the surrender of the federal garrison at Plymouth, North Carolina. Soldiers at Fort Monroe making final campaign preparations bore this news in mind when writing to their next of kin. One of Hinks' staff officers told his wife:

> Everything is in readiness. . . . The next ten days are to witness a fearful struggle. If we succeed, it will be the beginning of better things. We *must* succeed, failure for *us* is death or worse. This Division will never surrender, for officers and men expect no mercy from the foe. . . . [A]lthough we know that some of us

---

[75] *OR*, ser. 1, 33: 1046; Verplanck to Dear Mother, 2 Apr 1864.

[76] *OR*, ser. 3, 4: 448; Scroggs Diary, 30 Mar (quotation) and 25 Apr 1864; R. N. Verplanck to Dear Mother, 22 Apr 1864, Verplanck Papers; Edwin S. Redkey, ed., *A Grand Army of Black Men: Letters from African-American Soldiers in the Union Army, 1861–1865* (New York: Cambridge University Press, 1992), pp. 229–48.

[77] *OR*, ser. 1, 33: 1055; Scroggs Diary, 20 Apr 1864 ("an easy"); C. G. G. Merrill to Dear Father, 2 May 1864 ("There are"), Merrill Papers. For another complaint about unexamined recruits, see J. Fee to Capt C. C. Pom[e]roy, 24 Mar 1864, 29th USCI, Entry 57C, RG 94, NA.

will in all probability never come back again, . . . I have yet to see the first long face or hear the first regret.

Soon after Hinks arrived, Lieutenant Verplanck left the 6th USCI to join his staff. One evening, Verplanck remarked to the other officers that "he felt just as he used to [as] a boy when his folks were going to take him to the theater." To his mother, he wrote: "We are organizing our division as fast as possible . . . and then the first large body of black troops will go in together and will make an impression I believe such as has never been felt before."[78]

---

[78] S. A. Carter to My own darling wife, 1 May 1864 ("Everything is," "he felt"), S. A. Carter Papers, MHI; R. N. Verplanck to Dear Mother, 26 Apr 1864 ("We are"), Verplanck Letters; *New York Tribune*, 26 April 1864 ("taken out"). The most exhaustive study of events at Plymouth is Weymouth T. Jordan Jr. and Gerald W. Thomas, "Massacre at Plymouth: April 20, 1864," *North Carolina Historical Review* 73 (1995): 125–93.

CHAPTER 11

VIRGINIA, MAY–OCTOBER 1864

From before sunup until after sundown, soldiers at Fort Monroe during the early days of May 1864 busied themselves preparing for the spring campaign. In the 4th United States Colored Infantry (USCI), Sgt. Maj. Christian A. Fleetwood interrupted his paperwork to spend a morning at target practice. "Fair shooting," he thought, "not extra." Officers marveled at orders that restricted their baggage to fifteen pounds: "as well none as so little," wrote 2d Lt. Joseph J. Scroggs of the 5th USCI. "The bustle of preparation goes on vigorously and soon both men and officers will be divested of everything except their accoutrements and the clothes on their backs." Also in the 5th, Lt. Col. Giles W. Shurtleff noted that orders assigned each regiment only one wagon to haul its gear; officers had to store their roomy wall tents and sleep in pairs in shelter tents like the men. "This seems hard," he told his fiancée, "but I am rejoiced to see the commanding general go about his work as if he meant to effect his object. . . . It will cause us great inconvenience and some hardship and exposure; but what matter if we can more speedily accomplish the work to be done?"[1]

The new commanding general of all Union armies, Lt. Gen. Ulysses S. Grant, had arrived in Washington that March from west of the Appalachians, where federal troops had spent the previous two years advancing continually into Confederate territory. While they satisfied day-to-day needs by stripping hostile country of food for soldiers and animals, they moved ever farther from the depots that supplied their clothing and munitions, neither of which could be replenished on the spot, hence their habit of traveling light. Grant brought that method of warfare east, for he intended to put all the Union's forces in motion. Maj. Gen. Nathaniel P. Banks, in Louisiana, would move up the Red River toward Texas. At the same time, Maj. Gen. William T. Sherman would strike south from Chattanooga: "Joe Johnston's [Confederate] army his objective point and the heart of Georgia his ultimate aim," as Grant explained it to Maj. Gen. George G. Meade, who commanded the Army of the Potomac. "Lee's army will be your objective point," Grant continued. "Wherever Lee goes, there you will go also." Grant issued orders that limited the number

[1] C. A. Fleetwood Diary, 2 and 3 (quotation) May 1864, C. A. Fleetwood Papers, Library of Congress (LC); J. J. Scroggs Diary, 1 ("as well") and 2 ("The bustle") May 1864, U.S. Army Military History Institute (MHI), Carlisle, Pa.; G. W. Shurtleff to Dearest Mary, 2 May 1864, G. W. Shurtleff Papers, Oberlin College (OC), Oberlin, Ohio.

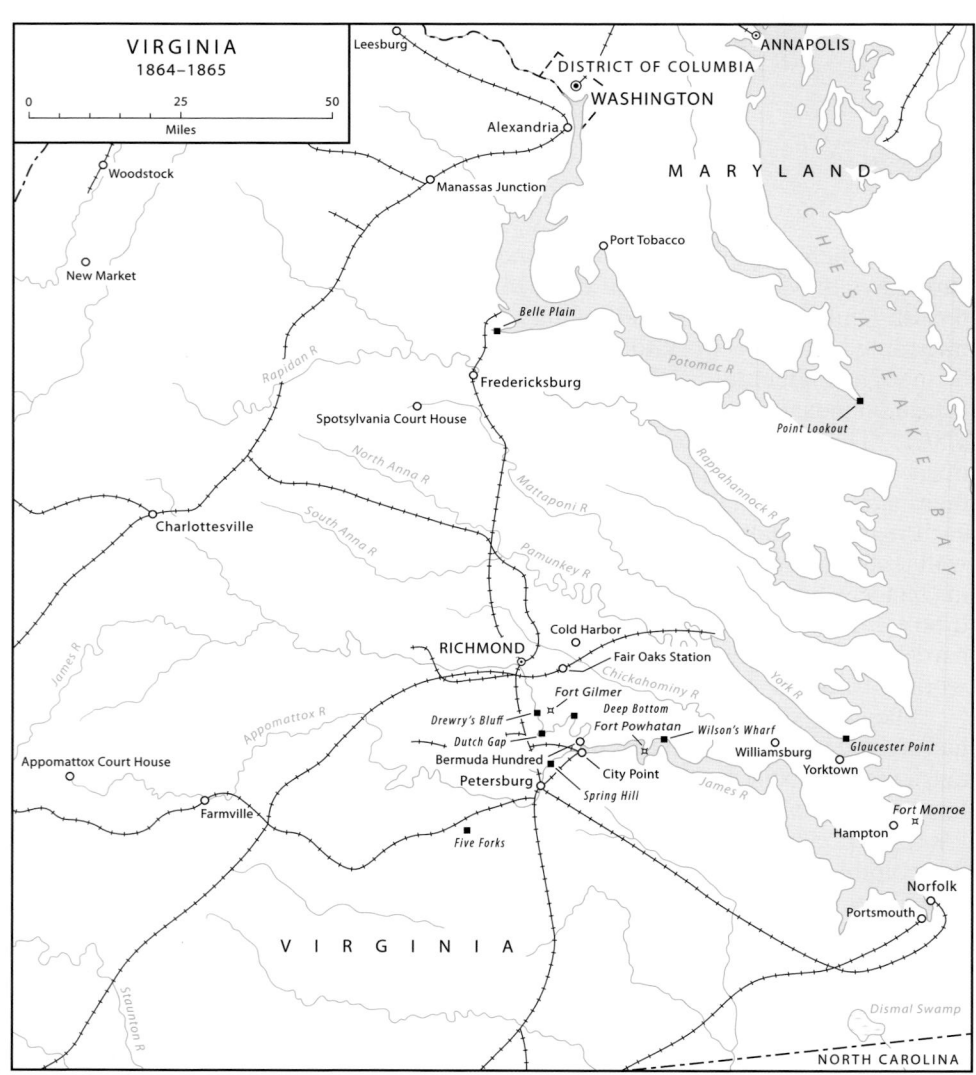

VIRGINIA
1864–1865

0   25   50
Miles

Leesburg

ANNAPOLIS

DISTRICT OF COLUMBIA

WASHINGTON

Alexandria

M A R Y L A N D

Woodstock

Manassas Junction

Port Tobacco

New Market

Belle Plain

Potomac R

Fredericksburg

Rapidan R

Spotsylvania Court House

Point Lookout

North Anna R

South Anna R

Mattaponi R

Rappahannock R

Charlottesville

Pamunkey R

C H E S A P E A K E   B A Y

Cold Harbor

RICHMOND

Fair Oaks Station

Chickahominy R

James R

Fort Gilmer

Deep Bottom

York R

Drewry's Bluff

Fort Powhatan

Wilson's Wharf

Appomattox R

Dutch Gap

Bermuda Hundred

City Point

Williamsburg

Gloucester Point

Yorktown

Appomattox Court House

Petersburg

Spring Hill

James R

Fort Monroe

Farmville

Five Forks

Hampton

V I R G I N I A

Norfolk

Portsmouth

Staunton R

Dismal Swamp

NORTH CAROLINA

Map 8

of baggage wagons allowed to each regiment and to each brigade, division, and corps headquarters. Meade's army needed its wheeled transport to haul rations and ammunition through the familiar, fought-over Virginia countryside between Washington and Richmond (*see Map 8*).[2]

While the Union's main armies were in motion, a fourth, led by Maj. Gen. Benjamin F. Butler, would advance from Fort Monroe up the James River toward Richmond. Grant himself visited Fort Monroe in early April to discuss the move, for Butler was a national figure, one of the nation's leading War Democrats—certainly the most prominent one in uniform—and too important to ignore in forming plans for the spring campaign. The two generals were in substantial agreement about an attack up the James, but Grant thought it best to confirm the results of their conference with a letter marked Confidential. Concentration of force was essential, he told Butler. As the Army of the Potomac advanced south toward the Army of Northern Virginia and Butler's Army of the James moved northwest toward the Confederate capital, the two would draw closer together and eventually coordinate their operations. Butler's army would receive a reinforcement of ten thousand men drawn from Union forces in South Carolina, Grant said. "All I want is all the troops in the field that can be got in for the Spring Campaign," he explained in a letter to Sherman. Since Butler had served only in administrative posts, Grant assigned Maj. Gen. William F. Smith, a former corps commander in the Army of the Potomac, to direct command of operations. Grant, who had graduated from West Point two years ahead of Smith, thought him "a very able officer, [but] obstinate."[3]

Butler's force included a division of six USCI regiments—the 1st, 4th, 5th, 6th, 10th, and 22d, along with Battery B, 2d United States Colored Artillery (USCA). Other black troops on the peninsula between the James and York Rivers included the 1st and 2d United States Colored Cavalries (USCCs), at Williamsburg. Some seventy miles to the north, but still within Butler's command, the 36th USCI guarded prisoners of war at Point Lookout, Maryland.[4]

Brig. Gen. Edward W. Hinks commanded the six regiments that accompanied the main force. A Massachusetts officer who had served with Butler in Maryland during the first weeks of the war, Hinks had received a severe wound while leading his regiment at Antietam in 1862 and had spent more than a year afterward in administrative posts. When he saw that Butler was to take charge of the Department of Virginia and North Carolina in the fall of 1863, he wrote to the general, requesting a field command. Hinks arrived at Fort Monroe in late April, just as news of the Fort Pillow massacre reached the East. Within a week, he asked to replace his division's "unreliable" weapons, which might, he said, "answer for troops who will be well cared for if they fall into [enemy] hands, but to troops who cannot afford to be beaten, and will not be taken, the best arms should be given that the country can afford." The 1st USCI regiment, its colonel complained, carried

---

[2] *The War of the Rebellion: A Compilation of the Official Records of the Union and Confederate Armies*, 70 vols. in 128 (Washington, D.C.: Government Printing Office, 1880–1901), ser. 1, 33: 827–29, 919–21 (quotation, p. 828) (hereafter cited as *OR*).

[3] *OR*, ser. 1, vol. 32, pt. 3, p. 305 ("All I want"); 33: 794–95 (Confidential); vol. 36, pt. 3, p. 43 ("a very able"). William G. Robertson, *Back Door to Richmond: The Bermuda Hundred Campaign, April–June 1864* (Newark: University of Delaware Press, 1987), pp. 18–24.

[4] *OR*, ser. 1, 33: 1055, 1057.

"second-hand Harper's Ferry smooth bore Muskets (cal .69)," a model that pre-dated the Mexican War. He asked for "the new improved Springfield muskets" to replace them. The regiment's correspondence gives no clear idea of when it received new weapons, but a few letters and orders that summer indicate that authorities took between six and eight months to act on the colonel's request. Whatever weapons Hinks' regiments carried, by early summer each was able to furnish men to form a company of divisional sharpshooters.[5]

The other large concentration of black soldiers in the Chesapeake region was the 4th Division of Maj. Gen. Ambrose E. Burnside's IX Corps. At the end of April 1864, it included the 19th, 23d, 27th, 30th, and 39th USCIs; five companies of the 43d; and four companies of the 30th Connecticut (Colored). Other regiments were on the way to join it, from as far away as Illinois and Indiana. Its commander was Brig. Gen. Edward Ferrero, who had served with Burnside since the North Carolina Campaign. In September 1862, he had led a brigade in the charge across Burnside's Bridge at Antietam. Ferrero had commanded a white division in the IX Corps for eight months before becoming the 4th Division's first commanding general on 19 April 1864.

All of the regiments in the 4th Division were of recent date. The senior one, the 19th USCI, had completed its organization in mid-January 1864; the 39th, only on the last day of March. The 43d USCI and the 30th Connecticut were still recruiting, sending companies to the front as men arrived to fill the ranks. After mustering in at army camps in Connecticut, Maryland, Ohio, and Pennsylvania, the regiments moved one by one to Annapolis, where Burnside had his headquarters. On 25 April, they marched through Washington to take station across the Potomac, near Manassas.[6]

Whether from a belief that military movements should be kept secret—as if nineteen thousand men passing a reviewing stand could be concealed—or out of racial spite, Washington newspapers nearly ignored the IX Corps. The *Evening Star* identified the troops as Burnside's only after other papers mentioned their identity. The *National Republican* confined itself to a sentence: "A large number of troops, infantry, artillery and cavalry, white and black, all in excellent condition, was reviewed in this city by the President to-day." The *Constitutional Union* devoted more space to mocking Republican patronage appointees than it did to describing the march itself: "As the column of colored soldiers passed down Fourteenth street, last evening, the office holders, from the Treasury and other places, whose number are legion, and who lined the

---

[5]Ibid., pp. 947, 1020–21 ("unreliable"); Col J. H. Holman to Maj C. W. Foster, 23 Dec 1863 ("second-hand"), 1st United States Colored Infantry (USCI), Regimental Books, Record Group (RG) 94, Rcds of the Adjutant General's Office, National Archives (NA). NA Microfilm Pub M594, Compiled Rcds Showing Svc of Mil Units in Volunteer Union Organizations, roll 205, 1st USCI; roll 206, 5th and 6th USCIs; roll 207, 22d USCI. *Private and Official Correspondence of Gen. Benjamin F. Butler During the Period of the Civil War*, 5 vols. ([Norwood, Mass.: Plimpton Press], 1917), 3: 136 (hereafter cited as *Butler Correspondence*). Examples of 1st USCI ordnance correspondence are Regimental Order 106, 28 Jun 1864, and Maj H. S. Perkins to Maj R. S. Davis, 23 Aug 1864, both in 1st USCI, Regimental Books, RG 94, NA.

[6]OR, ser. 1, 33: 1042. NA M594, roll 207, 19th USCI; roll 208, 30th USCI; roll 209, 43d USCI. Frederick H. Dyer, *A Compendium of the War of the Rebellion* (New York: Thomas Yoseloff, 1959 [1909]), pp. 116, 248–50.

Much of the District of Columbia was still rural during the Civil War. This photograph shows cattle grazing on the south bank of the Washington City Canal. The south portico of the White House is in the center of the picture, with the Treasury building to the east.

streets, set up a shout of exultation, at the picture before them. They had no shout for the white soldiers—no, none. Their hurras are for miscegenation and the new order of affairs." The writer may have thought the Treasury Department worth mentioning by name because its secretary, Salmon P. Chase, was the most outspoken abolitionist in the cabinet; but opponents of the administration were not the only spectators that day who were skeptical of the black troops. Elizabeth Blair Lee, sister of the postmaster general and wife of a naval officer, wrote: "I watched Genl Burnsides Corps for an hour today—counted five full negro Regts . . . & two full Regts of real soldiers. . . . [T]he Negroes were clad in new clothing marched well—every Regt had a good band of music—& they looked as well as Negroes can look—but Oh how different our Saxons looked in old war worn clothing—with their torn flags—but such noble looking men." Capt. Albert Rogall of the 27th USCI, which had left Ohio just seven days earlier, remembered the day differently. "Secesh white spitting at us," he wrote in his diary.[7]

The 19th USCI arrived in Virginia to find its campsite a charred ruin. The regiment's predecessors "were awful mad to think they were to be relieved by Colored Soldiers & they go to the front," Capt. James H. Rickard wrote; "they burned all their huts which they had all fixed up so we have got to make new ones. . . . Such is the feeling against Col. Troops." Rickard may well have

[7]*OR*, ser. 1, 33: 1045; (Washington) *Evening Star*, 26 April 1864; (Washington) *National Republican*, 25 April 1864 ("A large number"); (Washington) *Constitutional Union*, 27 April 1864 ("As the column"); Virginia J. Laas, ed., *Wartime Washington: The Civil War Letters of Elizabeth Blair Lee* (Urbana: University of Illinois Press, 1991), p. 372 ("I watched"); A. Rogall Diary, 26 Apr 1864 ("Secesh white"), A. Rogall Papers, Ohio Historical Society, Columbus.

Belle Plain, one of the river landings that served the Army of the Potomac's movement toward Richmond in May 1864. Wagons carried wounded from the fighting to waiting vessels and bore supplies back to the advancing troops.

been wrong; not every slight that the Colored Troops suffered was the result of racial prejudice. Union troops across the South burned their verminous winter quarters when the time came to leave them, although some pessimists in the often-defeated Army of the Potomac cautioned against the practice. "Leave things as they are," one veteran recalled hearing them say that spring. "We may want them before snow flies."[8]

The men of the 4th Division barely had time to improve their campsites, for the Army of the Potomac moved south on 4 May. The position of the IX Corps was awkward, for Burnside was senior to the army commander, Meade, yet led a smaller force. Grant solved the problem by assigning Burnside's corps to guard the roads in the wake of Meade's advance, from Manassas "as far south as we want to hold it." Within the corps, the 4th Division would guard wagon trains. The forty-three hundred wagons and eight hundred thirty-five ambulances that belonged to the Army of the Potomac required more than twenty-seven thousand horses and mules to draw them. If they had formed in single file, Grant estimated, the line that resulted would have been more than

---

[8] J. H. Rickard [no salutation], 29 Apr 1864, J. H. Rickard Papers, American Antiquarian Society (AAS), Worcester, Mass.; Frank Wilkeson, *Recollections of a Private Soldier in the Army of the Potomac* (New York: G. P. Putnam's Sons, 1886), p. 41 ("Leave things"); Charles W. Wills, *Army Life of an Illinois Soldier . . . Letters and Diaries of the Late Charles W. Wills* (Washington, D.C.: Globe Printing, 1906), p. 231; W. Springer Menge and J. August Shimrak, eds., *The Civil War Notebook of Daniel Chisholm: A Chronicle of Daily Life in the Union Army, 1864–1865* (New York: Orion Books, 1989), p. 12.

sixty miles long and would have stretched "from the Rapidan [River] to Richmond." This never happened, of course. Grant's movement plan called for an advance toward different fords of the Rapidan several miles apart. Besides, it was necessary to keep many wagons in reserve in order to deliver a constant flow of supplies to the army while wagons returning to base brought back men wounded in the fighting. One train that carried wounded from Spotsylvania Court House to Belle Plain, a landing on the Potomac River, included 256 ambulances and 164 wagons and was four miles long. Guarding these trains, the task assigned to Ferrero's 4th Division, was no trifling chore. During the course of the campaign, federal commanders reported that Confederate horsemen were active everywhere from Belle Plain to Fort Monroe.[9]

Two days of travel took Ferrero's command as far as the Rapidan River. Once across, the division passed through the Chancellorsville battlefield of 1863. Col. Delavan Bates of the 30th USCI saw "the ground . . . covered with bones of last year's dead." Also present were the corpses of more than three thousand soldiers, Union and Confederate, who had died during the previous three days. On 9 May, Captain Rogall recorded, "weather cloudy, gloomy, dusty, smell of dead bodies decaying from the last fight." For eleven days after Ferrero's division crossed the Rapidan, the sound of gunfire accompanied its march; not until 17 May did Rogall mention hearing songbirds in the woods. That day, the 30th USCI camped near where Bates had been taken prisoner during the Union debacle at Chancellorsville exactly fifty-four weeks earlier, while he was serving as a lieutenant in the 121st New York. That he had returned to his regiment from captivity within three weeks, well in time to take part in the battle of Gettysburg at the beginning of July 1863, showed how smoothly prisoner exchange worked during the middle part of the war, before the Confederate government mounted obstructions in response to federal enlistment of black soldiers.[10]

The gunfire that Captain Rogall recorded in his diary for eleven consecutive days was the sound of Grant's successive attempts to bring Lee's army to battle in the open, where greater federal numbers could decide the result. Lee's response, after the fighting near Wilderness Tavern on 5 May, was to fight from behind hastily prepared fortifications, forcing Grant to attack. Seventeen days' fighting, first in the Wilderness, then around Spotsylvania Court House, cost the Army of the Potomac more than thirty-seven thousand casualties—slightly more than 30 percent of its strength at the beginning of the month. Grant spent the rest of May edging southeast in recurring attempts to get around the Confederates' right flank, moving ever closer to Richmond. As he did so, his base of supplies moved down the Potomac from landing to landing, with wagons rolling "over narrow roads, through a densely wooded country," as Grant described it, "with a lack of wharves at each new base from which

        [9]*OR*, ser. 1, 33: 828 ("as far as"); vol. 36, pt. 1, pp. 230, 277, and pt. 2, pp. 779, 828, 856. Ulysses S. Grant, *Personal Memoirs of U. S. Grant,* 2 vols. (New York: Charles L. Webster, 1886), 2: 188 ("from the Rapidan"). Six horses or mules were usually sufficient to draw an army wagon. Reports do not state whether the ambulances required teams of two, four, or six animals.
        [10]*OR*, ser. 1, vol. 36, pt. 1, pp. 133, 987–91; NA M594, roll 208, 30th USCI; D. Bates to Father, 15 May (quotation) and 26 May 1863, both in D. Bates Letters, Historians Files, U.S. Army Center of Military History; Rogall Diary, 9 (quotation), 12, and 17 May 1864.

The 1864 battles of the Wilderness and Spotsylvania Court House took place on much of the same ground that the opposing armies had fought over just one year before. Marching through the woods, Union troops encountered many grisly relics of the earlier fighting.

In the spring of 1864, the Union advance on Richmond gave slaves like these in Hanover County, just north of the city, a chance at freedom.

to conveniently discharge vessels." During the month, by Grant's account, Ferrero's division had "but little difficulty" protecting the trains. Ferrero's reports claimed two attacks by "superior forces," both of which his troops repelled, but Rogall dismissed both incidents as the work of guerrillas. Two men of the 23d USCI suffered wounds. "The colored troops stand everything well that we have had to go through yet," Colonel Bates wrote. "How they will fight remains to be seen."[11]

The spring campaign was barely two weeks old on 19 May, when the Army of the Potomac finally penetrated beyond the site of its 1863 defeat. On that day, the first escaped slaves began to reach federal lines. The Union advance of 1864 did not lead to the release of hundreds of slaves at a time, as sometimes happened elsewhere in the South. The Tidewater and Piedmont counties of Virginia lacked the large plantations that characterized the cotton, rice, and sugar regions of the Confederacy. North of the Rapidan, moreover, the country had been the scene of continual fighting during the previous two years, and the bolder and more ingenious slaves had already found ways to flee bondage. In addition, many slaveholders had taken steps to remove their human property from the path of the federal army. Nevertheless, the turmoil created by the spring offensive offered the remaining black civilians another chance. Singly and in groups they made their way to the Union soldiers, often bringing intelligence of Confederate movements and troop strength that the liberating invaders found useful. Their numbers increased as the army reached the North Anna River, about twenty-five miles from Richmond. "Contraband[s] . . . flocking around us," Captain Rogall remarked at the end of the month.[12]

On 4 May, the day the Army of the Potomac crossed the Rapidan, General Butler's troops at Fort Monroe boarded transports for the voyage toward Richmond. "Start your forces on the night of the 4th," Grant had prompted Butler just six days earlier, "so as to be as far up the James River as you can get by daylight the morning of the 5th, and push from that time with all your might for the accomplishment of the object before you." Despite Grant's urging, the embarkation went slowly, especially that of the troops recently arrived from South Carolina, who did not finish loading until nearly midnight. While the newcomers struggled aboard, Hinks' division waited. "Embarked the Division and hauled into the Stream," Sergeant Major Fleetwood noted in his diary. "Lay there all night." In broad daylight the next morning, the fleet's departure resembled a regatta more than a landing force. "Crowd on all steam, and hurry up," Butler ordered Hinks, as his own boat, the *Greyhound*, chugged in and out among the other vessels. Upstream, Confederates on shore counted more than seventy-five gunboats and transports in the flotilla. The transports carried about thirty thousand soldiers. Hinks' division formed the vanguard, dropping off the 1st and 22d USCIs with four twelve-pounders of Battery B, 2d USCA, to seize Wilson's Wharf

[11] *OR*, ser. 1, 33: 1036, 1045; vol. 36, pt. 1, pp. 23 ("over narrow"), 986 ("superior forces"), 1070–71. Rogall Diary, 15 and 19 May 1864; D. Bates to Father, 15 May 1864, Bates Letters.

[12] *OR*, ser. 1, vol. 36, pt. 2, pp. 541, 918–19, and pt. 3, pp. 51, 84, 100, 121, 148; Rogall Diary, 29 May 1864; Ira Berlin et al., eds., *The Destruction of Slavery* (New York: Cambridge University Press, 1985), pp. 59, 69–70, and *The Wartime Genesis of Free Labor: The Upper South* (New York: Cambridge University Press, 1993), pp. 86, 110; Lynda J. Morgan, *Emancipation in Virginia's Tobacco Belt, 1850–1870* (Athens: University of Georgia Press, 1992), pp. 19–22, 111–12; Steven E. Tripp, *Yankee Town, Southern City: Race and Class Relations in Civil War Lynchburg* (New York: New York University Press, 1997), pp. 144–45.

*This view of General Butler's progress up the James River on 5 May 1864 captures
the bustling scene as two Union ironclads guard side-wheel transports and tugs and
rowboats ply back and forth between the flotilla and Fort Powhatan, on the bluff above
the water.*

on the north bank, several miles beyond the mouth of the Chickahominy River. Farther along, the 10th and the recently arrived 37th USCIs with four guns of Battery
M, 3d New York Light Artillery, landed at Fort Powhatan on the opposite shore. The
three remaining regiments of Col. Samuel A. Duncan's brigade and two guns of
each battery disembarked at City Point, on the south bank of the James, just below
the mouth of the Appomattox River and about seven miles from Petersburg, the rail
junction that connected Virginia with the states south of it.[13]

Having split Hinks' division into three parts, Butler landed the rest of the
expedition, some thirty thousand white troops organized in five divisions, on
a peninsula called Bermuda Hundred just across the Appomattox from City
Point. Not until the day after the landing did he push one of those brigades west
toward the Richmond and Petersburg Railroad. Four more brigades followed
the next day. By that time, the Confederates had been able to add twenty-six
hundred men to the garrisons of the two cities. Five days after the Union landing, reinforcements that arrived by rail from North Carolina doubled the defenders' numbers to more than fourteen thousand.[14]

Here began the collapse of the campaign. Rather than move at once up the
James toward Richmond against a Confederate garrison that numbered barely
seven thousand at first, Butler entertained the idea of moving on Petersburg.

---

[13]*OR*, ser. 1, 33: 1009 ("Start your"), 1053; vol. 36, pt. 2, pp. 165, 398, 432 ("Crowd on"), 956;
NA M594, roll 205, 2d U.S. Colored Artillery; Fleetwood Diary, 4 May 1864. Robertson, *Back Door
to Richmond*, pp. 57–60, conveys a vivid sense of the festive air on the morning of 5 May.

[14]Union strength from *OR*, ser. 1, 33: 1053–56, and Robertson, *Back Door to Richmond*, p.
59. Confederate returns from the Department of Richmond, 20 Apr 1864, show 7,265 officers and

Dispatches from Maj. Gen. Henry W. Halleck in Washington led him to believe that Grant had defeated Lee's army, which, he understood, was withdrawing toward Richmond. Inclined to wait for Grant's approach but unable to decide in the meantime whether to move on Petersburg or Richmond, Butler quarreled with his two corps commanders, Smith and Maj. Gen. Quincy A. Gillmore, who led the X Corps, made up of the recent arrivals from South Carolina. By the time the three generals managed to move four divisions toward Richmond, enough Confederates were present to stop them on 16 May at Drewry's Bluff, a height on the James River about eight miles north of the Union trenches at Bermuda Hundred. Butler's first venture at active operations had collapsed in less than two weeks.[15]

While the major portion of the campaign flagged, the men of Hinks' division began to entrench the places where they went ashore and to take part in what one company commander called "scouts and skirmishes too numerous to mention." These began the day after their arrival, when a detachment of Company B, 1st USCI, seized one of the Confederate signal stations that had reported the fleet's progress upriver, and continued with the capture of others later in the week. On 9 May, Colonel Duncan led the 4th and 6th USCIs on a reconnaissance from City Point about halfway to Petersburg. "Lay still all of the cool of the day," Sergeant Major Fleetwood recorded. "Started in the heat. . . . Countermarched and tried another road. [T]urned back[.] Arrived at City Point 11 eve." Three days later, Hinks took the same regiments and his four pieces of artillery to occupy Spring Hill, a site four miles up the Appomattox River. During the first two weeks of the occupation of City Point, the troops endured several attacks of a sort that one company commander dismissed with: "Rebs visited our pickets [with] no loss to us." Fire from gunboats in the river helped to disperse the attackers. Despite the troops' constant activity, disappointment hung in the air. "I am afraid there has been a fine opportunity . . . lost here by inexcusable tardiness," Lieutenant Scroggs wrote on 10 May. "We lay here four days without advancing a step and then on making a feeble attempt yesterday we found them prepared for us. Very courteous in us not to take them unawares."[16]

As soon as black residents along the James River saw that the newcomers intended to stay, they began escaping to the Union positions. Many were too old or too young to work, but those who were able found employment quickly with the expedition's quartermaster or as servants. They brought with them the kind of local knowledge that federal armies found invaluable throughout the South. "I have

---

men present for duty. *OR*, ser. 1, 33: 1299; Mark Grimsley, *And Keep Moving On: The Virginia Campaign, May–June 1864* (Lincoln: University of Nebraska Press, 2002), pp. 120–25.

[15] *OR*, ser. 1, 33: 1299; Grimsley, *And Keep Moving On*, pp. 126–28; Edward G. Longacre, *Army of Amateurs: General Benjamin F. Butler and the Army of the James, 1863–1865* (Mechanicsburg, Pa.: Stackpole Books, 1997), pp. 87–100; James M. McPherson, *Battle Cry of Freedom: The Civil War Era* (New York: Oxford University Press, 1988), pp. 722–24; Robertson, *Back Door to Richmond*, pp. 250–52.

[16] *OR*, ser. 1, vol. 36, pt. 2, pp. 22–24, 31, 165–66. NA M594, roll 205, 1st USCI; roll 206, 5th USCI ("scouts and skirmishes"), 6th USCI ("Rebs visited"). Fleetwood Diary, 9 May 1864; Scroggs Diary, 10 May 1864. For other criticism of Butler, see E. F. Grabill to My Darling Beloved, 28 May 1864, E. F. Grabill Papers, OC; G. W. Shurtleff to Dearest Mary, 12 May 1864, Shurtleff Papers; R. N. Verplanck to Dear Mother, 20 May 1864, R. N. Verplanck Letters typescript, Poughkeepsie [N.Y.] Public Library; Robertson, *Back Door to Richmond*, p. 251.

got a first rate fellow who left Petersburg [three days ago] & who knows every road & by path from here [to] there," 2d Lt. Robert N. Verplanck told his mother. Other slaves waited for Union troops to come to them. Assistant Surgeon James O. Moore accompanied a lieutenant and twenty enlisted men of the 22d USCI on a foraging expedition. "We halted at a house," he wrote, "or rather I should have said that a slave came in [and] wanted us to . . . get his Father Mother & six bros and sisters" from the farm of former President John Tyler. "We took all the slaves & ordered them to take a reasonable amount of clothing bedding &c whereupon they walked very deliberately into the best room took the best bed best pillows. . . . I never saw a happier lot [of] human beings than were those slaves when they were on their way to freedom."[17]

At least once, escaped slaves had the chance to accuse one of their former masters of mistreatment and to punish him for it. On 10 May, a planter named William H. Clopton, whose estate had been home to twenty-five slaves, came to Wilson's Wharf to take the oath of allegiance. "He gave a flattering account of his former treatment of his slaves," Surgeon Moore wrote. "In fact he considered himself [more] a public benefactor than otherwise." When some of his former slaves who had taken refuge in the Union camp accused him of whipping them for their reluctance to work on Confederate fortifications, Brig. Gen. Edward A. Wild had Clopton seized and tied. Sgt. George W. Hatton of the 1st USCI described the scene for readers of the *Christian Recorder*, the weekly newspaper of the African Methodist Episcopal Church:

> William Harris, a soldier in our regiment . . . , who was acquainted with the gentleman, and who used to belong to him, was called upon to undress him. . . . Mr. Harris played his part conspicuously, bringing the blood from his loins at every stroke, and not forgetting to remind the gentleman of the days gone by. After giving him some fifteen or twenty well-directed strokes, the ladies, one after another, came up and gave him a like number, to remind him that they were no longer his.

Reporting the incident to General Hinks, Wild told him, "I wish it to be distinctly understood . . . that I shall do the same thing again under similar circumstances." Hinks' response was to convene a general court-martial and prefer charges against Wild, for he would not "countenance . . . any Conduct on the part of my command not in accordance with the principles recognized for . . . modern warfare between Civilized Nations." Although the court convicted Wild, General Butler set the verdict aside, for Hinks had failed to follow a department order directing that a majority of U.S. Colored Troops officers sit on courts trying cases that involved black soldiers or their officers.[18]

Two weeks after Clopton's flogging, the garrison at Wilson's Wharf had to hold the post against an assault. On the afternoon of 24 May, Confederates appeared in the wood nearby, "evidently," Wild reported, "with the design of rushing

---

[17]R. N. Verplanck to Dear Mother, 12 May and 2 Jun ("I have got") 1864, Verplanck Letters; J. O. Moore to My Dearest Lizzie, 12 May 1864, J. O. Moore Papers, Duke University (DU), Durham, N.C.

[18]Moore to My Dearest Lizzie, 12 May 1864. Hinks and Wild quoted in Berlin et al., *Destruction of Slavery*, pp. 96–97; Hatton quoted in Edwin S. Redkey, ed., *A Grand Army of Black Men: Letters from African-American Soldiers in the Union Army, 1861–1865* (New York: Cambridge University Press, 1992), pp. 95–96. Butler's General Order 46, 5 Dec 1863, is in *OR*, ser. 3, 3: 1139–44; the

Many escaped slaves preferred to work as laborers rather than enlist as soldiers.
Employment with Union troops at Bermuda Hundred made it easy for these civilians to
come by greatcoats and other items of military uniform.

in upon us suddenly." An unknown number of attackers—perhaps as many as three thousand—fired on the Union trenches, the steamboat landing, and a nearby signal station for ninety minutes before their commander, Maj. Gen. Fitzhugh Lee, sent a flag of truce to the defenders with a demand for their surrender. If they submitted, he said, he would treat them as prisoners of war; if they did not, he could not guarantee that any of them would survive the final assault. Wild, commanding eleven hundred officers and men of the 1st and 10th USCIs, refused the offer and firing resumed, joined in by a Union gunboat in the river. The only Confederate attempt to storm the Union position left about two dozen bodies so close to the trenches that the attackers had to leave them behind when they withdrew during the night. As to other Confederate casualties, Wild could only guess. His own amounted to twenty-two officers and men killed, wounded, and missing.[19]

A month after Hinks took command, Lieutenant Verplanck wrote that the general "is becoming more & more attached to his division and has the greatest confidence in their fighting qualities. Indeed they have already shown themselves here in several little affairs." One of these affairs, Verplanck went on, occurred near City Point on 18 May, when pickets of the 4th and 6th USCI, although outnumbered by

clause governing the composition of courts-martial for U.S. Colored Troops enlisted men and officers is on p. 1144.

[19]*OR*, ser. 1, vol. 36, pt. 2, pp. 269–72 (quotation, p. 270). NA M594, roll 205, 1st USCI; roll 206, 10th USCI.

Confederate troops, "soon put them to fly, but not however without the loss of two killed & five wounded, but the rebels were awfully used up. These fellows fight awfully in earnest and will have to [be] restrained from treating the rebels as they were treated at Fort Pillow."[20]

The stalemate in front of Petersburg continued, punctuated by small fights. "Our regiment and the Fourth Colored made a sortie . . . to drive back some rebs who were approaching a little too close for good manners," 1st Lt. Elliott F. Grabill of the 5th USCI wrote on 1 June. "The movement was executed most splendidly. I never saw soldiers maneuver better than those two regiments did yesterday in the face of the enemy." While Grabill wrote, he could hear cannon fire from the Army of the Potomac, north of the James River. As Meade's force drew nearer to Richmond, General Smith led the two white divisions of the XVIII Corps across the river to assist them. General Hinks and the Colored Division stayed behind at City Point, Spring Hill, Fort Powhatan, and Wilson's Wharf.[21]

During the second week of the month, General Gillmore commanded the remainder of the Army of the James in an unsuccessful operation against Petersburg that caused recriminations between him and Butler. Hinks, who had been continually shuffling his regiments between their four bases as the occasion demanded, had some thirteen hundred men of the 1st and 6th USCIs on hand to contribute to Gillmore's attack. The two regiments moved forward during the night. As daylight came on 9 June, both Hinks and the brigadier who was to command the main body of troops viewed the Confederate works and judged them too strong for a successful assault. Gillmore agreed and withdrew the troops. When Butler received a report of the operation, he called it "unfortunate and ill-conducted," and relieved Gillmore of command.[22]

Meanwhile, Grant's Overland Campaign had ground to a halt northeast of Richmond, with the loss of more than five thousand men at Cold Harbor on the morning of 3 June. The commanding general returned General Smith and his two divisions of the XVIII Corps to Butler. As their leading regiments embarked once more for Bermuda Hundred on 13 June, another attack on Petersburg was in the works. Unable to break the Army of Northern Virginia by a frontal attack, Grant intended to capture the rail center and cut off his enemy's source of supplies. To accomplish this, he would bring the Army of the Potomac south of the James River to join Butler's Army of the James.[23]

Smith did not learn that he was to lead the attack until Butler told him, just as he and his troops reached Bermuda Hundred. The II Corps would follow Smith across the James by boat to take part in the operation while the rest of the army waited on the north bank for its engineers to complete a 1,240-foot pontoon bridge. The first of Smith's divisions arrived on the south bank late in the morning of 14 June. The second landed at 8:00 p.m., half an hour after sunset. Hinks, whose division of Smith's corps had never left its posts along the river, received his orders

---

[20] NA M594, roll 206, 4th and 6th USCIs; Verplanck to Dear Mother, 20 May 1864.

[21] E. F. Grabill to My Own Precious One, 1 Jun 1864, Grabill Papers; Robertson, *Back Door to Richmond*, pp. 240–41.

[22] *OR*, ser. 1, vol. 36, pt. 2, pp. 275 ("unfortunate"), 295, 306–08; NA M594, roll 205, 1st USCI, and roll 206, 6th USCI.

[23] *OR*, ser. 1, 33: 1053–55; vol. 36, pt. 1, p. 180; vol. 40, pt. 2, pp. 3, 17, 20. Brooks D. Simpson, *Ulysses S. Grant: Triumph over Adversity, 1822–1865* (Boston: Houghton Mifflin, 2000), pp. 335–37.

some time on 14 June, the day before the attack. He and his men were to take part in the assault and capture the Confederate works northeast of Petersburg. Three regiments of dismounted cavalry—the 1st and 2d USCCs and the 5th Massachusetts (Colored)—would augment the division's two brigades, although some of the regiments were absent at other posts along the river. With one battery—six guns— of artillery for each brigade, the troops present numbered 3,747 officers and men. They would act in concert with General Smith's divisions, which were en route to join them. "I do not want Petersburg visited, however," Grant warned Butler, "unless it is held, nor an attempt to take it unless you feel a reasonable degree of confidence of success. I think troops should take nothing with them except what they carry, depending upon supplies being sent after the place is secured."[24]

Any written instructions that Butler may have given Smith seem to have disappeared from the official record. Hinks' orders from Butler were merely to meet Smith at a landing on the south bank of the Appomattox River "at 2 a.m. precisely." He would receive further orders then. None of the surviving reports of Smith, the corps commander; of his divisional generals, Hinks and two others; or of six brigade commanders, convey any idea of the purpose of the attack. All agree that the troops awoke well before dawn, began moving south from the river, and then turned west toward the Confederate defensive line around Petersburg.[25]

Hinks met Smith and learned that his division was to follow the cavalry forward. The men of the division were up an hour or two before dawn and waited under arms until after sunrise for the twenty-five hundred troopers to pass them. Hinks was confident, even cocky: if Butler would return all the detachments of his division, he had written a few days earlier, "I will place Petersburg or my position [as divisional commander] at your disposal." When the cavalry came under fire from a Confederate battery about 7:00 a.m., the dismounted skirmishers and horse holders continued to move south, leaving a few men to keep an eye on the battery until Hinks' infantry arrived.[26]

The battery—observers disagreed as to the number of guns—fired from six hundred yards away, beyond woods full of fallen trees, vines, and brush. Hinks formed two lines: Colonel Duncan's brigade took the lead with the 5th USCI on the right and the 22d, 4th, and 6th USCIs to the left. Behind them came the 1st USCI with half of the dismounted 5th Massachusetts Cavalry on its left. The dismounted troopers caused some delay because the cavalry's dismounted drill had no commands for forming an infantry line of battle. Many of the troopers, besides, had been in the army for less than three months. At last, the lines plunged into what Colonel Duncan called "the blindness of the wood."[27]

First to emerge were three companies of the 4th USCI. The men set off with a yell for the enemy position. While their officers tried to restore order and Confederate artillerymen adjusted their guns to cover this new menace, the 5th Massachusetts Cavalry in the rear began firing into the troops just ahead of them—the

---

[24]*OR*, ser. 1, vol. 36, pt. 1, pp. 25–26, and pt. 3, p. 755 (quotation); vol. 40, pt. 1, pp. 236–37, 298, 720–21. Longacre, *Army of Amateurs*, pp. 141–45.

[25]*OR*, ser. 1, vol. 40, pt. 1, pp. 705, 714–15, 717, 719–26, 728–30 (quotation, p. 720); vol. 51, pt. 1, pp. 265–69, 1252–65. Grimsley, *And Keep Moving On*, pp. 227–28.

[26]*OR*, ser. 1, vol. 40, pt. 1, p. 721; vol. 51, pt. 1, pp. 263, 265. *Butler Correspondence*, 4: 361 (quotation).

[27]*OR*, ser. 1, vol. 40, pt. 1, p. 721 (Hinks counted a total of six guns in two positions), 725 (Kautz, three guns); vol. 51, pt. 1, pp. 265 (Duncan, four guns), 266 (quotation).

4th USCI and those companies of the 6th that were not lost in the woods. "Cut up badly. Regt broke and retreated," Sergeant Major Fleetwood wrote in his diary. Before the left of the Union line could recover itself, Col. Joseph B. Kiddoo on the right seized the opportunity to lead the 22d USCI forward, followed by the 5th USCI, while the enemy gunners' attention was elsewhere. While these two regiments crossed the three or four hundred yards between the edge of the woods and the Confederate position, the gunners finally noticed their approach and rode off with all but one of their twelve-pounders. Men of the 22d turned the remaining gun around and sent a few shots after them.[28]

By the time the entire division assembled, the hour was 9:00 a.m. Caught at the edge of the woods between the Confederate artillery in front and the 5th Massachusetts Cavalry in rear, the 4th USCI had lost one hundred twenty officers and men killed and wounded. The column moved on. Hinks put the 5th USCI in the lead as skirmishers, the men advancing in pairs to cover each other, one always having his rifle loaded. An hour's march brought them in sight of the enemy again. In front lay the eastern end of Petersburg's defenses, a ring of fifty-five artillery positions. Those directly in front of the skirmishers appeared as Batteries 7 through 11 on Union maps. Fire from their guns kept Hinks' two batteries from taking a position from which they could shell the Confederate line. About 1:00 p.m., Hinks relieved the 5th USCIs from the advance and moved the 4th, 22d, and 1st USCIs forward five hundred yards across a field to where a low crest offered partial protection from enemy fire. There they lay for five hours. "The situation was anything

---

[28] *OR*, ser. 1, vol. 40, pt. 1, pp. 721 (Hinks estimated the distance as 400 yards), 724; vol. 51, pt. 1, pp. 265 (Duncan, 300 yards), 266. Fleetwood Diary, 15 Jun 1864; James M. Paradis, *Strike the Blow for Freedom: The 6th United States Colored Infantry in the Civil War* (Shippensburg, Pa.: White Mane Press, 1998), pp. 52–53. Sgt. Maj. C. A. Fleetwood, of the 4th USCI, which received the fire of the 5th Massachusetts Cavalry, agreed with Col. S. A. Duncan that the dismounted cavalrymen fired into the troops ahead of them. *Anglo-African*, 9 July 1864. So did Chaplain H. M. Turner, of the 1st USCI, which was in line next to the cavalrymen. *Anglo-African*, 23 July 1864.

This panoramic view by the artist Edwin Forbes shows the ground across which the XVIII Corps attacked on 15 June 1865. The Confederate line ran along the widely spaced trees in the middle distance.

but a pleasant one to remain in," Sgt. Maj. John Arno of the 1st USCI wrote for readers of the *Anglo-African*, "with the scorching sun on the backs of the troops and the cannons belching forth their murderous missiles."[29]

At 7:00, half an hour before sundown, the entire XVIII Corps line, black soldiers and white, advanced. By General Smith's calculation, Hinks' division captured Batteries 7 and 8 in about twenty minutes. "They shouted 'Fort Pillow,' and the rebs were shown no mercy," Pvt. Charles T. Beman of the 5th Massachusetts Cavalry told his father. Night fell, but a three-quarter moon and muzzle flashes of the Confederate guns guided them to the next bastions by way of a 600-yard ravine choked with tree stumps, fallen timber, and water. Afterward, there were disputes about which regiment captured which position, but everyone was pleased with the day's results, including General Smith, who had been a notorious doubter of the Colored Troops' abilities. Lieutenant Verplanck sent his mother a diagram of the fight: "You can see that they enfiladed us and fronted us & generally ripped us but it didn't stop us," he wrote. "I have come through all right but I have smelt powder sure."[30]

Smith suspended operations at about 9:00 p.m. because of darkness. Even while his troops assaulted the ring of artillery positions outside Petersburg, the first Confederate reinforcements were arriving in the city by rail. By midmorning the next day, General Lee himself was at Drewry's Bluff, only fifteen miles north of Petersburg, with the rest of the Army of Northern Virginia close behind. Just arrived on the south bank of the James, Grant began to move the four corps of the Army of the Potomac toward the city, but the moment had passed when its capture by a single bold stroke had been possible. The attack might not have failed if Grant

---

[29] *OR*, ser. 1, vol. 40, pt. 1, pp. 721–22; vol. 51, pt. 1, pp. 266–67. *Anglo-African*, 9 July 1864; Paradis, *Strike the Blow for Freedom*, pp. 54–55.

[30] *OR*, ser. 1, vol. 40, pt. 1, pp. 705–06, 722; vol. 51, pt. 1, p. 267–68. Beman quoted in Redkey, *Grand Army of Black Men*, p. 99. R. N. Verplanck to Dear Mother, 17 Jun 1864, Verplanck Letters.

had given the orders directly to Smith, a career soldier, rather than transmitting them through Butler, a lawyer and politician who had never directed a successful military operation.[31]

Fighting went on for three more days, but Hinks' division did not play an active role. Its casualties during that time amounted to less than 10 percent of those it suffered in the morning and evening assaults on the first day. In all, Hinks' division lost more than five hundred officers and enlisted men killed, wounded, and missing. "For the last sixty-four hours I have had but ten hours sleep," Assistant Surgeon Charles G. G. Merrill wrote. "Today I brought in twenty-two wagons full of wounded and am going out tonight to bring in twelve wagons full more. We had lots of operations yesterday." The day after Hinks' division left the line, Capt. Solon A. Carter of the general's staff told his wife how, during the battle,

> Our Surgeon sat down to eat with us, just from the scene of his work (his operating table), with coat and vest off and his sleeves rolled up, his shirt and even his pantaloons besmeared with the blood of the poor fellows he had been carving up—We didn't any of us mind it so much but wondered what the folks at home would think of such an occurrence.[32]

Private Beman's remark that "the rebs were shown no mercy" was apparently no idle boast. The day after the battle, a reporter for the *New York Tribune* described a conversation he overheard: "'Well,' said Gen. Butler's Chief of Staff to a tall sergeant, 'you had a pretty tough fight there on the left.' 'Yes, Sir; and we lost a good many good officers and men.' 'How many prisoners did you take, sergeant?' 'Not any alive, sir,' was the significant response." The reporter quoted General Smith on the performance of Hinks' division: "They don't give my Provost Marshal [the staff officer responsible for prisoners of war] the *least trouble*, and I don't believe they contribute toward filling any of the hospitals with Rebel wounded." The antislavery, Republican *Tribune* headed the dispatch: "The Assault on Petersburg—Valor of the Colored Troops—They Take no Prisoners, and Leave no Wounded." Within a week, the story had spread throughout the army. Colonel Bates and the 30th USCI had marched with the Army of the Potomac to the James River from the Rapidan. "The colored troops in Butler's command took a line of very strong works . . . , fighting splendidly," he told his father. "They took no prisoners."[33]

Some of the black soldiers themselves talked, and even boasted, about what they had done. "The colored troops took five forts here on Tuesday," wrote a white soldier in the trenches at Petersburg. "I saw some of them to-day. They said the *white folks* took some prisoners, but they did not." Chaplain Henry M. Turner of the 1st USCI, one of the few black chaplains, deplored the practice and told read-

---

[31] *OR*, ser. 1, vol. 40, pt. 1, pp. 705, 749, 801.

[32] Ibid., vol. 51, pt. 1, p. 267. Civil War casualty figures vary widely. The total of 416 in Col. S. A. Duncan's report for 15–18 June 1864 (*OR*, ser. 1, vol. 51, pt. 1, p. 269), is greater than the 391 casualties for his brigade that appears in statistical tables covering the entire Union force around Richmond and Petersburg for the period 15–30 Jun 1864 (vol. 40, pt. 1, p. 237). C. G. G. Merrill to Dear Annie, 16 Jun 1864, C. G. G. Merrill Papers, Yale University (YU), New Haven, Conn.; S. A. Carter to My own precious wife, 20 Jun 1864, S. A. Carter Papers, MHI.

[33] *New York Tribune*, 21 June 1864; D. Bates to Father, 27 Jun 1864, Bates Letters.

ers of the *Christian Recorder* so. He described the attack, with Colored Troops and Confederates alike shouting "Fort Pillow!" "This seems to be the battlecry on both sides," Turner wrote. When the attackers got inside the forts, a few Confederates "held up their hands and pleaded for mercy, but our boys thought that over Jordan would be the best place for them, and sent them there, with a very few exceptions." The chaplain added that although "an immense number of both white and colored people" endorsed the practice of killing prisoners, he opposed it strongly. "True, the rebels have set the example, particularly in killing the colored soldiers; but it is a cruel one, and two cruel acts never make one humane act. Such a course of warfare is an outrage upon civilization and Christianity." In the end, experience as much as moral sentiment gradually diminished the number of massacres, region by region, as Confederates learned that black soldiers would impose the same terms on them, while black soldiers became more willing to take prisoners after their first battle, realizing how quickly fortune could reverse itself. But since the war extended from Virginia to Texas, and entire regiments were going into battle for the first time even during its last weeks, the cycle of atrocity and vengeance stopped only when the fighting ended.[34]

A future bishop of the African Methodist Episcopal Church, Henry M. Turner, was appointed chaplain of the 1st U.S. Colored Infantry in 1863.

By the end of June, the two armies had settled into parallel systems of trenches that skirted Petersburg and extended to the west. Union soldiers worked on the gun positions they had captured on the first day so that their thirty-pounders bore on the city and its railroad bridges. Confederate snipers encouraged men to keep their heads down, rather than admire the stretch of the Appomattox River that lay beyond the besieged city and the ripening grain in the fields. Other distractions from the view were "millions of savage flies" and the stench of the unburied corpses that their larvae fed on.[35]

In any case, the trenches required continual maintenance. "We have worked hard day & night most of the time, which has near worn us out," Captain Rickard of the 19th USCI wrote, "but after a few *days* of sleep we will be all right again."

---

[34] E. C. Mather to Dear Brother, 19 Jun 1864, E. C. Mather Papers, Dartmouth College, Hanover, N.H.; *Christian Recorder*, 9 July 1864. Prisoner-killing was not uncommon in Europe during both World Wars. Malcolm Brown, *The Imperial War Museum Book of the Western Front* (London: Pan Books, 2001), pp. 176–81; Gerald F. Linderman, *The World Within War: America's Combat Experience in World War II* (New York: Free Press, 1997), pp. 118–26.

[35] Rogall Diary, 13 Jul 1864.

When they were not shoring up the trenches, the men dug wells, for no appreciable rain fell between early June, before the beginning of the siege, and 19 July. Sergeant Major Fleetwood's diary recorded that he "washed and changed [clothes]" on 20 June, 7 July, and 29 July. With water and clean clothing in such short supply, it was no wonder that the Prussian-born Captain Rogall complained of "lices." Men inevitably grew bored and took chances, so that one diarist wrote that the "usual amount of sharpshooting" afforded "an occasional casualty to relieve the monotony." Captain Carter of Hinks' divisional staff found that the men became inured to cannon fire, "and it is really surprising how little attention any one pays to an artillery fight alone." Mortars were a different matter. Men liked to watch rounds fired by their own side. "The bomb presents a fine appearance in the night," Assistant Surgeon Merrill told his sister, "going up half a mile in the air—a red line of fire—then gradually falling & exploding after it reaches the ground." Men held the mortars in awe, and a round from the enemy would have troops diving for their "gopher holes." The reason for the name, Lieutenant Scroggs explained, was that "when a shell comes over, officers and men without distinction or 'standing upon the order,' incontinently 'go for' them." Lieutenant Verplanck took a day from his staff duties to visit his regiment, the 6th USCI, and found his old comrades "quite comfortable in their pits & holes. Everybody was as close to the ground as they could get."[36]

Since the first week of May, officers and enlisted men of the U.S. Colored Troops in the Army of the James had scanned the newspapers for items about Ferrero's division of the IX Corps, which had been guarding the wagons during Grant's overland march. Soldiers in Butler's army, some of them veterans of ten months' campaigning in North Carolina and Virginia, were anxious lest their unseasoned comrades bring discredit on black troops everywhere. "The Colored Division in Burnside's Corps has not yet taken active part in a single engagement," Lieutenant Grabill observed in June.[37]

Not only were Ferrero's men untested in battle; three months of continual activity—first during the march from the Rapidan to the James, then in the trenches around Petersburg—had left them no time to master the basic elements of soldiering. The 39th USCI had received rifles only when passing through Washington, D.C., in April. "Target practice, except for the five days at Manassas Junction, has been out of the question," the commanding officer wrote, "and this for men who have never been allowed the handling . . . of fire arms, has proved to be to[o] short to enable many to determine . . . whether the explosive part of the cartridge is the powder or the ball, many believing that because it is the ball that kills [it] should be put into the gun first. A few put in two or more loads at a time." Others merely fired from the shoulder without aiming. Many, like some rural white recruits, did

---

[36] S. A. Carter to My own darling Em, 3 Jul 1864, Carter Papers; Fleetwood Diary, 20 Jun (quotation), 7 and 29 Jul 1864; E. F. Grabill to My Own Little Puss, 24 Jun 1864, Grabill Papers; C. G. G. Merrill to Dear Annie, 4 Jul 1864, Merrill Papers; J. H. Rickard to Dear Brother, 21 Jul 1864, Rickard Papers; Rogall Diary, 25 Jun and 4 Jul 1864 ("lices"); Scroggs Diary, 7 ("an occasional"), 19, 20 ("when a shell"), and 26 ("usual amount") Jul 1864; R. N. Verplanck to Dear Mother, 26 Jun and 27 Jul 1864 (quotation), both in Verplanck Letters; Robert K. Krick, *Civil War Weather in Virginia* (Tuscaloosa: University of Alabama Press, 2007), pp. 130–33.

[37] E. F. Grabill to My Own Darling, 9 June 1864, Grabill Papers.

not know their left feet from their right. To these former slaves from Maryland, "every one is Captain or Boss and no amount of correction has so far rectified their knowledge of rank," the officer complained. Still, he thought, "I fully believe the material for good soldiers exists in the regiment, but that it takes longer to develop it, there can be no question."[38]

The lack of experience among General Ferrero's soldiers was evident, and noted by their own officers. The 30th USCI had "lost but few men yet," Colonel Bates wrote at the end of June. "Have been in no regular battle, but have been under sharp picket fire, shelling, &c. . . . The men do well so far." Grant, who had embraced the U.S. Colored Troops project a year earlier, displayed more confidence in his black soldiers and their commander. In mid-July, he wrote to Secretary of War Edwin M. Stanton that Ferrero "deserves great credit . . . for the manner in which he protected our immense wagon train with a division of undisciplined colored troops. . . . He did his work of guarding the trains and disciplined his troops at the same time, so that they came through to the James River better prepared to go into battle than if they had been in a quiet school of instruction during the same time."[39]

Ferrero's division spent the first three weeks of July away from the IX Corps, serving in turn with each of the other corps in the Army of the Potomac. The siege of Petersburg required flexibility of all the troops engaged in it that summer, for a Confederate raid into Maryland and Pennsylvania compelled Grant to withdraw one corps to defend Washington, leaving operations around Richmond and Petersburg to the remaining six, including the cavalry corps, that constituted Meade's Army of the Potomac and Butler's Army of the James. Fatigues formed a large part of the duties that fell to Ferrero's men, for Meade believed that the U.S. Colored Troops made better laborers than they did soldiers. Even so, he could promise one of the corps commanders to whom he lent Ferrero's division only that the black troops would "partially relieve your labor details." White troops continued to dig their own trenches along the Union line around Petersburg throughout the siege, and black soldiers manned advanced picket posts to keep an eye on the enemy as often as they dug or carried. By the time Ferrero's division returned to the IX Corps, on 22 July, General Burnside was nurturing a bold scheme to break the Confederate line: perhaps, even, to end the war. He intended to use black troops as the spearhead of this effort.[40]

The idea originated with an infantry regiment from the anthracite region of Pennsylvania. Some of the miners in its ranks proposed tunneling under the Confederate defenses and detonating a charge powerful enough to destroy a section of

[38]Maj Quincy McNeil to Brig Gen J. A. Rawlings, 13 Aug 1864, 39th USCI, Entry 57C, Regimental Papers, RG 94, NA.

[39]*OR*, ser. 1, vol. 40, pt. 3, p. 252 ("deserves great"); Bates to Father, 27 Jun 1864.

[40]*OR*, ser. 1, vol. 40, pt. 1, p. 595, and pt. 3, pp. 144, 304, 476–77. Meade's views on black soldiers are on pp. 187, 192; black soldiers on picket duty, pp. 166, 182, 234; fatigue details from Ferrero's division, pp. 236, 304–05; fatigue details from white divisions, pp. 231–33, 236–37, 262–62. For a division of white troops furnishing 250 to 700 men daily for road repair and construction of fortifications, see 2d Div, X Corps, Special Order 7, 6 Jun 1864, Entry 5195, 2d Div, X Corps, Special Orders, pt. 2, Polyonymous Successions of Cmds, RG 393, Rcds of U.S. Army Continental Cmds, NA. For a black regiment keeping 100 to 300 of its men in the front line around the clock, see Brig Gen P. A. Devin to Col F. B. Pond, 1 Jun 1864, Entry 5178, 2d Div, X Corps, Letters Sent (LS), pt. 2, RG 393, NA.

Delavan Bates had just turned twenty-four years old when he was appointed colonel of the 30th U.S. Colored Infantry in March 1864.

the enemy trench and enable Union troops to capture Petersburg. Their colonel took the plan to Burnside, who liked it and defended it against all doubters, chief among them Meade, while the Pennsylvanians dug. Beginning on 25 June, they took twenty-five days to complete a tunnel more than five hundred ten feet long from a ravine behind the Union trenches to a point under the Confederate line, which lay about one hundred fifty yards from the federal position. In the next few days, they finished a lateral passage seventy-five feet long across the head of the longer tunnel, making an underground T-shape with the head of the T roughly following the line of the Confederate trench above it. Along the lateral were eight small rooms, or magazines, each intended to hold between twelve hundred and fourteen hundred pounds of powder—some six tons in all. Meade had the entire charge reduced to four tons, or three hundred twenty kegs, citing the advice of his engineering officer, who was unenthusiastic about the project. On 26 July, Burnside asked for eight thousand sandbags to close the magazines and the lateral passage so that the full force of the blast would travel upward to the Confederate trench.[41]

On the same day, Burnside outlined for Meade the infantry advance that would come immediately after the explosion. His plan called for Ferrero's division to lead the attack, with both of its brigades advancing in column. The two columns would skirt the crater caused by the explosion, with the lead regiment of each stopping to secure the ruins of the Confederate trenches on either side of the crater while the regiments behind them moved on to seize a crest of ground that Union observers believed to be weakly held, some five hundred yards beyond the severely damaged Confederate front line. On the other side of this rise lay the city and its railroads. If Ferrero's division could gain the crest, Burnside thought, it could continue to

---

[41]*OR*, ser. 1, vol. 40, pt. 1, pp. 46, 59–60, 131, 136–37, and pt. 3, p. 354. The Pennsylvanians' commanding officer stated the dimensions in congressional testimony. *Report of the Joint Committee on the Conduct of the War*, 9 vols. (Wilmington, N.C.: Broadfoot Publishing, 1998 [1863–1865]), 2: 15–17, 113.

move downhill and "right into the town." The honor of capturing Petersburg would belong to black soldiers.[42]

Meade demurred. Just two weeks earlier, he had told his other corps commanders that he was reluctant to use Ferrero's men even for routine picket duty in front of the Union lines. That he would assent to the black division's leading a major assault was unimaginable. Having already told Grant his doubts about the entire mine project, he proposed to Burnside that they submit the question of the black troops' role in the attack to the commander of all the Union armies.[43]

Meade presented the matter as a political question, Grant told congressional investigators that December. "General Meade said that if we put the colored troops in front . . . and it should prove a failure, it would then be said, and very properly, that we were shoving those people ahead to get killed because we did not care anything about them. But that could not be said if we put white troops in front." A presidential election lay less than four months ahead. Grant, whose wife's family owned slaves, had adhered without a murmur to the Lincoln administration's policies of emancipation and black enlistment in the spring of 1863. Such loyalty, besides his victories at Fort Donelson, Vicksburg, and Chattanooga, helped to cement his good relations with the president. Grant saw Meade's point at once, and on the afternoon of 29 July, some twelve hours before the explosion and attack, Burnside received a message from Meade's chief of staff: "the lieutenant general commanding the armies . . . directs that [the attacking] columns be formed of the white troops."[44]

Burnside had three divisions of white infantry with which to carry out this order. The two closest to the site of the mine, led by Brig. Gen. Robert B. Potter and Brig. Gen. Orlando D. Willcox, were worn out from weeks of digging trenches under enemy fire. Somewhat better rested, Burnside thought, was Brig. Gen. James H. Ledlie's division, although it would have to undertake an overnight march in order to reach the next day's battlefield. "So I said, 'It will be fair to cast lots,'" Burnside recalled the scene. "And so they did cast lots, and General Ledlie drew the advance. He at once left my headquarters, in a very cheerful mood. . . . [N]o time could be lost in making the necessary arrangements, as it was then certainly 3 o'clock in the afternoon and the assault was to be made next morning."[45]

Within a few hours of Meade's conversation with Grant, Ferrero learned that the white divisions of the IX Corps, and not his own men, would lead the attack. Burnside had certainly revealed his own plans for the black division some time before 17 July, when Ferrero mentioned "the proposed assault" in a letter. A few weeks after the event, Burnside told a court of inquiry that he had "instructed [Ferrero] to drill his troops" in preparation for the attack. Survivors of the assault continued for the rest of their lives to debate the question of the division's readiness. Ferrero's report, dated two days after the assault, mentioned no special training. Captain Rogall wrote in his diary about the 27th

[42] *OR*, ser. 1, vol. 40, pt. 1, pp. 126, 136 (quotation).

[43] Ibid., pp. 60, 130–31, and pt. 3, pp. 187, 192.

[44] Ibid., pt. 1, p. 137 ("the lieutenant"); *Report of the Joint Committee*, 2: 18, 111 ("General Meade"). Brooks D. Simpson, *Let Us Have Peace: Ulysses S. Grant and the Politics of War and Reconstruction, 1861–1868* (Chapel Hill: University of North Carolina Press, 1991), pp. 3–5, 36–46.

[45] *OR*, ser. 1, vol. 40, pt. 1, p. 61.

USCI's "digging rifle pits, dangerous position," on 26 July, four days before the projected attack. The same day, Sgt. William McCoslin sent a letter to the *Christian Recorder*, saying that the 29th USCI had "built two forts and about three miles of breastworks, which shows . . . that we are learning to make fortifications, whether we learn to fight or not. We are now lying in camp, . . . resting a day or two. . . . We have worked in that way for eight or ten days without stopping." The drill that Burnside urged Ferrero to institute was probably barely enough to teach men who had seen only a few months' service to move from column into line "by the right companies, on the right into line wheel, the left companies on the right into line, and . . . the leading regiment of the left brigade to execute the reverse movement to the left," a sequence of movements to secure the wrecked enemy trenches on either side of the crater that would have bewildered untrained men. In any case, a shortage of officers hampered training of any kind. "The regiment by sickness and details is very short of officers for duty," the commanding officer of the 19th USCI complained just a week before the assault. "The labor upon the remaining officers . . . is so great, that it is almost impossible in so new a regiment, that they would do justice to themselves or their commands." The men of Ferrero's division might have been ill prepared to lead the assault, even if Meade's qualms had not sidelined them, but the other divisions of Burnside's corps had little more experience than Ferrero's, either on the drill field or in battle.[46]

The IX Corps was unique in the Army of the Potomac. It had its beginnings in the summer of 1862 and was composed of federal regiments withdrawn from the Carolinas to strengthen Union forces in Virginia after McClellan's failure to take Richmond that spring. This was the first instance of the Army's stripping other departments to reinforce operations closer to Washington, a practice that persisted for the next two years.

By the summer of 1864, only twelve of the forty-one white regiments in the corps had served with it since arriving from the Carolinas. Eight of the others had joined in time for the Virginia and Maryland campaigns during the summer and fall of 1862 and the IX Corps' expeditions to Mississippi and Tennessee in 1863. Of the remaining twenty-one regiments, seventeen dated from the summer of 1863 or later. Most of those had mustered in during the spring of 1864 and had no more experience than the black soldiers in Ferrero's division. Two of the seventeen were heavy artillery with twelve companies each rather than an infantry regiment's ten; three others were dismounted cavalry, also with twelve companies each. These regiments served to increase the size of the IX Corps, but they added little to its experience. The proportion of veteran soldiers was even smaller than the presence of the twenty older regiments would suggest, for disease and battle had thinned their ranks and the draft had only partly filled them again. "Imagine a thousand men, exposed to wind & weather, dust, smoke

---

[46]Ibid., pp. 58 ("instructed"), 136 ("by the right"), and pt. 3, p. 304 ("the proposed"); Lt Col J. Perkins to Maj C. W. Foster, 23 Jul 1864, 19th USCI, Entry 57C, RG 94, NA; Rogall Diary, 26 Jul 1864; *Report of the Joint Committee*, 2: 106; Edward A. Miller Jr., *The Black Civil War Soldiers of Illinois: The Story of the Twenty-ninth U.S. Colored Infantry* (Columbia: University of South Carolina Press, 1998), p. 55 ("built two"); Noah A. Trudeau, *Like Men of War: Black Troops in the Civil War, 1862–1865* (Boston: Little, Brown, 1998), p. 232.

& battle—for two years, . . . sifted down to a hundred & fifty sunburnt hardy fellows," Assistant Surgeon Merrill told his father, "and you will get an idea of one of [these] regiments."[47]

The IX Corps had added nearly thirteen thousand soldiers since the previous October, trebling its size to nineteen thousand two hundred fifty officers and men present for duty in April 1864. Nearly two-thirds of them, however, had spent only a few weeks in the Army. In this respect, the IX Corps was far worse off than the rest of the Army of the Potomac, which had increased in size by only 27.5 percent during the same six months to 102,869 of all ranks present for duty. As a result, the proportion of new men in the rest of Meade's army only slightly exceeded one-fourth. As the three-year enlistments of 1861 began to run out, the "sunburnt hardy fellows" in the IX Corps became increasingly rare, their places taken by conscripts, substitutes, and men who enlisted for bounty money. A sizable minority of the men in the ranks had been under arms no longer than those in the Union Army at Bull Run during the first summer of the war. This was the organization with which Burnside was supposed to capture Petersburg.[48]

Ledlie's division left its campground before 1:00 a.m. on 30 July and was in the Union front line when the mine exploded at about 4:45, a few minutes before sunrise. Captain Carter of General Hinks' staff watched the explosion from behind the Union lines. He saw the earth "rise gradually and as though it was hard work to start at first, and then leaping up to a height of 150 feet," he told his wife:

> Imagine a pile of earth the size of a half acre going up the distance I have described with cannon, horses, human beings and all, and then the whole falling together in a mass of ruins, men buried alive, others half-buried and some with their heads and upper part of their bodies buried and the rest remaining exposed. The rebs were completely surprised.[49]

The blast created a hole some two hundred feet long and fifty wide where the Confederate trench had been. The crater was twenty-five or thirty feet deep, with a lip of loose earth that rose about twelve feet above the ground that surrounded it. Stunned and fearful, the men of Ledlie's leading brigade lingered in their trenches for five minutes or more before climbing out and moving forward. The one veteran regiment in that brigade had joined the IX Corps only in April. Two of the others, both heavy artillery acting as infantry, had mustered in only seven months and three months earlier and had also joined the corps that spring. The fourth regiment

---

[47]*OR*, ser. 1, 6: 237; 9: 381; vol. 12, pt. 2, pp. 261–62; vol. 19, pt. 1, pp. 177–78; 21: 52–53; vol. 24, pt. 2, p. 149; vol. 29, pt. 1, p. 226. C. G. G. Merrill to Dear Father, 23 Jun 1864, Merrill Papers.

[48]*OR*, ser. 1, vol. 31, pt. 1, pp. 811–13; 33: 1036, 1045; vol. 40, pt. 1, pp. 228–30. For dates of service of individual regiments, see Dyer, *Compendium*. A social profile of the men who joined the new regiments is in Warren Wilkinson, *Mother, May You Never See the Sights I Have Seen: The Fifty-seventh Massachusetts Veteran Volunteers in the Army of the Potomac, 1864–1865* (New York: Harper & Row, 1990), pp. 10–12.

[49]S. A. Carter to My own darling Emily, 31 Jul 1864, Carter Papers.

This drawing by Alfred R. Waud shows the explosion of the Petersburg mine in the right-center distance.

in the brigade was still recruiting, having managed to fill only six of its companies by late May.[50]

Two of the five regiments in the second brigade of Ledlie's division had served with the IX Corps since 1862, but the other three had completed organization only in April. It was natural that these new troops, recalling the 35 percent casualties that the army had suffered during May and June followed by weeks of trench warfare, reverted to what Burnside called "the habit, which had almost become second nature, of protecting themselves from the fire of the enemy" by crowding into the crater. The men of Lieutenant Verplanck's old regiment in Hinks' division were not the only soldiers who wanted to stay "as close to the ground as they could get." General Ledlie's absence did not help. Surgeon Hamilton E. Smith testified afterward that Ledlie spent time that day at an aid station of General Willcox's division, asking for "stimulants" to treat his malaria. After a while, the general added a bruise from a spent rifle ball to the list of his maladies.[51]

The month had been dry and hot, with afternoon temperatures sometimes above 95 degrees. By 30 July, no rain had fallen around Richmond for six days, and the shower that fell then had been only the third of the month. Dust from the drought joined smoke from the explosion hanging in the air as two more divisions of the IX Corps tried to find

---

[50]*OR*, ser. 1, vol. 40, pt. 1, pp. 246, 527, 535, 539, 547, 558, 563 (diagram); *Report of the Joint Committee*, 2: 19, 39, 77, 79, 107; Dyer, *Compendium*, passim.

[51]*OR*, ser. 1, vol. 40, pt. 1, pp. 60 ("the habit"), 104, 118–19, 177, 527, 541, 547, 564. R. N. Verplanck to Dear Mother, 27 Jul 1864, Verplanck Letters.

their way forward. It was "almost impossible to see anything," the commander of the right-hand division later testified. By the time the two divisions advanced as far as the crater, nearby Confederates had recovered from the shock of the explosion and were firing on their attackers. On the left of the Union advance, General Willcox's division occupied about one hundred fifty yards of Confederate trench, a task that would have fallen to a single regiment of one of Ferrero's brigades if Burnside had been allowed to carry out his original plan. As matters stood, most of the gap that the explosion left in the Confederate line was "filled up with troops, all huddled together in the crater itself, and unable to move under the concentrated fire of the enemy, no other troops could be got in."[52]

Meanwhile, on the Union right, General Potter managed to keep enough control of his men to organize an attack on Confederates who were firing at his division; but as he was about to launch it, a message came from Burnside, ordering him to move forward at once and take the crest. Earlier, one of Ledlie's heavy artillery regiments had gone one hundred fifty yards in that direction but had to fall back under fire from the undamaged Confederate lines on either side of the crater. Rather than attack the Confederates who threatened the Union position, Potter obediently moved his men forward. A few dozen nearly reached the crest, but found themselves without support and came back.[53]

Although most officers' reports did not mention specific times between the explosion of the mine and the order to withdraw, which arrived about midday, Burnside probably ordered Potter to advance about 6:00 a.m. or not long afterward. At 5:40, nearly an hour after the blast, Meade's chief of staff had sent Burnside a message, saying that he understood that Ledlie's men were "halting . . . where the mine exploded," and that Burnside should push "all [his] troops . . . forward to the crest at once." Again at six, Meade himself ordered Burnside to "push your men forward at all hazards (white and black) and don't lose time . . . but rush for the crest." Meade's insistence on frequent information became so great that at 7:30 he asked, "Do you mean to say your officers and men will not obey your orders to advance? . . . I wish to know the truth and desire an immediate answer." Burnside replied about five minutes later that it was "very hard to advance to the crest. I have never in any report said anything different from what I conceived to be the truth. Were it not insubordinate I would say that the latter remark of your note was unofficerlike and ungentlemanly."[54]

By the time the generals began to quarrel, Ferrero's division of the IX Corps had been waiting for hours for the word to advance. The night before, the men of the 19th USCI "laid down after making all needful preparations," Captain Rickard wrote the next day. They expected to move toward the front trenches well before dawn, he continued, "but did not till sunrise when I was aroused from my slumbers by the most terrible cannonading I have ever heard." The division approached the old front line in time to receive an order from Burnside to advance, bypass the crater, and capture the crest beyond it. Ferrero did not like what he had been able to learn about the confusion ahead and protested that troops in front of his were

[52]*Report of the Joint Committee*, 2: 78 ("filled up"), 87 ("almost impossible"). On the weather, see Krick, *Civil War Weather*, pp. 133–34; Fleetwood Diary, esp. 24 Jul 1864; *Army and Navy Journal*, 6 August 1864.

[53]*OR*, ser. 1, vol. 40, pt. 1, pp. 541, 547–48, 554.

[54]Ibid., pp. 140 ("halting . . . where"), 141 ("push your"), 142 ("Do you mean"), 143 ("very hard").

Alfred R. Waud captured the confusion that prevailed among the Union attackers by the time the black soldiers of the IX Corps (in the foreground) joined the battle.

blocking the way. His division, just behind the second brigade of Willcox's, halted close by Surgeon Smith's aid station. Smith later testified that it took three orders from Burnside to set Ferrero's troops in motion. Having sent his division forward, Ferrero lingered near the aid station with General Ledlie. "I deemed it more necessary that I should see that they all went in than that I should go in myself," he told the court of inquiry.[55]

Not until after 8:00 a.m. were Ferrero's two brigades able at last to move into the open. Col. Henry G. Thomas' report said that the delay lasted half an hour, although he later testified that it was an hour and a half. Emerging from the Union trenches, Thomas' brigade, some twenty-four hundred men of the 19th, 23d, 28th, 29th, and 31st USCIs, headed left; that of Col. Joshua K. Sigfried, made up of the 27th, 30th, 39th, and 43d, about two thousand strong, went right. The 23d and 43d had completed organization only the month before; the 28th, 29th, and 31st went into battle with only six companies each, all that their recruiters had been able to fill so far. As the men attempted to pass the crater, the same daunting disorder faced each brigade. Colonel Sigfried saw "living, wounded, dead, and dying crowded so thickly that it was very difficult to make a passage way through." Captain Rickard and the 19th USCI

> advanced double quick over the breast works exposed to a galling fire & made towards the [crater.] I never expected to reach it men were falling all around me but I was not touched. Got into the Crater caused by the explosion & an awful sight it was filled

---

[55]Ibid., pp. 93 (quotation), 102–04, 118–19; *Report of the Joint Committee*, pp. 108–09; J. H. Rickard to Dear Sister, 31 Jul 1864, Rickard Letters.

with dead rebels dead union soldiers white & black wounded too of every description
& soldiers both white & black clambering through . . . over the shrieking wounded.

One staff officer in Sigfried's brigade claimed that only Colonel Bates' 30th USCI maintained a semblance of order on its way forward through the crater.[56]

This disorganization began to tell when officers tried to assemble their troops for an attack on the crest, which still remained in Confederate hands. Afterward, Ferrero told investigators that his men "went in without hesitation, moved right straight forward, passed through the crater that was filled with troops, and all but one regiment of my division passed beyond the crater." Two questions later, though, he had to admit that he was not present, but "at no time [was] farther [away] than eighty or ninety yards." If he remained in or behind the Union front trench, from which his men attacked, he would have been at least one hundred fifty yards from the crater, for the miners' tunnel was more than five hundred ten feet long. Ferrero's remarks also contradict the testimony of the officer who had been in the crater and claimed that only the 30th USCI moved through it without much confusion.[57]

The brigade commanders told a grimmer story. Brig. Gen. John F. Hartranft of Willcox's division said that Ferrero's men "passed to the front just as well as any troops; but they were certainly not in very good condition . . . , because in passing through the crater they got confused; their regimental and company organization was completely gone." In Sigfried's brigade, the only regiment that managed to close with the enemy was the 43d USCI, which took one Confederate battle flag from the enemy and recaptured colors that had been lost earlier in the day by a white regiment of the IX Corps. Sigfried recorded that the 43d returned with "a number" of prisoners, despite the men's earlier vows to "Remember Fort Pillow!" On the left, Thomas tried to order a charge, but the 31st USCI had just lost its three ranking officers and only about fifty of the men responded: "the fire was so hot that half the few [men] who came out of the works were shot," he reported. Thomas then spent some time trying to separate men of the 28th and 29th USCIs from the armed mob in the crater and form them into a coherent body. Just as he was about to accomplish this, he received a message from Ferrero, whom he had not seen since leaving the Union front trench: "Colonels Sigfried and Thomas . . . : If you have not already done so, you will immediately proceed to take the crest in your front." Accordingly, some one hundred fifty or two hundred men of the 23d, 28th, and 29th USCIs moved forward about fifty yards until they met "a heavy charging column of the enemy" of perhaps twice their strength "and after a struggle [were] driven back over our rifle pits. At this moment a panic commenced," Thomas reported. "The black and white troops came pouring back together." Many of them crowded into the crater. Sigfried's brigade held on "until pushed back by the

<hr />

[56] *OR*, ser. 1, vol. 40, pt. 1, pp. 105, 586, 590, 596 ("living, wounded"), 598; Rickard to Dear Sister, 31 Jul 1864. Brigade strengths based on figures for IX Corps, 30 June and 31 July 1864, in *OR*, ser. 1, vol. 40, pt. 2, p. 542, and pt. 3, p. 78; Field Return, 20 Jun 1864, and Casualty List, 30 Jul 1864, both in Entry 5122, 4th Div, IX Corps, LS, pt. 2, RG 393, NA.

[57] *OR*, ser. 1, vol. 40, pt. 1, p. 93.

mass of troops, black and white, who rushed back upon it, . . . until the enemy occupied the works to its left and the opposite side of the intrenchments, when, becoming exposed to a terrific flank fire, losing in numbers rapidly and in danger of being cut off, [the brigade] fell back behind the line . . . where it originally started from."[58]

That left hundreds of men still in the crater. These included about one hundred officers and men of the 19th USCI, still a disciplined force, who struggled into the crater, Thomas said, "and remained there for hours, expending all their own ammunition and all they could take from the cartridge boxes of the wounded and dead men that lay thick together in the bottom of this pit." Capt. Theodore Gregg, commanding one of the veteran regiments in Potter's division, was present for the aftermath of Thomas' unsuccessful charge. "A major of one of the negro regiments placed his colors on the crest of the crater, and the negro troops opened a heavy fire on the rebels," he reported.

> In a few moments, the rebel force . . . dashed into the pits among us, where a desperate hand-to-hand conflict ensued, both parties using their bayonets and clubbing their muskets. . . . During this brief contest the negroes in the crater kept up a heavy fire of musketry on the advancing enemy, compelling them to take shelter. Many of our men being killed and wounded, and the enemy pressing us hard, we were compelled to fall back into the crater in order to save our little band, while the negroes kept up a heavy fire on the rebels outside. . . . [Brig. Gen. William F.] Bartlett and one of his aides-de-camp . . . did everything in their power to rally the troops on inside the crater, but found it to be impossible, as the men were completely worn out and famished for water. He succeeded in rallying some twenty-five or thirty negroes, who behaved nobly, keeping up a continual fire. . . . The suffering for want of water was terrible. Many of the negroes volunteered to go for water with their canteens. A great part of them were shot in the head while attempting to get over the works; a few, more fortunate than others, succeeded in running the gauntlet and returned with water to the great relief of their suffering comrades.

As occurred throughout the IX Corps that day, the behavior of the men in Ferrero's division varied from panicked to heroic.[59]

Meade heard from an officer in a signal tower that two brigades of infantry were on their way to reinforce the Confederate defenders and sent a message at 9:30 to tell Burnside to withdraw the troops if he thought they could accomplish nothing more. Fifteen minutes later, the suggestion became an order, although Meade left it to Burnside's discretion whether to begin the withdrawal at once or wait till dark. General Bartlett of Ledlie's division replied at 12:40 p.m. from the crater, where he was the ranking officer: "It will be impossible to withdraw these men, who are a rabble without officers, before dark, and not even then in good order." Most of the men on the spot did not take time to

---

[58]Ibid., pp. 102 ("passed to"), 105 ("Colonels Sigfried"), 106–07, 596 ("a number"), 597 ("until pushed"), 598 ("the fire," "a heavy"), 599 ("and after").

[59]Ibid., pp. 554–55 ("A major"), 599 ("and remained").

The crater, not long after Union troops entered Petersburg in April 1865

consult their watches frequently, but Captain Gregg noted that it was 2:00 p.m. when he left the crater to rejoin the hundred men of his regiment who had been left behind some nine hours earlier to provide covering fire for the advance. Not long after that, Confederates swept into the crater, killing or capturing all the Union soldiers who remained.[60]

Casualties, as always, were hard to determine exactly. Ferrero's division suffered some thirteen hundred, about 38 percent of the thirty-five hundred casualties in the IX Corps that day. Almost one-third of the black casualties were dead, some of them under conditions similar to the killing of wounded and surrendered men at Fort Pillow nearly four months earlier. The difference this time was that three Confederate soldiers from different regiments, in private letters written days after the battle, mentioned the men of Ferrero's division shouting "No quarter!" and "Remember Fort Pillow!" The war was becoming as bloodthirsty as Lieutenant Verplanck had feared that spring. Still, Confederate deserters two days after the battle told Union officers that they had seen two hundred or two hundred fifty black prisoners of war at work for the Confederates, cleaning up the battlefield and unearthing for proper burial corpses that had been buried by the explosion of the mine. In October, Confederate authori-

---

[60] Ibid., p. 556, and pt. 3, pp. 661–64 (quotation, p. 663).

ties in Richmond reported that a total of 216 black Union soldiers had passed through the city's prisons.[61]

Three days after the attack, Grant asked that the War Department appoint a court of inquiry "to examine into and report upon the facts and circumstances attending" the operation. The court sat for seventeen days between 8 August and 8 September. Maj. Gen. Winfield S. Hancock, commander of the II Corps; two divisional commanders in the Army of the Potomac; and the inspector general of the Army questioned thirty-two witnesses ranging in rank from Grant himself to 1st Lt. Albert A. Shedd of the 43d USCI, a staff officer who had been present in the crater.[62]

The generals at once began to prepare their excuses for the catastrophe. Meade, in a sworn statement contradicted by routine messages he had sent to two corps commanders weeks earlier, tried to justify his substitution of one of Burnside's white divisions for Ferrero's to lead the attack. "Not that I had any reason to doubt . . . the good qualities of the colored troops, but that . . . he should assault with his best troops; not that I had any intention to insinuate that the colored troops were inferior to his best troops, but that I understood that they had never been under fire." Burnside referred to Ferrero's division when he said "no raw troops could have been expected to have behaved better," but the remark certainly applied to many other regiments in his corps as well. Ferrero told the court of inquiry that his men were "raw, new troops, and had never been drilled two weeks from the day they entered the service to that day." Although Ferrero had not been close enough to the battle to affect the result, he knew what training his men had and his statement seems to agree with the unofficial remarks of Captain Rogall and Sergeant McCoslin. Reports of the colonels who led brigades, and who actually spent time with the troops on 30 July, refer to "disorganized," "more or less broken" troops retiring in "confusion." Senior officers exerted so little control that day that it was easy for them, in their reports, to blame any troops other than their own for panicking and running. This was especially so for the divisional commanders. Colonel Thomas had seen Ferrero, Ledlie, and Willcox at the surgeons' station as he led his brigade forward that morning, which meant that Potter alone of the four generals had been close enough to see the fighting.[63]

The court found that most of the reasons for the failure fell under the heading of improper leadership, whether in preparation of the troops, in prompt execution of the plan, or in direct supervision at the scene of the operation. In its opinion, the court declared that Burnside, Ferrero, Ledlie, Willcox, and one brigade commander who had also been absent were "answerable" for the failure, although it absolved them of "any disinclination . . . to heartily co-operate in the attack." Only Burnside, who was relieved of his command two weeks after the battle, suffered

---

[61] Ibid., p. 248, gives a figure of 209 killed among 1,327 casualties in Ferrero's division and 3,475 casualties for the entire IX Corps. Bryce A. Suderow, "The Battle of the Crater: The Civil War's Worst Massacre," *Civil War History* 43 (1997): 219–24, revises the figure to 423 killed among 1,269 casualties in the division and also quotes the Confederate letters. For Lieutenant Verplanck, see above, note 10. The Confederate deserters' report is in *OR*, ser. 1, vol. 42, pt. 2, p. 5. Confederate authorities' report is in ser. 2, vol. 7, pp. 987–88.

[62] *OR*, ser. 1, vol. 40, pt. 1, p. 18 ("to examine").

[63] Ibid., pp. 46 ("Not that"), 93 ("raw, new"), 528 ("no raw"), 538 ("disorganized"), 542 ("confusion"), 567, 579 ("more or less").

any adverse consequences for the defeat. Meade remained at the head of the Army of the Potomac, which he led until the end of the war; Ledlie resigned in January 1865; Ferrero, Potter, and Willcox all received the brevet rank of major general at different times for their roles in the Overland Campaign and the siege. Potter's and Willcox's brevets were dated 1 August and had been in the works long before the failed attack; that Ferrero's did not come until December suggests that Grant still retained some confidence in his abilities.[64]

Yet another investigation remained, called for by Congress and conducted by the Joint Committee on the Conduct of the War. Radical Republicans had founded the committee in the fall of 1861 in response to early Union reversals. Four months after the Petersburg mine disaster, committee members traveled by boat from Washington to the Union base at City Point to gather testimony. A large part of their final report consisted of reprinting the proceedings of the Army's own court of inquiry, but the committee's conclusion held General Meade alone responsible for "the disastrous result." Republicans had been finding fault with Meade ever since his failure, as they saw it, to launch a vigorous pursuit of the retreating Confederate army after the battle of Gettysburg. The committee's conclusion was to be expected but, as with the earlier court of inquiry, it had no practical result.[65]

No one canvassed the opinions of General Hinks' officers and men about what their less-experienced comrades in Ferrero's division had done. Sergeant Major Fleetwood expressed disgust in his usual terse way: "Col[ore]d Div of 9th Corps charged or attempted [to,] broke and *run!*" In the 5th USCI, Lieutenant Grabill dismissed the entire operation as "a splendid fizzle." Colonel Shurtleff worried "that the blame will be laid upon the colored division of Burnside's corps. The truth is that the hardest part of the programme was assigned to them though they are comparatively inexperienced, many of them never before under fire. They went farther to the front than any white troops and were not routed until one brigade of white troops had first been driven back in panic." Members of Hinks' divisional staff were well informed, or claimed to be; Captain Carter knew that the mine contained four tons of powder, and Lieutenant Verplanck blamed the 112th New York specifically for causing the panic. Verplanck went on: "I saw many cases of bad management or rather want of interest on the part of division commanders in the 9th Corps. I know not if [it] was cowardice but they were not to be seen in the front where their brigades were fighting. . . . I believe faithfully that if corps & division commanders . . . had done their duty that day we would have gained a great victory." Disappointment in the result of the operation mingled with dread that the failure would cast all black soldiers in a bad light. Lieutenant Grabill wrote: "The selection of troops for the most difficult part was most blunderous. Ferrero's Colored Division, undisciplined, raw and unused to fighting were chosen to accomplish what should be expected only

---

[64]Ibid., p. 129 (quotation). The entire record of the court is on pp. 42–163. Generals' records in Francis B. Heitman, *Historical Register and Dictionary of the United States Army*, 2 vols. (Washington, D.C.: Government Printing Office, 1903), 1: 417, 622, 802, 1038.

[65]*Report of the Joint Committee*, 2: 11 (quotation); Bruce Tap, *Over Lincoln's Shoulder: The Committee on the Conduct of the War* (Lawrence: University Press of Kansas, 1998), pp. 18–19, 24, 187–92.

Behind the trenches, trees supplied both shelter and firewood. Stumps surround the camp of a black regiment from Ohio—either the 5th U.S. Colored Infantry or the 27th—during the siege of Petersburg.

of the best of veterans. . . . Of course the Copperhead press will now make a great blow about 'nigger troops' in the Abolition War."[66]

After a four-hour truce on the morning of 1 August to allow Union troops to bury their dead and remove their wounded, who had lain in the open for two nights and a day, the siege resumed its routine. In the 5th USCI, Lieutenant Grabill called it "easier times than we used to have. Now we are in the trenches but about half the time and our fatigue work is not so great as it used to be." He noted that the Confederates no longer tended to waste their ammunition, but that with the enemy lines "in plain sight . . . two or three hundred yards in our front," movement in the open was dangerous.[67]

Sniper fire presented a threat throughout the day. Men in the trenches saw sharpshooters "loafing about," as one officer put it, with special sights on their rifles, "peeping through the loop holes & watching for a shot." One of them ap-

[66]S. A. Carter to My own darling Emily, 31 Jul 1864; Fleetwood Diary, 30 Jul 1864; E. F. Grabill to My Own Loved One, 1 Aug 1864, Grabill Papers; G. W. Shurtleff to My darling Girl, 1 Aug 1864, Shurtleff Papers; R. N. Verplanck to Dear Mother, 1 Aug 1864, Verplanck Letters.

[67]OR, ser. 1, vol. 40, pt. 3, p. 821; E. F. Grabill to My own dear Anna, 12 Aug 1864, Grabill Papers.

proached the officer "with a careless lounging gait" and asked, "Isn't there a *cuss* with a black hat over here who bothers you a good deal?" "Yes he killed one of my men this morning," the officer replied. "Well said the sharpshooter I'll watch for him. He laid himself down by the loop hole & in ten minutes," the officer wrote, "I saw him slowly lift up[,] sight across his rifle & fire we were not troubled any more by the man with the black hat. . . . I get four or five good shots most every day he said as he lounged away."[68]

Not far away, Assistant Surgeon Merrill of the 22d USCI found himself in a relatively quiet part of the line. "There is nothing stirring here," he wrote. "We have a tacit truce on our front—neither party disturbs the other." From a hill behind the Union position, Merrill had "a fair view of the rebel lines for a mile or more . . . and we . . . can see both sides enjoying themselves during the day time. . . . There is a melon patch between them, it is said, and both parties visit it at night. Water melons are one of the greatest luxuries we have here now."[69]

Other men besides melon hunters crossed from one side to the other. Desertion plagued the Army of Northern Virginia after three months of continual fighting, a period of action that had no parallel in the war. Some dispirited Confederates merely turned toward home; others headed for the trenches opposite, where Union officers interrogated them and, if they took an oath and were willing to perform civilian work for the North, sent them to Washington, D.C., or even as far as Philadelphia. By mid-August, General Lee thought the problem so grave that he mentioned it to the Confederate secretary of war. During the two weeks before Lee wrote to the secretary, at least sixty-five of his soldiers crossed to the Union lines. "Deserters came in on our Picket line the last two nights," wrote Capt. Edward W. Bacon of the 29th Connecticut (Colored), "& were quite terrified when they found they had thrown themselves into the hands of the avenging negro."[70]

Union officers learned from these deserters that Lee had dispersed his army somewhat, detaching at least two divisions for service elsewhere while the rest held the trenches. Seeing an opportunity, Grant decided to send the II and X Corps to threaten Richmond. This would, he thought, cause Lee to withdraw troops either from the Shenandoah Valley or the trenches south of the James River to strengthen the defenses of the Confederate capital. A decision to draw reinforcements from south of the James, Grant told Meade, might "lead to almost the entire abandonment of Petersburg."[71]

The twelve thousand officers and men of General Hancock's II Corps took two days to withdraw from the trenches around Petersburg, board transport vessels at City Point, and disembark at Deep Bottom, on the north bank of the James. Maj. Gen. David B. Birney postponed the advance of his X Corps, a

---

[68] L. L. Weld to My dearest Mother, 29 Aug 1864, L. L. Weld Papers, YU.

[69] C. G. G. Merrill to Dear Father, 21 Aug 1864 ("There is") and C. G. G. Merrill [no salutation], 28 Aug 1864 ("a fair view"), both in Merrill Papers.

[70] *OR*, ser. 1, vol. 40, pt. 3, p. 693; vol. 42, pt. 2, pp. 4–5, 17, 28, 40–42, 53–54, 66, 76, 78, 84–85, 96–97, 103, 113–15, 125–28, 141–42, 1175–76. E. W. Bacon to Dear Kate, 26 Sep 1864, E. W. Bacon Papers, AAS; J. Tracy Power, *Lee's Miserables: Life in the Army of Northern Virginia from the Wilderness to Appomattox* (Chapel Hill: University of North Carolina Press, 1998), pp. 128, 182–83.

[71] *OR*, ser. 1, vol. 42, pt. 2, pp. 112, 114–15, 123, 136, 141 (quotation), 167.

force nearly as large as Hancock's, to wait for the new arrivals. The sun had been up for hours on 14 August by the time the troops of the II Corps all got ashore. Six days of inconclusive fighting followed, with the Union army failing to gain the advantage it sought.[72]

A recent addition to the X Corps was a brigade of black regiments withdrawn from the Department of the South and led by the corps commander's older brother, Brig. Gen. William Birney. The 7th, 8th, and 9th USCIs, along with the 29th Connecticut (Colored), had arrived at Deep Bottom on 13 August. These regiments would be the nucleus of an all-black division like those that were already serving in the IX and XVIII Corps. During the next few days, the brigade took part in an advance and repelled a Confederate counterattack. The 7th USCI "saw very little fighting" the morning after its arrival, Capt. Lewis L. Weld wrote:

> We were kept in reserve . . . & lay in the wood seeing the dead & wounded brought back through our lines. . . . About 3 [p.m.] or perhaps a little later the 7th was ordered to charge and take a line of Rebel rifle pits. . . . We formed in line of battle & moved across the open corn field in our front . . . , charged the works with a yell & took them in splendid style, so those who saw it say. My company is the extreme left company of the line & I was too busy to see much beside the work before me. The fire was very hot. . . . The Regt however did itself great credit both officers & men.

The next day, the brigade "did nothing but march & lie still waiting for developments." On 16 August, an "all day fight" was "very wearisome but our Regt was at no time under very severe fire. . . . About noon we were moved over on the right to charge a line of works there but after we had arrived we found the charge already made but partially unsuccessful[;] the lines had been taken but had to be abandoned. We lay nearly all night in a dense wood, all the latter part of the afternoon & early evening being under a fire not severe but annoying & not being able to return it."[73]

Skirmishers on both sides continued to exchange shots the next day. "Every few minutes," Weld wrote, "a bullet comes whistling over our heads." During five days' fighting, Birney's brigade lost 136 officers and men killed, wounded, and missing. Such casualties must have seemed light to those men of the 8th USCI who had survived the defeat at Olustee in February, when the loss of their regiment alone amounted to 343 killed, wounded, and missing. After a failed Confederate attack on 18 August, Birney reported to Hancock: "The colored troops behaved handsomely and are in fine spirits."[74]

The mid-August operation of Birney's brigade was the first to be covered by another new arrival along the James, the reporter Thomas M. Chester. His employer, the *Philadelphia Press*, had overcome enough of its past indiffer-

---

[72] Ibid., pt. 1, pp. 39, 119–20, 216, 249, 677.

[73] NA M594, roll 206, 7th, 8th, and 9th USCIs; roll 208, 29th Conn. L. L. Weld to My dearest Mother, 17 Aug 1864, Weld Papers.

[74] *OR*, ser. 1, vol. 35, pt. 1, p. 312; vol. 42, pt. 1, pp. 120, 219, 678 (quotation), 779–80. Weld to My dearest Mother, 17 Aug 1864.

ence or antagonism toward the city's black residents to hire and send south the first black war correspondent of a metropolitan newspaper. The fact that four regiments raised at Philadelphia—the 6th, 8th, 22d, and 43d USCIs—were serving near Richmond and Petersburg hardly seems like a probable reason for Chester's assignment. Although his employer's motive for sending him remains unclear, the reporter soon became a familiar figure in the camps of those and other black regiments—Lieutenant Verplanck, of the 6th USCI and General Hinks' staff, called him "our own correspondent"—and he soon caught the mood of the troops. "Between the negroes and the enemy it is war to the death," Chester told his readers. "The colored troops have cheerfully accepted the conditions of the Confederate Government, that between them no quarter is to be shown," he wrote on 22 August.

> Those here have not the least idea of living after they fall into the hands of the enemy, and the rebels act very much as if they entertained similar sentiments with reference to the blacks. Even deserters fear to come into our lines where colored troops may be stationed. Not unfrequently have they asked if there are any black troops near, and if there were the rebs have entreated that they should not be permitted to harm them.[75]

Official proclamations of the Confederate government, and the tendency of white people nationwide to hold black lives cheap, gave an especially vicious edge to the war even though both Confederates and Colored Troops continued to take prisoners at least as often as they killed surrendering enemies. Accounts by other witnesses indicate that Chester may have arrived in Virginia just as the spirit in the trenches was changing. The day before he filed his dispatch, Surgeon Merrill of the 22d USCI told his father: "We have a tacit truce on our front—neither party disturbing the other." On 10 September, Chaplain Turner of the 1st USCI wrote to the *Christian Recorder*:

> Having for some time heard that the colored and rebel pickets were exchanging words, and that the venom to each other had somewhat ameliorated, I was led to doubt its truthfulness from a previous knowledge of the uncompromising hostility they had hitherto cherished toward each other. But a short time since, my regiment was ordered to the trenches, where their proximity to the rebels was not more than a hundred yards. Here, to my great surprise, I saw the rebels and the soldiers of my regiment, talking, laughing, exchanging papers, tin-cups, tobacco, &c. Some of the rebels deserted and came into our lines, and cursed the rebellion, and then they had a jolly time with our boys. I learn that they are now acknowledging our soldiers as prisoners of war. This sudden

---

[75]R. J. M. Blackett, ed., *Thomas Morris Chester, Black Civil War Correspondent: His Dispatches from the Virginia Front* (Baton Rouge: Louisiana State University Press, 1989), pp. 38–39, 102–06, 109–10 ("Between the negroes"); R. N. Verplanck to Dear Mother, 8 Oct 1864, Verplanck Letters. Sgt. Maj. C. A. Fleetwood, 4th USCI, recorded his encounters with Chester in Fleetwood Diary, 5, 14, 17, 19, 23, 25, and 29 Oct 1864, and 8, 20, 29 Nov 1864.

transition, though, should be carefully watched; there is evidently some deep-laid treachery at the bottom of so singular a move.

Despite Chaplain Turner's misgivings, black soldiers and their enemies seem to have come to terms in a way that is not uncommon in trench warfare. In December, Chaplain Thomas S. Johnson of the 127th USCI wrote: "The enemy are on very friend-ly terms, talking . . . to our videttes and advanced pickets. . . . Our pickets in front of the works here are not more than two hundred paces from the rebs. . . . Last night four came in our lines as deserters." The friendly terms of which Johnson wrote did not mean that Confederate deserters escaped black soldiers' caustic wit. "As one [de-serter] passed through our inner trench on his way to the rear," Captain Bacon wrote, "a somewhat facetious darkey ventured to suggest, rather to the Deserter's chagrin 'Well Johnny! We're all brothers now, ain't we?' which made the whole line roar."[76]

The lull that followed Grant's failure to puncture the defenses of Richmond lasted several weeks, until nearly the end of September. In the meantime, west of Richmond, a Union army led by Maj. Gen. Philip H. Sheridan beat Confederate forces decisively in the Shenandoah Valley. Grain from the Valley had supplied Confederate armies dur-ing three years of warfare, but Sheridan's troops ended that and added to Lee's increas-ing worries. Five hundred miles to the southwest, General Sherman's army occupied Atlanta, giving a much-needed fillip to President Lincoln's chances of reelection.[77]

In line with his policy of keeping all Union forces in motion at once and press-ing the Confederacy simultaneously on several fronts, Grant decided to "make another stir," as he told his wife, around Richmond and Petersburg. According to his plan, Butler's Army of the James would attack north of the river, toward Richmond, while to the south the Army of the Potomac would hold the Confeder-ates around Petersburg in their trenches, unable to send reinforcements against the main assault lest Union troops walk into the undefended rail center. One city or the other, Grant told Butler, was apt to fall. Since quick movement was essential to success, "the troops will go light," carrying besides their rifles only blanket rolls, three days' rations, and sixty rounds of ammunition per man. Wagons would fol-low later with more rations and ammunition.[78]

Enough regiments of U.S. Colored Troops had joined the siege by late Septem-ber to form three small divisions. In the Army of the Potomac, Ferrero's division of the IX Corps included five infantry regiments from the free states and four raised in

---

[76]Merrill to Dear Father, 21 Aug 1864; *Christian Recorder*, 17 September 1864; Bacon to Dear Kate, 26 Sep 1864 ("As one"). This incident seems to have occurred in the 29th Connecticut, for both Bacon and 1st Lt. H. H. Brown, another officer in the regiment, mention it. H. H. Brown to Dear Friends at Home, 21 Sep 1864, H. H. Brown Papers, Connecticut Historical Society, Hartford. For another instance of jests at prisoners' expense, see Leon F. Litwack, *Been in the Storm So Long: The Aftermath of Slavery* (New York: Knopf, 1979), p. 102. Bell I. Wiley, *The Life of Billy Yank: The Common Soldier of the Union* (Indianapolis: Bobbs-Merrill, 1952), pp. 354–56, gives instances of fraternization between Confederates and white Union troops. On live-and-let-live in the First World War, see John Keegan, *The Face of Battle* (New York: Viking Press, 1976), pp. 209–10; a veteran's recollections are in Robert Graves, *Good-Bye to All That: An Autobiography* (London: Jonathan Cape, 1929), pp. 134, 181–82, 245.

[77]McPherson, *Battle Cry of Freedom*, pp. 774–80.

[78]*OR*, ser. 1, vol. 42, pt. 2, p. 1059 ("the troops"); Simpson, *Ulysses S. Grant*, p. 380 ("make another").

Maryland and Virginia. By some shuffling of regiments in the Army of the James, General William Birney became leader of a two-brigade division in the X Corps. The nucleus of his division remained Col. James Shaw's brigade, consisting of the 7th, 8th, and 9th USCIs and the 29th Connecticut. In the XVIII Corps, the 4th and 6th USCIs continued as Colonel Duncan's brigade, while the 5th USCI found itself brigaded with the 36th, from North Carolina, and the 38th, raised in Virginia, all under command of Col. Alonzo G. Draper, formerly of the 36th. Duncan's and Draper's brigades made up a division commanded by Brig. Gen. Charles J. Paine, a Massachusetts soldier who had served in Butler's 1862 expedition to Louisiana and led a brigade at the siege of Port Hudson the year after. For the attack on Richmond, Paine's division would operate with the X Corps. This addition brought the strength of the corps to some fourteen thousand men, about one-third of whom were black.[79]

On 24 September, Shaw's brigade withdrew from the Union trenches around Petersburg to spend five days out of the line, a period of inspections and replacing worn-out clothing and equipment. Officers spent time updating their company accounts. A new regiment, the 45th USCI, joined the brigade from Philadelphia. Rumors flew that transports in the James River would take a Union force to attack Wilmington, North Carolina. In midafternoon of 28 September, the brigade assembled and moved off by fits and starts along with the rest of the corps. By nightfall, it was on the south bank of the James, waiting to cross a pontoon bridge that engineers were just beginning to lay. Not until four the next morning did the column halt at Deep Bottom, on the north bank, fifteen miles from its previous camp. "Be ready to march at 4 A.M. were our orders," wrote 1st Lt. Henry H. Brown of the 29th Connecticut. "It was then after 4 but knowing that we would bring up the rear we lay down & slept till 7. We then turned out[,] eat a few hard-tack but had no time for coffee."[80]

The Confederate position lay along a road that ran southeast from Richmond to New Market, between two and three miles north of the Union troops' resting place at Deep Bottom. Butler had assured his men that the garrison of Richmond numbered no more than three thousand, of whom fewer than fifteen hundred were infantry capable of manning the trenches. The enemy's weakness meant that there was "no necessity of time spent in reconnoitering or taking special care of the flanks of the moving columns," the confident general wrote. His estimate of the total number of the city's defenders fell short by half; facing his troops alone were more than two thousand rifles. Well before the sun rose at 6:00, the leading brigades of the X Corps began to move toward the Confederate trenches.[81]

In Paine's division, on the left, some three hundred twenty officers and men of the 4th USCI were awake in time to get coffee before advancing to attack. Followed by the 6th USCI, roughly equal in strength, they moved through some woods that

---

[79]OR, ser. 1, vol. 42, pt. 2, pp. 617–22, and pt. 3, pp. 463–67; Dyer, *Compendium*, pp. 159, 247–50, 552; Heitman, *Historical Register*, p. 765.

[80]OR, ser. 1, vol. 42, pt. 1, pp. 106, 772, 780, 793, and pt. 2, p. 1083; H. H. Brown to Dear Friends at Home, 5 Oct 1864, Brown Papers; Longacre, *Army of Amateurs*, p. 211.

[81]OR, ser. 1, vol. 42, pt. 1, pp. 702, 708, 715, and pt. 2, pp. 1083–84, 1087 (quotation), 1243. "Barely 6,000" is one authority's tabulation of the total, with "nearly 2,900" of them facing Butler's attack. Richard J. Sommers, *Richmond Redeemed: The Siege at Petersburg* (Garden City, N.Y.: Doubleday,

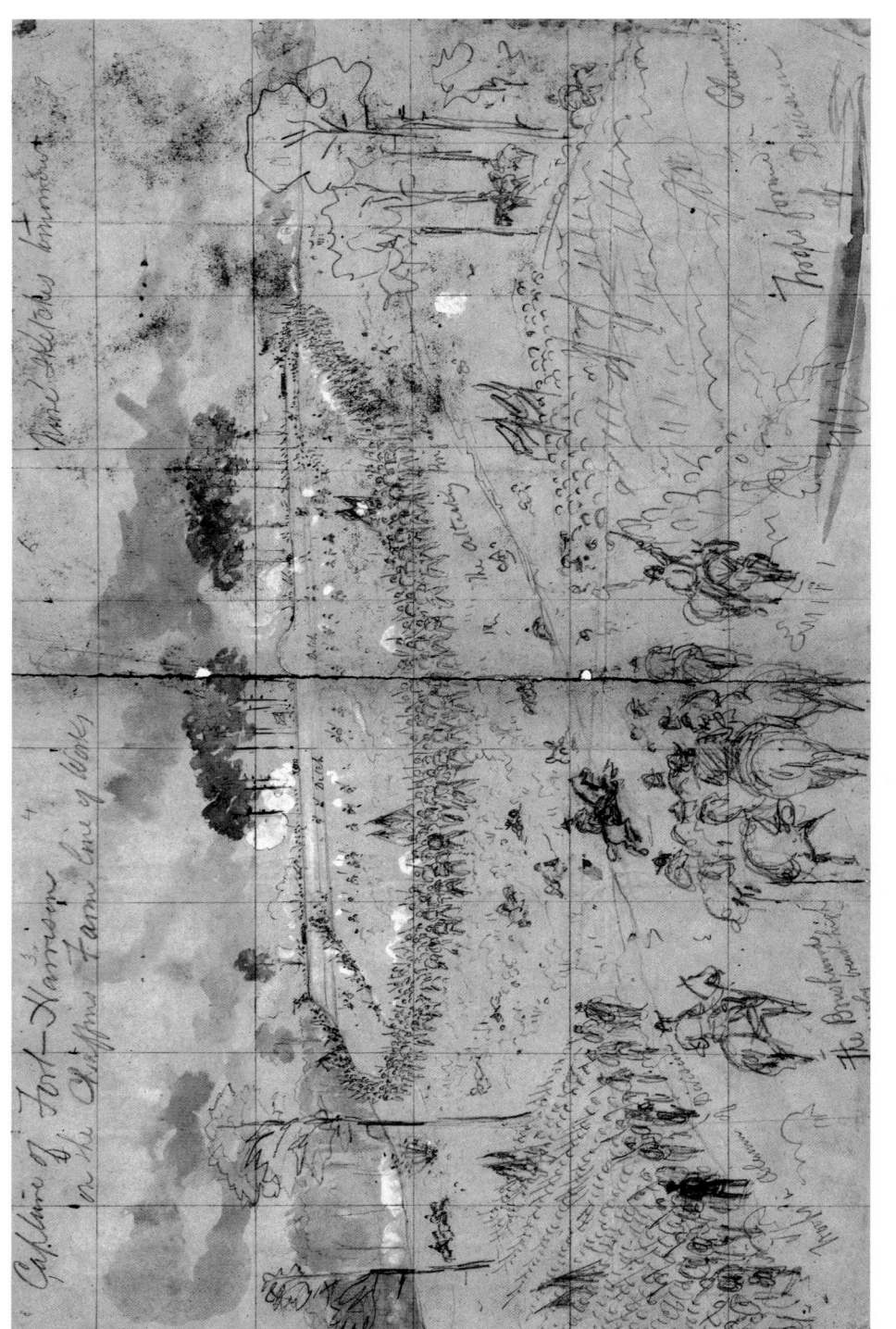

Union troops attack the Confederate line north of the James River, 29 September 1864, in this drawing by William Waud.

Terrain across which Union troops attacked on 29 September 1864. The trees in the distance mark the Confederate position, as shown also in the William Waud drawing.

lined a creek, formed line in front of the Confederate trenches, and attacked. The defenders met the assault with crushing fire. "Charged with the 6th at daylight and got used up," Sergeant Major Fleetwood entered in his diary. "Saved colors." Blocked by barriers of felled trees and chevaux-de-frise, the Union survivors fell back, leaving more than three hundred dead and wounded on the field. "We were all cut to pieces," Capt. James H. Wickes of the 4th USCI wrote. "We got up to the second line of abatis, . . . but by that time the line was so cut up that it was impossible to keep the men any longer in their places. . . . I tried to force my men to make a dash over the work, but there were [only] five left out of the twenty-five that I started up with, and they gave way." After the remnant of the regiment fell back through the woods, only 3 of 8 officers and 75 of 325 enlisted men answered roll call.[82]

Five days after the battle, Wickes was able to tell a more connected story:

It happened that when the advance was first made along the whole line Thursday morning, our regiment led the assault against the works where the enemy most expected an attack. We advanced about five hundred yards under a terrific fire of

1981), p. 17. Another writes that the force opposed to Butler was "barely 2000." Douglas S. Freeman, *R. E. Lee: A Biography*, 4 vols. (New York: Charles Scribner's Sons, 1934–1935), 3: 500.

[82]*OR*, ser. 1, vol. 42, pt. 1, p. 136; Field Return, 28 Sep 1864, Entry 1659, 3d Div, XVIII Corps, LS, pt. 2, RG 393, NA; Fleetwood Diary, 29 Sep 1864; J. H. Wickes to My dear Father, 2 Oct 1864, J. H. Wickes Papers, Boston [Mass.] Public Library; Sommers, *Richmond Redeemed*, pp. 31–35.

musketry. . . . The whole line seemed to wilt down under the fearful fire. . . . A few of our men fired their pieces—this was against orders, as we were to charge with fixed bayonets, without firing a shot. This led others to fire too, and then they stopped to load again[;] this was just what we tried to avoid, for it was death to us to halt in that place. I shouted to my men to push forward without loading, but my voice could not be heard. The line was growing to[o] weak and thin to make an assault. It began to waver and fall back. I did not leave till I found not a man on my part of the line to back me and then I retreated too.

It may be that the Confederates weakened neighboring parts of their line in order to withstand this attack, for as it was going on some veteran regiments of the division, on Paine's right, were able to seize the enemy trenches in front of them while suffering fifty-seven killed, wounded, and missing.[83]

The next brigade in Paine's column was Draper's, three regiments that fielded about 1,375 officers and men. Paine allowed an hour to pass before he sent Draper into action at 8:00 a.m. "When we received the order we were lying . . . in a deep ravine," wrote Lieutenant Scroggs of the 5th USCI. Along with the 36th and 38th USCIs, the 5th moved forward in a column two companies wide and five deep, to within five hundred yards of the Confederate trenches.

At the word "Charge" we moved forward at a double quick in good order: a thick jungle on our way deranged our ranks slightly . . . but [the men] pressed forward. . . . The color bearer was killed on one side of me and my orderly Sergt. wounded on the other, two of my Sergts killed and my company seemingly annihilated, yet on we went through the double line of abatis, and over their works. . . . The rebels retreated rapidly and we secured but few prisoners. We continued the pursuit a short distance then halted to reform the battalion. On getting my Co. (H) together I found I had lost 18 in killed and wounded . . . out of 50 the number I started with in the morning.[84]

Instead of advancing with both his brigades or using one in close support, Paine had put them in sequentially, each seemingly without reference to the other. Shaw's brigade stayed in reserve most of the morning. "I thought at first we were to assault the works we knew must be in front of us," Lieutenant Brown wrote, "but we stacked arms & lay down to rest." Later in the morning, the brigade moved forward to the Confederate position that Paine's division had just stormed. "Here we rested, filled our canteens & as soon [as] the road was cleared for us moved around to the breastworks," Brown continued. "Here we again rested till the Artillery & Cavalry might pass." So Shaw's brigade spent the morning.[85]

Having taken the heights, the X Corps moved northwest in the direction of Richmond. By midafternoon, advanced regiments in one division of the X Corps were able to set eyes on the city itself, only three miles distant. There they halted for the

---

[83] *OR*, ser. 1, vol. 42, pt. 1, pp. 133, 708, 713; J. H. Wickes to My dear Father, 4 Oct 1864, Wickes Papers.

[84] Scroggs Diary, 29 Sep 1864; Field Return, 28 Sep 1864, Entry 1659, pt. 2, RG 393, NA.

[85] Brown to Dear Friends at Home, 5 Oct 1864.

rest of the day, too few to push on without support. Meanwhile, the other division of the corps reached a point just south of the New Market Road, about four miles northwest of the Confederate trenches captured that morning. From its new position, the division was to attack Fort Gilmer, a Confederate bastion in the line of Richmond's outer defenses. It approached the fort from the north while Shaw's brigade, led by its divisional commander, General William Birney, moved against it from the east.[86]

Birney held the untested 45th USCI and 29th Connecticut in reserve, in a position from which they could watch part of the attack. "The Balles did whistle aroun our heads dreadfulley," Sgt. Joseph O. Cross of the 29th Connecticut told his wife. "Wee all expected that it was our last time. . . . [W]ee had orders to drop under abank in which w[e] did very freeley and glad to get off so wee Just set their & look at the woonded men as they passed By." The other three regiments of the brigade, the 7th, 8th, and 9th USCIs, each sent four companies forward to the attack at about 2:00 p.m. Under artillery and rifle fire, they crossed open ground that Captain Brown of the 29th Connecticut gauged at half a mile in width. The survivors plunged into a ditch at the base of the wall. Seeing what was happening to the first four companies of the 8th USCI, the major commanding the regiment refused to commit his remaining companies without a direct order; Birney told him to stay where he was. Captain Brown, from his position in the reserve, was able to see what happened to the attacking party of the 9th: "They climb upon each others shoulders & some few off them thus enter the fort but the rebs have been reinforced & they must not ever hope for success. . . . [W]e heard [the Confederates] picking them off with their rifles till dark when all who were not able to escape were taken." The afternoon's work cost the brigade 35 killed, 243 wounded, and 152 missing.[87]

Reports from Birney's subordinates agree that their attack began at about 2:00 p.m., while reports from the division that approached from the north indicate two assaults on that side between about 1:35 and 3:00. Within three weeks, Birney and Colonel Shaw began quarreling about which of them bore responsibility for the failed assault. They maintained the dispute for the rest of their lives. The lack of coordination in the afternoon attacks on Fort Gilmer was similar to General Paine's sequential assaults on the Confederate trenches earlier in the day. Such ineptitude was not limited to the leaders of black troops: one of the XVIII Corps generals, along with his division, got lost as well that morning in some woods between the James River bridgehead and the division's objective. A greater proportion of men with no military background—and without much aptitude for conducting operations—seems to have risen to higher rank in General Butler's Army of the James than in most other Union field armies. Even if more troops had been available to Butler's generals on 29 September, there was little chance that they would have moved quickly

---

[86] *OR*, ser. 1, vol. 42, pt. 1, p. 708; Sommers, *Richmond Redeemed*, pp. 93–94.

[87] *OR*, ser. 1, vol. 42, pt. 1, pp. 134, 772–75, 780–81, and pt. 3, p. 253–54; Kelly Nolin, ed., "The Civil War Letters of J. O. Cross," *Connecticut Historical Society Bulletin* 60 (1995): 211–35 (quotation, p. 220); Brown to Dear Friends at Home, 5 Oct 1864; Sommers, *Richmond Redeemed*, pp. 83–93.

enough or attacked with sufficient vigor to break through the Confederate lines and occupy Richmond.[88]

Sergeant Major Fleetwood's terse diary entry, "Charged . . . at daylight and got used up. Saved colors," contained a catch phrase that could mean "took heavy casualties" as well as "became depleted" or "exhausted." A set of colors consisted of one national flag and one distinctive regimental flag. When Sgt. Alfred B. Hilton, carrying the national color of the 4th USCI, saw the regimental standard-bearer shot, he picked up that flag, too, "and struggled forward with both . . . , until disabled by a severe wound at the enemy's inner line," an officer wrote. Fleetwood then took the national color, and Pvt. Charles Veal the regimental color, and they carried them through the rest of the fight. On 6 April 1865, Fleetwood, Hilton, and Veal were awarded Medals of Honor. Hilton's was one of the few posthumous awards in the nineteenth century; his wound necessitated amputation of his right leg, and he died three weeks afterward.[89]

Theirs were among twelve Medals of Honor earned by the men of Paine's division on 29 September. Sgt. Maj. Milton M. Holland, Sgt. Powhatan Beaty, Sgt. James H. Bronson, and Sgt. Robert Pinn each received a medal for taking command of a company of the 5th USCI when eight of the regiment's officers were wounded. In the middle of the battle, "we got mixed," Pinn wrote in a letter supporting Bronson's pension application.

> Bronson then personally in command of his Co. passed me I then saw . . . blood on the calf of his left leg, . . . noticed that he limped and sup[p]orted himself on his gun in answer to me he said he had been struck by a piece of a shell—This all took place in less time than it takes to write it, there was no time then to more than glance at a wounded man, as I was personally in command of my company and was suffering severely from two wounds, was soon after wounded a third time.[90]

In the 6th USCI, 1st Sgt. Alexander Kelly "seized the colors, which had fallen near the enemy's inner line . . . , raised them, and rallied the men, at a time of confusion and a place of the greatest possible danger," his citation read. Pvt. William H. Barnes and 1st Sgt. Edward Ratcliff had been among the first men of Company C, 38th USCI, to enter the Confederate trenches in their part of the line. Pvt. James Gardner of the 36th USCI "shot a rebel officer, who was on the parapet cheering his men, and then ran him through with his bayonet." In the same regiment, Cpl. Miles James "loaded and discharged his piece with one hand" after being wounded in the arm, "and urged his men forward . . . within 30 yards of the enemy's works." These soldiers' acts were of the kind for which most Medals of Honor were awarded during

---

[88] *OR*, ser. 1, vol. 42, pt. 1, pp. 761, 767, 769, 772, 774, 793–94; Longacre, *Army of Amateurs*, p. xi. A specimen of the Birney-Shaw controversy is William Birney, *General William Birney's Answer to Libels Clandestinely Circulated by James Shaw, Jr. . . .* (Washington, D.C.: privately printed, 1878).

[89] *OR*, ser. 1, vol. 42, pt. 3, p. 169; U.S. Department of the Army, *The Medal of Honor of the United States Army* (Washington, D.C. Government Printing Office, 1948), 174–75; *Butler Correspondence*, 5: 622.

[90] *OR*, ser. 1, vol. 42, pt. 1, p. 136; R. A. Pinn to Commissioner of Pensions, 14 Mar 1883, in Pension File SO343751, James H. Bronson, CWPAF.

the Civil War: saving the regiment's colors or capturing the enemy's, being the first to enter the enemy's position, or refusing to leave the fight after being wounded.[91]

The men whose awards came in April 1865 were the first black soldiers to be honored with a military decoration. A few others received medals after the war. In November 1865, Sgt. Decatur Dorsey of the 39th USCI received one for bravery at the Petersburg Crater fifteen months earlier. His medal was one of only four awarded for that battle until long after the war. Sgt. James H. Harris of the 38th USCI distinguished himself on 29 September but did not receive a medal for his actions until 1874, although his name appeared in the same orders as those of the other men. Sgt. William H. Carney of the 54th Massachusetts had to wait until 1900 to be decorated for his bravery at Fort Wagner in July 1863. Sgt. Andrew J. Smith of the 55th Massachusetts received a medal as recently as 2001. Such delays were not unusual in the nineteenth century. Criteria for award of the Medal of Honor have changed over the years; a survey of 121 medals awarded for valor at Gettysburg, the Wilderness, and Spotsylvania Court House shows that sixty-nine of them, or 57 percent, were issued during the 1890s.[92]

Christian A. Fleetwood in an undated photograph taken long after the war. He wears the uniform of an officer in the Washington, D.C., militia and the Medal of Honor awarded him for saving the colors of the 4th U.S. Colored Infantry at New Market Heights, 29 September 1864.

It is obvious that all of the medals awarded to black soldiers during the war stemmed from one action and went to men of the 3d Division, XVIII Corps, in General Butler's Army of the James. None of the medals for New Market Heights went to members of the black division of the X Corps. This is not surprising, for only three of the seventeen medals awarded to white troops for the action went to X Corps soldiers. Butler undertook his own project to overcome discrimination against black troops. He designed a medal with the motto *ferro iis libertas*

---

[91] *OR*, ser. 1, vol. 42, pt. 3, pp. 168 ("shot a"), 169 ("seized"); Department of the Army, *Medal of Honor*, p. 176 ("loaded and").

[92] *OR*, ser. 1, vol. 42, pt. 3, p. 169; Department of the Army, *Medal of Honor*, pp. 137–43, 151–52, 154–57, 166.

perveniet ("freedom attained by the sword"), and may have distributed as many as two hundred of them. Yet geographical as well as racial factors were at work in the distribution of decorations. Soldiers in Virginia received the vast majority of medals. Not one went to a soldier who took part in the disastrous Red River Expedition, or the defeat at Brice's Crossroads, Mississippi, or the victory at Tupelo, all in 1864. The crushing Union victory at Nashville in December of that year resulted in the issuance of fourteen medals the following February. The successful assault on Fort Blakely, at Mobile, in April 1865, brought only six medals two months afterward, although eight more were recommended and awarded in later years.[93]

General Grant himself had come from City Point, across the James River, to watch the attack on 29 September. Although he was impressed by the strength of the Confederate positions that Union troops captured, he concluded by midday that the Union advance was not sufficiently rapid to reach Richmond before dark or numerous enough to hold the city. "If our troops do not reach Richmond this afternoon," he told Butler, it might be best to withdraw those farthest in advance, and to select a defensible line "now." With the attack stalled in front of Fort Gilmer, Butler's men began to dig in opposite the Confederate trenches. Sporadic counterattacks, which seldom involved the black regiments, ceased by mid-October. Another episode of the great siege began.[94]

Throughout October, daytime temperatures, which had reached the mid-eighties during the battle of 29 September, gradually cooled. The second week of the month brought the first perceptible frost. And on 18 October, a new regiment of Colored Troops, the 117th USCI, arrived at City Point. It was the first regiment of black soldiers to report from a reservoir of manpower that the Lincoln administration had long been reluctant to tap: the slaveholding but unseceded state of Kentucky.[95]

[93]Benjamin F. Butler, *Autobiography and Personal Reminiscences of Major-General Benj. F. Butler* (Boston: A. M. Thayer, 1892), pp. 742–43; Department of the Army, *Medal of Honor*, pp. 166–68, 181–82, 202–03.

[94]*OR*, ser. 1, vol. 42, pt. 1, p. 20, and pt. 2, pp. 1090–92, 1110 (quotation); Sommers, *Richmond Redeemed*, pp. 418–19.

[95]*OR*, ser. 1, vol. 42, pt. 3, p. 269; Lt Col S. B. Lawrence to Brig Gen H. H. Lockwood, 15 Oct 1864, 117th USCI, Entry 57C, RG 94, NA; Krick, *Civil War Weather*, pp. 140–41.

CHAPTER 12

KENTUCKY, NORTH CAROLINA AND VIRGINIA, 1864–1865

The last state in which the Union recruited black troops was Kentucky. Stretching from the Appalachian Mountains to the Mississippi River, Kentucky touches the boundaries of seven other states. Two of these, Tennessee and Virginia, had joined the Confederacy; two others, Missouri and West Virginia, maintained slavery but stayed in the Union; and three—Illinois, Indiana, and Ohio—were free states. Kentucky's neighbors, therefore, reached from Norfolk, Virginia, to St. Joseph, Missouri; from Chattanooga to Chicago; from Cleveland to Memphis. North or South, whichever side held Kentucky could strike at its opponent from several different directions. For good reason then, Abraham Lincoln told a confidant during the first autumn of the war: "I think to lose Kentucky is nearly the same as to lose the whole game."[1]

The federal census of 1860 counted 38,645 slaveholding Kentuckians in the state's white population of 919,517. Their human property amounted to 225,483 persons. Slaves—and nearly all black Kentuckians were enslaved—accounted for 20 percent of the state's population. Most of them lived in the fertile western and central parts of the state, where production of grains, hemp, livestock, and tobacco made their employment profitable.[2]

The sheer number of slaveholding whites in Kentucky—more than in any other state but Virginia and Georgia—imposed extreme caution on Union policymakers during the early months of the war. The governor refused to answer Lincoln's call for militia in the spring of 1861, and the legislature declared the state's neutrality. Only in September, after a Confederate army fortified Columbus, Kentucky, which commanded navigation on the Mississippi, did federal troops cross the Ohio River and occupy towns at the mouths of the Cumberland and Tennessee Rivers. Seven months later, they had moved up both rivers, occupied Nashville, and beaten back attacking Confederates at Pittsburg Landing, near the Mississippi state line. In October 1862, some of

---

[1]William L. Miller, *President Lincoln: The Duty of a Statesman* (New York: Knopf, 2008), p. 110.

[2]U.S. Census Bureau, *Population of the United States in 1860* (Washington, D.C.: Government Printing Office, 1864), p. 181, and *Agriculture of the United States in 1860* (Washington, D.C.: Government Printing Office, 1864), p. 229; Sam B. Hilliard, *Atlas of Antebellum Southern Agriculture* (Baton Rouge: Louisiana State University, 1984), pp. 34, 36–38, 49–50, 52, 54, 59, 61–62, 66–67, 73–77.

*An 1859 map shows the central position of Kentucky between two future Confederate
states, Tennessee and Virginia, and four that remained in the Union, Ohio, Indiana,
Illinois, and Missouri. Lincoln is reputed (but not proven) to have quipped, "I hope to
have God on my side, but I must have Kentucky."*

the same troops ended the last major invasion of Kentucky when they defeated
a Confederate force at Perryville. Although mounted raiders remained active
until the end of the war, never again did they pose a significant threat to Union
occupation of the state.[3]

When federal troops abandoned their advanced posts in northern Alabama
during the fall of 1862 and hurried north to intercept the invasion of Kentucky,
they brought with them thousands of black refugees from slavery in parts of
the South that the Union could no longer hold. White Kentuckians leaped at
the chance to reenslave the new arrivals. Local authorities arrested those who
strayed too far from the protection offered by Northern soldiers, who by this
time in the war often practiced emancipation, even though they might disagree
with it in theory. In Kentucky, black people without passes faced jail and the
auction block. By April 1863, the military Department of the Ohio, which ad-
ministered all but the westernmost part of the state, had to issue an order on

---

[3]Ira Berlin et al., eds., *The Destruction of Slavery* (New York: Cambridge University Press,
1985), p. 493; Richard M. McMurry, *The Fourth Battle of Winchester: Toward a New Civil War
Paradigm* (Kent, Ohio: Kent State University Press, 2002), pp. 93–96; James M. McPherson, *Battle
Cry of Freedom: The Civil War Era* (New York: Oxford University Press, 1988), pp. 516–22.

the subject and act to stop the abuse. Having found and freed for a second time perhaps as many as a thousand of these former slaves, military authorities put the adults among them to work, the men laboring on construction projects and the women in army hospitals.[4]

By early 1864, with a few dozen black regiments having already taken the field in other parts of the South, black Kentuckians' contribution to the Union war effort was still restricted to the role of civilian laborers, repairing roads between federal garrisons in the state or laying track for the Louisville and Nashville Railroad. Black men who wanted to enlist first had to escape from bondage and then make their way to the western tip of Kentucky, which lay in the Department of the Tennessee, or leave the state altogether. More than two thousand of them went south to Tennessee for that purpose. Others crossed the Ohio River to Northern states where the War Department was also raising black regiments.[5]

In the course of a trip to organize Colored Troops west of the Appalachians, Adjutant General Lorenzo Thomas had stopped for a few days in January at Frankfort to confer with leading politicians. "My presence at the State capital was the occasion of quite an excitement among all classes, male and female," he told Secretary of War Edwin M. Stanton, "the opinion being fully expressed that I could only be there to take their negroes from them and put arms in their hands." Thomas suggested that since the state's black men were enlisting in other states and being credited toward the draft quotas of those states, Kentucky might be well advised to raise a few black regiments of its own. The people he talked to did not care for that idea but appeared less agitated by the end of his visit, he told Stanton.[6]

The Enrollment Act of 24 February 1864 changed everything. An amendment to the act that had instituted conscription one year earlier, it specified that male slaves, even those of loyal masters, for the first time became eligible for the draft. Opposition flared at once in Kentucky, even though the act did not propose to take any slaves unless a state failed to meet its quota of white volunteers. The most notorious display of disaffection came on 10 March, when Col. Frank Wolford of the 1st Kentucky Cavalry addressed an audience that had gathered to present him with an award for service to the Union cause, urging "the duty of the people of Kentucky to resist" the measure. Two weeks later, Wolford received a dishonorable discharge without a trial. The governor likewise advised forcible resistance to the registration of slaves for the draft. He was about to issue a proclamation to that effect but relented after an all-night conference with Brig. Gen. Stephen G. Burbridge, who commanded the District of Kentucky. Meanwhile, guerrillas continued to be active in many parts of the state, and in April raiders

---

[4] *The War of the Rebellion: A Compilation of the Official Records of the Union and Confederate Armies*, 70 vols. in 128 (Washington, D.C.: Government Printing Office, 1880–1901), ser. 1, vol. 23, pt. 2, p. 287 (hereafter cited as *OR*); Allen C. Guelzo, *Lincoln's Emancipation Proclamation: The End of Slavery in America* (New York: Simon and Schuster, 2004), pp. 78–79; Ira Berlin et al., eds., *The Wartime Genesis of Free Labor: The Upper South* (New York: Cambridge University Press, 1993), pp. 628–30 (hereafter cited as *WGFL: US*).

[5] *OR*, ser. 1, vol. 32, pt. 2, p. 479; Ira Berlin et al., eds., *The Black Military Experience* (New York: Cambridge University Press, 1982), pp. 191–92.

[6] *OR*, ser. 3, 4: 60.

led by Confederate Maj. Gen. Nathan B. Forrest penetrated as far north as Paducah, on the Ohio River, before returning south.[7]

With so much controversy and turmoil, it is no wonder that the first attempt to enforce the February 1864 Enrollment Act in Kentucky failed. The next month, more drafted men ignored or evaded the summons than answered it. General Burbridge set to work to supply the deficit. That he was a native Kentuckian and a slaveholder typified Lincoln's kid-glove approach to Kentucky, where three-quarters of the Union troops in garrison belonged to regiments raised in the state. Despite his local ties or any personal inclinations he may have had, Burbridge announced on 18 April that the War Department had named him superintendent of recruiting in Kentucky and set forth the rules for enrolling black recruits: a slave could enlist only with his owner's consent; the owner would receive a certificate entitling him to as much as four hundred dollars' compensation for each slave enlisted. Once sworn in, slaves would travel to a central depot at Louisville and from there "with all possible dispatch" to "the nearest rendezvous or camp of instruction outside of the State." Burbridge repeated this provision in the last paragraph of the order. Stanton called the repetition superfluous but approved the rest of the order and directed that Kentucky recruits go to Nashville, where Capt. Reuben D. Mussey was organizing black regiments in the Department of the Cumberland.[8]

In a state with Kentucky's turbulent history during the previous three years, the response of prospective black recruits to the federal initiative was quick and enthusiastic. By the first week in June, three hundred forty of them had reached Mussey's headquarters in Nashville, so many that he asked Stanton for authority to increase the number of recruiters and to set up receiving centers in Kentucky rather than ship recruits outside the state. A week later, Adjutant General Thomas authorized the increase of recruiters and the establishment of eight camps, with Camp Nelson, some twenty miles south of Lexington, receiving recruits from two of the state's nine congressional districts. Before the end of the month, General Burbridge reported that five regiments could be ready "in a very short time" if the War Department would name the officers. According to Thomas, eighteen hundred recruits had arrived at Louisville and Camp Nelson and awaited assignment to regiments.[9]

Many would-be volunteers headed for the nearest army camp without observing the legal requirement by obtaining their owners' permission. Recruiting officers accepted some of them, but those who could not pass the physical examination and had to return home faced whippings and other physical punishment, including mutilation. Moreover, the families of men who were able to convince recruiters to accept them also found themselves facing ill treatment. Because of these "cruel-

---

[7] *OR*, ser. 1, vol. 32, pt. 3, pp. 88, 132–33, 146–47, 172–73, 418; ser. 3, 4: 132, 146, 174–75. *WGFL: US*, p. 625; James W. Geary, *We Need Men: The Union Draft in the Civil War* (DeKalb: Northern Illinois University Press, 1991), pp. 64, 130–31; Victor B. Howard, *Black Liberation in Kentucky: Emancipation and Freedom, 1862–1884* (Lexington: University Press of Kentucky, 1983), pp. 57–62 (quotation, p. 58).

[8] *OR*, ser. 1, vol. 32, pt. 3, p. 572; ser. 3, 4: 132, 233–34 (quotations), 248–49. Howard, *Black Liberation in Kentucky*, p. 63. An account of Mussey's efforts in Tennessee is in Chapter 7, above.

[9] *OR*, ser. 1, vol. 39, pt. 2, p. 140 (quotation); ser. 3, 4: 423, 429–30, 460. Howard, *Black Liberation in Kentucky*, pp. 65–67.

ties," Burbridge was able to urge successfully, early in June, that recruiters be authorized to accept any man who presented himself for enlistment. Those who were not fit for operations in the field could perform garrison duty in an "invalid" regiment composed of men with similar disabilities, like others in service elsewhere in the South. The 63d and 64th United States Colored Infantries (USCIs) were already guarding plantations along the Mississippi River, and the 42d and 100th USCIs were performing guard and garrison duties at Chattanooga and Nashville.[10]

Although the Army eventually set up camps to house soldiers' dependents, slaveholders' abuse of the earliest recruits' families slowed the pace of enlistment during late spring. By summer, Burbridge found it necessary to send recruiting parties through the state, as authorities in Tennessee had had to do a year earlier. These groups faced active opposition. At Covington, across the Ohio River from Cincinnati, the officer commanding the 117th USCI reported that a "small squad" of his men led by a sergeant suffered one wounded and "several captured" in late July. The next month, the size of recruiting parties had increased, by order, to no fewer than fifty men. An expedition through Shelby County, halfway between Louisville and the state capital, required three hundred fifty. Larger, well-armed parties were better able to defend themselves against the "marauding Bands" mounted on "fleet Horses" that operated in most parts of Kentucky. Seventy men of the 108th USCI routed a group of about sixty guerrillas northeast of Owensboro in mid-August, wounding seven and capturing nine of them. Within three weeks, the officer of the 118th USCI who commanded the garrison at Owensboro reported the murder of three of his men by guerrillas. Despite such violent opposition, a recruiter at Henderson, an Ohio River town some twenty-five miles west of Owensboro, reported enlisting "from forty to sixty men daily." By mid-September, Adjutant General Thomas was able to tell the secretary of war that fourteen thousand black Kentuckians had joined the Army.[11]

General Burbridge wanted to mount two of his new black regiments and use them to hunt guerrillas. He spoke of this to Brig. Gen. Joseph Holt, the judge advocate general, who happened to be in Louisville and sent an enthusiastic telegram to the secretary of war: "These regiments, composed of men almost raised . . . on horseback, of uncompromising loyalty, and having an intimate knowledge of the topography of the country, would prove a powerful instrumentality in ridding the state of those guerrilla bands of robbers and murderers which now infest and oppress almost every part of it." After conferring with Lt. Gen. Ulysses S. Grant, Stanton wrote back to suggest that mounted infantry might prove a more versatile force than cavalry. He approved Burbridge's proposal to mount the troops on horses confiscated from disloyal owners. Despite Stanton's suggestion, Burbridge went ahead and organized

---

[10] *OR*, ser. 3, 4: 422 (quotations); Frederick H. Dyer, *A Compendium of the War of the Rebellion* (New York: Thomas Yoseloff, 1959 [1908]), pp. 1731, 1733–34, 1738; Berlin et al., *Black Military Experience*, pp. 193–96; Howard, *Black Liberation in Kentucky*, p. 64.

[11] *OR*, ser. 1, vol. 39, pt. 1, p. 492; ser. 3, 4: 733. Col L. G. Brown to Capt J. B. Dickson, 23 Jul 1864, 117th United States Colored Infantry (USCI); Lt Col J. H. Hammond to Col W. H. Revere, 30 Aug 1864, and 30 Aug 1864, both in 107th USCI; Capt J. L. Bullis to Maj Gen S. G. Burbridge, 17 Sep 1864 (quotations), 118th USCI; Capt J. C. Cowin to 1st Lt T. J. Neal, 17 Aug 1864, 108th USCI; all in Entry 57C, Regimental Papers, Record Group (RG) 94, Rcds of the Adjutant General's Office, National Archives (NA).

two twelve-company regiments of cavalry, the 5th and 6th United States Colored Cavalries (USCCs). Adjutant General Thomas saw several companies of the 5th at Lexington in mid-September. "The men are all selected with reference to weight and riding qualities," he told Stanton. "This will make one of the very best regiments in the service."[12]

Although the 5th USCC was not completely mustered in by late September 1864, it was one of the first of the new black regiments from Kentucky to go into action. Earlier that month, some of General Burbridge's white regiments "utterly routed and dispersed" an unusually large band of guerrillas, estimated at more than one hundred fifty men, that had recently murdered "a squad of 8 or 10 colored troops" near Ghent, halfway between Louisville and Cincinnati. With the threat of irregular warfare somewhat abated, Burbridge turned his attention to a large salt-works across the state line in southwestern Virginia. Saltville, the closest town, lay near the tracks of the East Tennessee and Virginia Railroad, the only line through the mountains between Harpers Ferry and Chattanooga. It connected with other roads that led east to Richmond and carried the saltworks' product to the Confed-erate Army of Northern Virginia. When word of this project reached Atlanta, Maj. Gen. William T. Sherman scoffed, "I doubt the necessity your sending far into Virginia to destroy the salt works, or any other material interest; we must destroy their armies." At that point in the war, Sherman's Military Division of the Missis-sippi included all the territory south of the Ohio River between the Appalachians and the Mississippi River and stood two organizational levels above the District of Kentucky. Nonetheless, Burbridge continued to plan his attack on Saltville.[13]

On 20 September, a division that included nine regiments of Kentucky cavalry and mounted infantry and one cavalry regiment each from Michigan and Ohio left Mount Sterling, Kentucky. A four-day march brought it to Prestonburg, some nine-ty miles to the southeast. There, a mixed force of some six hundred hastily armed and mounted black recruits joined it. The new troops had just covered more than one hundred miles from Camp Nelson. Col. James S. Brisbin, commanding officer of the 5th USCC, called these men "a detachment" of his regiment, although an officer of the 6th USCC led them and they included recruits of the 116th USCI as well. On 27 September, the column continued toward Virginia. Brisbin complained of the abuse that his men suffered from the overwhelmingly Kentuckian white troops of the command, "petty outrages, such as . . . stealing their horses, . . . as well as the jeers and taunts that they would not fight."[14]

As the federal column drew closer to its objective, it met some slight opposi-tion from a small Confederate cavalry brigade. The troopers of the 5th USCC, one Confederate wrote, were "the first [black soldiers] we ever met." The colonel commanding the brigade with which the regiment marched mentioned only two exchanges of shots, although General Burbridge claimed to have fought all the way

---

[12] *OR*, ser. 1, vol. 39, pt. 2, pp. 208 ("These regiments"), 231; ser. 3, 4: 733 ("The men").

[13] *OR*, ser. 1, vol. 39, pt. 2, pp. 323 ("a squad"), 335, 341, 360 ("utterly routed"), 447 ("I doubt"); NA Microfilm Pub M594, Compiled Rcds Showing Svc of Mil Units in Volunteer Union Organizations, roll 204, 5th United States Colored Cavalry (USCC).

[14] *OR*, ser. 1, vol. 39, pt. 1, pp. 553, 556–57 (quotations, pp. 556–57), and pt. 2, p. 436; NA M594, roll 204, 5th USCC; George S. Burkhardt, *Confederate Rage, Yankee Wrath: No Quarter in the Civil War* (Carbondale: Southern Illinois University Press, 2007), p. 194.

"from the Virginia line up to the salt works." By 2 October, local militia and rein-forcements brought by rail had increased the defenders' numbers to about twenty-eight hundred, more than half the strength of the attacking force. That morning, the Union column approached the North Fork of the Holston River. Saltville lay behind a range of hills on the south bank.[15]

Seeing the Confederate position about halfway up the slope, the Union troops moved forward that morning with the 5th USCC on the extreme left of the line. The black recruits "behaved well for new troops," the division commander wrote afterward. By afternoon, Union attackers had occupied most of the enemy position but soon found themselves with empty cartridge boxes. General Burbridge did not explain his failure to provide enough ammunition for this, his pet project. As dark-ness fell, the federal troopers withdrew as quietly as possible, leaving the saltworks largely undamaged. They marched all night, putting as much distance as possible between themselves and the enemy.[16]

Just what happened after the battle is hard to determine. "Nearly all the wounded were brought off, though we had not an ambulance in the command," Colonel Brisbin reported. "The negro soldiers preferred present suffering to being murdered at the hands of a cruel enemy." The chief medical officer, on the other hand, claimed to be able to give only an estimate of casualties because four of the surgeons who accompanied the expedition had stayed behind on the field with the wounded. What figures he was able to offer showed clearly that the 5th USCC and the Michigan and Ohio regiments brigaded with it had the hardest fight, suffering 129 killed and wounded, more than two-thirds of the attacking force's casualties. Fifty-three men in the 5th USCC constituted more than half the total of missing for the entire division. This figure probably reflected the troops' inexperience, since some of those missing found their way back to the regiment later in the war.[17]

Confederates certainly murdered some of the wounded they found after the battle, even invading their own hospitals to do it. Kentucky guerrillas who joined forces temporarily with the defenders of Saltville committed a number of these acts; their leader, a notorious figure named Champ Ferguson, shot several wounded soldiers, black and white, including a Unionist Kentucky officer. A spirit of rage against Unionist Southerners, whom General Forrest called "renegade[s]" and "Tories," moved Confederate Kentuckians at Saltville, as it had Forrest's troopers at Fort Pillow nearly six months earlier. Viewed by the Confederates as merely rebellious slaves, black soldiers were an equally inviting target. One of the Union surgeons who stayed behind with the wounded mentioned that seven black soldiers were murdered in Confederate hospitals. Left on the field, other wounded also died, but their number is uncertain. The day after the fight, a Confederate officer noted in his diary, "Great numbers of them were killed yesterday and today," although it is not clear whether he based this remark on hearsay, the sound of indiscriminate firing after the battle, or personal observation. Another Confederate's reminiscence

---

[15] *OR*, ser. 1, vol. 39, pt. 1, p. 552 ("from the"); Thomas D. Mays, "The Battle of Saltville," in *Black Soldiers in Blue: African American Troops in the Civil War Era*, ed. John David Smith (Chapel Hill: University of North Carolina Press, 2002), pp. 200–226 ("the first," p. 210).

[16] *OR*, ser. 1, vol. 39, pt. 1, pp. 552–53, 556 (quotation).

[17] Ibid., pp. 553–54, 557 ("Nearly all"); Mays, "Battle of Saltville," p. 218.

of a wounded trooper nimble enough to dodge, so that it took two shots to kill him, is at odds with Colonel Brisbin's insistence that every man who was able to move by himself accompanied the Union retreat.[18]

Saltville was the largest expedition that black troops from Kentucky took part in west of the Appalachians. From October 1864 to the end of the war, military activity in the state took the form of constant patrols and infrequent but sometimes fatal clashes with guerrillas. The two cavalry and four heavy artillery regiments raised in Kentucky did not leave the state; most of the seventeen infantry regiments did.[19]

When Burbridge returned to his headquarters at Lexington on 9 October, he found Adjutant General Thomas there making arrangements to move some of the new black regiments to Virginia. At Covington and Louisville, officers and men of these regiments boarded steamboats for travel to one of the West Virginia river ports, Wheeling or Parkersburg. From there, they moved to Baltimore by rail. The last leg of the journey was again by water, down the Chesapeake Bay to Fort Monroe and City Point. Five organizations from Kentucky—the 107th, 109th, 116th, 117th, and 118th USCIs—were in Virginia by the end of the month. The Union's ability at this stage of the war to raise five regiments in as many months and ship them hundreds of miles to where it meant to use them was a vivid display of its superiority to the Confederacy in men and machinery. Although black soldiers in the field, nationwide, did not number as many as ninety thousand until January 1865, their presence in the trenches of Virginia, along railroads west of the Appalachians, and at Mississippi River garrisons was a powerful influence on the outcome of the war.[20]

The new arrivals found themselves assigned to General Butler's Army of the James. Lt. Col. John Pierson of the 109th USCI found this a pleasant change from Kentucky. "The Colored Troops are as much thought of here by the white soldiers and officers as any men in this Department and treated as well," he told his daughter, "and all that I have seen seems glad to see us come and the white Regiments are anxious to have us Brigaded with them they say the Darkies are Bully fellows to fight and all the predjudice seems to be gone Officers of colored men are as much thought of as any." Some old hands in the Army of the James took a more critical view. "Those . . . new regiments are perfect donkeys," 2d Lt. Joseph M. Califf of the 7th USCI wrote in his diary just one day after Pierson addressed his daughter, "not only with regard to picket [duty] but almost every thing else military."[21]

There can be no doubt that the men of the Kentucky regiments arrived in Virginia with little grasp of a soldier's duties; they had few officers to instruct them. General Thomas filled the regiments destined for Virginia with recruits and reas-

---

[18] *OR*, ser. 1, vol. 32, pt. 1, pp. 607 ("renegade[s]"), 610 ("Tories"); vol. 39, pt. 1, p. 554. Mays, "Battle of Saltville," pp. 212 ("Great numbers"), 214–16.

[19] *OR*, ser. 1, vol. 39, pt. 1, pp. 857–58, 876; vol. 45, pt. 1, p. 876; vol. 49, pt. 1, pp. 9, 49. NA M594, roll 204, 6th USCC; roll 212, 72d USCI; roll 217, 121st USCI.

[20] *OR*, ser. 1, vol. 39, pt. 3, pp. 157, 200, 219. Monthly mean strength of "Colored Troops in the United States Army" from *The Medical and Surgical History of the War of the Rebellion*, 2 vols. in 6 (Washington, D.C.: Government Printing Office, 1870–1888), vol. 1, pt. 1, pp. 664–65, 684–85, 704–05.

[21] J. Pierson to Dear Daugter [*sic*], 30 Oct 1864, J. Pierson Letters, Clements Library, University of Michigan, Ann Arbor; J. M. Califf Diary, 31 Oct 1864, Historians files, U.S. Army Center of Military History (CMH).

signed to them a few officers from regiments that were to stay in Kentucky a while longer. He could do nothing, though, about officers who failed, for whatever reason, to report at all. All five of the ten-company regiments from Kentucky arrived in Virginia lacking at least one-fourth of the captains and lieutenants that each required to reach full strength.[22]

Maj. Edward W. Bacon joined the 117th USCI in January 1865. Two months later, he observed "considerable improvement in the command, but much remains to be done before it reaches even tolerable proficiency." Sickness had reduced the regiment's strength to below the minimum number necessary to muster in new officers to drill the men and see to their food, clothing, and shelter. The 118th USCI needed twenty-one to make up its complement. Absence of instruction and discipline would handicap the Kentucky regiments throughout their service.[23]

Lack of officers was common, too, in older regiments that had been in the field for months. By early fall, Lieutenant Califf himself was one of only eleven officers on duty with his regiment. An officer in the 45th USCI wrote at the end of October:

> During the last six weeks the company has neither marched nor drilled except a small squad each day, being the number relieved from guard. At 7 1/2 o'clock a.m. each day the line is formed for fatigue duty and the men (all except the sick & a guard) . . . work until 5 o'clock P.M. There are so few officers . . . that each has to take his turn on fatigue about every third day. The amount of labor required of the command and the lack of officers to give the necessary supervision, has rendered the company less efficient . . . than any well-wisher of our cause would hope.[24]

Officers throughout the army were aware of the problem. When Maj. Lewis L. Weld brought six companies of the 41st USCI from Philadelphia to Virginia in October, he reported to General Butler, who was surprised to learn of the regiment's arrival. Butler had requested that five companies of the 45th USCI, detached at Washington, D.C., be sent to join their regiment. "You see, Major," Butler said, "I didn't ask for you at all. . . . I suppose your men are perfectly green." "Perfectly so, sir," Weld replied. "Well, I'll give you a chance to drill," Butler said. "Send the major to Deep Bottom," he told an aide, "with orders to . . . put him on no duty that can be helped & let him alone till further orders. . . . By the way, Major, teach your men carefully the loadings & firings." "Certainly, General, but had I not better teach them how to make a right face first?" "Yes, yes, that is the first essential," Butler agreed, "but don't forget the other." Weld took his regiment to Deep Bottom on the James River, a place he knew well from his time as a captain in the 7th

---

[22]*OR*, ser. 1, vol. 39, pt. 3, p. 219; Brig Gen L. Thomas to Col P. T. Swaine, 6 Oct 1864, 117th USCI, and Col O. A. Bartholomew to "Captain," 3 Nov 1864, 109th USCI, both in Entry 57C, RG 94, NA; Edward A. Miller Jr., *The Black Civil War Soldiers of Illinois: The Story of the Twenty-ninth U.S. Colored Infantry* (Columbia: University of South Carolina Press, 1998), p. 114.

[23]E. W. Bacon to Dear Kate, 9 Mar 1864, E. W. Bacon Papers, American Antiquarian Society (AAS), Worcester, Mass.; Col A. A. Rand to Capt I. R. Sealy, 24 Oct 1864, 118th USCI, Entry 57C, RG 94, NA. Bacon was appointed major in the 117th USCI on 5 January 1865; he had been a captain in the 29th Connecticut and is mentioned in that grade later in this chapter.

[24]NA M594, roll 210, 45th USCI; Califf Diary, 17 Oct 1864.

USCI. His divisional commander, Brig. Gen. William Birney, "promise[d] that I shall not be put into the field until I have had time to organize & drill somewhat," Weld told his mother, "several weeks at least." Two more companies of the 41st joined later in the year, but the last two did not arrive until February. Only then was the regiment up to strength.[25]

Butler was not alone in wanting his men prepared for battle. The 127th USCI also reached Virginia in October and at once took up fatigue duty at Deep Bottom. General Birney, to whose division the regiment belonged, asked for it to be relieved from this duty and sent to him. "The regiment is new, and the men have not yet been drilled in the 'loadings and firings,'" he wrote. "If it is the intention to have them take an active part in the present campaign, it is absolutely necessary that opportunity be afforded for drilling and disciplining them. . . . I would prefer not to put this regiment under fire, until the men are taught how to load and fire, and have attained some proficiency in drill." Both the 127th USCI and Weld's 41st came from Camp William Penn, and the officers and men probably had heard of the disaster that resulted when another untried Philadelphia regiment, the 8th USCI, went into action at Olustee, Florida, that February.[26]

When General Butler told his aide that Weld's newly arrived troops should be "put . . . on no duty that can be helped," he was probably referring to the Dutch Gap Canal, an excavation that occupied labor details from at least seven black regiments in the Army of the James during the late summer and fall of 1864. Five hundred feet long, the canal cut across a neck of land formed by one of the many bends in the river. Its purpose was to afford passage for U.S. Navy gunboats past a stretch where the water at low tide was only eight feet deep, half as much as the draft of the vessels required, and where the fire of Confederate batteries could reach them. Such a canal, Union generals hoped, would also allow them to move troops more quickly by water than the Confederates could by land.[27]

Butler tried to begin his project with a call on 6 August for twelve hundred volunteers "to do laborious digging[,] to work 7 1/2 hours a day for not more than twenty days." Two shifts would labor all the daylight hours. Volunteers would receive eight cents an hour, an amount that would nearly double a private's monthly pay, and an eight-ounce ration of whiskey daily or its cash equivalent. Company commanders were to read the order to their men at two consecutive daily parades,

[25]*OR*, ser. 1, vol. 42, pt. 2, p. 1044. Lt Col L. Wagner to Maj C. W. Foster, 10 Oct 1864 (W–811–CT–1864); 21 Oct 1864 (W–848–CT–1864); 7 Dec 1864 (W–950–CT–1864); all in Entry 360, Colored Troops Div, Letters Received (LR), RG 94, NA. NA M594, roll 209, 41st USCI; L. L. Weld to My dearest Mother, 17 Oct 1864 (quotations), L. L. Weld Papers, Yale University, New Haven, Conn.

[26]Brig Gen W. Birney to 1st Lt W. P. Shreve, 8 Oct 1864, Entry 7035, 3d Div, X Corps, Letters Sent (LS), pt. 2, Polyonymous Successions of Cmds, RG 393, Rcds of U.S. Army Continental Cmds, NA.

[27]*OR*, ser. 1, vol. 42, pt. 1, p. 657. NA M594, roll 206, 4th and 6th USCIs; roll 208, 22d USCI; roll 216, 118th USCI; roll 217, 127th USCI. Weld to My dearest Mother, 17 Oct 1864 (quotation); *Official Records of the Union and Confederate Navies in the War of the Rebellion*, 30 vols. (Washington, D.C.: Government Printing Office, 1894–1922), ser. 1, 10: 345 (hereafter cited as *ORN*); Dyer, *Compendium*, pp. 1724, 1727, 1730, 1739; Benjamin F. Butler, *Autobiography and Personal Reminiscences of Major-General Benj. F. Butler* (Boston: A. M. Thayer, 1892), pp. 743–44; John Y. Simon, ed., *The Papers of Ulysses S. Grant*, 30 vols. to date (Carbondale and Edwardsville: Southern Illinois University Press, 1967–), 12: 446.

White troops as well as black toiled from August through December 1864 to dig the Dutch Gap Canal, a shortcut for Union shipping to avoid Confederate batteries on the James River.

record the names of volunteers by 8 August, and have the party ready to march the next day. "Anyone who is lazy or inattentive will be sent back to his company without pay," the order warned. Soon afterward, men of the 4th, 6th, and 22d USCIs reported to Dutch Gap and began to dig.[28]

Butler meant well, but he underestimated greatly both the number of men and the length of time the job required. Work dragged on into the fall, and took many men, not all of them volunteers. In mid-October, the commanding officer of the 4th USCI complained that his regiment was short seven of the ten second lieutenants it was entitled to. Moreover, 196 recruits who had been assigned to him were instead "at work in the canal at Dutch Gap. These men are wholly without drill or discipline and in their present condition totally unfit for service against the enemy and with our present depleted list of officers, I am unable to do ought to improve their condition." The situation remained unchanged at the end of the month. Before

---

[28] *OR*, ser. 1, vol. 42, pt. 2, p. 70; Edward G. Longacre, *A Regiment of Slaves: The 4th United States Colored Infantry, 1863–1866* (Mechanicsburg, Pa.: Stackpole Books, 2003), pp. 110–14; James M. Paradis, *Strike the Blow for Freedom: The 6th United States Colored Infantry in the Civil War* (Shippensburg, Pa.: White Mane Books, 1998), pp. 61–67.

the project was done, it would involve the efforts of soldier and civilian laborers from as far away as Roanoke Island, North Carolina.[29]

Military authorities expected that canal workers would undergo what the senior naval officer on the James River called "annoyances and interruptions" from enemy artillery, and Confederate batteries did not take long to open fire. What neither side foresaw was that Dutch Gap would become the scene of a test of will between the federal and Confederate governments about the treatment of prisoners of war. Federal interrogators learned from enemy deserters that more than one hundred black prisoners of war were at work on Confederate defenses north of the James River, under fire from Union artillery. Col. Samuel A. Duncan, commanding the all-black brigade at Dutch Gap, wrote to General Butler on 21 September: "Is it not established with sufficient certainty that the rebels have . . . put to hard labor, colored prisoners of war . . . , to warrant the use of rebel prisoners upon the work . . . at Dutch Gap, where the shells of the enemy are beginning to tell with considerable effect upon our laboring soldiers? My men would take pleasure in acting as guards; would perform the duty, I think, with unusual pride and efficiency."[30]

Not only did Butler command the Army of the James and the Department of Virginia and North Carolina; he also served as commissioner for the exchange of prisoners of war. Early in October, he wrote to his Confederate counterpart in Richmond, enclosing four depositions by deserters who swore that black Union prisoners were at work under fire in the trenches and adding that he had ordered one hundred ten prisoners held by his own side "into the canal at Dutch Gap . . . at hard labor, . . . until this practice is stopped." Uncertain of the exact number of black prisoners of war at work for the Confederates, or perhaps reckoning on future casualties, he asked the Union provost marshal general at City Point to send one hundred fifty of the prisoners in his care to the canal. Grant approved this proceeding. The next day, having received no reply from Richmond, Butler put his prisoner-hostages to work.[31]

The Confederate secretary of war wrote to General Robert E. Lee, outlining the situation. Government policy, he maintained, was to treat black soldiers as prisoners of war, unless they had been slaves before enlistment. Confederate authorities advertised the names of former slaves captured in uniform and hoped that their owners would reclaim them. The secretary compared their special status to that of turncoats caught wearing the uniform of the other side. The whole episode, he told Lee, became more complicated because the Confederate government was reluctant to deal with General Butler, whom Jefferson Davis had pronounced not "simply . . . a public enemy of the Confederate States of America, but . . . an outlaw and common enemy of mankind" because of what he regarded as Butler's high-handed and illegal behavior while commanding at New Orleans in 1862. Any Confederate

---

[29] Maj A. S. Boernstein to Lt Col E. W. Smith, 16 Oct 1864 (quotation), and 29 Oct 1864, both in 4th USCI, Regimental Books, RG 94, NA; Patricia C. Click, *Time Full of Trouble: The Roanoke Island Freedmen's Colony, 1862–1867* (Chapel Hill: University of North Carolina Press, 2001), pp. 130–33.

[30] *OR*, ser. 1, vol. 42, pt. 2, pp. 158, 959 ("Is it not"); *ORN*, ser. 1, 10: 345 ("annoyances").

[31] *OR*, ser. 1, vol. 42, pt. 3, pp. 216–17; ser. 2, 7: 967 (quotation). *Private and Official Correspondence of Gen. Benjamin F. Butler*, 5 vols. ([Norwood, Mass.: Plimpton Press], 1917), 5: 250.

officer who captured Butler was to hang him forthwith. Lee would have to correspond about the prisoners directly with General Grant.[32]

Lee sent Grant a long letter in which he began by citing precedents about slave property during wartime that went back to the Revolutionary War. Almost incidentally, he mentioned that the black prisoners of war were put to work by mistake and against his orders and had been withdrawn. He also insisted that "the negroes employed upon our fortifications are not allowed to be . . . exposed to fire," and asked whether Grant approved of Butler's retaliatory treatment of the Confederate prisoners. As soon as the letter reached Grant, he ordered Butler to return the Confederates to City Point, and wrote the next day to Lee:

> I shall always regret the necessity of retaliating for wrongs done our soldiers, but regard it my duty to protect all persons received into the Army of the United States, regardless of color or nationality. . . . I have nothing to do with the discussion of the slavery question, therefore decline answering the arguments adduced to show the right to return to former owners such negroes as are captured from our Army. In answer to the question at the conclusion of your letter, . . . all prisoners of war falling into my hands shall receive the kindest possible treatment consistent with securing them, unless I have good authority for believing any number of our men are being treated otherwise. Then, painful as it may be to me, I shall inflict like treatment on an equal number of Confederate prisoners.[33]

By the time Grant's letter arrived, Lee had withdrawn the black prisoners from their exposed position. Three more months would pass before the Confederate government agreed to equal consideration for "all prisoners . . . held by either party." The exchange system, which had ground to a halt more than a year earlier when the Confederacy refused to recognize black soldiers as legitimate combatants, then began to function again. Colonel Duncan's idea, Butler's implementation of it, and Grant's support of his action all served to put black soldiers on a par with a group of captive Union generals at Charleston four months earlier. The Confederate defenders had placed the generals in the way of artillery fire but had withdrawn them when the besiegers ordered prisoners of equal rank sent from Northern prison camps to work in exposed positions.[34]

Excavation of the Dutch Gap Canal also raised again the question of the disproportionate use of black soldiers for fatigue duty. Commanding officers of black regiments complained often about excessive fatigues, but white troops also performed such chores. The response to Butler's offer of additional pay was favorable: in one white regiment, six hundred men volunteered. Elsewhere in the Union trenches, when brigade commanders in white divisions received orders to build a road or to clear a field

---

[32] *OR*, ser. 1, 15: 906 (quotation); ser. 2, 7: 990–93.

[33] *OR*, ser. 2, 7: 1010–12 ("the negroes," p. 1012), 1018–19 ("I shall always").

[34] Ibid., 7: 1012, 1018; 8: 98 (quotation). McPherson, *Battle Cry of Freedom*, pp. 799–800; Brooks D. Simpson, *Let Us Have Peace: Ulysses S. Grant and the Politics of War and Reconstruction, 1861–1868* (Chapel Hill: University of North Carolina Press, 1991), pp. 66–67; Richard J. Sommers, "The Dutch Gap Affair: Military Atrocities and the Rights of Negro Soldiers," *Civil War History* 21 (1975): 51–64. On the use of captive generals as hostages at Charleston, see Chapter 2, above. The June 1864 correspondence about the Charleston prisoner-hostages between Maj. Gen. John G. Foster, commanding the Department of the South, and the War Department is in *OR*, ser. 1, vol. 35, pt. 2, pp. 141–45.

of fire in front of their trenches, their own troops did the job. In mid-October, one white division in the Army of the James was furnishing three hundred men a day for such fatigues.[35]

While it is clear that white troops undertook many onerous fatigues, the equitable distribution of these tasks is much less so. Late in August, the X Corps issued an order tapping its black division and one of its white divisions for three hundred men each to go on fatigue duty. The X Corps, though, was in General Butler's Army of the James. Butler was a hearty proponent of the Lincoln administration's Colored Troops policy. Things looked somewhat different in the Army of the Potomac, where General Meade deprecated the military ability of black soldiers. In Meade's army that fall, the only black division (Brig. Gen. Edward Ferrero's 4th Division of the IX Corps) sometimes furnished details of as many as twenty-two hundred men—half its strength—for work on fortifications and roads. Daily drafts of five, six, or seven hundred men, which white divisions also furnished routinely, were far more usual; even so, no division could hold its trenches for long with half of its men on pick-and-shovel duty. The root of the problem of unequal assignments, and its solution, lay in the practices that high authorities at the scene would encourage or allow.[36]

Fatigues were not the only form of labor that took men from their regiments. Black and white divisions alike detailed men as hospital attendants and as teamsters in the Quartermaster Department and elsewhere. That summer, Brig. Gen. Charles J. Paine noticed that eighty black infantrymen from his division were absent as teamsters in the XVIII Corps artillery brigade and that 192 men were with the corps ambulance train. He wrote to corps headquarters, asking for the return of all "except the fair proportion of this division. I make this application, not on account of particular need for the men with their companies, but because I consider it of the greatest importance to the Colored Regiments that they should be made to think themselves soldiers, and should not feel that they are only to be soldiers when they are not wanted as teamsters."[37]

For Union troops on both banks of the James River, October was a month of routine siege duty. "Dig, dig, dig is again the order of the day and night," remarked Capt. Elliott F. Grabill of the 5th USCI. The 4th USCI stood to arms at 4:00 a.m. daily, Sgt. Maj. Christian A. Fleetwood recorded in his diary. Capt. Solon A. Carter, a staff officer in the all-black 3d Division of the XVIII Corps, went nineteen days without "an opportunity to take a bath *all over*, or change my underclothing," he told his wife. On the same divisional staff, 2d Lt. Robert N. Verplanck kept an eye on the weather, which turned "real cold & windy" on 8 October after a week of rain. "There is one consola-

---

[35] Maj Gen D. B. Birney to Maj R. S. Davis, 8 Aug 1864, Entry 345, X Corps, LS, pt. 2, RG 393, NA. Capt C. A. Carleton to Col J. C. Abbott, 11 Oct 1864; to Brig Gen J. R. Hawley, 17 and 19 Oct 1864; to Col F. B. Pond, 18 and 20 Oct 1864; to Col H. M. Plaisted, 23 Oct 1864; all in Entry 376, 1st Div, X Corps, LS, pt. 2, RG 393, NA.

[36] X Corps, Special Orders (SO) 108, 28 Aug 1864, Entry 359, X Corps, Special Orders, pt. 2, RG 393, NA. Capt G. A. Hicks, daily Ltrs to Col O. P. Stearns and Col C. S. Russell, 5–11 Oct 1864, and Capt G. A. Hicks to Col O. P. Stearns, 12 and 13 Oct 1864, all in Entry 5122, 4th Div, IX Corps, LS, pt. 2, RG 393, NA. For fatigue details in white divisions, see Capt W. R. Driver to Lt Col W. Wilson, 6 and 7 Oct 1864, and to Lt Col J. E. McGee, 6 and 7 Oct 1864, all in Entry 86, 1st Div, II Corps, LS, pt. 2, RG 393, NA. 3d Div, V Corps, SO 91, 23 Oct 1864, and Circular 24, 26 Oct 1864, both in Entry 4357, 3d Div, V Corps, Orders and Circulars, pt. 2, RG 393, NA.

[37] Brig Gen C. J. Paine to Maj W. Russell Jr., 11 Aug 1864, Entry 1659, 3d Div, XVIII Corps, LS, pt. 2, RG 393, NA. For such assignments in a white division, see 3d Div, V Corps, SO 74, 4 Oct 1864, Entry 4357, pt. 2, RG 393, NA.

tion," he wrote, "that it will dry up the roads and we will get our supplies regularly and the ration will be full."[38]

By the third week in October, Grant had conceived a plan that he would put into action at the end of the month. Attacking from its trenches around Petersburg, the Army of the Potomac would seize the South Side Railroad, a line that ran west more than one hundred miles to Lynchburg, where there was a further rail link to Tennessee. Taking part in this movement would be Ferrero's nine-regiment division of the IX Corps. To prevent Confederates around Richmond from sending reinforcements to help defend the railroad, Butler's troops would launch a simultaneous attack north of the James River with the X Corps, which included Brig. Gen. William Birney's division of seven black regiments, and the XVIII Corps, with its all-black division of nine regiments led by the senior officer, Col. Alonzo G. Draper.[39]

Compared to earlier attacks that year, especially the fiasco at Cold Harbor in June, the move against the South Side Railroad was almost tentative. "Let it be distinctly understood . . . that there is to be no attack made against defended, intrenched positions," Grant told Butler on 24 October, and sent a similar warning to Meade. Butler's men were to "feel out" the enemy line "and, if you can, turn it." In Meade's army, the IX Corps commander in particular, "if he finds the enemy intrenched and their works well manned," was "not to attack but confront him, and . . . advance promptly" if the other two corps, operating on either flank, were able to shift the Confederates. With the presidential election two weeks away, Grant did not want to risk following recent Union successes in Georgia and the Shenandoah Valley with a bloody defeat.[40]

Southwest of Petersburg, Ferrero's division was awake and on the road at 3:30, three hours before sunrise on 27 October. Each man carried six days' rations and two hundred rounds of ammunition. The ammunition alone weighed about sixteen pounds. When daylight came, the division formed line of battle and plunged into what Col. Delavan Bates called "the worst piece of woods I ever saw." Bates, who had been captured in a forest near Chancellorsville in 1863 and had led the 30th USCI through some of the same country the next spring, commanded a brigade in the division. His men struggled forward to within one hundred yards of the enemy position. "The underbrush, briars, logs &c. made it . . . almost impenetrable," he told his father, "and when we halted in front of the enemy works a line of breastworks had to be thrown up and the timber slashed to prevent a surprise and be able to resist an attack if the rebs should undertake one. It was an awful job. . . . But fortunately the affair terminated without great loss to our Division or corps. . . . As usual when we make a move it rained like fury all night." On the west end of the Union advance, the II Corps failed to turn the

[38]E. F. Grabill to Dearly Loved One, 3 Oct 1864, E. F. Grabill Papers, Oberlin College (OC), Oberlin, Ohio; C. A. Fleetwood Diary, entries for Oct 1864, C. A. Fleetwood Papers, Library of Congress (LC); S. A. Carter to My own darling, 17 Oct 1864, S. A. Carter Papers, U.S. Army Military History Institute (MHI), Carlisle, Pa.; R. N. Verplanck to Dear Mother, 8 Oct 1864, R. N. Verplanck Letters typescript, Poughkeepsie [N.Y.] Public Library; Robert K. Krick, *Civil War Weather in Virginia* (Tuscaloosa: University of Alabama Press, 2007), pp. 140–41.

[39]*OR*, ser. 1, vol. 42, pt. 3, pp. 317–18, 331–32, 463, 465–66.

[40]Ibid., pp. 317 ("if he finds"), 331–32 ("Let it be"); Brooks D. Simpson, *Ulysses S. Grant: Triumph over Adversity, 1822–1865* (Boston: Houghton Mifflin, 2000), pp. 386–87.

enemy's flank, and the next day the IX Corps, along with the rest of the Army of the Potomac, retired to its previous position.[41]

North of the river, Butler's troops found themselves in a similar predicament. Birney's division of the X Corps was moving an hour before sunrise. Passing through the Union front line, it formed line of battle and moved almost at once into woods choked with underbrush. Capt. Edward W. Bacon was in the lead with the 29th Connecticut, acting as skirmishers and covering the entire division front, which stretched for nearly three-quarters of a mile. Turning to look around just before the advance began, he saw "two whole Corps of as fine troops as there are in the country. . . . It was the grandest display of men I ever saw." The regimental adjutant, 1st Lt. Henry H. Brown, rode along the line from end to end, and saw things differently: "Co[mpany] H . . . I found in a very bad fix. It had never drilled the skirmish & the 2nd Lt comdg knew as little of it as they & he was so hoarse with a cold he could not be heard so mounting a stump I deployed them & then wheeled the line to the left clearing the right from the swamp."[42]

At length, the 29th Connecticut "advanced slowly through dense woods and a bad swamp for nearly a mile when we encountered the videttes of the enemy who promptly fired upon us," Bacon wrote. The rest of the brigade followed. "The line moved forward in excellent order but in a few moments received a severe fire from the gopher holes of the picket—which were very numerous and well built," he continued.

> I answered with my front rank and on we ran at full speed—for the land was more clear just there and when the men understood the design they showed their appreciation of it by the most horrible howls—very similar to those with which the enemy love to charge—the gopher holes still sent out bullets into our faces until their inmates saw that we were black & close on them when they dropped all and ran. . . . A short half mile further through the meanest of under growth—slipping on the clayey ground wet by the last nights rain, dodging from the shrapnel which began to reach us now & from the branches which they were cutting from the bigger pines, wondering what we would find and how soon we would find it, on we went until at the edge of the woods.

There they saw a cornfield full of tree stumps and beyond that "a chain of redoubts connected in the usual manner by strong breast works. Into these the pickets which we had driven before us went pell mell and as they rose to cross the works we took delight in hitting them."[43]

After the Confederates reached their trenches, the attackers had to lie down to seek cover. Despite the awkwardness of loading and firing a muzzle-loading rifle while not standing erect, the men of the 29th Connecticut managed to

---

[41] *OR*, ser. 1, vol. 42, pt. 1, p. 592, and pt. 3, p. 350; D. Bates to Father, 25 May 1863 and 28 Oct 1864 (quotation), both in D. Bates Letters, Historians files, CMH; *The Ordnance Manual for the Use of the Officers of the United States Army* (Philadelphia: J. B. Lippincott, 1862), pp. 270, 487.

[42] *OR*, ser. 1, vol. 42, pt. 1, p. 771; E. W. Bacon to Dear Kate, 31 Oct 1864, Bacon Papers; H. H. Brown to Dear friends at Home, 29 Oct 1864, H. H. Brown Papers, Connecticut Historical Society, Hartford. Brown's account agrees with Bacon's in other respects, especially regarding the Confederate troops' terror of black soldiers.

[43] Bacon to Dear Kate, 31 Oct 1864.

Swampy woods near Petersburg. "The worst piece of woods I ever saw," one Union officer remarked.

discharge at least one hundred fifty rounds each in the course of the day. By evening, their rifle barrels were foul; some men dismantled their weapons on the spot to clean them. The regiment's commander, Capt. Frederick E. Camp, asked for relief. Rain fell through the night. Before dawn, the 7th USCI moved forward to relieve the skirmishers. In twenty hours, the 29th Connecticut had suffered eleven killed and sixty-nine wounded, more than the rest of the division combined.[44]

Lieutenant Califf commanded a company in the 7th USCI. "It was clear and cold," he noted in his diary, "with a keen wind from the S.E.

> Long before we reached the line, we could hear the continual, crack, crack, crack of the skirmishe[r]s. When we reached the line, by feeling our way through the dripping undergrowth, the bullets began to whistle past, or crash among the limbs above us. Before daylight we had our line established. . . . When day broke the rebs opened a sharp fire with musketry. Within two hours I had five men wounded & one killed. . . . The last man wounded was Isaac Cooper, "K," while lying in a place I had just quitted, at the reserve. The ball struck him just below the small of the back—He rolled and screamed for a moment & then became quiet. We were losing so many men that the order was

---

[44]*OR*, ser. 1, vol. 42, pt. 1, pp. 149–50, 777, 779; Bacon to Dear Kate, 31 Oct 1864.

> given to fall back with most of the line. . . . We occupied a line of rebel gopher holes farther back in the woods until about 3 o'ck when the order came to prepare to fall back. We waited a long while . . . for the order but none came— Soon we discovered that the entire line had fallen back leaving us alone. I advised falling back . . . for the John[n]ies were evidently advancing their lines. [1st Lt. Charles G.] Teeple opposed it until it became evident that we should have to fall back without orders or go to Richmond. . . . We fell back & after we had got inside our cavalry picket line we met Gen. Birney with the remainder of the brigade going out to fight us in if necessary.

During more than ten hours in its advanced position, Califf's party of twenty-five accounted for seven of the regiment's thirty-two casualties. This rate of casualties, between one-quarter and one-third of the men engaged, was nearly as great as the 29th Connecticut had suffered the day before.[45]

The XVIII Corps left its camp near the James River at 5:00 a.m. on 27 October and marched about eight miles north to Fair Oaks, the site of a battle during McClellan's Peninsula Campaign of 1862. By midafternoon, both divisions of white troops were in action and soon learned that the Confederate line was too stoutly defended to be captured by anything less than an all-out attack. While this was going on, Maj. Gen. Godfrey Weitzel, the corps commander, ordered Col. John H. Holman's brigade of Draper's division to take position on the extreme right of the Union line, a few hundred yards north of the Williamsburg Road. The fifteen hundred officers and men of the brigade were to attack west toward Richmond along the line of the York River Railroad.[46]

The 37th USCI crossed the tracks to guard the right flank. South of the rail line, the 1st USCI advanced with the 22d USCI on its left. After the two regiments had moved forward about a mile, they saw Confederate cavalry. Two enemy twelve-pounders unlimbered and opened fire. Holman ordered a charge. The 1st USCI advanced across cleared space close to the railroad tracks, reached the guns, and spiked them. The 22d USCI had to make its way through woods and never came close to the enemy. Two different stories of its misadventure began to circulate at once.[47]

According to Colonel Draper's account, a misunderstood order caused confusion. Only one company of the 22d USCI heard it properly and managed to execute the maneuver. The regiment's commanding officer, Lt. Col. Ira C. Terry, was more explicit:

> Had the regiment left its recruits behind I think we could have gone in. They kept firing their muskets while advancing, and in the midst of the excitement broke and ran, causing the worst of confusion. I will say on behalf of these recruits that they did well so far as they knew how, never having any drill of

---

[45]*OR*, ser. 1, vol. 42, pt. 1, pp. 149–50; Califf Diary, 28 Oct 1864.

[46]*OR*, ser. 1, vol. 42, pt. 1, pp. 795–97, 802–03, 807–08; Field Return, 27 Oct 1864, Entry 1659, pt. 2, RG 393, NA.

[47]*OR*, ser. 1, vol. 42, pt. 1, pp. 814–17.

any account. They did not know how to act, and their conduct might have been foreseen.

Unable to count on support from the 22d USCI, the 1st USCI had to leave the Confederate guns and fall back along the railroad line. The 1st suffered 124 casualties in the afternoon's fighting (20 percent of about six hundred twenty officers and men), and the 22d fifty of about five hundred present. It was the second time in as many months that poor fire discipline had slowed the pace of a charge by one of the black regiments.[48]

Stymied by Grant's instructions not to press attacks on defended Confederate positions, the second and final fall attack on Richmond sputtered out. By 29 October, Butler's and Meade's armies had returned to their earlier positions. "Everyone is fixing up for winter," Colonel Bates of Ferrero's division wrote a week later, "building fireplaces, logging up tents, . . . and preparing for cold weather as much as possible. We have no orders to prepare winter quarters but there are many little things in the management of the army that looks like staying where we are for some time." Weather would play a large part in determining the extent of operations for the next few months. "No fighting since we have been here," Colonel Pierson of the newly arrived 109th USCI told his daughter, "and unless we have some very soon we cannot do much this fall or winter as the Roads will be so bad we cannot move." As the men began to prepare their quarters for the winter, the generals looked around for a new avenue of attack, one that would not involve movement by land.[49]

Wilmington, North Carolina, some two hundred fifty miles south of Petersburg, had been the Confederacy's only seaport since Union regiments had seized the islands that blocked Mobile Bay that August. It lay twenty miles from the ocean, protected by thirteen Confederate batteries: five along the banks of the Cape Fear River, two at the river's mouth, and six more on nearby islands and promontories. The largest of these, Fort Fisher, ran across a spit of land between the east bank of the river and the ocean. On the seaward side, rifled cannon dissuaded Union warships from close pursuit of blockade runners making a final dash into the river's mouth. Although the U.S. Navy had attempted to blockade Wilmington for more than three years, it had managed to capture, sink, or drive ashore only about one hundred thirty of the many fast vessels that carried Confederate cotton to the Bahamas and Bermuda and returned with military stores. Through the port passed most of the 925 tons of saltpeter, 745 tons of lead, and 420,000 pairs of shoes—besides blankets,

---

[48] Ibid., pp. 815–16, 818–19 (quotation); Field Return, 27 Oct 1864, Entry 1659, pt. 2, RG 393, NA.

[49] OR, ser 1, vol. 42, pt. 1, pp. 78, 107, 109; D. Bates to Father, 6 Nov 1864, Bates Letters; J. Pierson to Dear Daugter [sic], 20 Nov 1864, Pierson Letters; Edward G. Longacre, *Army of Amateurs: General Benjamin F. Butler and the Army of the James, 1863–1865* (Mechanicsburg, Pa.: Stackpole Books, 1997), pp. 228–31.

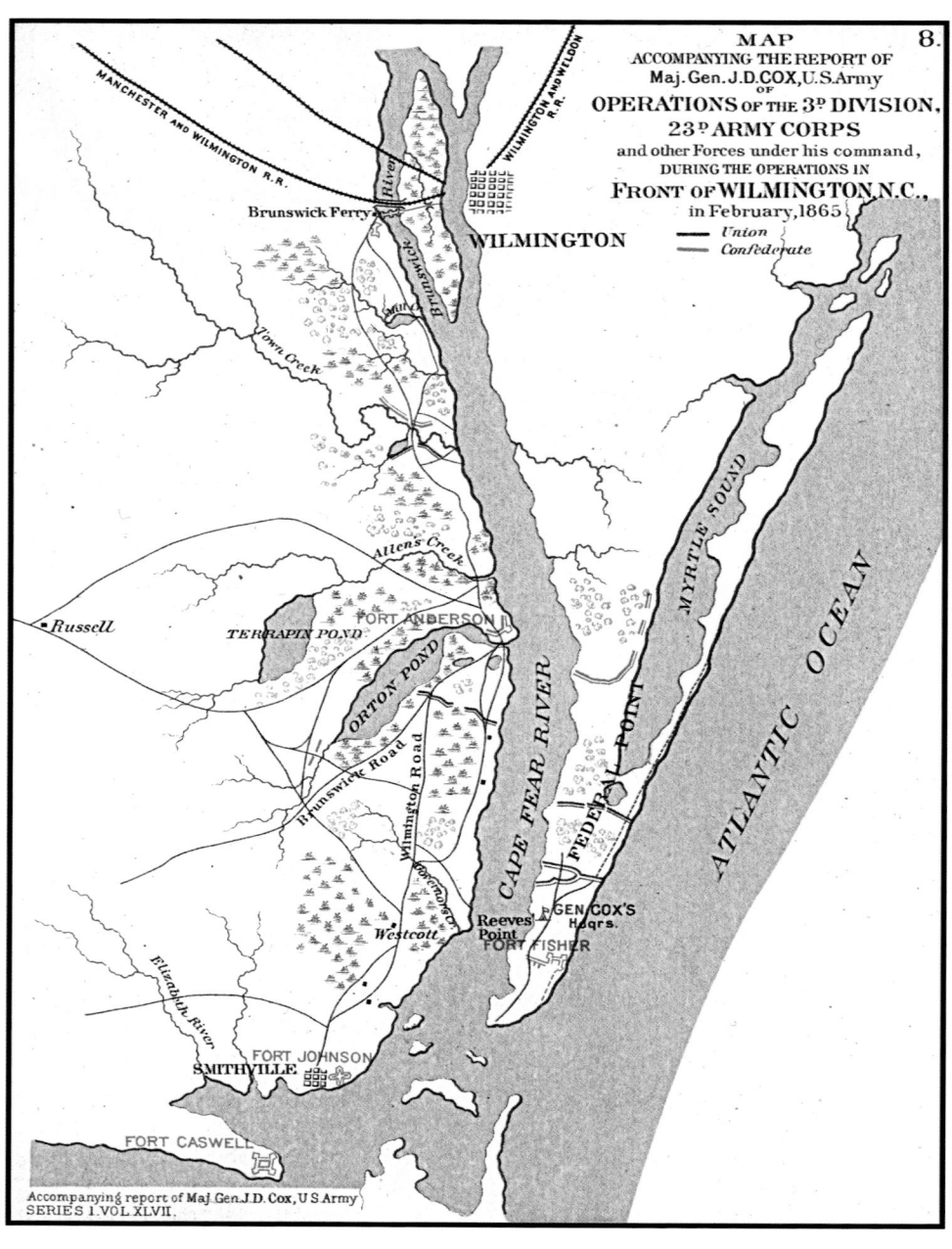

This map from the Official Atlas *shows Fort Fisher at the tip of Federal Point and other Confederate positions between Wilmington and the mouth of the Cape Fear River.*

medicine, and other supplies—that entered the Confederacy between November 1863 and October 1864.[50]

Secretary of the Navy Gideon Welles had long urged an expedition to reduce Fort Fisher and capture Wilmington. By mid-September, Grant had acceded to the idea, but attacks on Richmond and Petersburg remained uppermost in his mind. Days after the second attack failed in late October, General Butler was under orders for New York City with more than six thousand troops to keep order there during the presidential election. When he returned, Colonel Pierson's prediction about the weather had come true: "Roads nearly impassable," Butler wrote to Grant, who had himself gone north for a few days.[51]

As the troops waited for the roads to dry, it became time to implement an administrative change that had been under consideration for months. A few weeks after the IX Corps defeat at the Petersburg Crater that summer, Butler had suggested to Grant that Ferrero's division and its nine black regiments should transfer from Meade's Army of the Potomac to his own Army of the James. "From all that I can hear the colored troops . . . have been very much demoralized by loss of officers and by their repulse of [July] 30th," he wrote, adding the next day: "If they could be sent to me, . . . they might be recruited up and got into condition." Grant replied that at that time every one of his soldiers was occupied, either holding the trenches or preparing an offensive move. Not until mid-November did he consider the pace of events slow enough to make the change.[52]

The reorganization turned out to be more profound than the movement of nine regiments from Meade's army to Butler's authorized on 25 November. Eight days later came an order discontinuing the X and XVIII Corps. The white infantry divisions of those commands would constitute the XXIV Corps; the three black divisions, the XXV Corps. At the head of the XXV Corps was Maj. Gen. Godfrey Weitzel, the same officer who had asked Butler to remove black troops from his command in Louisiana more than two years earlier. Whether it was because of the hard campaigning that black soldiers had done since his complaint or because of his accession to a second star and with it command of a corps rather than the brigade that he had led in Louisiana, Weitzel voiced no qualms when he took command of the largest organization of black soldiers in the war (*Table 2*).[53]

One of the regiments that joined Butler's command was the 30th USCI. "General Meade had agreed with Gen Butler to trade us off for white troops," Colonel Bates wrote. "I am glad of it for I have always thought the colored troops ought to be placed together, and under Butler there is no doubt but that

---

[50]Robert M. Browning Jr., *From Cape Charles to Cape Fear: The North Atlantic Blockading Squadron During the Civil War* (Tuscaloosa: University of Alabama Press, 1993), pp. 220, 228–29, 266–68; McPherson, *Battle Cry of Freedom*, pp. 380–82.

[51]*OR*, ser. 1, vol. 39, pt. 1, pp. 364–65; vol. 42, pt. 3, pp. 492, 503–04, 517, 638, 669 (quotation). John G. Barrett, *The Civil War in North Carolina* (Chapel Hill: University of North Carolina Press, 1963), pp. 262–63.

[52]*OR*, ser. 1, vol. 42, pt. 2, pp. 323 ("From all"), 349 ("If they"), 350, and pt. 3, p. 619.

[53]*OR*, ser. 1, vol. 42, pt. 3, pp. 702, 791. For Weitzel in Louisiana, see Chapter 3, above; his 1862 letter to Butler is in *OR*, ser. 1, 15: 171–72.

TABLE 2—XXV CORPS ORDER OF BATTLE, 3 DECEMBER 1864
XXV Corps (Maj. Gen. Godfrey Weitzel)
1st Division (Brig. Gen. Charles J. Paine)
1st Brigade (Bvt. Brig. Gen. Delavan Bates)—1st, 27th, and 30th USCIs
2d Brigade (Col. John W. Ames)—4th, 6th, and 39th USCIs
3d Brigade (Col. Elias Wright)—5th, 10th, 37th, and 107th USCIs
2d Division (Brig. Gen. William Birney)
1st Brigade (Bvt. Brig. Gen. Charles S. Russell)—7th, 109th, 116th, and 117th USCIs
2d Brigade (Col. Ulysses Doubleday)—8th, 45th (six companies), and 127th USCIs
3d Brigade (Col. Henry C. Ward)—28th, 29th, and 31st USCIs
3d Division (Brig. Gen. Edward A. Wild)
1st Brigade (Bvt. Brig. Gen. Alonzo G. Draper)—22d, 36th, 38th, and 118th USCIs
2d Brigade (Col. Edward Martindale)—29th Connecticut; 9th and 41st USCIs
3d Brigade (Brig. Gen. Henry G. Thomas)—19th, 23d, and 43d USCIs
USCC = United States Colored Cavalry; USCI = United States Colored Infantry.
Note: The 2d USCC was in the corps but not assigned to a brigade; the ten artillery batteries in the XXV Corps were white. Companies of the 1st USCC and Battery B, 2d U.S. Colored Artillery, were at Newport News, Norfolk, Portsmouth, and posts along the James River.
Source: The War of the Rebellion: A Compilation of the Official Records of the Union and Confederate Armies, 70 vols. in 128 (Washington, D.C.: Government Printing Office, 1880–1901), ser. 1, vol. 42, pt. 3, pp. 791, 1126–29 (hereafter cited as *OR*).

they will have credit for all they do." A major general leading an entire corps of black soldiers could keep them from being assigned chores that would fall to civilian employees of the Quartermaster Department. A commander of a single black regiment in an otherwise all-white brigade could offer his men no such protection.[54]

While the troops were moving to new camps and becoming acquainted, Grant wrote to Butler, urging the importance of the move against Wilmington. The last week of November brought news, via Augusta and Savannah newspapers, that the Confederate General Braxton Bragg had left Wilmington to oppose Sherman's march through Georgia. Bragg had taken with him "most of

---

[54] D. Bates to Father, 20 Nov 1864, Bates Letters.

the troops" in garrison there, Grant told Butler. Four days later, he expressed "great anxiety to see the Wilmington expedition off."[55]

One element remained to be added to the campaign: Butler himself decided to go along. In January 1865, he testified before the Joint Committee on the Conduct of the War that he did not trust Weitzel because of his youth. The 29-year-old West Point graduate had led brigades and divisions in the field for two years; Butler had spent half of that period at home, between his administrative commands in Louisiana and Virginia, awaiting assignment. Although Butler's attempt to direct the work of another field commander, Maj. Gen. William F. Smith, on the James River earlier that year had ended badly, Grant approved the arrangement and Butler accompanied the expedition to Wilmington. Grant testified later that he had "never dreamed of [Butler's] going" until the expedition was under way; he had merely transmitted orders to Weitzel through Butler as the senior general commanding the geographical department where the younger man was to operate.[56]

Although Butler and the senior naval officer in the region, Rear Adm. David D. Porter, had grown to detest each other during their service in Louisiana two years earlier, both men saw the end of the war approaching and wanted to finish their roles in it with a resounding victory. Butler directed Weitzel to tell General Paine of the XXV Corps and one division commander from the XXIV Corps to "select their best men" for a force of 6,500 infantry, 50 cavalry, and 2 batteries of artillery. For Paine's all-black division, this meant leaving behind 25 percent of its strength, the least fit of its one hundred sixty officers and forty-one hundred men. While their leaders tried to complete arrangements, the chosen troops boarded transports at Bermuda Hundred on 8 December. The next day, they floated downstream to Fort Monroe, where they waited. By 14 December, when the expedition finally steamed south, knowledge of its destination had spread throughout the fleet. "The other vessels . . . with their designating lights of blue and white flashing and dancing with the modulations of the waves, formed a beautiful scene," 1st Lt. Joseph J. Scroggs of the 5th USCI observed. "Plenty of pitch but not sick," Sergeant Major Fleetwood recorded in his diary. He, Scroggs, and about thirty-two hundred other members of Paine's division stayed aboard ship for the next eleven days.[57]

The troops waited at sea while Butler, the amateur general, carried out a pet scheme. He planned to destroy Fort Fisher with an enormous explosive charge, seventy-five times the size of the one used at Petersburg in July. Instead of tunneling under the Confederate works, he hoped to use a condemned vessel to float three hundred tons of powder within half a mile of the fort. After the explosion, his troops would walk into the ruins and accept the surrender of any survivors. As it turned out, the charge failed to detonate properly on 23 December and did no damage to Fort Fisher. Grant afterward derided the idea, referring to it as "the gunpowder plot," after the failed seventeenth-century

---

[55] *OR*, ser. 1, vol. 42, pt. 3, pp. 760 ("most of the"), 799 ("great anxiety").

[56] *Report of the Joint Committee on the Conduct of the War*, 9 vols. (Wilmington, N.C.: Broadfoot Publishing, 1998) [1863–1865], 5: 11, 52 (quotation).

[57] *OR*, ser. 1, vol. 42, pt. 3, p. 837 ("select their"); 3d Div, XVIII Corps, Field Return, 4 Dec 1864, Entry 1659, pt. 2, RG 393, NA; J. J. Scroggs Diary, 8 and 14 (quotation) Dec 1864, MHI; Fleetwood Diary; Chester G. Hearn, *Admiral David Dixon Porter* (Annapolis: Naval Institute Press, 1996), pp. 116–17, 274; Hans L. Trefousse, *Ben Butler: The South Called Him Beast!* (New York: Twayne, 1957), pp. 124, 170.

Union transports in a heavy sea, en route to attack Wilmington, North Carolina. "Plenty of pitch but not sick," Sgt. Maj. Christian A. Fleetwood wrote in his diary.

conspiracy to blow up the English parliament. He told congressional investigators that he approved the idea only because the Navy seemed to be interested in it, too.[58]

At last, on Christmas Day, Butler's expedition put a small landing force ashore. Men of both divisions took part. "Co. 'H' [of the 5th USCI] was ordered into the launches," Scroggs wrote.

> We landed amid a shower of bullets from the enemy concealed in the bushes skirting the shore, deployed and advanced, a few well directed shots scattering the Johnnies like chaff. In the meantime the White troops had landed farther down the beach and a small party of 60 rebs had surrendered to them. . . . [Brig. Gen. N. Martin] Curtis was about making an assault on the main works when he received Butler's order to fall back. The fort was weakly defended and could have easily been taken but the order had to be obeyed and we all fell back to the beach. . . . We were all on board the transports again shortly after dark and heading seaward.

Sergeant Major Fleetwood spent the afternoon between the transports and the shore. "Got three companies off and ordered back," he entered in his diary. "Got a drenching in the surf coming off." The fleet steamed north to the James River and deposited the

---

[58]*Report of the Joint Committee*, 5: 51 (quotation); Browning, *From Cape Charles to Cape Fear*, pp. 288–89; Longacre, *Army of Amateurs*, p. 237.

troops there during the last week of the year. "Probably we will be permitted to hibernate unmolested the remainder of the winter," Lieutenant Scroggs wrote. "Hope so."[59]

In defense of his decision to withdraw the troops despite specific instructions to establish a permanent beachhead at Fort Fisher, Butler pleaded that he had sought to avoid a repetition of the horrendous repulses of Union assaults on Port Hudson and Fort Wagner eighteen months earlier. The president relieved him on 7 January 1865. With the election won and another four years in office to look forward to, Lincoln had no further need to conciliate Butler or to tolerate any more of his attempts at military leadership. Maj. Gen. Edward O. C. Ord, former commander of the XXIV Corps, replaced Butler as head of the Department of Virginia and North Carolina the next day. Maj. Gen. Alfred H. Terry, previously a division commander, had already assumed responsibility for the expedition to Fort Fisher.[60]

Paine's division boarded ships again on 5 January for what Captain Carter of the staff told his wife was apt to be "another wild goose chase to Wilmington. . . . [S]omebody is bound to get *hurt* this time for I don't suppose that this expedition will be given up if the last man should perish. . . . The season of the year and the character of the coast where we are to operate . . . make me very uneasy for the result." As it turned out, the division suffered no casualties in the landing and fifteen during the six days after.[61]

The troops disembarked on 13 January. Paine's division headed west across the peninsula while the white troops and a force of marines and sailors turned south toward the fort. The 5th and 37th USCIs led the way from the landing beach to the banks of the Cape Fear River. There they began to dig a defensive line, using "bayonets, tin plates, cups, boards & whatever would hold sand and rock," wrote Capt. Henry H. Brown, promoted from the adjutancy of the 29th Connecticut to lead a company in the 1st USCI, "and in less than an hour a strong breast work [was] thrown up." A relieving force of some six thousand Confederates faced Paine's division on 15 January during the assault on Fort Fisher; but to the chagrin of its leaders, General Bragg, in overall command of the defense of Wilmington, refused to order an all-out attack. "The pickets of my division held their ground resolutely," Paine reported. By evening Fort Fisher was in Union hands. The attackers had taken more than two thousand prisoners and one hundred sixty-nine cannon at a cost of six hundred fifty-nine killed, wounded, and missing.[62]

Sergeant Major Fleetwood wandered through the fort a few days later and viewed the results of the seven-hour naval bombardment that had preceded the final assault. "Scarcely a square foot of ground without some fragment of unexploded shell," he told his father:

Heavy guns bursted, others knocked to pieces as though made of pipeclay, heavy gun carriages knocked to splinters and dead bodies of rebels lying as they fell with wounds horrible enough to sicken the beholder, some with half of their heads off, others cut

---

[59] Scroggs Diary, 25 ("Co. 'H'") and 31 Dec 1864 ("Probably we"); Fleetwood Diary, 25 (quotation) and 28 Dec 1864; Browning, *From Cape Charles to Cape Fear*, pp. 290–91; Longacre, *Army of Amateurs*, pp. 249–53.

[60] *OR*, ser. 1, vol. 42, pt. 1, pp. 968, 972; vol. 46, pt. 2, pp. 46, 60, 71.

[61] *OR*, ser. 1, vol. 46, pt. 1, p. 424; S. A. Carter to My own darling Em, 3 Jan 1865, Carter Papers; Scroggs Diary, 5 Jan 1865.

[62] *OR*, ser. 1, vol. 46, pt. 1, pp. 399, 405, 423, 424 (quotation), 431; H. H. Brown to Dear Mother, 17 Jan 1865, Brown Papers; Barrett, *Civil War in North Carolina*, pp. 272, 279–80.

Fort Fisher

in two, disemboweled and every possible horrible wound that could be inflicted. Oh this terrible war! . . . Yet we must go ahead somehow, and we will. . . . Ten blockade runners have already walked quietly into our hands much to their surprise and disgust. The blockade is now effectual.

Captain Carter, like many others, had been too close to the action to grasp its significance. He wrote to his wife: "We have today just rec[eive]d papers . . . containing the ac[coun]ts and are just beginning to find out what we have done here. . . . I can hardly realize that we have achieved so much with so slight a loss."[63]

The day after Fort Fisher fell, the Confederates abandoned their other forts near the mouth of the river and withdrew some ten miles north to Fort Anderson, on the west bank. The force that had failed to relieve the besieged garrison entrenched on the opposite bank. Together, they outnumbered Terry's army. The Union force, for its part, sat still for three weeks. "Nothing but sand, thicket and swamp," Fleetwood complained: "Can't dig two feet under the surface without striking water." The men soon exhausted the sweet potatoes and cornmeal that they had captured at Fort Fisher and had to survive on the basic army ration of hardtack, coffee, beans, and salt pork, "with a rarity occasionally of fresh beef" and fish from the river, Captain Brown wrote. As late as the last week in January, no sutlers

---

[63] *OR*, ser. 1, vol. 46, pt. 1, p. 398; C. A. Fleetwood to Dear Pap, 21 Jan 1865, Fleetwood Papers; S. A. Carter to My own precious wifey, 22 Jan 1865, Carter Papers.

had followed the troops to sell supplements to the monotonous diet. Reinforcements and a new general arrived in the second week of February: Maj. Gen. John M. Schofield and a division of the XXIII Corps. Fifty days earlier, they had been pursuing Hood's ruined army south from Nashville. Since then, they had traveled by rail and river steamer to Annapolis and taken ship there for North Carolina. With one division of his corps landed and two more on the way, Schofield ordered a move toward Wilmington.[64]

Schofield's instructions from Grant were to seize the city; prepare a supply base for Sherman's army, which was marching north from Savannah; and advance to Goldsborough and the railroad there—the original objective of Burnside's expedition three years earlier. On 10 February, after ordering four hundred thousand rations and twenty thousand pairs of shoes for Sherman's men, Schofield instructed his own troops to begin their advance the next morning. Terry's force was to move against the Confederates east of the river. "It is not expected to gain possession of the enemy's works," Schofield explained. "Nevertheless, if the demonstration develops such weakness at any point of the enemy's line as to indicate that an attack would be successful it will be made at once." The troops "started out with the idea of taking up a new line of works and ascertaining the position of the enemy," Captain Carter told his wife. "We ascertained that without much difficulty," he added drily, "drove the rascals out of their rifle pits back into their main line of works and immediately threw up breastworks, in some places within 300 yards of their main line." It was "quite a nasty little fight," Carter wrote, and cost the division ninety-two killed and wounded.[65]

The men of Paine's division stayed in their new position across the river from Fort Anderson, about twelve miles downstream from Wilmington, until the morning of 19 February, when they learned that the Confederate trenches opposite them had emptied during the night. They moved forward that afternoon in cautious pursuit, meeting no resistance. The next morning, they began to exchange shots with the enemy. About 3:00 p.m., they set eyes on the defenses of Wilmington, "an earth-work well manned and showing artillery," Paine reported. He ordered the 5th USCI forward to reconnoiter.[66]

Lieutenant Scroggs told the story somewhat differently. "Moved forward at noon (the 5th still on the skirmish line)," he recorded in his diary, "and soon found the enemys rear guard. Drove them before us until 3 P.M. when they fell behind a strong line of works and refused to be driven further. Gen. Terry ordered the 5th to charge the works and we done it, but were not able to take works manned by 4500 troops and mounted with six pcs. of artillery. . . . I suppose it was fun for Terry but not for us." The regiment lost fifty-three officers and men killed and wounded.[67]

Meanwhile, Union divisions on the other side of the river waded through a swamp on the Confederates' flank and routed them, continuing the pursuit the next day. On the night of 21 February, Bragg's remaining troops set fire to the ships, bales

---

[64]*OR*, ser. 1, vol. 46, pt. 2, p. 74; vol. 47, pt. 1, p. 909. Fleetwood to Dear Pap, 21 Jan 1865; H. H. Brown to Dear Mother, 29 Jan 1865, Brown Papers; Barrett, *Civil War in North Carolina*, pp. 280–81.

[65]*OR*, ser. 1, vol. 47, pt. 1, p. 925, and pt. 2, p. 384 (quotation); S. A. Carter to My own darling Emily, 12 Feb 1865, Carter Papers.

[66]*OR*, ser. 1, vol. 47, pt. 1, p. 925.

[67]Ibid.; Scroggs Diary, 20 Feb 1865.

of cotton, and military supplies that remained in Wilmington and evacuated the city. As Paine's division marched in the next morning, the city's black residents rushed to greet them. "Men and women, old and young, were running through the streets, shouting and praising God," Commissary Sergeant Norman B. Sterrett of the 39th USCI wrote to the *Christian Recorder*. "We could then truly see what we had been fighting for." Captain Brown noticed "very few white people . . . as we came through but the contrabands filled the streets & welcomed us by shouts of joy. 'We're free! We're free!' 'The chain is broke!' &c. 'This is *my* boy now' said one old man as he held his child by the hand." The troops did not stop in the city, but pushed on another ten miles before dark, securing a bridgehead on the Wilmington and Weldon Railroad across the Northeast Branch of the Cape Fear River. There they waited for supplies to reach Wilmington and for General Schofield to gather a train of wagons to move them inland.[68]

The occupation of Wilmington presented Army officers, especially those of the U.S. Colored Troops, with new opportunities and difficulties. As occurred everywhere in the South, the arrival of a Union Army attracted thousands of black residents from the surrounding country. In February, the Subsistence Department issued rations to 7,521 black adults and 1,079 children at six sites along the North Carolina coast. Two days after federal troops entered the city, the officer commanding the 6th USCI asked permission to enlist one hundred twenty men to bring his regiment up to strength. General Terry approved the request, and the regimental chaplain, one captain, and five enlisted men began recruiting. New men from North Carolina would provide useful local knowledge for a newly arrived regiment that hailed from Philadelphia.[69]

Less helpful was General Terry's suggestion a few weeks later that he could organize three new regiments among the black refugees gathered at Wilmington. Union authorities were unprepared for the influx, as they so often were throughout the war and in every part of the South. "They are pressing upon us severely, exhausting our resources and threatening pestilence," the district commander complained. Terry proposed to use the refugees to strengthen Paine's division, which contained only ten regiments. Unfortunately for his plan, high-ranking Union generals had known since 1862 that organizing new regiments was an inefficient way to use recruits and that it was far better to put the new men in existing regiments and let them learn by example from their comrades. Besides, at this stage of the war, the last thing the Union army wanted was large masses of untrained men who did not know their officers and whose officers did not know them. Nothing came of Terry's suggestion.[70]

By 8 March, Sherman's army was in North Carolina. He wrote to Terry in Wilmington, saying that he would reach Fayetteville in three days and asking for bread, sugar, and coffee. Terry sent as much as he could load in a shallow-

[68]*OR*, ser. 1, vol. 47, pt. 1, pp. 911, 925, and pt. 2, pp. 559, 593–94, 619, 635–36, 654, 672, 683, 693–94; *Christian Recorder*, 1 April 1865; H. H. Brown to Dear Parents, 27 Feb 1865, Brown Papers.

[69]Maj A. S. Boernstein to Capt A. N. Buckman, 24 Feb 1865 (B–42–DNC–1865), and Endorsement, Capt W. L. Palmer, 15 Mar 1865, on Surgeon D. W. Hand to Maj J. A. Campbell, 7 Mar 1865 (H–65–DNC–1865), both in Entry 3290, Dept of North Carolina and Army of the Ohio, LR, pt. 1, Geographical Divs and Depts, RG 393, NA.

[70]*OR*, ser. 1, vol. 47, pt. 2, pp. 625, 978 (quotation); Maj Gen A. H. Terry to Lt Col J. A. Campbell, 13 Mar 1865 (T–33–DNC–1865), Entry 3290, pt. 1, RG 393, NA. On leading Union

draft steamer up the Cape Fear River and prepared to march to meet Sherman at Goldsborough. Paine's division moved north, guarding what wagons Terry had been able to collect and a mobile pontoon bridge that was necessary to cross rain-swollen streams. Black residents along the route were no less enthusiastic than those of Wilmington had been. "Some would clap their hands and say, 'The Yankees have come! The Yankees have come!'" Chaplain Henry M. Turner of the 1st USCI told readers of the *Christian Recorder*. "Others would say, 'Are you the Yankees?' Upon our replying in the affirmative, they would roll their white eyeballs up to heaven, and, in the most pathetic strain, would say, 'Oh, Jesus, you have answered my prayer at last! Thankee, thankee, Jesus.' . . . Others would commence venting their revengeful desires by telling of their hardships and the cruelty of their owners, and wanting us to revenge them immediately."[71]

Occasionally, the tales of cruelty that slaves told soldiers had the desired effect. Terry warned Paine of reports that "a portion of your command is burning buildings and destroying property. . . . [W]hile proper foraging is not prohibited, . . . wanton destruction cannot be permitted, and you will please take measures to put a stop to it immediately." Within a week of Terry's letter, Chaplain Turner confirmed the charges unofficially for readers of the *Christian Recorder*, relating an incident on the march through North Carolina:

> There was one infamous old rebel who . . . owned three hundred slaves, and treated them like brutes. . . . Seeing his splendid mansion standing near the road, our boys made for it, and soon learned that he had just released a colored woman from irons, which had been kept on her for several days. Upon hearing of this and sundry other overt acts of cruelty . . . , the boys grew incensed, and they utterly destroyed every thing on the place. . . . With an axe they shattered his piano, bureaus, side-boards, tore his finest carpet to pieces, and gave what they did not destroy to his slaves—and on his speaking rather saucily to one of the boys, he was sent headlong to the floor by a blow across the mouth. . . . I heard afterward that the white soldiers burned his houses to the ground; but whether they did so or not, I cannot say. But this much I do know—that I have seen numbers of the finest houses turned into ashes.

Turner and other observers claimed that black soldiers learned burning and looting from Sherman's men, but most of the soldiers in Paine's force had been born and raised in slave states. Of the division's regiments, the 1st USCI came from Washington, D.C.; the 4th, 30th, and 39th from Maryland; the 10th from Virginia; the 37th from North Carolina and Virginia; and the 107th from Kentucky. Only the 5th, 6th, and 27th had been raised in the free states, and many of the men in them had grown up in slavery. The advance into rebel territory that had remained unscathed by the war—unlike the often fought-over part of

---

generals' attitudes toward new regiments, see Maj Gen W. T. Sherman to Maj Gen U. S. Grant, 2 Jun 1863, in *OR*, ser. 1, vol. 24, pt. 3, pp. 372–73; Grant to the President, 19 Jun 1863, in *OR*, ser. 3, 3: 386; Maj Gen H. W. Halleck to Grant, 14 Jul 1863, in *OR*, ser. 3, 3: 487.

[71] *OR*, ser. 1, vol. 47, pt. 2, pp. 735, 791, 819, 839–42; *Christian Recorder*, 15 April 1865.

Virginia where they had served earlier—gave them, at last, a chance to exact retribution.[72]

Col. Giles W. Shurtleff, an Ohio abolitionist, tried to keep order in the 5th USCI. "The plundering and pillaging have been fearful," he told his wife.

> The country is full of "*foragers.*" They have stripped *everything* from the people. . . . Now I am not at all sure but the people merit this and it is perhaps the just retribution of the Almighty. Still I believe it is cruel and wicked on the part of our army. I have prevented this sort of action in my own regiment, and have gained the ill will of many officers and men in doing so. While on the march, the men in the regiments next to ours would break from the ranks and rush into houses and strip them of every particle of provision. . . . I detailed men—placed them under an officer and sent them to plantations away from the road with instructions to leave all that was necessary for the subsistence of families. In this way I obtained all that was necessary for my men and injured no one while I maintained the discipline of my regiment.

Shurtleff was proud of his attempt to keep foraging from degenerating into robbery and arson.[73]

Late on 21 March, Paine's division reached the Neuse River at Cox's Bridge, some ten miles west of Goldsborough. One brigade crossed the river that night and entrenched; a second followed the next day. The XIV and XX Corps, half of Sherman's army, came up the road from Fayetteville and crossed on the pontoon bridge that Paine's division had brought from Wilmington. Paine's men had caught sight of Sherman's cavalry and foragers before, but not so large a body of infantry. It was "a sight equally novel to both" forces, Turner wrote.

> We all desired to see Sherman's men, and they were anxious to see colored soldiers. . . . [T]hey were not passing long before our boys thronged each side of the road. There they had a full view of Sherman's celebrated army. Soldiers without shoes, ragged and dirty, came by thousands. Bronzed faces and tangled hair were so common, that it was hard to tell if some were white. . . . Some of their generals looked worse than our second lieutenants.[74]

During the previous three days, Sherman's men had driven General Joseph E. Johnston's Confederates back from Bentonville. The road to Goldsborough and the railroad finally lay open. On 23 March, Sherman issued a congratulatory order to his army, promising "rest and all the supplies that can be brought from the rich granaries and store-houses of our magnificent country." Active military operations

---

[72]*OR*, ser. 1, vol. 47, pt. 2, pp. 625, 966 (Terry quotation); *Christian Recorder*, 15 April 1865. For opinions of Sherman's army, see Barrett, *Civil War in North Carolina*, pp. 293–300, 344–48; Mark L. Bradley, *This Astounding Close: The Road to Bennett Place* (Chapel Hill: University of North Carolina Press, 2000), pp. 26–28. On members of free-state regiments who were born in slavery, see Paradis, *Strike the Blow for Freedom*, p. 112.

[73]G. W. Shurtleff to My darling little Wife, 29 Mar 1864, G. W. Shurtleff Papers, OC.

[74]*OR*, ser. 1, vol. 47, pt. 1, p. 925. NA M594, roll 205, 1st USCI; roll 206, 6th USCI; roll 208, 30th USCI; roll 209, 37th USCI; roll 215, 107th USCI. *Christian Recorder*, 15 April 1865.

in North Carolina were nearly over. On 24 March, Confederate cavalry made what General Paine described as "a reconnaissance in considerable force . . . and . . . a vigorous attack," but which several company commanders who took part in it dismissed as "a skirmish" and "a slight attack." Paine's men held the bridge at the cost of about a dozen casualties. The division marched twenty-five miles south the next day, to Faison's Station on the Wilmington and Weldon Railroad, where it made camp and waited for the generals to make peace. It stayed in the central part of the state until early June, when it sent one brigade to Wilmington and the other two to Beaufort for occupation duty.[75]

While Union troops in North Carolina moved into new territory and marveled at peach orchards abloom in March, soldiers one hundred miles to the north continued to occupy the bleak trenches around Petersburg and Richmond. Quartermaster Sergeant James H. Payne of the 27th USCI assured readers of the *Christian Recorder* that "all [was] quiet along the James." Grant's men spent the time strengthening their positions and threatening communications between the besieged cities and the rest of the Confederacy. Rain, snow, and mud had impeded military operations by both sides all winter. "The roads are bad," Payne wrote, "the mud deep, and a great deal of water in the woods and fields, render[s] travel of any kind almost impossible." Chaplain Thomas S. Johnson of the 127th USCI was glad when warmer weather arrived about mid-March, for troops had stripped the country of firewood for three miles behind the lines. Late in the winter, an order had been necessary to make sure that the teams and wagons allotted to each regiment carried firewood instead of being "diverted to other uses, such as hauling for sutlers and the private uses of officers." Enlisted men had to gather their own wood on foot. The practice was common to both divisions in the XXV Corps.[76]

A shortage of fuel compounded by the behavior of venal or selfish officers was not the only trial that the men of the XXV Corps endured. The sheer absence of officers could be as damaging as the callous or inattentive actions of those who were present. In February, three regiments reported unfilled vacancies for five officers on average besides those absent on detached duty or sick leave. The colonel of a fourth regiment, newly arrived from Kentucky, blamed a recent unfavorable inspection report on absent officers and a consequent lack of opportunity to drill, which prevented the troops from learning the commands necessary to move bodies of men in battle. Commanding officers also continued to complain of the Enfield rifles issued to their troops. Indeed, some regiments did not receive the newer

[75] *OR*, ser. 1, vol. 47, pt. 1, p. 44 ("rest and all"); pt. 2, p. 925 ("a reconnaissance"); pt. 3, p. 609. NA M594, roll 205, 1st USCI ("a slight attack"); roll 206, 6th USCI ("a skirmish"); roll 208, 30th USCI ("a skirmish"). Bradley, *This Astounding Close*, pp. 34–35. Dyer, *Compendium*, p. 825, lists the Union casualties on 24 March as nine wounded. Colonel Bates listed one man killed and eleven wounded in his brigade; Captain Carter said the division lost five killed and nine wounded, presumably for the entire division. D. Bates to Dear Parents, 26 Mar 1865, Bates Letters; S. A. Carter to My dearest Emily, 28 Mar 1865, Carter Papers.

[76] *OR*, ser. 1, vol. 46, pt. 1, p. 31; Brig Gen G. F. Shepley to Col J. Shaw, 27 Feb 1865 ("diverted to"), Entry 533, XXV Corps, Ltrs, Orders, and Rpts Recd by Divs, pt. 2, RG 393, NA; Brig Gen E. A. Wild to Capt D. D. Wheeler, 13 Feb 1865, Entry 549, 1st Div, XXV Corps, LS, pt. 2, RG 393, NA; *Christian Recorder*, 25 February 1865 ("all [was]"); T. S. Johnson to Dear Sister, 15 Mar 1865, Thomas S. Johnson Papers, Wisconsin Historical Society, Madison; Krick, *Civil War Weather*, pp. 147–53. For North Carolina peach blossoms in March, see D. Bates to Mother, 12 Mar 1865, Bates Letters; Scroggs Diary, 18 Mar 1865.

Late in the war, recruiting agents from Northern states tried to enlist black Southerners to fill their states' draft quotas. The recruits in the right background are undergoing the kind of cursory physical examination that one medical officer complained was doing more to fill state draft quotas than it was to fill the ranks of the Union Army.

model Springfields until after the fighting had ended. Thus, the men's training suffered, as did instruction in the basic requirements of living in large groups. Hundreds of rural recruits continued "committing nuisances" and "easing themselves," not only "between the huts" where they lived, but "in front of the earthworks, . . . all along the line."[77]

There were other threats to the troops' health besides filthy surroundings in their camps. A medical officer in the Army of the James that January condemned the unscrupulous recruiting and lack of physical examinations that had helped to

[77]On vacancies, see Col H. C. Ward to Capt J. H. Evans, 1 Feb 1865; Col L. F. Haskell to 1st Lt W. M. Burrows, 15 Feb 1865; Col O. A. Bartholemew to 1st Lt J. B. West, 15 Feb 1865; all in Entry 533, pt. 2, RG 393, NA. Col L. G. Brown to Capt D. D. Wheeler, 9 Feb 1865, Entry 517, XXV Corps, LR, pt. 2, RG 393, NA. On weapons, see Col S. B. Yeoman to 1st Lt G. H. Ropes, 8 Feb 1865, Entry 517, pt. 2, RG 393, NA; Brig Gen E. A. Wild to Capt W. Von Doehn, 2 Apr 1865, Entry 533, pt. 2, RG 393, NA; Capt R. F. Andrews to Maj D. D. Wheeler, 22 May 1865, 118th USCI, Entry 57C, RG 94, NA. On sanitation, see Capt J. H. Metcalf to Col G. W. Cole, 12 Feb 1865 ("easing themselves," "between the huts"), and Maj D. D. Wheeler to Brig Gen E. A. Wild, 5 Feb 1865 ("committing nuisances," "in front of"), both in Entry 533, pt. 2, RG 393, NA. For general background on military sanitation, see Bell I. Wiley, *The Life of Billy Yank: The Common Soldier of the Union* (Indianapolis: Bobbs-Merrill, 1952), pp. 124–28.

fill the ranks of the 117th USCI. The purpose of raising the regiment, he wrote, seemed to have been "to enable the Kentuckians to avoid the draft, and it has done more service in filling the [state's draft] quota than it will in filling the army." He blamed sickness in the regiment on "excessive exposure in the wet and the cold of the last month," and recommended that pickets be allowed to build fires in "severe weather" and that "new troops be relieved from fatigue duty in excess that exhausts their strength, . . . and depresses their power of resisting disease. The health of the troops appears to be in direct proportion to the intelligence of the men and the care taken by the Company Commanders."[78]

While one of the division commanders in the XXV Corps worried about the effect of fatigue assignments and picket duty during the winter on the health of black soldiers ("the . . . consequence of this exposure in the Negro is Pneumonia"), the other expressed more concern about rations, and the "total and sudden change of [the troops'] habit of life." "The derangement of the physical system by a change of food without any transition is the abundant cause of sickness among those new to the army," wrote Brig. Gen. Edward A. Wild, who had been a physician before the war.

> It seems to be well established, that those recruits whose food had been for some time the same as that used by soldiers do not suffer much from sickness. The men who have labored in large numbers under contractors on the public works soon enjoy the immunity of the veterans. . . . A larger mortality occurs among the young men who come from our northern farms; but the severest effects are witnessed among the class known as 'contrabands,' the freedmen from the rebellious or the border states, who do not obtain in the army a single article of their usual diet. Habituated to subsist on corn meal, fresh fish, yams, potatoes and on the varied vegetable products of their garden patches, they have suffered greatly from being placed suddenly under the regimen of the army ration.[79]

Both generals were justified in their concern. During the last year of the war, the likelihood of a black soldier contracting pneumonia was nearly four times greater than that of a white soldier and the mortality rate among black soldiers was more than 19 percent higher than among whites. The incidence of diarrhea and dysentery was more than 36 percent higher in black regiments than in white, and black sufferers were 25 percent more likely to die. The state of medical knowledge at the time was of little help in treating these ailments: the surgeon general classed diarrhea and dysentery with malaria and yellow fever as "miasmatic diseases" caused by unhealthy air. Not until 1886 did medical research identify the organism that causes pneumonia.[80]

Early that spring, with Sherman's army on the move and Union troops in the Carolinas moving inland from the coastal enclaves that they had so long occupied, Mobile under siege, and a strong cavalry raid headed toward central Alabama,

---

[78] Asst Surgeon A. A. Woodhull to Surgeon G. Suckley, 31 Jan 1865, Entry 517, pt. 2, RG 393, NA.

[79] Brig Gen E. A. Wild to Capt I. R. Sealy, 18 Jan 1865 ("the . . . consequence"), Entry 518, XXV Corps, Misc LR, pt. 2, RG 393, NA; Wiley, *Life of Billy Yank*, pp. 135–37.

[80] *Medical and Surgical History*, vol. 1, pt. 1, pp. 637, 639, 710–11; William Bulloch, *The History of Bacteriology* (London: Oxford University Press, 1960 [1938]), p. 237.

TABLE 3—XXV CORPS IN THE APPOMATTOX CAMPAIGN, 27 MARCH–9 APRIL 1865
XXV Corps (Maj. Gen. Godfrey Weitzel)
1st Division (Brig. Gen. August V. Kautz)
1st Brigade (Bvt. Brig. Gen. Alonzo G. Draper)—22d, 36th, 38th, 118th USCIs
2d Brigade (Brig. Gen. Edward A. Wild)—29th Connecticut, 9th, 115th, 117th USCIs
3d Brigade (Brig. Gen. Henry G. Thomas)—19th, 23d, 43d, 114th USCIs
Attached Brigade (Bvt. Brig. Gen. Charles S. Russell)—10th, 28th USCIs
Cavalry—2d USCC
2d Division (Brig. Gen. William Birney)
1st Brigade (Col. James Shaw Jr.)—7th, 109th, 116th USCIs
2d Brigade (Col. Ulysses Doubleday)—8th, 41st, 45th, 127th USCIs
3d Brigade (Col. William W. Woodward)—29th, 31st USCIs
Eight white artillery batteries
USCC = United States Colored Cavalry; USCI = United States Colored Infantry.
Source: OR, ser. 1, vol. 46, pt. 1, pp. 579–80.

Grant decided that it was time at last to make a decisive move in Virginia. On 24 March, he issued orders. Two corps of the Army of the Potomac were to move west from their positions in front of Petersburg, outflank the Confederate right, and make sure that the enemy did not thwart a planned cavalry attack on Lee's last two remaining rail links to the rest of the Confederacy. Ord's Army of the James manned the trenches on the Richmond side of the river. Three of Ord's divisions— William Birney's from Weitzel's XXV Corps and two from the XXIV Corps— were to cross from the Richmond side of the river and move to the left of the Union line, west of Petersburg. Weitzel would stay north of the river with the remaining two divisions of the Army of the James. The operation was to begin on 29 March. Ord's mobile divisions would need two days to cover the thirty-six miles to their starting positions (*Table 3*).[81]

In order to conceal the movement from the Confederates, Ord's force began its march after dark on Monday, 27 March. Leaving tents standing and campfires burning, the men crossed the James River on bridges strewn with "moist straw and

---

[81] *OR*, ser. 1, vol. 46, pt. 1, pp. 50–51, 1160, and pt. 3, pp. 210–11.

compost" to muffle the sound of their leather soles on the boards. "We marched all night," Chaplain Johnson told his brother. "The next day we marched & broke camp as many as three times in the rain and laid down with no shelter, or fire, through a cold, rainy night." On Wednesday morning, they crossed the Wilmington and Weldon Railroad tracks and went into camp near a stream called Hatcher's Run. "Waiting anxiously," Lieutenant Califf wrote in his diary on Thursday, 30 March, "for the morning and the morrow's events."[82]

The next day did not bring the anticipated attack. "Occasionally a shell would burst or a bullet whistle near our heads but none of us hurt," Califf wrote on Friday. "A great deal of skirmish fire and considerable shelling most of the time." The firing continued all through Saturday, increasing until almost one hundred fifty Union cannon were firing on the Confederate lines. "The Earth shook & trembled like a frightened brute," Califf wrote. "Our batteries were in a semicircular range of hills and were pouring in a continual shower of shell into the rebel works." Unknown to Califf and most of the others in Birney's division, Maj. Gen. Philip H. Sheridan's cavalry drove Confederate troops from the South Side Railroad that day, defeating them near a junction of country roads called Five Forks, some fifteen miles southwest of Petersburg.[83]

The victory blocked one possible route out of Petersburg and Richmond for Lee's army, which by mid-March was losing more than one hundred men each day by desertion, the troops either going over to the Union lines or returning to their homes. On 2 April, the day after Five Forks, Lee wrote to the Confederate secretary of war: "I see no prospect of doing more than holding [Richmond and Petersburg] till night. I am not certain that I can do that." The Confederate government at once began preparations to abandon its capital, and Lee to withdraw the Army of Northern Virginia from its trenches and march to Amelia Court House, some fifty miles to the west. There he expected to find supplies and a railroad that would allow him to unite his army with the remaining Confederate force in North Carolina. Evacuating Petersburg, Confederates set fire first to warehouses full of leaf tobacco, then to military stores, and, last of all, to the bridges by which they left the city.[84]

So it was that in the predawn hours of 3 April, Union troops discovered the Confederate trenches empty and began to move cautiously, piecemeal, into Petersburg. Lieutenant Califf of the 7th USCI was on picket duty. "No firing occurred after 12 o'ck," he recorded in his diary. "A heavy explosion took place about 2 1/2 & then several large fires. . . . About daylight . . . our skirmishers entered the city of Petersburg. I missed it myself. They were the first troops in without a doubt." Thomas Morris Chester agreed, telling readers of the *Philadelphia Press* that Califf's regiment and the 8th USCI, raised in Philadelphia, "were the first to enter Petersburg"; but reports from the IX Corps show that some Michigan troops had run up their regimental colors in the city an hour before first light and were patrolling the streets by sunrise, when Califf said that his own men reached the city. A

---

[82]Ibid., pt. 1, p. 1160 ("moist straw"); T. S. Johnson to My Dear Brother Barnabas, [3] Apr 1865, Johnson Papers; Califf Diary, 30 Mar 1865.

[83]Califf Diary, 30 Mar ("Occasionally") and 1 ("The Earth") and 2 Apr ("Our batteries") 1865; A. Wilson Greene, *Civil War Petersburg: Confederate City in the Crucible of War* (Charlottesville: University of Virginia Press, 2006), p. 243.

[84]*OR*, ser. 1, vol. 46, pt. 3, pp. 1353, 1378 (quotation); Greene, *Civil War Petersburg*, pp. 245, 249–51.

few Union regiments stayed in Petersburg to fight fires and prevent looting. Most pressed on westward in pursuit of Lee's army.[85]

North of the James River on 3 April, Confederate deserters began to reach Union outposts well before dawn with news of the evacuation of Richmond. As the sky began to lighten, General Weitzel reported "explosions and fires in the enemy's lines. . . . I will move at daybreak." His two divisions, one from the XXIV Corps and another from Weitzel's own XXV Corps, were ready. In the 19th USCI, Capt. James H. Rickard jotted additions to a letter home during spare moments throughout the day. Before leaving camp, he composed a few pages with pen and ink:

> Standing in line this morning a little past four o clock I witnessed one of the grandest sights I ever beheld . . . a great heavy column of bright blaze & smoke rose high in the heavens followed by a crash that shook the ground[.] [A]t daylight another similar in the direction of Richmond. . . . We have just got orders to be ready to move immediately. We go for them to-day I guess. I must stop & eat my breakfast.[86]

Later in the morning, he continued in pencil:

> 7.45 o clock passing through the rebel line they have evacuated our front[;] fires still burning. [T]hey have left their tents standing torpedoes [land mines] in front of their works 11 [a.m.] waiting in front of the city . . . to find a place to cross the river Richmond is in flames constant explosions are taking place continuous roar the rebels are just ahead of us we are after them close Fine day, one of the most glorious of my life. . . . [O]ur troops are filled with the greatest enthusiasm. 12 o clock M. in Richmond we have now entered Richmond the city is on fire we are going now on board a Steamer to cross the river. . . . 2 1/2 P.M. we are now in the city of Manchester [on the south bank of the James, opposite Richmond] the people very glad to see us come the negros flock around us in thousands & are in Extacies It is thought we may stay here a while.

That evening, Rickard reverted to ink: "Manchester 8 P.M. We are now encamped on the south side of the city. I have just ridden into the town to see about going back to morrow for our knap sacks which we left behind coming away in such a hurry. I have no time to write any more, will give you more details some other time."[87]

The advance on Richmond that morning was a race. The officer who commanded the XXIV Corps pickets "noticed that the pickets of the Twenty-fifth Corps were advancing to the [Confederate trenches] on their front. Our skirmishers were at once set in motion. . . . We had moved about two miles when General Wild and staff overtook us with about a company of colored soldiers. . . . I sent

---

[85]*OR*, ser. 1, vol. 46, pt. 1, pp. 1040, 1047, 1049; Califf Diary, 3 Apr 1865; R. J. M. Blackett, ed., *Thomas Morris Chester, Black Civil War Correspondent: His Dispatches from the Virginia Front* (Baton Rouge: Louisiana State University Press, 1989), p. 313.

[86]*OR*, ser. 1, vol. 46, pt. 3, p. 533; J. H. Rickard to Dear Brother, 2–3 Apr 1865, J. H. Rickard Letters, AAS.

[87]Rickard to Dear Brother, 2–3 Apr 1865.

Richmond, April 1865

word . . . to move past the colored troops, . . . and for the skirmishers to advance more rapidly." The race stopped at the city's edge. Weitzel had already sent a small party of cavalry into Richmond to find the civil authorities and receive a formal surrender. Mounted patrols stopped the infantry advance until the general and the mayor had completed their arrangements. Weitzel found "the greatest confusion, pillaging and disorder reigning, and the city on fire in several places." The arson and disorder were far greater than what greeted Union troops when they first entered a Confederate city, Nashville, in February 1862. Soldiers and city residents were not able to bring the fires under control until midafternoon. Weitzel left one brigade of the XXIV Corps in Richmond to preserve order and distributed the rest of his force in the old Confederate positions around the outskirts.[88]

Southward, along the Appomattox River, the men of Birney's division rested that night about ten miles west of Petersburg. The next day, they pushed on with the rest of the Army of the Potomac in pursuit of Lee. General Ord's three divisions aimed for Farmville, where they expected to find Confederate supply trains on the railroad. By the time Ord's men arrived, the boxcars had moved on to Appomattox Court House. One brigade of Birney's division followed the wrong road for most of 4 April and had to retrace its steps. As a result, its men may well have covered, during the entire march, the ninety-six miles that their commanding officer claimed in his report. For the rest of Birney's division, the average was somewhat shorter, but each day's march was by no means of equal length. On 8 April, the two brigades covered some thirty miles, to arrive near Appomattox Court House at about 1:30 a.m. the next day.[89]

Sheridan's cavalry had reached there the day before and captured three trainloads of Confederate supplies. Just before daybreak, Sheridan conferred with Ord, who agreed to bring his infantry forward while the cavalry, dismounted, engaged the Confederates. Those men in Birney's division who managed to get any sleep

---

[88] *OR*, ser. 1, vol. 46, pt. 1, pp. 1212 ("noticed that"), 1227 ("the greatest confusion").
[89] Ibid., pp. 1162, 1235–36, 1239.

at all had a couple of hours at most before the next day's work. Moving forward soon after 7:00 a.m., they met Sheridan's cavalry skirmishers retreating in what one brigade commander called "a panic-stricken mob" that "pressed . . . along my line, through which they vainly tried to break." One of the cavalry division commanders admitted having been "forced back by overwhelming numbers." Col. Samuel C. Armstrong summarized tersely the reaction of the 8th USCI: "Formed line of battle; arrested the progress of the enemy." By 9:30, Birney's two brigades had advanced about one mile, driving the Confederates from some thick woods. Not long after that, word arrived of a Confederate flag of truce and the guns fell silent. Rumors of surrender had been running through the ranks of the army since Tuesday, 4 April, but Sunday's truce was no rumor.[90]

Several commanding officers in Birney's division took care to praise their men's conduct during the final campaign. "The majority of the officers . . . proved themselves worthy of the trust reposed in them," wrote Lt. Col. James Givin, of the 127th USCI, whose regiment had spent seven months in the trenches before Petersburg and Richmond. "The men, though short of rations and almost worn out with fatigue, moved on without a murmur as long as there was an enemy to follow." The chief medical officer praised Chaplain Johnson's "untiring attention and care in providing for [the men's] wants, . . . in strong contrast with the other chaplains of the division." Even the men of the brigade that lost its way showed "the true spirit and fortitude of the soldier" in "their endurance of . . . hard marches, and short rations."[91]

The fighting may have ended, but the hard marching had not. Ord relieved Birney of command on 10 April, "for mismanagement of various sorts," surmised Major Bacon of the 117th USCI. Under a new commander, Brig. Gen. Richard H. Jackson, the division started for Richmond the next day, following, much of the way, the road it had just traveled. The chief quartermaster described the next six days as "arduous in the extreme, a great deal of rain falling . . . making the roads muddy and heavy." As though bad weather were not impediment enough, Confederate and Union armies had picked over the country during their westward march the week before and had left nothing for the division's draft animals. "Our rations were short and our horses were some of the time with nothing to eat at all," Chaplain Johnson wrote. On the third day of the march, orders arrived directing the division to Petersburg. It reached its old campgrounds there on 17 April. "We hope now that we are in a region where we can get enough to eat for ourselves and our horses and can be comfortable while we [recuperate] a while," Chaplain Johnson wrote the next day. "Some think we shall be sent to Texas. . . . We cannot tell what may be and simply must abide the issue."[92]

At Richmond, the occupation regime began in earnest the day after the fall of the city. General Grant ordered Weitzel to arrest all newspaper editors and publishers and send them to Fort Monroe under guard. In camp across the river, Brig. Gen.

---

[90]Ibid., pp. 1121 ("forced back"), 1132, 1136, 1236 ("a panic-stricken"), 1237 ("Formed line"), 1239; Califf Diary, 4 and 8 Apr 1865.

[91]*OR*, ser. 1, vol. 46, pt. 1, pp. 1231 ("untiring attention"), 1235 ("the true spirit"), 1241 ("The majority").

[92]Ibid., p. 1233 ("arduous"), and pt. 3, pp. 694, 763; E. W. Bacon to Dear Kate, 26 Apr 1865, Bacon Papers; T. S. Johnson to My Dear People, 18 Apr 1865, Johnson Papers; Califf Diary, 14 Apr 1865.

August V. Kautz's 1st Division of the XXV Corps received an order that adjured company commanders to make sure that "every man appears at Guard-mounting Inspections and Parades in the best possible condition, clean hands and face, shoes blacked, accoutrements properly adjusted, clothing brushed clean, caps on, coats buttoned, pants turned down, guns and equipments clean, and every thing pertaining to a good soldier strictly adhered to." On 5 April, Weitzel assigned an officer to supervise repair and maintenance of the municipal gasworks. The next day, the medical inspector warned that a "low estimate" credited Richmond with "a hundred houses of prostitution, and probably a thousand prostitutes, many of them foully diseased." He called for licensed brothels and medical inspections paid for by license fees.[93]

The order to Kautz's division about daily routine, dress, and deportment also tried to restrict the number of absences by issuing passes to one officer in each regiment and two enlisted men in each company. Soldiers who had been under fire only a few days before tended to ignore the rule. As the chaplain of the 29th USCI observed, "forced marches and short rations" encouraged "a decided tendency to recklessness and profanity."[94]

On the night of 11 April, an event occurred that helped to set the course of the XXV Corps for Texas. The troops' after-hours jaunts had already caused complaints at divisional headquarters, where General Kautz warned two of his brigade commanders about "soldiers . . . going beyond our lines committing depredations upon private property and . . . other disorderly conduct," and urged "prompt measures to prevent such irregularities." Union soldiers, black and white, were apt to stray from camp during spells of inactivity throughout the war and in all parts of the South. While the XXIV Corps division in Richmond also issued orders about clean clothing and passes to visit the city and warned its soldiers against despoiling nearby civilians, General Weitzel felt obliged on 11 April, after one week of occupation, to tell Colonel Draper of his "regrets that so many complaints are being made in regard to the colored troops of his command."[95]

Some time after 10:00 that night, two sergeants, a corporal, and five privates of the 38th USCI talked their way past regimental sentries and made their way to a nearby house. Along the way, four of the privates left the party. The other four men entered the house and took some food and clothing. While the remaining private made off with the loot, the three noncommissioned officers raped the two white

---

[93] OR, ser. 1, vol. 46, pt. 3, p. 567; 36th USCI, General Orders (GO) 43, 4 Apr 1865, 36th USCI, Regimental Books, RG 94, NA; Detachment Army of the James, SO 92, 5 Apr 1865, Entry 522, XXV Corps, Special Orders, pt. 2, RG 393, NA; 1st Div, XXV Corps, GO 29, 5 Apr 1865, Entry 533, pt. 2, RG 393, NA; Surgeon N. Folsom to Lt Col W. A. Conover, 6 Apr 1865 (F–96–DV–1865), Entry 5063, Dept of Virginia and Army of the James, LR, pt. 1, RG 393, NA.

[94] Chaplain G. S. Barnes to Adj Gen USA, 30 Apr 1865, 29th USCI, Entry 57C, RG 94, NA. A week after General Orders 43 ordered cleanliness in arms, uniform, and person, 36th USCI, GO 44, 11 Apr 1865, noted that "several non-commissioned officers of the regiment have been absent from camp without permission." 36th USCI, Regimental Books, RG 94, NA.

[95] Capt W. von Doehn to Commanding Officers, 1st and 2d Brigades, 9 Apr 1865 ("soldiers . . . going"), Entry 549, pt. 2, RG 393, NA; Maj D. D. Wheeler to Col A. G. Draper, 11 Apr 1865 ("regrets that"), Entry 512, XXV Corps, LS, pt. 2, RG 393, NA; Wiley, *Life of Billy Yank*, pp. 197–98. For examples of XXIV Corps orders, see Circular, 5 Apr 1865, Entry 7026, XXIV Corps, 3d Bde, 3d Div, General Orders, pt. 2, RG 393, NA; 2d Bde, 3d Div, XXIV Corps, GO 17, 14 Apr 1865, Entry 6946, 2d Bde, 3d Div, XXIV Corps, General Orders, pt. 2, RG 393, NA.

women who lived there. The younger of the two victims was only thirteen years old. Colonel Draper, one of the brigade commanders who had received a warning letter, learned of the crime within hours and took only a few days to identify the culprits, partly by stolen goods in their possession and partly by their own remarks to other soldiers. A general court-martial made up of seven officers who belonged to regiments in the division convened to try three of the men on charges of rape, assault, and "plundering and pillaging." By the first week in May, the court had condemned them to hang and the president had approved the sentences. The fourth man was tried only on the last charge. He finished his enlistment at hard labor, wearing a ball and chain, and received a dishonorable discharge.[96]

Black soldiers, individually and in small groups, had committed felonies in Virginia and other parts of the South, but never before had they committed such a sensational crime almost under the noses of the Union's senior generals. Halleck, who had succeeded Ord in command of the Department of Virginia on 16 April, told Grant that Ord thought "want of discipline and good officers in the Twenty-fifth Corps renders it a very improper force for the preservation of order in this department. A number of cases of atrocious rape by these men have already occurred. Their influence on the colored population is also reported to be bad." Halleck concurred with his predecessor's opinion. From the camp of the 117th USCI near Petersburg, Major Bacon wrote:

> I think the suspension of hostilities is going to rid the service of many incapable officers. . . . I wish very much that our Colored Service could be put through a sieve. The atrocities which disgraced the Corps at Richmond (not so numerous, happily, as to amount to a rule) were due chiefly to the fact that our officers are as a rule not officer like enough to teach their men . . . or discipline them into a proper respect for those entitled to it or worthy of it.

As if to prove these allegations, the Department of Virginia announced the dismissal of three officers of the 38th USCI: the regiment's lieutenant colonel for "borrowing money from enlisted men and suppressing the order prohibiting the same" and two lieutenants for "peddling candy, tobacco and trinkets to enlisted men." The dismissals came on the same day Bacon committed his thoughts to paper and three days before Halleck wrote to Grant.[97]

Although knowledge of the rapes was widespread among troops in eastern Virginia, not even a crime so sensational could find space in the black-bordered columns of newspapers during the week after the president's assassination. Grant was in Washington during the confused days just after the event, while armed parties sought the assassin and conspirators and administrators arranged the procession that would take Lincoln's body to the railroad station to begin its journey to

---

[96]Cases of Sgt Dandridge Brooks (MM–1972), Sgt William Jackson (MM–1984), Cpl John Shepard (MM–2006), and Pvt John Adams (OO–753), Entry 15A, General Court Martial Case Files, RG 153, Rcds of the Judge Advocate General's Office, NA. AGO, General Court Martial Order 268, 7 Jun 1865, which includes presidential approval of the death sentences, is in the regimental order book, 38th USCI, Regimental Books, RG 94, NA.

[97]OR, ser. 1, vol. 46, pt. 3, pp. 788, 1005 (quotation); Dept of Virginia, GO 48, 26 Apr 1865, 38th USCI, Regimental Books, RG 94, NA; Bacon to Dear Kate, 26 Apr 1865.

Pennsylvania Avenue in Washington, D.C., spring 1865

Springfield, Illinois. On 16 April, one of Grant's aides sent a telegram to Ord in Richmond: "Please send . . . immediately one of the best regiments of colored troops you have, to attend the funeral ceremonies. . . . One that has seen service should be selected." Weitzel's choice was the 22d USCI, a regiment raised in Philadelphia that had taken part in the previous year's fighting around Petersburg and Richmond. "We felt highly complimented," Assistant Surgeon James O. Moore told his wife, "to be among the first organized troops to march thru Richmond & now . . . to participate in the funeral obsequies of the President."[98]

The regiment embarked before dawn on 18 April and reached Washington at about noon the next day. Marching north from the wharf as all the church bells in the city tolled and cannon fired every sixty seconds, the 22d USCI met the funeral procession at Seventh Street and Pennsylvania Avenue, making its way east from the White House to the Capitol. "Halted[,] wheeled into col[umn]," one officer of the regiment noted, "and became the head of [the] procession. After funeral [the] men were quartered at Soldiers' Rest. Officers at Hotels." A Washington newspaper commented that the troops "appeared to be under the very best discipline, and displayed admirable skill in their various exercises."[99]

Three days later, they boarded a boat for Charles County, Maryland, to join the hunt for the president's assassin. Surgeon Moore surmised that they had been sent because the men of the regiment "would be more likely [than white troops] to get information from the colored population." Officers and men spent the next four days splashing through swamps until, on 26 April, news reached them of the assas-

---

[98] *OR*, ser. 1, vol. 46, pt. 3, pp. 797 (quotation), 816; J. O. Moore to My Dearest Lizzie, 20 Apr 1865, J. O. Moore Papers, Duke University, Durham, N.C.

[99] NA M594, roll 8, 22d USCI; (Washington) *Daily National Intelligencer*, 20 April 1865.

sin's death. They returned to their landing place on the Potomac and waited there until late May, when they took ship again for City Point, Virginia.[100]

While the 22d USCI camped by the Potomac, arguments flew along the James about the future of the XXV Corps. Maj. Gen. George L. Hartsuff, commanding at Petersburg, complained to Weitzel on 13 May about the conduct of Weitzel's men, especially "destruction of buildings and . . . exciting the colored people to acts of outrage against the persons and property of white citizens. Colored soldiers . . . [have] straggled about advising negroes not to work on the farms," and offering to arm the former slaves. Weitzel replied that the destruction was the work of "black and white cavalry, which . . . did not belong to my corps," or of "convicts in soldiers' clothing" who had been freed by retreating Confederates during the evacuation of Petersburg and Richmond. He enclosed a telegram in which Ord had told him: "I do not consider the behavior of the colored corps . . . to be bad, considering the novelty of their position and the fact that most of their company officers had come from positions where they were unaccustomed to command" and that occupation duty offered "perhaps the first great temptation to which [the] men were exposed. In the city of Richmond their conduct is spoken of as very good."[101]

That was not what Ord had said to Halleck three weeks earlier, when Halleck succeeded him in command of the Department of Virginia. On 29 April, Halleck had told Grant about Ord's poor opinion of Weitzel's troops, adding the next day: "On further consultation with . . . Ord, I am more fully convinced of the policy of the withdrawal of the [XXV] Corps from Virginia. Their conduct recently has been even worse than I supposed yesterday." General Meade agreed, telling Grant that his troops, "hearing of marauders, . . . succeeded in capturing a camp with several wagons loaded with plunder. The party consisted of negroes, mostly belonging to this army." Even though white cavalry commanders had received warnings to "use great care that no depredations are committed" and Ord himself had removed Col. Charles Francis Adams Jr. from command of the 5th Massachusetts Cavalry (Colored) for letting his men "straggle and maraud," even though officers of the 22d USCI, riding in the country near Richmond, had met a group of cavalrymen (race unspecified, therefore probably white) looting a house and had driven them off; still blame settled on the men of the XXV Corps. The recent gang rape and court-martial did nothing to dispel it.[102]

Throughout the war, Halleck had favored sweeping solutions and peremptory orders. In the fall of 1861, rather than deal with escaped slaves and the claims of their supposed owners in Missouri, he had issued an order that barred commanding officers from admitting any black people to military posts. When he arrived in Virginia in the spring of 1865, his plan for getting crops planted and preventing famine later in the year was to prevent recently freed black people from moving to the cities, forcing them to work on the land. With the war over and black men admitted to the Army, the quickest way for him to dispose of complaints about their miscon-

---

[100] NA M594, roll 8, 22d USCI; J. O. Moore to My Dearest Lizzie, 23 Apr 1865, Moore Papers.

[101] *OR*, ser. 1, vol. 46, pt. 1, pp. 1148 (Hartsuff), 1160–61 (Weitzel, Ord).

[102] Ibid., pt. 3, pp. 811 (Meade), 1016 (Halleck). Asst Adj Gen to Col E. V. Sumner, 16 Apr 1865 ("use great care"), Entry 6977, 3d Div, XXIV Corps, LS, pt. 2, RG 393, NA; J. O. Moore to My Dearest Lizzie, 9 Apr 1865, Moore Papers; Worthington C. Ford, ed., *A Cycle of Adams Letters*, 2 vols. (Boston: Houghton Mifflin, 1920), 1: 267 ("straggle and maraud").

duct was to remove them from his department. On 18 May, after consultation with Halleck, Grant ordered Weitzel to prepare his command to take ship for Texas.[103]

By that time, hundreds of thousands of soldiers of every rank, black and white, were eager to get out of uniform. Some officers, who found themselves better off in the Army than they had ever been in civilian life, wanted to remain. "You had better approve applications to resign when there is no great advantage in retaining the officer," Ord told Weitzel in early May, "as we can get first rate men now from the white troops being mustered out. I have already had applications of officers . . . highly recommended to transfer to Colored Corps—and there is nothing gained by retaining discontented officers."[104]

Unlike an officer, an enlisted men could not submit a resignation on the chance that it would be accepted. Sixty-three officers managed to resign from regiments of the XXV Corps between 9 April, when Lee surrendered, and 25 May, when the first transports sailed for Texas, but all enlisted men except those declared unfit by a surgeon were obliged to wait for their discharges until their regiments mustered out of service. In 1864, when thousands of white soldiers who had volunteered in 1861 refused to reenlist for another three years, entire regiments disappeared from the Union Army. The white volunteers of 1862 would be ready for discharge in the fall of 1865; but since nationwide recruiting of black soldiers had only begun early in 1863, even the longest-serving veteran among them had nearly a year of his enlistment left by the spring of 1865, if the government should decide to retain his regiment. Other black regiments, raised in 1864, might continue to serve well into 1867. That the troops' obligation was completely legal did nothing to improve their mood.[105]

Black soldiers worried especially about their families. The white regiments of 1861 and 1862 had recruited and organized locally, and local committees made arrangements to help sustain their dependents. West of the Appalachians and in Union beachheads along the Atlantic coast, many black soldiers' families lived in contraband camps maintained by the federal government. About half of the soldiers in the XXV Corps, though, came either from the free states or from unseceded Maryland, where such institutions did not exist. Even the equalization of pay for black and white soldiers in 1864 was only of small help, for six or eight months might pass between paymasters' visits. The 114th USCI saw no pay from 1 September 1864 until 20 April 1865. Irregular pay damaged the morale of black and white soldiers alike, in all parts of the South. General Ord suggested that soldiers' wives could be appointed laundresses in their husbands' companies, for each company in the Army was entitled to several laundresses, paid by deductions from the men's pay. Laundresses could accompany their husbands to Texas, the government bearing the expense of their travel,

---

[103] *OR*, ser. 1, 8: 370; vol. 46, pt. 1, pp. 1005–06, 1168–69, 1172–73.

[104] Maj Gen E. O. C. Ord to Maj Gen G. Weitzel, Entry 5046, Dept of Virginia and Army of the James, LS, pt. 1, RG 393, NA.

[105] The number of resignations was calculated by consulting records of the 1st and 2d USCCs; 7th, 8th, 9th, 19th, 22d, 23d, 29th, 31st, 36th, 38th, 41st, 43d, 45th, 109th, 114th, 115th, 116th, 117th, 118th, and 127th USCIs; 5th Massachusetts Cavalry; and 29th Connecticut Infantry in *Official Army Register of the Volunteer Force of the United States Army*, 8 vols. (Washington, D.C.: Adjutant General's Office, 1867), vol. 8.

which it would not do for officers' wives. Although this solution might work for soldiers whose wives were already close by, it clearly would not help those whose families were in Maryland or the North.[106]

When the order to prepare for a move reached the troops, rumors burgeoned. Early in 1863, when the 1st South Carolina Volunteers received orders for Florida, stories circulated that the men would be sold into Cuban slavery to raise money for the war. This time, rumor had it that the men of the XXV Corps would go south to pick cotton until the war was paid for. Officers assured their men that it was not so, but many remained suspicious. Nevertheless, few deserted before boarding the transports, and only a handful of incidents occurred that amounted to mutiny.[107]

Embarkation began on 25 May and ended at noon on 7 June, when the transport with General Weitzel and his staff aboard weighed anchor. Unlike the responsibilities that faced the Union force in most of the occupied South, those of the XXV Corps in southern Texas had less to do with the reestablishment of civil government and protection of the rights of new black United States citizens than with international diplomacy and simple law enforcement. During the war, the regiments that belonged to the corps had spent periods that varied from four months to eighteen months in Virginia, the least typical theater of operations in the South. Before they mustered out, they would serve for similar periods in the most unusual region of the postwar occupation—the Rio Grande border with Mexico.

---

[106] Maj Gen E. O. C. Ord to Brig Gen G. H. Gordon, 12 May 1865, Entry 5046, pt. 2, RG 393, NA. For the 114th USCI, see W. Goodale to Dear Children, 20 Apr 1865, W. Goodale Papers, Massachusetts Historical Society, Boston; Berlin et al., *Black Military Experience*, pp. 656–61; Wiley, *Life of Billy Yank*, pp. 49, 291–92. Miller, *Black Civil War Soldiers of Illinois*, pp. 153–54, offers a good, brief summary of morale in the XXV Corps in May 1865.

[107] *OR*, ser. 1, vol. 46, pt. 3, p. 1262; Berlin et al., *Black Military Experience*, pp. 723–27; Glatthaar, *Forged in Battle*, p. 219; Miller, *Black Civil War Soldiers of Illinois*, p. 153. For the rumor about black soldiers being sold in Cuba, see Chapter 1, above.

CHAPTER 13

SOUTH TEXAS, 1864–1867

When the Republic of Texas joined the United States in 1845, its admission to the union allowed President James K. Polk to move an American army into the southern tip of the new state, past the Nueces River and all the way to the Rio Grande. Since Mexico had disputed Texan claims to the region south of the Nueces throughout the ten years since Texas had achieved its independence, Polk's aggressive maneuver plunged the United States and Mexico into war. The Treaty of Guadalupe Hidalgo ended the conflict officially in early 1848, fixing the international boundary and the southern edge of Texas on the Rio Grande (*see Map 9*).[1]

Slaves in Texas were few along the international boundary but more numerous farther north in river valleys where cotton and sugar cultivation made "the institution" profitable. These staple crops left the state by way of its main seaport, Galveston, which also served as a landing place for thousands of immigrants each year. Galveston and its inland neighbor Houston together numbered more than twelve thousand residents, black and white, in 1860. Farther south, on Matagorda Bay, lay the state's second seaport, Indianola, with some eleven hundred inhabitants. Only 357 of the state's 182,921 black residents lived south of the Nueces River in a semiarid land where range cattle outnumbered people by at least ten to one. More than one-third of this region's black residents were free, a sharp contrast with the rest of Texas. Fifty-three free men and women and only seven slaves lived in Brownsville, a border town some twenty miles up the Rio Grande from the Gulf of Mexico.[2]

Brownsville and other towns along the lower Rio Grande continued to grow during the years after the Mexican War. As merchants and ranchers from the United States arrived in the region, they wrested economic and political power from native Spanish-speakers. This ethnic conflict occasionally erupted in gunfire, as during the "Merchants War" of 1851, which concerned trade; the "Cart War" of 1857, touched off by freight rates; and, most serious, the "Cortina War" of 1859, occasioned by ill will between Spanish-speaking *Tejanos* and the ascendant

---

[1]K. Jack Bauer, *The Mexican War, 1846–1848* (New York: Macmillan, 1974), pp. 4–7, 11–12, 17–21, 28–29.

[2]U.S. Census Bureau, *Population of the United States in 1860* (Washington, D.C.: Government Printing Office, 1864), pp. 484–87, and *Agriculture of the United States in 1860* (Washington, D.C.: Government Printing Office, 1864), pp. 140, 144, 148; Daniel D. Arreola, *Tejano South Texas: A Mexican American Cultural Province* (Austin: University of Texas Press, 2002), pp. 11–19.

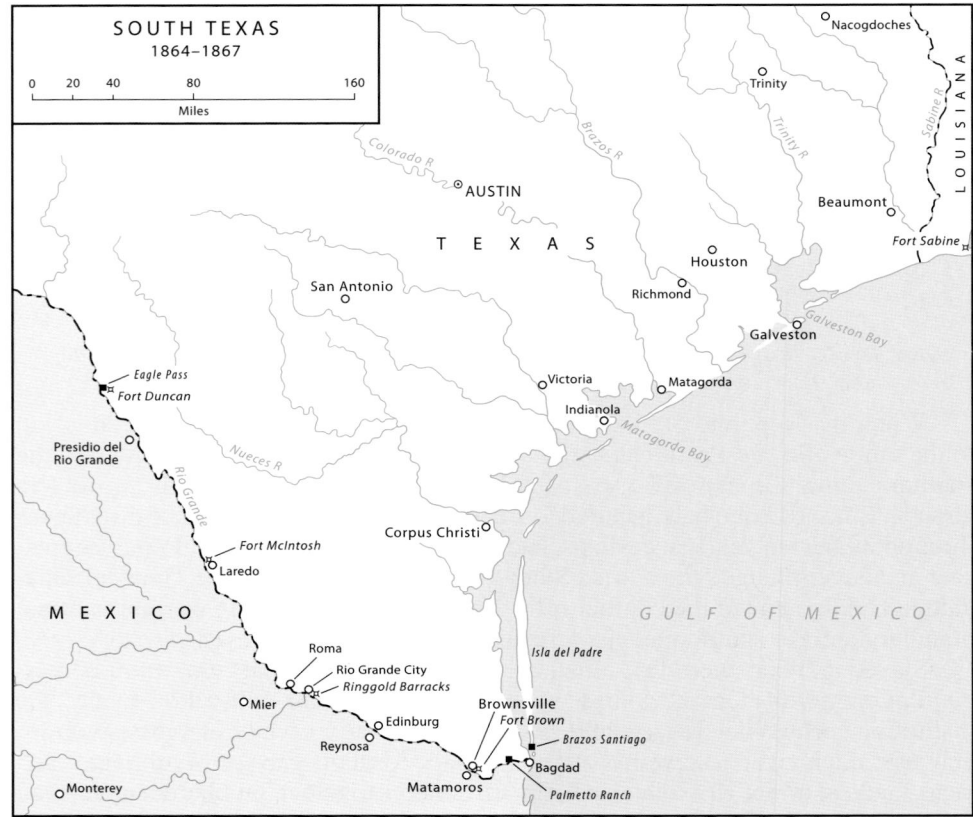

Map 9

English-speaking Texans. Although this last outbreak, named for the landowner Juan N. Cortina, involved only a few dozen men on each side, United States troops had to quell the disturbance. Despite these violent episodes, Brownsville thrived during the 1850s. By the end of the decade, its 2,347 residents made it the fifth-largest city in Texas.[3]

On 2 February 1861, thirteen years to the day after diplomatic representatives of the United States and Mexico signed the Treaty of Guadalupe Hidalgo, the state of Texas adopted an ordinance of secession from the Union. First on its list of grievances were Northern schemes to abolish "the institution known as negro slavery." With that, the Rio Grande became the Confederacy's only land frontier with

---

[3]Census Bureau, *Population of the United States in 1860*, pp. 486–87; Benjamin H. Johnson, *Revolution in Texas: How a Forgotten Rebellion and Its Bloody Suppression Turned Mexicans into Americans* (New Haven: Yale University Press, 2003), pp. 10–25; David Montejano, *Anglos and Mexicans in the Making of Texas, 1836–1986* (Austin: University of Texas Press, 1987), pp. 26–33; Jerry Thompson, *Cortina: Defending the Mexican Name in Texas* (College Station: Texas A&M University Press, 2007), pp. 22–23, 35.

Brownsville, Texas, from across the Rio Grande. The bales of cotton stacked on the Mexican shore indicate Brownsville's economic importance to the Confederacy.

a neutral country. Shipping boomed, with wagons carrying baled cotton across the forbidding landscape of southern Texas to pay for munitions of war that entered Mexican seaports. One merchant in England delivered forty-two hundred Enfield rifles for $24.20 each, for which he expected payment in cotton at thirty cents a pound: in all, more than fifteen tons of cotton. In the course of the war, as many as three hundred fifty thousand bales may have left the Confederacy by crossing the Rio Grande. The Mexican town of Matamoros, opposite Brownsville, swelled to a population of some forty thousand. Its seaport, Bagdad, also thrived.[4]

A few weeks before Texas left the Union, rival Mexican parties known as Liberals and Conservatives concluded a civil war of their own that had lasted for more than two years. At issue was the constitution of 1857, a secular document favored by the Liberals that, among its other provisions, disestablished the Catholic Church. Guerrilla warfare, massacres, and reprisals characterized the conflict. By the time the Liberals won, the country lay exhausted. An empty treasury caused Benito Juárez, the new president, to suspend repayment of Mexico's foreign loans. This prompted the creditor nations, Britain, France, and Spain, to take direct action. In December 1861, a naval fleet from the three powers landed troops at Veracruz and occupied the port. When Britain and Spain learned a few months later that the French emperor, Napoleon III, intended to conquer the entire country and install a puppet government, they withdrew their contingents. Lacking the legitimacy conferred by prominent allies, French troops nevertheless marched inland, meeting fierce resistance that blocked their path to Mexico City for a year and a

[4]*The War of the Rebellion: A Compilation of the Official Records of the Union and Confederate Armies*, 70 vols. in 128 (Washington, D.C.: Government Printing Office, 1880–1901), ser. 4, 3: 569–70, 572–74 (hereafter cited as *OR*); Ernest W. Winkler, ed., *Journal of the Secession Convention of Texas, 1861* (Austin: Texas Library and Historical Commission, 1912), pp. 61–66 (quotation, p. 62); David G. Surdam, *Northern Naval Superiority and the Economics of the American Civil War* (Columbia: University of South Carolina Press, 2001), p. 178; Jerry Thompson and Lawrence T. Jones III, *Civil War and Revolution on the Rio Grande Frontier: A Narrative and Photographic History* (Austin: Texas State Historical Association, 2004), p. 17; Stephen A. Townsend, *The Yankee Invasion of Texas* (College Station: Texas A&M University Press, 2006), pp. 5–7.

half. Archduke Maximilian of Austria, a relative of Napoleon's by marriage, arrived in the spring of 1864 to ascend the throne as emperor of Mexico.[5]

In order to forestall French occupation of the mouth of the Rio Grande and to stop the traffic in military stores and cotton, the Union's Maj. Gen. Nathaniel P. Banks dispatched a force from the Department of the Gulf to seize the lower river in the fall of 1863. On 6 November, federal troops raised the United States flag over Brownsville for the first time since March 1861. The few hundred Confederates in the region withdrew north of the Nueces River, or up the Rio Grande toward Eagle Pass. As they moved upriver, the route of Southern cotton for export had to shift westward more than three hundred miles, adding further expense to already heavy freight costs. With two contending parties, Union and Confederate, on the north side of the river and two, the Liberals (Juárez) and the Imperialists (Maximilian), on the south, the lower Rio Grande soon attracted a class of men whose ethics were elastic, often in the extreme.[6]

Events far from the Rio Grande valley also had a decisive influence on Union operations there, the kind of effect that outlying military departments on both sides of the conflict felt throughout the war. The failure of General Banks' Red River Expedition in the spring of 1864 and the withdrawal that summer of the XIX Corps from Louisiana to Virginia led to the abandonment of all but one of the federal beachheads in Texas in order to reinforce garrisons along the Mississippi River. Texas and its cotton were alluring targets for a Union expedition, but the agriculture and commerce of a dozen loyal states, from western Pennsylvania to Kansas, depended on federal control of the Mississippi.[7]

As Union troops withdrew from the Texas coast, a Confederate force reentered Brownsville on 30 July, once again affording cotton shipments a short but still arduous route to Mexico. Only the federal post at Brazos Santiago, near the mouth of the Rio Grande, remained. It was a secure position on an island, approachable from the mainland by only one route. In the fall of 1864, four regiments constituted the garrison: the 91st Illinois and the 62d, 87th, and 95th United States Colored Infantries (USCIs). The 62d had begun its existence as the 1st Missouri Colored Infantry, organized near St. Louis in December 1863. The 87th and 95th USCIs were Louisiana regiments, raised in and around New Orleans as part of General Banks' Corps d'Afrique.[8]

At the beginning of November 1864, a new commanding general arrived at Brazos Santiago: Brig. Gen. William A. Pile, who had helped Adjutant General Lorenzo Thomas recruit black troops, including the 1st Missouri Colored Infantry,

---

[5] Enrique Krause, *Mexico: Biography of Power: A History of Modern Mexico, 1810–1996* (New York: HarperCollins, 1997), pp. 169–74; Paul Vanderwood, "Betterment for Whom? The Reform Period, 1855–1875," pp. 371–96 in *The Oxford History of Mexico*, eds. Michael C. Meyer and William H. Beezley (New York: Oxford University Press, 2000), especially pp. 375–83.

[6] Surdam, *Northern Naval Superiority*, p. 177; Townsend, *Yankee Invasion of Texas*, pp. 14–19; Ronnie C. Tyler, "Cotton on the Border, 1861–1865," *Southwestern Historical Quarterly* 73 (1970): 461–63. Examples of rascality on both sides of the border in early 1864 are in *OR*, ser. 1, vol. 34, pt. 2, pp. 8–10, 216–17.

[7] Stephen A. Dupree, *Planting the Union Flag in Texas: The Campaigns of Major General Nathaniel P. Banks in the West* (College Station: Texas A&M University Press, 2008), pp. 6–7.

[8] *OR*, ser. 1, vol. 41, pt. 1, pp. 185–86, and pt. 4, pp. 266–67, 366; Frederick H. Dyer, *A Compendium of the War of the Rebellion* (New York: Thomas Yoseloff, 1959 [1908]), pp. 1718–19, 1733, 1736–37.

a year earlier. Pile found conditions at Brazos Santiago far from satisfactory and blamed his predecessor in command, the colonel of the 91st Illinois. The previous ordnance officer, Pile reported, had been "inefficient and negligent. In this he took pattern from the Comdg Officer of these Forces. The whole command except the 62d USCI (just arrived) being without discipline . . . and performing their duties very inefficiently." The garrison lacked a shallow-draft boat for travel along the coast; its horses were "broken down and diseased," left behind by the expedition that had seized the island a year earlier; hospital patients lay in tents that were often blown down and shredded by squalls from the Gulf of Mexico; the commissary officer sold Army beef to civilians; the quartermaster provided passage to New Orleans on government steamers for civilians who paid in gold. Pile set to work at once to clean house.[9]

He ought to have known better than to expect that any supplies he requested, such as lumber to build a windbreak for the hospital tents, would come at once to a backwater outpost like Brazos Santiago. After a month on the island, Pile asked for another infantry regiment to replace the 91st Illinois and additions of cavalry and heavy artillery to his command. "If I had 500 cavalry I could inflict material damage" on the Confederates at Brownsville, he wrote to Department of the Gulf headquarters in New Orleans. "Is it desired that I do anything on the mainland? I would like to take a command to Brownsville, if it is the intention of the military authorities to occupy this coast; if not, I desire to be transferred to another command." Pile's letter passed on to even higher headquarters, the Military Division of West Mississippi. There, Maj. Gen. Edward R. S. Canby remarked that "the first duty of an officer is to do the best he can with the means at his command, and not to ask to be relieved because his superior officers may find it impracticable or inexpedient to increase his resources."[10]

Despite Canby's rebuke, Pile received a few things he had asked for. On 26 November, in one of the consolidations that befell understrength Louisiana regiments, the enlisted men of the 95th merged with those of the 87th. The new organization at first received the number 81, until word arrived that there was already a regiment of that number. Since the consolidation had left the number 87 vacant, the new regiment became the 87th USCI (New). Slow communications and conflicting regional authorities ensured that such confusion occurred repeatedly throughout the war. The decision to discharge nearly three-quarters of the officers of the old 87th and 95th, retaining only fourteen of the forty-eight, seemed to confirm Pile's assessment of their aptitude. Late in December, the 91st Illinois left Brazos Santiago for New Orleans, trading places with the 34th Indiana.[11]

Pile got another of his wishes in February 1865, when he received orders to join General Canby's expedition against Mobile. Arriving in New Orleans, he requested the assignment of two regiments to the expedition: the 81st USCI, which

---

[9] *OR*, ser. 1, vol. 41, pt. 4, pp. 448–49, 676 ("broken down"); Brig Gen W. A. Pile to Maj G. B. Drake, 28 Nov 1864 ("inefficient and"), Entry 5515, Mil Div of West Mississippi, Letters Received (LR), pt. 1, Geographical Divs and Depts, Record Group (RG) 393, Rcds of U.S. Army Continental Cmds, National Archives (NA).

[10] *OR*, ser. 1, vol. 41, pt. 4, pp. 767–68.

[11] Dyer, *Compendium*, pp. 1085, 1133, 1737; *Official Army Register of the Volunteer Force of the United States Army*, 8 vols. (Washington, D.C.: Adjutant General's Office, 1867), 8: 267–68, 276

he had recently inspected at Port Hudson and thought was "perhaps the best colored regiment in this department," and the 62d USCI at Brazos Santiago, "also a well drilled and disciplined regiment and well fitted for field service." He asked that they be sent "if necessary, in the place of other regiments not in so good condition, and that one of [them] be assigned to my brigade." Such praise came not from a politician or newspaper correspondent, nor from a politically appointed major general at the head of a geographical department, but from a brigadier seeking to improve his own command with troops whose performance could make or mar his reputation and perhaps even cost him his life. This time, authorities refused to grant even part of Pile's request. The two regiments he asked for remained at their stations in Louisiana and Texas while Pile and his brigade set off for Mobile on the last major campaign of the war.[12]

The 62d USCI spent the winter on Brazos Santiago. Its commanding officer, Lt. Col. David Branson, took measures to maintain and improve regimental discipline and morale. He admonished "several officers" of the regiment for hitting the men with their fists or the flat of a sword. "An officer is not fit to command who cannot control his temper sufficiently to avoid the habitual application of blows to enforce obedience," he wrote. "Men will not obey as promptly an officer who adopts the systems of the slave driver to maintain authority as they will him who punishes by a system consistent with . . . the spirit of the age." Branson allowed that "generally, the men who have received such punishment have been of the meanest type of soldiers; lazy, dirty & inefficient." Still, he insisted, "such treatment will not produce reform in them, while it has an injurious effect on all good men, from its resemblance to their former treatment while slaves." By mid-April, Branson reported the regiment "in a good state of discipline [and] in excellent health," while having "attained an unusual degree of efficiency in Battalion Drill and in the Bayonet Exercise." He asked for 437 recruits to augment the 543 men that remained of the 1,050 who had entered the ranks of the regiment during its sixteen months of service. Eighty-six of the missing men had died of disease before they left Missouri. More than two hundred lay buried at Port Hudson and Morganza, Louisiana, where the health of the regiment had suffered severely. Scores more had died elsewhere in the state.[13]

In April 1865, news of the Confederate surrender in Virginia traveled by telegraph, reaching St. Louis within twenty-four hours. Separated from the telegraph by miles of enemy-held territory, soldiers at Union beachheads on the Gulf of Mexico received that news, and word of the surrender in North Carolina, a week or more later. While Confederate generals in Alabama made similar arrangements, those west of the Mississippi River considered their situation. Maj. Gen. John B.

(hereafter cited as *ORVF*). For the organization, consolidation, and disbandment of Corps d'Afrique regiments, see Chapters 3 and 4, above.

    [12] *OR*, ser. 1, vol. 48, pt. 1, pp. 846, 964 (quotations).

    [13] 62d United States Colored Infantry (USCI), General Orders (GO) 36, 9 Nov 1864; Lt Col D. Branson to Adj Gen, USA, 20 Apr 1865; Company Descriptive Books; all in 62d USCI, Regimental Books, RG 94, Rcds of the Adjutant General's Office (AGO), NA. NA Microfilm Pub M594, Compiled Rcds Showing Svc of Mil Units in Volunteer Union Organizations, roll 212, 62d USCI; Ira Berlin et al., eds., *The Black Military Experience* (New York: Cambridge University Press, 1982), pp. 513–14; Margaret Humphreys, *Intensely Human: The Health of the Black Soldier in the American Civil War* (Baltimore: Johns Hopkins University Press, 2008), pp. 116–17.

Magruder had his headquarters at Houston. The port of Galveston was closed by the Union blockade, he told General E. Kirby Smith, who commanded the Confederate Trans-Mississippi Department, at the end of April.

> We have thus left only the Rio Grande as our outlet, and the occupation of Brownsville . . . becomes a prime necessity. As long as we can receive supplies by that route, and as long as the door is left open for us to co-operate with Mexico against the United States, our army will possess a moral influence very disproportioned to its numbers. . . . Our relations with the Imperial authorities are of the most cordial nature.[14]

One week after Magruder wrote, the last Confederate Army east of the Mississippi River surrendered. General Smith's troops in Arkansas and Louisiana, many of them Texans, began to desert in droves, simply heading home and taking their weapons with them. Along the way, they helped themselves to whatever they found at military supply depots or could take by force from farmers and townspeople. Some officers with better-disciplined commands, such as the cavalry force led by Brig. Gen. Joseph O. Shelby, began to ponder a move to Mexico. Meanwhile, the small Confederate garrisons on the lower Rio Grande waited to see what would happen.[15]

The Union commander at Brazos Santiago, Col. Theodore H. Barrett, made the next move. On 8 May, he ordered Colonel Branson with eleven officers and 250 men of the 62d USCI to the mainland. Barrett's reasons remain unclear; neither his nor Branson's report offers an explanation. It may have begun as a raid to gather mounts for the 2d Texas Cavalry, two officers and fifty men of which went along on foot. It may have been, as Barrett later described it, "a foraging expedition." One of his detractors later asserted that he merely wanted "to establish for himself some notoriety before the war closed." It was true that Barrett's previous service had been unremarkable, consisting mostly of frontier duty in Minnesota after the Sioux uprising of 1862; but an impulse to distinguish himself during the last days of the war should have prompted him to accompany the 62d USCI to the mainland in command of the expedition, rather than to send it and stay behind.[16]

Whatever Barrett's reasoning, foul weather and the mechanical failure of a steamboat that was supposed to ferry the troops kept them confined to Brazos Santiago for most of 8 May. It was 9:30 p.m. before they all reached the mainland. Moving off the beach, Branson had led them about six miles toward Brownsville by 2:00 a.m., as far as White's Ranch, near the Rio Grande. There, finding no Confederates, they lay down on the riverbank to rest. Not until 8:30, well after daylight

---

[14] *OR*, ser. 1, vol. 48, pt. 2, pp. 64, 187, 1289 (quotation).

[15] Brad R. Clampitt, "The Breakup: The Collapse of the Confederate Trans-Mississippi Army in Texas," *Southwestern Historical Quarterly* 108 (2005): 498–534; Carl H. Moneyhon, *Texas After the Civil War: The Struggle of Reconstruction* (College Station: Texas A&M University Press, 2004), p. 6; William L. Richter, *The Army in Texas During Reconstruction, 1865–1870* (College Station: Texas A&M University Press, 1987), p. 13.

[16] *OR*, ser. 1, vol. 48, pt. 1, pp. 265–69; NA M594, roll 212, 62d USCI; Jeffrey W. Hunt, *The Last Battle of the Civil War: Palmetto Ranch* (Austin: University of Texas Press, 2002), pp. 54–59 (quotations, p. 57).

revealed their presence to watchers on the opposite shore, did they move on. Later in the morning, they met a few enemy cavalry, followed them several miles west to their camp at a place called Palmetto Ranch, and drove them from it. At this point, the expedition had marched some seventeen miles inland from Brazos Santiago. The approach at midafternoon of "a considerable force of the enemy," as Branson called it, made him order his men back to White's Ranch, where they spent the night again.[17]

The Confederate officer commanding at Brownsville, Col. John S. Ford, was a Texan of nearly thirty years' residence and a man renowned throughout the state for his service with the Texas Rangers during the Mexican War and the years after it. A former state senator besides, Ford was able to rally the few hundred soldiers who still remained at their posts within a day's ride of Brownsville. A sixty-man cavalry picket downstream from the town sent word on 12 May that its men had exchanged shots with a force of three hundred Union troops. Late the next morning, Ford led two hundred cavalry troopers and a battery of six mismatched cannon served by thirty gunners—five or six of them French volunteers from across the river—to meet the invaders.[18]

Meanwhile, Colonel Barrett had come ashore with two hundred men of the 34th Indiana. They reached Branson's camp at White's Ranch about daylight on 13 May. Assuming command of the entire force, Barrett ordered an advance with the 62d USCI in the lead. A march of an hour or two brought the force to Palmetto Ranch again—Barrett's report recorded their arrival "by 7 or 8 a.m."—where the troops finished their interrupted work of destroying the Confederate camp. Sporadic firing had occurred during the advance. Perhaps in order to discover its source, Barrett ordered two companies of the 34th Indiana to seize the only nearby hill, which stood in a bow in the river a mile or two south of the ranch. When they met resistance in the underbrush along the river, he sent the 62d USCI to their assistance. There the regiment suffered its first casualty of the expedition, one man wounded. All the while, Barrett seemed uncertain of his purpose, asking one company commander, 2d Lt. Charles A. Jones, "What do you think should be done?" Breaking off the action about midafternoon, he told Jones, who had helped to take the hill a little while earlier, "Well, if you think best, we will [retire] and eat supper." Such remarks did not infuse Barrett's subordinates with confidence.[19]

The Confederates neared the field about 3:00 p.m., as Barrett's men were disengaging from the skirmish that had occupied them all day. By this time, Barrett had apparently decided that his force would return to the coast. His reason for this decision is as obscure as his reason for undertaking the expedition in the first place. Ford, for his part, decided that the best chance of defeating his opponents was to catch them on the march before they reached their goal. He ordered some of his horsemen and two cannon forward to block the road at Palmetto Ranch ahead of

---

[17]*OR*, ser. 1, vol. 48, pt. 1, pp. 267–68; Case of Lt Col R. G. Morrison (MM–2967), transcript, p. 20, Entry 15A, General Court Martial Case Files, RG 153, Rcds of the Judge Advocate General's Office, NA; Hunt, *Last Battle*, pp. 58–59; Townsend, *Yankee Invasion*, p. 127.

[18]Hunt, *Last Battle*, pp. 7–8, 62–63, 82, 171.

[19]*OR*, ser. 1, vol. 48, pt. 1, pp. 266–68; Hunt, *Last Battle*, pp. 68–71, 73 ("What do you"), 79 ("Well, if you").

the retreating Union force. Meanwhile, the rest of his cavalry dismounted to attack through the riverside undergrowth.[20]

Ford's mounted men hastened toward the ranch while his remaining guns opened fire on the Union troops, still in the bow of the river where they had enjoyed a brief rest from the day's skirmishing. Barrett's infantry scrambled to form ranks while the Confederate artillery, about one mile distant, sought their range. Branson led the 62d USCI off first, followed by the 34th Indiana and the few dozen men of the 2d Texas Cavalry, all moving at the double. The Indiana regiment left behind two companies, an officer and forty-eight men, to cover the retreat. These the Confederates soon captured. Meanwhile, Barrett, in order to avoid a headlong rout, ordered Branson to slow his regiment's pace. Branson obeyed, but the 34th Indiana, continuing at the double on a separate trail through the undergrowth that lined the riverbank, ran into and through the 62d USCI a little way short of Palmetto Ranch. While officers separated the men of the two regiments and formed the line of march again, Barrett detailed the two companies of the 2d Texas Cavalry as a rear guard despite their officers' protests that their men had only one or two rounds of ammunition left. When they had discharged those, the horseless troopers sneaked into the undergrowth and hid. There the Confederates captured them later in the afternoon.[21]

The Confederate horsemen had swung wide, hoping to reach Palmetto Ranch unobserved; but an officer of the 62d USCI spotted them soon after they started out, and the federal troops made for the ranch by a more direct route. The mixup of the 62d with the 34th Indiana had left the white troops at the head of the retreat, covered by half of the companies of the 62d USCI acting as skirmishers in a line that stretched for some twelve hundred yards. "Every attempt of the enemy's cavalry to break this line was repulsed with loss to him," Barrett wrote, "and the entire regiment fell back . . . in perfect order, under circumstances that would have tested the discipline of the best troops." Only two hours of daylight remained by the time Barrett's force reached Palmetto Ranch and the road to the coast, ahead of the Confederates. The 62d, nearly intact, and some one hundred twenty men of the 34th Indiana reached the coast half an hour after nightfall, Branson's regiment "marching as from Dress Parade, 28 inch step, music playing." All the troops were back on Brazos Santiago before dawn the next day. Most of the expedition's losses were by capture. That the 62d USCI had suffered five wounded in two days and two men taken prisoner indicates the desultory nature of the fighting.[22]

Branson's report praised the conduct of the 62d, his own regiment. "The men did their duty nobly," he reported. "First Sergeants [Willis] Shipley, Company E, and [Henry] Brown, Company D, proved themselves, as far as field duty . . . , fit to command companies." Unlike many regiments that enlisted former slaves from the Mississippi Valley, the 1st Missouri Colored Infantry had from the beginning filled all noncommissioned positions with black soldiers rather than appoint a white first sergeant in each

---

[20]*OR*, ser. 1, vol. 48, pt. 1, pp. 266, 268; Hunt, *Last Battle*, pp. 84–90.

[21]*OR*, ser. 1, vol. 48, pt. 1, p. 268; Case of Lt Col R. G. Morrison (MM–2967), transcript, p. 21, Entry 15A, RG 153, NA; NA M594, roll 212, 62d USCI; Hunt, *Last Battle*, pp. 91–100, 102–03.

[22]*OR*, ser. 1, vol. 48, pt. 1, p. 267 ("Every attempt"); Morrison Case, p. 92 ("marching as from"); Hunt, *Last Battle*, pp. 104–05.

company to assist the officers with drill and necessary paperwork. The attempt to appoint black soldiers as company first sergeants in the 62d USCI had resulted in some poor choices at first, as company commanders selected men in December 1863 on the basis of a few weeks' acquaintance. By May 1865, only one of the original ten first sergeants still held that rank. Brown and Shipley had both taken the places of men who had been found unsuitable for one reason or another. Like more than nine-tenths of the men in the regiment, both sergeants had been slaves before the war. Nor were they the only noncommissioned officers who distinguished themselves on 13 May: Sgt. Isham Boggs was appointed first sergeant of Company F "for gallantry in action," and Sgt. William A. Messley became first sergeant of Company G.[23]

Even before the defeat at Palmetto Ranch, Department of the Gulf headquarters had planned to send an officer more senior than Colonel Barrett to command the troops at the mouth of the Rio Grande. Brig. Gen. Egbert B. Brown, a veteran of campaigns in Arkansas and Missouri, arrived not long after the battle. He soon wrote to New Orleans, requesting rations and reinforcements, but before either could arrive he ordered another advance inland. When his troops reached Brownsville on 30 May, they found the Confederates gone. The final Union reoccupation of Brownsville meant that any Confederates seeking an escape route to Mexico would have to travel far out of their way to find a sanctuary south of the Rio Grande.[24]

Meanwhile, the Army was rushing troops to Texas, although not in response to General Brown's request. On 17 May, three days after Barrett's expedition returned to Brazos Santiago, Lt. Gen. Ulysses S. Grant sent Maj. Gen. Philip H. Sheridan from Virginia to take charge of a new geographical division. Called the Military Division of the Southwest (after 27 June, the Military Division of the Gulf), Sheridan's new command stretched from the Florida Keys to the Rio Grande. At his disposal were three corps, predominantly of infantry, and two cavalry divisions. The XIII Corps started from Mobile, where it had helped to capture the city the month before. One of its divisions moved by river to northeastern Texas. Another took possession of Houston and Galveston. The third division of the corps steamed for the Rio Grande. From Tennessee, the IV Corps, veterans of the previous year's battle of Nashville, took riverboats to New Orleans and ships from there to Indianola on the Texas coast. Two columns of Union cavalry marched overland from Shreveport and Alexandria in Louisiana to San Antonio and Houston, while from Virginia, nearly sixteen thousand officers and men of Maj. Gen. Godfrey Weitzel's XXV Corps, black infantry, cavalry, and artillery, took ship for southern Texas.[25]

Preparations for the voyage from Virginia were as thorough as possible. Regiments left sick men behind to be cared for at Army hospitals. Besides the usual Army ration, ships carried foods such as pickles, sauerkraut, and dried apples to ward off scurvy. Still, Assistant Surgeon James O. Moore of the 22d USCI complained that the water on board his ship "fairly stunk." This was hardly surprising after the convoy touched at New Orleans, where at least one vessel replenished its casks with river

---

[23] *OR*, ser. 1, vol. 48, pt. 1, pp. 268–69 (quotation); Company Descriptive Books, 62d USCI, Regimental Books, RG 94, NA; Col T. H. Barrett to Brig Gen L. Thomas, 30 Apr 1864, 62d USCI, Entry 57C, Regimental Papers, RG 94, NA.

[24] *OR*, ser. 1, vol. 48, pt. 2, pp. 300, 381–82, 564–65, 827–28.

[25] Ibid., vol. 46, pt. 3, p. 1032; vol. 48, pt. 2, pp. 476, 1004. Richter, *Army in Texas*, pp. 14–17. For Union operations around Mobile in 1865, see Chapter 4, above.

water while steaming into the mouth of the Mississippi, below the city. Whatever the difficulties of life afloat, few men died during the voyage—only eight in the entire 1st Division, the commanding general reported: "No more than might have been expected had we remained in camp." Those who died on board ship were buried at sea.[26]

However diligent medical authorities had been in providing antiscorbutics for the voyage, the Quartermaster Department did not take equal care when it hired transport ships. While no mishaps occurred during the trip, the oceangoing vessels that brought two brigades of the XXV Corps to Indianola had hulls too deep to pass over a seven-foot bar that kept them out of the harbor. They remained there, pitching in a high sea for six days before steaming back to New Orleans for more coal and water. By the time they returned, the weather had calmed and the troops were able to land in light-draft vessels; but the pickles, sauerkraut, and dried apples had long since run out, and signs of scurvy had begun to appear.[27]

Once ashore, the troops at Indianola found themselves in a populated region and were able to supplement their rations with local produce. Those who landed at Brazos Santiago, nearly two hundred miles to the south, had no such luck, but they were able to disembark more promptly than the other force and so postponed the threat of scurvy for a little while. On Brazos Santiago, "as far as the eye can reach nothing but sand is seen," Chaplain Thomas S. Johnson of the 127th USCI wrote. "There is not a spear of vegetation growing within sight of my tent," 1st Lt. Oliver W. Norton told his sister. The sole water condenser on the island had a capacity of six thousand gallons a day. It provided only three pints per man, "boiling hot," Pvt. Samuel H. Smothers of the 45th USCI told readers of the *Christian Recorder*. Another contributor to the paper, who signed his letter "M. R. Williams" and claimed to belong to the 41st USCI, alleged that the water ration was one cup per day and that men had to pay one dollar for a piece of hardtack. An investigation of the complaint revealed that there was no man by that name on the rolls of the regiment. The lack of water necessitated moving the regiments inland to Brownsville as quickly as possible. This meant, in the words of one of General Weitzel's aides, "as soon as the condition of the roads will permit."[28]

The same foul weather that had met the transports at Indianola had turned the road from Brazos Santiago to Brownsville into "a dozen miles of swamp," as Surgeon Charles G. G. Merrill of the 22d USCI called it. It was Merrill's job

---

[26]Col M. R. Morgan to Capt C. Wheaton Jr., 21 May 1865, Entry 518, XXV Corps, Misc Ltrs, Orders, and Rpts Recd, pt. 2, Polyonymous Successions of Cmds, RG 393, NA. Maj Gen G. A. Smith to Lt Col D. D. Wheeler, 24 Jul 1865 ("No more"); Col J. C. Moon to Maj A. Ware, 19 Jul 1865; Col T. D. Sedgwick to Maj A. Ware, 20 Jul 1865; Col S. B. Yeoman to Maj A. Ware, 21 Jul 1865; all in Entry 525, XXV Corps, LR Relating to Troop Movements, pt. 2, RG 393, NA. J. O. Moore to My Dearest Wife, 9 Jul 1865 ("fairly stunk"), J. O. Moore Papers, Duke University, Durham, N.C.; W. Goodale to Dear Children, 8 June 1865, W. Goodale Papers, Massachusetts Historical Society, Boston. For burials at sea, see J. M. Califf Diary, 6 and 14 Jun 1865, Historians files, U.S. Army Center of Military History; Oliver W. Norton, *Army Letters, 1861–1865* (Chicago: privately printed, 1903), p. 266.

[27]Col J. Shaw to Maj E. B. Parsons, 20 Jun 1865, and to Capt R. C. Shannon, 8 Jul 1865, both in Entry 533, XXV Corps, LR by Divs, pt. 2, RG 393, NA; Califf Diary, 13–17 and 25 Jun 1865.

[28]Maj J. F. Lacey to Maj Gen G. Weitzel, 26 Jun 1865, Entry 533; Col J. Shaw to Capt R. C. Shannon, 8 Jul 1865, Entry 518; Maj Gen F. Steele to Maj Gen P. H. Sheridan, 15 Jun 1865, Entry 2063, U.S. Forces on Rio Grande, Letters Sent (LS); all in pt. 2, RG 393, NA. T. S. Johnson to Dear

to pick up stragglers, following the division with two four-mule ambulances. "The roads are horrible," wrote the division commander. "The wagons were ordered to load only eight hundred pounds and they have had an awful time at that. Some of the way we were obliged to have the men carry the loads and then twelve mules [double teams] stalled with empty wagons." The men marched "sometimes over shoe tops in mud, and again through water up to our waists," Sgt. Charles W. Cole of the 29th Connecticut told readers of the *Christian Recorder*. The division took two days to cover twenty-odd miles to Brownsville. Assistant Surgeon Moore, who cared for the 22d USCI while Surgeon Merrill brought up the rear of the march, told his wife that the town was "one of the most forsaken looking holes you ever saw."[29]

Once in camp at Brownsville, the commanding officer of the 43d USCI wrote to divisional headquarters to explain why the provost guard had arrested fifty of his men—the equivalent of an entire company—as stragglers during the march. In the first place, the men were "much debilitated" from twenty-five days' close confinement on shipboard. Going ashore, they were "ordered to camp on ground which became flooded . . . after each shower, completely drenching" their clothing and blankets. The regiment had had to change its campsite three times in two days because of flooding. On the march, wagons "were continually . . . compelling the men to dive into the dense chapperel which grew close to each side of the road." Finally, there was the matter of rations, which had arrived at regimental headquarters too late to be distributed to the men. Companies detailed men to fetch the rations and follow the column, and the provost guard arrested them as stragglers. The 43d was last in the line of march, "subject to all the difficulties of halting on account of delays at the front and rapid marching to regain lost distances." If the regiment had been farther ahead, the men with the rations could have "passed along the flanks of the other regiments unnoticed," but, being so far behind, they were arrested instead. The march to Brownsville was not as urgent as some that the XXV Corps had undertaken in Virginia, but it was no less exasperating.[30]

Lieutenant Norton had an opportunity to observe the country as his regiment followed the route several days later, after the road had dried somewhat. He saw

> a boundless prairie, dotted here and there with prickly pears and Spanish bayonet. . . . Part of the way the road lay through mesquit chaparral, impenetrable thickets of scrubby, thorny trees, too small for shade and too dense to admit a breath of air. . . . In passing through some parts of the country, the chaparral

---

People, 24 Jun 1864, T. S. Johnson Papers, Wisconsin Historical Society, Madison; W. Goodale to Dear Children, 4 Jul 1865, Goodale Papers; *Christian Recorder*, 29 July and 11 November 1865; Norton, *Army Letters*, pp. 267–68; Edwin S. Redkey, ed., *A Grand Army of Black Men: Letters from African-American Soldiers in the Union Army, 1861–1865* (New York: Cambridge University Press, 1992), p. 197.

[29] Maj Gen G. A. Smith to Lt Col D. D. Wheeler, 29 Jun 1865, Entry 525, pt. 2, RG 393, NA; 1st Div, XXV Corps, GO 49, 27 Jun 1865, Entry 533, pt. 2, RG 393, NA; NA M594, roll 216, 114th USCI; *Christian Recorder*, 9 September 1865; C. G. G. Merrill to Dear Father, 2 Jul 1865, C. G. G. Merrill Papers, Yale University, New Haven, Conn.; J. O. Moore to My Dearest Lizzie, 30 Jun 1865, J. O. Moore Papers.

[30] Lt Col H. S. Hall to Maj A. Ware, 2 Jul 1865, 43d USCI, Regimental Books, RG 94, NA.

cleared up and the mesquit trees with the wild grass under them, looked exactly like an old orchard of half-dead apple trees in a field of half-ripe oats.

To a Northern eye, the vegetation seemed to be either not quite mature or long past ripeness, and "take it all in all, I would not live in this country if I could own a whole county."[31]

This view was widespread among Union troops. Capt. James H. Rickard of the 19th USCI thought that southern Texas offered "some of the hardest soldiering I have ever seen & in the meanest part of the world. [N]othing grows here except a few short stunted brush covered with thorns & the cactus in its different varieties." It was a view shared by 1st Lt. Warren Goodale of the 114th USCI. "All vegetable life seems thorny, & insect & reptile life venomous," he told his children. Soldiers had expressed such sentiments since the Army first marched to the Rio Grande in 1846, at the start of the Mexican War, and would continue to do so for decades.[32]

In overall command of southern Texas was Maj. Gen. Frederick Steele, who had seen action during the war in Arkansas and, in April 1865, at Mobile. General Grant's instructions to Steele were to "occupy as high up [the Rio Grande] as your force and means of supplying them will admit of." With two brigades at Indianola and Corpus Christi and the balance of the XXV Corps camped near the mouth of the river, Steele ordered the reoccupation of prewar forts that had not seen a federal garrison since the spring of 1861. The principal sites were Ringgold Barracks, at Rio Grande City, some one hundred miles upriver from Brownsville; Fort McIntosh, at Laredo, another hundred miles farther on; and Fort Duncan, at Eagle Pass, roughly three hundred miles above Brownsville. Troops also established posts at the little settlement of Roma, some fifteen miles west of Ringgold Barracks; Edinburg, a town about sixty-five miles west of Brownsville; and White's Ranch, on the Rio Grande between Brazos Santiago and Brownsville. Light-draft steamboats carried supplies up the river as far as Ringgold Barracks.[33]

In order to move those supplies eleven miles inland from the saltwater port at Brazos Santiago to a wharf on the Rio Grande at White's Ranch, thus bypassing a treacherous bar at the mouth of the river, troops of the XXV Corps began in July to lay track for a rail line. Weitzel had thought about bringing civilian laborers from Virginia, but Grant overruled the idea. "There are plenty of negroes in Texas," he told General Weitzel, but Grant was thinking of the agricultural part of the state, far from the Rio Grande. Instead, the work fell to soldiers. With details that varied from four hundred fifty to six hundred fifty men a day, they finished the line by the end of the year. While they did this, troops at Indianola repaired an existing forty-mile line between that port and the inland town of Victoria to get supplies across

---

[31] Norton, *Army Letters*, pp. 271, 275.

[32] J. H. Rickard to Dear Friends, 2 Jul 1865, J. H. Rickard Papers, American Antiquarian Society (AAS), Worcester, Mass.; Goodale to Dear Children, 4 Jul 1865. For an example of Army officers' opinions of the lower Rio Grande, see Thomas T. Smith et al., eds., *The Reminiscences of Major General Zenas R. Bliss, 1854–1876* (Austin: Texas State Historical Association, 2007), pp. 11, 426; Arnoldo De Leon, *They Called Them Greasers: Anglo Attitudes Toward Mexicans in Texas, 1821–1900* (Austin: University of Texas Press, 1983), pp. 53–62.

[33] *OR*, ser. 1, vol. 48, pt. 2, p. 525. Brig Gen R. H. Jackson to Lt Col D. D. Wheeler, 23 Jul 1865, Entry 517, XXV Corps, LR; Maj Gen H. G. Wright to Maj Gen G. Weitzel, 18 Sep 1865, Entry 518; both in pt. 2, RG 393, NA.

a waterless stretch of eighteen miles that lay between the two. General Sheridan reported that the Army eventually sold both lines to civilian operators at a profit.[34]

The headquarters of Steele's District of the Rio Grande and Weitzel's XXV Corps remained at Brownsville. The stations of most troops along the river, from Brazos Santiago inland to Ringgold Barracks, lay in the lower valley, which was less sparsely populated than the stretch upriver, northwest of Ringgold Barracks. From their posts, the Americans kept an eye on the struggle between Imperial and Liberal forces that flared up from time to time in the Mexican state of Tamaulipas, which ran along the opposite bank of the Rio Grande from a point just north of Laredo to the mouth of the river. Steele's orders from Grant were to "observe a strict neutrality." The first step in that direction was to prohibit all enlisted men and officers without passes from crossing the river at Clarksville to visit the Mexican port of Bagdad. Prohibition or not, rumors soon gained circulation that black cavalrymen were selling carbines and revolvers to Mexicans. Moreover, a German-speaking officer of the 45th USCI stood accused of crossing the river to urge Austrian troops in the Imperial army to desert. Attempts to restrict troops' movements during off-duty hours were never entirely effective.[35]

Long before the XXV Corps arrived, one of the reasons for enlarging the Union force on the Rio Grande had become outdated. On 10 May, Union cavalry in Georgia had captured the fleeing Jefferson Davis. Still, the whereabouts of other Confederates and their plans were less well known. Several hundred horsemen, all that remained of General Shelby's command, accompanied their leader across the Rio Grande in early July. The tiny force made its way to Mexico City, where Shelby offered its services to the Imperialist cause. When Maximilian declined, the group dispersed. Other former Confederates had bolder ideas. Lt. Gen. Jubal A. Early hoped to inspire a war between France and the United States that would drain the South of occupying troops and make possible a Confederate military revival. After a few weeks' stay in the Mexican capital, he pronounced the Imperialist movement "an infernal humbug" and returned eventually to the United States.[36]

The end of Confederate military activity left several tasks for the Union occupiers of southern Texas. Since the Rio Grande lay hundreds of miles from the center of the state's population, few of these duties had to do with the work of Reconstruction that military and civilian officials pursued elsewhere in the South. Relations between local residents and occupying troops along the Rio Grande, where few black people had lived before the war, certainly differed from those far-

---

[34]*OR*, ser. 1, vol. 46, pt. 3, p. 1193 (quotation); vol. 48, pt. 1, p. 299. 3d Div, XXV Corps, Special Orders (SO) 7, 18 Jul 1865, and Maj F. D. Kent to Maj O. O. Potter, 18 Sep 1865, both in Entry 533, RG 393, NA; Capt J. M. Lee to Maj L. S. Barnes, 15 Dec 1865, Entry 539, XXV Corps, Ltrs and Rpts Recd by Inspector General, both in pt. 2, RG 393, NA; NA M594, roll 209, 38th USCI.

[35]*OR*, ser. 1, vol. 48, pt. 2, p. 525 (quotation); Cav Bde, XXV Corps, GO 5, 5 Jul 1865, 5th Mass Cav, Regimental Books, RG 94, NA; Col J. G. Jenkins to Lt Col D. D. Wheeler, 5 Apr 1866, 19th USCI, Regimental Books, RG 94, NA. Brig Gen G. W. Cole to Brig Gen R. H. Jackson, 11 Jul 1865, Entry 533; Maj Gen G. Weitzel to Commanding Officer, Bagdad, 12 Jul 1865, Entry 512; Lt Col D. D. Wheeler to Brig Gen W. T. Clarke, 11 Sep 1865, Entry 2073, U.S. Forces on Rio Grande, LR; all in pt. 2, RG 393, NA.

[36]Andrew F. Rolle, *The Lost Cause: The Confederate Exodus to Mexico* (Norman: University of Oklahoma Press, 1965), pp. 17–18, 74–77, 122–24 (quotation, p. 124); Thomas D. Schoonover, *Dollars over Dominion: The Triumph of Liberalism in Mexican–United States Relations, 1861–1877* (Baton Rouge: Louisiana State University Press, 1978), pp. 189–90.

ther north. Sergeant Cole of the 29th Connecticut praised the hospitality of Brownsville's Mexican residents in the pages of the *Christian Recorder*, and Sgt. Maj. Thomas Boswell of the 116th USCI predicted a few weeks later, "If our regiment stays here any length of time we will all speak Spanish, as we are learning very fast." The commanding officer of the 19th USCI reported, "The Mexicans are without much prejudice against the negroes on account of color and if let alone by the whites would give no trouble."[37]

The situation was different north of the Nueces River, where slavery had been the basis of the social and economic order. One of Grant's staff officers on a tour of Sheridan's command landed in Galveston and wrote to the chief of staff:

German-speaking Edelmiro Mayer (shown here as major of the 7th U.S. Colored Infantry) was lieutenant colonel of the 45th U.S. Colored Infantry when he crossed the Rio Grande to harangue Austrian troops in the Imperialist army. The 45th, like other regiments raised in the North, mustered out not long afterward, and Mayer never faced punishment for his breach of neutrality.

One man an ex-Confederate navy officer was very savage on a negro regiment brought here for fatigue duty—denounced it as an outrage and intended humiliation of the people—would evidently like the privilege of shooting them. . . . A squad of them were marching down [a] street the other day and met some white men who did not give way. . . . [O]ne of the citizens thinking a negro hit him with his elbow in passing, struck the soldier with his cane whereupon soldier No. 2 hit citizen an astonisher under the ear. Of course this was an outrage and in good old times the negroes would have been lynched—in the present case investigation showing the negroes not in fault the citizens were advised to let the soldiers alone in future—to their great indignation and disgust.

Officers of the XXV Corps regiments at Corpus Christi, Indianola, and towns inland meanwhile busied themselves with administering loyalty oaths to former Confederates who sought full restoration of their civil rights. In contrast, troops along the Rio Grande merely kept an eye on the conflict between Imperialists and

---

[37]Col J. G. Perkins to Lt Col D. D. Wheeler, 7 Apr 1866 ("The Mexicans"), 19th USCI, Regimental Books, RG 94, NA; *Christian Recorder*, 9 September 1865; Redkey, *Grand Army of Black Men*, p. 203 ("If our regiment").

Liberals for control of the region across the river and tried to prevent or punish the activities of those perennial border worries, livestock thieves and Indian raiders.[38]

Land and cattle were the two principal sources of wealth along the lower Rio Grande. With recently arrived English-speaking Texans owning an ever-increasing share of the land, extended families of Mexican origin occupying both banks of the river, and an easily forded stream serving as the international boundary, theft of livestock thrived. Although the trade in stolen cattle had not reached the heights that it would a few years later, it occupied the attention of officers and men scattered along the river in one-company posts at tiny settlements with names like Rancho Barrancas, Rancho Cortina, and Rancho Santa Maria. The XXV Corps had been in Texas only one month when its commissary officer called attention to the porous border and its effect on the local beef supply. In a vain attempt to stop the illicit traffic, the black regiments patrolled the river until the last of them left Texas. Although a patrol from Fort McIntosh managed to impound a herd of 137 head in November 1865, such efforts more often failed, as would any such attempts by people new to a country they were trying to police.[39]

Unlike the central and northern plains, Texas did not see many armed clashes between whites and Indians in 1865. Maj. Gen. Wesley Merritt, commanding a division of cavalry at San Antonio, called "this part of the country at least . . . very quiet." Nevertheless, the Department of Texas asked General Steele to dispatch "a regiment of colored troops" to Fort McIntosh, at Laredo, "to look after the frontier between Ringgold Barracks and Eagle Pass." When the choice settled on the 62d USCI a few weeks later, Colonel Barrett received the caution that "it is just possible that Indians may pass for raiding or other evil purposes"; his instructions were "to defeat & frustrate their doings."[40]

Although Indian disturbances were rare while the XXV Corps served in southern Texas, rumors were plentiful. A report of one occurrence in the summer of 1865 affords an instance abounding with difficulties of the sort that would dog the Army in the West for a generation. Late in the afternoon of 11 August 1865, Maj. Thomas Wright led a party of four companies from the 31st and 116th USCIs, some 175 officers and men, out of Roma "in pursuit of a party of Hostile Indians,

---

[38]Lt Col C. B. Comstock to Maj Gen J. A. Rawlins, 7 Feb 1866 (quotation), Entry 35, Letters Sent and Recd by General Grant, RG 108, Rcds of the Headquarters of the Army, NA. For loyalty oaths, see 2d Lt R. A. Kent to Maj Gen G. Weitzel, 11 Aug 1865, Entry 533, pt. 2, RG 393, NA; Califf Diary, 12, 27, and 28 Jul 1865.

[39]Capt R. C. Shannon to Col T. H. Barrett, 31 Oct 1865; 1st Lt H. H. Miller to 1st Lt T. C. Barden, 12 Nov 1865, and to Capt J. H. Looby, 18 Nov 1865; all in Entry 533; Lt Col C. Wheaton to Capt L. Rhoades, 28 Jul 1865, Entry 2073; Brig Gen R. H. Jackson to Lt Col D. D. Wheeler, 13 Aug 1865, Entry 517; all in pt. 2, RG 393, NA. Col T. D. Sedgwick to 1st Lt G. C. Potwin, 18 Nov 1866; Col J. G. Perkins to Capt T. C. Barden, 11 Oct 1866; Capt A. McIntyre to Col T. D. Sedgwick, 31 Oct 1866; all in 114th USCI, Entry 57C, RG 94, NA. Capt J. H. Looby to Commanding Ofcr, 116th USCI, 30 Oct 1865; 2d Lt M. Himes to Capt R. C. Shannon, 9 Nov 1865; Maj Gen H. G. Wright to Maj Gen G. W. Getty, 14 May 1866; all in 116th USCI, Entry 57C, RG 94, NA. NA Microfilm Pub M617, Returns from U.S. Mil Posts, roll 681, Fort McIntosh, Nov 1865; Montejano, *Anglos and Mexicans in the Making of Texas*, pp. 30–53; Thompson, *Cortina*, pp. 22–23, 31–33, 200–202. Place names from Weekly Station and Effective Force Rpt, 10 Sep 1866, Entry 4790, Dept of Texas, Ltrs and Misc Rpts Recd, pt. 1, RG 393, NA.

[40]Maj Gen W. Merritt to Brig Gen G. A. Forsyth, 31 Oct 1865 ("this part of"), Entry 4495, Mil Div of the Southwest, LR, pt. 1, and Maj Gen H. G. Wright to Maj Gen F. Steele, 18 Sep 1865 ("a regiment of"), Entry 2073, pt. 2, both in RG 393, NA; Capt R. C. Shannon to Col T. H. Barrett, 31 Oct 1865 ("it is just"), 62d USCI, Entry 57C, RG 94, NA.

supposed to be in the vicinity of Redmond's Ranche," about forty miles upriver. When the troops reached there on the morning of 14 August, residents could tell them nothing of importance, but that afternoon "a Mexican came in" with the news that he had seen Indians at his ranch, more than forty miles to the northeast, far from the river. Having gone part of the way, and hearing that "a large force of Cavalry" was moving from San Antonio toward the Rio Grande, Wright decided the next morning to move northwest again, toward Laredo and the river. On the morning of 17 August, the party arrived at a ranch some twenty-five miles from Laredo. "There I found a post of one Sergt and six men of the 2d Texas Cavalry, who were scouting around the country," Wright reported. This may have been the "large force of Cavalry" he had heard about.[41]

Having marched his men more than one hundred miles in six days, Wright decided to let them rest while he rode on to Laredo. There, the lieutenant commanding a garrison of some two dozen men told him that the raiders were Mexican Kickapoos. These Indians had been forced from their lands east of the Mississippi River two generations earlier. Many had settled in Kansas, but some had moved to Texas, only to be driven from there into Mexico ten or fifteen years later. Others from Kansas had joined them recently, disgusted by an 1862 treaty that demanded further land cessions. The lieutenant at Laredo said that small bands of raiders had driven off herds of cattle and horses and killed more than a dozen residents along the river. Wright rejoined his command and marched back down the river to Roma, arriving on 24 August. During the expedition he had learned that while residents along the Rio Grande were clamoring for protection, raiding in Texas by Indians amounted to little, compared to thefts by residents who drove herds across the river. The commanding officer at Roma reported a band of marauders "painted and disguised as Indians" killing residents and stealing livestock. Vague information, demands for military protection, and complaints blaming property losses on Indian raiders would all become familiar to soldiers charged with implementing federal Indian policy in the West during the following decades.[42]

Army officers soon learned to discount what General Sheridan called "exaggerated reports, gotten up in some instances by frontier people to get a market for their produce, and in other instances by army contractors to make money." Sheridan believed in any case that warnings of raids on the Texas frontier were merely a ruse to remove troops from the settlements so that former slaveholders could have a free hand with the black population. The general commanding the Department of Texas told Sheridan in July 1866 that he received "frequent complaints . . . of the barbarities practiced towards . . . freedmen" but could do nothing about it for want of troops.[43]

While staff officers planned the distribution of soldiers and supplies, enlisted men and medical officers on the lower Rio Grande confronted scurvy, brought about yet again by a lack of fresh meat and vegetables at Brazos Santiago. "You can have no idea of our desperate situation," Surgeon Merrill wrote to his father. "The idea of

---

[41] Maj L. Wright to Capt R. C. Shannon, 24 Aug 1865, Entry 533, pt. 2, RG 393, NA.

[42] Ibid.; Jackson to Wheeler, 13 Aug 1865 ("painted and disguised"); Craig Miner and William E. Unrau, *The End of Indian Kansas: A Study of Cultural Revolution, 1854–1871* (Lawrence: Regents Press of Kansas, 1978), pp. 45–49, 96–98.

[43] *OR*, ser. 1, vol. 48, pt. 1, p. 301 ("exaggerated reports"); "Condition of Affairs in Texas," 39th Cong., 2d sess., H. Ex. Doc. 61 (serial 1,292), p. 4 ("frequent complaints").

putting ten thousand men in such a country without . . . making any provision is more than preposterous—it is damnable—and I am perfectly disgusted with . . . the whole affair. If they ask my opinion I shall tell them plainly. . . . I do not want to see my men murdered by inches, when there is no necessity for any such thing." Officers, Chaplain Johnson explained in a letter home, could afford supplements to their diet and thus avoided the scurvy that afflicted enlisted men. "We could buy canned Peaches and Tomatoes . . . but the soldiers without money not being paid for six months had to confine themselves to the regular army ration."[44]

The Quartermaster Department, which arranged shipping and hauling of military supplies, had suffered from corruption on the lower Rio Grande since the Union army had landed in the fall of 1863 and was slow to recover after General Weitzel and the XXV Corps arrived. Neither were military administrators in Washington of much help. The Adjutant General's Office in Washington assured Sheridan, in New Orleans, that the Subsistence Department would ship "a large quantity of potatoes and onions . . . from St. Louis, Boston and New York, . . . which may be issued in lieu of other rations allowed by law. The law does not authorize extra issues of these articles and the Commissary General of Subsistence considers the authorized ration sufficient." Rather than abide by a bureaucrat's comments on "the law" and "the authorized ration," the officer commanding at Ringgold Barracks sent an expedition to the Nueces valley, some one hundred fifty miles to the north, that returned with two hundred fifty head of cattle bearing "brands of the late Rebel Government . . . and of one [Richard] King, late a contractor for the so-called Confederate States." The United States Sanitary Commission, a private charitable organization that operated under a federal charter, contributed a barrel of pickles that traveled by boat from Brownsville to Ringgold Barracks and from there fifty miles overland to the garrison at Edinburg.[45]

As happened wherever regiments, black or white, camped in one place for long, enlisted men on the Rio Grande soon took measures of their own to supplement dietary deficiencies. By 7 August, "thieving and plundering" had become so common that the brigade commander at Roma threatened to allow neighboring civilians "to shoot any soldiers caught marauding or . . . molesting the citizens by the killing of their cattle, destruction of water melon gardens, or trespassing upon their premises." Residents of Brownsville also complained, but the general in command there merely appointed a board of officers to investigate claims and offered cash payments for proven damages. In one case, three companies of the 8th United States Colored Artillery (USCA) split a fine of seventy-five dollars for "potatoes pillaged" from a local farmer.[46]

Fortunately for the health of the troops, a remedy was available in native plants of the region. As early as 10 July, Lieutenant Norton saw men of the 8th USCI eating the prickly pear, "a sort of cactus that grows all over this country. It looks like

---

[44]Maj L. S. Barnes to Lt Col D. D. Wheeler, 5 Aug 1865, Entry 533, pt. 2, RG 393, NA; Merrill to Dear Father, 2 Jul 1865; T. S. Johnson to My Dear People, 15 Aug 1865, Johnson Papers; Humphreys, *Intensely Human*, pp. 125–41.

[45]Maj Gen G. Weitzel to Maj G. Lee, 21 Dec 1865, and Col E. D. Townsend to Maj Gen P. H. Sheridan, 25 Aug 1865 ("a large quantity"), both in Entry 4495, pt. 1, RG 393, NA; Jackson to Wheeler, 13 Aug 1865 ("brands of the"); Brig Gen L. F. Haskell to Capt R. C. Shannon, 21 Aug 1865, Entry 533, pt. 2, RG 393, NA.

[46]3d Bde, 2d Div, XXV Corps, GO 20, 7 Aug 1865 (quotations), 116th USCI, Entry 57C, RG 94, NA; 1st Div, XXV Corps, Circular, 1 Jul 1865, Entry 533, pt. 2, RG 393, NA; Central Dist of Texas, SO 177, 1 Sep 1865, 8th United States Colored Artillery (USCA), Regimental Books, RG 94, NA.

a set of green dinner plates, the edge of one grown fast to the next. . . . The pears grow round the edge of the plates, about the size and shape of pears, covered with thorns and of a beautiful purple color when ripe, and full of seeds like a fig. Most of the men devoured them greedily, but I did not fancy their insipid taste." Enlisted men with a nutritional craving were not as fastidious as their better-fed officers.[47]

Two weeks later, a letter went from XXV Corps headquarters to generals commanding divisions, extolling the properties of "the 'Agave Americana' or American Aloe, which is found in groves of greater or less sizes [and] will cure scurvy or prevent it." After giving instructions for rendering the juice, Weitzel ordered his generals to "send out detachments from each post or brigade . . . to collect this tree and make this drink, called by common people 'Pulque.' . . . Ascertain where the trees can be found before starting the expedition, it is worth while even to send even a hundred miles off for it." By mid-August, regiments were sending entire companies fifty or sixty miles in search of aloes, otherwise known as maguey. The incidence of scurvy decreased the next month, although some officers attributed this to the recent arrival of potatoes in quantity. Still the disease persisted; in early October, the surgeon of the 43d USCI reported that of 539 men in the regiment, 163 were excused from duty, "nearly all being cases of scurvy."[48]

The surgeon was concerned about the effect on scurvy patients of a few weeks' shipboard diet, for the regiment was due to muster out and return to Philadelphia, where it had been raised and where its officers and men would receive their discharges and final pay. Orders had arrived recently for the muster-out of all black regiments from the free states. This was part of the program dismantling the Union Army and cutting government expenses.[49]

That June, a month after the last Confederate surrender, the War Department had discontinued the Army of Georgia and the Army of the Potomac, two of the Union's premier fighting forces, mustering out most of the regiments in each. In the same month, across the South, mustering out began of volunteer artillery batteries and cavalry regiments, the two most costly arms of the service. With nearly all of the soldiers who had marched with Sherman discharged and paid off, the War Department discontinued the Army of the Tennessee and nearly all of the wartime corps organizations on 1 August. The next step was to begin reducing the number of infantry regiments that had not been part of the major field armies but were subordinate to regional commands or organized as corps, divisions, or brigades.[50]

Although even the most senior of the black regiments was not due for muster-out until early 1866, War Department administrators decided to begin with those that had been raised in the free states, from Massachusetts and Rhode Island to Illinois and

---

[47] Surgeon D. Mackay to Capt R. C. Shannon, 13 Aug 1865, Entry 533, pt. 2, RG 393, NA; Norton, *Army Letters*, p. 271.

[48] Maj Gen G. Weitzel to Maj Gen G. A. Smith et al., 26 Jul 1865 ("send out"), Entry 512, XXV Corps, LS, pt. 2, RG 393, NA. Asst Surgeon J. L. Chipman to 1st Lt E. S. Dean, 2 Oct 1865, 43d USCI, and Capt H. G. Marshall to Col T. D. Sedgwick, 25 Aug 1865, 114th USCI, both in Entry 57C, RG 94, NA; W. Goodale to Dear Children, 22 Aug 1865 ("nearly all"), Goodale Papers; T. S. Johnson to My Dear People, 5 Jul 1865, Johnson Papers; E. W. Bacon to Dear Kate, 9 Sep 1865, E. W. Bacon Papers, AAS.

[49] *OR*, ser. 3, 5: 516–17; Mark R. Wilson, *The Business of Civil War: Military Mobilization and the State, 1861–1865* (Baltimore: Johns Hopkins University Press, 2006), pp. 191–96.

[50] *OR*, ser. 1, vol. 46, pt. 3, pp. 1301, 1315; vol. 47, pt. 3, p. 649.

Iowa. At that time, some of those regiments occupied the Carolinas; some manned posts along the Mississippi River; and eleven were in Texas. These were the 8th, 22d, 41st, 43d, 45th, and 127th USCIs, all from Philadelphia; the 28th USCI, from Indiana; the 29th, from Illinois; the 31st, from New York; the 29th Connecticut Infantry; and the 5th Massachusetts Cavalry. All of them left Texas that fall.[51]

With the free-state regiments of the XXV Corps gone and other reductions to come, the general commanding the Department of Texas made an unusual request. He asked Weitzel to provide a list of the remaining regiments "in the order in which they should be retained, according to your judgment of their qualities." Seldom, if ever, had the commander of more than a dozen black regiments been asked to rate them in order of merit. Weitzel thought for a few days before replying and toward the end of November submitted a list in descending order of merit (*Table 4*). At the top stood the 7th USCI, followed by the 9th, 46th, 62d, 38th, and 114th USCIs; the 2d United States Colored Cavalry (USCC); the 36th, 19th, 10th, 117th, 109th, 116th, 118th, 115th, and 122d USCIs; the 1st USCC; and the 8th United States Colored Artillery (USCA).[52]

What made the difference between a good regiment and a bad one, an organization that Weitzel wanted to keep and one that he would gladly be rid of? One difference, clearly, was sheer length of service, the number of months since a regiment had mustered in. The first nine regiments, those at the top half of Weitzel's list, averaged nearly two years of service. The nine in the bottom half of the list averaged slightly more than one year and a quarter. Each regiment's history of active service also influenced its efficiency. According to records compiled by the adjutant general, the 7th USCI, at the head of the list, had taken part in eleven engagements, including some full-scale battles around Richmond in the fall of 1864. The nine regiments in the top half of the list averaged slightly more than four engagements each; those in the bottom half, fewer than two. Length of time and variety of service therefore counted for a great deal.

Table 4 shows at once that some regiments varied wildly from the average. The circumstances of each regiment's service, and the personalities of its senior officers, could have appreciable effects. After two companies of the 1st Arkansas (African Descent [AD]) surrendered to a Confederate force at the Mound Plantation in Louisiana, in May 1863, the remaining companies moved across the Mississippi River to Vicksburg, where they became part of a large garrison. There, brought up to strength and with all its companies stationed together, the 1st Arkansas (AD) had ample opportunity to improve its drill; but the Mound Plantation remained its only engagement throughout the war. In April 1864, it received a new designation as the 46th USCI. Brig. Gen John P. Hawkins, who commanded at Vicksburg, called it "my 'show Regiment,'" and attributed its proficiency in large part to the efforts of its commanding officer.[53]

Another forceful personality was Lt. Col. David Branson of the 62d USCI. Branson took severe measures to promote literacy in his command. He ordered that any soldier found playing cards would "be placed standing in some prominent

---

[51] XXV Corps, GO 63, 28 Sep 1865, Entry 520, XXV Corps, General Orders, pt. 2, RG 393, NA.

[52] Maj Gen H. G. Wright to Maj Gen G. Weitzel, 16 Nov 1865, Entry 2073, U.S. Forces on the Rio Grande, LR; Maj Gen G. Weitzel to Col C. H. Whittlesey, 26 Nov 1865, Entry 2063, U.S. Forces on the Rio Grande, LS; both in pt. 2, RG 393, NA.

[53] Brig Gen J. P. Hawkins to Maj Gen G. Granger, 24 Jun 1865, 46th USCI, Entry 57C, RG 94, NA. For the Mound Plantation fight, see Chapter 6, above.

TABLE 4—GENERAL WEITZEL'S RANKING OF REGIMENTS IN XXV CORPS, NOVEMBER 1865

Regiment	Mustered In	No. Engagements
7th USCI	September–November 1863	11
9th USCI	November 1863	4
46th USCI	May 1863	1
62d USCI	December 1863	2
38th USCI	January–March 1864	2
114th USCI	July 1864	0
2d USCC	December 1863	8
36th USCI	October 1863	6
19th USCI	December 1863–January 1864	3
10th USCI	November 1863–September 1864	4
117th USCI	July–September 1864	1
109th USCI	July 1864	0
116th USCI	June–July 1864	1
118th USCI	October 1864	2
115th USCI	July–October 1864	0
122d USCI	December 1864	0
1st USCC	December 1863	6
8th USCA	October 1864	1

USCA = United States Colored Artillery; USCC = United States Colored Cavalry; USCI = United States Colored Infantry.

Source: Frederick H. Dyer, *A Compendium of the War of the Rebellion* (New York: Thomas Yoseloff, 1959 [1909]), and *Official Army Register of the Volunteer Force of the United States Army*, 8 vols. (Washington, D.C.: Adjutant General's Office, 1867), vol. 8.

position in the camp with book in hand, and required then and there to learn a considerable lesson in reading and spelling; and if unwilling to learn, he will be compelled by hunger to do so. . . . No freed slave who cannot read well has a right to waste the time and opportunity . . . to fit himself for the position of a free citizen." After January 1865, illiterate noncommissioned officers of the regiment faced reduction to the ranks. Branson also took measures to promote personal cleanliness: "The dirtiest man in each Company shall be thoroughly washed. . . . Each Company Commander will detail one Corporal and two men for this purpose. The practice will be repeated as often as it may be thought necessary." Few commanding officers, if any, imposed such a vigorous program of personal improvement on their men.[54]

Among the regiments on the low end of Weitzel's list, the 122d USCI had suffered since its inception from most of the ills that afflicted black regiments. Late in October 1864, its four hundred fifty armed and equipped recruits had had only six company officers (captains and lieutenants) present and fit for duty. The situation had barely improved by February, when the regiment was on the move to Virginia. "Many of the officers have not yet reported," Col. John H. Davidson complained. "There is considerable sickness in the command, and . . . several of the companies have but a single officer." Arriving in Virginia, the individual companies found themselves "scattered at various points, too remote from Head Quarters to receive medical attendance from the Surgeon," so sickness continued unabated. In the same letter, Davidson asked that officers who had not yet reported have their appointments revoked and that others be named in their place. The regiment, he explained, had never had more than half its full complement of thirty company officers.[55]

With the possibility of instruction so limited, many of the men never learned to care for their weapons. By the end of February 1865, 152 of the regiment's Enfield rifles, some 20 percent, had been condemned as "unserviceable," Colonel Davidson complained, "and each day adds to the number." Furthermore, since companies of the regiment guarded lighthouses and other important sites miles from the trenches around Richmond and Petersburg, "the Commissary of Subsistence only issues the ration prescribed for troops in garrison duty, and the men really do not get enough to eat." Men and officers alike complained of the limited fare, and Davidson asked that they receive the usual ration for troops in the field. Finally, although the regiment had begun organizing the previous October, a paymaster did not visit it until the following March. "The . . . Officers are mostly men promoted from the ranks and have performed the duties of Officers so long without pay, that they are entirely destitute of funds to clothe themselves properly or meet their incidental expenses," Davidson wrote. The colonel's neglect to mention any possible inconvenience to the enlisted men suggests that officers' attitudes were yet another

---

[54] 1st Missouri Inf (African Descent), GO 9, 11 Feb 1864 ("the dirtiest man"); 62d USCI, GO 31, 3 Jul 1864, and GO 35, 29 Oct 1864 ("be placed"); all in 62d USCI, Regimental Books, RG 94, NA. Keith P. Wilson, *Campfires of Freedom: The Camp Life of Black Soldiers During the Civil War* (Kent, Ohio: Kent State University Press, 2002), pp. 82–108.

[55] Lt Col D. M. Layman to Col J. S. Brisbin, 23 Oct 1864; Col J. H. Davidson to Adj Gen, Army of the James, 1 Feb 1865 ("Many of"), and to Maj C. W. Foster, 15 Feb 1865 ("scattered at"); all in 122d USCI, Regimental Books, RG 94, NA.

way, besides inadequate weapons and rations or infrequent paydays, in which the 122d USCI fell far short of bare adequacy.[56]

The ability and character of a regiment's officers was just as important for training and discipline as the sheer number of officers present for duty—perhaps more so. The longer service, on average, that was common to the top nine regiments on Weitzel's list meant that most of their officers had been appointed earlier in the war and seemed to be of better quality than many of those who joined the Kentucky infantry regiments (most of which received numbers between 107 and 125) during the autumn of 1864. While inept officers could be found in various proportions in black regiments from all parts of the country, incidents of fraud and theft seemed to occur mostly during the last months of the war and to concentrate in the Kentucky regiments. These involved regimental officers of all grades. Especially odious was Col. William W. Woodward, of the 116th USCI, who diverted $3,300 of his soldiers' bank deposits to his own use during the regiment's eight months in Virginia and made off with more money in December 1865, when he managed to leave the Army with an honorable discharge. Efforts to track down the former colonel resulted only in a report, months later, that he was "leading a 'sporting' life on a Mississippi Steamboat." After consulting former officers and enlisted men of the regiment, an investigator concluded that professional gambling was "an occupation rendered probable by [Woodward's] life while with the command." The lieutenant colonel of the 124th USCI, a regiment organized early in 1865 that spent its entire ten-month service in Kentucky, received a sentence of three years' imprisonment for embezzling $7,350 of his soldiers' bounty money. Little wonder, then, that seven Kentucky regiments were among the nine that made up the bottom half of Weitzel's list.[57]

Department of Texas headquarters apparently paid serious attention to Weitzel's advice, for when it issued the next order for mustering out regiments, six of the eight named came from the bottom nine on the general's list: the 1st USCC; the 8th USCA; and the 109th, 115th, 118th, and 122d USCIs. Also on the list were the 2d USCC, in accordance with the War Department's practice of mustering out cavalry and artillery regiments, which were more expensive to maintain than infantry, and the 46th USCI, the senior black regiment in Texas. The first to be raised by Adjutant General Lorenzo Thomas in May 1863, the 46th had only eight months

---

[56]Col J. H. Davidson to Lt Col E. W. Smith, 28 Feb 1865 ("unserviceable"); to Capt S. L. McHenry, 3 Mar 1865 ("the Commissary"); to Brig Gen B. W. Brice, 9 Mar 1865 ("The . . . Officers"); all in 122d USCI, Regimental Books, RG 94, NA.

[57]A. M. Sperry to J. W. Alvord, 18 Dec 1866, NA Microfilm Pub M803, Rcds of the Education Div of the Bureau of Refugees, Freedmen, and Abandoned Lands, roll 14; Endorsement, Lt Col D. H. McPhail, 18 Feb 1867 (quotation), on S–53–DG–1867, Entry 1756, Dept of the Gulf, LR, pt. 1, RG 393, NA. The files of the Freedmen and Southern Society Project at the University of Maryland, which contain photocopied material from the National Archives, include at least seven instances of officers suspected of, and even tried for, defrauding enlisted men. All but one of them occurred in Kentucky regiments: the 12th USCA (file G44), 109th USCI (B214), 114th USCI (B318), 117th USCI (CC14), 123d USCI (G178), and 124th USCI (H19). Problems of officer replacement at the end of a long war were not unique to the Union Army. For a British reminiscence of the First World War, see Robert Graves, *Good-Bye to All That: An Autobiography* (London: Jonathan Cape, 1929), pp. 304–05. For the U.S. Army in the Second World War, see Jeffrey J. Clarke and Robert R. Smith, *Riviera to the Rhine*, U.S. Army in World War II (Washington, D.C.: U.S. Army Center of Military History, 1993), p. 569.

of its three-year term left to serve. The departure of these regiments left only ten in the entire XXV Corps, with a strength of fewer than five thousand officers and men present for duty.[58]

With barely enough black regiments in southern Texas to constitute one division, General Sheridan recommended the discontinuance of the XXV Corps. Communications were so difficult in Texas, he told Grant, that a regional chain of command allowing post commanders to report directly to district headquarters rather than through the hierarchy of brigade, division, and corps, would move messages more quickly. Grant agreed to the proposal, and the XXV Corps ceased to exist on 8 January 1866.[59]

While more than half of the regiments in the corps were mustering out, the conflict across the Rio Grande that was the cause of their presence wore on. In the late winter of 1865, the Imperialists dominated all of Mexico except for four states on the Pacific coast and the northern border, but by the following winter the tide had turned. Influenced by the collapse of the Confederacy and the presence of more than forty-five thousand United States troops in Texas, by the Imperialists' inability to subdue the Liberals and impose order on the country, and by worries about his increasingly bellicose neighbor Prussia, Napoleon III announced on 15 January 1866 his intention to withdraw by October 1867 the thirty thousand French troops that were the most reliable support of the Imperialist regime.[60]

"About ninety eight out of every hundred officers and men are strongly in favor of the Liberals," General Weitzel told department headquarters in early January 1866. For many United States citizens in the region, commercial interests outweighed allegiance to one side or another in a foreign country's politics, but some Americans saw opportunities to be gained by favoring the Liberals. Two of these were R. Clay Crawford and Arthur F. Reed, adventurers who had gravitated to the Rio Grande after the war. Crawford was an honorably discharged former captain in the Union Army who claimed to hold a major general's commission in the Liberal forces. Reed was a former lieutenant colonel of the 40th USCI. A general court-martial had cashiered him in June 1865 for neglect of duty, insubordination, insulting his commanding officer, absence without leave, breaking arrest, and "utter incompetence for military command." To be cashiered meant ineligibility for further military office in the United States. Reed claimed to be a colonel in the Liberal forces.[61]

Matamoros had been in the hands of the Imperialists since September 1864. In the fall of 1865, its garrison withstood a sixteen-day siege by the Liberals. Suffering more than five hundred casualties in their attempt to take the city, the Liberals

[58] Dept of Texas, SO 8, 9 Jan 1866, Entry 2073, and Trimonthly Inspection Rpt, 31 Oct 1865, Entry 539, both in pt. 2, RG 393, NA. On the muster-out policy, see War Department, GO 144, 9 Oct 1865, which authorized muster-out of all volunteer cavalry regiments east of the Mississippi River. Entry 44, Orders and Circulars, RG 94, NA.

[59] Maj Gen P. H. Sheridan to Lt Gen U. S. Grant, 30 Dec 1865 (G–1056–AGO–1865), NA Microfilm Pub M619, AGO, LR, 1861–1870, roll 360.

[60] Krause, *Mexico*, pp. 177–86; Vanderwood, "Betterment for Whom?" pp. 386–91; James E. Sefton, *The United States Army and Reconstruction, 1865–1877* (Baton Rouge: Louisiana State University Press, 1967), p. 261.

[61] Maj Gen G. Weitzel to Maj Gen H. G. Wright, 7 Jan 1866, filed with (f/w) Maj Gen H. G. Wright to Col G. L. Hartsuff, 14 Jan 1866, Entry 4495, pt. 1, RG 393, NA; Case of A. F. Reed (OO–1302), Entry 15, RG 153, NA.

Palm trees and the twin spires of a Roman Catholic church gave Frank Leslie's *readers a sense of the foreignness of the Mexican port of Matamoros, across the Rio Grande from Brownsville.*

withdrew and contented themselves during the weeks that followed with harassing river traffic and ambushing small detachments of Imperialists. Late in December, Crawford and Reed made plans with the Liberal leader Mariano Escobedo to seize the port of Bagdad. Crawford was sure that this would force the Imperialists out of Matamoros.[62]

Across the Rio Grande from Bagdad, the camp of the 118th USCI stood near the town of Clarksville. Some time between 3:00 and 4:00 a.m. on 5 January 1866, the regiment's commanding officer awoke to the sound of cannon fire from a French gunboat on the river. Enlisted men on guard speculated that "the French were fighting among themselves." Reed, with a force estimated at between sixty and one hundred fifty men, had taken Bagdad. The Imperialist garrison surrendered quickly, many of the men changing sides on the spot. Among Reed's force were about thirty men of the 118th USCI.[63]

The gunfire also alerted 1st Lt. Joseph J. Fierbaugh, the officer of the day, stationed on a steamer moored at the Clarksville landing. He sent part of the guard to arrest any returning absent soldiers and to stop any more from crossing. About 6:00, an hour before first light, Fierbaugh himself crossed the river to Bagdad. Since he did not have a sufficient force to return men to camp under an armed guard, he merely sent those he found to the riverbank, where a small boat took

[62] R. C. Crawford to M. Escobedo, 23 Dec 1865 (f/w A–909–AGO–1866), and A. F. Reed to R. C. Crawford, 28 Dec 1865, both in NA M619, roll 452; Thompson, *Cortina*, pp. 147, 162–66.

[63] "Proceedings of a Military Commission," f/w A–909–AGO–1866, and Lt Col I. D. Davis to Col R. M. Hall, 5 Jan 1866, both in NA M619, roll 452.

them across. Most returned to camp in time to answer reveille roll call. Two who did not were Cpl. William Oates and Pvt. Dade Davis, who were among the four killed on the Liberal side during the night's fighting.[64]

When Surgeon Russell D. Adams went to Bagdad later that morning, he found another soldier of the regiment lying wounded but did not bother to learn his name. This seems to have been typical of the officers of the 118th USCI. Fierbaugh was unable to name any of the soldiers he rounded up in Bagdad. Capt. Lewis Moon, who succeeded him as officer of the day, told a military commission that he did not know the name of any soldier outside his own company. Moreover, both Fierbaugh and Moon told the commission that the regiment had never kept a record of which of its soldiers were arrested or of how they were punished. Since Moon had no specific instructions to record the names of men he arrested, he did not feel obliged to do so. Evidently, the 118th USCI had not improved during the two months since it had ranked fifth from the bottom on General Weitzel's list.[65]

By daybreak, refugees from the fighting packed both banks of the river, with boats plying back and forth to carry them across. When Surgeon Adams visited Bagdad later that morning to care for the wounded, he found "considerable commotion around town," with soldiers "running around the streets. . . . [E]verything seemed to be in confusion." Mexican authorities soon saw that they were unable to restore order and asked the commanding officer at Clarksville for assistance. The next day, two hundred officers and men of the 118th USCI crossed the river to occupy Bagdad. A force from the 46th USCI, a regiment that General Weitzel considered much more reliable, replaced them within a few days.[66]

On 17 January, one hundred fifty officers and men of the 2d USCC arrived at Bagdad to relieve the 46th; the rest of the cavalry, some three hundred strong, remained on the opposite bank. A Liberal general assured the commanding officer of the 2d USCC that he was not yet able to guarantee order in the town. The cavalry stayed on, patrolling the streets while Liberal troops manned defenses around the outskirts, for another five days until an order recalled them to Brazos Santiago. On 25 January, an attack by a mixed force of more than five hundred Austrian, French, and Mexican troops drove the Liberals from Bagdad and the Imperialists regained a tenuous control of the south bank of the Rio Grande.[67]

Affairs on the Mexican side of the river remained turbulent for the next five months, with the Imperialists holding the major towns. A New Orleans newspaper summed up the situation flippantly, naming several local generals and would-be generals: "Canales outlaws Cortina, Escobedo & Co. outlaws both, and Mejía outlaws the whole gang." Sheridan took a more serious tone in a letter to Grant: "The Liberals are in good spirit, and are doing very well. They are divided in Tamaulipas, and there waste their strength, but all are contending against the common enemy." In mid-June, a Liberal force attacked an Imperialist supply train, killing or capturing nearly all of the train's 1,400-man escort. Within a week, the Imperial-

---

[64] "Proceedings of a Military Commission"; Descriptive Book, 118th USCI, Regimental Books, RG 94, NA.

[65] "Proceedings of a Military Commission."

[66] Ibid.; F. de Leon to Lt Col I. D. Davis, 5 Jan 1866; Col J. C. Moon to Col D. D. Wheeler, 6 Jan 1866; Lt Col F. J. White to Capt W. D. Munson, 22 Jan 1866; all in NA M619, roll 452.

[67] White to Munson, 22 Jan 1866; Thompson, *Cortina*, p. 169.

ists evacuated Bagdad and Matamoros. In the course of the summer, the Liberals finally gained control of all of northern Mexico.[68]

The expulsion of the Imperialists by no means resulted in a reign of law and order. The new governor of Tamaulipas imposed a policy of forced "loans" and confiscation that hurt the leading merchants of Matamoros, many of whom were United States citizens who had favored the Imperialists and had grown rich trading in cotton and arms on behalf of the Confederacy. The president of Mexico, Benito Juárez, himself disowned the governor's actions. Another local strongman proclaimed himself governor, but before he could march on Matamoros, other parties there overthrew the incumbent, who escaped across the river to Brownsville. Juárez detested the new regime in Matamoros as much as he had the old one, and in November Escobedo led an army of thirty-five hundred men toward the city.[69]

With a battle imminent, the merchants of Matamoros looked for means of staving off the new governor's defeat until they could collect debts amounting to some $600,000 that he had accrued during his three months in office. The merchants found their means in Col. Thomas D. Sedgwick, of the 114th USCI, who commanded the post at Brownsville. The merchants convinced Sedgwick that the governor's troops might riot and pillage the town. No doubt remembering the days of disorder at Bagdad in January, the colonel agreed to send a small force across the river. Although he wrote to Sheridan on 22 November, telling him of his plan, his letter could barely have reached Sheridan's desk in New Orleans by the time he acted.[70]

The black infantry companies in the Brownsville garrison were responsible for a military pontoon bridge that they had brought from Virginia. On the night of 24 November, two companies of the 19th and 114th USCIs crossed the Rio Grande in boats and secured a site on the Mexican bank. The next day, they assembled the structure of boats and planks and 118 officers and men of the 4th U.S. Cavalry clattered across it to occupy Matamoros. The black infantrymen guarded the south end of the bridge and a ferry landing two miles from the city while a battery of the 1st U.S. Artillery positioned its guns at the north end of the bridge. No longer responsible for patrolling the town themselves, the defenders of Matamoros were able to repel a Liberal attack on 27 November, inflicting some one thousand casualties on Escobedo's force.[71]

Weeks earlier, Sheridan had warned Sedgwick that the United States pursued a course of strict neutrality in Mexico's quarrels but contradicted himself somewhat by emphasizing that the policy was in force especially "against the adherents of the imperial buccaneer representing the so-called Imperial Government." When Sheridan learned that Sedgwick had acceded to the request of the Imperialist sympathizers of Matamoros, he ordered him to withdraw United States troops across the river at

---

[68] Maj Gen P. H. Sheridan to Lt Gen U. S. Grant, 7 May 1866 ("The Liberals"), NA Microfilm Pub M1635, Headquarters of the Army, LS, roll 94; Thompson, *Cortina*, pp. 175–81 ("Canales outlaws," pp. 175–76).

[69] "Occupation of Mexican Territory," 39th Cong., 2d sess., H. Ex. Doc. 8 (serial 1,287), p. 3; Thompson, *Cortina*, pp. 181–85.

[70] Col T. D. Sedgwick to Maj Gen P. H. Sheridan, 22 Nov 1866, and Maj Gen P. H. Sheridan to Gen U. S. Grant, 27 Nov 1866, both in Andrew Johnson Papers, Library of Congress; "Mexico," 39th Cong., 2d sess., H. Ex. Doc. 17 (serial 1,288), p. 177; Thompson, *Cortina*, pp. 185–86.

[71] NA M594, roll 216, 114th USCI; NA M617, roll 152, Fort Brown, Nov 1866; "Present Condition of Mexico," 39th Cong., 2d sess., H. Ex. Doc. 76 (serial 1,292), pp. 550–52, 554; Thompson, *Cortina*, pp. 186–88.

The pontoon bridge at Brownsville

once. Sedgwick complied. The day he withdrew his troops, Escobedo and the self-proclaimed governor entered negotiations. On 1 December, the Liberal army took possession of Matamoros, peacefully and for the final time. A few days later, Sheridan took ship for the mouth of the Rio Grande. Once there, he relieved Sedgwick of command and placed him in arrest. Nevertheless, the general was hardly displeased with the result of "this unauthorized and harmless intervention," as he called it in a letter to Grant's chief of staff. He released Sedgwick from arrest in January.[72]

While all these events were taking place, the muster-out of volunteer regiments continued. The 10th and 62d USCIs left Texas in the spring of 1866, the officers and men of both regiments traveling north for final payment and discharge. That fall, the 7th, 9th, and 36th USCIs followed them. The 19th, 38th, and 116th USCIs left Texas in January 1867, the 19th sailing for Maryland, the 38th for Virginia, and the 116th for Kentucky. By that time, the War Department had undertaken a new project. On 28 July 1866, in an act that determined the size of the Army's post-war establishment, Congress for the first time authorized all-black regiments for peacetime service. Two of these, the 9th Cavalry and the 39th U.S. Infantry, were recruiting in New Orleans, the port where the men of the 116th USCI landed on their way home to Kentucky.[73]

Before the Civil War, the Army's responsibilities had amounted for the most part to maintaining the country's coastal defenses and keeping the peace in the West. With the occupation of the South added to these tasks, Congress in July 1866 authorized a sixty-regiment peacetime force. Two cavalry and four infantry regiments

---

[72]Maj Gen P. H. Sheridan to Col T. D. Sedgwick, 23 Oct 1866 (quotation) (f/w G–204–AUS–1866), NA M1635, roll 94; "Mexico," pp. 3–5 (quotation); Thompson, *Cortina*, pp. 188–89.
[73]*ORVF*, 8: 176, 179–80, 190, 207, 209, 235, 297.

were to be "composed of colored men." Sheridan was to organize one regiment of each branch in the Division of the Gulf, both of them headquartered at or near New Orleans. A War Department order offered immediate discharges to men of volunteer regiments who intended to join the regulars, and one hundred thirty men of the 116th availed themselves of it. The vast majority of them went directly into the 39th U.S. Infantry. In cities from New Orleans to Boston, about twenty-five hundred veterans of the U.S. Colored Troops joined the six black regular regiments in 1866 and 1867, contributing more than 40 percent of the total number of recruits and providing most of the noncommissioned officers. Two companies of the 9th U.S. Cavalry arrived at Brownsville in April 1867, just four months before the 117th USCI, the last regiment of the U.S. Colored Troops in Texas, mustered out. In July, companies of the 41st U.S. Infantry, another of the new black regular regiments, relieved companies of the 117th at Fort McIntosh and Ringgold Barracks.[74]

Throughout the first few months of 1867, the Imperialist cause in Mexico continued to collapse. Sheridan thought that Maximilian might embark for Europe as his foreign troops withdrew from Mexico, but the emperor decided to make a stand at Querétaro, some one hundred thirty miles northwest of Mexico City. Besieged there for more than two months, he surrendered in mid-May. A firing squad shot him on 19 June. A few days later, the garrison of Brownsville was able to see fireworks and hear the sounds of celebration in Matamoros.[75]

Within six weeks, the 117th USCI mustered out and its officers and men took ship for Kentucky to receive final payment and discharges. Since that spring, the 117th had been the last volunteer regiment in Texas. Its duties on the Rio Grande seemed far removed from the cause for which its officers and men had joined the Army, but Sheridan was convinced that the successful suppression of the Confederacy and the Liberal victory in Mexico ran parallel to each other. "While we were struggling for a republican existence against organized rebellion," he wrote in his report of November 1866,

> the Emperor of the French undertook the bold expedition to subvert the Republic of Mexico. . . . The effect of the presence of our troops in Texas and on the Rio Grande . . . on the destiny of imperialism was great . . . , so much so, that . . . had a demand been made for the withdrawal of the Imperial troops, on the ground that the invasion of Mexico was part of the rebellion, it would have been granted and the miseries of that country for the last year avoided.

While officers and men of the black regiments openly favored the Liberal party in the struggle for control of Mexico, they managed to avoid direct involvement in all but a few episodes. Nevertheless, their presence on the north bank of the Rio Grande influenced the calculations of Napoleon III when he announced the

---

[74] 116th USCI, Entry 57, Muster Rolls of Volunteer Organizations, RG 94, NA. NA M617, roll 155, Post of Brownsville, April 1867; roll 681, Fort McIntosh, Jul 1867; roll 1020, Ringgold Barracks, Jul 1867. William A. Dobak and Thomas D. Phillips, *The Black Regulars, 1866–1898* (Norman: University of Oklahoma Press, 2001), pp. xii–xv, 1–2, 13, 24.

[75] Maj Gen P. H. Sheridan to Maj Gen J. A. Rawlins, 4 Jan 1867 (G–7–AUS–1867), NA M1635, roll 98; Thompson, *Cortina*, pp. 189–92.

withdrawal of French troops from Mexico. In that sense, it helped to hasten the end of the conflict there.[76]

Mustered-out regiments of black soldiers sailed from Texas for Philadelphia, Baltimore, or Louisville, where officers and men received their final pay and discharges. As the veterans reached home, they found life there changed because of their efforts during the war. For many former enlisted men, the most dramatic change was in their status, and that of their families', from slave to free. This was especially true in the states of the former Confederacy that came under military occupation. While some black regiments stood guard on the Rio Grande, others served in posts across the defeated South, assisting the federal attempt to impose a new regime of freedom.

---

[76]*OR*, ser. 1, vol. 48, pt. 1, p. 300 (quotation); Krause, *Mexico*, pp. 177–86; Vanderwood, "Betterment for Whom?" pp. 386–91.

CHAPTER 14

RECONSTRUCTION, 1865–1867

The business of Reconstruction began before the federal government had settled on a policy of Emancipation or organized a single regiment of black soldiers. The chief concern at first was to create stable, loyal governments in states that had left the Union. Efforts to install such governments began early in 1862, not long after Nashville became the first capital of a seceded state to fall to a federal army. On 4 March, Andrew Johnson, who had remained in the U.S. Senate when Tennessee seceded, received an appointment as brigadier general of U.S. Volunteers and assumed the post of military governor of that state. Later in the war, other attempts to install Unionist state governments gave impetus to federal military offensives in Florida and Louisiana (*see Map 10*).[1]

As Union armies moved south, they met the black residents of each state. On the Sea Islands of South Carolina, soldiers found slaves tending their own garden plots on plantations from which white owners had fled. In other parts of the Confederacy, escaped slaves thronged the camps of the advancing troops or settled in shantytowns on the outskirts of occupied cities. Whether black Southerners waited for the liberators to arrive or rushed to meet them, Union soldiers saw the former slaves as a problem that required food, shelter, and direction in performing useful labor. While putting to work the able-bodied residents of plantations and camps and providing food and shelter for others, federal administrators also had to decide what to do with the plantations of disloyal owners. Congress had declared these lands forfeit to the federal government and provided for their sale or lease in a series of laws enacted between August 1861 and July 1864. Often, administrators used these plantations as settlement sites for former slaves, who

[1]*The War of the Rebellion: A Compilation of the Official Records of the Union and Confederate Armies,* 70 vols. in 128 (Washington, D.C.: Government Printing Office, 1880–1901), ser. 1, 7: 424–33; vol. 10, pt. 2, p. 612 (hereafter cited as *OR*). Leroy P. Graf et al., eds., *The Papers of Andrew Johnson,* 16 vols. (Knoxville: University of Tennessee Press, 1967–2000), 5: 177, 182 (hereafter cited as *Johnson Papers*); Eric Foner, *Reconstruction: America's Unfinished Revolution, 1863–1877* (New York: Harper & Row, 1988), pp. 35–37, 43–50; Peter Maslowski, *Treason Must Be Made Odious: Military Occupation and Wartime Reconstruction in Nashville, Tennessee, 1862–65* (Millwood, N.Y.: KTO Press, 1978), pp. 19–20; Ted Tunnell, *Crucible of Reconstruction: War, Radicalism, and Race in Louisiana, 1862–1877* (Baton Rouge: Louisiana State University Press, 1984), pp. 44–50.

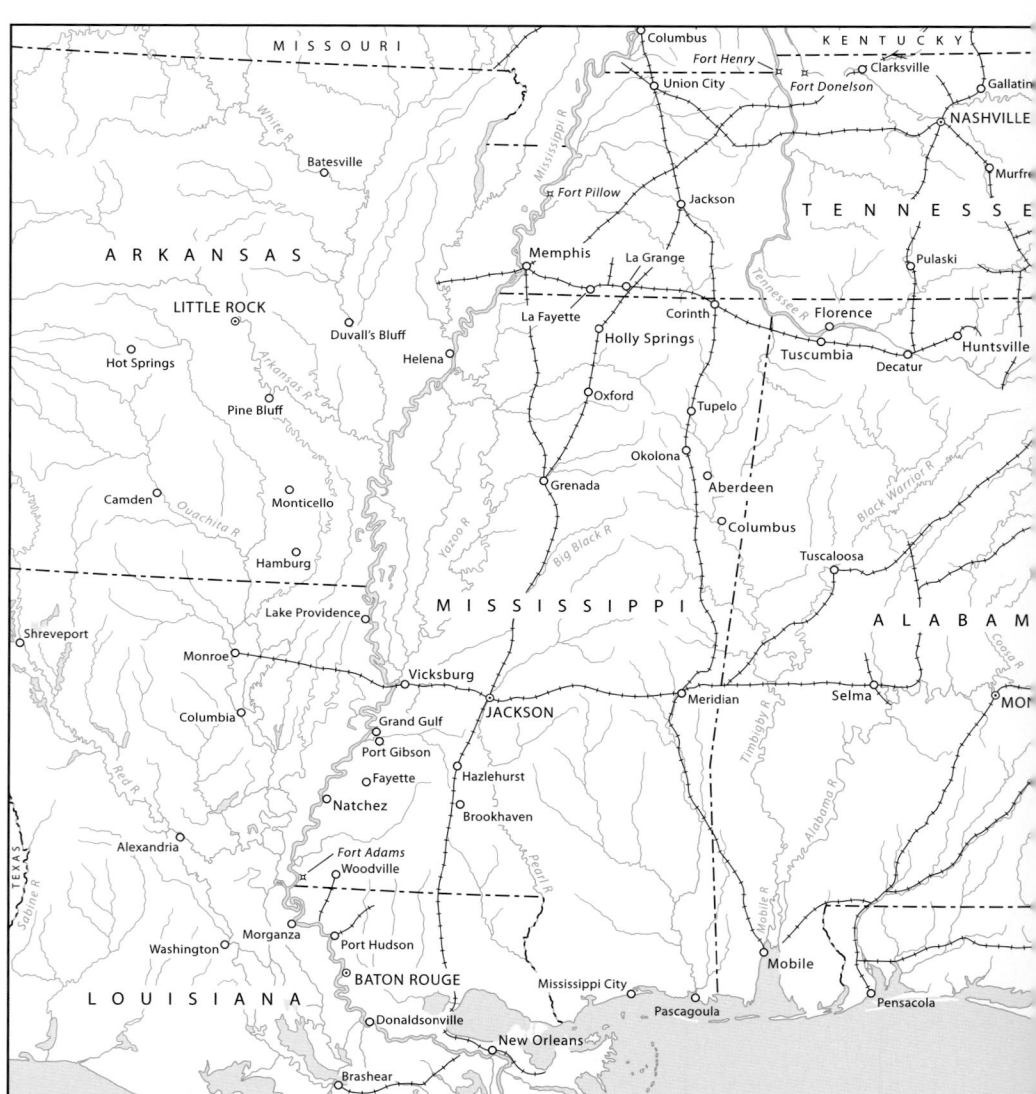

Map 10

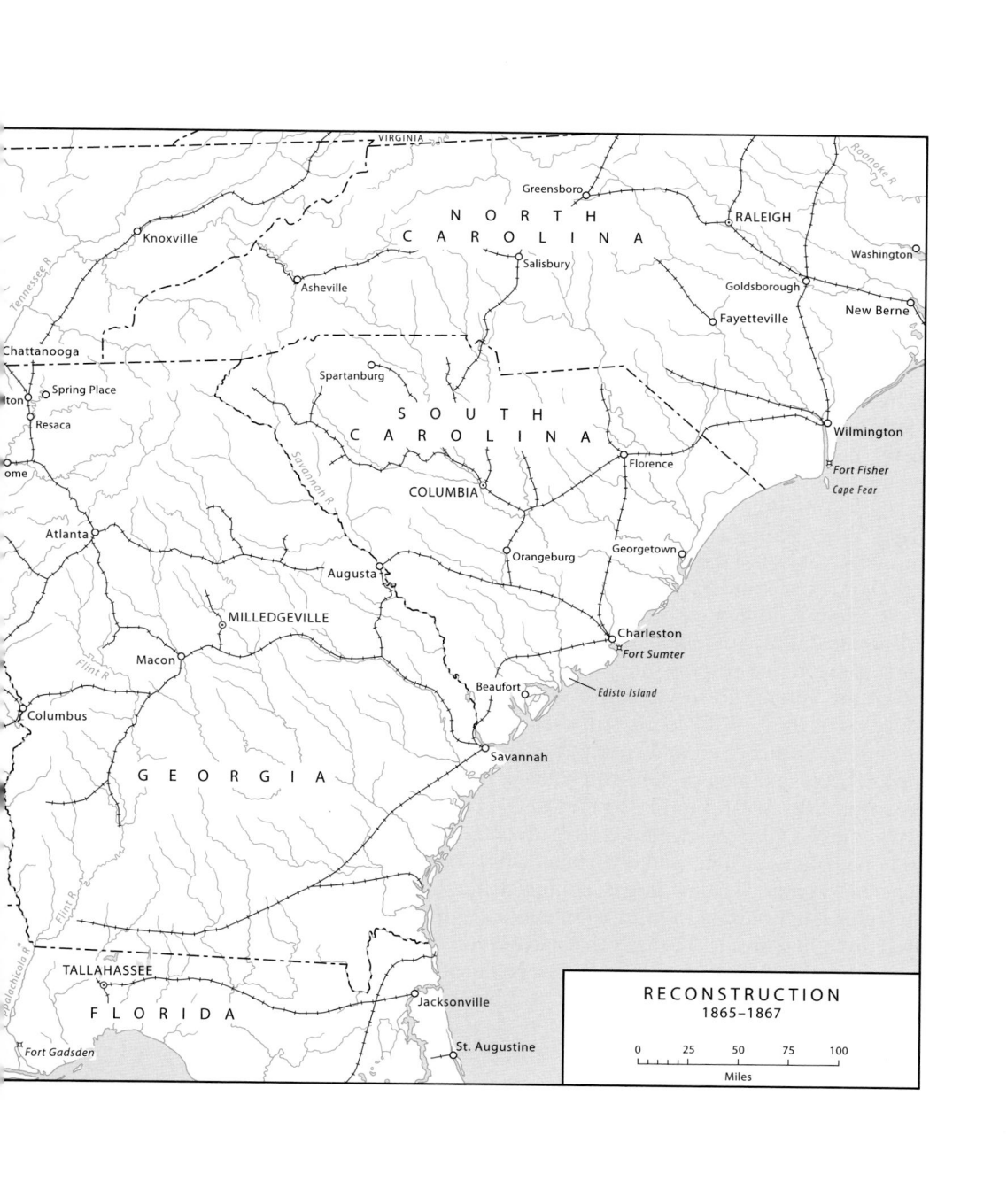

VIRGINIA

Roanoke R.

**N O R T H
C A R O L I N A**

Knoxville

Greensboro

RALEIGH

Washington

Salisbury

Asheville

Goldsborough

Fayetteville

New Berne

Chattanooga

Spring Place

Ilton

Resaca

Spartanburg

**S O U T H
C A R O L I N A**

Wilmington

Fort Fisher

Cape Fear

ome

Florence

COLUMBIA

Atlanta

Augusta

Orangeburg

Georgetown

MILLEDGEVILLE

Macon

Charleston

Fort Sumter

Beaufort

Edisto Island

Columbus

G E O R G I A

Savannah

Tennessee R.

Savannah R.

Flint R.

Flint R.

Apalachicola R.

TALLAHASSEE

Jacksonville

F L O R I D A

Fort Gadsden

St. Augustine

RECONSTRUCTION
1865–1867

0   25   50   75   100

Miles

grew food for themselves as well as staple crops, chiefly cotton, that helped pay for the Union war effort.

To govern the freedpeople and the land on which they lived, and to provide for thousands of white Unionist refugees forced from their homes, Congress passed and President Lincoln signed on 3 March 1865 an act that established the Bureau of Refugees, Freedmen, and Abandoned Lands, a title soon shortened in popular usage to the Freedmen's Bureau. Deliberations on the bill had extended through two sessions of Congress. Introduced in December 1863 to establish a "Bureau of Emancipation," its provisions grew during the next fourteen months to include responsibility both for destitute white Unionists in the South and for plantations that had fallen to the federal government for nonpayment of taxes, or through abandonment by a disloyal owner, or because the owner was a civil or military officer of one of the seceded states or of the Confederacy itself. In the end, legislators felt so confident that revenues from management of abandoned and forfeited lands would suffice to fund the new agency that they failed to appropriate any money for its operations and its agents' salaries. This lack of budget meant that the Bureau had to be staffed by Army officers who were already on the federal payroll. The new agency itself became part of the War Department.[2]

At the Bureau's head was a commissioner, Maj. Gen. Oliver O. Howard, who had led the Army of the Tennessee on its march through Georgia and the Carolinas during the last months of the war. "I hardly know whether to congratulate you or not," Maj. Gen. William T. Sherman wrote when he learned of his subordinate's appointment, "but . . . I cannot imagine that matters that may involve the future of 4,000,000 of souls could be put in more charitable and more conscientious hands." Assistant commissioners reporting to Howard in Washington would be in charge of the Bureau's affairs in the states. Local administration would be in the hands of field agents, each one responsible for several counties. Most of these agents were officers of the Veteran Reserve Corps, an organization of wounded soldiers fit for light duty, or of the U.S. Colored Troops.[3]

As paroled Confederate soldiers returned home in the spring of 1865, one hundred thousand officers and men of the Army's black regiments occupied dozens of camps scattered from Key West, Florida, to Fort Leavenworth, Kansas. The largest body of troops was the XXV Corps, twenty-nine regiments of cavalry, infantry, and heavy artillery and one battery of light artillery, aboard ships bound for Texas, leaving no black regiments in Virginia. The next-largest command numbered 21 regiments, with companies of 3 others, in Louisiana and 21 regiments and 3 batteries in Tennessee. Mississippi played unwilling host to 12 regiments and several companies of another, as well as 2 batteries; North Carolina, to 10 regiments; Kentucky and South Carolina, to 9 each; Arkansas, to 8 regiments and companies of 2 others, as well as 2 batteries; Florida, to 6 regiments; and Alabama and Georgia, to 4 regiments each. A little farther north, the 123d United States Colored Infantry (USCI), recently raised in Kentucky, guarded

---

[2] George R. Bentley, *A History of the Freedmen's Bureau* (New York: Octagon Books, 1974 [1944]), pp. 36–49; Steven Hahn et al., eds., *Land and Labor, 1865* (Chapel Hill: University of North Carolina Press, 2008), pp. 17–19. The text of the Freedmen's Bureau Act appears in *OR*, ser. 3, vol. 5, pp. 19–20; the two Confiscation Acts (August 1861 and July 1862), the Direct Tax Act (June 1862), and subsequent acts implementing them are in *U.S. Statutes at Large* 12: 319, 422–26, 589–92; 13: 320–21, 375–78.

[3] *OR*, ser. 1, vol. 47, pt. 3, p. 515 (quotation); Hahn et al., *Land and Labor*, pp. 19–20.

the quartermaster depot at Jefferson-ville, Indiana, and the 24th USCI, a Philadelphia regiment, monitored the repatriation of Confederate prisoners of war at Point Lookout, Maryland, while guarding public property there.[4]

Wherever soldiers were sta-tioned, safeguarding government buildings and supplies was an im-portant part of their duties, for nineteenth-century Americans were quick to appropriate for themselves whatever might be described as public, whether movable goods or real estate. As a result, soldiers in many black regiments spent most of their time as sentinels during the months after the Confederate surrender. Men of the 59th USCI, veterans of Brice's Crossroads and Tupelo in the summer of 1864, stood watch over the navy yard at Memphis ten months later. The 81st USCI, a regiment that evoked favor-able comment from both generals

Maj. Gen. Oliver O. Howard, Commissioner of the Bureau of Refugees, Freedmen, and Abandoned Lands from 1865 to 1872

and inspectors, guarded warehouses, ordnance depots, and government offices at eighteen sites in and near New Orleans. The Freedmen's Bureau headquarters in Washington became the responsibility of the 107th USCI, one of the last volunteer regiments, black or white, to muster out. Along with surplus ordnance stored at several of the forts that ringed the capital, the 107th also guarded Freedmen's Vil-lage, which stood across the Potomac on the Virginia estate of Confederate Gener-al Robert E. Lee. Apart from sentry duty at settlements of displaced former slaves and the informal off-duty relations of enlisted men with nearby residents during the months before mustering out, these regiments had little to do with enforcing federal Reconstruction policies.[5]

The exact nature of those policies remained unclear as spring turned to sum-mer. The Congress that had been elected in 1864 was not scheduled to convene until December 1865, leaving the initiative to President Andrew Johnson. A Demo-

---

[4]Mean strength of black troops in May 1865 was 98,316; in June, 105,009. *The Medical and Surgical History of the War of the Rebellion*, 2 vols. in 6 (Washington, D.C.: Government Printing Office, 1870–1888), 1: 685. Troop stations, 30 Jun 1865, in National Archives (NA) Microfilm Pub M594, Compiled Rcds Showing Svc of Mil Units in Volunteer Union Organizations, rolls 204–17. This count differs slightly from that provided by the map in Noah A. Trudeau, *Like Men of War: Black Troops in the Civil War, 1862–1865* (Boston: Little, Brown, 1998), p. 457, which portrays the stations in May.

[5]Capt C. P. Brown to Col I. G. Kappner, 29 Aug 1865, 59th United States Colored Infantry (USCI); Maj W. Hoffman to Lt Col B. Gaskill, 11 Jun 1865, and Capt H. K. Smithwick to Capt B. B. Campbell, 14 Aug 1865, both in 81st USCI; Dept of Washington, Special Orders (SO) 196, 18 Oct

crat from the mountains of eastern Tennessee and wartime military governor of the state, Johnson had seemed a good choice for Lincoln's running mate on the National Union ticket, a Republican Party surrogate, the previous year. When the nominating convention met in June 1864, Northern newspapers had been printing long casualty lists from Lt. Gen. Ulysses S. Grant's Virginia Campaign for a month and Sherman's attempt to seize Atlanta was still far from achieving a result. The administration needed every vote it could get, so the Tennessean replaced Vice President Hannibal Hamlin, a Republican from Maine, on the ticket. The election of Lincoln and Johnson and Lincoln's assassination in April 1865 put Johnson in a position to reconstruct the conquered South by himself, without congressional interference, for nearly eight months.[6]

The new president embodied an observation expressed by many federal officers during the war and after, that a staunch Southern Unionist was not necessarily an abolitionist, or even well intentioned toward black people. Having risen from poverty himself, Johnson as an elected official represented the interests of the white residents of the poorest section of his state. As a candidate for the vice presidency in October 1864, he had told an audience of black Tennesseans, "I will indeed be your Moses, and lead you through the Red Sea of war and bondage, to a fairer future of liberty and peace." Yet nearly sixteen months later—ten of them spent as president following Lincoln's assassination—after meeting a delegation headed by the black abolitionist Frederick Douglass, he told his secretary, "I know that d——d Douglass; he's just like any nigger, and he would sooner cut a white man's throat as not." In the fall of 1865, a captain of the 40th USCI serving as Freedmen's Bureau agent at Knoxville reported his inability to accomplish much among "a people so hostile to the negroe as are the East Tennesseans." The new president was true to the type.[7]

Johnson's first weeks in office confused onlookers. Late in April, he disowned the too-lenient surrender agreement General Sherman had offered to Confederate troops in North Carolina and sent Grant south to impose more stringent terms. Southerners, black and white, awaited the president's next move with anxiety. Then, on 29 May, Johnson issued an amnesty proclamation and announced a plan to install state governments throughout the former Confederacy. The amnesty terms were generous, exempting only certain categories of persons, among them the Confederacy's highest-ranking officials, civil and military officers of the federal government who had embraced the Confederate cause, and owners of more than twenty thousand dollars' worth of property. Such persons could apply to the president for individual pardon. In a second proclamation that day, Johnson appointed a provisional governor for North Carolina, whose duty it would be to summon a convention to draft a new state constitution that would repudiate secession

---

1866, 107th USCI; all in Entry 57C, Regimental Papers, Record Group (RG) 94, NA. On the 59th USCI at Brice's Crossroads and Tupelo, see above, Chapter 7; on the reputation of the 81st USCI, see above, Chapter 13.

[6] Foner, *Reconstruction*, pp. 43–45, 176–84, 228.

[7] David W. Bowen, *Andrew Johnson and the Negro* (Knoxville: University of Tennessee Press, 1989), pp. 6 ("I know"), 51, 81 ("I will"); Capt D. Boyd to Capt W. T. Clarke, 5 Oct 1865 (B–136), NA Microfilm Pub T142, Selected Rcds of the Tennessee Field Office of the Bureau of Refugees, Freedmen, and Abandoned Lands (BRFAL), roll 25.

and slavery and pave the way for the state's representation in Congress. Delegates to the convention had to have been eligible voters in the 1860 election—that is, white—and to have taken an oath of allegiance to the United States since the fighting ended. During the next six weeks, he issued similar proclamations for Alabama, Florida, Georgia, Mississippi, Texas, and South Carolina. These seven proclamations, and the Unionist state governments established in Arkansas, Louisiana, Tennessee, and Virginia during the war, set all the former Confederate states on the road to reunion.[8]

More pressing even than political matters was the business of tending and harvesting that year's crops, for the federal government was already feeding thousands of destitute Southerners, black and white, and sought to reduce the financial burden. Efficient management of the agricultural labor force would help to diminish government expenditures just as surely as did the rapid mustering out of Union regiments and might forestall a famine that was otherwise sure to come with winter. Unfortunately for those who hoped to manage the laborers, many of the South's former slaves were absent from their home plantations that spring and summer. Reasons for the mass movement were many. Some of the migrants searched for relatives from whom they had been separated, whether by slave sales before the war or by forced removal from the paths of advancing Union armies during the fighting. Other migrants wished to avoid the kind of confrontation with former masters that the change from slave to free labor was sure to bring. Still others merely sought safety in numbers within growing black urban communities, for freedom meant that former slaves were no longer protected property, but instead were fair game for any evil-tempered white man with a deadly weapon.[9]

Chaplain Homer H. Moore of the 34th USCI traveled across northern Florida in May and June. When the official announcement of freedom in the Department of the South came in late May, he said, "large numbers of negroes left their homes, & began flocking into the towns, causing great inconvenience to the Military Authorities, & great danger to the growing crops." Moore and two civilian officials set out across the state to investigate conditions and to try to explain the workings of a free labor system to former masters and former slaves alike. "In so far as it was the purpose of our mission to induce the negroes to remain at home, & work for wages, we think we were very successful," he reported, "for having heard from their masters that they were free, but still having to work very much the same as before, they naturally believed they were imposed upon; & that to secure perfect freedom they must get to some place occupied by U.S. troops. But hearing from us, unquestionable Yankees, that they were free wherever they were, & that the Government would protect them,

---

[8] Brooks D. Simpson, *The Reconstruction Presidents* (Lawrence: University Press of Kansas, 1998), pp. 73–75; Hans L. Trefousse, *Andrew Johnson: A Biography* (New York: W. W. Norton, 1989), pp. 210–11, 216–22. Texts of the amnesty and state government proclamations are in *OR*, ser. 2, 8: 578–80, and ser. 3, 5: 37–39.

[9] Leon F. Litwack, *Been in the Storm So Long: The Aftermath of Slavery* (New York: Knopf, 1979), pp. 305–16; Hahn et al., *Land and Labor*, pp. 7, 80; statistic in Dan T. Carter, *When the War Was Over: The Failure of Self-Reconstruction in the South* (Baton Rouge: Louisiana State University Press, 1985), p. 157.

but that they would have to work nevertheless to live they became reconciled to the new state of things."[10]

While only the tiniest fraction of former slaves—those whose masters had allowed them to hire out their labor before the war—had any idea of the workings of a free labor system, many former masters had little better understanding. One of the Northern reporters who flocked to the South in 1865 had an illuminating discussion with a former slaveholder in South Carolina. "All we want," the planter told him, "is that our Yankee rulers should give us the same privileges with regard to the control of labor which they themselves have. . . . In Massachusetts, a laborer is obliged by law to make a contract for a year. If he leaves his employer without his consent, or before the contract expires, he can be put in jail. . . . All we want is the same or a similar code of laws here." The reporter denied that such a law existed in any Northern state. "How do you manage without such laws?" the planter asked. "How can you get work out of a man unless you *compel* him in some way?" Even a leading politician like James W. Throckmorton of Texas expressed privately his yearning "to adopt a coercive system of labor."[11]

Although Northerners had a better idea of how a free labor system operated than the planters did, many of them, including high-ranking Army officers and Freedmen's Bureau officials, were unsure about the future of free labor in the South. At Memphis, the field agent reported in mid-August:

> Many freed people prefer a life of precarious subsistence and comparative idleness in the suburbs of the city, to a more comfortable home and honest labor in the country. . . . I propose . . . to take efficient steps to remove that portion . . . who have no legitimate means of support, and distribute them in the Country, where their labor is wanted, and where they will have much better opportunities of leading useful and happy lives.

Six weeks later, a new Bureau official in the city noted that "quite a large number of vagrants were arrested by the colored troops, & by force of arms, were sent to the country to work on plantations."[12]

At the same time that black soldiers at Memphis were rounding up reluctant plantation labor, a Freedmen's Bureau inspector found successful cotton crops in Arkansas counties where black regiments had guarded the workers for more than two years. Three officers from those regiments were serving as Bureau agents at places the inspector visited. Near Helena, he noticed that cotton "on the small leases worked by colored lessees on their own accounts is decidedly superior to that cultivated by them as hired hands." Freedmen on a plantation that had belonged to Confederate Brig. Gen. Gideon J. Pillow hoped to clear enough money from the 1865 crop to buy the land they had been farming. Near Pine Bluff, a government farm with 876 residents, "mostly disabled men, women and children," managed to farm 250 acres of cotton and 150 of

---

[10]H. H. Moore et al. to N. C. Dennett, 12 Jun 1865 (E–521), NA Microfilm Pub M752, Registers and Letters Received (LR) by the Commissioner of the BRFAL, roll 20.

[11]John T. Trowbridge, *The South: A Tour of Its Battle-Fields and Ruined Cities* (New York: Arno Press, 1969 [1866]), p. 573; Throckmorton quoted in Eric Foner, *Nothing But Freedom: Emancipation and Its Legacy* (Baton Rouge: Louisiana State University Press, 1981), p. 49.

[12]Brig Gen D. Tillson to Capt W. T. Clarke, 18 Aug 1865 (T–54) ("Many freed"), NA T142, roll 27; Brig Gen N. A. M. Dudley to Capt W. T. Clarke, 30 Sep 1865 (D–66) ("quite a large"), NA T142, roll 25.

corn. "The cotton . . . elicits the praise of every body, and old planters say it is as fine a crop as was ever produced on the farm." Free labor seemed successful where former slaves had been allowed self-direction in their work, but one inspector's report could not have been expected to budge the deeply ingrained prejudices of so many white Southerners and Northerners alike.[13]

In the summer of 1865, with the year's crops still growing and the efficacy of free labor still unproven, Southern planters clung stubbornly to old beliefs. As a captain of the 113th USCI reported from Monticello, Arkansas, "many of the rebels do not conceed that the 'negro' is yet free." Similar reports came from all over the South. A chaplain at Beaufort, South Carolina, told the department commander that local planters viewed the Emancipation Proclamation as a wartime measure that had lapsed with the Confederate surrender. West of the Appalachians, although Union soldiers had occupied parts of Tennessee for more than three years, a captain of the 83d USCI reported that "slavery, or the next thing to it," was widespread. At Helena, Arkansas, which federal troops had also held since 1862, Capt. Henry Sweeney of the 60th USCI offered an even gloomier view. Black Mississippians who brought complaints to his office, he told the assistant commissioner for that state, said "that there was nothing in the worst days of slavery to compare with the present persecutions."[14]

Indeed, white Southerners bent every effort to impose a new social and economic order that resembled the old as closely as possible. President Johnson's provisional governors called state conventions to repudiate secession and slavery, but the elections that followed relied on voter qualifications that had been in force before the war, when all voters had been white men and most of them secessionist. The results were not surprising. When the new Mississippi legislature convened in October, its members quickly passed a set of laws to govern black residents that together became known as the Black Code. The principal law bore the title "An Act to confer Civil Rights on Freedmen," but most of its sections limited, rather than conferred, any rights that former slaves hoped to enjoy. First among these was the prohibition of freedmen leasing or renting farmland. This measure forced the overwhelming majority of former slaves, who were too poor to own their own land, to work on the large farms and plantations that were then being returned to possession of their former owners by the president's program of amnesty and individual pardon.[15]

The Mississippi legislature also decreed that former slaves had to obtain proof of residence and occupation in the form of annual contracts for farm laborers or licenses for self-employed workers. Other laws defined vagrancy so as

---

[13]Lt Col D. H. Williams to Maj Gen O. O. Howard, 18 Sep 1865 (W–4), NA M752, roll 22; Nathan C. Hughes and Roy P. Stonesifer, *The Life and Wars of Gideon J. Pillow* (Chapel Hill: University of North Carolina Press, 1993), pp. 142–43; Ira Berlin et al., eds., *The Wartime Genesis of Free Labor: The Lower South* (New York: Cambridge University Press, 1990), pp. 622–50; Hahn et al., *Land and Labor*, pp. 681–96.

[14]Barker quoted in Maj W. G. Sargent to Capt G. E. Dayton, 31 Aug 1865, NA Microfilm Pub M979, Rcds of the Asst Commissioner for the State of Arkansas, BRFAL, roll 23; Capt H. Sweeney to Col S. Thomas, 11 Sep 1865, NA M979, roll 6; Chaplain M. French to Maj Gen Q. A. Gillmore, 6 Jun 1865, Entry 4109, Dept of the South, LR, pt. 1, Geographical Divs and Depts, RG 393, Rcds of U.S. Army Continental Cmds, NA; Capt R. J. Hinton to "General," 8 Sep 1865 (H–90), NA T142, roll 26.

[15]William C. Harris, *Presidential Reconstruction in Mississippi* (Baton Rouge: Louisiana State University Press, 1967), pp. 130–31; Edward McPherson, ed., *The Political History of the United States of America During the Period of Reconstruction* (New York: Da Capo Press, 1972 [1871]), p. 81.

to limit the mobility of black laborers and consigned black orphans and some other children to unpaid labor, euphemistically called apprenticeship, until a girl's eighteenth birthday or a boy's twenty-first. Yet another forbade black civilians from possessing "fire-arms of any kind, or any ammunition, dirk, or bowie-knife." The penalties were forfeiture of the weapon and a ten-dollar fine. Local companies of the state militia, largely composed of Confederate veterans, began enforcing the law. Black people were alarmed. "They talk of taking the armes a way from (col) people and arresting them and put[ting] them on farms next month," Pvt. Calvin Holly of the 5th United States Colored Artillery (USCA) wrote directly to General Howard from his post at Vicksburg. "They are doing all they can to prevent free labor, and reestablish a kind of secondary slavery."[16]

Still other Mississippi legislation governed the testimony of black witnesses, limiting their competence to cases that involved at least one black party. During the fall and winter, legislatures of other Southern states enacted similar laws. South Carolina charged black shopkeepers one hundred dollars for an annual license. The most sobering feature of these laws was that they were not drafted by ignorant rabble-rousers but by some of the most respected jurists in the South. They reflected the opinion of the most educated and well-to-do white men.[17]

The passage of laws by state legislatures was no business of the Army's. What concerned federal occupiers was the preservation of public order, for much of the South continued under martial law until President Johnson declared the rebellion at an end on 2 April 1866. Even then, General Howard received instructions that the Freedmen's Bureau might resort to military tribunals "in any case where justice [could not] be attained through the medium of civil authority." The disorders that concerned the Army were violent for the most part and fell into several broad categories: those that occurred between white plantation owners and black laborers; rowdy misbehavior, when individual whites bullied freedpeople, or attempted to; and, finally, the kind of violence for which the South became notorious, organized bands of night riders whose purpose was to terrorize the black population into subservience. To counter this violence, those black regiments that were not guarding federal property or fortifications moved detachments of one or two companies into scattered county seats across the South. As a staff officer at Shreveport, Louisiana, told the commanding officer of the 61st USCI, the purpose of the troops was "to keep the country quiet, arrest criminals, protect the weak and defenceless from wrong and outrage, and generally to enforce obedience to the laws and orders."[18]

The relationship of plantation owners to their workers had become that of employers to employees rather than that of masters to slaves, but planters were slow to adapt to changed circumstances. They had "the idea firmly fixed in their minds that the negroes will not work[,] are impatient with them, and see no

---

[16]McPherson, *Political History*, pp. 29–32 ("fire-arms," p. 32); Holly quoted in Ira Berlin et al., eds., *The Black Military Experience* (New York: Cambridge University Press, 1982), pp. 755–56.

[17]McPherson, *Political History*, pp. 31, 36; Carter, *When the War Was Over*, pp. 187–92; Foner, *Nothing But Freedom*, pp. 49–53; Richard Zuczek, *State of Rebellion: Reconstruction in South Carolina* (Columbia: University of South Carolina Press, 1996), pp. 15–16.

[18]Capt B. F. Monroe to Colonel [Lt Col J. Foley], 24 Jul 1865, 61st USCI, Entry 57C, RG 94, NA; McPherson, *Political History*, pp. 13–17 ("in any case," p. 17).

way to induce faithfulness but by a resort to there old usages—the lash," Maj. George D. Reynolds of the 6th USCA reported from Natchez. Near Vicksburg, the colonel of the 64th USCI wrote, "old masters . . . would abuse and shoot their [former] slaves on the slightest provocation." Since black laborers no longer represented a substantial capital investment, some plantation owners inflicted whippings more severe than those they had laid on before emancipation.[19]

Although Bureau agents tried to investigate as many reports of wrongdoing as they could, black soldiers sometimes took matters into their own hands. Near Columbia, Louisiana, where "the cruel punishment of all colored people [was] indulged in to the heart's content" of white residents, Col. Alonzo W. Webber reported, men of the 51st USCI threatened the life of a former slaveholder who had "shot and killed one of his negroes." The man's former slaves had reportedly told the soldiers about the incident and urged them to act. White residents were "making a great howl over" the incident, the officer reported, for although they "believe[d] it to have been originated by their own slaves," they wanted a documented disturbance as a means of getting rid of a Union garrison in their midst, especially one made up of black soldiers.[20]

Incidents of fraud were also common. In North Carolina, Chaplain Henry M. Turner of the 1st USCI told readers of the *Christian Recorder* that "freedmen . . . have been kept at work until the crops were gathered, under the promise of pay or part of the crop, but when the time for reward came, they were driven away, without means, shelter or homes." Many freedmen and their families gravitated to Raleigh, the state capital, where they came under the care of Brig. Gen. Eliphalet Whittlesey, former colonel of the 46th USCI, who was serving as assistant commissioner of the Freedmen's Bureau.[21]

While labor relations gave rise to a great deal of violence during the months just after the Confederate surrender, any encounter between persons of different races could spark an incident. An Army uniform was no guarantee of immunity from an attack; rather, it might provoke one if the soldiers were few in number. An official inquiry into a street affray in Vicksburg elicited this statement from one of the participants, Pvt. Berry Brown of the 5th USCA:

> I was coming a cross the road . . . and three white men were going along the road, one of them was ahead of the other two. And as I crossed the road he triped me up. I then got up and asked him what he ment by triping a person up when he was not medling with him. He then said you god dam black yankee son of a bitch I will cut your dam guts out, and drew out his knife. . . . The orderly Sergeant then came down to see what the fuss was about when he commenced cuting at the orderly Sergeant. One of the boys then knocked him down with

---

[19]Maj G. D. Reynolds to 1st Lt S. Eldridge, 31 Aug 1865, NA Microfilm Pub M1907, Rcds of the Field Offices for the State of Mississippi, BRFAL, roll 34; Col S. Thomas to Maj Gen O. O. Howard, 12 Oct 1865, NA M752, roll 22; Hahn et al., *Land and Labor*, pp. 40–41, 80–81.

[20]Col A. W. Webber to Capt S. B. Ferguson, 12 Sep 1865 (L–270–DL–1865), Entry 1757, Dept of the Gulf, LR, pt. 1, RG 393, NA; Hahn et al., *Land and Labor*, p. 165 ("the cruel punishment").

[21]*Christian Recorder*, 2 September 1865.

a brick, and he got up and came after me again, and then I knocked him down with a brick.

The investigator concluded, "I shall endeavor to teach the inlisted men . . . to avoid if possible difficulty with citizens, yet I will at the same time teach them never to do so at the expense of their dignity and mand-hood and to disgrace the uniform they wear." Although such attacks made up only a small part of the violence directed against freedmen, they became more frequent in the last months of 1865. In December, reports appeared of black soldiers shot dead by white civilians at Atlanta and in Calhoun and Hinds Counties, Mississippi.[22]

Besides white Southerners, another group that was often hostile to black soldiers and civilians was the body of white federal troops in the South. Most of these men did not differ in their attitudes from the unfavorable national consensus regarding black people, and they often used their authority as members of the occupying force to annoy and injure black civilians and, at times, the black men who were their own comrades in arms. One such incident occurred in Washington, D.C., in October 1865. The 107th USCI had just arrived from North Carolina to take up garrison duties around the capital and pitched its tents near the Soldier's Rest, a transit camp at the Baltimore and Ohio Railroad depot, near the Capitol. On the morning of 14 October, 3 officers and 1,576 enlisted men of the 6th U.S. Cavalry arrived, having just turned in their horses before taking ship for Texas. The officers quickly "left for points 'up town,'" the quartermaster in charge of the Soldier's Rest learned, presumably in search of amusement. Within hours, "a difficulty occurred . . . followed by blows, showers of stones and one gun shot" that killed a soldier of the 107th. Authorities summoned five other regiments to the scene before the riot subsided. Similar conflicts occurred in Charleston, South Carolina, and in other cities where black and white soldiers with too few officers and too much time on their hands encountered each other.[23]

Most of the violence directed against black people in the South came on impulse from individual whites. According to one count of more than fifteen hundred attacks on black Texans during the years from 1865 to 1868, nearly 70 percent were individual acts. The unpredictable nature of such violence made it all the more intimidating, but what drew national attention to the campaign to subjugate the freedmen was its most distinctive feature: groups of men who rode disguised,

[22] Maj D. Conwell to Capt R. Wilson, 20 Dec 1865 (quotations verbatim), 5th USCA, Regimental Books, RG 94, NA; Lt Col G. Curkendall to Brig Gen D. Tillson, 26 Dec 1865 (G–18–1866), NA M752, roll 20; Maj Gen M. F. Force to Maj M. P. Bestow, 12 Dec 1865 (F–226–MDT–1865), Entry 926, Dept of the Cumberland, LR, pt. 1, RG 393, NA; Lt Col M. H. Tuttle to 1st Lt W. H. Williams, 21 Dec 1865, 50th USCI, Entry 57C, RG 94, NA; Joe G. Taylor, *Louisiana Reconstructed, 1863–1877* (Baton Rouge: Louisiana State University Press, 1974), p. 421.

[23] Capt W. W. Rogers to Capt A. H. Wands, 15 Oct 1865 (R–655–DW–1865); Capt E. M. Camp to Colonel Taylor [Col J. H. Taylor], 17 Oct 1865 (quotations), filed with (f/w) RG–655–DW–1865; Brig Gen F. T. Dent to General [Brig Gen A. V. Kautz], 14 Oct 1865; all in Entry 5382, Dept of Washington, LR, pt. 1, RG 393, NA. 6th U.S. Cavalry return, Oct 1865, NA Microfilm Pub M744, Returns from Regular Army Cav Rgts, roll 61; Mark L. Bradley, *Bluecoats and Tarheels: Soldiers and Civilians in Reconstruction North Carolina* (Lexington: University Press of Kentucky, 2009), pp. 66–67, 123–24; Robert J. Zalimas, "A Disturbance in the City: Black and White Soldiers in Postwar Charleston," in *Black Soldiers in Blue: African American Troops in the Civil War Era*, ed. John David Smith (Chapel Hill: University of North Carolina Press, 2002), pp. 361–90.

The 107th U.S. Colored Infantry served in Virginia and North Carolina before spending its last year, 1865–1866, guarding ordnance stores and other public property around Washington, D.C. In this cracked image, men of the regiment form in front of the guardhouse at Fort Corcoran, across the Potomac from Georgetown.

often at night. These local bands, often called "regulators," did not belong to the Ku Klux Klan—the Klan's founding meeting did not come until the spring of 1866, and its popularity did not sweep the South until after the last black volunteer regiments had mustered out—but their aims and methods were those adopted later by the Klan, and many of the participants must have joined the new organization. The Klan may have begun as a social group of fun-loving young men in Pulaski, Tennessee, but racial concerns were inevitably uppermost in its members' minds, so their club was not long in adopting the program of race warfare that had begun almost as soon as Confederate armies surrendered.[24]

Terrorism directed against black Southerners grew naturally out of the lawlessness that prevailed during the dying weeks of the Confederacy. Away from towns occupied by the armies of either side, bands of "guerrillas and stray robbers and thieves," as one Union general called the forces of disorder, thrived. Near Mor-

---

[24] Allen W. Trelease, *White Terror: The Ku Klux Klan Conspiracy and Southern Reconstruction* (Baton Rouge: Louisiana State University Press, 1971), pp. 3–21; Barry Crouch, *The Dance of Freedom: Texas African Americans During Reconstruction* (Austin: University of Texas Press, 2007), pp. 95–117, esp. pp. 100–102; Paul A. Cimbala, *Under the Guardianship of the Nation: The Freedmen's Bureau and the Reconstruction of Georgia, 1865–1870* (Athens: University of Georgia Press, 1997), p. 204.

ganza, Louisiana, the opposing sides arranged an armistice in the spring of 1865 "to enable the rebs to catch and hang a band of outlaws who infest the woods near our lines, fire into steamboats, [and] plunder citizens," 2d Lt. Duren F. Kelley of the 67th USCI wrote to his wife. "The rebs caught four of them day before yesterday and hung them on a tree. They got ten yesterday and I don't know how many they have got today. They are hanged as fast as captured." After surrenders across the South, disbanded soldiers on their way home added to the confusion. When Confederate troops in North Carolina laid down their arms that April, "most of [the] cavalry refused to surrender," the Union general commanding the Department of the South reported. He predicted that "they will scatter themselves over South Carolina and Georgia & commit all sorts of depredations, particularly upon the colored people."[25]

Union occupation authorities inclined at first to blame disbanded Confederate soldiers for the unrest that roiled the South. The commanding officer of the 75th USCI, for one, noted "large numbers of armed men of the late rebel army roaming about" near Washington, Louisiana. Fifty miles to the east, a captain of the 65th USCI serving as provost marshal at Port Hudson drew up charges for the military trial of a Confederate veteran who had been robbing and killing freedmen nearby. Maj. Gen. Peter J. Osterhaus at Jackson, Mississippi, thought that the marauders' abundant stock of military arms proved conclusively that they were "Rebel soldiers."[26]

It was not long, though, before the occupiers began to detect other influences at work. Maj. Gen. Rufus Saxton, whose dealings with freedmen and their affairs went back to the spring of 1862, reported in June that "guerrillas" around Augusta, Georgia, included "young men of the first families in the State, . . . bound together by an oath to take the life of every able bodied negro man found off his plantation." Two months later, a lieutenant of the 4th United States Colored Cavalry (USCC) told the officer commanding at Morganza, Louisiana, about "a secret society" of Confederate veterans in a nearby parish "organized . . . to drive out or kill all persons whom they term Yankees." Americans' well-known fascination with secret societies suited perfectly the requirements of resistance to Reconstruction. Many terrorists did not disguise themselves with masks or white sheets. A few simply blackened their faces, donned cast-off Union uniforms, and told their victims that they were U.S. Colored Troops. It was impossible for civil authorities to try them, a district judge told the assistant commissioner, for the offenders "are unknown to

---

[25] *OR*, ser. 1, vol. 47, pt. 3, p. 64 ("guerrillas"); Richard S. Offenberg and Robert R. Parsonage, eds., *The War Letters of Duren F. Kelley, 1862–1865* (New York: Pageant Press, 1967), p. 153. For official correspondence about outlaws and guerrillas in North Carolina, see *OR*, ser. 1, vol. 47, pt. 3, pp. 502, 543–45, 587; in Kansas, Mississippi, and Missouri, vol. 48, pt. 2, pp. 46, 346, 355–56, 571–72; in Alabama, Georgia, Mississippi, and Tennessee, vol. 49, pt. 2, pp. 418–19, 504, 1256–57. Maj Gen Q. A. Gillmore to Adj Gen, 7 May 1865 (S–1077–AGO–1865), NA Microfilm Pub M619, LR by the Adjutant General's Office, 1861–1870, roll 410. A good, brief synopsis of lawlessness throughout the South in 1865 is Stephen V. Ash, *When the Yankees Came: Conflict and Chaos in the Occupied South, 1861–1865* (Chapel Hill: University of North Carolina Press, 1995), pp. 203–11.
[26] Lt Col J. L. Rice to Capt B. B. Campbell, 7 Jun 1865, 75th USCI, Entry 57C, RG 94, NA; Capt A. D. Bailie to T. Conway, 30 Jul 1865 (B–36), and Charges and Specifications, 1 Aug 1865 (B–39), both in NA Microfilm Pub M1027, Rcds of the Asst Commissioner for the State of Louisiana, BRFAL, roll 7; Maj Gen P. J. Osterhaus to Capt J. W. Miller, 19 Aug 1865 (M–345–DM–1865), Entry 2433, Dept of Mississippi, LR, pt. 1, RG 393, NA.

us except through negro testimony," which was not admissible in court, "and we cannot therefore punish them." Before legislatures met that fall to revise the laws, Southern states limited severely the competence of black witnesses, if they did not rule out their testimony altogether.[27]

White Southerners had a strong aversion to federal occupiers in general and to black soldiers in particular, for the latter represented not simply military defeat, but the beginning of a social revolution. "The negroes congregate around the garrisons, and are idle and perpetrate crimes," the governor of Mississippi told General Howard. "It is hoped the black troops will be speedily removed." The governor anticipated "a general revolt" of the freedmen, which he thought black troops would support. From Clarksville, Tennessee, a state Supreme Court justice complained to Maj. Gen. George H. Thomas about the 101st USCI stationed there. The regiment's commanding officer, the judge said, "regards himself as the guardian of the negroes and this necessarily makes them insolent. . . . If the colored soldiers were removed, the negro population would be more obedient to the laws." It seemed clear that the former rulers of the South intended "to accomplish by state legislation and by covert violation of law what they . . . failed to accomplish by Rebellion," the assistant commissioner for Missouri and Arkansas wrote. As a Bureau official in Tallahassee put it, white Floridians expected that after state conventions met in the fall, "military forces will be withdrawn & the negroes will be again in their power, to do with as they may see fit."[28]

Unfortunately for the efficacy of the military occupation and the reputation of the black regiments, there was a kernel of truth in some of the complaints about the troops' conduct. Like soldiers after other wars, veterans of the Civil War tended to become unruly with the onset of peace. In one instance, the general commanding in Alabama during the summer of 1865 had to ask that disaffected white regiments of the XVI Corps be mustered out quickly and replaced by "troops that can be depended on." Two months later, an officer at Vicksburg placed an extra guard on railroad yards to prevent looting by homeward-bound troops. In Georgia, a Bureau official reported that "the worst acts committed . . . upon negroes [near Augusta] have been committed by . . . white soldiers."[29]

With time on their hands, black soldiers also misbehaved. A freedman showed the Bureau agent at Helena his wounded scalp, cut by a brick in the hand of a soldier of the 56th USCI during a street brawl. Along the river between Savannah and

---

[27]Maj Gen R. Saxton to Maj Gen O. O. Howard, 4 Jun 1865 (S–14) ("guerrillas"), NA M752, roll 17; N. M. Reeve to Brig Gen D. Tillson, 27 Nov 1865 ("are unknown"), f/w Brig Gen D. Tillson to Maj Gen O. O. Howard, 28 Nov 1865 (G–37), NA M752, roll 20; 1st Lt J. W. Evarts to 1st Lt L. B. Jenks, 22 Aug 1865 (f/w F–97–DL–1865), Entry 1757, pt. 1, RG 393, NA. On terrorists in blackface, see Maj J. M. Bowler to Capt C. E. Howe, 15 Oct 1865, Entry 269, Dept of Arkansas, LR, pt. 1, RG 393, NA; Maj J. M. Bowler to Maj W. S. Sargent, 31 Oct 1865, NA M979, roll 23; Cimbala, *Under the Guardianship*, p. 204.

[28]W. L. Sharkey to Maj Gen O. O. Howard, 10 Oct 1865 (M–45), NA M752, roll 22; J. O. Shackelford to Maj Gen G. H. Thomas, 18 Jul 1865 (S–18), NA T142, roll 27; Brig Gen J. W. Sprague to Maj Gen O. O. Howard, 17 Jul 1865 ("to accomplish"), NA M979, roll 23; Col T. W. Osborn to Maj Gen O. O. Howard, 21 Sep 1865 (F–4) ("military forces"), NA M752, roll 20.

[29]Maj Gen C. R. Woods to Brig Gen W. D. Whipple, 20 Sep 1865 (A–443–MDT–1865), Entry 926, pt. 1, RG 393, NA; Maj E. B. Meatyard to 1st Lt C. W. Snyder, 10 Nov 1865, (M–394–DM–1865), Entry 2433, pt. 1, RG 393, NA; Brig Gen E. A. Wild to Maj Gen R. Saxton, 14 Jul 1865, NA Microfilm Pub M869, Rcds of the Asst Commissioner for the State of South Carolina, BRFAL,

Augusta, Georgia, men of the 33d USCI looted houses. Thefts from garden plots near Brookhaven and Vicksburg, Mississippi, became frequent as soldiers of the 58th and 108th USCIs tried to supplement the inadequate Army ration. An officer at Brookhaven recognized the connection. "It is absolutely necessary in order to maintain discipline, and prevent depredation," he urged, "that supplies should be forwarded more regularly." Neither black nor white civilians were exempt from pillage. In Nashville, a black street vendor complained to the Bureau that men of the 15th USCI "forceably took from him watermelons" valued at twenty-one dollars. A lieutenant of the 101st USCI serving as Freedmen's Bureau agent at Gallatin, Tennessee, wrote to the assistant commissioner to request the removal of one company from his own regiment and the assignment of another to the garrison there. The discipline of the company he wanted removed was so lax, he explained, "that it is utterly impossible to have them perform their various duties correctly. When they are sent on duty away from the Post, they cannot be depended upon. Their lawless acts are becoming a disgrace to the public service."[30]

While black soldiers used their off-duty hours to supplement their diet, often at the expense of black and white civilians, they also helped neighboring freedpeople adjust to their new status, both with advice and in more substantial ways. At Helena, Arkansas, men of the 56th USCI cleared ground and erected buildings for an orphanage; at Okolona, Mississippi, black civilians elected two noncommissioned officers of the 108th USCI as their financial agents in starting a school. Enlisted men and officers of the 62d and 65th USCIs—originally the 1st and 2d Missouri Infantries (African Descent)—raised $5,346 toward the founding of the Lincoln Institute, the forerunner of Lincoln University, in Jefferson City.[31]

The shortage of officers in the black regiments was one reason for a lack of discipline that many observers noticed. This problem became apparent as soon as the fighting died down and the troops took up occupation duties. Even before the Freedmen's Bureau organized fully, an inspector at New Orleans warned that "a large number of officers" of the 81st USCI "have been detached and placed on duties in this city," in addition to five assigned to various staff jobs at Port Hudson. "The 81st is a very fine regiment," he wrote, "and should have the requisite number of officers to maintain its present reputation by constant attention." Three days after the inspector's warning, a general in Louisi-

---

roll 34. Instances of misbehavior by troops of another American occupying force are in Earl F. Ziemke, *The U.S. Army in the Occupation of Germany, 1944–1946,* U.S. Army in World War II (Washington, D.C.: U.S. Army Center of Military History, 1975), pp. 323–25, 421–23.

[30] Capt H. Sweeney to 1st Lt S. J. Clark, 13 Jul 1865, 56th USCI; Maj L. Raynolds to 1st Lt J. A. Stevens, 6 Sep 1865, 58th USCI; 1st Lt C. Wright to Commanding Officer (CO), 108th USCI, 10 Jul 1865, and 2d Lt A. F. Cook to CO, 108th USCI, 30 Aug 1865, both in 108th USCI; Endorsement, Lt Col N. S. Gilson, 21 Sep 1865, on Maj L. Raynolds to Lt Col J. W. Miller, 19 Sep 1865 (R–137–DM–1865), 58th USCI; all in Entry 57C, RG 94, NA. 1st Lt A. J. Harding to Col R. W. Barnard, 16 Aug 1865 ("forceably took"), NA T142, roll 27; Brig Gen E. L. Molineux to Maj W. L. M. Burger, 22 Jun 1865, Entry 4109, Dept of the South, LR, pt. 1, RG 393, NA; 1st Lt A. L. Hawkins to Brig Gen C. B. Fisk, 2 Sep 1865 (H–102 1/2) ("that it is"), NA T142, roll 26.

[31] 1st Lt S. J. Clark to J. Dickenson and T. Harrison, 11 Jun 1866, 56th USCI, Regimental Books, RG 94, NA; HQ 108th USCI, Regimental Order 137, 25 Oct 1865, 108th USCI, Regimental Books, RG 94, NA; W. Sherman Savage, *The History of Lincoln University* (Jefferson City, Mo.: Lincoln University, 1939), pp. 2–3.

ana listed twelve officers from four black regiments in his division who were absent, filling positions that ranged from acting mayor of New Orleans to post quartermaster at Jackson, Mississippi.[32]

In the spring of 1865, the Freedmen's Bureau itself had to be staffed. Although one early call for Louisiana field agents requested four officers from black regiments and four from white, the constant mustering out of white volunteers that summer shifted the burden of providing agents increasingly to officers of the U.S. Colored Troops. When the assistant commissioner for Mississippi sent General Howard his roster of Bureau officers in mid-August, thirty-nine of his forty-eight headquarters staff and field agents came from ten of the black regiments stationed in the state. Elsewhere, the same situation prevailed. At Alexandria, Louisiana, the 80th USCI had only six officers on duty with the regiment's ten companies. At Nashville, Tennessee, command of the 101st USCI fell to a captain who had to report that only eight of the regiment's officers were present while fifteen were on detached service. The general commanding at Jackson, Mississippi, complained that "in some instances, by no means rare, subaltern officers have to take charge of two companies, in one instance of three."[33]

Since the cost of horses, tack, and fodder made cavalry expensive to maintain, the adjutant general issued an order during the first week of May 1865, just days after the surrender of Confederate armies between the Appalachians and the Mississippi River, for the muster-out of all volunteer cavalry troopers whose enlistments would expire in the next four months. The remaining men would reorganize as full-strength regiments. Officers and noncommissioned officers declared surplus by local commanders were also to muster out. The order did not affect the black cavalry regiments, in which the men's three-year enlistments would not begin to run out until late 1866, but it reduced drastically the size of the mounted force available to patrol the occupied South. Only eight days after the order, the colonel of the 49th USCI wrote from Jackson, Mississippi, that "there ought to be at least two hundred well mounted Cavalry at this Post for the purpose of protecting the inhabitants from . . . the 'Bushwhackers' who are very numerous in this vicinity." At the beginning of June, the general commanding at Jacksonville, Florida, made a similar request.[34]

Dwindling troop strength detracted from the efficacy of the occupying force. The Southern District of Mississippi, headquartered at Natchez, published a list of posts and their garrisons at the beginning of September. In the

---

[32]Lt Col J. M. Wilson to Lt Col C. T. Christensen, 12 Jun 1865 (I–81–DG–1865), and Brig Gen J. P. Hawkins to Lt Col C. T. Christensen, 15 Jun 1865 (H–193–DG–1865), both in Entry 1756, Dept of the Gulf, LR, pt. 1, RG 393, NA.

[33]T. W. Conway to Lt Col C. T. Christensen, 15 Jun 1865 (C–360–DG–1865), Entry 1756; Lt Col A. W. Webber to Brig Gen L. Thomas, 22 Aug 1865 (W–147–DL–1865), Entry 1757; Maj Gen P. J. Osterhaus to Capt J. W. Miller, 15 Aug 1865 (M–359–DM–1865), Entry 2433; all in pt. 1, RG 393, NA. Col S. Thomas to Maj Gen O. O. Howard, 15 Aug 1865 (T–123), NA M752, roll 18; Roster of Ofcrs, 101st USCI, 10 Sep 1865 (R–76), NA T142, roll 27.

[34]Col V. E. Young to Maj Gen G. K. Warren, 16 May 1865 (Y–B–27–DM–1865) ("there ought"), Entry 2433, RG 393, NA; Brig Gen I. Vogdes to Maj W. L. M. Burger, 4 Jun 1865 (V–40–DS–1865), Entry 4109; both in pt. 1, RG 393, NA. Orders disbanding volunteer cavalry and horse-drawn artillery between May and Oct 1865 are in *OR*, ser. 3, 5: 11–12, 48–49, 94–97, 516–17.

eighteen counties that constituted the district, 4,110 officers and men were responsible for policing more than fifteen thousand square miles. Less than one-third of the district was farmland, concentrated at the western edge of the state in the rich alluvial soil of the plantation country along the Mississippi River. The rest of the district consisted of sandy soil and pine forest that extended east through the Florida panhandle, the same forest that Brig. Gen. John P. Hawkins' division of Colored Troops had marched through earlier that year on its way from Pensacola to the siege of Mobile. The thick piney woods of the region were inviting to those fleeing from authority and difficult for pursuers to penetrate. In the southern district, only 359 soldiers were mounted, and they were scattered at five posts that ranged in size from 149 troopers at Port Gibson to 12 at Fayette. They belonged to a white regiment from New Jersey that mustered out on 1 November, leaving the district with no trained cavalry. All a local commander could do was to mount his infantry on horses or mules that belonged to the quartermaster and hope for the best.[35]

Throughout the summer, as the War Department continued to disband volunteer mounted regiments, pleas for cavalry reached state headquarters of the Army and the Freedmen's Bureau. An inspector in South Carolina reported that infantry troops on duty in the state "show a very creditable efficiency but they frequently have to march long distances to quell disturbances and often arrive too late to do good. A small force of cavalry would be of infinite service." A captain of the 6th USCA, serving as Bureau agent at Woodville, Mississippi, welcomed the arrival of some cavalry. "I got along quietly without them," he told the assistant commissioner, "but I could not do much business." At Mississippi City, a major of the 66th USCI sent "a scout" of mounted infantry to arrest a gang of returned Confederates who were murdering and abusing freedpeople; the Bureau agent, another officer of the regiment, recommended assignment of "a small squad of Cavalry" to the post. In Arkansas, "many acts of brutality are perpetrated upon the unfortunate and unprotected negroes," a captain of the 83d USCI reported. As a Bureau agent, he added that the white population in the southwestern part of the state was "most bitter, and hostile in the extreme, nothing deters them from . . . the foulest crimes, but the dread of our soldiers, for whom they entertain feelings of 'holy horror.' . . . The importance of . . . small forces of Cavalry can not be fully realized until one has had to do with these half whiped barbarians." The recommendations of agents did not matter. By September, the inexorable process of mustering out left only one mounted regiment in all of Arkansas. Throughout the fall, the War Department continued to muster out volunteer cavalry regiments across the South. Of thirteen mounted regiments serving in North Carolina during April, all were

---

[35] Station List of Troops, 1 Sep 1865, NA M1907, roll 33; U.S. Census Bureau, *Agriculture of the United States in 1860* (Washington, D.C.: Government Printing Office, 1864), p. 84; William Thorndike and William Dollarhide, *Map Guide to the U.S. Federal Censuses, 1790–1920* (Baltimore: Genealogical Publishing, 1987), p. 187; *Rand McNally Commercial Atlas and Marketing Guide, 2008*, 2 vols. (Chicago: Rand McNally, 2008), 2: 147. For instances of local commanders raising companies of mounted infantry, see Osterhaus to Miller, 19 Aug 1865; Brig Gen C. H. Morgan to Capt C. E. Howe, 16 Sep 1865 (M–129 [Sup] DA–1865), Entry 269, pt. 1, RG 393, NA. On the march of General Hawkins' division, see Chapter 5, above.

gone by the end of October; of eleven at Vicksburg and other posts on the lower Mississippi River, only one remained by December.[36]

Meanwhile, the War Department further accelerated the disbandment of volunteers by ordering the muster-out of all black regiments raised in Northern states. The order went out on 8 September. By mid-December, men from thirteen regiments at garrisons in Arkansas, Florida, Louisiana, the Carolinas, and Virginia had returned home. Besides eleven regiments that mustered out in Texas, those affected by the order were the 11th USCA (Rhode Island); the 1st USCI (Washington, D.C.); the 3d, 6th, 24th, and 25th USCIs (Pennsylvania); the 5th and 27th USCIs (Ohio); the 20th USCI (New York); the 60th USCI (Iowa); the 79th and 83d USCIs (Kansas); and the 102d USCI (Michigan). Mustering out had begun even earlier in South Carolina, with the 26th USCI (New York), the 32d USCI (Pennsylvania), and the 54th and 55th Massachusetts leaving by the end of August.[37]

The impetus for disbanding these troops was certainly not electoral, for while tens of thousands of voters in the Union's main field armies had received their discharges in the summer of 1865, black men could not vote in most Northern states. Rather, the reason may have been complaints about black soldiers from the provisional governors of Southern states, the president's own appointees. On 10 August, the governor of South Carolina reported "dissatisfaction" among the white population "on account of colored troops garrisoning the country villages & town. . . . [T]he black troops are a great nuisance & do much mischief among the Freed men." He followed this complaint with another two weeks later. The same month also saw the arrival of similar letters from the governors of Mississippi, North Carolina, and Tennessee. By the end of the year, a total of fifty black regiments had mustered out, consolidated, or otherwise left the Army (*Table 5*).[38]

An incident at Hazlehurst, Mississippi, in October showed the recalcitrance of those Southern whites whom the Arkansas agent had called "half whiped barbarians." The town had sprung up a few years before the war when a railroad from New Orleans to Jackson bypassed Gallatin, the seat of Copiah County. Since then, Hazlehurst had prospered. It stood some thirty-five miles south of Jackson and about twice that distance east of Natchez, headquarters of the military Southern

---

[36]Capt H. S. Hawkins to 1st Lt J. W. Clous, 13 Aug 1865 ("show a very"), NA M869, roll 34; Capt W. L. Cadle to Maj G. D. Reynolds, 31 Aug 1865 ("I got"), NA M1907, roll 34; Capt J. R. Montgomery, quoted in Maj W. G. Sargent, 31 Aug 1865 ("most bitter"), NA M979, roll 23. *OR*, ser. 1, vol. 48, pt. 2, pp. 265–67, lists cavalry regiments in Arkansas on 30 April 1865; cavalry regiments in the Department of the Gulf are on pp. 256, 260; in North Carolina, vol. 47, pt. 1, p. 55. Muster-out dates are in Frederick H. Dyer, *A Compendium of the War of the Rebellion* (New York: Thomas Yoseloff, 1959 [1908]), pp. 113, 118–19, 127–28, 131, 141, 144, 146, 150, 165–66, 177, 180, 200, 215, 230, 237. For the extent of Northern demobilization, see Mark R. Wilson, *The Business of Civil War: Military Mobilization and the State, 1861–1865* (Baltimore: Johns Hopkins University Press, 2006), pp. 191–95, 202–03.

[37]The text of the War Department order is in *OR*, ser. 3, 5: 108. Dyer, *Compendium*, pp. 1266, 1728–29.

[38]Letters from the governor of South Carolina to Andrew Johnson are in *Johnson Papers*, 8: 558 (quotation), 651; complaints from other governors are on pp. 556, 653, 666–68, 686. On white Southerners' abhorrence of black soldiers, see Chad L. Williams, "Symbols of Freedom and Defeat: African American Soldiers, White Southerners, and the Christmas Insurrection Scare of 1865," in *Black Flag over Dixie: Racial Atrocities and Reprisals in the Civil War*, ed. Gregory J. W. Urwin (Carbondale: Southern Illinois University Press, 2004), pp. 210–30, esp. pp. 213–17.

TABLE 5—MUSTER-OUT DATES OF BLACK REGIMENTS

1865	
20 Aug	54th Mass Infantry
22	32d USCI
28	26th USCI
29	55th Mass Infantry
20 Sep	5th and 6th USCIs
21	27th USCI
27	73d USCI
29	1st USCI
30	102d USCI
1 Oct	24th and 79th USCIs
2	11th USCA
7	20th USCI
9	83d USCI
11	74th USCI
15	60th USCI
16	22d and 123d USCIs
20	43d and 127th USCIs
23	135th USCI
24	124th USCI
	29th Conn Infantry
31	5th Mass Cavalry
	3d USCI
4 Nov	45th USCI
6	29th USCI
7	31st USCI
8	28th USCI
10	8th USCI
18	13th USCA
25	75th USCI
30	23d USCI
4 Dec	39th USCI
6	25th USCI
10	30th and 41st USCIs

11	14th USCA
26	100th USCI
30	61st USCI
31	55th, 76th, and 92d USCIs

1866	
4 Jan	48th and 136th USCIs
5	2d and 47th USCIs
6	78th and 138th USCIs
9	63d USCI
10	13th USCI
12	11th USCI
15	137th USCI
16	12th USCI
21	101st USCI
26	3d USCC
29	96th USCI
30	46th USCI
31	33d, 42d, and 59th USCIs
4 Feb	1st USCC
5	68th and 104th USCIs
6	109th, 110th, and 118th USCIs
8	122d USCI
10	8th USCA, 115th USCI
12	2d USCC
21	18th USCI
25	4th USCA
28	34th USCI
7 Mar	70th USCI
8	53d USCI
13	64th USCI
14	84th USCI
16	5th USCC
20	4th USCC; 50th and 66th USCIs
21	108th USCI
22	49th USCI

TABLE 5—MUSTER-OUT DATES OF BLACK REGIMENTS—CONTINUED

26	14th USCI
31	1st USCA, 62d USCI
2 Apr	114th USCI
6	97th USCI
7	15th USCI
9	113th USCI
10	86th USCI
15	6th USCC
15–20	103d USCI
23	99th USCI
24	12th USCA
25	17th, 21st, and 40th USCIs
27	119th USCI
30	3d USCA; 16th, 44th, 58th, and 111th USCIs
4 May	4th USCI
5	52d USCI
13	6th USCA
17	10th USCI
20	5th USCA
1 Jun	35th USCI
16	51st USCI
10 Sep	82d USCI
15	56th USCI
10 Oct	128th USCI
13	7th USCI
28	36th USCI
22 Nov	107th USCI
26	9th USCI

30	81st USCI
13 Dec	57th USCI

1867	
8 Jan	65th USCI
15	19th USCI
17	116th USCI
25	38th USCI
11 Feb	37th USCI
22	10th USCA
1 Mar	80th USCI
10 Aug	117th USCI
20 Dec	125th USCI

USCA = United States Colored Artillery; USCC = United States Colored Cavalry; USCI = United States Colored Infantry.

Notes: The 54th USCI "mustered out of service by companies at different dates from August 8 to December 31, 1866." *Official Army Register of the Volunteer Force of the United States Army*, 8 vols. (Washington, D.C.: Adjutant General's Office, 1868), 8: 227 (hereafter cited as *ORVF*). The 2d USCI batteries mustered out as follows: A, 13 January 1866; B, 17 March 1866; C, D, and F, 28 December 1865; E, 26 September 1865; G, 12 August 1865; H, 15 September 1865; I, 10 January 1866; Independent Battery, 22 July 1865. *ORVF*, 8: 165–68.

District of Mississippi. The 1860 census had counted 7,432 whites; 7,963 slaves; and one free black man living in the county.[39]

In the fall of 1865, Hazlehurst was the site of a Freedmen's Bureau office. The agent was Capt. Warren Peck of the 58th USCI, a regiment that had been raised at Natchez two years earlier. Regimental headquarters was at Brookhaven, twenty miles to the south; one company garrisoned Hazlehurst, partly to help Captain Peck in his work and partly to guard cotton gathered there from the surrounding country. In Mississippi, the Confederate government had owned more than 127,000 bales of cotton, worth nearly $8 million. When the fighting ceased, U.S. Treasury agents began impounding what they could find of it while private citizens and government officials, civilian and uniformed, stole what they could. At Natchez, Major Reynolds complained of "high-handed and extensive cotton thefts" throughout the country, engineered by "white men, who employ negroes to steal for them. The large scale on which their operations are conducted shows that it is an organized affair."[40]

Crime in Mississippi went largely unchecked that summer as the state endured a tug-of-war between its civilian governor and the military authorities. In June, President Johnson had appointed William L. Sharkey, a Mississippi politician who had opposed secession in 1860, as provisional governor of the state. Two months later, while the reconstruction convention debated reform of the state constitution, Sharkey asked the president to repeal martial law. He had recently issued a call to raise companies of militia in each county, ostensibly "to suppress crime, which is becoming alarming," he told Johnson.[41]

When General Osterhaus, at Jackson, saw a newspaper advertisement that urged the formation of a local militia company, he wrote to the provisional governor, reminding him that the state was still under martial law "and that no military organizations can be tolerated which are not under control of United States officers." The same day, the general told department headquarters that Sharkey had mentioned in conversation that the main purpose of the militia was "to suppress any acts of violence, which the negroes may attempt to commit during next winter." Osterhaus had retorted, he went on, that all the violent criminals awaiting trial in the state were white, "young men . . . lately returned from military service, just the very same men, who in all probability would join the . . . companies of militia. The result of the organization of such companies, while the state is occupied by U.S. troops, mostly colored, cannot be doubted." After ten days of correspondence between the governor, department headquarters, and Washington, the president decided to support Sharkey in organizing state militia. Col. Samuel Thomas, the Freedmen's Bureau assistant commissioner for Mississippi, thought that a transfer of authority from federal to state officials could not "be smoothly managed in the present temper of Mississippi. . . . [W]e are in

---

[39]U.S. Census Bureau, *Population of the United States in 1860* (Washington, D.C.: Government Printing Office, 1864), p. 270.

[40]Station List of Troops, 1 Sep 1865, NA M1907, roll 33; Lt Col N. S. Gilson to Maj Gen P. J. Osterhaus, 16 Nov 1865, and Affidavits, Sgt William Gray, n.d., and Pvt Lewis Donnell, 31 Oct 1865, all in Warren Peck file (P–84–CT–1863), Entry 360, Colored Troops Div, LR, RG 94, NA; Reynolds to Eldridge, 31 Aug 1865; Harris, *Presidential Reconstruction*, pp. 63–68.

[41]*Johnson Papers*, 8: 628 (quotation); Harris, *Presidential Reconstruction*, pp. 72–73.

honor bound to secure to the helpless people we have liberated a republican form of government, and . . . we betray our trust when we hand these freedmen over to their old masters."[42]

This was the uneasy state of affairs in Mississippi on the morning of 13 October, when a white resident of Copiah County entered the Hazlehurst Freedmen's Bureau office "in a boisterous and defiant manner," as Captain Peck later testified. Drury J. Brown, a planter who had led a regiment of Confederate infantry during the war, accused Peck of extorting money under the pretense of collecting a tax from employers of freedmen. Brown then left but returned in the afternoon and became quarrelsome and abusive. When he shoved Peck, the captain called a private of the 58th USCI into his office and ordered Brown's arrest. The planter was drunk, "which I did not notice until he refused to respect the arrest," Peck said. It took three soldiers to drag Brown out of the office. "We took hold of Mr. Brown and with considerable struggling . . . got him out of the back door," Sgt. William Gray testified. They dragged Brown by his legs to the veranda of a nearby house that served the Freedmen's Bureau as a jail, "not having any more appropriate place," Peck explained. Within an hour, the captain released his prisoner on the understanding that Brown would go home.[43]

The next day, Peck took a train some seventy-five miles to department headquarters at Vicksburg, where he hoped to collect copies of some recent orders that had not reached Hazlehurst. Returning on 18 October, he found the infantry company withdrawn to regimental headquarters at Brookhaven, leaving a sergeant and six privates to keep watch over impounded cotton. On the same day, Drury Brown took his complaint of being manhandled by black soldiers to a justice of the peace, who issued an order to the sheriff for Peck's arrest. About half an hour after the captain reached Hazlehurst, a deputy tried to serve the warrant on him, but he refused to acknowledge the right of the county to interfere with a federal official in the execution of his duties.[44]

That evening, Pvt. Lewis Dowell stood guard over the cotton that was piled near the railroad tracks. He heard a group of men pass by; one of them said, "He thinks he cannot be taken because he has got a few Yankee niggers with him." About nine, Dowell heard Peck call for the guard. Sgt. Dilman George brought the six privates at the double and found the captain some distance from his office, surrounded by fifteen or twenty men. Dowell counted four shotguns or revolvers trained on Peck and six pointed toward the advancing soldiers. Three or four dozen more men, most of them armed, stood "scattered down the road . . . in a sort of scrmish line [sic]," Dowell remembered. As the first of the soldiers came within ten paces of the group, the sheriff cocked both hammers of his shotgun and ordered

---

[42]Maj Gen P. J. Osterhaus to W. L. Sharkey, 21 Aug 1865, and Maj Gen P. J. Osterhaus to Capt J. W. Miller, 21 Aug 1865 (M–347–DM–1865), both in Entry 2433, pt. 1, RG 393, NA; Col S. Thomas to Maj Gen O. O. Howard, 21 Sep 1865 (M–5), NA M752, roll 22; Harris, *Presidential Reconstruction*, pp. 73–74.

[43]Affidavits, Capt W. Peck, 1 Nov 1865, and Gray, n.d., in Peck file.

[44]Capt W. Peck to Maj G. D. Reynolds, 31 Oct 1865, NA M1907, roll 34. Affidavits, Dowell, 31 Oct 1865, and Peck, 1 Nov 1865; T. Jones to Sheriff, 18 Oct 1865, Peck file.

him to stop, "or I will blow your brains out you black son of a bitch." The soldiers finally halted about ten yards from Peck, the sheriff, and the posse.[45]

"We did not look behind us to see . . . whither there were any men or not," Dowell testified. "We had our guns levelled—each man of us had his man picked out in the crowd." Dowell aimed at the sheriff. While Peck talked to his captors, one of them used his shoulder as a rest for the barrel of a shotgun pointed at the soldiers. After a few minutes' conversation that Peck's men could not overhear, the captain agreed to submit to arrest. As the posse and its prisoner left Hazlehurst, Pvt. Peter Williams followed them for a while to learn whether the sheriff's men intended to murder Peck. Instead, they took him to Gallatin, the decaying county seat some four miles west of the railroad, where Justice Thomas Jones held court. Required to post a $2,000 bond, Peck refused to acknowledge the authority of county officials. When he declined to post bond, they "locked [him] up in an *iron* cage in a very filthy room," Peck testified. "I was left in the cage from the 19th until the 23d Oct after which I was allowed to walk about the room in the day time—and locked up in the cage during the night."[46]

How word of Peck's arrest got out is not clear. He sent a note to his clerk in Hazlehurst before entering the Gallatin jail, but the Bureau assistant commissioner at Vicksburg got the news in a telegram from an Army staff officer at Jackson on 22 October. Then began five days of correspondence between Colonel Thomas, the assistant commissioner; General Osterhaus, commanding the Southern District; Provisional Governor Sharkey; and the new popularly elected governor, Benjamin G. Humphreys. When Humphreys asserted finally that any attempt by the executive (himself) to influence a judicial proceeding (Peck's arrest and trial) would be unconstitutional, the general acted, ordering four companies of the 58th USCI from Brookhaven to secure the captain's release. To lead the expedition, Osterhaus sent his judge advocate general, Maj. Norman S. Gilson of the 58th USCI.[47]

At the same time Gilson released Peck, he arrested Judge Jones and Leonard H. Redus, the deputy sheriff who had taken Peck from Hazlehurst to Gallatin. Present at the arrests was another Freedmen's Bureau agent, Capt. James T. Organ of the 6th USCA. "When the said Redus was arrested and placed under guard, he grew violent," Organ testified, "saying that he had arrested Captain Peck and By God if he had the power, he would get out a posse that night to arrest [Gilson] and his whole party. . . . The father of the aforesaid Redus who was arrested at the same time and place used very insulting and treasonable language saying I always have been a Rebel and I am Rebel now." How long Gilson held the justice and the deputy is not clear.[48]

Peck returned to Hazlehurst to find that his office had been ransacked. He blamed the entire affair on public opinion in Mississippi, which held that the federal government would withdraw its troops after the state elections, "that all au-

---

[45] Affidavits, Dowell, 31 Oct 1865, Sgt D. George, 31 Oct 1865, and Peck, 1 Nov 1865, Peck file.
[46] Ibid.
[47] Lt Col R. S. Donaldson to Col S. Thomas, 21 Oct 1865 (D–56), NA Microfilm Pub M826, Rcds of the Asst Commissioner for the State of Mississippi, BRFAL, roll 9; Col S. Thomas to Maj Gen O. O. Howard, 31 Oct 1865 (M–61), and B. G. Humphreys to Lt Col R. S. Donaldson, 23 Oct 1865, both in NA M752, roll 22; Maj N. S. Gilson to Maj Gen P. J. Osterhaus, 4 Nov 1865, and Maj Gen P. J. Osterhaus to Maj Gen E. D. Townsend, 6 Nov 1865, both in Peck file.
[48] Affidavits, Peck, 1 Nov 1865, and Capt J. T. Organ, 31 Oct 1865, Peck file.

thority had been taken from the Freedmen's Bureau, and that the Officers of the Bureau were subject to trial before civil courts for their actions in any case where they were not in accordance with the Code of Miss[issippi]." Osterhaus' action did much to correct that impression, and General Howard confirmed it later in the year when he told Colonel Thomas:

> Use all the power of the Bureau, to see that the Freedmen are protected . . . , and to that end . . . make application to the Dept. Commander, for such military force to assist you, as you may deem necessary; the whole power of the Government being pledged to sustain the actual freedom of the negro. . . . [W]henever [state] authorities show a disposition to infringe upon any of [the freedmen's] rights, . . . or refuse them equal justice with other citizens, then you will take such measures as may seem best to guard and protect their interests.[49]

Captain Peck's arrest had occurred without gunfire, but indignant white Southerners took many shots at their occupiers during the months after the Confederate surrender. The gunmen were not necessarily former Confederates: a drunken soldier of the 1st Louisiana Infantry, a white Union regiment recruited in the state, shot dead Sgt. Joseph Smith of the 11th USCA as Smith's regiment arrived to join the Donaldsonville garrison in July. In August, a civilian in South Carolina gunned down 2d Lt. James T. Furman of the 33d USCI with one round in the back followed by another in the head.[50]

Assassinations continued during the fall. In October, persons near Okolona, Mississippi, killed Pvt. James Roberts of the 108th USCI and wounded a white cavalryman. Efforts to arrest the culprits failed. Days later, Sgt. George Montgomery and Pvt. William Howell, both of the 42d USCI, were waylaid en route from Decatur, Alabama, to a nearby town and bludgeoned to death. Again, the killers escaped. Opportunistic killings continued through the following months, with civil juries unwilling to convict and Army officers, sometimes uncertain of their own authority, reluctant to act decisively. Black soldiers and their white officers were by no means the only victims, but as their regiments came to form the bulk of the occupation force, they offered a conspicuous target even as they stoked white Southerners' racial ire. Infantry, well suited to accompany Freedmen's Bureau agents on routine visits to plantations, was seldom able to catch fleeing murderers, and the last volunteer cavalry regiments were rapidly mustering out.[51]

Meanwhile, state militias across the South enforced laws that deprived freedmen of weapons. At La Grange, Tennessee, the Bureau agent thought that it was part of a program "to reduce the Freedmen to their former condition." An officer

---

[49]Peck to Reynolds, 31 Oct 1865; Maj Gen O. O. Howard to Col S. Thomas, 27 Dec 1865 (R–148), NA M826, roll 11.

[50]Col J. H. Sypher to Asst Adj Gen, 10 Jul 1865, Entry 402, Post of Donaldsonville, Letters Sent (LS), pt. 4, Mil Installations, RG 393, NA; Descriptive Book, Co E, 11th USCA, Regimental Books, RG 94, NA. Joseph T. Glatthaar, *Forged in Battle: The Civil War Alliance of Black Soldiers and White Officers* (New York: Free Press, 1990), p. 215, describes Furman's death. An account of a white soldier's murder in South Carolina is in the *New York Tribune*, 25 November 1865.

[51]Post of Columbus, SO 92, 5 Oct 1865, and 2d Lt A. Noble to 1st Lt W. Clendennin, 7 Oct 1865, both in 108th USCI; Maj G. W. Grubbs to Maj J. B. Sample, 13 Oct 1865, 42d USCI; Capt S. Marvin

in Louisiana reported that in parishes southwest of New Orleans, the militia was a "great source of annoyance and irritation to the blacks," who believed that the purpose of the militia was "to crush out what freedom they now enjoy." White Unionists in West Feliciana Parish petitioned the general commanding federal troops in the state to establish a garrison there to counteract the local militia company, "its legitimate purposes subverted to subserve the wicked designs of those malicious persons, who only strike in the dark." The petitioners praised the men of the 4th USCC who had camped nearby for a month, imposing "an unwonted quiet and orderly state of affairs." In South Carolina, the militia worried Army officers as well as freedmen. "All of the officers and men of these companies have seen service," the general commanding at Darlington wrote. Most members of the twelve militia companies in his district had "arms of some description," the general wrote, "and . . . they are superior in numbers to the total Military force of the United States." The commanding officer at Camden tried to constrain the local militia company by forbidding it to assemble with arms.[52]

The militia companies clearly represented an effort by white Southerners to revive the antebellum system of mounted rural patrols that restricted travel by slaves and punished summarily those who left their homes without passes. The intention was to reduce black Southerners to subservience. State officials preferred to ignore the obvious parallel, claiming instead that the purpose of the militia, apart from the suppression of general lawlessness, was to avert a black rebellion at the end of the year.[53]

In October, news of an uprising by black Jamaicans that left more than twenty persons of European or mixed ancestry dead inflamed fears of a racial insurrection in the American South. From coastal North Carolina to Arkansas, worried white residents petitioned civil and military authorities for protection. Just as common were reports from officers of black regiments deriding the idea of an uprising that, according to rumor, the freedmen planned for Christmas or New Year's Day. Col. Frederick M. Crandal of the 48th USCI dismissed "the fears of the people" around Shreveport, Louisiana, and attributed the rumors to recalcitrant former Confederates "who are anxious that all the trouble possible should be made . . . and who get up these stories for the purpose of embarrassing the Government." At Memphis, Maj. Arthur T. Reeve of the 88th USCI was "confident that no conspiracy exists." The Freedmen's Bureau agent at Washington, North Carolina, 2d Lt. Josiah G. Hort of the 30th USCI declared the rumors "utterly groundless," and the state assistant commissioner, General Whittlesey, called "these fears . . . relics of the past, nervous convulsions of the dead body of slavery." As the end of December approached, and with it the imagined insurrection, even the governor of South

---

to Capt A. S. Montgomery, 20 Nov 1865, with Endorsement, Brig Gen C. A. Gilchrist, 27 Nov 1865, 58th USCI; all in Entry 57C, RG 94, NA. Tuttle to Williams, 21 Dec 1865.

[52] S. H. Melcher to Brig Gen C. B. Fisk, 12 Dec 1865 (K–59), NA M752, roll 21; Capt T. Kanady to 1st Lt Z. K. Wood, 23 Dec 1865 (L–896–DL–1865), and John Wible et al. to Maj Gen E. R. S. Canby, 29 Nov 1865 (F–262–DL–1865), both in Entry 1757, pt. 1, RG 393, NA; Brig Gen W. P. Richardson to Lt Col W. L. M. Burger, 7 Dec 1865, Entry 4112, Dept of the South, LR Relating to Freedmen, pt. 1, RG 393, NA; J. L. Orr to Maj Gen D. E. Sickles, 13 Dec 1865, Entry 4109, pt. 1, RG 393, NA; Zuczek, *State of Rebellion*, pp. 13, 20.

[53] Carter, *When the War Was Over*, pp. 191–203.

Carolina admitted that he did not expect an organized disturbance, although he coupled this denial with a request that federal troops "be vigilant and watchful keeping the negroes in perfect order and arresting every one of them who may be turbulent or drunk."[54]

Warnings from Southern whites became more frantic as the holidays neared. The sheriff of St. Helena Parish, on the Louisiana-Mississippi state line, claimed in a Christmas Eve telegram to have "information from white & black persons that the negro troops at Baton Rouge intend to come out to the country for insurrectionary purposes on Christmas." The commanding officer of the 47th USCI, at the state capital, dismissed the report as having "no shadow of foundation." In the end, the season passed quietly throughout the South.[55]

Although the rumors of insurrection arose from white peoples' generations-old fear of slave rebellions as much as from the novel sights of black men in uniform patrolling towns and former slaves associating freely, some white observers had predicted an uprising when black Southerners' hopes of land redistribution collapsed after the war. In fact, expectations of free land were as widespread among black Southerners as fears of an uprising were among whites. Andrew Johnson himself, in a speech to black Tennesseans during the presidential campaign of 1864, had hinted at postwar confiscation of large estates and their division among "loyal, industrious farmers." In early September 1865, during the days between the muster-out of the 55th Massachusetts at Charleston, South Carolina, and its voyage to Boston for final payment and discharge, Capt. Charles C. Soule, at his commanding officer's insistence, sent a letter to General Howard that addressed the subject. During that brief period, when the regiment was out of service but officers and men had not entirely become civilians, Soule and his colonel thought that "one or two subjects may be addressed, upon which an officer in the army could hardly touch with propriety." Among these was black Carolinians' idea "that all the land is to be partitioned out to them in January." "In this belief they have been encouraged by some of the colored troops," Soule told Howard. "Even if justice is had in the division of the crops [between laborers and landowners], which cannot in every case be expected, they will be disappointed and dissatisfied at . . . getting none of the stock or other property upon the farms. There is a discontented and riotous feeling among them, which must culminate at some time or other, and this feeling is not directed against their former masters alone, but also, in some instances, against the United States forces." Early that summer, when officers of the 55th Massachusetts and other regiments had visited plantations near Orangeburg to impress on the freedpeople the necessity for labor contracts with their former masters, "the idea . . . gained universal currency among the negroes, . . . that these envoys were not

---

[54]Col F. M. Crandal to Maj Gen J. P. Hawkins, 30 Oct 1865 (H–300–DL–1865), Entry 1757, pt. 1, RG 393, NA; Maj A. T. Reeve to Maj Gen C. B. Fisk, 23 Dec 1865 (F–231–MDT–1865), Entry 926, pt. 1, RG 393, NA; 2d Lt J. G. Hort to Capt H. James, 30 Nov 1865, NA Microfilm Pub M1909, Rcds of the Field Offices for the State of North Carolina, BRFAL, roll 35; Col [sic] E. Whittlesey to Maj Gen O. O. Howard, 8 Dec 1865, NA M752, roll 23; Orr to Sickles, 13 Dec 1865 ("be vigilant"); Hahn et al., *Land and Labor*, pp. 131–33 (North Carolina), 834–40 (Arkansas); Gad Heuman, *"The Killing Time": The Morant Bay Rebellion in Jamaica* (Knoxville: University of Tennessee Press, 1994).

[55]J. W. Dodd to Capt E. R. Ames, 24 Dec 1865 (D–191–DL–1865), and Col H. Scofield to "Lieut Wood," 26 Dec 1865 (L–885–DL–1865), both in Entry 1757, pt. 1, RG 393, NA.

United States officers, but planters in disguise," trying "to cajole them into 'signing away their freedom.'"[56]

Some observers attributed the freedpeople's faith in imminent land redistribution to tales spread by black soldiers, but Soule blamed "Sherman's men," who had traversed the Carolinas early in the year. When white officers brought different news, he wrote, black residents refused to believe "so unpalatable an announcement," so the regiment sent parties of "intelligent and judicious" enlisted men instead to set up camps, transmit information, and preserve order throughout the Orangeburg District. "The system worked much better than anticipated," Soule told Howard. By November, the 35th USCI had fifteen enlisted men "visiting plantations" more than ninety miles east of Orangeburg, the commanding officer wrote. The squad reported to regimental headquarters at Georgetown on Saturdays, received instructions for the coming week, and set off again on its rounds.[57]

Sherman's soldiers could not have been solely responsible for the idea of a massive redistribution of farmland, of course. The belief was widespread across the South. A more plausible source was the conversation of slaveholders themselves, as they urged each other to greater wartime effort with assertions that Yankee abolitionists were hell-bent on freeing their slaves and dividing the plantations among them. Overhearing a rant like this, house servants carried the news to the slave quarters, where it gained wide circulation. This was the explanation that General Saxton, who had longer experience with freedpeople than anyone in the Army, offered to General Howard.[58]

Desire for land ownership was universal among rural black Southerners. "They ask 'what is the value of freedom if one has nothing to go on?' That is to say, if property in some shape or other is not to be given us, we might as well be slaves," Chaplain Thomas Smith of the 53d USCI reported from Jackson, Mississippi. "Nearly all of them have heard, that at Christmas, Government is going to take the planters' lands and other property . . . and give it to the colored people," the chaplain continued. As a result, few freedmen were willing to sign a labor contract for the coming year. The South Carolina Sea Islands formed part of the coastal tract that General Sherman had reserved for black settlement in January 1865. Nearly a year later, white landowners with presidential pardons were returning to reclaim their plantations. "The [freedmen] are exceedingly anxious to buy or lease land, rather than to hire themselves to their former owners. They . . . will gladly pay any

[56]Capt C. C. Soule to Maj Gen O. O. Howard, [8 Sep 1865], NA M752, roll 17; *Johnson Papers*, 7: 251 ("loyal, industrious"); Hahn et al., *Land and Labor*, pp. 814–16, 856; Eugene D. Genovese, *Roll, Jordan, Roll: The World the Slaves Made* (New York: Pantheon Books, 1974), pp. 588–89, 592–96. The 35th USCI detailed three officers as a "Special Commission for Making Contracts." 35th USCI, SO 40, 20 Jun 1865, 35th USCI, Regimental Books, RG 94, NA.

[57]Soule to Howard, [8 Sep 1865]. General Howard's brother also thought the freedmen's ideas of land redistribution came from Sherman's army. Brig Gen C. H. Howard to Maj Gen R. Saxton, 17 Nov 1865, and Maj A. J. Willard to Maj W. H. Smith, 13 Nov 1865 (quotation), both in NA M869, roll 34; Maj A. J. Willard to Capt G. W. Hooker, 19 Nov 1865, Entry 4112, pt. 1, RG 393, NA; Hahn et al., *Land and Labor*, p. 381; Foner, *Reconstruction*, p. 68.

[58]Maj Gen R. Saxton to Maj Gen O. O. Howard, 6 Dec 1865, NA M752, roll 24. A letter from Secretary of War Edwin M. Stanton assigned Saxton to manage plantations on the South Carolina Sea Islands in April 1862. *OR*, ser. 3, 2: 27–28. See also Steven Hahn, *A Nation Under Our Feet: Black Political Struggles in the Rural South from Slavery to the Great Migration* (Cambridge: Harvard University Press, 2003), pp. 130–31.

reasonable or unreasonable price for it," Brig. Gen. James C. Beecher reported from Edisto Island, "but if they must give up the land they will do it peaceably. A large number . . . will go to the main land preferring to hire out there" rather than work for their former masters, "if they must hire out at all." Capt. William L. Cadle of the 6th USCA reported in December that freedmen in southern Mississippi were "still hopeful that something will turn up about Christmas that will be to their interest." Yet Christmas came and went without realizing the hopes or fears of either black or white Southerners, and in January freedmen began making contracts to work during the coming year.[59]

With incidents of assault and murder occurring every day and rumors of an impending uprising by freedmen circulating widely, it is not surprising that tales of other conspiracies reached federal officers. In September, the general commanding at Mobile reported hearing from the governor of Alabama and the Freedmen's Bureau assistant commissioner for the state that white men north of the city were luring freedmen to the Florida coast with promises of work, then taking them aboard ship to Cuba, where slavery still thrived, and selling them to sugar planters. The general's report resulted in months of investigation by officers of the 34th and 82d USCIs, who reported no evidence of any "cargo of negroes" going to Cuba. The Cuban slave ships proved to be as insubstantial as the freedmen's uprising.[60]

While the military occupation of the South wore on through the fall of 1865, Northerners turned increasingly worried eyes on political developments in the region. On 20 November, the new, popularly elected governor of Mississippi told the state legislature: "Under the pressure of Federal bayonets, . . . the people of Mississippi have abolished the institution of slavery. . . . The negro is free, whether we like it or not. . . . To be free, however, does not make him a citizen, or entitle him to political or social equality with the white man." He then recommended several laws intended "for the protection and security . . . of the freedmen . . . against evils that may arise from their sudden emancipation." One law would declare the testimony of black witnesses admissible in court; another would establish a state militia; a third law or set of laws would "encourage" black workers "to enter in some pursuit of industry . . . and then, with an iron will and the strong hand of power, take hold of the idler and the vagrant and force [them] to some profitable employment." By passing these laws, the governor assured the legislators, "we may secure the withdrawal of the Federal troops."[61]

As news of this and other developments in the South appeared in Northern newspapers, discharged Union veterans of both political parties and their families began to join Radical Republicans and abolitionists in wondering whether their four years of striving and sacrifice had been in vain. "Has the South any statesmen

---

[59]Chaplain T. Smith to Capt J. H. Weber, 3 Nov 1865 (M–82), NA M752, roll 22; Brig Gen J. C. Beecher to Capt T. D. Hodges, 2 Dec 1865, Entry 4112, pt. 1, RG 393, NA; Capt W. L. Cadle to Maj G. D. Reynolds, 10 Dec 1865, NA M1907, roll 32.

[60]Maj Gen C. R. Woods to Brig Gen W. D. Whipple, 20 Sep 1865 (A–455–MDT–1865), Entry 926, pt. 1, RG 393, NA; Maj Gen J. J. Foster to Col G. L. Hartsuff, 6 Mar 1866 (G–186–AGO–1866) (quotation), and 1st Lt D. M. Hammond to 1st Lt J. M. J. Sanno, 18 Feb 1866, both in NA M619, roll 473; Capt G. H. Maynard to Maj Gen J. G. Foster, 25 Apr 1866 (f/w G–295–AGO–1866), NA M619, roll 474.

[61]Governor's message quoted in *New York Times*, 3 December 1865; Foner, *Reconstruction*, pp. 224–25.

still living?" an editorialist at the Republican *New York Tribune* wondered. After citing alarming developments in Mississippi, Florida, and South Carolina, the writer concluded that other Southern states would enact similar laws in an effort to be rid of federal troops. "The incessant and general outcry against Negro Soldiers forebodes this. . . . The Government is now pressed by the ex-Rebels to disband its Black soldiers forthwith. It is doing so as fast as it can. But what is to become of these soldiers? Many if not most of them dare not return to the homes they left to enter the Union service. They know they would be hunted down and killed by their badly reconstructed White neighbors." These white neighbors, a *Philadelphia Inquirer* editorial said, were "slow to learn. Our Southern brethren evidently need much instruction. . . . They have suffered some humiliation, but it is evident that they will be required to endure much more before they can understand exactly the situation which they occupy." Even the *New York Times*, a staunch supporter of President Johnson and his policies, called results of the recent elections in the South "unsatisfactory."[62]

The *Times* pronounced its judgment as members of the Thirty-ninth Congress gathered in Washington. All of the representatives and one-third of the senators had been elected the previous year, during the last autumn of the war. All came from states that had stayed in the Union. They numbered 176 Republicans, 49 Democrats, and 22 Unionists from the border states and Tennessee. Since it is the prerogative of Congress to review the credentials of its members, the first order of business was to decide whether to seat the twenty senators and fifty-six representatives recently elected in the ten occupied states. One of Georgia's senate choices was Alexander H. Stephens, who eight months earlier had been vice president of the Confederacy; ten of the other prospective members had served as generals in the Confederate Army. On the first day of the session, Thaddeus Stevens, the leading Radical Republican in the House, moved that seating the Southerners be postponed until a joint committee had investigated "the condition of the States which formed the so-called Confederate States of America, and report[ed] whether they, or any of them are entitled to be represented in either house of Congress." The legal basis for the inquiry was the constitutional guarantee to each state of a republican form of government. That Southern voters had elected so many candidates who had played prominent parts in the rebellion proved to many Republicans that all was not yet well in that part of the country.[63]

The House approved Stevens' motion by a vote of 133 to 36, with 13 abstentions; as did the Senate, 33 to 11. A committee of six senators and nine representatives began examining witnesses in January and continued into May. It questioned Union and Confederate leaders, among them Robert E. Lee and Alexander H. Stephens; less prominent Union generals, some of whom had commanded black troops during the war; General Saxton, who had supervised freedmen's affairs for years in the Department of the South; the adjutant general, Brig. Gen. Lorenzo Thomas, who had organized black regiments in the Mississippi Valley in 1863; and

---

[62] *New York Tribune*, 24 November 1865; *Philadelphia Inquirer*, 28 November 1865; *New York Times*, 2 December 1865.

[63] *Report of the Joint Committee on Reconstruction . . .* (Washington, D.C.: Government Printing Office, 1866), pp. iii, ix; Foner, *Reconstruction*, pp. 196, 225–26.

lesser soldiers and civilians, in person and by letter. Among those testifying were recently discharged officers who had served with black regiments in most parts of the South. Some were still serving there as agents of the Freedmen's Bureau.[64]

Committee members wanted to know how the withdrawal of federal troops would affect public order in the South. Two former officers of the 101st USCI expressed their views. Robert W. Barnard, the regiment's colonel, said that an old Unionist resident had told him, "If you take away the military from Tennessee, the buzzards can't eat up the niggers as fast as we'll kill 'em." John H. Cochrane, the lieutenant colonel, agreed that in parts of the state, freedmen, northerners, and southern Unionists would be in danger if federal troops left. George O. Sanderson, who had served with the 1st USCI as a lieutenant in North Carolina, said that without supervision, planters would reduce farmworkers' wages to less than thirty-eight cents a day, "to make it worse for them . . . than before they were freed." Poor whites, Sanderson said, "feel bitter towards the free class. . . . They say that they will drive them out of the country; they will not . . . live side by side with them." From Mississippi, Capt. James H. Mathews, of the 66th USCI, serving as a Bureau agent, contributed a letter that told how one soldier from his regiment had been assaulted and run out of town during a visit to his home. The commanding officer of the 113th USCI wrote from Arkansas that "if the troops should be withdrawn, . . . civil government would be too weak to protect society, and terror and confusion would be the result."[65]

For the most part, the statements of these and other witnesses divided sharply along lines drawn during the war, with Unionists demanding further military occupation and former secessionists denying the need for it. The division was the same as the one the committee noted in the recent state elections, which "had resulted, almost universally, in the defeat of candidates who had been true to the Union, and in the election of notorious and unpardoned rebels, men who could not take the prescribed oath of office and who made no secret of their hostility to the government and the people of the United States." The committee found that the conventions summoned by provisional governors had made only the most superficial attempts to reconstitute state government before calling elections. "Hardly is the war closed," the committee reported, "before the people of these insurrectionary States come forward and haughtily claim, as a right, the privilege of participating at once in that government which they had for four years been fighting to overthrow."[66]

While the committee heard testimony and wrote its report, Congress became increasingly estranged from the president. In February, Johnson vetoed a bill that would have extended the existence of the Freedmen's Bureau for another year, until early 1867. An effort to override that veto failed, but the president's conduct continued to alienate moderate Republicans, who made up the bulk of the party's membership in Congress. In April, they contributed to the majority necessary to override Johnson's veto of a civil rights bill that guaranteed freedpeople

---

[64]Lee's testimony is in *Report of the Joint Committee*, pt. 2, pp. 129–36; Stephens', in pt. 3, pp. 158–66; Saxton's, in pt. 2, pp. 216–31, and pt. 3, pp. 100–102; Thomas', in pt. 4, pp. 140–44. House and Senate votes on Stevens' motion are in *Congressional Globe*, 39th Cong., 1st sess., pp. 6, 30.

[65]*Report of the Joint Committee*, pt. 1, p. 121 ("If you"); pt. 2, pp. 175 ("to make it"), 176 ("feel bitter"); pt. 3, pp. 146–47, 170 ("if the troops").

[66]*Report of the Joint Committee*, pp. x (quotation), xvi ("Hardly is").

Black veterans were as eager to get out of uniform as most American soldiers have been at the end of every war. Alfred R. Waud recorded this scene in Little Rock, where the 113th U.S. Colored Infantry mustered out in April 1866.

"full and equal . . . security of person and property as is enjoyed by white citizens." Three months after that, two-thirds of both houses passed a second version of the Freedmen's Bureau bill hours after another veto. The president's vetoes and his intemperate speeches attacking opponents in Congress, coupled with the actions of white Southerners, had driven the moderate Republicans to ally with the Radicals, creating a veto-proof majority in both houses.[67]

As Congress and the president sparred in Washington, a dwindling number of black regiments undertook an even greater share of occupation duties. On 11 December, the War Department issued an order to muster out all remaining white volunteer regiments in Alabama, Georgia, and Mississippi, leaving an occupying force of about seven thousand U.S. Colored Troops and white regulars. Later that month, the Freedmen's Bureau assistant commissioner for Georgia, Brig. Gen. Davis Tillson, wrote to General Howard requesting direct command of the remaining troops in the state, since "their duties will consist almost wholly in aiding officers of the bureau." In January, after the last white volunteers had left, Tillson reported that Bureau officers in more than seven

---

[67]Bentley, *History of the Freedmen's Bureau*, pp. 115–20, 133–35; Foner, *Reconstruction*, pp. 243–51; Trefousse, *Andrew Johnson*, pp. 240–53. Text of the Civil Rights Bill is in McPherson, *Political History*, pp. 78–80 (quotation, p. 78).

towns sorely missed "the presence of at least a few troops," and that agents were "powerless without them." "In almost every case, . . . the withdrawal of troops has been followed by outrages upon the freed people," he wrote. "A large number of troops is not required, but . . . unless small garrisons are kept at many points, most unfortunate results will certainly follow." Tillson was right: reports of murders in Georgia during 1866, although sketchy, indicate a sevenfold increase after the 103d USCI mustered out in April, leaving only eight companies of regular infantry in the state. A report from South Carolina shows a similar, although less pronounced, trend after June, when the muster-out of white volunteers there left the 128th USCI, thirteen companies of regular infantry, and two companies of regular cavalry as the occupying force in the state. Although South Carolina was smaller than Georgia, its garrisons included nearly 25 percent more federal troops. While white peace officers were reluctant to arrest white murderers of black people and white juries refused to convict them, the increase of reported murders in both states after troop withdrawals suggests that even an occupation force of infantry served as some deterrent to racial violence.[68]

At the beginning of 1866, some sixty-five thousand black soldiers were still in service, representing slightly more than 53 percent of the remaining Civil War volunteers. Two months later, after more white regiments mustered out, the number of black troops had shrunk to fewer than forty thousand, but their proportion of the force had grown to nearly 60 percent. By early summer, only 17,320 black volunteers remained, constituting nearly three-quarters of the men still in service who had volunteered "for three years or the war." Sharing their duties were companies of the Regular Army—more than 70 percent of the regular infantry force, one regiment of cavalry, and one of artillery—but some eighteen thousand regulars could hardly compensate for the mustering out of nearly one hundred thousand volunteers, white and black, during the first six months of the year.[69]

Despite pleas and protests from commanding officers and Freedmen's Bureau agents, troop numbers in the South continued to dwindle. General Beecher asked for a company of his old regiment, the 35th USCI, to escort him while he settled labor contracts near the South Carolina coast that winter. In Kentucky and Tennessee, the assistant commissioner for those states told General Howard, troops had become so scarce by spring that they "could do but little else than guard the government property and garrison the chief cities." The Bureau agent at Hamburg, Arkansas, an officer of the 5th USCC, had to abandon his station until "troops sufficient to protect him from personal violence" could be sent there. In the southwest corner of the state, a former officer of the 113th USCI acting as a Bureau agent feared an armed conflict. "The most direct cause is the colored troops stationed here—the feeling is very bitter, and I daily look for a conflict," he reported. "It is

---

[68] *OR*, ser. 3, 5: 13; "Freedmen's Bureau," p. 315 ("their duties"), p. 328 ("the presence"); Rpts of Persons Murdered, Dists of Atlanta, Brunswick, Columbus, Griffin, Macon, Marietta, Rome, Savannah, Thomasville, Entry 642, Georgia: Rpts of Murders and Outrages, RG 105, Rcds of the BRFAL, NA; Rpt of Outrages, NA M869, roll 34.

[69] *OR*, ser. 3, 5: 138–39, 932, 973; *Army and Navy Journal*, 28 July 1866.

strongly threatened, and . . . the troops would all be killed . . . if I sent them out to make any arrest. There are but 13 of them not enough to enforce respect to the authority of the U.S. nor defend themselves if the conflict comes. . . . Either white troops should be sent here or enough colored ones to enable them to enforce order & protect themselves."[70]

The effectiveness of the occupying force continued to decline through the winter. Freedmen's Bureau agents in Kentucky and Arkansas needed military escorts to make arrests for murder and theft, and could not get them. Where black infantry regiments were available, officers had requests of their own. Post commanders at Grenada, Mississippi, and Baton Rouge asked for horses enough to mount a few infantrymen. Without an escort, the commanding officer of the 84th USCI explained, it was dangerous for a federal official to travel more than eight or ten miles outside the state capital of Louisiana. The Bureau's assistant commissioner for Arkansas asked the department commander to send a company of cavalry to Hamburg, which he said was "controlled by unsubdued rebels." In the northern part of the state, an officer and two enlisted men of the 113th USCI, the only mounted force available, tried to arrest a man for assaulting a Bureau agent. They followed the assailant to his home, where he shot at them and, since his three pursuers were not enough to cover all sides of the house, rode off in the night. The Bureau agent at Duvall's Bluff, an officer of the same regiment, concluded that it was "almost impossible . . . to enforce the regulations of the Bureau without troops." Nevertheless, the War Department continued to disband the volunteer force. Forty-one more black regiments mustered out during the winter.[71]

Events in Georgia during the first postwar fall and winter illustrate the sort of relations that prevailed between white planters, black farmworkers, defiant former Confederates, Freedmen's Bureau agents, and soldiers in the ever-dwindling occupation force. Maj. William Gray of the 1st USCA was a Bureau inspector in the state. In counties northwest of Augusta, he found:

> Many of the farmers have not yet settled with, and say they do not intend to pay, the freed people for their last year's work. The ignorance of the freed people has been taken advantage of . . . , and many of the white people have coerced them into making contracts at from $2 to $4 and $6 per month—stating that, if they did not . . . go to work after New Year, they would all be taken away, sent

---

[70]Brig Gen J. C. Beecher to Lt M. N. Rice, 9 Jan 1866 (f/w D–26), NA M752, roll 20; Maj Gen C. B. Fisk to Maj Gen O. O. Howard, 30 Apr 1866 (F–30–MDT–1866) ("could do"), Entry 926, pt. 1, RG 393, NA; Capt E. G. Barker to Brig Gen J. W. Sprague, 28 Apr 1866 (S–66–DA–1866) ("troops sufficient"), and A. W. Ballard to Col D. H. Williams, 30 Apr 1866 (B–10 [Sup] DA–1866) ("The most"), Entry 269, pt. 1, RG 393, NA.

[71]2d Lt R. W. Thing to 2d Lt J. T. Alden, 8 Jan 1866 (T–121), NA T142, roll 27; W. G. Bond to Maj Gen C. B. Fisk, 23 Jan 1866 (B–26), NA T142, roll 28; Maj E. Boedicker to 1st Lt J. K. Wood, 12 Jan 1866 (B–26–DL–1866), Entry 1757, pt. 1, RG 393, NA; Capt S. Marvin to Col M. P. Bestow, 10 Feb 1866 (S–25–DM–1866), Entry 2433, pt. 1, RG 393, NA; Brig Gen J. W. Sprague to Maj Gen J. J. Reynolds, 17 Jan 1866 ("controlled by"), NA M979, roll 1; Capt E. P. Gillpatrick to Maj J. M. Bowler, 16 Jan 1866, NA M979, roll 6; 1st Lt W. S. McCullough to Capt D. H. Williams, 31 Jan 1866 ("almost impossible"), NA M979, roll 23.

to Cuba, and sold into slavery. I spoke of this to the white people, and they did not deny it.

Cheating farmworkers and lying to them were widespread practices in the postwar South, but the Georgia planters, being unfamiliar with a free labor system, had not reckoned on differences in the availability of labor, both within the state and in the region as a whole. That fall, General Tillson foresaw great suffering in the months to come and promised "immediate and vigorous efforts to provide all freed people . . . with opportunities for labor where fair compensation and kind treatment will be secured to them. This is the only practicable and comprehensive plan of providing for their necessities." By winter, recruiters from Arkansas, Mississippi, and Missouri had arrived in the state, offering twenty and even twenty-five dollars a month to workers who were willing to migrate.[72]

By the first week in December 1865, several hundred freedmen and their families had signed up to work on plantations in Arkansas and Tennessee, but in a few weeks, the flow slowed to a trickle. Farmworkers were "afraid, and justly so," Major Gray reported, "that, if they attempt to leave, they will be in danger of bodily injury." Among the agents of fear were bands of self-styled "regulators" that had operated for months in the northeastern part of the state. Their members were "not mere outlaws but sons of wealthy and influential families," Tillson told General Howard. "They openly declare that no negro shall live upon land owned or rented by himself, but that he shall live with some white man or leave the country." West of Augusta, farmworkers told another Freedmen's Bureau officer in January 1866 "that the white people would not allow them to leave," and local planters asserted "that they have always had their labor and they intend to have it now and at their own price."[73]

White Georgians threatened Freedmen's Bureau officers as well as black farmhands. Before leaving Augusta on an inspection tour in January, Gray received warning from a Bureau agent "that it would be unsafe for me to go . . . without protection and I found on my arrival . . . that this was a necessary precaution. . . . I felt myself unsafe during my entire stay." Arthur T. Reeve, former major of the 88th USCI, met the inspector en route. Reeve's regiment had been consolidated with the 3d USCA at Memphis a month earlier. He was no longer in the Army, but instead

---

[72]Maj W. Gray to Maj Gen D. Tillson, 31 Jan 1866 ("many of"), NA Microfilm Pub M798, Rcds of the Asst Commissioner for the State of Georgia, BRFAL, roll 27; "Freedmen's Bureau," 39th Cong., 1st sess., H. Ex. Doc. 70, p. 57 ("immediate and"); Maj W. Gray to W. M. Haslett, 22 Jan 1866, NA M798, roll 1; Cimbala, *Under the Guardianship*, p. 148. For instances of cheating farmworkers, see Roberta S. Alexander, *North Carolina Faces the Freedman: Race Relations During Presidential Reconstruction, 1865–67* (Durham: Duke University Press, 1985), pp. 101–02; James T. Currie, *Enclave: Vicksburg and Her Plantations* (Jackson: University Press of Mississippi, 1980), p. 156; Robert T. McKenzie, *One South or Many? Plantation Belt and Upcountry in Civil War–Era Tennessee* (New York: Cambridge University Press, 1994), pp. 127–28; C. Peter Ripley, *Slaves and Freedmen in Civil War Louisiana* (Baton Rouge: Louisiana State University Press, 1976), p. 196; Zuczek, *State of Rebellion*, p. 29.

[73]Maj W. Gray to Lt Col G. Curkendall, 6 Dec 1865, and Maj W. Gray to Capt P. Slaughter, 6 Dec 1865, both in NA M798, roll 1; W. F. Avent to Brig Gen D. Tillson, 8 Dec 1865, NA M798, roll 24; Maj W. Gray to Brig Gen D. Tillson, 30 Jan 1866 ("afraid, and"), NA M798, roll 27; Capt G. H. Pratt to Brig Gen D. Tillson, 1 Feb 1866, NA M798, roll 28 ("that the white"); Tillson to Howard, 28 Nov 1865 ("regulators").

was acting as a labor recruiter for planters in western Tennessee. Traveling himself with an escort of two white soldiers from the 1st Battalion, 16th U.S. Infantry, he agreed with Gray's assertion, telling General Tillson that the inspector met with "undisguised disrespect and was at one period . . . in danger of mob violence."[74]

Gray ventured some ninety miles west of Augusta in March, accompanied by ten soldiers from the same regular battalion that had provided Reeve's escort in January. The purpose of this trip was to inspect labor contracts for fair wages and other terms of employment and to spread the word that if wages were too low in central Georgia, there were "abundant opportunities" for men to earn fifteen dollars a month, and women twelve, in the southwestern counties. The day after Gray arrived at the first county seat on his itinerary, he reported, some of the black residents told him "that a number of the [white] citizens intended to notify me that I should have a certain time in which to leave, and that if I did not . . . I should be mobbed." When crowds of farmhands gathered to have their contracts inspected, white employers grew alarmed and threatened Reeve, who was hiring laborers along with several other recruiters. Overhearing the threats, Gray marshaled his tiny escort and spoke to "several of the leading citizens," telling them, "'Look here Gentlemen . . . you can't intimidate me. . . . If my little garrison of Ten men is not strong enough, I shall get more troops, and let me tell you, that you are bidding fair to have your Town garrisoned by a Battalion of Colored troops for the remainder of the year.' [T]his latter remark worked like a charm." The threat averted immediate violence, but Reeve and the other labor recruiters asked for and received the protection of Gray's escort on the next leg of their journey.[75]

Although Gray's threat of "a Battalion of Colored troops" had the desired effect, it was transparent bluster. The Army had been withdrawing troops from Georgia steadily since the previous summer, as it had done throughout the South. In August 1865, the occupying force in Georgia had been twenty-one white volunteer infantry regiments; four recently raised black infantry regiments, the 103d USCI complete and the other three still organizing; one regiment of regular cavalry, and one battery of regular artillery. These formed the garrisons of nine towns, scattered in all parts of the state. By the end of the year, their number had dwindled to five volunteer infantry regiments, including the 103d USCI, and a newly arrived eight-company battalion of regular infantry. These amounted to a total of 3,758 officers and men posted at Atlanta, Augusta, Macon, and Savannah, leaving large tracts of the state without a nearby garrison. In April 1866, the last volunteers mustered out, leaving the all-white 1st Battalion, 16th U.S. Infantry—four hundred ten officers and men scattered at six towns and Fort Pulaski, at the mouth of the Savannah River—to police the entire state, an area of nearly fifty-eight thousand square miles.[76]

As more black regiments mustered out during the first half of the year, white residents of several Southern cities attacked the freedpeople in their midst. The worst of these occurrences, and the only one that involved an appreciable number

---

[74]Gray to Tillson, 30 Jan 1866; A. T. Reeve to Brig Gen D. Tillson, 31 Jan 1866, NA M798, roll 28.

[75]Maj W. Gray to Brig Gen D. Tillson, 14 Mar 1866, NA M798, roll 27.

[76]Maj Gen J. B. Steedman to Maj Gen W. D. Whipple, 8 Aug 1865, and Maj Gen C. R. Woods to "General," 2 May 1866, Entry 1708, Dept of Georgia, LS, pt. 1, RG 393, NA; Maj Gen C. R. Woods

of black soldiers, occurred in Memphis, a major port on the Mississippi River that had seen its black population quadruple, to eleven thousand of the city's twenty-eight thousand residents, since Union troops arrived there in May 1862. The 3d USCA had been part of the Memphis garrison since the regiment was raised in 1863, and the soldiers' dependents lived in shantytowns near Fort Pickering and other posts on the edge of the city. Their presence gave rise to "bitterness of feeling . . . between the low whites and blacks," a Freedmen's Bureau inspector reported. The 3d USCA mustered out on the last day of April 1866.[77]

The trouble began that evening with a hostile encounter between four city policemen and a few black soldiers who were waiting for their discharges. The next day the conflict became more serious, with city police arresting soldiers who were drinking while they awaited their final pay and discharges. A little later, police fired on shantytown residents. By afternoon, a mob of white rioters had arrived on the scene. The muster-out of the 3d USCA had left Maj. Gen. George Stoneman, the department commander, with only 150 regulars of the 3d Battalion, 16th U.S. Infantry, in the Memphis garrison. Stoneman later told congressional investigators that the troops numbered barely enough to protect government property in the city, and that this had kept him from intervening in the riot. Just after the riot, a Freedmen's Bureau agent reported, the department commander had said that the newly recruited infantry could not be trusted to restore order—that he feared that they would join the white mob.[78]

By 3 May, when civic leaders finally asked Stoneman to declare martial law, two white men and at least forty-six black people lay dead. More than thirteen of them were soldiers of the 3d USCA or discharged veterans of other black regiments. Besides attacking the shantytown and its residents, the mob had destroyed three black churches, eight schools, and about fifty freedpeople's homes. The *Memphis Avalanche* was a newspaper with a national reputation for its inflammatory prose. "Soon we shall have no more black troops among us," its editor exulted. "Thank heaven the white race are once more rulers of Memphis."[79]

By mid-June 1866, only eighteen black regiments continued in service, the last vestige of the Union armies that had occupied the South a year earlier. Seven of them had gone from Virginia to Texas with the XXV Corps and still manned posts along the lower Rio Grande and the Gulf Coast; two regiments, the 10th USCA and the 80th USCI, were at New Orleans and the forts around the city; two, the 57th and 125th USCIs, were scattered at small posts in New Mexico; the 107th USCI guarded government property in and near Washington, D.C.; and the 37th USCI

---

to Maj Gen W. D. Whipple, n.d. (T–814–AGO–1866, f/w Annual Rpts), NA M619, roll 533; Return, 16th U.S. Inf, Jun 1866, NA Microfilm Pub M665, Returns from Regular Army Inf Rgts, roll 174.

[77]Maj Gen G. Stoneman to Lt Gen U. S. Grant, 13 May 1866 (T–328–AGO–1865, f/w T–287–AGO–1866), NA M619, roll 519; Maj T. W. Gilbreth to Maj Gen O. O. Howard, 22 May 1866, NA Microfilm Pub M999, Rcds of the Asst Commissioner for the State of Tennessee, BRFAL, roll 34 (quotation); Carter, *When the War Was Over*, pp. 248–50; Foner, *Reconstruction*, pp. 261–63; Kevin R. Hardwick, "'Your Old Father Abe Lincoln Is Dead and Damned': Black Soldiers and the Memphis Riot of 1866," *Journal of Social History* 27 (1993): 109–28.

[78]Brig Gen B. P. Runkle to Maj Gen C. B. Fisk, 23 May 1866, NA M999, roll 34; "Memphis Riots and Massacres," 39th Cong., 1st sess., H. Rpt. 101 (serial 1,274), p. 2.

[79]"Memphis Riots and Massacres," pp. 50–52; John H. Franklin, *Reconstruction After the Civil War*, 2d ed. (Chicago: University of Chicago Press, 1993), p. 63 (quotation).

An artist imagines the destruction of the shantytown near Fort Pickering where dependents and hangers-on of the 3d U.S. Colored Artillery lived. The Memphis Riot began hours after the regiment mustered out, 30 April 1866. It was one of several similar occurrences—white-on-black violence with a lopsided casualty list—that occurred in the former Confederacy that spring and summer.

manned coastal forts in North Carolina. Only five of the regiments that remained in the former Confederate states had much to do with enforcement of Reconstruction policies: the 56th USCI, headquartered at Helena, Arkansas; the 65th, at Lake Providence in northeastern Louisiana; the 80th, at towns along the Red River in western Louisiana and northeastern Texas; the 82d, at Pensacola; and the 128th, in South Carolina.[80]

The presence of black regiments as far west as New Mexico resulted from General Grant's wish, expressed to General Sherman early in 1866, "to get some colored troops out on the plains." White volunteers, many of them from western states and territories, had manned forts along major routes to California, New Mexico, and Oregon for most of the war, and they brought with them their local attitudes toward American Indians. Colorado militia had attacked a village of peaceful Cheyennes in 1864, igniting more than two years of warfare. Grant hoped that "colored and regular troops," with no special axe to grind, could guarantee "the rights of the Indian . . . [so] as to avoid much of the difficulties . . . heretofore experienced." As it turned out, only two black regiments were available for assignment, and they served in New Mexico at a time when it was one of the quietest parts of the West. Scattered companies of the regiments undertook repairs on the forts where they served and sometimes pursued Indian stock thieves. In this, they were no more successful than the black infantry regiments on the lower Rio Grande or infantry in the South chasing mounted white terrorists.[81]

Early in the summer of 1866, two noteworthy events occurred in Washington. On 3 July, General Howard wrote to General Grant from Freedmen's Bureau headquarters in Washington, mentioning three shootings of Bureau officers and freedmen that had occurred recently in Georgia, Mississippi, and Virginia. "The civil authorities have failed, and are afraid to act," Howard told Grant. "The simple issuing of an order . . . would go far to prevent these attacks upon officers of the Government." Three days later, Grant issued a general order that authorized "Department, District and Post Commanders" in the South to arrest and detain anyone charged with "offenses against officers, agents . . . and inhabitants of the United States, irrespective of color," when civil authorities failed to act. Army officers were to hold the prisoners "until . . . a proper judicial tribunal may be ready and willing to try them." The legal status of the occupation force in the South had been ambiguous since the president had declared the rebellion at an end in April. Grant's language left the execution of the order to the judgment of local commanders and did little to clarify the situation while exposing Army officers to endless civil law-

---

[80] Dyer, *Compendium*, pp. 1720–40; see also order books and letter books of regiments named in Regimental Books, RG 94, NA.

[81] Lt Gen U. S. Grant to Maj Gen W. T. Sherman, 3 Mar 1866, in *The Papers of Ulysses S. Grant*, ed. John Y. Simon, 30 vols. to date (Carbondale and Edwardsville: Southern Illinois University Press, 1967–), 16: 93 ("to get some") (hereafter cited as *Grant Papers*); Lt Gen U. S. Grant to Maj Gen W. T. Sherman, 14 Mar 1866, in *Grant Papers*, 16: 117 ("colored and"). For black soldiers in the field in New Mexico, see Capt G. W. Letterman to Post Adj Ft Cummings, 5 Oct 1866, and Capt R. B. Foutts to Maj C. H. De Forrest, 24 Nov 1866, 125th USCI, Entry 57C, RG 94, NA. Francis B. Heitman, *Historical Register and Dictionary of the United States Army*, 2 vols. (Washington, D.C.: Government Printing Office, 1903), 2: 427–30, shows only six engagements in New Mexico during the time the 57th and 125th USCIs served there.

suits. The order might have had greater effect if there had been enough troops to cover the region, but there were not.[82]

Congress attempted to remedy this lack on 28 July, the last day of the session, by passing an act that increased the size of the Army. The peacetime establishment expanded by four regiments of cavalry, two of them with black enlisted men. The nine infantry regiments that had been raised in 1861, with three battalions of eight companies each, were broken up into twenty-seven ten-company regiments to match the organization of the ten senior infantry regiments. This added fifty-four infantry companies to the force. In addition, the act created four new infantry regiments with black enlisted men (another forty companies) and four regiments of wounded veterans, which, when organized, garrisoned Washington, D.C.; Nashville, Tennessee; and posts along the Canadian border, releasing regiments of able-bodied troops for service in the South or West. In all, the act added 48 companies of cavalry and 134 of infantry—more than fourteen thousand officers and men—to the Regular Army as it had existed since the spring of 1861. Still, the new organization added little to the enforcement of congressional Reconstruction measures; for while more than one-third of the infantry served in the South for at least a few years, all of the new mounted regiments went west.[83]

As commanding officers in the South looked around them in the summer of 1866, what they saw was not encouraging. Lt. Col. Orrin McFadden of the 80th USCI reported "very little change " around Alexandria, in central Louisiana. "Union men whether of northern or southern birth are living in extreme jeopardy of their lives." He mentioned "extremely bitter feeling" against Henry N. Frisbie, former colonel of the 92d USCI, who ran a plantation some twenty miles from Alexandria. "The only ground . . . for this hostility," McFadden wrote, "is the fact that Col. F. treats his laborers decently, and accords to them the common rights of humanity." Besides legal harassment in the courts, Frisbie had received threats that led him to arm his plantation hands that spring.[84]

The number of former Union officers who stayed in the South to farm after the war is uncertain, but there were certainly scores, if not hundreds, of them among the thousands of Northerners who took up plantation agriculture. Frisbie was not the only one to arm his workers; some thirty-five miles northeast of Vicksburg, Morris Yeomans' plantation was home to fifty veterans of his former regiment, the 70th USCI. Surrounded by "those who have not ceased to be our constant and unrelenting foes," they went "thoroughly armed," Yeomans told a staff officer at

---

[82]Maj Gen O. O. Howard to Lt Gen U. S. Grant, 3 Jul 1866, quoted in *Grant Papers*, 16: 229. The text of Grant's order is on p. 228. Queries from officers in the South about the effects of Johnson's proclamation and Grant's order appear on p. 229 and in McPherson, *Political History*, p. 17. See also James E. Sefton, *The United States Army and Reconstruction, 1865–1877* (Baton Rouge: Louisiana State University Press, 1967), pp. 77–82, 92–94; Foner, *Reconstruction*, pp. 239–51; Simpson, *Reconstruction Presidents*, pp. 92–99.

[83]Heitman, *Historical Register*, 2: 601, 604. Troop stations appear in the *Army and Navy Journal*, 28 July 1866 and 20 July 1867. Heitman, *Historical Register*, 2: 601, shows five of six mounted regiments as having ten companies each, but the Army standardized the size of cavalry regiments at twelve companies in 1862. Mary L. Stubbs and Stanley R. Connor, *Armor-Cavalry, Part 1: Regular Army and Army Reserve*, U.S. Army Lineage Series (Washington, D.C.: Office of the Chief of Military History, 1969), p. 16.

[84]Lt Col O. McFadden to 1st Lt N. Burbank, 12 Jul 1866, Entry 25, Post of Alexandria, LS, pt. 4, RG 393, NA; H. N. Frisbie to Maj W. Hoffman, 22 May 1866, Entry 1757, pt. 1, RG 393, NA.

department headquarters. A gang had been stealing mules from plantations run by Unionists and "disarming all Negroes that come within their reach." Some of its members had been seen reconnoitering Yeomans' plantation. The former colonel also reported the murders of seven freedmen in his neighborhood since the beginning of the year.[85]

Although it made sense for a former officer of U.S. Colored Troops to buy or lease land where discharged soldiers from his regiment offered a disciplined labor force well acquainted with the use of firearms, the prospects of success were still not great. Floods and insect pests combined to ruin many Northern planters before three growing seasons had passed. Frisbie left his plantation for New Orleans, and Yeomans returned to Ohio, where he had first joined a volunteer regiment in 1862.[86]

The handful of black regiments that remained on duty in the rural South tried to maintain order. "Many abuses to the freedmen are being perpetrated," the colonel of the 80th USCI complained to department headquarters from Shreveport that September, "and the parties go free from punishment . . . , as we are powerless to reach them with infantry troops. . . . Civil authorities will not protect the negro when calling for justice against a white man. The people are as strongly united here against . . . the U.S. Government as . . . [at] any time during the rebellion." Despite the ineffective performance of infantry, the colonel wrote, "Take away the troops and northern men must leave or foreswear every principle of true loyalty and manhood and truckle to the prejudices of the masses." As if to underscore his point, officers of the 65th USCI on the other side of Louisiana reported failures throughout the summer to arrest mounted lawbreakers around Lake Providence, on the Mississippi River. Officers of the regular infantry, which had necessarily taken on an increasing share of occupation duty as black regiments mustered out throughout the year, complained of similar unsatisfactory results.[87]

While federal troops in the South struggled to control what seemed to be a rising tide of disorder during 1866, Congress and the president became increasingly estranged. Although the fall elections had increased Republican majorities in both houses, Johnson continued to veto Reconstruction laws and to see his vetoes overridden. He tried to obstruct passage of the Fourteenth Amendment, a carefully worded measure that conferred citizenship on native-born freedmen and reduced the congressional delegations of states that barred them from the polls because of their race. When his opposition further excited northern editorial opinion against

---

[85]M. Yeomans to Col M. P. Bestow, 20 Jun 1866, Entry 2433, pt. 1, RG 393, NA; Lawrence N. Powell, *New Masters: Northern Planters During the Civil War and Reconstruction* (New Haven: Yale University Press, 1980), pp. xiii, 28–29, 50.

[86]Currie, *Enclave,* pp. 151–52, 156–59; Taylor, *Louisiana Reconstructed,* pp. 343–45; Michael Wayne, *The Reshaping of Plantation Society: The Natchez District, 1860–80* (Urbana: University of Illinois Press, 1990), pp. 61–66; *Roster, Surviving Members of the 95th Regiment, O.V.I.* [Columbus, Ohio: Champlin Press, 1916].

[87]Col W. S. Mudgett to Maj J. S. Crosby, 6 Sep 1866, 80th USCI, and 1st Lt W. P. Wiley to 1st Lt N. Burbank, 8 Jul 1866, 65th USCI, both in Entry 57C, RG 94, NA; Capt A. D. Bailie to AAG [Assistant Adjutant General] Dept of the Gulf, 27 Sep 1866, Entry 1756, pt. 1, RG 393, NA. For regular officers bemoaning the lack of cavalry in Florida, see Col J. T. Sprague to Brig Gen C. Mundee, 31 Aug 1866, f/w Maj Gen J. G. Foster to Lt Col G. Lee, 11 Sep 1866 (F–25–DG–1866), Entry 1756, pt. 1, RG 393, NA; in South Carolina, 1st Lt C. Snyder to Lt Col H. W. Smith, 21 Jul 1866, NA M869, roll 34.

him, General Grant urged him to modify his stance, but to no effect. Southern state legislatures refused to ratify the amendment. In turn, Congress passed the first of several Reconstruction Acts. It assigned ten Southern states to five military districts, within each of which an Army general would oversee the administration of justice until the constitutions of the occupied states were judged to conform to the federal constitution. On 2 March 1867, Johnson vetoed the bill and Congress once again overrode his veto.[88]

The Reconstruction Act and the events that occurred after it do not figure in the history of the U.S. Colored Troops. The day before the act became law, the last black regiment on Reconstruction duty, the 80th USCI, mustered out in Louisiana. Still in service were the 117th USCI, the last regiment of the long-since disbanded XXV Corps on the lower Rio Grande, and the 125th USCI at posts in New Mexico. The 117th mustered out in August and headed for Louisville for final payment and discharge. In the fall, companies of the 125th gathered in northern New Mexico and Colorado and followed the Santa Fe Trail east to Fort Leavenworth, Kansas, where the regiment mustered out on 20 December 1867. The last regiments of Civil War volunteers were out of service. About three thousand enlisted men, with representatives from most U.S. Colored Troops organizations, tried the life of the peacetime Army in one of the new black regiments of cavalry or infantry, as did roughly one hundred of the officers. The vast majority—more than 95 percent—returned to civilian life. For the tens of thousands who had served in the ranks, their discharges released them into a new world in which most of them were free for the first time; a world that, whatever its imperfections, their own efforts had helped to shape.[89]

[88] Foner, *Reconstruction*, pp. 251–80; Simpson, *Reconstruction Presidents*, pp. 109–15; Trefousse, *Andrew Johnson*, p. 274. A complaint of increasing violence in Florida is Maj Gen J. G. Foster to Maj Gen G. L. Hartsuff, n.d. [early Oct 1866] (F–28–DG–1866) (quotation), Entry 1756, pt. 1, RG 393, NA; in South Carolina, Col G. W. Gile to Lt Col H. W. Smith, 1 Jul 1866, NA M869, roll 34; in Arkansas, Maj Gen J. W. Sprague to Maj Gen O. O. Howard, 1 Sep 1866, NA M979, roll 23.

[89] 125th USCI, Regimental Books, RG 94, NA; William A. Dobak and Thomas D. Phillips, *The Black Regulars, 1866–1898* (Norman: University of Oklahoma Press, 2001), pp. 24, 293; Dyer, *Compendium*, p. 1739.

CHAPTER 15

CONCLUSION

Although the presence of nearly 4 million slaves in the Confederacy and the loyal border states made it inevitable that black people would play a prominent role in the Civil War, the federal government's eventual decision to enlist black soldiers was as hesitant as its approach to the entire question of emancipation. In the first place, the prevailing racial attitudes of white Americans meant that the presence of black people would be discounted, if not ignored, as much as possible and for as long as possible. Moreover, the geopolitical necessity of securing the loyalty of slaveholding border states ensured that the approach would be hesitant and oblique. Rail connections to the nation's capital ran through Maryland; beyond the Mississippi River, the state of Missouri controlled routes to the Pacific Coast and the Rocky Mountains, both sources of wealth necessary to the federal treasury; between Maryland and Missouri lay Kentucky, with its river boundary shared by three large and populous free states. Until the border states were secured to the Union, Abraham Lincoln and his cabinet believed that they had to proceed cautiously. Early attempts to preserve the Union were thus tentative and soft. In the opening months of the conflict, Union generals assured white Southerners that they came only to reassert federal authority, not to free slaves. Only in July 1861, when a Confederate army rebuffed an attempt to oust it from the vicinity of Washington, D.C., did the Northern public accept the fact that the country faced a long war.[1]

During the next year, Union armies advanced on all fronts, despite well-publicized reverses in Virginia. They occupied Nashville, New Orleans, Norfolk, and Memphis; marched through Arkansas; and established beachheads in the Carolinas and Florida. Everywhere they went, the region's enslaved black residents thronged their camps, hoping for an escape from bondage. Army quartermasters and engineers quickly put the new arrivals to work, often competing for their services with agents of the Treasury Department who wanted the freedpeople settled on plantations and producing cotton to finance the war. Meanwhile, the president rejected attempts by generals in Missouri, South Carolina, and elsewhere to free slaves or to enlist them as soldiers. In the summer of 1862, when the federal advance had

---

[1] U.S. Census Bureau, *Agriculture of the United States in 1860* (Washington, D.C.: Government Printing Office, 1864), pp. 223–45; Mark Grimsley, *The Hard Hand of War: Union Military Policy Toward Southern Civilians, 1861–1865* (New York: Cambridge University Press, 1995), pp. 8–11, 23–46.

moved beyond the still-loyal border states and reached well into the Confederacy, public opinion in the North had matured enough to allow Congress to pass an act that prohibited soldiers from returning escaped slaves to their masters.[2]

By that summer, Lincoln had decided on a policy of Emancipation. He waited to announce it until Union arms had turned back a Confederate thrust into Maryland. Even then, he declined to alienate the white population in parts of the South that federal troops had already occupied by freeing slaves there. The Emancipation Proclamation applied only to those slaves who were beyond the reach of Union authority. Nevertheless, the steady advance of federal armies assured that many more of the thousands still enslaved would be free before another year ended. Vicksburg and Port Hudson fell in July 1863, allowing Union control of the Mississippi River; Chattanooga, a rail center on the upper Tennessee River, followed two months later. In January 1864, federal soldiers crossed the state of Mississippi from west to east and back again before boarding riverboats and railroad cars to join a Union drive into northwestern Georgia. Each of these advances added thousands more names to the rolls of freedpeople working for the Union, whether on plantations growing food and cotton; as teamsters and longshoremen for Army staff officers; or, finally, as soldiers themselves.

The question arose at once: what functions should these new troops perform? Moving as cautiously as ever, Lincoln specified in the Emancipation Proclamation that they were "to garrison forts . . . and other places." Yet black soldiers in Kansas and South Carolina had already undertaken duties of a different kind, escorting wagon trains and conducting raids well outside the limits of federal garrisons. Several times, they had exchanged shots with the enemy. As happened often during a war in which federal policy evolved in reaction to events, practices in the field were far in advance of pronouncements from Washington.[3]

Assignment of new black regiments to stations in the wake of the federal advance had sound precedents. Union generals had always taken great care to protect their lines of communications. Even before the first shots were fired, Lt. Gen. Winfield Scott thought that one-third of the force necessary to crush secession would have to serve at garrisons in occupied territory. In December 1863, the Army of the Potomac counted 94,151 officers and men present, while those assigned to the Defenses of Washington numbered 33,905, including 12 white regiments of heavy artillery—more than the number of black artillery regiments raised to protect river ports from Paducah to New Orleans. Together with federal garrisons in Maryland and along the line of the Baltimore and Ohio Railroad in West Virginia, soldiers guarding the rear of the Army of the Potomac amounted to more than two-thirds the strength of the offensive force. The situation was similar west of the Appalachians, where the XVI Corps, at Memphis and other points in Tennessee, nearly equaled in size to the rest of Maj. Gen. William T. Sherman's army, camped at more advanced posts in Alabama and Mississippi. Stationed around Nashville were more

---

[2] On competition between military and civilian demands for black laborers, see above, Chapters 2, 5–8.

[3] The text of the Emancipation Proclamation in *The War of the Rebellion: A Compilation of the Official Records of the Union and Confederate Armies*, 70 vols. in 128 (Washington, D.C.: Government Printing Office, 1880–1901), ser. 3, 3: 2–3 (hereafter cited as *OR*).

than twelve thousand soldiers, roughly the same number as served in one of the corps that made up the Army of the Cumberland, which wintered at Chattanooga.[4]

To suppose that garrison duty or guarding a railroad removed troops from the likelihood of fighting is to ignore the fluid nature of the war, especially west of the Appalachians. Infantry escorting a wagon train might receive little warning before finding itself heavily engaged with Confederate raiders, as could happen anywhere from Arkansas to Virginia. The Confederate cavalry leader Nathan B. Forrest was able to raid as far north as the Ohio River, where the 8th U.S. Colored Artillery served in the garrison of Paducah, Kentucky, in the spring of 1864. That December, the Confederate Army of Tennessee camped outside Nashville for more than a week before being driven off, although Union troops had occupied the city for nearly three years. Black soldiers who had spent the previous year guarding the Nashville and Northwestern Railroad helped to repel this last Confederate offensive. Even as late as the last twelve months of fighting, Union troops far in the rear of advancing federal armies might receive a visit from a formidable body of Confederates at almost any time.[5]

While the Lincoln administration may have intended a defensive role for the new black regiments, Union generals in the field did not hesitate to put them into action. The best results came at first from operations for which the troops were already well adapted, such as the early riverine expeditions in South Carolina and Florida, where locally recruited black soldiers were operating on their home ground. New regiments tended to do less well when their first battle was an assault on enemy trenches: witness the disasters that befell the Louisiana Native Guards at Port Hudson in May 1863 and the 54th Massachusetts at Fort Wagner less than two months later. Still, the survivors of those misconceived attacks became seasoned campaigners. In February 1864, seven months after the reverse at Fort Wagner, the 54th Massachusetts helped to save the Union army at Olustee, Florida, while a new black regiment in the same fight, the 8th United States Colored Infantry (USCI), had trouble simply loading and firing its weapons. The 8th, in its turn, did well eight months later during the fall campaign in Virginia. So did the 73d USCI (the 1st Louisiana Native Guards of the Port Hudson assault) when it helped to capture Fort Blakely, near Mobile, in the last days of the war.[6]

Black soldiers clearly had little trouble carrying out assignments when they relied on knowledge they already possessed or when they received adequate training. Unfortunately for them, that training could be a matter of chance. It might depend on the preoccupations of a colonel commanding a new regiment who led his men into battle without having taught them to load and fire their weapons or on the racial beliefs of a general commanding a garrison, who might see black soldiers only as a source of manual labor and deny them time for drill. Although white

---

[4] *OR*, ser. 1, vol. 29, pt. 2, pp. 598, 608–09, 611, 614; vol. 31, pt. 3, pp. 548–49, 564. Winfield Scott, *Memoirs of Lieut.-General Scott* (New York: Sheldon, 1864), p. 627.

[5] For the attack on a Union wagon train at Poison Spring, Arkansas, see above, Chapter 8; for Forrest's attack on Paducah, Chapter 7; for black soldiers' part in the battle of Nashville, Chapter 9. Other Confederate raids on wagon trains are in Chapters 7, 9, and 11.

[6] On riverine operations in South Carolina and Florida, see above, Chapters 2 and 3; on Fort Wagner, Chapter 2; on Port Hudson, Chapter 4; on Olustee, Chapter 3; on the 8th USCI in Virginia, Chapters 11 and 12; on Mobile, Chapter 5.

soldiers and black civilian laborers also wielded axes, picks, and shovels, written complaints from commanders of black regiments show that high-ranking officers were apt to put their racial opinions into practice wherever Union troops served.[7]

An important factor in the training of new black regiments was the selection of officers. Most of these regiments were raised locally in the South. Their officers came from whatever white regiments happened to be on the spot. Most of these officers received their appointments long before an examining board met to judge their qualifications. The system could be effective, as when Col. Embury D. Osband picked men from his previous regiment to lead the 3d U.S. Colored Cavalry or when Brig. Gen. Edward A. Wild drew up his list of officers for the 35th USCI. At other times, the results could be scandalously bad. The 79th, 83d, 88th, 89th, and 90th USCIs—mustered in between August 1863 and February 1864— had to be disbanded on 28 July 1864, with the enlisted men reassigned and the officers mustered out. Officers of the disbanded regiments who thought they were competent to face an examining board could apply for reinstatement. Those who passed the examination joined a list of names to fill vacancies in the remaining black regiments within the Department of the Gulf. Competent or incompetent, nearly all of the mustered-out officers had served for between five and eleven months before the shabby state of their regiments became evident enough to move authorities to act.[8]

Prevalent racial attitudes in the nineteenth-century United States determined that white men would lead the new regiments. Since the prejudices of white Americans dictated that the country would begin the war with an all-white Army, when the time came two years later to enlarge the force by more than one hundred new black regiments the only veterans available to fill officers' posts were white men. Moreover, officers had to be literate, and generations of unequal education had made book learning rare among black people even in the North. Although War Department policy at this time excluded potential black officers from consideration, there were few alternatives, anyway; the immediate need for several thousand experienced men to lead the black regiments dictated that the successful applicants would come from the all-white army that already existed.[9]

In September 1864, with Sherman's army in Atlanta at last and prospects for the fall election looking up, Lincoln still maintained that his "sole avowed object" in prosecuting the war was "preserving our Union, and it is not true that it has since been, or will be, prossecuted . . . for any other object." That sole aim had driven the president to many shifts, emancipation among them. Emancipation launched black

---

[7]On lack of preparedness going into battle, see above, Chapters 3, 6, 11, and 12. On the disproportionate amount of fatigue duty allotted to black troops, see Chapters 2, 5, 7, and 12.

[8]*Official Army Register of the Volunteer Force of the United States*, 8 vols. (Washington, D.C.: Adjutant General's Office, 1868), 8: 261, 269–71.

[9]Dudley T. Cornish, *The Sable Arm: Negro Troops in the Union Army, 1861–1865* (New York: Longmans Green, 1956), p. 201; Joseph T. Glatthaar, *Forged in Battle: The Civil War Alliance of Black Soldiers and White Officers* (New York: Free Press, 1990), pp. 35–36; Ira Berlin et al., eds., *The Black Military Experience* (New York: Cambridge University Press, 1982), pp. 18–20, 303–12. Leon F. Litwack, *North of Slavery: The Negro in the Free States, 1790–1860* (Chicago: University of Chicago Press, 1961), pp. 113–17, 131–39, describes educational opportunities for blacks in the North.

Americans on the path to citizenship. The military service that some two hundred thousand of them rendered during the Civil War gave them and their descendants an undeniable claim on that citizenship, as Lincoln recognized. "Any different policy in regard to the colored man," he continued, "deprives us of his help, and this is more than we can bear." With black troops positioned all across the occupied South, from the outskirts of Richmond to the mouth of the Rio Grande:

> We can not spare the hundred and forty or fifty thousand now serving as soldiers, seamen, and laborers. This is not a question of sentiment or taste, but one of physical force. . . . Keep it and you can save the Union. Throw it away, and the Union goes with it. Nor is it possible for any Administration to retain the service of these people with the express or implied understanding that upon the first convenient occasion, they are to be re-inslaved. It *can* not be; and it *ought* not to be.[10]

Yet within twelve months of Lincoln drafting that letter, a new administration had set aside his judgment and begun to abet just such a process. This was not merely the result of Andrew Johnson's personal views; other matters occupied the nation's attention, as well. During the war, the national debt had soared past $2.5 billion in the dollars of that day, about half of the gross national product. In the third quarter of 1865, it increased by another $60 million. Restoring the economy to a peacetime footing and beginning to pay off that debt seemed to be the most pressing tasks at hand. In Johnson's first annual message to Congress that December, he praised "measures of retrenchment in each bureau and branch" of the War Department that had brought expenditure down by 93 percent, from more than $516 million the previous year to a projected total of less than $34 million. These measures, including reduction of the cavalry force, "exhibit[ed] a diligent economy worthy of commendation," Johnson said. Meanwhile, Southern night riders terrorized freedpeople and evaded Union infantry.[11]

In the end, the federal government was unwilling to pay the price necessary to sustain the social revolution that it had begun so hesitantly during the war. In the summer of 1865, it took steps to dismantle the military structure that it had painfully, although not always carefully, assembled. Among the first to go were the mounted regiments, necessary to maintain order among the South's disaffected white population but expensive to maintain. In 1866, most of the remaining Civil War volunteers turned over occupation duties to hastily recruited infantry regiments of the Regular Army. The year after the last of the veterans mustered out, the

---

[10]Roy P. Basler et al., eds., *Collected Works of Abraham Lincoln*, 9 vols. (New Brunswick, N.J.: Rutgers University Press, 1953–1956), 8: 1–2.

[11]"Annual Message of the President," 39th Cong., 1st sess., H. Ex. Doc. 1 (serial 1,244), p. 13; *New York Times*, 3 October 1865. For public opinion on the national debt, see *New York Times*, 28 October 1865; Walter N. K. Nugent, *The Money Question During Reconstruction* (New York: W. W. Norton, 1967), pp. 28–30; Robert T. Patterson, *Federal Debt-Management Policies, 1865–1879* (Durham, N.C.: Duke University Press, 1954), pp. 51–58; Irwin Unger, *The Greenback Era: A Social and Political History of American Finance, 1865–1879* (Princeton: Princeton University Press, 1964), p. 16.

number of lynchings in one state, Kentucky, nearly doubled, from eleven in 1867 to twenty-one in 1868.[12]

Programs to ensure the well-being of freedpeople also lost the forceful backing of public opinion. As the attention of federal officials shifted from the South to the West, so did that of many Quakers and New England intellectuals who had formed the backbone of the abolitionist movement. The object of these philanthropists was not economic expansion, but reform of the Office of Indian Affairs. Civil service reform and other causes also attracted the attention of former abolitionists. During 1869, while the states went through the process of ratifying the Fifteenth Amendment to the Constitution, intended to safeguard the voting rights of black men, reformers engaged in acrimonious debates about the voting rights of women. In 1870, the year the Fifteenth Amendment was adopted, the American Anti-Slavery Society announced its own dissolution. After the achievement of their main goal, the society's members may not have seen a clear road ahead. Indeed, regarding "the Negro's . . . position in the political arena," the editor of *The Nation* could write as early as July 1865, "everybody is heartily tired of discussing his condition and his rights."[13]

How did black soldiers themselves fare after they received their discharges? Most lived quietly as private citizens. By 1890, when the federal census counted 53,799 surviving black Civil War veterans, more than twelve thousand of them were still working as common laborers, with nearly twice that many employed in agriculture, either as hired hands or as farmers in their own right. More than seventeen hundred were teamsters, and a like number domestic servants. Skilled laborers included 1,250 carpenters, 596 masons, and 559 blacksmiths.[14]

The census also recorded 844 surviving black soldiers as clergymen. A comparative handful of veterans also went into politics at various levels. Of the men named in this book, the only officeholder was Prince Rivers, one of the noncommissioned officers who accepted the colors of the 1st South Carolina on New Year's Day 1863. The regimental surgeon described him as "black as the ace of spades and a man of remarkable executive ability." While in uniform, Rivers exerted his influence off duty to encourage the men of his regiment to save their pay. After the war, he was a delegate to South Carolina's constitutional convention and served three terms in the legislature. There, he was no more venal than other members, insisting that he and other members from the Piedmont sold their votes only to keep Low Country delegates from getting all the money. Rivers also was involved in

---

[12]George C. Wright, *Racial Violence in Kentucky, 1865–1940: Lynchings, Mob Rule, and "Legal Lynchings"* (Baton Rouge: Louisiana State University Press, 1990), pp. 307–08.

[13]Eric Foner, *Reconstruction: America's Unfinished Revolution, 1863–1877* (New York: Harper & Row, 1988), pp. 446–49; Francis P. Prucha, *The Great Father: The United States Government and the American Indians* (Lincoln: University of Nebraska Press, 1984), pp. 496–500; Michael L. Benedict, "Reform Republicans and the Retreat from Reconstruction," in *The Facts of Reconstruction: Essays in Honor of John Hope Franklin*, eds. Eric Anderson and Alfred A. Moss Jr. (Baton Rouge: Louisiana State University Press, 1991), pp. 53–77; *The Nation* quoted in David W. Blight, *Race and Reunion: The Civil War in American Memory* (Cambridge: Harvard University Press, 2001), p. 53.

[14]*Report of the Eleventh Census of the United States, 1890, Part 2*, 52d Cong., 1st sess., H. Misc. Doc. 340, pt. 19 (serial 3,019), pp. 807–09.

railroad construction and in 1871 helped to found Aiken County, where he served as a judge in later years.[15]

Somewhat more typical of black veterans was Harry Williams of the same regiment, who had led twenty-seven South Carolina slaves to freedom in November 1863. He moved to Savannah after the war and worked with his brother cleaning houses and offices. He "taught a night school one year," as he told a pension examiner in 1889, "and he was in politicks and stumped as a speaker in political campaigns and [was] interested in public affairs." His political activities may have been the reason he moved north after the 1876 presidential election heralded the end of Reconstruction. Williams worked as a waiter and boarding-house keeper in Philadelphia and a laundryman in New Jersey until his death in 1917.[16]

About three thousand veterans of the U.S. Colored Troops enlisted in the six new black regiments of the Regular Army in 1866 and 1867. While they represented only 2 percent of black Civil War veterans, they made up half the strength of the new regiments and furnished them with most of their noncommissioned officers. For the vast majority of these soldiers, a single enlistment in the regulars was enough. One such was Henry James, former sergeant major of the 3d USCI, who had led an expedition into the interior of Florida during the last days of the war. In October 1866, he joined the 9th U.S. Cavalry. On a scout in western Texas three years later, he contracted an infection of the urinary tract that necessitated his discharge for disability. He died at Carlisle, Pennsylvania, in 1895.[17]

That was longer than most black veterans survived the war, as the federal census of 1890 showed. Successful pension applicants tended to be among the longer lived, for as successive Congresses expanded eligibility, the ranks of pensioners grew. William A. Messley was one such applicant. As a first sergeant in the 62d USCI, Messley had taken command of a company at Palmetto Ranch, Texas, when the commissioned officers were out of action. After the war, rheumatism crippled him. He wrote to the Commissioner of Pensions in 1887: "Hundreds of Times have I wished for *death* to relieve me of this Everlasting disease." Yet he lived on for nearly thirty more years, dying at Chicago in 1916. Dick Brown, taken prisoner in September 1864 along with half of the 100th USCI, tried to continue blacksmithing after the war, but rheumatism prevented it. "I have not been able to make more than half a hand at my trade since my discharge," he attested in 1891. "Some days

---

[15]"War-Time Letters from Seth Rogers," p. 7 (quotation), typescript at U.S. Army Military History Institute, Carlisle, Pa.; *Report of the Eleventh Census, Part 2*, p. 807; Foner, *Reconstruction*, pp. 62, 570; Glatthaar, *Forged in Battle*, p. 246; Thomas Holt, *Black Over White: Negro Political Leadership in South Carolina During Reconstruction* (Urbana: University of Illinois Press, 1977), pp. 76–80; Joel Williamson, *After Slavery: The Negro in South Carolina During Reconstruction, 1861–1877* (Chapel Hill: University of North Carolina Press, 1965), pp. 27, 393–94.

[16]Pension File SC738833, Harry Williams, Civil War Pension Application Files (CWPAF), Record Group (RG) 15, Rcds of the Veterans Admin, National Archives (NA). Quotation from applicant's affidavit, 11 Jun 1889.

[17]Pension File C2747723, Henry James, CWPAF; William A. Dobak and Thomas D. Phillips, *The Black Regulars, 1866–1898* (Norman: University of Oklahoma Press, 2001), pp. 13, 24; Donald R. Shaffer, *After the Glory: The Struggles of Black Civil War Veterans* (Lawrence: University Press of Kansas, 2004), p. 39.

I can do a good day's work and then again I cannot work at all." Nevertheless, Brown lived to the age of 105, dying near Athens, Alabama, in 1926.[18]

Large questions about the effectiveness of the U.S. Colored Troops and their influence on the outcome of the Civil War require several answers. On the institutional level, the recruitment of black soldiers and the organization of their regiments developed during a period of about two years, from the first efforts of individual Union generals to the final opening of Kentucky for black enlistments in 1864. The process went as well as could be expected, given the means of communication that were available and the Lincoln administration's wary approach to the entire subject of emancipation during its first year and a half in office. Some abnormalities continued until the end of the conflict, with the adjutant general himself supervising black recruiting in the Mississippi Valley and communicating directly with the Secretary of War even after a separate bureau had been created in his own Washington office to oversee black troops throughout the country. Far more important to the soldiers themselves, Congress failed to state unequivocally that their pay would be equal to that of white troops rather than to that of black laborers, and the War Department, on the advice of its solicitor, failed to rectify the oversight. In the spring of 1864, Congress began a series of halting steps to correct the inequality, but it did not extend full pay to all black regiments until March 1865.[19]

Matters of that sort aside, from the standpoint of numbers alone, black soldiers constituted about 12 percent of the Union's men under arms by the end of the war. Besides representing a significant addition to federal armies, their presence in the Union ranks denied to the Confederacy the labor of some eighty thousand former slaves recruited in the South who might have been forced to work for the enemy if they had remained in bondage. Their enlistments also nearly equaled the number of soldiers drafted by the Union and thus helped to quell anticonscription protest and to ensure the continued functioning of Northern industry and agriculture.[20]

Black soldiers' service varied from headlong assaults on the Confederate lines around Richmond to garrison duty at river ports or along railroad lines that were important to Union strategy. As with white Union troops, their proficiency improved with training and experience. Maj. Gen. Godfrey Weitzel's ranking of the regiments under his command in 1865 demonstrates the importance to the troops' abilities of time spent both on the parade ground and in the field. Regimental officers were keenly aware that post commanders' orders detailing their men to fatigue duty interfered with military instruction, and they sought a remedy through official complaints. Often, these were successful. The absence of a contiguous front line and the constant threat of violence made it imperative that men knew at least how

---

[18]William A. Messley to Commissioner of Pensions, 18 Feb 1887, in Pension File SC908536, William A. Messley, and Deposition, Dick Brown, 19 Mar 1891, in Pension File SC569893, Dick Brown, both in CWPAF; *Report of the Eleventh Census, Part 2*, p. 801.

[19]The Militia Act of 17 July 1862, *OR*, ser. 3, 2: 280–82, established the ten-dollar wage for black laborers. The Enrollment Act of 3 Mar 1863 (3: 90), promised that new soldiers would be "on the same footing, in all respects, as volunteers for three years." See also Cornish, *Sable Arm*, pp. 190–95.

[20]Cornish, *Sable Arm*, p. 288; William W. Freehling, *The South vs. the South: How Anti-Confederate Southerners Shaped the Course of the Civil War* (New York: Oxford University Press, 2001), pp. 141–47.

to load and fire their weapons and to form line of battle. The determinants of performance were training and practical experience.[21]

The most enduring accomplishment of the Union's black soldiers was to assert their right to full citizenship and, by extension, that of all their kin. Lincoln recognized this claim as early as March 1864, when he urged the new governor of Louisiana to extend the franchise to "the very intelligent" among the freedmen, "and especially those who have fought gallantly in our ranks." This was merely a private suggestion, he told the governor, but hundreds of black Southerners reached the same conclusion independently during the months that followed. "We want two more boxes, beside the cartridge box," Sgt. Henry J. Maxwell told a convention at Nashville in August 1865, "the ballot box and the jury box." In the years to come, black veterans in other parts of the country would base petitions for full civic participation on their military service during the war. They had answered fully the question that Treasury Agent Edward Pierce had posed in the summer of 1863: "Will they fight for their freedom?" Another century and five more wars would pass before most Americans began to acknowledge the answer.[22]

---

[21]Maj Gen G. Weitzel to Col C. H. Whittlesey, 26 Nov 1865, Entry 2063, U.S. Forces on the Rio Grande, Letters Sent, pt. 2, Polyonymous Successions of Cmds, RG 393, U.S. Army Continental Cmds, NA. On fatigue duty, training, and discipline, see above, Chapters 2–5, 7, 9, 11, 12.

[22]Basler et al., *Collected Works of Abraham Lincoln*, 7: 243; *Colored Tennessean* (Nashville), 12 August 1865; Edward L. Pierce, "The Freedmen at Port Royal," *Atlantic Monthly* 12 (September 1863): 291–315 (quotation, p. 291). Petitions of black veterans and remarks of black orators are in Berlin et al., *Black Military Experience*, pp. 817–18, 822–23; Leon F. Litwack, *Been in the Storm So Long: The Aftermath of Slavery* (New York: Knopf, 1979), pp. 532–33, 537–38.

BIBLIOGRAPHICAL NOTE

Documentation for this book comes mostly from official sources written soon after the events they record. Personal letters add further detail to the narrative. Secondary sources corroborate and aid the interpretation of evidence furnished by contemporary sources. I have avoided memoirs and reminiscences, for time tends to dull the edge of memory. Although there is no guarantee that an official report was entirely truthful, the Articles of War forbade filing false musters or returns and offenders were to be cashiered, that is, "utterly disabled to have or hold any office or employment in the service of the United States." This tended to encourage a degree of honesty not always found in accounts rendered by old men who are not under oath.[1]

In selecting sources, I have tried to cite the most easily accessible version of a document that exists in both manuscript and published forms: for instance, when a manuscript report or letter housed at the National Archives also appears in *The War of the Rebellion: A Compilation of the Official Records of the Union and Confederate Armies*—published in 128 volumes between 1880 and 1901 and widely available in two paper reprints, a CD-ROM, and an online edition—I have cited the published version (commonly abbreviated *OR*, for *Official Records*). The Adjutant General's Office in the War Department was responsible for compiling the *Official Records*, and most of the editorial work was done by Army officers detailed from their regiments. Compilers took reports and correspondence from War Department files to document military operations (Series 1 of the *Official Records*, fifty-three volumes bound as 111); prisoners of war and related matters (Series 2, eight volumes); Union recruitment, including the draft (Series 3, five volumes); and records of the Confederate government (Series 4, four volumes). Some of the documents were returned to their original files; others were not. This latter class constitutes the ninety-one shelf feet of the National Archives' "Civil War Records Retained by the War Records Office" (Record Group 94, Records of the Adjutant General's Office, Entries 729–33). The idea of "objective" or "scientific" history written by professionals was in its infancy during the last two decades of the nineteenth century, confined for the most part to a few graduate schools, and the editors of the *Official Records* therefore felt free to alter punctuation and paragraphing, practices which compilers of modern

---

[1]*Revised United States Army Regulations of 1861* (Washington, D.C.: Government Printing Office, 1863), p. 488.

documentary collections avoid. Readers planning to consult the *Official Records* extensively should read the Adjutant General's own history of the editorial project in the General Index volume of the series, as well as Dallas D. Irvine's essay, "The Genesis of the *Official Records*," *Mississippi Valley Historical Review* 24 (1937): 221–29.

The compilers of the *Official Records* did not return the documents they used to the War Department files from which they were taken, but kept them separate. During the 1940s, the National Archives received old War Department documents. Archivists classified the manuscripts that formed the basis of most of the *Official Records* as Record Group 94, Records of the Adjutant General's Office, Entry 729, Union Battle Reports.

Other manuscript documents consulted while writing this book were:

National Archives, College Park, Maryland
Record Group 217, Records of Accounting Officers of the Department of the
  Treasury
    Entry 732, Settled Case Files for Claims Approved by the Southern Claims
      Commission

National Archives, Washington, D.C.

Manuscripts
Record Group 15, Records of the Veterans Administration
    Civil War Pension Application Files
Record Group 94, Records of the Adjutant General's Office
    Entry 44, Orders and Circulars
    Entry 57, Muster Rolls of Volunteer Organizations, Civil War
    Entry 57C, U.S. Colored Troops Regimental Papers
    Entry 159BB, Generals' Papers and Books, Lorenzo Thomas
    Entry 159DD, Generals' Papers and Books, Daniel Ullmann
    Entry 159GG, Generals' Papers and Books, David Hunter
    Entry 352, Colored Troops Division, Letters Sent
    Entry 360, Colored Troops Division, Letters Received
    Entry 363, Letters Received by Adjutant General Lorenzo Thomas
    Entry 519, Carded Records, Volunteer Organizations, Civil War
    Entry 729, Union Battle Reports
      Regimental Books, Civil War Volunteers
Record Group 105, Records of the Bureau of Refugees, Freedmen, and
  Abandoned Lands
    Entry 642, Georgia: Reports of Murders and Outrages
Record Group 108, Records of the Headquarters of the Army
    Entry 35, Letters Sent and Received by General Grant
Record Group 153, Records of the Judge Advocate General's Office
    Entry 15, General Court Martial Case Files
Record Group 393, Records of U.S. Army Continental Commands, 1821–1920
    Part 1, Geographical Divisions and Departments

Entry 269, Department of Arkansas, Letters Received

Entry 323, Department of Arkansas, Monthly Retained Copies of Inspection Reports

Entry 926, Department of the Cumberland, Letters Received

Entry 1141, Department of the Cumberland, Organization of Colored Troops, Letters Sent

Entry 1149, Department of the Cumberland, Records of Capt. R. D. Mussey

Entry 1708, Department of Georgia, Letters Sent

Entry 1756, Department of the Gulf, Letters Received, 1862–1865 and 1866–1867

Entry 1757, Department of the Gulf, Letters Received, 1865–1866

Entry 1767, Department of the Gulf, Special Orders

Entry 2269, Department and District of Key West, Letters Received

Entry 2433, Department of Mississippi, Letters Received

Entry 3290, Department of North Carolina and Army of the Ohio, Letters Received

Entry 4109, Department of the South, Letters Received

Entry 4112, Department of the South, Letters Received Relating to Freedmen

Entry 4495, Division of the Southwest and Department of the Gulf, Letters Received

Entry 4720, Department of Tennessee, Letters Received

Entry 4790, Department of Texas, Letters and Miscellaneous Reports Received

Entry 5046, Department of Virginia and Army of the James, Letters Sent

Entry 5063, Department of Virginia and Army of the James, Letters Received

Entry 5382, Department of Washington, Letters Received

Entry 5515, Military Division of West Mississippi, Letters Received

Part 2, Polyonymous Successions of Commands

Entry 86, 1st Division, II Corps, Letters Sent

Entry 345, X Corps, Letters Sent

Entry 359, X Corps, Special Orders

Entry 376, 1st Division, X Corps, Letters Sent

Entry 512, XXV Corps, Letters Sent

Entry 517, XXV Corps, Letters Received

Entry 518, XXV Corps, Miscellaneous Letters Received

Entry 520, XXV Corps, General Orders

Entry 522, XXV Corps, Special Orders

Entry 525, XXV Corps, Letters Received Relating to Troop Movements

Entry 533, XXV Army Corps, Letters, Orders, and Reports Received by 1st–3d Divisions, December 1864–January 1866

Entry 539, XXV Corps, Letters and Reports Received by the Inspector General

Entry 549, 1st Division, XXV Corps, Letters Sent

Entry 646, Military District of Washington, Letters Received
Entry 649, Military District of Washington, Special Orders
Entry 1659, 3d Division, XVIII Corps, Letters Sent
Entry 1860, Defenses of New Orleans, Letters Received
Entry 1976, U.S. Forces at Morganza, Letters Received
Entry 2014, District of Northeast Louisiana, Letters Sent
Entry 2063, U.S. Forces on the Rio Grande, Letters Sent
Entry 2073, U.S. Forces on the Rio Grande, Letters Received
Entry 2254, South Carolina Expeditionary Corps, Letters Received
Entry 2844, District of Memphis, Special Orders, January 1863–September
  1865
Entry 4357, 3d Division, V Corps, Orders and Circulars
Entry 5122, 4th Division, IX Corps, Letters Sent
Entry 5178, 2d Division, X Corps, Letters Sent
Entry 5195, 2d Division, X Corps, Special Orders
Entry 6300, XVII Corps, Letters, Reports, and Orders Received
Entry 6946, 2d Brigade, 3d Division, XXIV Corps, General Orders
Entry 6977, 3d Division, XXIV Corps, Letters Sent
Entry 7026, 3d Brigade, 3d Division, XXIV Corps, General Orders
Entry 7035, 3d Division, X Corps, Letters Sent
Part 4, Military Installations
Entry 25, Post of Alexandria, Letters Sent
Entry 402, Post of Donaldsonville, Letters Sent

Microfilm Publications
M594, Compiled Records Showing Service of Military Units in Volunteer Union
  Organizations
M617, Returns from U.S. Military Posts, 1820–1916
M619, Letters Received by the Office of the Adjutant General, 1861–1870
M665, Returns from Regular Army Infantry Regiments
M711, Register of Letters Received, Adjutant General's Office
M744, Returns from Regular Army Cavalry Regiments
M752, Registers and Letters Received by the Commissioner of the Bureau of
  Refugees, Freedmen, and Abandoned Lands (BRFAL)
M798, Records of the Assistant Commissioner for the State of Georgia, BRFAL
M803, Records of the Education Division of the BRFAL
M826, Records of the Assistant Commissioner for the State of Mississippi,
  BRFAL
M869, Records of the Assistant Commissioner for the State of South Carolina,
  BRFAL
M979, Records of the Assistant Commissioner for the State of Arkansas,
  BRFAL
M999, Records of the Assistant Commissioner for the State of Tennessee,
  BRFAL
M1027, Records of the Assistant Commissioner for the State of Louisiana,
  BRFAL

M1619, Headquarters of the Army, Letters Sent
M1635, Headquarters of the Army, Letters Received
M1818, Compiled Military Service Records of Volunteer Union Soldiers Who Served in the U.S. Colored Troops: Artillery Organizations
M1820, Compiled Military Service Records of Volunteer Union Soldiers Who Served in the U.S. Colored troops: 2d through 7th United States Colored Infantries (USCIs)
M1907, Records of the Field Offices for the State of Mississippi, BRFAL
M1909, Records of the Field Offices for the State of North Carolina, BRFAL
T142, Selected Records of the Tennessee Field Office of the BRFAL
T289, Organization Index to Pension Files of Veterans Who Served Between 1861 and 1900

Private diaries and letters quoted in this book are housed at the following institutions:

American Antiquarian Society
    Edward W. Bacon Papers
    James H. Rickard Letters
Boston Public Library
    James H. Wickes Papers
Connecticut Historical Society
    Henry Harrison Brown Papers
Dartmouth College
    Elias C. Mather Papers
    Andrew H. Young Papers
Duke University
    Frederick and Sarah M. Cutler Papers
    Edward W. Kinsley Papers
    James O. Moore Papers
    Alonzo Reed Papers
Emory University
    Henry M. Crydenwise Letters
    William M. Parkinson Letters
Harvard University, Schlesinger Library
    James C. Beecher Papers
Huntington Library
    George W. Buswell Journals
Indiana Historical Society
    Caleb Mills Papers
Library of Congress
    Matthew C. Brown and John C. Brown Papers
    Christian A. Fleetwood Papers
    Samuel M. Quincy Papers
Massachusetts Historical Society
    Warren Goodale Papers

Michigan State University
    Wilbur Nelson Diary typescript
Minnesota Historical Society
    Christopher C. Andrews Papers
    James M. Bowler Papers
    Benjamin Densmore Papers
New Hampshire Historical Society
    Duncan-Jones Family Papers
New-York Historical Society
    Daniel Ullmann Papers
Oberlin College
    Eliott F. Grabill Papers
    Giles W. Shurtleff Papers
Ohio Historical Society
    Jacob Bruner Papers
    Evans Family Papers
    Albert Rogall Papers typescript
Poughkeepsie Public Library
    Robert N. Verplanck Letters typescript
Rutgers University
    Aaron K. Peckham Letters
Smith College
    James S. Rogers Letters typescript
State Historical Society of Iowa, Iowa City
    John L. Mathews Papers
U.S. Army Center of Military History, Historians files
    Delavan Bates Letters
    Joseph M. Califf Diary typescript
    Henry C. Merriam Diary typescript
U.S. Army Military History Institute
    John W. M. Appleton Diary photocopy
    Solon A. Carter Papers
    John Habberton Papers
    "War-Time Letters from Seth Rogers" typescript
    Joseph J. Scroggs Diary typescript
    Edward A. Wild Papers
University of Arkansas
    Milton P. Chambers Papers
    Minos Miller Papers
University of Iowa
    John L. Mathews Letters
University of Maryland
    Freedmen and Southern Society Project, indexes and photocopied material
University of Michigan
    William Elgin Journal—Clements Library
    Morris S. Hall Papers—Bentley Library

Harrison Soule Papers—Bentley Library
John Pearson Letters—Clements Library
University of North Carolina
Jonathan L. Whitaker Papers—Southern Historical Collection
Wabash College
Henry Campbell Journal
Wisconsin Historical Society
Thomas S. Johnson Papers
Yale University, Sterling Library
Walter A. Chapman Papers
Charles G. G. Merrill Papers typescript
Lewis L. Weld Papers

Nineteenth-century American newspapers were more overtly political than the relatively bland sheets produced by later generations of journalists. James Gordon Bennett's Democratic *New York Herald*, for instance, took a view of black Americans noticeably different from that of Horace Greeley's Republican *New York Tribune*. Other newspapers and periodicals quoted are:

Anglo-African (New York)
Army and Navy Journal (New York)
Atlantic Monthly (Boston)
Baltimore Sun
Christian Recorder (Philadelphia)
Colored Tennessean (Nashville)
Congressional Globe (Washington, D.C.)
Constitutional Union (Washington, D.C.)
Daily National Intelligencer (Washington, D.C.)
Evening Star (Washington, D.C.)
Janesville [Wis.] *Daily Gazette*
Kansas Daily Tribune (Lawrence)
Leavenworth [Kans.] *Conservative*
National Republican (Washington, D.C.)
National Tribune (Washington, D.C.)
New York Herald
New York Times
New York Tribune
Philadelphia Evening Bulletin
Philadelphia Inquirer

Since the earliest sessions of Congress, committees of both houses have collected testimony and documents and published them in the thousands of volumes that constitute the Congressional Serial Set. Documents cited in this work are:

Alldredge, J. Haden. "A History of Navigation on the Tennessee River System." 75th Cong., 1st sess., H. Doc. 254 (serial 10,119).

"Annual Message of the President." 39th Cong., 1st sess., H. Ex. Doc. 1 (serial 1,244).

"Condition and Treatment of Colored Refugees." 38th Cong., 2d sess., S. Ex. Doc. 28 (serial 1,209).

"Condition of Affairs in Texas." 39th Cong., 2d sess. H. Ex. Doc. 61 (serial 1,292).

"Diary and Correspondence of Salmon P. Chase." *Annual Report of the American Historical Association for . . . 1902.* 57th Cong., 2d sess., H. Doc. 461, pt. 2 (serial 4,543).

"Fort Pillow Massacre." 38th Cong., 1st sess., H. Rpt. 65 (serial 1,206).

Journal of the Congress of the Confederate States of America, 1861–1865. 58th Cong., 2d sess., S. Doc. 234 (7 vols., serials 4,610–4,616).

"Memphis Riots and Massacres." 39th Cong., 1st sess, H. Rpt. 101 (serial 1,274).

"Mexico." 39th Cong., 2d sess., H. Ex. Doc. 17 (serial 1,288).

"Occupation of Mexican Territory." 39th Cong., 2d sess., H. Ex. Doc. 8 (serial 1,287).

"Present Condition of Mexico." 39th Cong., 2d sess., H. Ex. Doc. 76 (serial 1,292).

Report of the Eleventh Census of the United States, 1890, Part 2. 52d Cong., 1st sess., H. Misc. Doc. 340, pt. 19 (serial 3,019).

Report of the Secretary of War for 1863. 38th Cong., 1st sess., H. Ex. Doc. 1, vol. 5 (serial 1,184).

Report of the Secretary of War for 1864. 38th Cong., 2d sess., H. Ex. Doc. 83 (serial 1,230).

Report of the Secretary of War for 1865. 38th Cong., 1st sess., H. Ex. Doc. 1, vol. 3, pt. 1 (serial 1,249).

Among the scholarly works cited in this book, three in particular stand out: Dudley T. Cornish's *The Sable Arm*; Joseph T. Glatthaar's *Forged in Battle*; and the series of documentary collections produced by the Freedmen and Southern Society Project at the University of Maryland, beginning in 1982, which runs to five volumes so far.[2]

Cornish's book was the first scholarly work devoted entirely to the U.S. Colored Troops. While the book has attained the status of a classic, Cornish's research at the National Archives was apparently limited to the papers of Adjutant General Lorenzo Thomas, correspondence of the Colored Troops Bureau, and the regimental books of the 79th and 82d U.S. Colored Infantries (formerly the 1st and 2d Kansas Colored Infantries). Only some 10 percent of Cornish's citations are of newspapers and unpublished material not available at the Kansas State Historical Society, but that is to be expected in a work that the author produced while teaching at a state teacher's college during the pre-Sputnik era, before travel grants were widely available and when passenger jets and interstate highways had not yet made visits to the National Archives almost routine for historians.

---

[2] Full bibliographical citations appear below.

Forged in Battle, the next comprehensive treatment of the U.S. Colored Troops, appeared thirty-three years after Cornish's book. Not surprisingly, Glatthaar was able to consult manuscripts at forty-four repositories in twenty-four states, besides the Library of Congress and the National Archives and two private collections, and his book reflects the change between his generation and Cornish's. Both authors are leading figures among the historians who, as Brooks D. Simpson put it, "have concentrated on the consequences of military service for blacks and for the whites who commanded them." Cornish wrote before, and Glatthaar during, the increasing amount of attention historians have paid in recent decades to irregular tactics in the Civil War, a literature summarized by Daniel E. Sutherland in "Sideshow No Longer: A Historiographical Review of the Civil War." *Freedom by the Sword*, on the other hand, attempts to place black soldiers in the larger operational context of the Civil War and to take account of the irregular nature of the conflict in parts of the country where many black regiments served, at some distance from the Union's main armies.[3]

The output of the Freedmen and Southern Society Project's documentary history of emancipation at the time of writing includes four volumes under the general editorship of Ira Berlin: *The Destruction of Slavery*; two about *The Wartime Genesis of Free Labor*, one dealing with the Upper South and one with the Lower South; and a fourth, *The Black Military Experience*. Most recently, the first volume about the postwar period has appeared, under the general editorship of Steven Hahn: *Land and Labor, 1865*. Documents found at the National Archives by a team of researchers constitute the bulk of these volumes. Each begins with a long, unsigned essay on the subject of the volume. Shorter essays introduce each chapter throughout the book.

Published works cited in this book include:

Books

Alexander, Roberta S. *North Carolina Faces the Freedman: Race Relations During Presidential Reconstruction, 1865–67*. Durham, N.C.: Duke University Press, 1985.

Ambrose, Stephen E., ed. *A Wisconsin Boy in Dixie: The Selected Letters of John K. Newton*. Madison: Wisconsin State Historical Society, 1961.

Anderson, Mary A., ed. *The Civil War Diary of Allen Morgan Geer, Twentieth Regiment, Illinois Volunteers*. Denver: R. C. Appleman, 1977.

Annual Report of the Adjutant General of the State of Maine. Augusta: Stevens and Sayward, 1863.

Appendix D of the Report of the Adjutant General of the State of Maine for the Years 1864 and 1865. Augusta: Stevens and Sayward, 1866.

Arreola, Daniel D. *Tejano South Texas: A Mexican American Cultural Province*. Austin: University of Texas Press, 2002.

Ash, Stephen V. *Firebrand of Liberty: The Story of Two Black Regiments That Changed the Course of the Civil War*. New York: W. W. Norton, 2008.

---

[3] Brooks D. Simpson, "Quandaries of Command: Ulysses S. Grant and Black Soldiers," in *Union and Emancipation: Essays on Politics and Race in the Civil War Era*, eds. David W. Blight and Brooks D. Simpson (Kent, Ohio: Kent State University Press, 1997), pp. 123–49 (quotation, p. 123); Daniel E. Sutherland, "Sideshow No Longer: A Historiographical Review of the Guerrilla War," *Civil War History* 46 (2000): 5–23.

———. *Middle Tennessee Society Transformed, 1860–1870: War and Peace in the Upper South*. Baton Rouge: Louisiana State University Press, 1988.

———. *When the Yankees Came: Conflict and Chaos in the Occupied South, 1861–1865*. Chapel Hill: University of North Carolina Press, 1995.

Bailey, Anne J. *The Chessboard of War: Sherman and Hood in the Autumn Campaigns of 1864*. Lincoln: University of Nebraska Press, 2000.

Barrett, John G. *The Civil War in North Carolina*. Chapel Hill: University of North Carolina Press, 1963.

Basler, Roy P., et al., eds. *Collected Works of Abraham Lincoln*, 9 vols. New Brunswick, N.J.: Rutgers University Press, 1953–1956.

Bauer, K. Jack. *The Mexican War, 1846–1848*. New York: Macmillan, 1974.

Bentley, George R. *A History of the Freedmen's Bureau*. New York: Octagon Books, 1974 [1944].

Bergeron, Arthur W., Jr. *Confederate Mobile*. Jackson: University Press of Mississippi, 1991.

Berlin, Ira. *Generations of Captivity: A History of African-American Slaves*. Cambridge: Harvard University Press, 2003.

———, et al. *Slaves No More: Three Essays on Emancipation and the Civil War*. New York: Cambridge University Press, 1992.

———, et al., eds. *The Black Military Experience*. New York: Cambridge University Press, 1982.

———, et al., eds. *The Destruction of Slavery*. New York: Cambridge University Press, 1985.

———, et al., eds. *The Wartime Genesis of Free Labor: The Lower South*. New York: Cambridge University Press, 1990.

———, et al., eds. *The Wartime Genesis of Free Labor: The Upper South*. New York: Cambridge University Press, 1993.

Bernstein, Iver. *The New York City Draft Riots: Their Significance for American Society and Politics in the Age of the Civil War*. New York: Oxford University Press, 1990.

Black, Robert C., III. *The Railroads of the Confederacy*. Chapel Hill: University of North Carolina Press, 1998 [1952].

Blackett, R. J. M., ed. *Thomas Morris Chester, Black Civil War Correspondent: His Dispatches from the Virginia Front*. Baton Rouge: Louisiana State University Press, 1989.

Blight, David W. *Race and Reunion: The Civil War in American Memory*. Cambridge: Harvard University Press, 2001.

Borchert, James. *Alley Life in Washington: Family, Community, Religion, and Folklore in the City, 1850–1970*. Urbana: University of Illinois Press, 1980.

Bowen, David W. *Andrew Johnson and the Negro*. Knoxville: University of Tennessee Press, 1989.

Bradley, Mark L. *Bluecoats and Tarheels: Soldiers and Civilians in Reconstruction North Carolina*. Lexington: University Press of Kentucky, 2009.

———. *This Astounding Close: The Road to Bennett Place*. Chapel Hill: University of North Carolina Press, 2000.

Brinkman, Harold D., ed. *Dear Companion: The Civil War Letters of Silas I. Shearer*. Ames, Iowa: Sigler Printing, 1996.

Brown, Canter, Jr. *Florida's Peace River Frontier*. Orlando: University of Central Florida Press, 1991.

Brown, Malcolm. *The Imperial War Museum Book of the Western Front*. London: Pan Books, 2001.

Brown, William W. *The Negro in the American Rebellion: His Heroism and His Fidelity*. Boston: Lee and Shepard, 1867.

Browning, Robert M., Jr. *From Cape Charles to Cape Fear: The North Atlantic Blockading Squadron During the Civil War*. Tuscaloosa: University of Alabama Press, 1993.

———. *Success Is All That Was Expected: The South Atlantic Blockading Squadron During the Civil War*. Washington, D.C.: Brassey's, 2002.

Bulloch, William. *The History of Bacteriology*. London: Oxford University Press, 1960 [1938].

Burkhardt, George S. *Confederate Rage, Yankee Wrath: No Quarter in the Civil War*. Carbondale: Southern Illinois University Press, 2007.

Burlingame, Michael, and John R. T. Ettlinger, eds. *Inside Lincoln's White House: The Complete Civil War Diary of John Hay*. Carbondale and Edwardsville: Southern Illinois University Press, 1997.

Burton, William L. *Melting Pot Soldiers: The Union's Ethnic Regiments*. New York: Fordham University Press, 1998.

Butler, Benjamin F. *Autobiography and Personal Reminiscences of Major-General Benj. F. Butler*. Boston: A. M. Thayer, 1892.

———. *Private and Official Correspondence of Gen. Benjamin F. Butler During the Period of the Civil War*, 5 vols. [Norwood, Mass.: Plimpton Press], 1917.

Carter, Dan T. *When the War Was Over: The Failure of Self-Reconstruction in the South*. Baton Rouge: Louisiana State University Press, 1985.

Castel, Albert. *A Frontier State at War: Kansas, 1861–1865*. Ithaca, N.Y.: Cornell University Press, 1958.

Cecelski, David S. *The Waterman's Song: Slavery and Freedom in Maritime North Carolina*. Chapel Hill: University of North Carolina Press, 2001.

Chronicle of the Union League of Philadelphia, 1862–1902. Philadelphia: Union League, 1902.

Cimbala, Paul A. *Under the Guardianship of the Nation: The Freedmen's Bureau and the Reconstruction of Georgia, 1865–1870*. Athens: University of Georgia Press, 1997.

Cimprich, John. *Fort Pillow, A Civil War Massacre, and Public Memory*. Baton Rouge: Louisiana State University Press, 2005.

Clarke, Jeffrey J., and Robert R. Smith. *Riviera to the Rhine*, U.S. Army in World War II. Washington, D.C.: U.S. Army Center of Military History, 1993.

Click, Patricia C. *Time Full of Trouble: The Roanoke Island Freedmen's Colony, 1862–1867*. Chapel Hill: University of North Carolina Press, 2001.

Cobb, James C. *The Most Southern Place on Earth: The Mississippi Delta and the Roots of Regional Identity*. New York: Oxford University Press, 1992.

Coffman, Edward M. *The Old Army: A Portrait of the American Army in Peacetime, 1784–1898*. New York: Oxford University Press, 1986.

Connelly, Thomas E. *Autumn of Glory: The Army of Tennessee, 1862–1865*. Baton Rouge: Louisiana State University Press, 1971.

Cornish, Dudley T. *The Sable Arm: Negro Troops in the Union Army, 1861–1865*. New York: Longmans, Green, 1956.

Cowden, Robert. *A Brief Sketch of the Organization and Services of the Fifty-ninth Regiment of United States Colored Infantry*. Freeport, N.Y.: Books for Libraries Press, 1971 [1883].

Cox, Jacob D. *The March to the Sea: Franklin and Nashville*. New York: Charles Scribner's Sons, 1882.

Cozzens, Peter. *The Shipwreck of Their Hopes: The Battles for Chattanooga*. Urbana: University of Illinois Press, 1994.

Crouch, Barry. *The Dance of Freedom: Texas African Americans During Reconstruction*. Austin: University of Texas Press, 2007.

Cullum, George W. *Biographical Register of the Officers and Graduates of the U.S. Military Academy*, 3d ed., 3 vols. Boston: Houghton Mifflin, 1891.

Currie, James T. *Enclave: Vicksburg and Her Plantations*. Jackson: University Press of Mississippi, 1980.

Davis, George B., et al., eds. *The Official Military Atlas of the Civil War*. New York: Barnes & Noble, 2003 [1891–1895].

Davis, Stephen. *Atlanta Will Fall: Sherman, Joe Johnston, and the Yankee Heavy Battalions*. Wilmington, Del.: Scholarly Resources, 2001.

De Leon, Arnoldo. *They Called Them Greasers: Anglo Attitudes Toward Mexicans in Texas, 1821–1900*. Austin: University of Texas Press, 1983.

DeForest, John W. *A Union Officer in the Reconstruction*. New Haven: Yale University Press, 1948.

———. *A Volunteer's Adventures: A Union Captain's Record of the Civil War*. New Haven: Yale University Press, 1946.

Dew, Charles B. *Apostles of Disunion: Southern Secession Commissioners and the Causes of the Civil War*. Charlottesville: University Press of Virginia, 2001.

Dobak, William A. *Fort Riley and Its Neighbors: Military Money and Economic Growth, 1853–1895*. Norman: University of Oklahoma Press, 1998.

———, and Thomas D. Phillips. *The Black Regulars, 1866–1898*. Norman: University of Oklahoma Press, 2001.

Dougan, Michael B. *Confederate Arkansas: The People and Policies of a Frontier State in Wartime*. University: University of Alabama Press, 1976.

Du Bois, W. E. B. *The Philadelphia Negro: A Social Study*. New York: Schocken Books, 1967 [1899].

Duncan, Russell. *Where Death and Glory Meet: Colonel Robert Gould Shaw and the 54th Massachusetts Infantry*. Athens: University of Georgia Press, 1999.

Dupree, Stephen A. *Planting the Union Flag in Texas: The Campaigns of Major General Nathaniel P. Banks in the West*. College Station: Texas A&M University Press, 2008.

Durrill, Wayne K. *War of Another Kind: A Southern Community in the Great Rebellion*. New York: Oxford University Press, 1990.

Dusinberre, William. *Civil War Issues in Philadelphia, 1856–1865*. Philadelphia: University of Pennsylvania Press, 1965.

————. *Them Dark Days: Slavery in the American Rice Swamps*. New York: Oxford University Press, 1996.

Dyer, Frederick H. *A Compendium of the War of the Rebellion*. New York: Thomas Yoseloff, 1959 [1908].

Edwards, William B. *Civil War Guns: The Complete Story of Federal and Confederate Small Arms*. Gettysburg, Pa.: Thomas Publications, 1997.

Einolf, Christopher J. *George Thomas: Virginian for the Union*. Norman: University of Oklahoma Press, 2001.

Emilio, Luis F. *A Brave Black Regiment: History of the Fifty-fourth Regiment of Massachusetts Volunteer Infantry*. New York: Arno Press, 1969 [1894].

Engs, Robert F. *Freedom's First Generation: Black Hampton, Virginia, 1861–1890*. Philadelphia: University of Pennsylvania Press, 1979.

Etcheson, Nicole. *Bleeding Kansas: Contested Liberty in the Civil War Era*. Lawrence: University Press of Kansas, 2004.

Farrow, Edward S. *Farrow's Military Encyclopedia*, 3 vols. New York: privately printed, 1885.

Fleming, Walter L. *Civil War and Reconstruction in Alabama*. Gloucester, Mass.: Peter Smith, 1949 [1905].

Foner, Eric. *Nothing But Freedom: Emancipation and Its Legacy*. Baton Rouge: Louisiana State University Press, 1981.

————. *Reconstruction: America's Unfinished Revolution, 1863–1877*. New York: Harper & Row, 1988.

Ford, Worthington C., ed. *A Cycle of Adams Letters*, 2 vols. Boston: Houghton Mifflin, 1920.

Franklin, John H. *Reconstruction After the Civil War*, 2d ed. Chicago: University of Chicago Press, 1993.

Frazer, Robert W. *Forts of the West: Military Forts and Presidios, and Posts Commonly Called Forts, West of the Mississippi River to 1898*. Norman: University of Oklahoma Press, 1965.

Fredrickson, George M. *The Black Image in the White Mind: The Debate on Afro-American Character and Destiny, 1817–1914*. Middletown, Conn.: Wesleyan University Press, 1971.

Freehling, William W. *The South vs. the South: How Anti-Confederate Southerners Shaped the Course of the Civil War*. New York: Oxford University Press, 2001.

Freeman, Douglas S. *R. E. Lee: A Biography*, 4 vols. New York: Charles Scribner's Sons, 1934–1935.

French, David. *Military Identities: The Regimental System, the British Army, and the British People, c. 1870–2000*. New York: Oxford University Press, 2005.

Gallman, J. Matthew. *Mastering Wartime: A Social History of Philadelphia During the Civil War*. New York: Cambridge University Press, 1990.

Geary, James W. *We Need Men: The Union Draft in the Civil War*. DeKalb: Northern Illinois University Press, 1991.

Genovese, Eugene D. *Roll, Jordan, Roll: The World the Slaves Made*. New York: Pantheon Books, 1974.

Gerteis, Louis S. *From Contraband to Freedman: Federal Policy Toward Southern Blacks, 1861–1865*. Westport, Conn.: Greenwood Press, 1973.

Gibbs, C[arroll] R. *Black, Copper, and Bright: The District of Columbia's Black Civil War Regiment*. Silver Spring, Md.: Three Dimensional Publishing, 2002.

Glatthaar, Joseph T. *Forged in Battle: The Civil War Alliance of Black Soldiers and White Officers*. New York: Free Press, 1990.

Graf, Leroy P., et al., eds. *The Papers of Andrew Johnson*, 16 vols. Knoxville: University of Tennessee Press, 1967–2000.

Grant, Ulysses S. *Personal Memoirs of U. S. Grant*, 2 vols. New York: Charles L. Webster, 1886.

Graves, Robert. *Good-Bye to All That: An Autobiography*. London: Jonathan Cape, 1929.

Gray, John C., and John C. Ropes. *War Letters, 1862–1865*. Boston: Houghton Mifflin, 1927.

Gray, Lewis C. *History of Agriculture in the Southern United States to 1860*. Gloucester, Mass.: Peter Smith, 1958 [1932].

Green, Constance M. *The Secret City: A History of Race Relations in the Nation's Capital*. Princeton: Princeton University Press, 1967.

Greene, A. Wilson. *Civil War Petersburg: Confederate City in the Crucible of War*. Charlottesville: University of Virginia Press, 2006.

Griffith, Paddy. *Battle Tactics of the Civil War*. New Haven: Yale University Press, 1987.

Grimsley, Mark. *And Keep Moving On: The Virginia Campaign, May–June 1864*. Lincoln: University of Nebraska Press, 2002.

———. *The Hard Hand of War: Union Military Policy Toward Southern Civilians, 1861–1865*. New York: Cambridge University Press, 1995.

Guelzo, Allen C. *Lincoln's Emancipation Proclamation: The End of Slavery in America*. New York: Simon and Schuster, 2004.

Hahn, Steven. *A Nation Under Our Feet: Black Political Struggles in the Rural South from Slavery to the Great Migration*. Cambridge: Harvard University Press, 2003.

———, et al., eds. *Land and Labor, 1865*. Chapel Hill: University of North Carolina Press, 2008.

Haller, John S. *American Medicine in Transition, 1840–1910*. Urbana: University of Illinois Press, 1981.

Harrington, Fred H. *Fighting Politician: Major General N. P. Banks*. Philadelphia: University of Pennsylvania Press, 1948.

Harris, William C. *Presidential Reconstruction in Mississippi*. Baton Rouge: Louisiana State University Press, 1967.

Hearn, Chester G. *Admiral David Dixon Porter*. Annapolis: Naval Institute Press, 1996.

———. *When the Devil Came Down to Dixie: Ben Butler in New Orleans*. Baton Rouge: Louisiana State University Press, 1997.

Heitman, Francis B. *Historical Register and Dictionary of the United States Army*, 2 vols. Washington, D.C.: Government Printing Office, 1903.

Heuman, Gad. *"The Killing Time": The Morant Bay Rebellion in Jamaica*. Knoxville: University of Tennessee Press, 1994.

Hewett, Janet B., et al., eds. *Supplement to the Official Records on the Union and Confederate Armies*, 93 vols. Wilmington, N.C.: Broadfoot Publishing, 1994–1998.

Hewitt, Lawrence L. *Port Hudson, Confederate Bastion of the Mississippi*. Baton Rouge: Louisiana State University Press, 1987.

Higginson, Thomas W. *Army Life in a Black Regiment*. East Lansing: Michigan State University Press, 1960 [1870].

Hilliard, Sam B. *Atlas of Antebellum Southern Agriculture*. Baton Rouge: Louisiana State University Press, 1984.

Hollandsworth, James G., Jr. *The Louisiana Native Guards: The Black Military Experience During the Civil War*. Baton Rouge: Louisiana State University Press, 1995.

———. *Pretense of Glory: The Life of General Nathaniel P. Banks*. Baton Rouge: Louisiana State University Press, 1998.

Holt, Thomas. *Black Over White: Negro Political Leadership in South Carolina During Reconstruction*. Urbana: University of Illinois Press, 1977.

Howard, Victor B. *Black Liberation in Kentucky: Emancipation and Freedom, 1862–1884*. Lexington: University Press of Kentucky, 1983.

Hughes, Nathan C., and Roy P. Stonesifer. *The Life and Wars of Gideon J. Pillow*. Chapel Hill: University of North Carolina Press, 1993.

Humphreys, Margaret. *Intensely Human: The Health of the Black Soldier in the American Civil War*. Baltimore: Johns Hopkins University Press, 2008.

Hunt, Jeffrey W. *The Last Battle of the Civil War: Palmetto Ranch*. Austin: University of Texas Press, 2002.

Hurt, R. Douglas. *Agriculture and Slavery in Missouri's Little Dixie*. Columbia: University of Missouri Press, 1992.

Instructions for Heavy Artillery: Prepared by a Board of Officers for the Use of the Army of the United States. Washington, D.C.: Gideon, 1851.

Irwin, Richard B. *History of the Nineteenth Army Corps*. New York: G. P. Putnam's Sons, 1892.

Jackson, Harry F., and Thomas F. O'Donnell. *Back Home in Oneida: Hermon Clarke and His Letters*. Syracuse: Syracuse University Press, 1965.

Jefferson, Thomas. *Notes on the State of Virginia*, ed. William Peden. Chapel Hill: University of North Carolina Press, 1954.

Johnson, Benjamin H. *Revolution in Texas: How a Forgotten Rebellion and Its Bloody Suppression Turned Mexicans into Americans*. New Haven: Yale University Press, 2003.

Johnson, Ludwell H. *The Red River Campaign: Politics and Cotton in the Civil War*. Baltimore: Johns Hopkins University Press, 1958.

Johnson, Russell L. *Warriors into Workers: The Civil War and the Formation of Urban-Industrial Society in a Northern City*. New York: Fordham University Press, 2003.

Joiner, Gary D. *Through the Howling Wilderness: The 1864 Red River Campaign and Union Failure in the West*. Knoxville: University of Tennessee Press, 2006.

Jordan, Thomas, and J[ohn] P. Pryor. *The Campaigns of Lieut.-Gen. N. B. Forrest, and of Forrest's Cavalry*. New York: Da Capo Press, 1996 [1868].

Kautz, August V. *Customs of Service for Non-Commissioned Officers and Soldiers.* Philadelphia: J. B. Lippincott, 1865.

Keegan, John. *The Face of Battle.* New York: Viking Press, 1976.

Kinard, Jeff. *Lafayette of the South: Prince Camille de Polignac and the American Civil War.* College Station: Texas A&M University Press, 2001.

Klein, Maury. *History of the Louisville & Nashville Railroad.* New York: Macmillan, 1972.

Krause, Enrique. *Mexico, Biography of Power: A History of Modern Mexico, 1810–1996.* New York: HarperCollins, 1997.

Krick, Robert K. *Civil War Weather in Virginia.* Tuscaloosa: University of Alabama Press, 2007.

Laas, Virginia J., ed. *Wartime Washington: The Civil War Letters of Elizabeth Blair Lee.* Urbana: University of Illinois Press, 1991.

Lane, Roger. *Roots of Violence in Black Philadelphia, 1860–1900.* Cambridge: Harvard University Press, 1986.

Lawson, Melinda. *Patriot Fires: Forging a New American Nationalism in the Civil War North.* Lawrence: University Press of Kansas, 2002.

Lerwill, Leonard L. *The Personnel Replacement System in the United States Army.* Washington, D.C.: Department of the Army, 1954.

Levine, Lawrence W. *Black Culture and Black Consciousness: Afro-American Folk Thought from Slavery to Freedom.* New York: Oxford University Press, 1977.

Lighter, J. E., ed. *Random House Historical Dictionary of American Slang,* 2 vols. New York: Random House, 1994–1997.

Linderman, Gerald F. *Embattled Courage: The Experience of Combat in the American Civil War.* New York: Free Press, 1987.

———. *The World Within War: America's Combat Experience in World War II.* New York: Free Press, 1997.

Litwack, Leon F. *Been in the Storm So Long: The Aftermath of Slavery.* New York: Knopf, 1979.

———. *North of Slavery: The Negro in the Freed States, 1790–1860.* Chicago: University of Chicago Press, 1961.

Livermore, Thomas L. *Numbers and Losses in the Civil War in America, 1861–65.* Boston: Houghton Mifflin, 1901.

Longacre, Edward G. *Army of Amateurs: General Benjamin F. Butler and the Army of the James, 1863–1865.* Mechanicsburg, Pa.: Stackpole Books, 1997.

———. *A Regiment of Slaves: The 4th United States Colored Infantry, 1863–1866.* Mechanicsburg, Pa.: Stackpole Books, 2003.

———. *A Soldier to the Last: Maj. Gen. Joseph Wheeler in Blue and Gray.* Washington, D.C.: Potomac Books, 2007.

Looby, Christopher, ed. *The Complete Civil War Journal and Selected Letters of Thomas Wentworth Higginson.* Chicago: University of Chicago Press, 2000.

Lowe, Richard. *Walker's Texas Division C.S.A.: Greyhounds of the Trans-Mississippi.* Baton Rouge: Louisiana State University Press, 2004.

Mackey, Robert R. *The Uncivil War: Irregular Warfare in the Upper South, 1861–1865.* Norman: University of Oklahoma Press, 2004.

Main, Edwin M. *The Story of the Marches, Battles and Incidents of the Third United States Colored Cavalry.* New York: Negro Universities Press, 1970 [1908].

Marvel, William. *Andersonville: The Last Depot.* Chapel Hill: University of North Carolina Press, 1994.

Maslowski, Peter. *Treason Must Be Made Odious: Military Occupation and Wartime Reconstruction in Nashville, Tennessee, 1862–65.* Millbrook, N.Y.: KTO Press, 1978.

Massachusetts Soldiers, Sailors, and Marines in the Civil War, 8 vols. and index. Various places and publishers, 1931–1937.

McDonald, Roderick A. *The Economy and Material Culture of Slaves: Goods and Chattels on the Sugar Plantations of Jamaica and Louisiana.* Baton Rouge: Louisiana State University Press, 1993.

McDonough, James L. *Nashville: The Western Confederacy's Final Gamble.* Knoxville: University of Tennessee Press, 2004.

McKay, Ernest A. *The Civil War and New York City.* Syracuse: Syracuse University Press, 1990.

McKenzie, Robert T. *One South or Many? Plantation Belt and Upcountry in Civil War–Era Tennessee.* New York: Cambridge University Press, 1994.

McMurry, Richard M. *Atlanta 1864: Last Chance for the Confederacy.* Lincoln: University of Nebraska Press, 2000.

———. *The Fourth Battle of Winchester: Toward a New Civil War Paradigm.* Kent, Ohio: Kent State University Press, 2002.

———. *John Bell Hood and the War for Southern Independence.* Lexington: University Press of Kentucky, 1982.

———. *Two Great Rebel Armies: An Essay in Confederate Military History.* Chapel Hill: University of North Carolina Press, 1989.

McNeilly, Donald P. *The Old South Frontier: Cotton Plantations and the Formation of Arkansas Society, 1819–1861.* Fayetteville: University of Arkansas Press, 2000.

McPherson, Edward, ed. *The Political History of the United States of America During the Great Rebellion.* Washington, D.C.: Philp and Solomons, 1864.

———. *The Political History of the United States of America During the Period of Reconstruction.* New York: Da Capo Press, 1972 [1871].

McPherson, James M. *Battle Cry of Freedom: The Civil War Era.* New York: Oxford University Press, 1988.

———. *For Cause and Comrades: Why Men Fought in the Civil War.* New York: Oxford University Press, 1997.

———. *The Negro's Civil War: How American Negroes Felt and Acted During the War for the Union.* New York: Pantheon Books, 1965.

———. *The Struggle for Equality: Abolitionists and the Negro in the Civil War and Reconstruction.* Princeton: Princeton University Press, 1964.

The Medical and Surgical History of the War of the Rebellion, 2 vols. in 6. Washington, D.C.: Government Printing Office, 1870–1888.

Menge, W. Springer, and J. August Shimrak. *The Civil War Notebook of Daniel Chisholm: A Chronicle of Daily Life in the Union Army, 1864–1865.* New York: Orion Books, 1989.

Messner, William F. *Freedmen and the Ideology of Free Labor: Louisiana, 1861–1865*. Lafayette: University of Southwest Louisiana, 1978.

Military History of Kansas Regiments During the War for the Suppression of the Rebellion. Leavenworth, Kans.: W. S. Burke, 1870.

Miller, Edward A., Jr. *The Black Civil War Soldiers of Illinois: The Story of the Twenty-ninth U.S. Colored Infantry*. Columbia: University of South Carolina Press, 1998.

———. *Lincoln's Abolitionist General: The Biography of David Hunter*. Columbia: University of South Carolina Press, 1997.

Miller, William L. *President Lincoln: The Duty of a Statesman*. New York: Knopf, 2008.

Miner, Craig, and William E. Unrau. *The End of Indian Kansas: A Study of Cultural Revolution, 1854–1871*. Lawrence: Regents Press of Kansas, 1978.

Moneyhon, Carl H. *The Impact of the Civil War and Reconstruction on Arkansas*. Baton Rouge: Louisiana State University Press, 1994.

———. *Texas After the Civil War: The Struggle Over Reconstruction*. College Station: Texas A&M University Press, 2004.

Montejano, David. *Anglos and Mexicans in the Making of Texas, 1836–1986*. Austin: University of Texas Press, 1987.

Morgan, Lynda J. *Emancipation in Virginia's Tobacco Belt, 1850–1870*. Athens: University of Georgia Press, 1992.

Nalty, Bernard C. *Strength for the Fight: A History of Black Americans in the Military*. New York: Free Press, 1986.

Niven, John. *Salmon P. Chase: A Biography*. New York: Oxford University Press, 1995.

———, et al., eds. *The Salmon P. Chase Papers*, 5 vols. Kent, Ohio: Kent State University Press, 1993–1998.

Norton, Oliver W. *Army Letters, 1861–1865*. Chicago: privately printed, 1903.

Nugent, Walter T. K. *The Money Question During Reconstruction*. New York: W. W. Norton, 1967.

Nulty, William H. *Confederate Florida: The Road to Olustee*. Tuscaloosa: University of Alabama Press, 1990.

O'Brien, Sean M. *Mobile, 1865: Last Stand of the Confederacy*. Westport, Conn.: Praeger, 2001.

———. *Mountain Partisans: Guerrilla Warfare in the Southern Appalachians, 1861–1865*. Westport, Conn.: Praeger, 1999.

Ochs, Stephen J. *A Black Patriot and a White Priest: André Cailloux and Claude Paschal Maistre in Civil War New Orleans*. Baton Rouge: Louisiana State University Press, 2006.

Öfele, Martin W. *German-Speaking Officers in the U.S. Colored Troops, 1863–1867*. Gainesville: University Press of Florida, 2004.

Offenberg, Richard S., and Robert R. Parsonage, eds. *The War Letters of Duren F. Kelley, 1862–1865*. New York: Pageant Press, 1967.

Official Army Register of the Volunteer Force of the United States Army, 8 vols. Washington, D.C.: Adjutant General's Office, 1867.

Official Records of the Union and Confederate Navies in the War of the Rebellion, 30 vols. Washington, D.C.: Government Printing Office, 1894–1922.

Ordnance Manual for the Use of Officers of the United States Army. Philadelphia: J. B. Lippincott, 1862.

Palmer, Beverly W., ed. *Selected Letters of Charles Sumner*, 2 vols. Boston: Northeastern University Press, 1990.

Paradis, James M. *Strike the Blow for Freedom: The 6th United States Colored Infantry in the Civil War*. Shippensburg, Pa.: White Mane Press, 1998.

Patterson, Robert T. *Federal Debt-Management Policies, 1865–1879*. Durham: Duke University Press, 1954.

Pearson, Elizabeth W., ed. *Letters from Port Royal, 1862–1868*. New York: Arno Press, 1969 [1909].

Powell, Lawrence N. *New Masters: Northern Planters During the Civil War and Reconstruction*. New Haven: Yale University Press, 1980.

Power, J. Tracy. *Lee's Miserables: Life in the Army of Northern Virginia from the Wilderness to Appomattox*. Chapel Hill: University of North Carolina Press, 1998.

Prucha, Francis P. *The Great Father: The United States Government and the American Indians*. Lincoln: University of Nebraska Press, 1984.

Quarles, Benjamin. *The Negro in the Civil War*. Boston: Little, Brown, 1953.

Rand McNally Commercial Atlas and Marketing Guide, 2008, 2 vols. Chicago: Rand McNally, 2008.

Redkey, Edwin S., ed. *A Grand Army of Black Men: Letters from African-American Soldiers in the Union Army, 1861–1865*. New York: Cambridge University Press, 1992.

Reid, Richard M. *Freedom for Themselves: North Carolina's Black Soldiers in the Civil War Era*. Chapel Hill: University of North Carolina Press, 2008.

Report of the Joint Committee on the Conduct of the War, 9 vols. Wilmington, N.C.: Broadfoot Publishing, 1998 [1863–1865].

Report of the Joint Committee on Reconstruction. Washington, D.C.: Government Printing Office, 1866.

Reuss, Martin. *Designing the Bayous: The Control of Water in the Atchafalaya Basin*. Alexandria, Va.: U.S. Army Corps of Engineers, 1998.

Revised United States Army Regulations of 1861. Washington, D.C.: Government Printing Office, 1863.

Richter, William L. *The Army in Texas During Reconstruction, 1865–1870*. College Station: Texas A&M University Press, 1987.

Ripley, C. Peter. *Slaves and Freedmen in Civil War Louisiana*. Baton Rouge: Louisiana State University Press, 1976.

———, et al., eds. *The Black Abolitionist Papers*, 5 vols. Chapel Hill: University of North Carolina Press, 1985–1992.

Robertson, William G. *Back Door to Richmond: The Bermuda Hundred Campaign, April–June 1864*. Newark: University of Delaware Press, 1987.

Rodrigue, John C. *Reconstruction in the Cane Fields: From Slavery to Free Labor in Louisiana's Sugar Parishes, 1862–1880*. Baton Rouge: Louisiana State University Press, 2001.

Rolle, Andrew F. *The Lost Cause: The Confederate Exodus to Mexico*. Norman: University of Oklahoma Press, 1965.

Rose, Willie Lee. *Rehearsal for Reconstruction: The Port Royal Experiment.* Indianapolis: Bobbs-Merrill, 1964.

Roster, Surviving Members of the 95th Regiment, O.V.I. [Columbus, Ohio: Champlin Press, 1916].

Royster, Charles F. *The Destructive War: William Tecumseh Sherman, Stonewall Jackson, and the Americans.* New York: Knopf, 1991.

Sanders, Charles W., Jr. *In the Hands of the Enemy: Military Prisons of the Civil War.* Baton Rouge: Louisiana State University Press, 2005.

Savage, W. Sherman. *The History of Lincoln University.* Jefferson City, Mo.: Lincoln University, 1939.

Schoonover, Thomas D. *Dollars over Dominion: The Triumph of Liberalism in Mexican–United States Relations, 1861–1877.* Baton Rouge: Louisiana State University Press, 1978.

Schwalm, Leslie A. *Emancipation's Diaspora: Race and Reconstruction in the Upper Midwest.* Chapel Hill: University of North Carolina Press, 2009.

Scott, Henry L. *Military Dictionary.* New York: D. Van Nostrand, 1864.

Scott, Winfield. *Memoirs of Lieut.-General Scott.* New York: Sheldon, 1864.

Sears, Cyrus. *Paper of Cyrus Sears.* Columbus, Ohio: F. J. Heer, 1909.

Sebag-Montefiore, Simon. *Dunkirk: Fight to the Last Man.* Cambridge: Harvard University Press, 2006.

Sefton, James E. *The United States Army and Reconstruction, 1865–1877.* Baton Rouge: Louisiana State University Press, 1967.

Shaffer, Donald R. *After the Glory: The Struggles of Black Civil War Veterans.* Lawrence: University Press of Kansas, 2004.

Shannon, Fred A. *The Organization and Administration of the Union Army, 1861–1865,* 2 vols. Cleveland: Arthur H. Clark, 1928.

Sherman, William T. *Memoirs of General William T. Sherman,* 2 vols. New York: D. Appleton, 1875.

Shofner, Jerrell H. *Nor Is It Over Yet: Florida in the Era of Reconstruction, 1863–1877.* Gainesville: University Press of Florida, 1974.

Sifakis, Stewart. *Compendium of the Confederate Armies,* 11 vols. New York: Facts on File, 1992–1995.

Simon, John Y., ed. *The Papers of Ulysses S. Grant,* 30 vols. to date. Carbondale and Edwardsville: Southern Illinois University Press, 1967–.

Simpson, Brooks D. *Let Us Have Peace: Ulysses S. Grant and the Politics of War and Reconstruction, 1861–1868.* Chapel Hill: University of North Carolina Press, 1991.

———. *The Reconstruction Presidents.* Lawrence: University Press of Kansas, 1998.

———. *Ulysses S. Grant: Triumph over Adversity, 1822–1865.* Boston: Houghton Mifflin, 2000.

———, and Jean V. Berlin, eds. *Sherman's Civil War: Selected Correspondence of William Tecumseh Sherman, 1860–1865.* Chapel Hill: University of North Carolina Press, 1999.

Sitterson, J. Carlyle. *Sugar Country: The Cane Sugar Industry in the South, 1753–1950.* Lexington: University of Kentucky Press, 1953.

Smith, John David, ed. *Black Soldiers in Blue: African American Troops in the Civil War Era*. Chapel Hill: University of North Carolina Press, 2002.

Smith, Thomas T., et al., eds. *The Reminiscences of Major General Zenas R. Bliss, 1854–1876*. Austin: Texas State Historical Association, 2007.

Sommers, Richard J. *Richmond Redeemed: The Siege at Petersburg*. Garden City, N.Y.: Doubleday, 1981.

Speer, Lonnie R. *War of Vengeance: Acts of Retaliation Against Civil War POWs*. Mechanicsburg, Pa.: Stackpole Books, 2002.

Stubbs, Mary L., and Stanley R. Connor, *Armor-Cavalry, Part 1: Regular Army and Army Reserve*, U.S. Army Lineage Series. Washington, D.C.: Office of the Chief of Military History, 1969.

Surdam, David G. *Northern Naval Superiority and the Economics of the American Civil War*. Columbia: University of South Carolina Press, 2001.

Sutherland, Daniel E. *A Savage Conflict: The Decisive Role of Guerrillas in the American Civil War*. Chapel Hill: University of North Carolina Press, 2009.

Tap, Bruce. *Over Lincoln's Shoulder: The Committee on the Conduct of the War*. Lawrence: University Press of Kansas, 1998.

Taylor, Joe G. *Louisiana Reconstructed, 1863–1877*. Baton Rouge: Louisiana State University Press, 1974.

Taylor, Orville W. *Negro Slavery in Arkansas*. Durham, N.C.: Duke University Press, 1958.

Taylor, Robert A. *Confederate Storehouse: Florida in the Confederate Economy*. Tuscaloosa: University of Alabama Press, 1995.

Thomas, Benjamin P., and Harold M. Hyman. *Stanton: The Life and Times of Lincoln's Secretary of War*. New York: Knopf, 1962.

Thompson, Jerry. *Cortina: Defending the Mexican Name in Texas*. College Station: Texas A&M University Press, 2007.

———, and Lawrence T. Jones III. *Civil War and Revolution on the Rio Grande Frontier: A Narrative and Photographic History*. Austin: Texas State Historical Association, 2004.

Thornbrough, Emma L. *Indiana in the Civil War Era, 1850–1880*. Indianapolis: Indiana Historical Society, 1965.

Thorndike, William, and William Dollarhide. *Map Guide to the U.S. Federal Censuses, 1790–1920*. Baltimore: Genealogical Publishing, 1987.

Throne, Mildred, ed. *The Civil War Diary of Cyrus F. Boyd, Fifteenth Iowa Infantry, 1861–1863*. Baton Rouge: Louisiana State University Press, 1998.

Tomblin, Barbara B. *Bluejackets and Contrabands: African Americans and the Union Navy*. Lexington: University Press of Kentucky, 2009

Townsend, Stephen A. *The Yankee Invasion of Texas*. College Station: Texas A&M University Press, 2006.

Trefousse, Hans L. *Andrew Johnson: A Biography*. New York: W. W. Norton, 1989.

———. *Ben Butler: The South Called Him Beast!* New York: Twayne, 1957.

Trelease, Allen W. *White Terror: The Ku Klux Klan Conspiracy and Southern Reconstruction*. Baton Rouge: Louisiana State University Press, 1971.

Tripp, Steven E. *Yankee Town, Southern City: Race and Class Relations in Civil War Lynchburg*. New York: New York University Press, 1997.

Trowbridge, John T. *The South: A Tour of Its Battle-Fields and Ruined Cities*. New York: Arno Press, 1969 [1866].

Trudeau, Noah A. *Like Men of War: Black Troops in the Civil War, 1962–1865*. Boston: Little, Brown, 1998.

Tunnell, Ted. *Crucible of Reconstruction: War, Radicalism and Race in Louisiana, 1862–1877*. Baton Rouge: Louisiana State University Press, 1984.

U.S. Census Bureau. *Agriculture of the United States in 1860*. Washington, D.C.: Government Printing Office, 1864.

———. *Historical Statistics of the United States: Colonial Times to 1970*, 2 vols. Washington, D.C.: Government Printing Office, 1975.

———. *Population of the United States in 1860*. Washington, D.C.: Government Printing Office, 1864.

———. *Statistics of the Population of the United States*. Washington, D.C.: Government Printing Office, 1872.

U.S. Department of the Army. *The Medal of Honor of the United States Army*. Washington, D.C.: Government Printing Office, 1948.

U.S. Statutes at Large.

Unger, Irwin. *The Greenback Era: A Social and Political History of American Finance, 1865–1879*. Princeton: Princeton University Press, 1964.

Unruh, John D., Jr. *The Plains Across: The Overland Emigrants and the Trans-Mississippi West, 1840–1860*. Urbana: University of Illinois Press, 1979.

Urwin, Gregory J. W., ed. *Black Flag over Dixie: Racial Atrocities and Reprisals in the Civil War*. Carbondale: Southern Illinois University Press, 2004.

Walker, Henry P. *The Wagonmasters: High Plains Freighting from the Earliest Days of the Santa Fe Trail to 1880*. Norman: University of Oklahoma Press, 1966.

The War of the Rebellion: A Compilation of the Official Records of the Union and Confederate Armies, 70 vols. in 128. Washington, D.C.: Government Printing Office, 1880–1901.

Washington, Versalle F. *Eagles on Their Buttons: A Black Infantry Regiment in the Civil War*. Columbia: University of Missouri Press, 1999.

Wayne, Michael. *The Reshaping of Plantation Society: The Natchez District, 1860–80*. Urbana: University of Illinois Press, 1990.

Wearmouth, John, ed. *The Cornwell Chronicles: Tales of an American Life . . . in the Volunteer Civil War Western Army. . . .* Bowie, Md.: Heritage Books, 1998.

Weaver, C. P., ed. *Thank God My Regiment an African One: The Civil War Diary of Colonel Nathan W. Daniels*. Baton Rouge: Louisiana State University Press, 1998.

Welcher, Frank J. *The Union Army, 1861–1865: Organization and Operations*, 2 vols. Bloomington: University of Indiana Press, 1989–1993.

Whitman, William E. S. *Maine in the War for the Union*. Lewiston, Me.: Nelson Dingley Jr., 1865.

Wiley, Bell I. *The Life of Billy Yank: The Common Soldier of the Union*. Indianapolis: Bobbs-Merrill, 1952.

———. *The Life of Johnny Reb: The Common Soldier of the Confederacy*. Indianapolis: Bobbs-Merrill, 1943.

————. *Southern Negroes, 1861–1865*. New York: Rinehart, 1938.

Wilkeson, Frank. *Recollections of a Private Soldier in the Army of the Potomac*. New York: G. P. Putnam's Sons, 1886.

Wilkinson, Warren. *Mother, May You Never See the Sights I Have Seen: The Fifty-seventh Massachusetts Veteran Volunteers in the Army of the Potomac, 1864–1865*. New York: Harper & Row, 1990.

Williams, Austin B. *Shrimps, Lobsters, and Crabs of the Atlantic Coast of the Eastern United States, Maine to Florida*. Washington, D.C.: Smithsonian Institution Press, 1984.

Williams, George W. *A History of the Negro Troops in the War of the Rebellion, 1861–1865*. New York: Harper and Brothers, 1888.

Williamson, Joel. *After Slavery: The Negro in South Carolina During Reconstruction, 1861–1877*. Chapel Hill: University of North Carolina Press, 1965.

Wills, Charles W. *Army Life of an Illinois Soldier*. Carbondale and Edwardsville: Southern Illinois University Press, 1996 [1906].

Wilson, Joseph T. *The Black Phalanx*. Hartford: American Publishing, 1890.

Wilson, Keith P. *Campfires of Freedom: The Camp Life of Black Soldiers During the Civil War*. Kent, Ohio: Kent State University Press, 2002.

Wilson, Mark R. *The Business of Civil War: Military Mobilization and the State, 1861–1865*. Baltimore: Johns Hopkins University Press, 2006.

Winkler, Ernest W., ed. *Journal of the Secession Convention of Texas, 1861*. Austin: Texas State Library and Historical Commission, 1912.

Winschel, Terrence J., ed. *The Civil War Diary of a Common Soldier: William Wiley of the 77th Illinois Infantry*. Baton Rouge: Louisiana State University Press, 2001.

Winters, Donald L. *Tennessee Farming, Tennessee Farmers: Antebellum Agriculture in the Upper South*. Knoxville: University of Tennessee Press, 1994.

Winters, John D. *The Civil War in Louisiana*. Baton Rouge: Louisiana State University Press, 1963.

Wise, Stephen R. *Gate of Hell: Campaign for Charleston Harbor, 1863*. Columbia: University of South Carolina Press, 1994.

Woodward, William E. *Meet General Grant*. Garden City, N.Y.: Garden City Publishing, 1928.

Wright, George C. *Racial Violence in Kentucky, 1865–1940: Lynchings, Mob Rule, and "Legal Lynchings."* Baton Rouge: Louisiana State University Press, 1990.

Ziemke, Earl F. *The U.S. Army in the Occupation of Germany, 1944–1946*, U.S. Army in World War II. Washington, D.C.: U.S. Army Center of Military History, 1975.

Zuczek, Richard. *State of Rebellion: Reconstruction in South Carolina*. Columbia: University of South Carolina Press, 1996.

Articles

Bailey, Anne J. "The USCT in the Confederate Heartland." In *Black Soldiers in Blue: African American Troops in the Civil War Era*, ed. John D. Smith. Chapel Hill: University of North Carolina Press, 2002, pp. 227–48.

Benedict, Michael L. "Reform Republicans and the Retreat from Reconstruction." In *The Facts of Reconstruction: Essays in Honor of John Hope Franklin*, eds. Eric Anderson and Alfred A. Moss Jr. Baton Rouge: Louisiana State University Press, 1991.

Clampitt, Brad R. "The Breakup: The Collapse of the Confederate Trans-Mississippi Army in Texas." *Southwestern Historical Quarterly* 108 (2005): 498–534.

Dirck, Brian. "By the Hand of God: James Montgomery and Redemptive Violence." *Kansas History* 27 (2004): 100–15.

Frazier, Donald S. "'Out of Stinking Distance': The Guerrilla War in Louisiana." In *Guerrillas, Unionists, and Violence on the Confederate Home Front*, ed. Daniel E. Sutherland. Fayetteville: University of Arkansas Press, 1999, pp. 151–70.

Glatthaar, Joseph T. "The Civil War Through the Eyes of a Sixteen-Year-Old Black Soldier: The Letters of Lieutenant John H. Crowder of the 1st Louisiana Native Guards." *Louisiana History* 35 (1994): 201–16.

Hardwick, Kevin R. "'Your Old Father Abe Lincoln Is Dead and Damned': Black Soldiers and the Memphis Riot of 1866." *Journal of Social History* 27 (1993): 109–28.

Hess, Earl J. "Confiscation and the Northern War Effort: The Army of the Southwest at Helena." *Arkansas Historical Quarterly* 44 (1985): 56–75.

Irwin, Richard B. "The Capture of Port Hudson." In *Battles and Leaders of the Civil War*, 4 vols. New York: Century Company, 1887–1888, 3: 586–98.

Jordan, Weymouth T., Jr., and Gerald W. Thomas. "Massacre at Plymouth: April 20, 1864." *North Carolina Historical Review* 73 (1995): 125–93.

Kaye, Anthony E. "Slaves, Emancipation, and the Powers of War: Views from the Natchez District of Mississippi." In *The War Was You and Me: Civilians in the American Civil War*, ed. Joan E. Cashin. Princeton, N.J.: Princeton University Press, 2002.

Kemp, Thomas R. "Community and War: The Civil War Experience of Two New Hampshire Towns." In *Toward a Social History of the American Civil War: Exploratory Essays*, ed. Maris A. Vinovskis. New York: Cambridge University Press, 1990.

Kohl, Rhonda M. "'This Godforsaken Town': Death and Disease at Helena, Arkansas, 1862–63." *Civil War History* 50 (2004): 109–44.

Mays, Thomas D. "The Battle of Saltville." In *Black Soldiers in Blue*, ed. Smith, pp. 200–26.

Meier, Michael T. "Lorenzo Thomas and the Recruitment of Blacks in the Mississippi Valley, 1863–1865." In *Black Soldiers in Blue*, ed. Smith, pp. 249–75.

Moran, Frank E. "Colonel Rose's Tunnel at Libby Prison." *The Century Magazine* 35 (1888): 770–90.

Nolin, Kelly, ed. "The Civil War Letters of J. O. Cross." *Connecticut Historical Society Bulletin* 60 (1995): 211–35.

Pierce, Edward L. "The Freedmen at Port Royal." *Atlantic Monthly* 12 (September 1863): 291–315.

Redkey, Edwin S. "Brave Black Volunteers: Profile of the Fifty-fourth Massachusetts Regiment." In *Hope and Glory: Essays on the Legacy of the Fifty-fourth Massachusetts Regiment*, ed. Martin H. Blatt et al. Amherst: University of Massachusetts Press, 2001, pp. 21–34.

Reid, Richard. "Raising the African Brigade: Early Black Recruitment in Civil War North Carolina." *North Carolina Historical Review* 70 (1993): 266–301.

Ripley, C. Peter. "The Black Family in Transition: Louisiana, 1860–65." *Louisiana History* 41 (1975): 369–80.

Robertson, William G. "From the Crater to New Market Heights: A Tale of Two Divisions." In *Black Soldiers in Blue*, ed. Smith, pp. 169–99.

Schafer, Daniel L. "Freedom Was as Close as the River: African-Americans and the Civil War in Northeast Florida." In *The African American Heritage of Florida*, ed. David R. Colburn and Jane L. Landers. Gainesville: University Press of Florida, 1995, pp. 157–84.

Sheridan, Richard B. "From Slavery in Missouri to Freedom in Kansas: The Influx of Black Fugitives and Contrabands into Kansas, 1854–1865." *Kansas History* 12 (1989): 28–47.

Simpson, Brooks D. "Quandaries of Command: Ulysses S. Grant and Black Soldiers." In *Union and Emancipation: Essays on Politics and Race in the Civil War Era*, ed. David W. Blight and Brooks D. Simpson. Kent, Ohio: Kent State University Press, 1997, pp. 123–49.

Sommers, Richard J. "The Dutch Gap Affair: Military Atrocities and the Rights of Negro Soldiers." *Civil War History* 21 (1975): 51–64.

Suderow, Bryce A. "The Battle of the Crater: The Civil War's Worst Massacre." *Civil War History* 43 (1997): 219–24.

Sutherland, Daniel E. "Sideshow No Longer: A Historiographical Review of the Guerrilla War." *Civil War History* 46 (2000): 5–23.

Tyler, Ronnie C. "Cotton on the Border, 1861–1865." *Southwestern Historical Quarterly* 73 (1970): 456–477.

Urwin, Gregory J. W. "'We Cannot Treat Negroes . . . As Prisoners of War': Racial Atrocities and Reprisals in Civil War Arkansas." *Civil War History* 42 (1996): 193–210.

Vanderwood, Paul. "Betterment for Whom? The Reform Period, 1855–1875." In *The Oxford History of Mexico*, eds. Michael C. Meyer and William H. Beezley. New York: Oxford University Press, 2000, pp. 371–96.

"War Letters of Charles P. Bowditch." *Proceedings of the Massachusetts Historical Society* 57 (1924): 414–95.

Westwood, Howard C. "Captive Black Soldiers in Charleston—What To Do?" *Civil War History* 28 (1982): 28–44.

———. "The Cause and Consequence of a Union Black Soldier's Mutiny and Execution." *Civil War History* 31 (1985): 222–36.

Williams, Chad L. "Symbols of Freedom and Defeat: African American Soldiers, White Southerners, and the Christmas Insurrection Scare of 1865." In *Black Flag Over Dixie: Racial Atrocities and Reprisals in the Civil War*, ed. Gregory J. W. Urwin. Carbondale: Southern Illinois University Press, 2004, pp. 210–30.

Zalimas, Robert J. "A Disturbance in the City: Black and White Soldiers in Postwar Charleston." In *Black Soldiers in Blue*, ed. Smith, pp. 361–90.

Pamphlets and Ephemera

Birney, William. *General William Birney's Answer to Libels Clandestinely Circulated by James Shaw, Jr. . . .* Washington, D.C.: privately printed, 1878.

Colyer, Vincent. *Report of the Services Rendered by the Freed People to the United States Army, in North Carolina. . . .* New York: privately printed, 1864.

Free Military School for Applicants for Command of Colored Troops, 2d ed. Philadelphia: King and Baird, 1864.

U.S. Sanitary Commission. *A Report to the Secretary of War of the Operations of the Sanitary Commission, and upon the Sanitary Condition of the Volunteer Army. . . .* Washington, D.C.: McGill & Witherow, 1861.

Yeatman, James E. *A Report on the Condition of the Freedmen of the Mississippi.* St. Louis: Western Sanitary Commission, 1864.

ABBREVIATIONS

AAG	Assistant Adjutant General
AAS	American Antiquarian Society
AD	African Descent
Adj. Gen.	Adjutant General
AGO	Adjutant General's Office
Arty	Artillery
Bde	Brigade
Bn	Battalion
BRFAL	Bureau of Refugees, Freedmen, and Abandoned Lands
Brig.	Brigadier
Brig. Gen.	Brigadier General
Btry	Battery
Capt.	Captain
Cdr	Commander
Cmd	Command
CMH	U.S. Army Center of Military History
CMSR	Compiled Military Service Record
CO	Commanding officer
Col.	Colonel
Cong.	Congress
Cpl.	Corporal
CWPAF	Civil War Pension Application Files
Dept	Department
Dist	District
Div	Division
DU	Duke University
ed(s).	editor(s), edition
esp.	especially

f/w	filed with
Gen.	General
GO	General Orders
H. Ex. Doc.	House Executive Document
H. Rpt	House Report
HA	Heavy Artillery
HQ	Headquarters
Inf	Infantry
Jnl	Journal
LC	Library of Congress
LR	Letters Received
LS	Letters Sent
Lt. Col.	Lieutenant Colonel
Lt. Gen.	Lieutenant General
Ltr	Letter
Maj.	Major
Maj. Gen.	Major General
MDW	Military District of Washington
MHI	U.S. Army Military History Institute
MHS	Minnesota Historical Society
Mil	Military
n.d.	no date
NA	National Archives
no.	number
OC	Oberlin College
Ofcr	officer
OHS	Ohio Historical Society
pt.	part
Pub	publication
Pvt.	Private
Rcd	Record
Rear Adm.	Rear Admiral
RG	Record Group
Rpt	Report

S. Doc.	Senate Document
S. Ex. Doc.	Senate Executive Document
ser.	series
sess.	session
Sgt.	Sergeant
Sgt. Maj.	Sergeant Major
SO	Special Orders
Svc	Service
UA	University of Arkansas
USCA	United States Colored Artillery
USCC	United States Colored Cavalry
USCI	United States Colored Infantry
vol.	volume
YU	Yale University

INDEX